SINGLE PC LICENSE AGREEMENT

READ THIS LICENSE CAREFULLY BEFORE OPENING THIS
THE TERMS AND CONDITIONS OF THIS LICENSE. IF YOU DO NOT AGREE, DO NOT OPEN THE PACKAGE. PROMPTLY RETURN THE UNOPENED PACKAGE AND ALL ACCOMPANYING ITEMS TO THE PLACE YOU OBTAINED THEM.

1. GRANT OF LICENSE and OWNERSHIP: The enclosed computer programs <<and data>> ("Software") are licensed, not sold, to you by Pearson Education, Inc. publishing as Pearson Prentice Hall ("We" or the "Company") and in consideration of your purchase or adoption of the accompanying Company textbooks and/or other materials, and your agreement to these terms. We reserve any rights not granted to you. You own only the disk(s) but we and/or our licensors own the Software itself. This license allows you to use and display your copy of the Software on a single computer (i.e., with a single CPU) at a single location for <u>academic</u> use only, so long as you comply with the terms of this Agreement. You may make one copy for back up, or transfer your copy to another CPU, provided that the Software is usable on only one computer.

2. RESTRICTIONS: You may <u>not</u> transfer or distribute the Software or documentation to anyone else. Except for backup, you may <u>not</u> copy the documentation or the Software. You may <u>not</u> network the Software or otherwise use it on more than one computer or computer terminal at the same time. You may <u>not</u> reverse engineer, disassemble, decompile, modify, adapt, translate, or create derivative works based on the Software or the Documentation. You may be held legally responsible for any copying or copyright infringement that is caused by your failure to abide by the terms of these restrictions.

3. TERMINATION: This license is effective until terminated. This license will terminate automatically without notice from the Company if you fail to comply with any provisions or limitations of this license. Upon termination, you shall destroy the Documentation and all copies of the Software. All provisions of this Agreement as to limitation and disclaimer of warranties, limitation of liability, remedies or damages, and our ownership rights shall survive termination.

4. LIMITED WARRANTY AND DISCLAIMER OF WARRANTY: Company warrants that for a period of 60 days from the date you purchase this SOFTWARE (or purchase or adopt the accompanying textbook), the Software, when properly installed and used in accordance with the Documentation, will operate in substantial conformity with the description of the Software set forth in the Documentation, and that for a period of 30 days the disk(s) on which the Software is delivered shall be free from defects in materials and workmanship under normal use. The Company does <u>not</u> warrant that the Software will meet your requirements or that the operation of the Software will be uninterrupted or error-free. Your only remedy and the Company's only obligation under these limited warranties is, at the Company's option, return of the disk for a refund of any amounts paid for it by you or replacement of the disk. THIS LIMITED WARRANTY IS THE ONLY WARRANTY PROVIDED BY THE COMPANY AND ITS LICENSORS, AND THE COMPANY AND ITS LICENSORS DISCLAIM ALL OTHER WARRANTIES, EXPRESS OR IMPLIED, INCLUDING WITHOUT LIMITATION, THE IMPLIED WARRANTIES OF MERCHANTABILITY AND FITNESS FOR A PARTICULAR PURPOSE. THE COMPANY DOES NOT WARRANT, GUARANTEE OR MAKE ANY REPRESENTATION REGARDING THE ACCURACY, RELIABILITY, CURRENTNESS, USE, OR RESULTS OF USE, OF THE SOFTWARE.

5. LIMITATION OF REMEDIES AND DAMAGES: IN NO EVENT, SHALL THE COMPANY OR ITS EMPLOYEES, AGENTS, LICENSORS, OR CONTRACTORS BE LIABLE FOR ANY INCIDENTAL, INDIRECT, SPECIAL, OR CONSEQUENTIAL DAMAGES ARISING OUT OF OR IN CONNECTION WITH THIS LICENSE OR THE SOFTWARE, INCLUDING FOR LOSS OF USE, LOSS OF DATA, LOSS OF INCOME OR PROFIT, OR OTHER LOSSES, SUSTAINED AS A RESULT OF INJURY TO ANY PERSON, OR LOSS OF OR DAMAGE TO PROPERTY, OR CLAIMS OF THIRD PARTIES, EVEN IF THE COMPANY OR AN AUTHORIZED REPRESENTATIVE OF THE COMPANY HAS BEEN ADVISED OF THE POSSIBILITY OF SUCH DAMAGES. IN NO EVENT SHALL THE LIABILITY OF THE COMPANY FOR DAMAGES WITH RESPECT TO THE SOFTWARE EXCEED THE AMOUNTS ACTUALLY PAID BY YOU, IF ANY, FOR THE SOFTWARE OR THE ACCOMPANYING TEXTBOOK. BECAUSE SOME JURISDICTIONS DO NOT ALLOW THE LIMITATION OF LIABILITY IN CERTAIN CIRCUMSTANCES, THE ABOVE LIMITATIONS MAY NOT ALWAYS APPLY TO YOU.

6. GENERAL: THIS AGREEMENT SHALL BE CONSTRUED IN ACCORDANCE WITH THE LAWS OF THE UNITED STATES OF AMERICA AND THE STATE OF NEW YORK, APPLICABLE TO CONTRACTS MADE IN NEW YORK, EXCLUDING THE STATE'S LAWS AND POLICIES ON CONFLICTS OF LAW, AND SHALL BENEFIT THE COMPANY, ITS AFFILIATES AND ASSIGNEES. THIS AGREEMENT IS THE COMPLETE AND EXCLUSIVE STATEMENT OF THE AGREEMENT BETWEEN YOU AND THE COMPANY AND SUPERSEDES ALL PROPOSALS OR PRIOR AGREEMENTS, ORAL, OR WRITTEN, AND ANY OTHER COMMUNICATIONS BETWEEN YOU AND THE COMPANY OR ANY REPRESENTATIVE OF THE COMPANY RELATING TO THE SUBJECT MATTER OF THIS AGREEMENT. If you are a U.S. Government user, this Software is licensed with "restricted rights" as set forth in subparagraphs (a)-(d) of the Commercial Computer-Restricted Rights clause at FAR 52.227-19 or in subparagraphs (c)(1)(ii) of the Rights in Technical Data and Computer Software clause at DFARS 252.227-7013, and similar clauses, as applicable.

Should you have any questions concerning this agreement or if you wish to contact the Company for any reason, please contact in writing: Legal Department, Prentice Hall, 1 Lake Street, Upper Saddle River, NJ 07450 or call Pearson Education Product Support at 1-800-677-6337.

TENTH EDITION

AMERICAN GOVERNMENT

WALTER E. VOLKOMER
Hunter College of the City University of New York

PEARSON

Prentice
Hall

Upper Saddle River, New Jersey 07458

Library of Congress Cataloging-in-Publication Data
Volkomer, Walter E.
    American government election update edition/ Walter E. Volkomer.—10th ed.
        p. cm.
    Includes bibliographical references and index.
    ISBN 0-13-185635-9
    1. United States—Politics and government. I. Title.
JK276.V65 2004
320.473—dc21
                                        2003049828

Editorial director: *Charlyce Jones Owen*
Acquisitions editor: *Glenn Johnston*
Editorial assistant: *Suzanne Remore*
**VP/Director of production and
    manufacturing:** *Barbara Kittle*
Production editor: *Barbara Reilly*
Prepress and manufacturing manager:
    Nick Sklitsis
Prepress and manufacturing buyer: *Sherry Lewis*
Creative design director: *Leslie Osher*
Art director: *Anne Bonanno Nieglos*
Interior and cover designer: *Laura Gardner*
Cover image specialist: *Karen Sanatar*

Cover photo: *Getty Images, Inc.*
Electronic art manager: *Guy Ruggiero*
Line art: *Mirella Signoretto*
Director, Image Resource Center: *Melinda Reo*
Interior image specialist: *Beth Boyd Brenzel*
Manager, rights and permissions: *Zina Arabia*
Photo researcher: *Kathy Ringrose*
Image permission coordinator: *Michelina Viscusi*
Marketing director: *Beth Mejia*
Marketing assistant: *Jennifer Bryant*
Media editor: *Kate Ramunda*
Media production manager: *Lynn Pearlman*

This book was set in 10/11 Garamond Book by Pine Tree Composition, Inc.,
and was printed and bound by RR Donnelley & Sons Company.
The cover was printed by Phoenix Color Corp.

© 2005 by Pearson Education, Inc.
Upper Saddle River, New Jersey 07458

Printed in the United States of America

10 9 8 7 6 5 4 3 2 1

ISBN: 0-13-185635-9

Pearson Education LTD., *London*
Pearson Education Australia PTY, Limited, *Sydney*
Pearson Education Singapore, Pte. Ltd
Pearson Education North Asia Ltd, *Hong Kong*
Pearson Education Canada, Ltd., *Toronto*
Pearson Educación de Mexico, S. A. de C.V.
Pearson Education—Japan, *Tokyo*
Pearson Education Malaysia, Pte. Ltd
Pearson Education, *Upper Saddle River, New Jersey*

Brief Contents

Contents

PART IV   THE RIGHTS OF THE INDIVIDUAL

Preface

It was early in a new century and a new millennium. I was working on the revisions of the tenth edition of this textbook on American government. My thoughts turned to the political system of the United States one hundred years ago. How did it compare with the system that operated at the start of the twenty-first century? Had we improved American democracy in the past hundred years?

A detailed examination of these questions would require the production of a book-length manuscript and I was faced with publishing deadlines for this volume. But I have put together a few thoughts on the state of American democracy then and now. My overall conclusion is that despite some weaknesses in our present system, our political system is markedly improved and far more democratic today than it was a hundred years ago. Consider the following facts.

In 1900, African Americans in the South lived in a segregated society. Separation of the races existed in both the private and public spheres. Private companies and individuals were free to discriminate and government laws required racial segregation in all public facilities from schools and parks to bathrooms and drinking fountains. The entire system of segregation was given legal sanction by the 1896 decision of the United States Supreme Court in *Plessy v. Ferguson*. This case held that government could require the separation of the races so long as the facilities provided to each group were equal. In reality, "separate but equal" meant separation but not equality for black Americans. It was only with the 1954 Supreme Court case of *Brown v. Board of Education* and the enactment of the Civil Rights Act of 1964 that racial segregation was gradually brought to an end in this country.

Voting rights in the United States were also restricted in 1900. Despite the Fifteenth Amendment to the Constitution that protected African Americans from being denied the right to vote because of their race, very few voted in the American South. Devious legal schemes, intimidation, and violence kept most African Americans from voting in this region of the nation. It was not until after the passage of the Voting Rights Act of 1965 that blacks were freely able to vote in the South.

Similarly, few women voted in the United States at the beginning of the twentieth century. Although women had been granted the right to vote in a number of states, no constitutional provision existed to bar the states from denying them the right to vote. That changed in 1920 with the adoption of the Nineteenth Amendment. In the decades since this change occurred, more and more women have participated in American politics. Indeed, in recent presidential elections, more women have voted than men.

In 1900, United States senators were chosen by the state legislatures. Most often this meant that a few influential state political leaders made these important decisions. In 1913, the Seventeenth Amendment to the Constitution was adopted, making United States senators popularly elected by the voters in each state.

Finally, in 1900, there was little in the way of social legislation to protect Americans when they became unemployed, disabled, ill, or when they retired. They were forced to depend on relatives or on charity provided by churches and other private organizations. The country did not even have child labor laws to protect children from working long hours in factories and mines. Although some European countries had established social security systems by 1900—Germany, for example—it was not until 1935 that the United States adopted legislation that established the Social Security retirement system. Later in the same decade, Congress also enacted laws that established the maximum number of hours a person could work each week, created a minimum wage, outlawed child labor, and formulated a program of unemployment insurance. And it was not until the 1960s that Congress passed legislation that provided government programs of medical care for the elderly and the poor.

The fact that in the twentieth century the United States eliminated much of the blight of racial and gender discrimination and created a safety net of social legislation does not mean that we have solved all of our problems. Much remains to be done to eliminate the remaining traces of discrimination in our society. Further, perhaps 30 percent of the people living in the United States do not have any medical insurance. We are a rich nation that should be able to provide health protection for all of our citizens.

To enumerate two problems—discrimination and the lack of medical insurance for many people—that have not yet been solved is not to suggest that there are no other difficulties confronting the nation in this new century. The economic gap between rich and poor that exists in the United States today is not a healthy condition for our democracy. Other shortcomings in our society exist that have not yet been identified. Their discovery is the work of coming generations, including the generation that is currently attending America's colleges and universities.

In writing each edition of this textbook I have always attempted to keep students in the forefront of my thinking. It has been my goal to write a book that is both readable and interesting to undergraduates. Without these qualities, there is small hope that its readers will develop a concern for this nation's governmental system and its public problems. Although I have attempted to interest students in American government, I have never been willing to lower the intellectual level of the book below what I believe to be appropriate for an introductory college level course.

I would like to thank Professor Cynthia A. Roberts, a colleague of mine in the Political Science Department of Hunter College, for providing invaluable help to me in the writing of the chapter on foreign affairs. My work has also been aided by the contributions of the Prentice Hall reviewers who offered suggestions for improving the quality of the book: Janet Campbell, Mt. Hood Community College; Paul Goren, Arizona State University; Thomas Keating, Arizona State University; E. Terrence Jones, University of Missouri-St. Louis; David Steiniche, Missouri Western State College; Robert Ballinger, South Texas Community College; Joanna L. Briganti, Monroe County Community College; Jennifer B. Clark, South Texas Community College; Chris Bourdouvalis, Augusta State University; Steven J. Shone, South Texas Community College; and Ann Kelleher, Pacific Lutheran University. Needless to say, I assume all responsibility for any errors of fact that might be present in this textbook.

WALTER E. VOLKOMER

LIST OF SUPPLEMENTS

For the Instructor

INSTRUCTOR'S MANUAL For each chapter, a summary, review of major concepts, lecture suggestions and topic outlines, suggestions for classroom discussions, additional resource materials, and a detailed content outline for lecture planning are provided.

TEST ITEM FILE Thoroughly reviewed and revised to ensure the highest level of quality and accuracy, the test item file offers over 1000 multiple-choice, true/false, and essay questions covering factual, conceptual, and applied information from the text.

PRENTICE HALL TEST GENERATOR A computerized version of the test item file, this program allows full editing of the questions and the addition of instructor-generated test items. Other special features include random generation, scrambling question order, and test preview before printing. Available in Windows and Macintosh formats.

AMERICAN GOVERNMENT TRANSPARENCIES, SERIES VI AND VII Over 100 four-color transparency acetates reproduce illustrations, charts, and maps taken from the text as well as from additional sources.

PRENTICE HALL CUSTOM VIDEO: HOW A BILL BECOMES A LAW This 25-minute video chronicles an environmental law in Massachusetts—from its start as one citizen's concern to its passage in Washington, D.C. Students see step-by-step the process of how a bill becomes a law. Contact your local Prentice Hall representative for details.

FILMS FOR THE HUMANITIES AND SOCIAL SCIENCES With a qualifying order of textbooks from Prentice Hall, you may select from a high quality library of political science videos from Films for the Humanities and Social Sciences. Contact your local Prentice Hall representative for a complete listing.

For the Student

REVIEW GUIDE AND LECTURE COMPANION This study aid includes chapter review tests and lecture notetaking pages designed to reinforce information in the text. It provides a thorough study and review resource to help students develop a greater understanding of American government and politics.

THE PRENTICE HALL GUIDE TO EVALUATING ONLINE RESOURCES WITH RESEARCH NAVIGATOR™ This timely supplement provides an introduction to the Internet and the numerous political sites on the World Wide Web. The guide keeps students and instructors abreast of the latest news and information and helps students create top quality research papers. The guide is available free to students upon adoption and purchase of *American Government*. Contact your local Prentice Hall representative for information.

Media Resources

COMPANION WEBSITE™ This unique resource tool makes it easy for students and instructors to integrate the text with an online experience. The site is a comprehensive resource that is organized according to the chapters within the text. It features a variety of learning and teaching modules, including self-tests, surveys, destinations to other sites, news updates, and a faculty section with illustrations from the text available for downloading into PowerPoint slides and other resources. Address: **http://www.prenhall.com/volkomer**.

POLISIM VERSION 2.0 This new CD-ROM of multi-level simulations requires students to make politically charged decisions based on the evaluation of real data and information obtained from a variety of authentic sources. Using information such as real election results, demographics, maps, and voting score cards of actual senators, students complete simulations in a highly interactive, full multimedia environment. The **PoliSim2** CD-ROM is included free with all new copies of *American Government* and is referenced to chapters on tabs included in the textbook.

RESEARCH NAVIGATOR™ This exciting new Internet resource helps students make the most of their research time. From finding the right articles and journals to citing sources, drafting and writing effective papers, and completing research assignments, **Research Navigator**™ simplifies and streamlines the entire process. Free access to the site is available when packaged with *American Government*. Contact your local sales representative for more details or take a tour on the web at **http://www.researchnavigator.com**.

PoliSim2

Think Politics Is Just a Game? Think Again.

Prentice Hall is proud to bring you—included free with this textbook—**PoliSim: Simulations in American Government, Version 2.0.** With this unique CD-ROM, you will experience the power of real politics with fully animated and interactive simulations in American Government. **PoliSim2** presents you with politically charged situations where the outcome depends on the choices YOU make.

PoliSim2 challenges you with multi-level simulations that require you to make simple and complex decisions based on information drawn from

- REAL election results
- REAL demographics, including gender, age, education level, race, and income data
- REAL maps, including ones that show political persuasion (Democratic and Republican) for specific areas
- REAL score cards from actual Senate members showing their votes on public interest issues . . . and much more!

Based on real situations discussed in the textbook, **PoliSim2** encourages you to experience hands-on application of the concepts presented. **PoliSim2** gives you the political power to

- Act as one of America's founding fathers to make decisions that impact the country's political development for centuries to come
- Balance the nation's budget to gain popularity in the public eye
- Spend foreign aid dollars most effectively to reduce wars, terrorism, drug trade, and brutal dictatorship, and to improve the U.S. standing from an international perspective
- Get legislation passed by lobbying the Senate on a realistic budget and time frame—and use links to actual U.S. senators' websites that include their real views . . . and much more!

PoliSim2 Contents

The Map of Freedom
The Constitution
Political Culture and Ideology
Political Opinion
The Political Horizon
Interest Groups
Election 2004
The Great American Divide
Running for Congress
Who's Got the Power?
Presidential Greatness: How Do We Judge Them?
Bureaucracy
Balancing the Nation's Checkbook: What Can You Get for $4 Trillion?
Civil Liberties
Travel the Civil Rights Timeline
The Impact of Foreign Aid

Read this text. Experience the simulations on the free **PoliSim2** CD-ROM that accompanies this text. Become an informed decision-maker who considers the impact of political decisions before they are made. After all, isn't that what politics is all about?

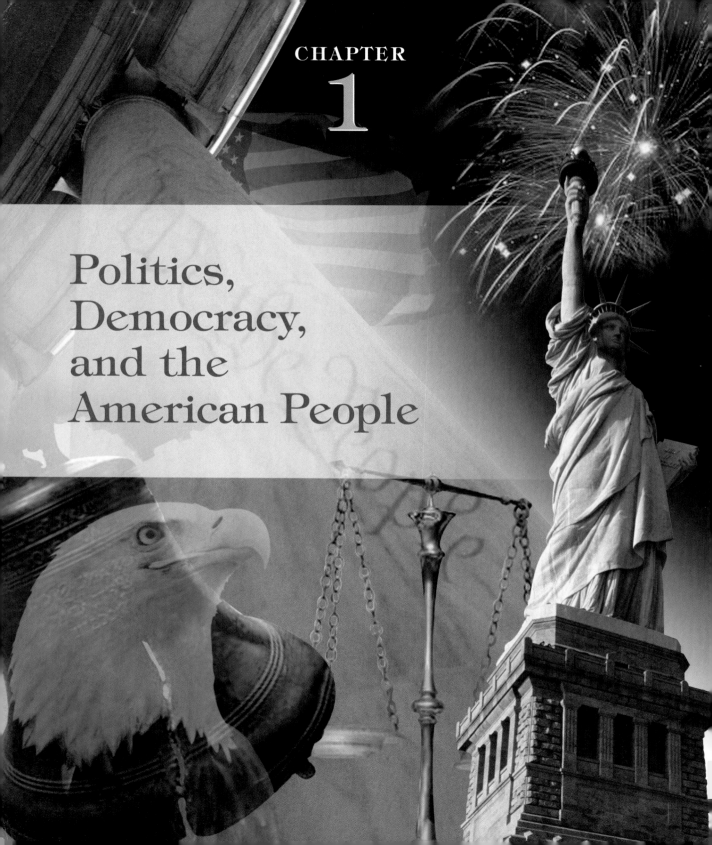

Politics, Democracy, and the American People

The main purpose of this book is not to provide answers to today's political questions; instead, it is to convey basic facts about the structure and functioning of American government. Like Tocqueville, the young French aristocrat who made the comment quoted here after visiting the United States in the early 1830s, the book will examine "the image of a democracy"—not only its governmental structure but also its politics and its people. Armed with this information, you will be better able to understand—and perhaps participate in—American politics.

"I confess that in America I saw more than America; I sought there the image of a democracy itself, with its inclinations, its character, its prejudices, and its passions, in order to learn what we have to fear or to hope from its progress."

—*Alexis de Tocqueville,*
Democracy in America

THE NATURE OF POLITICS

Politics has been defined as the art of governing humanity by deceiving it. It has also been seen as the conduct of public affairs for private advantage. Such definitions reflect a view of politics as synonymous with deception and dishonesty. Many Americans today do not trust either government or politicians. It was not always so. In 1964, 76 percent of Americans said that they had confidence that the federal government would do "what is right" most of the time. By the mid-1990s this figure had dropped to only 22 percent.[1] And in 1999, when Americans were asked whether they "trust politicians when they talk about social and moral values," 42 percent indicated that they strongly distrusted politicians, and another 33 percent said that they generally distrusted them.[2]

The September 11, 2001, attack on the United States by terrorists produced a dramatic turnabout in public sentiment toward government. In the months after the attack, opinion polls showed that 57 percent of Americans believed that the federal government could be trusted to do what is right all or most of the time. But by May 2002 the level of trust in government had declined to 40 percent.[3]

Negative ideas about politicians and government may arise in good measure from a tendency to confuse politics as a whole with the activities of certain politicians. Examples of scandal and corruption in government increase the prevalence of this type of cynicism toward politics. To people who hold this view, all political activities are suspect, and politics serves as a convenient whipping boy for the problems and wrongs of society.

Not everyone is cynical about politics, however. Many people have a different and more positive view of the subject. Most political leaders and private citizens show genuine interest in bringing about needed changes and improving the welfare of all members of

1

society. By demonstrating that the actions of concerned citizens can have a positive effect in solving social and political problems, they have encouraged others to develop a favorable opinion of politics and to participate in political activity at the local, state, or national level.

Politics and Power

More than sixty years ago, political scientist Harold Lasswell spoke of **politics** as the study of "who gets what, when, and how."[4] A generation later, another political scientist refined that definition when he described politics as a process by which values are authoritatively allocated for a society—in other words, a method of deciding who gets what.[5] These definitions go to the heart of what politics is about and point to the concerns of political scientists as they study this area of human activity.

Closely related to the concept of politics is that of **political power**—the ability to influence the political behavior of others. Political power is sought for the sake of the rewards and benefits that can be gained from it. A political candidate tries to influence voters to win an election; an interest group tries to influence key members of Congress in the hope that they will support or oppose a particular bill. Politics, then, is concerned with the use of power to achieve specific benefits and with the way in which those benefits are distributed among individuals and groups in society.

We all deal with "politics" in our daily lives—office politics, school politics, family politics. These are the areas in which ordinary people compete for personal advantage. The power at stake in such contests is usually limited, and the size of the group affected is relatively small. The politics that are of interest to political scientists, on the other hand, have an impact on large numbers of people and involve significant amounts of power. These activities can—and often do—affect the entire society.

Any person or group can seek to exercise political power. For example, church groups normally engage in nonpolitical activities of a spiritual and social nature. But some churches have become active in opposing or supporting legalized abortion, which is a political issue as well as a moral and ethical one.

The Bases of Political Power

In discussing political power, we are not referring to power that is based solely on force or coercion. Instead, we are referring to *legitimate* power. A political official can exercise legitimate power only if most people accept that power and believe that the rules and decisions stemming from it are right and proper. According to the German sociologist Max Weber (1864–1920), **legitimacy** in politics is derived from three sources: tradition, charisma, and legality.[6]

Weber believed that positions of power become legitimate over time; that is, they become *traditional*. American political parties provide an example of this kind of legitimacy. The U.S. Constitution contains no mention of a two-party system or even of political parties, yet a two-party system has existed almost from the beginning of the nation's history. So-called third parties have rarely won elections and have had a very limited effect on election results.

Weber also stressed the importance of personality in creating political

The popular search engine "Google," whose corporate offices are shown here, symbolizes the rapidly developing information technology of the twenty-first century.

legitimacy. The great popularity of some leaders is due in part to their personal magnetism, or *charisma*. Such twentieth-century political leaders as Dwight Eisenhower, Winston Churchill, and Charles de Gaulle acquired acceptance for their ideas through sheer force of personality. Some—such as the Reverend Martin Luther King, Jr.—held no formal political position but because of their charisma were able to win the loyalty of large numbers of people not only to themselves but also to their ideas.

Finally, Weber pointed to the importance of law in creating legitimacy. Some political activities are considered legitimate simply because they are legal—that is, based on an accepted body of laws. In the United States, the written constitutions of the national and state governments and the laws passed by Congress and state and local legislatures provide the foundation on which legitimate authority is exercised by government over the people.

Politics and Government

It is important to understand that *government* is not the same as *politics*. The term **government** refers to the institutions and processes by which rules are made and enforced for all members of a society. Congress, the Supreme Court, and the president are all parts of the government of the United States. They have the power to make decisions or rules for all the members of society, and they have the power to enforce those decisions. For the government to exercise this power over citizens, the citizens must accept it as legitimate. Without such acceptance, a government cannot function effectively. In contrast, the governing units of labor unions, schools, churches, and social clubs are far more limited both in their jurisdictions and in their power to enforce their regulations.

The Reverend Martin Luther King, Jr. (1929–1968), minister, civil rights le[...] and recipient of the 1964 Nobel Pe[...] Prize.

A key phrase in the definition of government is *all members of a society.* If a few people break the rules of a union or a club, at worst they may be dismissed from the organization; after that, its rules no longer apply to them. Nonmembers do not view the organization as having legitimate power over them. But if the same people break the rules of government, they can be punished whether they agree with those rules or not.

Individuals and groups may be deeply involved in politics but not be part of government. A labor union, a corporation, or a group concerned with protecting civil liberties and civil rights can influence government decisions that will affect society as a whole. These organizations, therefore, have political power but cannot make and enforce rules for all members of society.

THE MEANING OF DEMOCRACY

Now that we have distinguished between government and politics, let us turn to the nature of government in the United States. Most Americans would agree that their nation is a democracy, but few have a clear understanding of what that means. **Democracy** is a form of government in which the policy decisions of the government are based on the freely given consent of the people and the people are guaranteed certain basic rights. For the most part, democracy in the United States is **representative democracy** as opposed to **direct democracy.** In a direct democracy, each voter is able to participate directly and personally in the decision-making process. The town meeting is a form of direct democracy that has survived from colonial times in some small rural areas of New England. In this system of government, citizens gather to make decisions for their community.

Twentieth-century versions of direct democracy include the processes of referendum, initiative, and recall, which are widely used in the western states of

CLOSE-UP

BALLOT INITIATIVES

Ballot initiatives are a contemporary form of direct democracy. The initiative has its origins in the progressive reform movement of the early twentieth century. The progressives had a deep distrust of professional politicians, and in many states they succeeded in creating a device that gives the people the ability to change state policies. In its purest form, ballot initiatives occur when the required number of registered voters in a state sign a petition supporting a particular proposal. The proposal is then automatically placed on the election ballot and, if it obtains the backing of a majority of voters, it becomes state policy.

Today, twenty-four of the fifty states permit the use of some form of ballot initiative. The majority of initiatives take place in Alaska, Nevada, Oregon, Washington, and California. Some initiatives deal with relatively minor issues, and many initiatives are not approved. But the voters in states that provide for the use of initiatives have adopted policies on important and often very controversial issues. Most of these states have imposed term limits on members of the state legislatures. In recent years Alaska, Nevada, Oregon, and Washington have legalized the use of marijuana for medical use. Voters in California and Washington ended the use of all racial and sexual preference programs by the state in hiring and contracting and in college and university admissions. California voters have also barred the use of bilingual education programs in public schools, permitted casino gambling, and restricted the use of the word *marriage* in state laws to unions between men and women.

this nation at both the state and the local levels. Where *referendums* are permitted, voters may vote for or against the adoption of particular laws. The *initiative* system permits citizens to place a proposal on the ballot by obtaining a required number of petition signatures; then the proposal is voted on in the next election. In a *recall,* citizens collect signatures on a petition to recall a public official; if enough signatures are obtained, a vote is held on whether that official may continue to hold office.

In a representative democracy (sometimes referred to as *republican government*), citizens transfer their decision-making power to people whom they elect to represent them. These elected representatives are held responsible for their official acts through the election system. Representative democracy thus requires that there be regularly scheduled elections that cannot be postponed or suspended by the government. It also requires the freedom to discuss political ideas and the freedom to form political parties and contest elections. The American social and economic theorist Joseph Schumpeter (1883–1950) once defined modern democracy as an "institutional arrangement for arriving at political decisions in which individuals acquire the power to decide by means of a competitive struggle for the people's vote."[7]

The Bases of Democracy

SELF-GOVERNMENT   A basic principle of American democracy is the belief that people are capable of governing themselves. This idea of **self-government** was set forth by the British philosopher John Locke (1632–1704) in his *Two Treatises of Government,* which had a strong influence on the political leaders of eighteenth-century America. Locke believed that people are rational enough to

Town meeting in Hebron, Maine. Town meetings are a form of direct democracy.

perceive and understand the higher law—the so-called *natural law*—that pro-vides a standard of human conduct. This leads to the recognition of certain *natural rights,* such as the rights to life, liberty, and property. These rights exist separately from society and government and, as such, should not be abridged by any political state; the state, in fact, exists solely to protect them. Locke's views on law were in sharp contrast to those of many other political and legal theorists, who viewed law as a creation of people and government, not as a system derived from nature.

Locke not only stressed the natural rights of all people but also believed that the individual has the reasoning ability needed to participate in a govern-ment established to protect those rights. He understood that some restraints must be placed on people's conduct. But he rejected the idea that people are not capa-ble of governing themselves and that strong government is necessary to control their activities and maintain order.

The men who drafted the United States Constitution in 1787 believed that people were rational enough to govern themselves and did not need a king or a tyrant to regulate their conduct. Despite that belief, however, they were not overly optimistic about human nature, tending to agree with the political ideas of two other British writers: Thomas Hobbes (1588–1679) and David Hume (1711–1776). To varying degrees, both Hobbes and Hume were skeptical of human reason. They stressed the role of passion and self-interest in human behavior and the need for a government strong enough to control these irrational impulses. Thus, James Madi-son, the most important figure in the writing of the United States Constitution, stated his views on human nature and government as follows:

John Locke (1632–1704), British philosopher and author of *Two Treatises of Government* (1689), which strongly influenced the thought of late-eighteenth-century America and the writing of the United States Constitution.

But what is government itself, but the greatest of all reflections on human nature? If men were angels, no government would be necessary. If angels were to govern men, neither external nor internal controls on government would be necessary. In framing a government which is to be administered by men over men, the great difficulty lies in this: you must first enable the government to control the governed; and in the next place oblige it to control itself.[8]

THE SOCIAL CONTRACT　Locke's belief that people are capable of governing themselves became a basic principle of American democracy. But why should there be a government at all? Why not simply let each person govern himself or herself?

Locke's political philosophy was based on the idea that early in human existence people lived in a "state of nature" in which neither organized society nor government existed. That state was unsatisfactory precisely because it was unorganized. There were no laws, judges, or penalties to prevent some people or groups from oppressing others. Eventually this chaotic situation led to the formation of *civil society,* in which there exists a method to preserve the property rights of each individual—"that is, his life, liberty, and estate. . . ."

Those who are united into one body and have a common established law and judicature to appeal to, with authority to decide controversies between them and punish offenders, are in civil society one with another.[9]

According to Locke, civil society was created by a **social contract,** an agreement among members of the society in which they accepted existing laws and penalties as binding. A second contract created government. It went into effect when a majority of the people agreed on the form of government that was to be created by the contract.

Government, in Locke's view, can possess only limited powers. It is established to protect people's natural rights to life, liberty, and property. If the government should fail to do this, the people have the right to replace it. They can then create a new government that will perform its proper function of protecting individuals and not oppressing them. This right was eloquently expressed by Thomas Jefferson (1743–1826) in the Declaration of Independence, which set forth the philosophical basis for the right of the American colonies to assert their independence from Great Britain and stated the many grievances that justified that action.

> To secure these Rights, Governments are instituted among Men, deriving their just Powers from the Consent of the Governed; that, whenever any Form of Government becomes destructive of these Ends, it is the Right of the People to alter or abolish it, and institute new Government, laying its Foundation on such Principles, and organizing its Powers in such Forms, as to them shall seem most likely to effect their Safety and Happiness.

MAJORITY RULE   According to Locke's social contract theory, a person who lives in a civil society no longer has to fear the arbitrary use of power by other people, as was the case in the state of nature. But Locke did not believe that people are totally free in a civil society. They are now governed by the will of the majority. Locke believed that the decisions of government should be based on this principle. The doctrine of **majority rule** is an extension of his idea that people are able to make rational decisions and that they understand what policies would best serve their interests.

The concept of majority rule has been criticized, however. A well-known challenge to this idea came from the French nobleman and social historian Alexis de Tocqueville, who was concerned about the possibility of a "tyranny of the majority." In the course of his extensive travels in the United States in the early 1830s, Tocqueville observed American democracy in operation throughout the country. In his brilliant analysis of the American political system, *Democracy in America,* he warned that

> if ever the free institutions of America are destroyed, that event may be attributed to the omnipotence of the majority, which may at some future time urge the minorities to desperation and oblige them to have recourse to physical force.[10]

For Tocqueville, absolute power was a danger in any form of government:

> When I see that the right and the means of absolute command are conferred on any power whatever, be it called a people or a king, an aristocracy or a democracy, a monarchy or a republic, I say there is the germ of tyranny, and I seek to live elsewhere, under other laws.[11]

It has been argued that one wise and benevolent leader, or a group of such leaders, would be better qualified to decide public policy than a majority. This argument is based on the idea that people do not have the ability to make rational decisions about public affairs. It cannot be denied that many citizens vote on the basis of a candidate's appearance or religious and ethnic background rather than on the basis of informed judgment. Supporters of majority rule argue, however, that error and injustice are much less likely under a system of majority rule.

Alexis de Tocqueville (1805–1859), French liberal politician, historian, and author of *Democracy in America* (1835).

Although the public may often be uninformed or misinformed about political issues, it can quickly become involved and even outraged if it believes an injustice or a wrong has taken place.

Majority rule as a governing principle may sometimes result in unwise decisions. Unlike nondemocratic systems of government, however, it does permit the correction of errors and the removal of ineffective public officials from office. Moreover, it can be argued that a correct policy is more likely to emerge from the opinions of many than from the judgment of a few leaders.

MINORITY RIGHTS   At his first inauguration in 1801, Thomas Jefferson made the following statement: "All too well, bear in mind the sacred principle, that though the will of the majority is in all cases to prevail, that will, to be rightful, must be reasonable; that the minority possess their equal rights, which equal laws must protect." Although majority rule prevents tyranny by the few, the majority can violate the rights of individuals and groups in society. In a democracy, majority rule is legitimate only if it respects and protects the rights of the minority. The preservation of **minority rights** does not, of course, mean that the policies of the minority must be accepted by the majority. Rather, it means that the minority must be granted certain basic freedoms. These basic freedoms are what people usually mean when they link democracy and liberty. *Liberty* means freedom to express one's opinions even if they differ from those of the majority; freedom to worship—or not worship—as one chooses; freedom to join social, economic, or political organizations of almost any description; and many other such freedoms. Even the freedom to travel from one place to another, both within one's own country and outside it, is a right of Americans that is not possessed by citizens of some nondemocratic nations.

LIMITED GOVERNMENT The idea of limited government is closely related to the belief in minority rights. Both Locke and the political leaders of late-eighteenth-century America stressed the need to place limits on the power of government, even when that government is a democracy in which the majority rules. The idea of limited government has a long history in this country. It was very popular in colonial America and during the decades after the end of the Revolutionary War. Today Americans who distrust "big government" and the concentration of governmental power in Washington are expressing the same belief in the value of limited government.

The idea of limited government is associated with the principle of *constitutionalism,* which holds that the powers of government should be defined and limited in a written document that serves as the basic law of the land. The written constitution outlines the institutions of the government, their relationship to one another, and their specific powers. It puts limits on the authority of the government, and it may also guarantee certain rights to the individual. The basic structure and power of government created by the constitution can be altered only through a formal amendment process that is also stated in the document. A written constitution thus attempts to achieve the goal of limited government by stating the limits and making them legally binding on all officials of the government. The form of government that exists in the United States is often referred to as a **constitutional democracy,** meaning one that places written legal limits on the power of the majority to act.

The United States Constitution is an attempt to put into practice the ideas of limited government, constitutionalism, and minority rights. Many of its sections define and limit the power of government; others stress the need to protect the rights of individuals and minorities. Nowhere is this more evident than in the Bill of Rights—the first ten amendments to the Constitution. Adopted in 1791, two years after the Constitution was ratified, the Bill of Rights sought to protect the individual against abuses of the power of government, even if the government had the support of the majority. The First Amendment, for example, guarantees freedom of speech, freedom of the press, the right to assemble, and the right to petition the government. The Fourth, Fifth, and Sixth Amendments grant important rights to people who are accused of having committed crimes, such as the right to a trial by jury and the right to have an attorney. These rights, usually referred to as **civil liberties,** will be discussed in detail in Chapter 11.

DEMOCRATIC INSTITUTIONS To be practical, democratic principles have to be translated into actual institutions. The United States Constitution established a government with three branches—executive, legislative, and judicial—run by officials with specific terms of office who were to be chosen in specific ways. It set forth the relationships among the three branches, as well as their powers and limitations, and created a system of elections. In addition, it divided power between a central government and the state governments.

Not all democratic governments take this form. Often power is centralized in a single national government and not divided along geographic lines. Nor do all democracies separate the powers of the government into three branches. In Great Britain, for example, the legislature (Parliament) is supreme and the executive and judicial functions are legally subordinate to it.

The complex system of separation of powers created by the United States Constitution is largely due to the influence of the eighteenth-century French philosopher Montesquieu (1689–1755). The basic functions of government (legislative, executive, and judicial) had been recognized by political theorists before the eighteenth century, but it was Montesquieu who argued that if any two of these functions were held by the same person or group, political liberties would be destroyed. He therefore advocated that the three functions of government be separated. The authors of the U.S. Constitution adopted this theory of government. The ways in which they built Montesquieu's ideas into the Constitution will be discussed more fully in Chapter 2.

FREE ELECTIONS Free elections are essential in a government based on the will of the people. In the United States, elections are regularly scheduled and open to citizens over the age of 18 who meet certain brief residency requirements. In addition, all states conduct primary elections, in which citizens nominate the candidates who will run in the general election.

In the course of the nation's history, the right to vote has been granted to increasing numbers of people. At first it was restricted to white male property owners; later it was granted to white males who did not own property, then to blacks, to women, and in the 1970s to 18-year-olds.

Another important aspect of the American electoral system is the secret ballot. Voters may be urged to vote for a particular candidate, but they cannot be forced to do so. The frequency of elections is also significant. Presidential elections are held every fourth year; U.S. senators are elected every six years, and members of the House of Representatives every two years. This means that elected officials must repeatedly win the approval of their constituents and respond to the challenges of opposing candidates.

Free elections fulfill several functions. They give citizens a chance to select policy-making officials and to express their preferences on public policy, and they encourage elected officials to be responsive to the desires of their constituents. Clearly, these functions are basic to a representative democracy. An additional effect of the electoral process is that it solves the difficult problem of determining how the power of government will pass from one group of rulers to another. If the election system is operating properly, its results will be accepted by the officials who have been removed from power and by the citizens who supported the losing candidates. Nations that rely on elections avoid violence as a means of replacing rulers.

AN ORGANIZED OPPOSITION One feature that distinguishes a democracy from other forms of government is the presence of an organized opposition that is free to criticize people in positions of power. In the United States this is done primarily by **political parties**—organized groups that support candidates for public office. When the Democrats control the presidency, for example, the Republicans serve as the organized opposition; they examine the policies of the Democratic administration and attempt to persuade the public that their programs would be superior.

Some critics of the American two-party system claim that the parties do not offer real policy choices and thus do not truly oppose each other. Whether the political parties differ significantly is a matter of some debate, but one cannot deny that each party performs the valuable service of criticizing the other, especially at election time. The party in power is highly sensitive to accusations by the opposition, and such charges are answered—not silenced, as they are in nations that do not possess a democratic form of government.

FREE EXPRESSION OF IDEAS The First Amendment to the U.S. Constitution guarantees freedom of speech, press, and assembly and the right to petition government. The freedom to express opinions on issues and to hear the opinions of others is what makes democratic dialogue possible. Such exchanges of opinion can range from presidential press conferences to informal discussions among friends. In the United States the primary channel for the discussion and debate of politics is the mass media—newspapers, magazines, television, and radio.

Although political discussion may not bring all the facts of an issue into the open, it gives people a basis for making decisions, forces them to think about public problems in new ways, challenges them to defend their points of view, and encourages them to develop more rational opinions. Moreover, the free expression of ideas forces public officials to defend their policies to the citizenry. The result may be not only responsive government but a more responsible public as well.

EQUALITY Like the concept of liberty, that *of equality* is often mentioned in connection with democracy. The concept of equality is one of the noblest and perhaps least understood aspects of democratic theory. In a democracy, equality should apply in many areas of human life: equality before the law, equality of political rights, equality of economic and social opportunity, and equality of economic condition. Democratic theory has always stressed legal and political equality and the right of each person to have an equal chance to advance economically and socially. The idea that economic equality is necessary for the existence of a democratic society—that every person should have an adequate income and there should not be wide disparities in wealth between members of a society—is fairly recent. It became an important idea only in the twentieth century.[12]

During the 1990s the U.S. economy grew at a steady rate, and most Americans found themselves much better off economically at the end of this decade. But the prosperity did not extend to all segments of the society. In 2001 the Census Bureau reported that 31 million people, or 11.3 percent of the nation's total population, lived below the official poverty line (defined as $17,960 for a family of four.)[13] While this number is disconcerting, Census Bureau information indicates that the total number of poor people in the United States actually dropped in the five years between 1996 and 2001. In 1996 the Bureau reported that 36.5 million people, or 13.7 percent of all Americans, lived below the poverty level.[14] This decline in poverty took place even though a record number of immigrants came to this country during the 1990s, and most of them arrived here poor.

Income equality, however, was not a matter of concern to the nation's founders. When Thomas Jefferson, the author of the Declaration of Independence, wrote that "all men are created equal," he was not expressing the belief that all people are equal in intellectual ability or that they should be equal in income and possessions. The equality Jefferson spoke of was *a moral equality,* one that would give each individual equality of opportunity. This kind of equality would

Thomas Jefferson (1743–1826), diplomat, philosopher, author of the Declaration of Independence, vice president (1797–1801), and the third president of the United States (1801–1809).

not result in equality of wealth or position. It seemed obvious to Jefferson that people are born with different talents and that they respond differently to the opportunities life offers them. But he believed strongly that people should not be kept from realizing their full potential by arbitrary laws or by distinctions based on factors like religion or family background.

Jefferson's view of equality included equality under the law. Jefferson also believed in broad political rights, such as the right to vote and the right to express political ideas. It should be noted, however, that like other late-eighteenth-century thinkers, he did not apply the concept of equality to all human beings. In particular, black slaves and women did not share in the legal and political equality possessed by American citizens.

Abraham Lincoln (1809–1865) expressed a view of equality similar to Jefferson's in a speech given while he was a member of the House of Representatives on June 26, 1857:

> I think the authors of [the Declaration of Independence] intended to include all men, but they did not intend to declare all men equal in all respects. They did not mean to say all were equal in color, size, intellect, moral developments, or social capacity. They defined with tolerable distinctness, in what respects they did consider men created equal—equal in "certain inalienable rights, among which are life, liberty, and the pursuit of happiness." . . . They meant to set up a standard maxim for free society, which would be familiar to all, and revered by all; constantly looked to, constantly labored for, and even though never perfectly attained, constantly approximated, and thereby constantly spreading and deepening its influence, and augmenting the happiness and value of life to all people of all colors everywhere.

Some observers have expressed the fear that an excessive devotion to equality in a democratic society can lead to the loss of liberty. Tocqueville, for example, believed that democracy is more strongly linked to equality than to liberty and that people might tend to choose equality at the expense of liberty. "Equality every day confers a number of small enjoyments on every man," and as a result "the passion for equality penetrates. . .into men's hearts, expands there, and fills them entirely." Any challenge to equality will arouse their fury and distract them so that they will not notice "freedom escaping from their grasp."[15]

UNIVERSAL EDUCATION   Thomas Jefferson claimed that a nation cannot be both ignorant and free. An early advocate of public education, he defended the cost of such a system on the grounds that it would prepare citizens to make wiser political choices and would instill in them the values of democracy. A few nations, however, have succeeded in maintaining a democratic political system despite widespread illiteracy and poverty; India is a good example. But such conditions only make the task of establishing and maintaining democratic institutions more difficult.

The importance of education to democratic government is evident. Democracy requires that citizens have some understanding of public issues and the ability to make electoral choices on the basis of that knowledge. It also requires tolerance, respect for the rights of others, and the ability to compromise on public issues. These are attitudes that are developed through education. For poor people in America, therefore, the quality of education is a matter of particular concern. Inadequate education acts as a major obstacle to an understanding of political issues, the ability to participate in the nation's political system, and the capacity to improve their economic and social participation in American society.

DEMOCRACY AND DIVERSITY

Democracy is said to have arisen in Athens in the fifth century B.C. There, for the first time in history, every citizen had an equal voice in government. But there is little similarity between democracy as it was practiced in ancient Athens and democracy as it exists in the United States today. For one thing, in Athens the privileges of democracy were granted only to free males, not to women or slaves. For another, Athens was a small, self-contained city-state, whereas the United States is an immense nation with a population whose diversity is almost beyond description.

Think of it! From a few small, rural, largely Protestant colonies with a fairly homogeneous population, the nation has expanded to cover an entire continent. Its population has grown by leaps and bounds and is likely to continue to do so in coming decades. As of August 4, 2004, the Census Bureau estimated that the population of the United States had grown to 293.8 million people, an increase of 12 million since the April 2000 census result. This came after a growth of over 33 million in the decade of the 1990s. The Census Bureau estimates that the American population will reach 337 million in 2025 and 403 million by 2050.[16]

The population is not growing at the same rate in all regions of the country. The most rapid increase is occurring in the West, with a 20 percent increase in population between 1990 and 2000. The two most rapidly growing states are Nevada, with a 66 percent increase, and Arizona with 40 percent. California had the largest numerical growth in population during this ten-year period—4.1 million people. The South placed second in regional growth with a 17 percent gain and

Immigration to the United States has reached one of its highest rates in American history in the past several decades. Here newly naturalized citizens take an oath of allegiance to the United States.

also had the biggest numerical gain of any area of the country—14.6 million people. Georgia, Texas, and Florida were the states in the South whose population grew at the fastest rate. Other parts of the country also grew in size but at a much slower rate. The Midwest increased by 8 percent and the Northeast by 6 percent.[17]

Another significant trend in the U.S. population is the shift from urban to suburban and metropolitan residence. The migration to the suburbs began immediately after World War II. By 1950 about one quarter of the population lived in suburbs, and by 1990 half of all Americans were suburban dwellers. This pattern of growth continued between 1990 and 2000. Metropolitan areas in the nation grew faster than non-metropolitan areas—14 percent to 10 percent. Metropolitan growth was especially strong in the South and West, which grew by about 19 percent. Metropolitan areas in the Midwest and Northeast also increased in size but at a much slower pace.[18]

Not only is the population growing but it is also aging. In 1900 about 4 percent of the population was over the age of 65, but by 1970 the proportion of elderly people had risen to 9 percent. The 2000 census showed that about 35 million Americans, or about 12.4 percent of the nation's population, were over the age of 65. But for the first time since the census has been taken, the rate of growth of the over 65 segment of the society was slower than that of the total

CLOSE-UP

HISPANIC AMERICANS

Hispanics are already the nation's largest minority group. They have come to the United States from many countries: Central and South America and from island nations in the Caribbean. By far the largest migration has come from Mexico (66 percent). The largest number of Hispanics have settled in the states of California, Texas, Florida, and New York, and in the large cities of Los Angeles, Chicago, Houston, New York, and Miami. These population trends have been evident for several decades. The most recent studies show that the Hispanic population is spreading into other parts of the United States. The fastest rates of dispersion have occurred in smaller metropolitan areas such as Dallas, Phoenix, Sacramento, Atlanta, and Raleigh-Durham.

Hispanic Americans are far from a homogeneous population, despite their treatment as a single group in census figures. In fact, Hispanics have come to the United States from twenty-two different nations. As a result, there are numerous sub-groups within the Hispanic population. The Cuban subgroup, centered in Miami, has different cultural traditions from those of the Puerto Ricans and Dominicans living in New York City or the Mexicans who predominate in Texas and California.

The political consequences of these population trends are already being felt. Between 1994 and 1999 the number of Hispanics registering to vote increased by 30 percent. Similarly, there has been an increase in the number of Hispanic elected and appointed officials, and both the Democratic and Republican parties have attempted to recruit more Hispanic voters as well as candidates to run for elective office. In states such as Florida, Texas, and California, Hispanic Americans have already become an important voting bloc. These trends will certainly continue in coming decades as the number of Americans with Hispanic backgrounds continues to grow.

population of the nation. Still, the median age of Americans increased between 1990 and 2000 from 32.9 to 35.3 percent.[19]

The U.S. population is not only expanding rapidly but is also becoming increasingly diverse. The largest ethnic and racial groups within the population are people of German, Irish, English, African American, Hispanic, and Italian ancestry. However, the percentage of foreign-born residents has risen rapidly in recent decades as millions of immigrants have arrived from the former Soviet Union, Mexico, the Philippines, the Dominican Republic, Korea, Vietnam, and China.[20]

The 2000 census showed that the largest minority group in the United States today are Hispanic/Latinos, who comprise 12.5 percent of the nation's population. They replaced African Americans as the largest group during the 1990s; today, African Americans are 12.3 percent of the population. Asians are the third largest minority group at 3.6 percent.[21] The Census Bureau estimates that while the African American population of the United States will increase only moderately to the year 2050, the Hispanic American population will more than double, and the Asian American population will almost triple.[22]

Like the population shifts described earlier and the aging of the population as a whole, the growing diversity of the population is having a tremendous impact on politics and government in the United States. Diversity creates special problems for a democracy; it leads to wide differences of opinion, making it difficult to obtain agreement on proposed solutions to political problems. Even Tocqueville, visiting the new nation more than 150 years ago, recognized this difficulty. "A confused clamor is heard on every side," he observed, "and a thousand simultaneous voices demand the immediate satisfaction of their social wants."[23] In sum, as we shall see throughout this book, the task of running a democracy as large and diverse as the United States is enormously challenging.

CONCLUSION

In this chapter we have described the philosophical bases of democratic government and sketched in general terms how the framers of the United States Constitution put those ideas into practice. We have also seen that in setting up a representative democracy based on a written constitution, the nation's founders did not merely establish a new political system. They believed that they were creating a better form of government because, for the first time, the rights of the citizen would be protected. By means of a written constitution that embodied such devices as the separation of powers, federalism, and a bill of rights, the nation's founders hoped to guarantee to each person freedom from the arbitrary exercise of governmental power.

We have also examined the roots of what political scientist Samuel P. Huntington has called the American creed: "liberty, equality, democracy, and the rule of law under a constitution."[24] Although this creed has been modified somewhat since it was first stated in the Declaration of Independence and the Constitution, its basic elements have not changed much in more than two centuries.

How has American democracy worked out in practice? Did the founders achieve their goal? In evaluating American democracy, we must keep in mind not only the intent of the founders but also the problems the nation faced at various times in its history. When we encounter instances in which democratic institutions have failed to protect the rights of the citizen or have failed to solve an important political, economic, or social problem, we must ask whether such failures are due to faults in the institutions of democracy, faults in human nature, or simply the difficulty of running a democracy in a nation as large as the United States.

QUESTIONS FOR THOUGHT

1. What is political power?
2. What is the difference between direct and representative democracy?
3. What are the main political ideas of John Locke, and how did they influence the framers of the United States Constitution?
4. Why are the principles of both majority rule and minority rights important in a democracy?

INTERNET ACTIVITY

Experiments in Direct Democracy: State Ballot Initiatives and Referenda. Go to **http://www.ncsl.org/public/ballotB.htm**. Select your home state. (Pick one if your state is not linked—California Proposition 215 will do.) Follow the link and review the actual text of the propositions. Choose one, go back to "Ballot Issues," and submit a query to see if the proposition passed or failed. Is direct democracy better than a republican form of government?

KEY TERMS

civil liberties
constitutional democracy
democracy
direct democracy
government

legitimacy
majority rule
minority rights
political parties
political power

politics
representative democracy
self-government
social contract

SUGGESTED READING

Crotty, William. ed. *The State of Democracy in America.* Washington, DC: Georgetown University Press, 2001.

Dahl, Robert A. *Democracy, Liberty, Equality.* New York: Oxford University Press, 1987.

———. *Democracy and Its Critics.* New Haven, CT: Yale University Press, 1989.

Frantzich, Stephen E. *Citizen Activism in a Cynical Age.* Lanham, MD: Rowman & Littlefield, 1999.

Hall, John A., and Charles Lindholm. *Is America Breaking Apart?* Princeton, Princeton University Press, 2001.

Hartz, Louis. *The Liberal Tradition in America.* New York: Harcourt, 1955.

Kingdon, John W. *America the Unusual.* New York: Worth, 1999.

Lipset, Seymour Martin. *American Exceptionalism: A Double-Edged Sword.* New York: Norton, 1996.

Lowi, Theodore J. *The End of Liberalism.* 2nd ed. New York: W.W. Norton & Co., 1979.

Nie, Norman H., Jane Junn, and Kenneth Stehlik-Barry. *Education and Democratic Citizenship in America.* Chicago: University of Chicago Press, 1996.

NOTES

1. University of Michigan National Election Study, 1958–1992. CBS/*New York Times* poll, October 1994.

2. *Wall Street Journal*/NBC poll, *Wall Street Journal,* June 24, 1999, p. A10.

3. Brookings Institute Press Release, "Post-9/11 Surge in Public Support of Government Reverses Course," May 30, 2002.

4. Harold D. Lasswell, *Politics: Who Gets What, When, How* (New York: McGraw-Hill, 1936).

5. David Easton, *The Political System* (New York: Knopf, 1953), pp. 129–34.

6. Max Weber, *The Theory of Social and Economic Organization,* trans. A. M. Henderson and Talcott Parsons (New York: Oxford University Press, 1947), p. 328.

7. Joseph Schumpeter, *Capitalism, Socialism, and Democracy,* 3rd ed. (New York: Harper, 1950), p. 269.

8. *The Federalist Papers,* No. 51.

9. John Locke, *The Second Treatise of Government* (New York: The Liberal Arts Press, 1952), pp. 48–49.

10. Alexis de Tocqueville, *Democracy in America,* vol. I, ed. Phillips Bradley (New York: Vintage, 1954), p. 279.

11. Ibid., p. 270.

12. See John Rawls, *A Theory of Justice* (Cambridge: Harvard University Press, 1971).

13. U.S. Bureau of the Census, *Poverty in the United States, 2000* (Washington, DC: 2001), p. 1; U.S. Bureau of the Census, *Poverty 2001* (Washington, DC: July 22, 2002).

14. U.S. Bureau of the Census, *Statistical Abstract of the United States, 1998,* 118th ed. (Washington, DC: 1998), Table 756, p. 477.

15. Tocqueville, *Democracy in America,* vol. II, pp. 101–2.

16. U.S. Bureau of the Census. Population Division, *Population Estimates* (Washington, DC: August 4, 2004). U.S. Bureau of the Census. Population Division, *Annual Projection of the Total Residency Population as of July 1, 1999 to 2100* (Washington, DC: 2001).

17. U.S. Bureau of the Census, *Census 2000 PHC-T-2: Ranking Tables for States: 1990 and 2000* (Washington, DC: 2001), Table 3, "States Ranked by Percentage Population Change: 1990 to 2000."

18. U.S. Bureau of the Census, *Census 2000 PHC-T-3: Ranking Tables for Metropolitan Areas: 1990 to 2000* (Washington, DC, 2001), Table 4, "Metropolitan Areas Ranked by Numeric Population Change: 1990 to 2000."

19. U.S. Bureau of the Census, *DP.1 Profile of General Demographic Characteristics: 2000* (Washington, DC: 2000).

20. U.S. Bureau of the Census, *Statistical Abstract of the*

United States, 2001, 121st ed. (Washington, DC: Government Printing Office, 2001), Table 7, p. 11.

21. U.S. Bureau of the Census, *Census 2000 PHC-T-1. Population by Race and Hispanic or Latino Origin for the United States* (Washington, DC: 2001), Table 3, "Population by Race Alone, Race in Combination Only, Race Alone or in Combination, and Hispanic or Latino Origin, for the United States: 2000."

22. *Statistical Abstract, 2001,* Table 15, p. 17.

23. Alexis de Tocqueville, *On Democracy, Revolution, and Society,* trans. J. Stone and S. Mennell (Chicago: University of Chicago Press, [1835] 1980), p. 78.

24. Samuel P. Huntington, *American Politics: The Promise of Disharmony* (Cambridge: Harvard University Press, Belknap Press, 1981), p. 14.

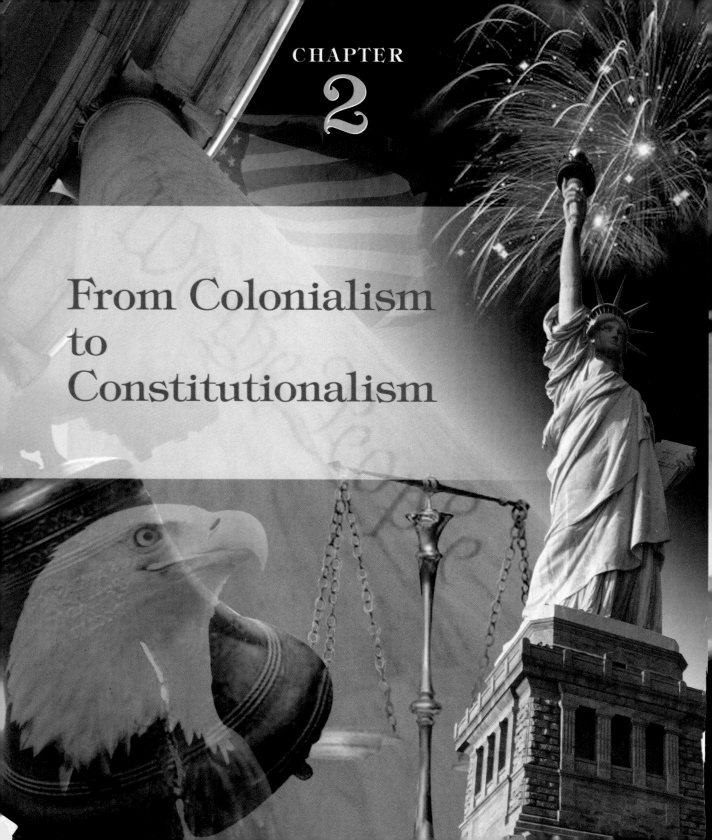

From Colonialism to Constitutionalism

How right Adams was, and how very wrong was King George! Every year for more than 225 years, the anniversary of the signing of the Declaration of Independence on July 4, 1776, has been celebrated "with shows, games, sports, guns, bells and illuminations." And the Declaration did indeed signify "deliverance." In a few paragraphs this unique document effectively ended British rule over the American colonies. True, the Revolutionary War would continue for another five years, but the tide had turned. The Declaration was followed by the drafting and adoption of the Articles of Confederation, and in 1787 by the writing of the United States Constitution. Colonialism had come to an end in the American states, although it would continue in other parts of the world until the second half of the twentieth century. But eventually the colonial empires ruled by Great Britain, France, Spain, and other European powers would disappear, and the right of self-government would become accepted in most parts of the globe. Far from a day on which "nothing of importance" took place, July 4, 1776, was a turning point in world history.

As we saw in Chapter 1, the American political experience had its roots in the traditions brought by the colonists from England in the seventeenth and eighteenth centuries. In fact, the colonists thought of themselves as English, and their ideas about politics, religion, law, and individual rights were rooted in their English background. The American legal system, for example, is derived from English ideas and practices. It is based on the English common law—a system of law built on judicial decisions and precedents that developed over many centuries.

Perhaps most important, the American political and legal system owes a tremendous debt to the English tradition of individual rights. According to the **Magna Charta** of 1215, the king was bound by the law and must respect the rights of his subjects. The **English Bill of Rights** of 1689 established basic guarantees, such as the right to trial by jury and the right to petition the

July 4, 1776 "Nothing of importance this day."

—*Diary of King George III of England*

"I am apt to believe that it [Independence Day] will be celebrated by succeeding generations as the great anniversary Festival. It ought to be commemorated, as the Day of Deliverance, by solemn acts of devotion to God Almighty. It ought to be solemnized with pomp and parade, with shows, games, sports, guns, bells and illuminations from one end of this continent to the other, from this time forward forever."

—*Letter from John Adams to his wife, Abigail, July 1776*

government. Thus, when the American colonists finally rebelled against British rule and demanded their rights, they were demanding that they be accorded the rights already possessed by English citizens.

THE ROAD TO INDEPENDENCE

The idea of a separate nation independent of English rule was not widely accepted by the colonists until just before the American Revolution, which began in 1775. There were, however, several instances in which the colonists cooperated in attempts to solve shared problems. These efforts were the first step along the road to independence.

Early Attempts at Cooperation

The first of the early efforts to cooperate occurred between 1643 and 1684, when four New England colonies formed the New England Confederation to deal with the danger of attacks by the Indians. Another attempt was made in 1754, when delegates from the Iroquois nation and several northern colonies met in Albany to discuss their common concerns. On his way to that meeting, Benjamin Franklin devised a proposal for colonial government known as the Albany Plan. The proposal called for the creation of a general government with the power to make treaties with the Native American tribes, to settle and purchase western lands, and to make war and peace and regulate trade with the Indians. But the British rulers of the colonies rejected Franklin's ideas, and the plan was never carried out.

After 1760 the cooperative efforts of the colonies were spurred by British policies, some of which were intended to raise revenue for England at the expense of the colonists. The first of these was the American Revenue Act, better known as the Sugar Act, which was adopted by the British Parliament in 1764. Among other things, this law placed import duties on coffee, certain wines, and other goods that were imported by the colonists. Shortly after Parliament passed this act, "taxation without representation" (that is, taxation without the consent of the colonists) was denounced at a Boston town meeting. One of the fundamental rights of English citizens was the guarantee that taxes could be imposed on them only by elected representatives. The colonists agreed that Parliament could make some laws for them, but they claimed that it did not have the power to tax them without their consent.

In 1765 the resentment aroused by the Sugar Act was intensified by the passage of the Quartering Act. This law required some of the colonies to provide supplies for the British troops that were stationed there and to house them in inns and unoccupied buildings. Even more exasperating to the colonists was the Stamp Act, also passed in 1765. This law, which imposed a tax on items such as newspapers, legal documents, and playing cards, met with strong opposition throughout the colonies.

In 1770 the growing tension between the citizens of Boston and the British soldiers quartered there came to a head. A fistfight between a colonist and a soldier developed into a riot that ended in the so-called Boston Massacre, in which five colonists were killed.

The grievances of the colonists led to the formation of "committees of correspondence" in several of the colonies. The purpose of the committees was to communicate with one another regarding actions of Parliament that were viewed as threatening to the colonies. One such action was the passage of the Tea Act of 1773, which gave the East India Company a monopoly on the American tea trade. This placed a hardship on American merchants, whose protests eventually led to the famous Boston Tea Party, in which a group of Bostonians disguised as Mohawk Indians boarded a ship loaded with tea and dumped much of its cargo into Boston Harbor.

After the Boston Tea Party there was little pretense of harmony between the colonists and the British government. In 1774 Parliament passed a series of measures that came to be known as the Coercive Acts, including a bill that prohibited the loading or unloading of ships in any part of Boston Harbor. About the same time, the Quartering Act was renewed and its provisions were extended to all the colonies. Americans began to feel that the colonies were being occupied rather than governed. The protest against British rule gathered momentum.

The First Continental Congress

The growing outcry against British control led to numerous calls for the creation of a congress at which the colonies might agree on a joint response to the actions of the British. In September 1774 delegates from all the colonies except Georgia met in Philadelphia for the **First Continental Congress.** The announced purpose of the congress was "to deliberate and determine on wise and proper measures . . . for the restoration of union and harmony between Great Britain and America." But, led by radical delegates like Samuel Adams of Boston, it ended up adopting a "Declaration of Rights and Grievances" that listed a number of violations of colonial rights and stated that Parliament had no authority over the colonies.

The British government was not impressed by the colonists' protests. The Continental Congress had little real power and did not appear to pose a serious threat to British rule. However, Britain's leaders failed to consider the colonists' growing sense of national identity, as expressed in Patrick Henry's statement that "the distinctions between Virginians, Pennsylvanians, New Yorkers, and New Englanders are no more. I am not a Virginian, but an American."

The Revolution

The colonists' frustration at the British government's attitude led to violent action. On the morning of April 19, 1775, six companies of British soldiers traveled west from Boston to Concord, Massachusetts, to search for hidden arms and arrest rebel leaders. The colonists had been warned the night before by Paul Revere, and when the British soldiers reached Lexington, they found the road blocked by about sixty Massachusetts minutemen armed with muskets. Historians cannot determine which side fired the first shot, but shots were fired and eight minutemen were killed. The war for independence had begun.

The **Second Continental Congress** met in Philadelphia in May 1775. It had no more authority than the first congress, but the reality of war had caused most of the colonists to see the need for at least a temporary central government: Troops had to be raised, money printed, and ambassadors sent to foreign powers. Congress became responsible for guiding the efforts of the colonists in their fight against the British.

The Battle of Lexington, Massachusetts, April 1775, was one of the first engagements of the American Revolutionary War.

The Declaration of Independence

Even with the American Revolution under way, some colonists continued to hope that peaceful relations with England could be restored. Thomas Paine's pamphlet *Common Sense,* which called the king a "royal brute" and claimed that "of more worth is one honest man . . . than all the crowned ruffians that ever lived," is credited with turning the tide of public opinion in favor of a formal break with England. By the summer of 1776, the idea of independence had become popular throughout the colonies.

On June 7, 1776, Richard Henry Lee of Virginia submitted two proposals to the Continental Congress, one recommending that the colonies form a permanent confederation and the other calling for a positive declaration that "these United Colonies are, and of right ought to be, Free and Independent States." The latter proposal was debated for nearly a month and was finally adopted on July 2. Thomas Jefferson had been asked to prepare a statement to be read to the public, and this document, the Declaration of Independence, was adopted on July 4.[1]

THE ARTICLES OF CONFEDERATION

Although the Declaration of Independence announced America's independence to the world, the "United Colonies" were recognized only by France and the Netherlands. To the rest of the world, the American states were still British colonies rebelling against British rule. In fact, from 1776 until 1781 they had no real common government but consisted of thirteen separate states. It was not until 1781, when the **Articles of Confederation** were ratified by the Continen-

The ringing of the Liberty Bell announced the signing of the Declaration of Independence on July 4, 1776. Today the bell is on display at Independence Hall in Philadelphia.

tal Congress, that the nation finally obtained a constitution that established a central government, though one with very limited authority.

The nation's first constitution created a Congress in which each state had one vote, but it did not provide for the creation of a separate executive branch or a national court system. Even Congress had very little authority; it did not have the power to regulate interstate commerce, and it could neither tax citizens nor draft them into the military during times of war. It could request money and soldiers from the states, but it had no authority to enforce its requests. Moreover, amendments to the Articles of Confederation required the unanimous consent of the states—a condition that was virtually impossible to meet.[2]

The Articles of Confederation was based on a theory of state sovereignty, which held that the ultimate legal authority resided in the thirteen states. This belief was clearly expressed in Article II of the document: "Each state retains its sovereignty, freedom and independence, and every Power, Jurisdiction and right, which is not by this confederation, expressly delegated to the United States in Congress assembled."

But the Articles was not consistent in its application of state sovereignty. The states were denied the right to negotiate treaties with foreign nations and to make war. To the contrary, the Articles of Confederation delegated these two important powers to the Congress. It further granted Congress additional authority in the area of foreign and military affairs, including the right to send and receive ambassadors, regulate Indian affairs, appoint military officers, and make rules governing the nation's army and navy.

Indeed, perhaps the most important successes of the government under the Articles of Confederation came in the area of foreign affairs. Representatives of Congress negotiated commercial treaties with several European nations and the Treaty of Paris (1783), which concluded the Revolutionary War with Great Britain and gained the new nation official recognition by its former enemy.

The domestic situation of the country, however, told a far different tale. Here the weaknesses of the Congress soon became apparent. The American Revolution ended two years after the adoption of the Articles of Confederation. The new nation had managed to survive the war, but with little help from its central government. The long years of fighting and the collapse of the British colonial system led to economic depression and a weakening of the national spirit. Most of the states failed to give the central government financial support, and the new nation had almost no standing among foreign powers. But the main problems facing the central government under the Articles of Confederation arose from the fact that it lacked the power to tax individuals and the power to regulate commerce. Thus, of the $10 million that Congress had requested from the states, it had collected only $1.5 million by the end of 1783. Unable to regulate commerce, it left the job to the states, and they handled it badly. To protect their own economies, they imposed tariffs on products imported from other states. A series of trade wars developed in which states used tariffs to keep out goods and produce of other states.

The situation within the states was no better. The economic problems of the time led the debtor class, mainly the poorer farmers, to demand action by the state legislatures. Some legislatures responded by passing laws that extended the period for making payments on mortgage debts. A majority also issued paper money, which increased the amount of money in circulation, making it easier to repay debts. But these actions angered creditors and failed to solve the economic problems of the states.

In Massachusetts the picture was especially bleak. Massachusetts had taxed its citizens so heavily that by 1786 its economy was crippled. Mortgage foreclosures were at an all-time high, and the prisons were full of debtors; whole towns were demanding tax reductions. Under the leadership of a former Revolutionary War captain named Daniel Shays, the Massachusetts debtors took action. They marched on the courthouse in Northampton and denied entrance to judges who were preparing to foreclose mortgages on local farms. **Shays's Rebellion** lasted for nearly a year until it was put down by the state militia.

THE CONSTITUTIONAL CONVENTION

The economic distress of the new nation and the inability of the existing government to deal with the problem were the main factors that led to the calling of a constitutional convention. But military concerns also fueled the growing desire for change. The presence of British, Spanish, and French military forces on the borders of the new nation produced anxiety and contributed to the desire for a stronger central government that would be better equipped to deal with these threats. The presence of sometimes hostile Indian tribes also contributed to the insecurity felt by the American people.

In 1785 the first step toward constitutional change was taken when Virginia and Maryland reached an agreement resolving the problem of commercial use of the Potomac River. The Virginia legislature then advanced the idea of a convention to deal with the interstate problems encountered by all the American states. Only five states sent delegates to the convention, which met at Annapolis, Maryland, in September 1786. But the representatives of those states—New York, New Jersey, Pennsylvania, Delaware, and Virginia—went far beyond simply dealing with commercial issues. They recommended that a convention be held for the purpose of devising remedies for all the nation's ills. This idea was approved by Congress, which called for a convention to be held in Philadelphia beginning May 14, 1787, "for the sole and express purpose of revising the Articles of Confederation."

The movement to alter the Articles of Confederation had broad support, but it also had opponents. Some groups favored the existing system, either because they benefited from it economically or because they were fearful of a more centralized form of government. As a result of these opposing views, drafting an acceptable constitution and obtaining public approval for the new document would prove to be a difficult process. Yet the outcome of these efforts has endured for two centuries. Today, more than two hundred years after it was written and ratified, the United States Constitution is the oldest written constitution still in use in the world.

Bad roads and heavy rains delayed the opening of the **Constitutional Convention** until May 29, 1787, when delegates from nine states were present and the first official session was held. The sessions were closed to the public, but James Madison kept records of the proceedings, and these have been of great value to historians and political scientists in putting together an account of what actually happened at the Convention.[3]

James Madison (1751–1836), fourth president of the United States (1809–1817). Madison represented Virginia in the Continental Congress and the Congress of the Articles of Confederation, and was a member of the House of Representatives from 1789 to 1797. He served as President Jefferson's secretary of state between 1801 and 1809. Madison wrote a majority of *The Federalist Papers* and was the principal drafter of the United States Constitution and the Bill of Rights. (Thomas Sully, "James Madison" 1809. In the Collection of The Corcoran Gallery of Art. Gift of Frederick E. Church. Washington, DC.)

The Delegates

The delegates who attended the Philadelphia convention were not the same individuals who had signed the Declaration of Independence. (Only six men signed both documents: Roger Sherman of Connecticut, George Read of Delaware, and Benjamin Franklin, Robert Morris, George Clymer, and James Wilson of Pennsylvania.) The delegates were selected by their respective state legislatures and not by popular vote. James Madison called them "the most respectable characters in the United States . . . the best contribution of talents the states could make for the occasion." Jefferson went further, calling them "an assembly of demigods." Indeed, they were an exceptional group. Among them were George Washington, commander-in-chief of the Revolutionary War army and one of the richest men in the nation; James Madison, who had served in the Virginia Assembly and had studied the governments of many nations; Benjamin Franklin, the noted statesman, scientist, inventor, and writer; Roger Sherman, a judge and legislator and the only person to sign the Declaration of Independence, the Articles of Confederation, and the Constitution; James Wilson of Pennsylvania, a lawyer and state legislator; Gouverneur Morris, also of Pennsylvania, who, because of his brilliant command of language, was called upon to draft the final version of the Constitution; and George Mason, author of the Virginia Bill of Rights.

As a group, delegates to the Constitutional Convention represented the nation's economic and social elite. All were white men. Many had served in Congress or as state governors; more than half had attended American colleges or received a university education in England; and most were wealthy. The middle class, on the other hand—the shopkeepers, artisans, and successful farmers—was not represented at the convention, nor was the lower class—hunters and trappers, less successful farmers, and laborers.

"George Washington." Oil on canvas, ca. 1790s, 53 × 47 cm. American, 18th c. (The Cleveland Museum of Art, Hinman B. Hurlbut Collection, 2552.21.)

The Issues

At the first official session of the convention, Governor Edmund Randolph of Virginia presented the so-called **Virginia Plan,** which included a proposal that "a national government ought to be established consisting of a supreme legislative, executive, and judiciary." This proposal clearly went beyond revising the Articles of Confederation, yet it was approved with little debate as a basis for starting the proceedings of the convention. The decision to scrap the Articles of Confederation and write a totally new constitution was probably the most important decision made at the convention.

A NATIONAL GOVERNMENT VERSUS STATES' RIGHTS The decision to write a new constitution was closely related to another basic problem faced by the convention delegates: Should they create a truly national government, or should they continue the system established by the Articles of Confederation, in which the states possessed most of the legal authority of government? Nationalist feelings were strong among the delegates. A large majority wanted to create a national government, one in which each citizen would have both national and state citizenship and would have a legal relationship to both governments. The Virginia Plan envisioned a strong central government composed of legislative, executive, and judicial branches with the power to veto state laws. In addition, the legislative power of Congress would be expanded, and it would gain the authority to make laws that directly affected the people and not just the state governments. It would, for example, have the power to tax citizens rather than to request funds from the states, as had been the case under the Articles of Confederation. This last feature clearly showed the national character of the government proposed by the Virginia Plan and its fundamental departure from the confederate system.

Not all the delegates favored a national form of government, however. Supporters of the Articles of Confederation made an attempt to prevent the adoption of the Virginia Plan. One of them, William Paterson, presented the **New Jersey Plan,** which would have preserved the basic elements of the confederate system. Under the New Jersey Plan, Congress would consist of one house, in which all the states would be represented equally. It would have to obtain the approval of the states to impose duties on foreign goods, regulate foreign and interstate commerce, impose postal fees, and the like. In presenting his proposal, Paterson said, "If the confederacy was radically wrong, let us return to our States, and obtain larger powers, not assume them of ourselves."

In reality, the decision to draft a new constitution and the decision to set up a national government could not be separated. The New Jersey Plan would not solve the problems that had brought the delegates to the convention. The two plans were debated for several days and then put to a vote. The New Jersey Plan was voted down, and the delegates undertook to establish a national system of government that would have the power to act directly on the people.[4]

LARGE STATES VERSUS SMALL STATES Another issue that divided the delegates was the nature of the proposed legislature. The Virginia Plan, which was generally supported by the larger states, called for a *bicameral,* or two-house, national legislature, with the number of representatives in both houses to be determined by population or by taxes paid; the members of the lower house would be elected by the people and those of the upper house would be appointed by the lower house. This arrangement favored large states, such as Virginia, New York,

Massachusetts, and Pennsylvania, which had larger populations and paid more taxes than smaller states, such as New Jersey, Delaware, and Maryland.

The small states generally objected to the adoption of such a legislative system. They favored the creation of a *unicameral,* or single-house, legislature, with each state having equal representation. When this idea was defeated, many small states insisted on equal representation in at least one house of a bicameral legislature.

The division over the issue of representation should not be viewed as solely a conflict between large and small states. The conflict also had a regional aspect. Most of the small states were in the North; they included New Jersey, Connecticut, New Hampshire, Maryland, and Delaware. New York, a state with a large population and territory, generally voted with the other northern states on questions of representation. On the other hand, the large states, which included Pennsylvania and Massachusetts, received the backing of the four southern states: populous Virginia as well as thinly settled North Carolina, South Carolina, and Georgia.

The convention almost collapsed because of the deep division on the subject of representation. To resolve the conflict, the delegates formed a committee to work out a compromise. The committee's proposal, known as the **Connecticut Compromise,** called for a bicameral legislature in which the number of representatives in the lower house (the House of Representatives) would be determined by population, but each state would have equal representation in the upper house (the Senate). This arrangement satisfied both sides and ended the conflict.

NORTH VERSUS SOUTH Other differences between the northern and southern states also created problems at the convention. The economies of the northern states were based on commerce, shipping, and industry, whereas those of the southern states were based on agriculture, slave labor, and the export of farm products. The southern states were afraid that the northern states, which outnumbered them, would interfere with their export trade. They therefore argued for a clause in the Constitution stating that "no tax or duty shall be paid on articles exported from any state." They also insisted that all treaties with foreign governments be approved by a two-thirds vote in the Senate. This would give the South the power to block any treaty that would harm the economic interests of that region. Both of these proposals were accepted by the convention delegates and included in the final draft of the Constitution.

Slavery was also a major concern of the southern states. They would not accept any constitution that would interfere with its continued existence. It is likely that a majority of the delegates opposed the slave trade and that some were morally opposed to slavery. Luther Martin of Maryland declared that slavery was "dishonorable to the American character." But North Carolina, South Carolina, and Georgia would not yield. John Rutledge of South Carolina pointed to the political reality that confronted the convention delegates: "The true question . . . is whether the Southern states shall or shall not be parties to the Union."

Although the framers of the Constitution never used the word *slavery,* the document sanctioned its existence at several points. One section of the original document required all states to return escaped slaves to their masters. In addition, the Constitution gave Congress the authority to outlaw the importation of slaves into the United States after 1808. But this deadline provided the South with a period of twenty years in which to continue the slave trade and build up the size of the slave population. (In 1808 Congress acted to outlaw the importation of slaves from outside the United States, but it did not legislate against the slave trade within the nation.)

The delegates to the Philadelphia convention also dealt with the question of how slaves were to be counted in determining a state's population for the purposes of allocating seats in the House of Representatives and levying direct taxes. The southern delegates failed in their attempt to have slaves included in the total population so that their states would obtain more seats in the House of Representatives. The convention ultimately agreed to adopt a *three-fifths rule,* by which each slave would be counted as three-fifths of a person in determining the number of representatives each state would send to the House and for purposes of imposing direct taxes.

The three-fifths rule certainly cannot be justified on moral grounds; it was one feature of the original Constitution that gave legal sanction to the existence of slavery. But the rule represented a partial victory for the delegates who objected to the slave system. Had the convention given in to the demand to have slaves counted as whole persons for the purpose of allocating seats in the House of Representatives, the political position of the South would have been greatly strengthened. With its large slave population, the South would have dominated the House of Representatives and would have been able to protect and expand the slave system. The three-fifths rule allowed the states without large slave populations to command a majority in the House and, hence, to check the expansion of slavery.

The provisions that sanctioned slavery remained in the Constitution until after the Civil War, when they were eliminated by two constitutional amendments: the Thirteenth Amendment abolished slavery; the Fourteenth Amendment repealed the three-fifths rule and required that representatives be apportioned among the states on the basis of the total number of people living in each state.

SELECTING GOVERNMENT OFFICIALS Delegates to the convention agreed on the need for a government based on the consent of the people, but they had difficulty agreeing on how that consent should be obtained. There was a division between those who favored a more democratic system of government, that would give greater authority to the people, and those who had a more aristocratic view and were afraid of giving too much power to the people.

In the debate over how members of the House of Representatives were to be elected, there was overwhelming backing for the idea of direct election by the citizenry. But the question of who would be eligible to vote for those members was bypassed. The convention was unable to agree on a national standard for voting. Instead, it was decided that the standards used by each state in choosing members for the lower house of its legislature would be used in determining who could vote for members of the House of Representatives. Under state law at the close of the eighteenth century, only adult white males were qualified to vote, and some states also imposed property requirements for voting.

The Convention resolved in a very different manner the question of how senators were to be chosen. A proposal that senators be chosen by the people was soundly defeated. The idea of having them selected by the state legislatures emerged during the debate on this subject and was ultimately adopted.[5] Supporters of this method of electing senators favored it because it would directly represent the state governments in Congress and would also serve as a check on the popularly elected House.[6]

The Constitutional Convention had made the important decision to create an executive branch of government headed by a president. But it had great difficulty deciding how the nation's chief executive would be chosen. Conflict developed between delegates who favored direct popular election and those who believed that the president should be selected by Congress. Most delegates did not believe that the people were wise enough to make such an important choice. In addition, delegates from the small states feared that direct election would give too much influence to the larger states. Moreover, it would have been impossible to hold a single national election, given the great difficulty of travel and the limited means of communication that existed at the close of the eighteenth century. Support for the idea of legislative election of the president was strong, but many delegates to the Philadelphia convention were unwilling to accept this system. They were afraid that it would make the president a captive of the legislative branch.

This problem was not resolved until the closing days of the convention and was one of the last major decisions made by the delegates. A specially appointed committee proposed an indirect system for selecting the president: an **Electoral College.** After some changes, this plan was accepted by the convention delegates. In accepting this proposal, the delegates rejected a parliamentary form of government, such as existed in Great Britain, and gave its support to a presidential model of government.

Under the Electoral College system, each state would choose a number of electors equal to its total number of senators and representatives in Congress. The state legislatures were free to decide how the electors were to be chosen. The electors would meet in each state and cast votes for two people, at least one of whom was not a resident of that state. The votes of each state would be sealed, sent to the U.S. Senate, and then opened and counted before a joint meeting of the two houses of Congress. The individual who obtained the largest number of electoral votes would become president as long as he received a majority of the total number of votes cast. If there was a tie in the electoral votes cast or if the candidate with the most votes did not receive a majority of the votes, the House of Representatives was given the power to select the president from among the candidates with the five highest vote totals. In voting for the president, the House would vote by state, with each state having a single vote. The candidate with the second-highest number of electoral votes would become vice president, but if two or more people had equal numbers of votes, the Senate was to make the choice.[7]

Ratification

The U.S. Constitution was signed by thirty-nine delegates on September 17, 1787. It was then submitted to the Congress of the Confederation and to the states for **ratification.** The Constitutional Convention had made an important decision when it required that ratification of the proposed Constitution be achieved when only nine of the thirteen states gave their approval. Moreover, the decision to ratify was to be made not by the state legislatures, in which opposition to the new system of government was likely to be strong, but by specially created conventions.

The supporters of the Constitution were called **Federalists** and its opponents **Antifederalists.** The latter were at a disadvantage because they could only voice opposition to the proposed Constitution; they did not have an alternative plan. Still, the contest was a very close one.

Supporters of the new Constitution tended to live in the states with small populations. With the exception of New Hampshire and Rhode Island, the small states—Delaware, New Jersey, Georgia, and Connecticut—were the first to ratify. These states were satisfied with the compromise that gave each state equal representation in the Senate, and they felt that a stronger central government would make them more secure against the threat posed by foreign governments that possessed territories on the nation's borders.

Opposition to the new Constitution was greatest in the most populous states. Most of the people in those states lived in rural areas, not in cities like New York and Philadelphia. Although city dwellers tended to favor the Constitution, farmers often opposed it because they were suspicious of the lawyers and merchants who had drafted it. As a result, by June 1788, when New Hampshire became the ninth state to ratify, Virginia and New York had not yet given their consent. Without the approval of these major states, the Constitution was doomed even though it had been ratified by the required number of states.

Age also influenced people's attitudes toward the Constitution. The leading Federalists were an average of ten to twelve years younger than the most prominent Antifederalists. As historian Samuel Eliot Morison has noted, "The warmest advocates were eager young men."[8]

The Federalists and the Antifederalists differed in other respects besides age and place of residence. For one thing, their careers were quite different. The Federalists had begun their public lives during the Revolutionary War and had developed a "continental" outlook as a result of serving in national institutions such as the Continental Army and the Continental Congress. The Antifederalists did not share this outlook. Their careers had begun in the years before the Revolution and had consisted largely of service in the state governments.[9]

THE DEMAND FOR A BILL OF RIGHTS   The ideas of the Antifederalists were stated during debates at the Philadelphia convention of 1787 and in the ratifying conventions held in the states in the following months. Appendix C contains an example: a speech given by George Mason, a delegate from Virginia, to the Philadelphia Convention. In this speech Mason gave the reasons why he, along with two other delegates, refused to sign the proposed Constitution. He pointed out that the Constitution did not adequately protect the people against the power of the central government because it lacked a **bill of rights.** Such a statement of individual freedoms was essential to prevent the new government from becoming either a monarchy or a tyrannical aristocracy, he argued.

The Antifederalists also wrote numerous pamphlets and newspaper articles setting forth their reasons for opposing the Constitution. The authors of these works often signed their work with the names of leading figures from the ancient Roman Republic. (The use of such pseudonyms was a common practice in political writings of the eighteenth century.) One of the best of these writings was signed "Brutus" and was probably the work of Robert Yates, a New York jurist and a delegate to the Philadelphia convention. In it "Brutus" expressed his fear that the proposed Constitution would create a highly centralized government that would exercise power over the entire nation. Such a government would inevitably become arbitrary and would ultimately eliminate the states altogether. To "Brutus" and other Antifederalists, a republic could not survive unless it was geographically small—like the Greek and Roman republics—and its citizens close to those who governed them.[10] A sample of writing by "Brutus" can be found in Appendix C.

The absence of a bill of rights was by far the most effective argument of the Antifederalists. While the Constitution did contain some protections—the right to a jury trial in criminal cases, a narrow definition of the crime of treason, and restrictions on the power of government to pass *ex post facto laws* and *bills of attainder* and to suspend the *writ of habeas corpus* (see Chapters 3 and 11)—the Antifederalists believed that these were not sufficient. Unless the basic rights of the people were enumerated in the Constitution, the national government would ignore them.

As a result of these criticisms, some of the leading supporters of the new Constitution promised that drafting a bill of rights would be the first action of the new Congress. This acceptance of the Antifederalists' primary criticism reduced opposition to the proposed Constitution and increased the chances of its ratification. After the Constitution was ratified, Congress did in fact adopt a Bill of Rights (the first ten amendments to the Constitution) by the necessary two-thirds vote and submit it to the states for consideration. The required number of states quickly ratified the amendments, and they became part of the nation's fundamental law.

THE FEDERALIST PAPERS   The most important arguments of the Federalists in favor of ratification were published in a series of eighty-five essays that appeared in New York newspapers and are collectively known as *The Federalist Papers*. They were written under the pseudonym "Publius" by James Madison, Alexander Hamilton, and John Jay.[11] The importance of *The Federalist Papers* cannot be overestimated. They have been translated into many languages and have been a source of ideas to scholars and writers of constitutions in many countries. But their greatest impact has been felt in the United States. Although they were written as propaganda tracts designed to gain support for the new Constitution, they have played a central role in American constitutional history for more than two hundred years. They are at the core of constitutional theory and have been cited and discussed by scholars and judges almost from the time the first essay appeared on October 27, 1787.

The authors of *The Federalist Papers* criticized the Articles of Confederation and argued that small republics tend to quarrel among themselves and to be easily dominated by more powerful nations. They favored a geographically large republic with a strong government, which they believed would be most likely to provide both security and liberty for its citizens. These goals could be achieved through the devices of federalism, separation of powers, checks and balances, national supremacy, and judicial review, all of which are embodied in the United States Constitution. (These devices are discussed in the next section of the chapter.)

Appendix D contains the two most famous and important of *The Federalist Papers*. No. 10 is a complex, closely argued essay that deals with the fundamental question of how government in a free society should be organized. In addressing this question, Madison ranges over a variety of topics: the problem of factions, the nature of man, the purpose of government, and the constitutional arrangements that can create the best possible form of government and still maintain freedom.

In *The Federalist,* No. 51, Madison presents a detailed discussion of why separation of powers and checks and balances are necessary parts of a constitution that will permit the existence of both freedom and a strong republican

A depiction of the inauguration of George Washington as the first president of the United States at Federal Hall, New York City, on April 30, 1789.

government. Madison explained that these constitutional devices were necessary because of the nature of human beings. "It may be a reflection on human nature," he wrote, "that such devices should be necessary to control the abuses of governments. But what is government itself, but the greatest of all reflections on human nature? If men were angels, no government would be necessary."

THE UNITED STATES CONSTITUTION

The delegates to the Constitutional Convention in Philadelphia were practical men who were willing to compromise on some issues to achieve their overall objective of writing a new document that would create a strong central government. But the delegates were also motivated by certain fundamental ideas, and those ideas shaped the character of the final document. Although they wanted to create a central government with adequate powers, they also wanted to restrain those powers. They sought to achieve this goal through the use of several constitutional devices: federalism, separation of powers, and checks and balances. The power of the courts to exercise judicial review, though not expressly stated in the Constitution, was also intended to act as a restraint on the power of government.

The delegates were fundamentally opposed to both monarchy and autocratic government. They desired to establish a republican form of government based on the concept of *popular sovereignty*. The idea that the people were sovereign—that they were the ultimate source of legal power in a nation—was a novel one at the end of the eighteenth century, but it was to have great influence from that time on as more governments throughout the world were established on this principle.

Finally, the authors of the Constitution wanted to guarantee that the newly created central government would be supreme within the area of its legal authority. To accomplish this purpose, they made the principle of *national supremacy* part of the new U.S. Constitution.[12]

Federalism

Federalism is a system for organizing government that is based on a geographic division of power. In a federal system, a national government has authority over the entire territory, whereas a regional government has authority only within its own area. Under the United States Constitution, the national government has specific powers, such as the right to regulate interstate commerce. States have the general power to legislate in areas that have not been delegated to the national government or denied them by the Constitution.

In a federal system, power can be divided in different ways. The constitutions of some countries, unlike that of the United States, delegate specific powers to the states or provinces and reserve all other authority to the central government. Regardless of how power is distributed, federalism always serves the basic purpose of limiting the power of government by dividing it along geographic lines.

Separation of Powers

Having divided the powers of government between the states and the national government, the writers of the U.S. Constitution went on to separate the operations of the national government into three distinct branches: legislative, executive, and judicial. This was accomplished in the first three articles of the Constitution. Article I states that "all legislative Powers herein granted shall be vested in a Congress of the United States"; Article II, that "the executive Power shall be vested in a President of the United States of America"; and Article III, that "the judicial Power of the United States, shall be vested in one Supreme Court, and in such inferior Courts as the Congress may from time to time ordain and establish." The framers believed that the concentration of powers in any one branch of government would inevitably lead to despotism. In *The Federalist,* No. 47, James Madison wrote: "The accumulation of all powers, legislative, executive, and judiciary, in the same hands, whether of one, a few, or many, and whether hereditary, self-appointed, or elective, may justly be pronounced the very definition of tyranny." The nation's founders believed that the system of **separation of powers** that they created in the Constitution would prevent any one of the three branches of government from dominating the other two. They were especially fearful of legislative power, since it was believed that in a popular form of government, power tends to flow to the legislature, which is most directly responsive to the wishes of the people.

Checks and Balances: Shared Powers

The authors of the Constitution did not believe in absolute separation of governmental powers. Once they had formally separated the three branches of government, they introduced a system of **checks and balances** in which the power of government is shared by the legislative, executive, and judicial branches. (The term *checks* here refers to controls or limits.) The main purpose of checks and balances is to limit the power of government by making each branch dependent on the others. Congress can pass laws, for example, but the president can veto them. The president has the power to negotiate treaties with foreign nations, but such agreements must be approved by a two-thirds vote of the Senate. The federal courts can interpret the meaning of laws and of the Constitution, but they are limited by the broad authority of Congress to shape the structure of the federal judicial system and to define the types of cases courts can hear.

IMPEACHMENT The checks-and-balances system is also illustrated by the methods found in the Constitution for removing public officials. The president, the vice president, federal judges, and other officials can be removed from office only by means of **impeachment** and conviction. The Constitution assigns these tasks to the House of Representatives and the Senate, respectively. The House is given the sole power to impeach—that is, to formally accuse a public official of wrongdoing. But the Senate alone has the authority to convict and remove the accused person, and this action requires a two-thirds vote of the members of the Senate who are present. Thus, in the removal process, the power of the House of Representatives is checked by that of the Senate.

The impeachment of President Clinton illustrates this aspect of the checks-and-balances system. On December 19, 1998, the House of Representatives impeached the president on two grounds: perjury and obstruction of justice. This made Clinton only the second president to be impeached in the nation's history, and the first elected president to be impeached. (Andrew Johnson, who was impeached in 1868, had been elected as vice president and became president after the assassination of Abraham Lincoln.)

A trial of the charges against Clinton was held in the Senate in early January 1999. As required by the Constitution, Chief Justice William Rehnquist presided. The Senate failed to achieve the two-thirds vote required for conviction on either of the two charges. Thus, despite having been impeached, Clinton remained in office to serve the remainder of his second term as president.

Thirteen federal judges have been impeached during the course of American history. Two resigned prior to trial by the Senate, four were acquitted, and seven convicted and removed from office. Three of these convictions were obtained against federal district court judges between 1986 and 1989.

A BICAMERAL LEGISLATURE The Constitution created a complex system for organizing the three branches of the national government and for choosing the people who will serve in each branch. The framers established a **bicameral legislature,** a legislature composed of two largely separate and independent bodies. The purpose of this two-house structure was to limit the power of both houses; each house would serve as a check on the other. To gain passage, a bill would have to satisfy the interests and beliefs of a majority of the legislators in both houses. It was expected that the House of Representatives would act more quickly, since it more directly represented the interests of the people, while the Senate would be more cautious. The conduct of the House and Senate during the impeachment of President Clinton illustrates the difference in attitude between the two houses of Congress.

SELECTION OF PUBLIC OFFICIALS Finally, the Constitution requires that members of the three branches of government be chosen in different ways, represent different interests in society, and serve for different lengths of time.

Senators always represent the people of an entire state; members of the House of Representatives usually represent the voters of smaller districts within a state; and the president represents all the citizens of the nation (though the president is actually elected by an Electoral College, which is organized by states). Federal judges are appointed by the president with the advice and consent of the Senate.

Moreover, the Constitution assigns different terms of office to representatives (two years); senators (six years, with one-third of the senators elected every two years); the president (four years); and federal judges (life). The staggered terms for the president and members of Congress were designed to prevent the government from being "captured" or totally controlled by the officials chosen in any one election year.

The nation's founders believed that this complex election system would limit government by introducing different points of view into debates on public issues. Local viewpoints would conflict with state and national viewpoints. Senators elected in one year would represent different interests from those of senators elected two years later, but they would serve together in the upper house of the legislature. The life tenure of federal judges would make them independent of public opinion and thus would give stability and continuity to the governmental system.

Judicial Review

The term **judicial review** refers to the power of courts to declare legislative and executive actions unconstitutional. Although judicial review is not mentioned in the Constitution, there is evidence that its authors intended the federal courts to have this authority. Judicial review had been used on a number of occasions by courts in colonial America and by state courts in the years following the Revolutionary War. The first time this power was exercised by the Supreme Court to nullify an act of Congress came in 1803 in the famous case of *Marbury* v. *Madison.*[13] Chief Justice John Marshall's opinion in that case established the precedent that judicial review could be used by the federal courts to limit the legislative power of Congress. He wrote: "It is emphatically the province and duty of the judicial department to say what the law is. Those who apply the rule to particular cases, must of necessity expound and interpret that rule. If two laws conflict with each other, the courts must decide on the operation of each."

The Supreme Court's power of judicial review extends not only to actions of the United States Congress and the president but also to acts of the state governments. As early as 1796 the U.S. Supreme Court invalidated a Virginia law that violated a provision of the peace treaty made by the United States with Great Britain after the Revolutionary War.[14] The federal courts have exercised the power of judicial review over state governments on many hundreds of occasions over the course of the nation's history.

Popular Sovereignty

The word *sovereignty*—ultimate legal authority—is not explicitly mentioned in the Constitution, but it is clear that the delegates to the Constitutional Convention had definite ideas on this subject. And those ideas were decidedly different

John Marshall (1755–1835), diplomat, Virginia congressman, and fourth Chief Justice of the United States. His opinion in *Marbury* v. *Madison* (1803) provided the precedent for the power of judicial review. Later opinions strengthened the authority of the central government in relation to the states.

from those that had been expressed by commentators on government up to that time. In England and Europe, sovereignty had been viewed as indivisible and as residing in a single source—usually the monarch. In the early history of this nation, the Articles of Confederation had declared that the American states were the ultimate source of legal authority.

But this conception of sovereignty was at odds with the new republican theory of government that developed in the United States after the Revolutionary War. This new theory was based on the idea of **popular sovereignty**—the belief that the people are the source of all legal authority.

The writers of the Constitution accepted the idea of popular sovereignty and rejected the notion that either the state or the federal government was the final source of legal authority. Critics argued that two systems of government could not function in the same geographic area, since this denied all traditional ideas of sovereignty. "But this was precisely what American federalism provided for, and the doctrine of popular sovereignty made it possible. Created by the people, state and federal government could legislate and govern concurrently over the same population in the same territory."[15]

National Supremacy

Article VI, Section 2, of the Constitution declares that

> This Constitution, and the Laws of the United States which shall be made in Pursuance thereof; and all Treaties made, or which shall be made, under the Authority of the United States, shall be the supreme Law of the Land; and the Judges in every state shall be bound thereby, any Thing in the Constitution or Laws of any State to the Contrary notwithstanding.

This important provision of the Constitution—originally proposed as part of the New Jersey Plan—established two major principles. First, the United States Constitution and all federal laws and treaties are superior to conflicting provisions of state constitutions and laws; this is the principle of **national supremacy.** Second, the "supremacy clause" makes clear that the Constitution is enforceable as law by judges and is not merely a statement of political or moral rules.

CONSTITUTIONAL CHANGE AND DEVELOPMENT

Amending the Constitution

If it is not to become obsolete, a constitution must include a procedure for changing or revising the original document—an **amendment** process. The nation's founders understood this need, but they also realized that there was a danger in making the amendment process too easy. The fundamental rules created by the U.S. Constitution could then be readily changed, and the document would take on the character of a lengthy legislative code. The delegates therefore made it difficult to amend the Constitution.

Article V establishes a two-step amendment procedure: *proposal* and *ratification.* Amendments can be proposed using either of two methods: by a two-thirds vote of both houses of Congress or by a national convention called by Congress at the request of the legislatures of two-thirds of the states. Only the first method has been used to date. Similarly, there are two procedures for ratifying an amendment: approval by the legislatures of three-fourths of the states or by specially elected ratifying conventions in three-fourths of the states. The latter method has been used for only one of the amendments ratified thus far—the Twenty-first, which repealed the Eighteenth (Prohibition) Amendment. Congress can determine which of the two ratifying procedures must be used. It can also set a time limit for ratification by the states, a practice it has consistently followed in proposing constitutional amendments in the past half-century.

The Constitution has been amended only twenty-seven times in all and only seventeen times since 1791. The first ten amendments, the Bill of Rights, were proposed by the First Congress to meet the popular demand for a written statement of rights that would protect individuals against oppression by the national government. The post–Civil War amendments—the Thirteenth (1865), Fourteenth (1868), and Fifteenth (1870)—abolished slavery and were intended to guarantee and protect the rights of black people. Many of the remaining amendments were designed to make the political system more responsive to the people. The Seventeenth Amendment (1913) provided for direct popular election of U.S. senators; the Nineteenth (1920) outlawed discrimination on the basis of sex in determining who shall have the right to vote; the Twenty-third (1961) gave the District of Columbia votes in the Electoral College; the Twenty-fourth (1964) barred the state and national governments from denying a person the right to vote in primary and national elections because of failure to pay a poll tax; and the Twenty-sixth (1971) denied the state and national governments the right to discriminate against people 18 years of age or over in granting the right to vote (age 21 had been the gen-

CLOSE-UP

A SECOND METHOD OF PROPOSING AMENDMENTS

All amendments to the Constitution have been proposed by a two-thirds vote of both houses of Congress. The Constitution, however, also provides for a second method of proposing an amendment: Two-thirds of the states can petition Congress to call a constitutional convention.

While this method of proposing an amendment has never been used, on one occasion a movement to hold a convention indirectly led to the adoption of a constitutional amendment. In the early years of the twentieth century, growing public support for the direct election of United States senators was resisted by the Senate. A movement to call a constitutional convention received the support of all but one of the necessary two-thirds of the states. Congress finally acted, thereby avoiding the need for a convention. In 1912 it proposed the Seventeenth Amendment, which provided for the popular election of senators; the required number of states quickly ratified the amendment.

erally accepted standard); and the Twenty-seventh (1992) restricted the power of Congress to put into effect an increase in its members' salaries until after an election has occurred.

Other amendments have dealt with a variety of matters. The Eighteenth (1919) prohibited the manufacture, sale, and transportation of alcoholic beverages. This "noble experiment"—Prohibition—ended with the adoption of the Twenty-first Amendment (1933), which repealed it. The Eleventh (1798), Twelfth (1804), Twentieth (1933), and Twenty-fifth (1967) Amendments dealt with constitutional problems of a technical and procedural nature. The Twenty-second Amendment (1951) prevented any person from being elected president more than twice. (It also provided that a vice president who becomes president as a result of the impeachment, death, or resignation of his predecessor can be elected to two full terms only if he has served less than two years of the former president's term of office.) (See Table 2.1.)

In every session of Congress, many constitutional amendments are introduced. A few of the proposed amendments have been subjects of serious national debate. One of these is the proposal to require Congress to balance the federal budget in each fiscal year. The Balanced Budget Amendment has been considered by Congress on a number of occasions over the past several decades, most recently during the Republican-controlled 104th Congress (1995–1997), when it was narrowly defeated. But the proposal has never received the necessary two-thirds vote in both houses of Congress.

Many less serious proposals are also introduced in Congress each year and receive little or no attention. For example, there have been suggestions to end congressional immunity from traffic citations received en route to and from the Capitol, to reduce the terms of federal judges to eight or ten years, and to allow voters in national elections to enact or repeal federal laws.[16]

Since the Civil War, almost all amendments proposed by Congress have been ratified by the states. Two of the three exceptions to this pattern occurred in the recent past. The Equal Rights Amendment, which would have barred all discrimination on the basis of gender, was proposed by Congress in 1972 but fell three

TABLE 2.1

AMENDMENTS TO THE CONSTITUTION: TIME BETWEEN CONGRESSIONAL APPROVAL AND RATIFICATION

Amendment	Year Ratified	Ratification Time
1–10 Bill of Rights	1791	1 year, 2½ months
11 Suits against states	1798	3 years, 10 months
12 Election of the president	1804	8½ months
13 Slavery	1865	10½ months
14 Civil rights	1868	2 years, 1½ months
15 Voting right for blacks	1870	1 year, 1 month
16 Income tax	1913	3 years, 7½ months
17 Direct election of senators	1913	1 year, ½ month
18 Prohibition	1919	1 year, 1½ months
19 Voting right for women	1920	1 year, 2½ months
20 Terms of office	1933	11 months
21 Repeal of Prohibition	1933	9½ months
22 Two-term limit for presidents	1951	3 years, 11½ months
23 Voting in presidential elections for Washington, D.C.	1961	9 months
24 Abolition of the poll tax	1964	1 year, 5½ months
25 Presidential succession	1967	1 year, 6½ months
26 Voting right for 18-year-olds	1971	4 months
27 Salary increases for members of Congress	1992	203 years

Perhaps 10,000 proposed constitutional amendments have been introduced in Congress since 1789, but only 27 have been ratified. Seven amendments were proposed by Congress but never ratified by the necessary number of states.

states short of the number needed for ratification. And in 1978 Congress proposed a constitutional amendment that would have given the citizens of the District of Columbia full voting representation in Congress. But by the time this proposal expired in 1985, only sixteen states had ratified it.

Other Means of Constitutional Development

The Constitution provides a written outline for the American political system. Some aspects of this system, however, are not found in the words of that document but are derived from experience and accepted practice. For example, there is no mention in the Constitution of political parties or the cabinet.

The political parties had their origins in the debate over the ratification of the Constitution. The Federalists and the Antifederalists evolved into two separate political parties during the years of Washington's presidency. Differences over economic policy and the interpretation of the Constitution led to the formation of the Republican party led by Thomas Jefferson and the Federalist party headed by more conservative politicians of the period such as Alexander Hamilton and

John Adams. The names of the two major political parties went through a number of changes during the first half of the nineteenth century. But since the close of the Civil War, American politics has been dominated by the Democratic and Republican parties.

The cabinet likewise is not mentioned in the Constitution and has no formal legal status, although some federal laws mention cabinet officers. Following the creation of the first three departments of government in 1789 (State, Treasury, and War), President George Washington began conferring with the secretaries of those departments on issues of public policy. In 1791 Washington began to meet with the secretaries as a group, and by 1794 he regularly sought their counsel on issues of state. During much of the nineteenth century, many presidents used the cabinet as their primary source of advice, but in the twentieth century it fell into disfavor, and few presidents have relied on it as an important source of guidance on public issues. And unlike the cabinet in a parliamentary system, the American cabinet has no formal legal authority. This is illustrated by President Lincoln's statement to his cabinet after he had cast a yes vote on an issue: "Seven nays and one aye, the ayes have it."[17]

The United States Supreme Court plays the most significant role in developing the meaning of the Constitution. Through its many decisions over two centuries, the Court has given life and force to the general rules set forth in the Constitution. Without judicial interpretation, such important but broad principles

CLOSE-UP

THE TWENTY-SEVENTH AMENDMENT

It took more than two hundred years, but the legislative pay amendment was finally added to the United States Constitution on May 7, 1992.

Originally proposed by James Madison in 1789, the amendment bars Congress from giving itself an immediate pay raise: "No law, varying the compensation for the services of the Senators and Representatives, shall take effect, until an election of Representatives shall have intervened," the amendment reads.

To become part of the Constitution, an amendment must be approved by a two-thirds majority of each house of Congress and then be ratified by three-fourths of the states. The legislative pay amendment originated as one of twelve amendments proposed by the First Congress; ten of those amendments were quickly ratified and became known as the Bill of Rights, but the legislative pay amendment was not one of them. Between 1789 and 1791 six states ratified the amendment; 82 years later, in 1873, Ohio ratified it; and 105 years after that, in 1978, Wyoming did so. In the next

decade numerous other states acted; the requisite three-fourths majority (38 states) was achieved with Michigan's ratification in 1992. Those actions by the states were directly related to public dissatisfaction with Congress—and particularly with pay raises that had been enacted for its members.

Immediately after Michigan's action, there was some doubt that the amendment had been properly ratified. In recent years Congress has imposed a time limit on ratification, usually seven years, but no such limit had been placed on Madison's proposal. Some legal scholars and members of Congress questioned the validity of a ratification process extending over two centuries. However, the head of the National Archives certified the amendment as legitimate, stating that it had become the Twenty-seventh Amendment to the Constitution on the day that Michigan ratified it. In addition, a resolution was introduced and approved in both houses of Congress asserting the validity of the amendment despite the long delay in its ratification.

as national supremacy, due process of law, equal protection of the laws, and freedom of speech would exist as mere words on paper, without specific meaning. The U.S. Constitution is a living instrument of government in large part because of the role played by the Supreme Court as its final interpreter.

In sum, the Constitution should be viewed as a document that includes not just the written text but the whole set of customs, traditions, practices, and understandings that have developed in the more than two centuries since its ratification in 1789.[18]

CONCLUSION

For over two hundred years the U.S. Constitution has served as the basic instrument of government for the United States. It has done so despite the nation's transformation from a largely rural country confined to the Atlantic seaboard to a heavily urban industrial society spread across a continent. The Constitution has survived these great changes because the nation's founders understood that it had to be made flexible enough to adapt to changing needs. At the same time, the basic principles embodied in the Constitution remain intact. Popular sovereignty, federalism, separation of powers, checks and balances, and judicial review continue to shape the political system of the United States.

Over the past two centuries the Constitution has survived a civil war, several international wars, economic depressions, and major scandals in government. In the future the nation will undoubtedly face new challenges both at home and abroad, and the Constitution will be tested again. During those crises some critics will say that the Constitution of 1789 is outdated and inadequate. But if American history is any guide, the critics will be proved wrong, and the document written during the hot Philadelphia summer of 1787 will be equal to the challenge.

QUESTIONS FOR THOUGHT

1. What were the main features of the Articles of Confederation?
2. What were the major weaknesses of the Articles of Confederation?
3. What issues most divided the delegates to the Constitutional Convention?
4. What arguments did the Antifederalists make against ratification of the Constitution?
5. What are the main principles embodied in the United States Constitution?
6. What procedures must be followed to amend the Constitution?

INTERNET ACTIVITY

Problems with Confederation. Go to the Library of Congress website at **http://lcweb.loc.gov/**. Access "American Memory," then access "The Continental Congress and the Constitutional Convention," review all links/documents, and follow the link to "Form a More Perfect Union" at **http://lcweb2.loc.gov/ammem/bdsds/bdexhome.html**. Access "Defects in the Confederation." Summarize the major defects of the government under the Articles. Check out the remainder of the site, especially its neat timelines. Review the American Memory homepage.

KEY TERMS

amendment
Antifederalists
Articles of Confederation
bicameral legislature
bill of rights
checks and balances
Connecticut Compromise
Constitutional Convention
Electoral College

English Bill of Rights
federalism
Federalists
First Continental Congress
impeachment
judicial review
Magna Charta
national supremacy
New Jersey Plan

popular sovereignty
ratification
Second Continental Congress
separation of powers
Shays's Rebellion
state sovereignty
Virginia Plan

SUGGESTED READING

Brinkley, Alan, Nelson B. Polsby, and Kathleen M. Sullivan. *New Federalist Papers: Essays in Defense of the Constitution.* New York: Norton, 1999.

Elkins, Stanley, and Eric McKitrick. *The Age of Federalism.* New York: Oxford University Press, 1993.

Kammen, Michael. *A Machine That Would Go of Itself: The Constitution in American Culture.* New York: Random House, 1986.

Kerber, Linda. *Women of the Republic: Intellect and Ideology in Revolutionary America.* New York: Norton, 1986.

MacDonald, Forrest F. *Novus Ordo Seclorum: The Intellectual Origins of the Constitution.* Lawrence: University Press of Kansas, 1985.

Rakove, Jack N. *Original Meanings: Politics and Ideas in the Making of the Constitution.* New York: Knopf, 1996.

Redish, Martin H. *The Constitution as Political Structure.* New York: Oxford University Press, 1995.

Rosen, Gary. *American Compact.* Lawrence: University Press of Kansas, 1999.

Simon, James F. *What Kind of a Nation: Thomas Jefferson, John Marshall and the Epic Struggle to Create a United States.* New York: Simon & Schuster, 2002.

Wood, Gordon S. *The Radicalism of the American Revolution.* New York: Knopf, 1996.

NOTES

1. The complete text of the Declaration of Independence appears in Appendix A.

2. The complete text of the Articles of Confederation appears in Appendix B.

3. The best brief study of the Constitutional Convention may be found in Max Farrand, *The Framing of the Constitution of the United States* (New Haven, CT: Yale University Press, 1913), which has been issued in a number of modern editions. Much of the discussion that follows is based on Farrand's study.

4. C. Herman Pritchett, *Constitutional Law of the Federal System* (Englewood Cliffs, NJ: Prentice Hall, 1984), p. 12.

5. The Seventeenth Amendment to the Constitution, adopted in 1913, provided for direct election of U.S. senators by the people.

6. See *The Federalist Papers,* No. 62, by James Madison.

7. Some features of this method of selecting the president and the vice president were changed by the Twelfth Amendment to the Constitution, ratified in 1804. See Chapter 6 for a more complete discussion of the present workings of the Electoral College.

8. Samuel Eliot Morison and Henry Steele Commager, *The Growth of the American Republic,* 5th ed. (New York: Oxford University Press, 1962), vol. 1, p. 194.

9. Stanley M. Elkins and Eric McKitrick, "Youth and the Continental Vision," in Leonard W. Levy, ed., *Essays on the Making of the Constitution,* 2nd ed. (New York: Oxford University Press, 1987), pp. 241–45.

10. Excerpts from George Mason's writings and the essay by "Brutus" appear in Appendix C.

11. The complete text of two of the most influential essays, No. 10 and No. 51, appears in Appendix D.

12. The complete text of the Constitution appears in Appendix E.

13. 1 Cranch 137 (1803).

14. *Ware* v. *Hylton,* 3 Dallas 199 (1796).

15. Alfred H. Kelly, Winfred A. Harbison, and Herman Belz, *The American Constitution,* 6th ed. (New York: Norton, 1983), pp. 105–6.

16. Francis J. Flaherty, "The Amend Corner," *National Law Journal,* March 26, 1984, p. 3.

17. James P. Pfiffner, *The Modern Presidency* (New York: St. Martin's Press, 1994), pp. 110–11.

18. Kelly, Harbison, and Belz, *American Constitution,* p. xv.

CHAPTER

3

The Federal
System

The United States Constitution created a federal form of government, one in which power is divided between the states and the national government. Many provisions of the Constitution deal with the federal system, but only in the Tenth Amendment does it provide a general definition of federalism.

One way to understand federalism is to compare it with other methods of organizing government. A federal government is somewhere between a unitary, or centralized, government and a confederation. In a **unitary government,** such as that of France, the United Kingdom, or Israel, the central government has ultimate legal authority over citizens. It grants specific powers to local governments, but in theory it can reclaim those powers at any time. In a **confederation,** by contrast, the limited powers possessed by the central government are granted to it by the state or provincial governments. The central government can make laws for the nation as a whole, but it cannot regulate the actions of citizens. For example, it may request financial support from the states, but it cannot impose a tax on individuals. Authority over individuals in any given area of policy is in the hands of the state government. Confederate governments are relatively rare. Such a system existed in the United States under the Articles of Confederation during the 1780s and in the Confederacy created by the southern states during the American Civil War; the government of Switzerland is a modern example of a confederacy.

Under **federalism,** neither the central government nor the state governments exercise the total power of government. Legal power is divided between them, usually in a written constitution. Today the word *federal* is used to refer to an activity or institution of the national (central) government, whereas *federalism* refers to a system in which decisions and functions are divided between two levels of government. In such a system each unit of government can make decisions separately from the other in its specific areas of authority.

It is important to understand that in a federal form of government the states are not merely administrative units that manage

"The powers not delegated to the United States by the Constitution, nor prohibited by it to the States, are reserved to the States respectively, or to the people."

—*United States Constitution, Amendment 10*

programs adopted in Washington. Although they may administer some national programs, they are separate entities acting independently within their legal sphere of activity. It should also be noted that the power to conduct foreign affairs rests exclusively with the central government; the states have no legal authority in this area. Federalism, therefore, applies only to the nation's internal, or domestic, affairs.

It is rare that a state government involves itself directly in foreign affairs. But one recent attempt by Massachusetts to dramatize civil rights abuses by the government of Burma (Myanmar) led to a Supreme Court decision on the subject. Massachusetts enacted a law that barred all state agencies from buying goods or services from any person or company doing business with Burma. A foreign trade association challenged the constitutionality of the law on the ground that it infringed on the federal government's foreign affairs power, interfered with the power of Congress to regulate foreign commerce, and violated existing federal law on the subject of imposing economic sanctions on Burma. The Supreme Court unanimously declared the Massachusetts law to be unconstitutional.[1]

Under federalism, different units of government theoretically have authority over different areas of life: The federal government makes decisions concerning broad national issues, such as foreign and military affairs and interstate commerce, and the state governments control local matters, such as education and road construction. In practice, however, the distribution of power in a federal system is less clear-cut, and the powers of various units overlap. Although the

United States troops from the 10th Mountain Division in eastern Afghanistan, March 2002.

Constitution makes no mention of city governments or other forms of local government, many other types of government exist within the nation's political system. They include cities, counties, villages, towns and townships, and a large number of special-purpose governments such as school districts. Indeed, two political scientists have observed that the structure of government in the United States is "chaotic."[2]

This chapter begins by outlining the main constitutional rules that govern this nation's federal system. We then discuss the major theories that have shaped the federal system during various periods of American history. Finally, we examine the actual operation of contemporary American federalism.

FEDERALISM IN THE CONSTITUTION

The colonists who came to America before the Revolution were fleeing from arbitrary, often oppressive, governments. When they found that political conditions in the colonies were not much better, they rebelled. Having won their independence from Great Britain after a long struggle, the colonists did not want to create another strong central government. Under the Articles of Confederation, therefore, power was distributed among a set of largely independent states. But the confederation was unable to deal with many of the problems facing the new nation. A primary goal of the Constitutional Convention of 1787 was to create a stronger central government. The result, after many compromises, was a federal form of government.

The Constitution, which was ratified by the states in 1789, established the basic pattern of American federalism, though later amendments have made some changes in this system. The nation's founders created a form of government that delegated specific powers to the national government and reserved most of the remaining powers for the states. In the words of James Madison, the framers of the Constitution created "neither a national nor a federal Constitution, but a composition of both."[3]

In addition to establishing a system of shared powers, the Constitution sets forth the limitations on the national government and its obligations to the states. It denies specific powers to the states, and it defines the obligations of one state to another as well as to the national government. It also provides for a Supreme Court. One of the main functions of the Court is to settle conflicts that arise from the distribution of powers among the fifty-one governments that make up the federal system. It therefore plays a key role in defining and shaping the American federal form of government.

Powers of the National Government

The Constitution gives two basic types of powers to the national government: **delegated powers** (also called expressed or enumerated powers) and **implied powers.** Delegated powers are stated at various points in the Constitution, but especially in Article I, Section 8; implied powers are derived from the **necessary and proper clause** that appears at the end of Article I, Section 8.

DELEGATED POWERS Article I, Section 8, of the Constitution lists many of the delegated powers of Congress. In domestic matters the most important of these are the authority to tax and spend and the power to regulate interstate

CLOSE-UP

COERCION BY CONGRESS

Before 1984 the minimum drinking age varied from state to state; in some states it was as low as 18, whereas in others it was 19, 20, or 21. These differences encouraged young people to drive to states where the drinking age was lower, and often they attempted to drive home after consuming significant amounts of alcohol. Rates of accidents, injuries, and fatalities from drunk driving by young people were very high, yet many states did not change their minimum drinking age.

In 1984 Congress used its constitutional spending power as a means of encouraging the states to raise their drinking age to 21. The National Minimum Drinking Age Amendment directed the secretary of transportation to withhold a percentage of federal highway funds from states that allowed individuals under 21 to purchase alcoholic beverages. The states were not required to change their laws; they could have made up the shortfall in highway funds by raising taxes or reducing spend-ing on highway construction and repairs. But from both a practical and a political standpoint, it was easier to raise the drinking age to 21.

Congress used a similar approach in 2000 to create another national driver safety standard. This time the issue was the blood alcohol level used by the states to determine if an automobile driver is legally intoxicated. Most states use a blood alcohol level of 0.1%. Congress established a new standard of 0.08%. (Some states, including Texas, California, and Florida, already use this figure in cases of alleged drunk driving.) States that fail to adopt the 0.08% test stand to lose up to 8% of federal highway money each year. These penalties are to be phased in gradually between the 2004 fiscal year and September 30, 2007. States can recover all lost highway money by adopting the change at any time before the September 2007 date. Those who fail to act stand to lose tens of millions of dollars in federal highway grants.

commerce. The expansion of the authority of the national government has been based largely on these powers. The taxing authority is used by Congress not only to obtain revenue but also to regulate certain types of behavior. The federal tax on tobacco products and alcoholic beverages, for example, is designed both to raise revenue and (because the tax increases the price) to discourage use of these products. Congress has also used its power to tax and spend to bring about changes in state policies it considers desirable.

The power to regulate interstate commerce has far-reaching effects. By the late 1930s the Supreme Court had interpreted this power in such a way as to support broad governmental regulation of business, labor, and agriculture. For example, it upheld the Fair Labor Standards Act of 1938, which set wage and hour standards for workers engaged in interstate commerce.[4] In the Civil Rights Act of 1964 Congress used the commerce clause to outlaw racial discrimination in hotels, motels, and many restaurants. Because their customers and the food they serve move from one state to another, discrimination reduces the flow of these forms of commerce. The Supreme Court ruled that these provisions of the act are constitutional.[5]

Many federal crimes are based on the power of Congress to regulate interstate commerce. For example, kidnapping a person and taking the victim across a state line is a federal crime. So is using the nation's interstate telephone lines to carry out fraudulent business practices.

Article I, Section 8, also grants Congress important powers in foreign and military affairs. Congress is given the authority to raise an army and a navy and to declare war. But in Article II the president is given the primary power to act in foreign affairs. The president is designated as commander-in-chief of the armed forces, granted the right to receive ambassadors from foreign nations and (with Senate approval) appoint American ambassadors, and authorized to negotiate treaties with foreign nations (with the advice and consent of two-thirds of the Senate).

IMPLIED POWERS Article I, Section 8, of the Constitution gives Congress the right "to make all laws which shall be necessary and proper for carrying into Execution the foregoing Powers, and all the powers vested by this Constitution in the government of the United States, or in any Department or Officer thereof." This clause can be cited to justify the use of an unstated, or implied, power as a means of carrying out an expressed power. For example, although the Constitution gives Congress the expressed power to raise an army and a navy, it does not say how that is to be done. Various methods have been adopted by Congress over the course of the past sixty years—including lotteries, selective service, and, currently, a volunteer system—all constitutionally justified by the "necessary and proper" clause.

The precedent for a broad interpretation of the implied powers of Congress was set in the important case of *McCulloch* v. *Maryland* (1819).[6] Congress had created a system of national banks that was extremely unpopular in some parts of the nation. Maryland had imposed a tax on the operation of the system's Baltimore branch, which the bank refused to pay. One of the central issues raised in the case was whether Congress had the power to create a national banking system. The Constitution does not expressly grant such a power, but the government argued that Congress had the implied power to do so to carry out its delegated authority to borrow and to coin money. The state maintained that the federal banking system was unconstitutional; it sought to persuade the Supreme Court to accept a very narrow reading of the "necessary and proper" clause.

Chief Justice John Marshall rejected Maryland's arguments and upheld the constitutionality of the banking system. He took a broad view of the implied-powers clause, one that has been accepted ever since. "Let the end be legitimate," he wrote, "let it be within the scope of the Constitution, and all means which are appropriate, which are plainly adapted to that end, which are not prohibited, but consistent with the letter and spirit of the Constitution, are constitutional."

Limitations on the National Government

In Article I, Section 9, the Constitution denies the national government specific powers. Among these is the power to pass **bills of attainder** (legislative acts that single out certain people for punishment without a judicial trial) and **ex post facto laws** (laws that make criminal an act that was legal when it was performed, or increase the penalty for a crime after it has been committed). The government is also limited in its power to suspend the **writ of habeas corpus,** a court order that protects people from arbitrary imprisonment by requiring officials of the government to bring them before a court and state the reasons for the detention. (This most ancient of Anglo-American legal rights has been suspended on only four occasions in U.S. history: in parts of the nation during the Civil War; in South Carolina during the post–Civil War Reconstruction period; in 1905 in the

Philippines during the American occupation of that nation; and in Hawaii during World War II.)

The Constitution also bars the national government from passing laws or engaging in activities that would deny rights guaranteed by the Constitution. The main limitations of this type are found in the Bill of Rights, the first ten amendments to the Constitution. For example, the First Amendment begins by declaring that Congress "shall make no law respecting an establishment of religion." Congress therefore may not pass legislation that favors one religion over another, nor may it grant federal funds to religious groups to advance their religious purposes. (This subject is discussed more fully in Chapter 11.)

Powers of the States

The Constitution does not assign specific powers to the states, but the Tenth Amendment makes it clear that all powers that are not delegated to the national government or denied to the states are reserved for the states or the people. The powers of the states under the United States Constitution are referred to as **reserved powers.** They give the states the authority to pass laws that promote the health, welfare, safety, and morals of their citizens. Education and fire and police protection are among the principal functions exercised by state governments as part of their reserved powers. The states, and not Washington, have the legal right to create and administer a public school system and police and fire departments.

The states may enact legislation under their reserved powers without express authority from the U.S. Constitution. They may not, however, invade areas that are assigned to the national government (foreign affairs and interstate commerce, for example). Nor may the states violate any specific limitations on their power found in provisions of either the United States Constitution (such as those having to do with ex post facto laws) or their own state constitutions.

Concurrent Powers

Concurrent powers are those that can be exercised by both the states and the federal government. A prime example is the power to tax and spend. The states may impose taxes on people and businesses within their jurisdiction. Without that power, they would be unable to function; they would be entirely dependent on the national government. Other concurrent powers include the power to borrow money, to take property for public purposes after compensating the owner (this is known as the power of *eminent domain*), to establish courts, and to enforce the laws. (See Figure 3.1.)

Limitations on the States

Certain powers are denied to the states by the Constitution. Article I, Section 10, contains a number of limitations. For example, the states may not pass bills of attainder or ex post facto laws. They are barred from acting in the field of foreign affairs by the provision that declares that states may not "enter into any Treaty, Alliance, or Confederation" with a foreign nation. (For example, Texas could not negotiate a treaty with Mexico to settle problems related to their common border.) States also cannot levy any tax on imports or exports without the approval

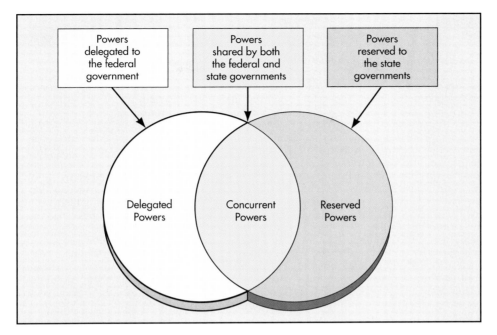

FIGURE 3.1 The Federal System.

of Congress. Several amendments to the Constitution—including the Thirteenth, Fourteenth, Fifteenth, Nineteenth, Twenty-fourth, and Twenty-sixth—impose limitations on the states in areas of civil rights such as voting.

    The **due process** and **equal protection clauses** of the Fourteenth Amendment have become especially important sources of restrictions on the states during the past half century. The Supreme Court has interpreted the due process clause as including most of the provisions of the Bill of Rights, thereby guaranteeing those freedoms against infringement by both the state and the federal governments. It has also used the equal protection clause of the Fourteenth Amendment to outlaw racial discrimination and most forms of gender discrimination by state governments. (A fuller discussion of these subjects is to be found in Chapters 11 and 12 of this book.)

Interstate Relations

The Constitution also sets forth a number of important rules governing relations among the states:

1. The **full faith and credit clause** of Article IV, Section 1, requires the states to honor the final civil rulings of other states, such as marriages, divorce decrees, and final court judgments. (This provision does not apply to criminal cases.) Thus, a marriage or a divorce that is validly granted under the laws of one state must be recognized in all other states.

2. According to Article IV, Section 2, "The citizens of each State shall be entitled to all privileges and immunities of citizens in the several States."

CLOSE-UP

GAY MARRIAGE AND FULL FAITH AND CREDIT

The full faith and credit clause of Article IV, Section 1, of the Constitution establishes an important rule for the nation's federal system, but it has rarely been a subject of controversy. Taken almost word for word from the Articles of Confederation, the clause guarantees that the legal decisions of one state must be accepted by the courts of other states. Thus, a person who has a judicially recognized debt in one state cannot move to another state to escape the liability. Similarly, a person who has obtained a divorce in the courts of one state is divorced in all the states of the nation.

In 1996 the clause was at the center of the public debate over marriages by same-sex partners. A court in Hawaii held that under the state's constitution it was illegal to deny persons of the same sex the right to marry. Many people in other states feared that the decision in Hawaii would cause gay couples to travel there, marry, and upon returning

to their home state seek to have the marriage recognized under the full faith and credit clause of the United States Constitution.

More than a dozen states enacted laws declaring that they would not acknowledge such marriages even if same-sex marriages were permitted in another state. Congress then entered the picture and exercised its legislative power under Article IV, Section 1, which states that Congress "may by general Laws prescribe the Manner in which such [state] Acts, Records and Proceedings shall be proved, and the Effect thereof." The Defense of Marriage Act, passed in the fall of 1996 and signed by President Clinton, provides that no state shall be required to give effect to any same-sex marriage that is treated as a marriage under the law of another state. (A state is free, however, to grant such recognition if it so chooses.)

Although this **privileges and immunities clause** has never been clearly defined, various Supreme Court decisions have created some general rules. The Court has held that the clause does not guarantee complete legal equality between citizens and noncitizens of a state. It protects only the "fundamental rights" that are "basic to the maintenance and well-being of the nation."[7] Thus, for example, a state may not discriminate against a noncitizen with respect to providing police protection and medical care. But a doctor or a lawyer who is licensed to practice in one state does not have a constitutional right to practice in another state without first meeting that state's licensing requirements.

3. The **interstate rendition clause** of Article IV, Section 2, states that "a person charged in any State with Treason, Felony, or other Crime, who shall flee from Justice, and be found in another State, shall on Demand of the executive Authority of the State from which he fled, be delivered up to be removed to the State having jurisdiction of the Crime." In the vast majority of situations, interstate rendition, or *extradition,* presents relatively few problems: Fugitives usually agree to be returned to the state where they are wanted. When prisoners do not agree to be returned, state governors routinely comply with the extradition requests of other states. For 125 years the Supreme Court interpreted the interstate rendition clause as denying to the federal courts the authority to compel a state governor to extradite a fugitive to another state. But in 1987 the Court reversed that precedent, holding that governors have no discretion to reject requests for extradition and that the federal courts may compel the extradition of fugitives to other states.[8]

4. Article I, Section 10, of the Constitution provides that "no State shall, without the consent of Congress, . . . enter into any Agreement or Compact with another State." In this indirect way, it permits the states to settle mutual problems through the use of **interstate compacts,** or agreements between two or more states. An interstate compact is normally negotiated by the states' governors and approved by their legislatures. The compact must then receive the approval of the United States Congress before it can go into effect.

   Throughout the nineteenth century interstate compacts were used almost exclusively to settle boundary disputes between states. In the twentieth century compacts were used to resolve more complex problems. Some compacts still deal with relatively minor issues, but a growing number are concerned with difficult interstate problems involving transportation, environmental issues, crime control, and a variety of commercial problems.

   Perhaps the best-known, and the largest, interstate compact is the one that created the Port Authority of New York and New Jersey in 1921. The Port Authority operates many aspects of transportation in the New York–New Jersey area, including interstate bridges and tunnels, port facilities for ships, bus terminals, and a small railroad system. The Port Authority also owned the 110-story twin towers (the World Trade Center) that were destroyed by a terrorist attack on September 11, 2001.

5. In the case of a dispute between two or more states (for example, when one state sues another over a disputed boundary line), Article III gives the Supreme Court **original jurisdiction;** that is, the Supreme Court sits as a trial court to settle the problem. The Court has, however, heard relatively few such cases in the course of the nation's history.

MUTUAL OBLIGATIONS OF THE NATIONAL AND STATE GOVERNMENTS

Article IV, Section 4, of the Constitution declares that the United States shall guarantee to the states a "Republican Form of Government." There is no definition of the term *republican* and nothing to indicate which branch of the federal government has the duty of applying this provision. The Supreme Court has always refused to become involved in issues arising under the so-called **guarantee clause.** It has claimed that all such questions are "political," not "judicial," and therefore must be decided by either Congress or the president. Thus, the Court would not decide whether the provisions of the Oregon Constitution, which permitted direct legislation by the people through the procedures known as initiative and referendum, denied the state a republican form of government.[9]

Article IV, Section 4, also requires the national government to protect the states against foreign invasion or internal violence. On the rare occasions in the nation's early history when a state was invaded by a foreign power (during the War of 1812 the British invaded Washington, DC, Baltimore, and New Orleans), the national government used its military forces to oppose the invasion.

Article IV, Section 4, also provides that upon the application of the state legislature (or the governor if the legislature cannot be convened), the United States

The George Washington Bridge, which spans the Hudson River between New York and New Jersey, is one of many transportation facilities operated by the Port Authority of New York and New Jersey.

shall protect the states against internal or domestic violence. The states have requested federal aid in suppressing domestic violence on about sixteen occasions since the nation's founding.

The federal government has the right to intervene within a state "in cases of domestic violence," even in the absence of a request by the state. Congress has delegated to the president the power to put down domestic violence by using federal troops or calling the state militia into federal service. The president can also act on the basis of his own constitutional authority. The president has the legal right to act to protect federal property and to prevent interference with the postal system and the movement of interstate commerce.[10] In addition, the president can act to uphold federal court orders. For example, in 1957, acting against the wishes of state officials, President Dwight Eisenhower used federal troops to subdue violence and enforce a federal court order requiring desegregation of public schools in Little Rock, Arkansas. In 1962 federal troops were used to maintain order at the University of Mississippi, which had been ordered by the federal courts to admit its first black student. And in 1965 President Lyndon Johnson sent federal troops to Selma, Alabama, to protect the participants in a voting rights march led by Rev. Martin Luther King, Jr.

The Constitution also imposes certain legal obligations on the states. They are required to maintain a republican form of government, preserve peace within their borders, hold elections for members of Congress, fill vacancies in their

CLOSE-UP

LIFE, DEATH, AND THE FEDERAL SYSTEM

In the fall of 1993 an interstate compact became the focus of a life-and-death struggle between two states. In 1990 Thomas Grasso had robbed and killed an 87-year-old woman in Tulsa, Oklahoma. A year later, after fleeing to New York City, he murdered an 81-year-old woman. Grasso was arrested in New York and pleaded guilty to the second crime, receiving a prison sentence of twenty years to life. New York State did not have a death penalty at that time.

After the conviction Grasso was sent to Oklahoma to be tried for the earlier homicide. Again he pleaded guilty, but this time he was sentenced to death by lethal injection. Grasso did not appeal the sentence, stating that he wished to die rather than face life in prison. The execution was scheduled for October 19, 1993.

Grasso had been returned to Oklahoma by New York under the terms of an interstate compact, the Interstate Agreement on Detainers, which had been adopted by forty-seven states and the District of Columbia. Under the terms of the compact, New York was required to send the prisoner to Oklahoma, but only for the purpose of prosecution for the pending criminal charges. Oklahoma was required to return the prisoner to New York before carrying out its sentence. However, corrections of-

ficials in Oklahoma declined to send Grasso back to New York.

A nine-month tug-of-war between the two states was finally resolved by a federal judge in Oklahoma. Twelve hours before Grasso was scheduled to be executed, the judge ordered Oklahoma to return Grasso to New York. He noted, however, that New York's governor could waive the return of the prisoner and allow Oklahoma to carry out its sentence.

The ruling posed a dilemma for New York's Governor Mario Cuomo, a staunch opponent of the death penalty. Should he waive Grasso's return and thereby allow Oklahoma to execute him? Or should he insist that the prisoner be sent back to New York, thereby preventing the execution and denying Grasso his wish? Governor Cuomo chose the latter course, and Grasso was returned to New York's Sing Sing Prison to serve his sentence.

The story did not end there, however. In November 1994 Republican George Pataki was elected governor of New York. Soon after he was elected, Pataki waived New York's right to maintain custody of Grasso and he was returned to Oklahoma. At 12:22 A.M. on March 20, 1995, Grasso was executed by lethal injection in the Oklahoma State Penitentiary.

delegations to Congress, choose presidential electors, and consider proposed constitutional amendments submitted by Congress or by a national convention under the provisions of Article V.

National Supremacy

In a federal system of government there is bound to be some conflict between the central and state governments over the exercise of various powers. In Article VI, the framers of the Constitution made a clear and unambiguous decision in favor of national supremacy when such a conflict exists: "This Constitution, the Laws of the United States which shall be made in Pursuance thereof; and all treaties made, or which shall be made, under the Authority of the United States, shall be the supreme Law of the Land."

Article VI does not make the states completely subordinate to the national government. Rather, it prevents the states from exercising power in areas that the Constitution has assigned to the national government. States may not, therefore, pass laws or establish policies that conflict with the Constitution, constitutional acts of Congress, or valid national treaties. When such a conflict arises, Article VI requires that the state policy give way to that of the national government.

One of the main functions of the United States Supreme Court is to resolve conflicts within the federal system. The Court is, in fact, the arbiter of American federalism. This role was firmly established early in the nineteenth century. In *McCulloch* v. *Maryland,* for example, Chief Justice Marshall, after upholding Congress's right to establish a national bank, declared unconstitutional a state law that taxed the bank on the ground that it violated the national supremacy clause of Article VI. Early in the nineteenth century the Supreme Court also upheld the right of Congress to create an appeals system in which decisions of state courts involving questions of federal law could be reviewed by the Supreme Court.[11] This method of appeal, which has been used throughout American history, permits the Supreme Court to serve as the ultimate interpreter of federal law. It guarantees that federal, not state, judges will have the final say on issues arising under the Constitution, federal law, and national treaties.

A modern example of the Supreme Court serving as arbiter of the federal system can be seen in the case of *Philadelphia* v. *New Jersey.*[12] A New Jersey law designed to protect the health of its citizens prohibited bringing into the state "any solid or liquid waste that originated or was collected outside [the] state." The Court declared the law to be "impermissible under the Commerce Clause of the Constitution," which bars one state from setting up discriminatory laws designed "to isolate itself in the stream of commerce from a problem shared by all."

The commerce clause also bars states from taxing interstate transactions. If, for example, you purchase an item by mail from an out-of-state company, you do not have to pay a sales tax on the transaction (unless the company has stores in your state). Such a tax would be an illegal interference with interstate commerce. Nor could a state impose an income tax on out-of-state commuters who work in the state but not require resident workers to pay the same levy.

FEDERALISM IN THEORY AND PRACTICE

As we noted at the beginning of the chapter, the framers of the Constitution created only an outline of a federal system. They allowed the details of its operations to be filled in by those who followed them and were charged with running the American governmental system.

From its earliest years under the Constitution, the United States has witnessed an ongoing struggle between advocates of a stronger national government and those who favor greater power for the states. During the 1790s, for example, a debate took place over whether the central government had the constitutional power to create a national bank that would function within the states. Secretary of the Treasury Alexander Hamilton argued forcibly that the Constitution permitted such an exercise of national authority. Thomas Jefferson, the Secretary of State, contended with equal force that the government lacked such authority and that the creation of a national bank would invade the powers that were reserved to the states under the Constitution.

Two major crises in American history have centered on the issue of federalism. The first arose over the issue of slavery and lasted from the 1820s to the 1860s. Southern defenders of slavery contended that the national government had no authority to interfere with this system and that the matter lay solely within the authority of the states. They argued that the Constitution had been created by the states and that the states could withdraw from the Union when the exercise of national power violated the rights of the states. After the election of Abraham Lincoln as president in 1860, the southern states asserted this presumed right to secede, an act that precipitated the Civil War.

Northern opponents of slavery viewed the constitutional system of federalism in a very different way. They believed that the national government had the power to regulate slavery, especially to prevent its expansion into the new states and territories of the West. Moreover, they contended that the Constitution had been created by the people of the nation and not by the states. States therefore had no right to secede from the perpetual Union of states that had been established in 1789.

The issue of slavery was ultimately decided on the battlefields of the Civil War (1861–1865). The victory of the North led to the destruction of the slave system and to the exercise of broad national power by Congress to reconstruct southern society. It also represented a triumph for the view that the Constitution was a national act and that states had no right to secede from the Union.

The second great crisis of American federalism came during the 1930s, when the United States and much of the world were ravaged by economic depression. The nation was convulsed by mass unemployment in the cities, the collapse of its banking system, and falling agricultural prices, which caused many small farmers to lose their land.

In 1932 Franklin Roosevelt was elected president with a broad, though ill-defined, public mandate to deal with the Depression. The problems created by the Depression clearly required national action. But the question remained as to whether the national government possessed the constitutional power to act. President Roosevelt and his Democratic supporters in Congress clearly believed that it did. Between 1933 and 1938 legislation was passed that for the first time imposed federal regulation on important parts of the American economy—for example, labor-management relations and the stock and commodity exchanges. Moreover, Congress enacted a broad program of economic and social legislation, including child labor legislation, unemployment insurance, minimum wage and maximum hours legislation, aid for dependent children, and the Social Security retirement system.

President Roosevelt's New Deal program was strenuously opposed by political conservatives, and its constitutionality was challenged in the courts. For a time the Supreme Court hindered the implementation of Roosevelt's program by declaring important parts of it unconstitutional. But by 1937 the Court altered its position, and it subsequently ruled against all challenges to the program. President Roosevelt and the Democratic Congress, with the overwhelming backing of the American public, emerged victorious in the struggle with the Supreme Court.

The success of the New Deal program profoundly changed the nature of the American federal system. The national government gained vast new power to regulate the economy, and new agencies were created to administer these regulations. Moreover, a network of social welfare programs had been created that provided a safety net for the American people in periods of economic slowdown or personal crisis.

Some of the programs created during the New Deal were operated entirely at the national level. The Social Security system, for example, is funded by a national payroll tax and administered by a national agency. But many other New

Deal programs involve cooperative efforts by state and national governments. An example is the unemployment insurance system, which was created by Congress but is funded and administered by the states.

The term **cooperative federalism** is often used to describe the relationship between the state and national governments that developed to administer much of the reform legislation passed during the 1930s and the following decades. Cooperative federalism was based on the recognition that not all problems are best solved by concentrating authority in Washington. This new view of federalism also recognized that the states lacked the financial ability to pay for the social welfare programs that the public demanded.

To understand the financial difficulties faced by the states and their subdivisions, it is necessary to understand the nature of the nation's complex system of taxation. The federal government benefits from the most productive and flexible tax, the personal income tax. As national wealth increases, federal tax revenues also rise. State revenue is collected from a variety of other taxes, which are not as responsive to increases in wealth. These include small personal and business income taxes, sales taxes, and excise taxes on products like liquor and tobacco. Local governments are forced to rely on an even less desirable tax—the tax on real property. (See Table 3.1.)

It is also important to recognize that significant differences exist in wealth among various states and regions of the United States. Mississippi and Arkansas, for example, are much less prosperous than Connecticut or Delaware. Moreover, within a state some cities or counties may be relatively affluent and others relatively poor.

The dilemma that has confronted American federalism is that demands for greater, and increasingly expensive, public services have been placed on local and state governments, which lack the taxing ability to pay for those programs. The

TABLE 3.1

FEDERAL GOVERNMENT RECEIPTS BY SOURCE (IN BILLIONS OF DOLLARS)

Source	2003 Actual	Estimated 2004	2005	2006	2007	2008	2009
Individual income taxes	793.7	765.4	873.8	956.5	1,049.3	1133.4	1,209.9
Corporation income taxes	131.8	168.7	230.2	250.0	251.0	252.1	255.7
Social insurance and retirement receipts	713.0	732.4	793.9	834.0	878.7	918.8	960.2
Excise taxes	67.5	70.8	73.2	75.8	77.9	80.0	82.2
Estate and gift taxes	22.0	23.9	21.4	23.9	21.5	22.2	23.6
Customs duties	19.9	22.6	22.1	24.4	26.2	27.6	30.0
Miscellaneous receipts	34.5	34.3	36.5	41.2	46.2	51.2	54.8
Adjustment for revenue uncertainty[1]	—	−20.0	—	—	—	—	—
Total receipts	**1,782.3**	**1,798.1**	**2,036.3**	**2,205.7**	**2,350.8**	**2,485.3**	**2,616.4**

Source: U.S. Office of Management and Budget. *The Budget for Fiscal Year 2005.* pp. 23–24.

federal government, on the other hand, has greater access to taxable wealth but relatively little responsibility for actually providing basic domestic services.

Efforts to resolve this dilemma resulted in the development of cooperative federalism, "a new style and new philosophy of federalism distinguished by *joint undertakings* between the federal and state governments and the expansion of the use of *federal grants-in-aid.*"[13] A **grant-in-aid** is a sum of money given by a higher level of government to a lower level to be used to pay for a specific program—for example, highway construction. Grants are said to be *categorical;* they are to be used for a specific, narrowly defined purpose. They also require *matching grants*—the state or local government receiving the grant is required to pay some percentage of the costs of the project.

In this approach to federalism, the emphasis is on cooperation between the state or local government and the national government in achieving goals determined by the national government. Although Congress does not have direct power to regulate public health, safety, or welfare, it can employ its power to tax and spend for the general welfare to establish a system that will reward the states for performing these functions.[14]

The Growth of the Grant System

Although grants have been employed throughout American history—beginning with land grants for such purposes as the establishment of public schools—in the twentieth century the use of grants increased dramatically. In 1902 the national government operated five grant programs that distributed a total of $3 million, or less than 1 percent of state and local government revenues. The number of federal grant programs reached fifty-one by 1964. As a result of President Lyndon Johnson's "Great Society" program, the number grew to 530 by 1971. The cost of these programs also multiplied rapidly: $10.9 billion was spent in 1965, $24.1 billion in 1970, $91.3 billion in 1980, and $105.9 billion in 1985. By fiscal year 2003 the total amount distributed under federal grant programs had risen to an estimated $384 billion. Over 34 percent of all state and local spending is derived from federal grant money.[15]

Federal grants are given to a wide assortment of programs in areas such as environmental protection, transportation (airports, highways, and mass transit) education, employment, training, social services, health, income security, veterans benefits, and for the administration of state justice systems. By far the largest of the federal grants are given for health (Medicaid) and income security programs (family support payments to states).

The primary reason for the growth of the grant system was dissatisfaction with state and local government actions. According to one authority: "People who wanted problems addressed and who were unsatisfied with state and local responses went to Washington. Responding to their problems through grants enabled officials at different levels of government to share the credit for fighting crime, combating poverty, or improving educational opportunities."[16]

Centralized Federalism

During the "Great Society" administration of President Lyndon Johnson, beginning in the mid-1960s, a new approach to federalism developed. Sometimes referred to as **centralized federalism,** this approach entailed more forceful control of

Federal grants help pay the cost of constructing much of America's highway system, such as this Los Angeles interchange.

grants by the federal government. The goal was to persuade state and local governments to adopt programs that they might otherwise not have undertaken. This approach was applied most fully in the areas of civil rights, job training, welfare, transportation, and housing for the poor. It abandoned any pretense of a state and local government role in making policy for the nation; the federal government assumed the power to define national problems and set national goals. In effect, therefore, centralized federalism was centralized government.[17]

During the 1980s the Supreme Court gave its approval to this highly centralized view of the federal system. In *Garcia* v. *San Antonio Metropolitan Transit Authority* (1985),[18] for example, the Court upheld the power of Congress to impose minimum wage and overtime provisions on employees of state governments who perform governmental functions. It rejected the claim that this 1974 legislation interfered with the sovereignty of the states and hence violated the Tenth Amendment to the Constitution. According to the Court, the rights of the states are protected through their representation in Congress and by their role in the election of the president, not by the Tenth Amendment or the Supreme Court.

The New Federalism

By the late 1960s many state and local officials were increasingly critical of the federal grant system. They claimed that it had become excessively complex and fragmented. Moreover, these officials believed that the grant system compelled them to adopt programs favored by the national government and not those needed by their communities. Federal officials were simply too far away to understand the unique problems of states and localities.

The election of Republican presidents—Nixon (1969–1974) and Reagan (1981–1989)—brought to power administrations that favored changes in the federal system. In 1994 the election of the first Republican-controlled Congress in more than forty years created further support for changes in the relationship between Washington and state and local governments. And as we shall see in the next section, changes in the makeup of the Supreme Court have also led to a number of significant decisions that have supported state interests as against those of the national government.

The changes brought about in the functioning of federalism in the past three decades are often referred to as the New Federalism. Presidents Nixon and Reagan and the Republican Congress of 1995–1997 agreed on a number of matters. "All three federalism reform efforts were responses to perceived policy failures of the past; all advanced decentralization as a goal for responding to those failures. . . ."[19]

The Republican presidents and Congress also agreed that block grants should replace the categorical grants-in-aid that had become the most salient feature of the American federal system. A **block grant** is a sum of money given by the federal government to a state or local government to be used for a broad, general purpose. A block grant might be given for any purpose related to law enforcement, for example, while a grant-in-aid would require that the money be spent for new police cruisers or police communication systems.

President Reagan was successful in increasing the federal government's use of block grants. He also reduced the number of federal grants-in-aid from approximately 539 in 1981 to 340 in 1986. During Reagan's first years as president, the total cost of federal grants actually declined. However, their cost has risen steadily since that time.

But there have also been significant differences in the approaches to New Federalism taken by different Republican presidents. Nixon attempted to implement managerial reforms in order to make the federal bureaucracy more efficient; Reagan's ultimate goal was the elimination of many federal aid programs. The centerpiece of Nixon's reform program was **general revenue sharing,** a system of financial aid to the states and localities with no strings attached; these governments could spend the money in whatever areas they wished. Reagan opposed revenue sharing, and the program was ended in 1986.[20]

The most significant change in the operation of the federal system came in the area of public welfare. Although welfare reform had been discussed for several decades, change did not come about until 1996, when Congress passed and President Clinton signed the Personal Responsibility and Work Opportunity Reconciliation Act. This legislation ended the Aid to Families With Dependent Children (AFDC) program begun in the 1930s as part of President Roosevelt's New Deal. Under AFDC, federal funds were given to the states to help pay for welfare benefits for eligible families. AFDC was an *entitlement* program; families with incomes below a specified level were automatically eligible to receive benefits.

The new welfare law became effective on October 1, 1996. It required that Congress appropriate a total of $16.4 billion to the states annually through 2002. After that date, federal financial support for this type of welfare program ended. The $16.4 billion was given to the states in the form of block grants based on the number of recipients in the states and was to be matched by the states. Most federal regulations on the use of the block grants were ended, but the law did set a five-year limit on the length of time any family can receive welfare benefits. The general purpose of the law was to move people off the welfare rolls and into jobs. The states are free to establish their own programs to achieve this goal. States have used a variety of approaches, including job training, providing child care, increasing educational opportunities, or some combination of methods.

While New Federalism achieved some significant changes in policy, its overall accomplishments have been limited. Federal aid to the states has increased since the end of the Reagan administration. Block grant spending has become a deceasing part of federal aid, and the number of categorical grants has grown significantly. Federal aid has also increased, both as a percentage of all federal outlays and as a percentage of state and local expenditures. (Much of the increase in federal aid money was a result of spending for Medicaid, the federal program that supports health costs for the needy.)

TABLE 3.2

FEDERAL BUDGET TOTALS BY FUNCTION AND SUBFUNCTION, FISCAL YEARS 2002–2006 (IN BILLIONS OF DOLLARS)

Function and Subfunction	2002	2003	Estimated 2004	2005	2006
National defense	348,555	404,920	453,684	450,586	436,147
Human resources	1,317,437	1,417,707	1,497,286	1,566,477	1,651,094
Education, training, employment, and social services	70,544	82,568	87,211	89,020	88,856
Health	196,544	219,576	243,501	252,597	267,719
Medicare	230,855	249,433	270,4512	294,249	341,028
Income security	312,530	334,432	339,495	348,149	353,180
Social Security	455,980	474,680	496,174	514,989	533,536
Veterans benefits and services	50,984	57,018	60,454	67,473	66,775
Physical resources	104,359	113,240	127,246	122,303	116,401
Energy	482	-775	957	1,774	1,877
Natural resources and environment	29,454	29,703	31,665	30,899	30,401
Commerce and housing credit	-391	-1,607	7,723	2,714	-1,243
Transportation	61,833	67,069	68,144	69,899	70,284
Community and regional development	12,981	18,850	18,757	17,017	15,082
Net interest	170,951	153,076	156,264	177,909	213,362
Other functions	117,060	123,076	143,675	145,676	133,716
International affairs	22,351	21,208	34,236	37,838	32,460
General science, space, and technology	20,767	20,873	22,291	24,353	24,666
Agriculture	21,957	22,600	20,121	22,322	20,895
Administration of justice	35,171	35,408	41,603	42,782	42,288
General government	16,814	22,987	25,424	19,148	19,445
Allowances	—	—	—	-767	-6,038
Undistributed offsetting receipts	−47,392	−54,382	−59,321	−63,108	−77,422
Tota, Federal outlays	2,010,970	2,157,637	2,318,834	2,399,843	2,473,298

Source: U.S. Office of Management and Budget. *Historic Tables, The Budget for Fiscal Year 2005.* p. 52.

America's war on terrorism that began with the attacks of September 11, 2001, will most certainly have an effect on the nation's federal system. Wars always have the consequence of increasing the size and power of the national government. This phenomenon can already be seen in the movement to reorganize and strengthen the nation's Homeland Security system through improved immigration control, better training and equipment of police, fire, and emergency medical personnel, increased aviation security, and the creation of medical programs to counter the threat of bioterrorism.

But the most dramatic changes in government policy will be found in the increase in military and defense spending to pay for the war on terrorism. Expenditures in this area will grow from $329 billion in the fiscal year that preceded the September 11, 2001, attacks to an estimated $396.8 billion in fiscal 2003 to $426.6 billion in fiscal 2005. (See Table 3.2.)

Future trends in the nation's federal system—whether toward greater centralization or devolution of power to the states and cities; whether continued growth of federal spending or the imposition of effective restraints on government—will depend on a number of factors. The election of Democratic or Republican presidents, as well as the political composition of Congress, will, of course, have a major effect on the character of federal legislation. But ultimately the direction of American federalism will depend on public attitudes toward government—whether Americans will continue to look to government for solutions to social problems or whether they will look more favorably to nongovernmental remedies.

Since much of the impact of federalism depends on rulings by the Supreme Court, we turn now to a discussion of the Court's role in the development and implementation of the contemporary federal system.

THE SUPREME COURT AND CONTEMPORARY FEDERALISM

In 1937 the Supreme Court abandoned the restricted view of the legislative power of Congress that it had defended during the first decades of the twentieth century.[21] In the spring of 1937 President Franklin Roosevelt proposed legislation that would permit him to increase the number of Supreme Court justices. Although he justified the change on other grounds (that the justices were older and therefore needed help), the real goal of the proposal was to alter the composition of the Court and thus produce a new majority that would accept the growth of national power. The president had a personal stake in this issue; the Supreme Court had declared unconstitutional much of his New Deal legislative program, which had been intended to combat the serious economic depression that gripped the United States during the 1930s.[22]

President Roosevelt's so-called "court packing plan" was not passed by Congress, but the Supreme Court began to alter its position regarding national power. It now began to approve Roosevelt's New Deal program. Soon the opponents of broad national power began resigning from the Court, and Roosevelt was able to appoint justices who sympathized with his domestic legislative agenda.

For almost sixty years the Supreme Court rejected constitutional challenges to all congressional legislation based on the commerce clause. Thus, for example, it upheld such major legislation as the National Labor Relations Act of 1935,[23] the

Fair Labor Standards Act of 1938,[24] and the Civil Rights Act of 1964.[25] During these years the Court swept aside all arguments that Congress's use of the commerce clause unconstitutionally invaded the reserve powers of the states. Specifically, it rejected the argument that manufacturing is not part of commerce[26] and the contention that the Tenth Amendment protected the states against federal laws designed to regulate activities that occurred within a state.[27]

But since 1995 the Supreme Court has on several occasions invalidated federal laws on the grounds that they exceeded Congress's power to regulate interstate commerce and illegally invaded the reserve powers of the states. Thus, in *United States* v. *Lopez* the Court, by a 5-to-4 vote, declared unconstitutional a statute that made it a federal crime to possess a weapon within 1000 feet of a school building. If the government's view of the commerce clause were accepted, Chief Justice Rehnquist wrote, "Congress could regulate any activity that it found was related to the economic activity of individual citizens: family law (including marriage, divorce, and child custody), for example."[28]

The Supreme Court has also imposed restrictions of the use of other forms of federal authority. It declared unconstitutional a provision of the Brady Handgun Violence Prevention Act of 1993 that required state and local officials to conduct background checks on prospective purchasers of handguns. By a 5-to-4 vote, the Court found that the law violated the sovereign power of the states. "The Federal Government may neither issue directives requiring the States to address particular problems, nor command the States' officials, or those of their political subdivisions, to administer or enforce a federal regulatory program," Justice Scalia wrote in the majority opinion.[29] The Court has also imposed restrictions on the use of the enforcement power of Congress set forth in Section 5 of the Fourteenth Amendment[30] and found that the federal government could not require state courts to hear private lawsuits involving federal claims.[31] Finally, the Court has asserted the sovereign immunity of states both from private lawsuits brought in federal court[32] and from administrative claims brought before federal agencies.[33]

At this point it is impossible to say whether these decisions represent merely isolated inroads on the powers of Congress or the beginning of a fundamental shift in power within the federal system of government. The future path of the Supreme Court in this area will depend largely on the kinds of individuals who are appointed to the Court in the early years of the twenty-first century. Since the Court's recent federalism cases have been decided by 5-to-4 votes, new appointments to the Court could reverse the trend toward decisions favorable to the interests of the state or extend the decisions already made to other areas of the federal system.

CONCLUSION

The United States Constitution created the world's first federal form of government. Other nations have since adopted it as a governing system; they include Canada, Mexico, Brazil, Australia, and Germany. Federalism has been popular in countries with large geographic areas and diverse populations, since it permits the decentralization of important governmental functions to states or provinces. It would be unimaginable for the central government to make all domestic political decisions for a huge and populous nation like the United States.

A constitution that creates a federal form of government cannot provide the details for the workings of that system; it can only establish a broad outline for governance. Political and legal forces provide the operational details for the working of a federal form of government. Moreover, tensions between the central and state governments are an inevitable aspect of federalism. The governments that compose that system will sometimes seek to expand their power at the expense of other governmental units.

The history of the United States shows that our federal system shares these characteristics. National and state governments have exercised their governmental power to provide details for the system and have frequently come into conflict. And throughout our history the Supreme Court has played an important part in defining the proper constitutional roles for Washington and the states.

Arguments over national and state power have continued from the nation's early years to the present. In different periods either national or state power has been in the ascendancy. Throughout the first 150 years of the nation's history, Americans looked primarily to their states and localities to provide governmental services. During the Great Depression of the 1930s, the public increasingly looked to Washington for answers to the country's economic and social problems. Moreover, state and local governments became dependent on federal money to pay for the cost of public services.

Centralization of government reached its peak during the 1960s and 1970s. The election of Ronald Reagan as president in 1980 signaled a change in the functioning of the federal system. The movement of power to Washington was slowed, if not entirely halted, and a trend toward greater state authority became evident. The enactment of welfare reform legislation in 1996 and decisions of the Supreme Court in the last years of the twentieth century are the most significant evidence of this change. It remains to be seen whether this trend will continue and produce a federal system very different from the centralized system that existed throughout much of the last century.

One powerful force that will work to create greater national power is the war on terrorism that began when the United States was attacked on September 11, 2001. Earlier wars in American history have always produced an increase in the power of the national government and a rapid growth in expenditures to support the military effort. Both characteristics have marked the early stages of the nation's war on international terrorism.

QUESTIONS FOR THOUGHT

1. What are the main features of a federal form of government?
2. How does a federal form of government differ from a confederacy? From a unitary government?
3. What types of powers are given to the national government by the Constitution?
4. What types of powers are given to the states by the Constitution?
5. What are federal grants-in-aid?
6. Why do grants-in-aid play such an important part in the operation of the American federal system?
7. What consequences will the war on terrorism likely have on the nation's federal system?

INTERNET ACTIVITIES

1. *The U.S. Constitution and Your State Constitution.* Access your home state constitution at **http://www.constitution.org/cons/usstcons.htm**. Access the U.S. Constitution at **http://www.law.cornell.edu/constitution/consti tution.overview.html**. Briefly compare the amendment procedures used by each.

2. *Complying with the Fed.* Go to the National Conference of State Legislatures at **http://www.ncsl.org/**. From "State-Federal Relations," **http://www.ncsl. org/statefed/humserv/welfareauth.htm**, briefly summarize the impact that recent federal regulations have for states that administer federal welfare programs for immigrants.

KEY TERMS

bill of attainder	ex post facto law	necessary and proper clause
block grant	federalism	original jurisdiction
centralized federalism	full faith and credit clause	privileges and immunities
concurrent powers	general revenue sharing	clause
confederation	grant-in-aid	reserved powers
cooperative federalism	guarantee clause	unitary government
delegated powers	implied powers	writ of *habeas corpus*
due process clause	interstate compacts	
equal protection clause	interstate rendition clause	

SUGGESTED READING

Greve, Michael S. *Real Federalism.* Washington, DC: AEI Press, 1999.

Grey, Virginia, Russell L. Hanson, and Herbert Jacob, eds. *Politics in the American States,* 7th ed. Washington, DC: Congressional Quarterly Press, 1999.

Haskins, Ron, Isabel V. Sawhill, R. Kent Weaver, and Andrea Kane. eds. *Welfare Reform and Beyond.* Washington, DC: Brookings Institution, 2002.

Nagel, Robert F. *The Implosion of American Federalism.* New York: Oxford University Press, 2001.

O'Toole, Laurence J., Jr. *American Intergovernmental Relations.* 3rd ed. Washington, DC: Congressional Quarterly Press, 2000.

Posner, Paul L. *The Politics of Unfunded Mandates: Whither Federalism?* Washington, DC: Georgetown University Press, 1998.

Walker, David B. *The Rebirth of Federalism,* 2nd ed. New York: Chatham House, 2000.

Wallin, Bruce A. *From Revenue Sharing to Deficit Sharing.* Washington, DC: Georgetown University Press, 1998.

Weaver, R. Kent. *Ending Welfare as We Know It.* Washington, DC: Brookings Institution, 2000.

Zimmerman, Joseph F. *Interstate Cooperation: Compacts and Administrative Agreements.* Westport, CT: Greenwood Publishing Group, 2002.

NOTES

1. *Crosby* v. *National Foreign Trade Council,* 530 U.S. 363 (2000).
2. Morton Grodzins and Daniel Elazar, "Centralization and Decentralization in the American Federal System," in Robert A. Goldwin, ed., *A Nation of States: Essays on the American Federal System,* 2nd ed. (Chicago: Rand McNally, 1974), p. 1.
3. *The Federalist Papers,* No. 39.
4. *United States* v. *Darby,* 312 U.S. 100 (1941).
5. *Heart of Atlanta Motel* v. *United States,* 379 U.S. 241 (1964).
6. 4 Wheat. 316 (1819).
7. *Baldwin* v. *Montana Fish and Game Commission,* 436 U.S. 371 (1978).
8. *Puerto Rico* v. *Branstad,* 483 U.S. 219 (1987).
9. *Pacific States Telephone and Telegraph Co.* v. *Oregon,* 223 U.S. 118 (1912). See also *Luther* v. *Borden,* 7 How. 1 (1849).
10. *In re Debs,* 158 U.S. 564 (1895).
11. *Martin* v. *Hunter's Lessee,* 1 Wheat. 304 (1816); *Cohens* v. *Virginia,* 6 Wheat. 264 (1821).
12. 437 U.S. 617 (1978).
13. Jeffrey R. Henig, *Public Policy and Federalism: Issues in State and Local Politics* (New York: St. Martin's Press, 1985), p. 15. Italics in original.
14. Thomas R. Dye, *American Federalism: Competition Among Governments* (Lexington, MA: Lexington Books, 1990), p. 7.

15. U.S. Bureau of the Census, *Statistical Abstract of the United States, 2003*, 123rd ed. (Washington, DC: Government Printing Office, 2003), Table 437 p. 280.

16. David C. Nice, *Federalism: The Politics of Intergovernmental Relations* (New York: St. Martin's Press, 1987), p. 55.

17. Dye, *American Federalism*, pp. 7–8.

18. 469 U.S. 528 (1985).

19. Timothy Conlan, *From New Federalism to Devolution* (Washington, DC: Brookings Institution, 1998), p. 2.

20. Ibid., p. 3.

21. See, for example, *Hammer* v. *Dagenhart*, 247 U.S. 251 (1918): (child labor legislation).

22. See, for example, *Schechter Brothers Poultry Corp.* v. *United States,* 295 U.S. 495 (1935) (National Industrial Recovery Act) and *Railroad Retirement Board* v. *Alton R.R.,* 295 U.S. 330 (1935) (Railway Pension Act).

23. *NLRB* v. *Jones & Laughlin Steel Corp.,* 301 U.S. 1 (1937).

24. *United States* v. *Darby,* supra.

25. *Heart of Atlanta Motel Co.* v. *United States,* supra.

26. *NLRB* v. *Jones & Laughlin Steel Corp.,* supra.

27. *United States* v. *Darby,* supra.

28. 511 U.S. 1029 (1995). See also *U.S.* v. *Morrison,* 529 U.S. 598 (2000).

29. *Printz* v. *United States* and *Mack* v. *United States,* 521 U.S. 898 (1997).

30. *City of Boerne* v. *Flores,* 521 U.S. 507 (1997).

31. *Alden* v. *Maine,* 527 U.S. 706 (1999).

32. *Seminole Tribe of Florida* v. *Florida,* 517 U.S. 44 (1996).

33. *Federal Maritime Commission* v. *South Carolina Ports Authority,* (May 28, 2002).

Public Opinion
and the
Mass Media

As we have seen in earlier chapters, the concept of self-government is fundamental to American democracy. But if the people are to govern themselves, they must form sound opinions on political issues and vote accordingly. In this chapter we explore how political opinions are formed; in particular, we examine the role of early experiences in the family, school, and community and the impact of the media, from which individuals acquire basic information about government. We also examine the techniques used to study public opinion, especially public-opinion polling. In the final sections of the chapter, we discuss the means through which Americans express their political opinions—that is, how Americans participate in politics.

> Sometimes it is said that Man cannot be trusted with the government of himself.—Can he then be trusted with the government of others? Or have we found angels in the form of kings to govern him?— Let History answer this question.
>
> —*Thomas Jefferson, First Inaugural Address, March 4, 1801*

THE AMERICAN POLITICAL CULTURE

Public opinion in the United States must be viewed within the context of the nation's **political culture**—the fundamental, widely supported values that hold American society together and give legitimacy to its political institutions. The American political culture is, obviously, democratic. The democratic goals of equality, individual freedom, and due process of law are among the most basic values of the American people.[1]

Although almost all Americans support the basic goals of democracy, there is less agreement when it comes to the application of democratic procedures. Over the course of American history, for example, majorities have been willing to deny freedom of speech to a variety of groups, including communists, fascists, atheists, racists, and artists. But most studies show that the American public has become more tolerant of unpopular political ideas in recent decades; this is especially true of citizens with more education.[2]

It should also be understood that the nation's political leaders support democratic goals and procedures more strongly than the general public does. The fact that public officials are especially likely to support democratic procedures is important. It means that they will generally make decisions that maintain those procedures even if they lack widespread public support. It is not at all certain that democratic political systems require public commitment to basic democratic principles:

> Hostility to democratic procedures is fatal, whether among the leaders or the public, but support of these procedures may prove essential only among leaders. Perhaps the public need not agree on basic principles so long as it does not demand disruptive policies and procedures.[3]

POLITICAL SOCIALIZATION

The process by which a society's political culture is transmitted from one generation to the next is known as **political socialization.** The process begins in early childhood, when children acquire a general orientation toward political issues from their parents that continues throughout life.[4] People's political ideas are influenced by all the groups of which they are members: immediate, personal groups such as family and friends as well as larger, less personal groups such as political parties or labor unions. They are also affected by social categories such as race, religion, place of residence, income level, and education. Of course, historical events and political issues may also affect a person's attitudes.

The Family

The earliest and perhaps most powerful influence on a person is the family. This is largely because young children have very little contact with people outside the family. Many youngsters learn about their parents' political party preference during the preschool years, and often that party identification persists in later life. The family also has a strong effect on a person's later interest in politics. Children of people who show interest in political matters generally express such an interest as adults.

The School

Many social scientists believe that the school's impact on the socialization process is almost as great as the family's. That is not surprising, for after their preschool years children spend much of their time in the classroom. Here they are taught discipline, patriotism, and respect for the law. In addition, teachers serve as models for many schoolchildren and influence their attitudes and behavior.[5]

The Peer Group

Children's friends, classmates, teammates, and other associates also influence their attitudes. As an adult, a person may belong to peer groups within his or her religious community, political party, and ethnic association, as well as other more or less formal groups such as bridge clubs and parent-teacher associations. Relations among the members of peer groups are often highly personal, and certain groups can have a lasting effect on a person's political opinions.

The daily recitation of the Pledge of Allegiance in public school classrooms is an example of political socialization.

The Media

Although many of the forces that socialize children and young adults have been around for centuries, the influence of the media on the socialization process is a product of the past several decades. Now that television is a regular part of most Americans' daily lives, the political messages presented on TV have become more important to our political culture.

The media can socialize through very direct methods, such as broadcast coverage of political campaigns and elections. This coverage gives the public direct contact with the political process. In addition, the media can socialize in much more subtle ways. Television shows for children can encourage tolerance of people of other races and religions, or they may encourage children to believe that violence is an acceptable solution to most problems. These more subtle and indirect forms of socialization are present in virtually all broadcast programming, even when the programming is ostensibly labeled as entertainment. The important role of television in socializing children is starkly shown by the fact that many children spend more time each day watching television than they spend being formally educated in school.

Social Class: Income, Occupation, and Education

Although the United States is sometimes thought to be a classless society, there are several fairly distinct social classes—"upper middle," "lower middle," "working"—based on income, occupation, education, and related factors. Americans can, and often do, move from one social class to another.

It is sometimes difficult to obtain information about the political opinions of members of various social classes. Some people, for example, do not consider themselves to be members of the class in which a social scientist might place them. Despite this difficulty, however, enough information has been gathered to permit some conclusions about the relationships between social class and political opinions. Generally, people with higher incomes, more education, and higher job status (doctors, business executives, lawyers) are more conservative in their political opinions and tend to support the Republican party. Unskilled workers, by contrast, are generally more liberal in their political views and support the Democratic party.

Race and Religion

Certain patterns of political opinion can be traced to race or religion. On such issues as civil rights, abortion laws, and aid to Israel, members of racial and religious groups have strong opinions, are very active, and in some cases have a significant influence on public policy. Most African Americans, for example, are concerned about civil rights issues; many Catholics and conservative Protestants oppose abortion; and Jews have been active in their support for Israel.

Place of Residence

The area in which people live can also influence their political opinions. Ever since World War II, the suburbs of America's large cities have been Republican, whereas most of the nation's largest cities have been strongly Democratic for more than a century. Certain sections of the country—the Rocky Mountain states, for example—have been Republican strongholds. By contrast, the Democratic party's almost complete dominance of the South for a century after the Civil War caused political analysts to refer to it as the "solid South." This dominance has gradually declined since the 1950s, and the Republican party is now either the majority party or competitive in all southern states.

History and Political Events

Attitudes are also influenced by the important events that occur in a person's lifetime. Military service in Vietnam during the 1960s and 1970s has probably had a long-term effect on the opinions of many Americans regarding issues of war and peace and American foreign policy in general. In the same manner, the September 11, 2001 terrorist attack on the United States will surely have long-term consequences on the way most Americans will think about issues of war and foreign policy. But the involvement with history need not be a direct, personal one. The opinions of most members of a society are influenced by the events of their time. This is especially true of major developments like wars, scandals, economic depressions, and periods of economic prosperity.

THE NATURE OF PUBLIC OPINION

As people grow older, they gather a variety of impressions of the political system in which they live. Very early in life they begin to develop their own attitudes toward political activities—attitudes that are influenced by the many different kinds of people with whom they come into contact, by factors in their society, and by historical events. These attitudes shape their political opinions.

Political opinion is a form of **public opinion,** the range of opinions expressed by citizens on any subject. The subject may be anything from their favorite television programs to which team is going to win the World Series. There is no single public opinion on any given issue; rather, there are as many public opinions as there are possible views on an issue. **Political opinion** is the set of opinions expressed by the members of a community on political issues (issues that involve some aspect of public policy). Issues such as taxation, welfare, health care, and foreign policy can, and usually do, generate political opinions, and those opinions are just as varied as opinions on nonpolitical issues. In this chapter, when we refer to public opinion, we are concerned with opinions on political subjects.

Although views on political subjects can vary greatly, even within the same family, it is possible to identify some general features of political opinions. These characteristics have been labeled *intensity, concentration, stability, distribution,* and *salience* (importance or relevance). Political opinions can also be either transitory or lasting.

Intensity refers to how strongly an opinion is held. It varies according to the individual; some people feel more strongly about certain issues than do others. Intensity also varies according to how important an issue seems to a person. Topics such as crime, education, and taxation tend to evoke stronger opinions among many Americans than do such matters as farm subsidies or antitrust law.

An opinion is said to be *concentrated* if it is held by a small portion of society. For example, corn and wheat farmers in the Midwest have benefited from federal farm subsidies. Accordingly, public opinion in favor of farm subsidies tends to be concentrated in that part of the nation.

When the intensity and concentration of a given political opinion are fairly constant over a long period, the opinion is said to be *stable.* The opinion that democracy is a good form of government is clearly a stable one; if it were not, radical attempts to change the American political system would have succeeded long ago. It should be noted, however, that opinions are never absolutely stable; change is always possible.

The *distribution* of opinion refers to the number of people who support various positions on a given issue. In the case of abortion, for instance, opinion is largely distributed between two major camps—those who are opposed and those who believe it is a matter for individual decision. In other cases, however, opinion may be distributed fairly evenly along a continuum. An example would be the opinions Americans hold on a subject such as the future of the American economy—that is, whether the nation will continue to prosper or decline in coming years.

The term *salience* refers to the importance or relevance of an issue to a person or group. To most Americans, such issues as the state of the economy or whether the United States should engage in military conflicts are salient, whereas for most Americans U.S. policy toward small businesses is not.

Some political opinions are short-lived or transitory, whereas others are lasting. Many political issues at the national, state, and local levels change fairly rapidly; political opinions on those issues will be formed and will last only as long as the issue is important. Some political opinions remain constant and are long-lived. People's core attitudes—whether they are liberal or conservative, for example—may remain basically the same throughout their lives.

MEASURING PUBLIC OPINION

In a democracy, politicians and public officials want to know what the public is thinking about issues and candidates. Historically, they found this out by talking to citizens directly and by reading the letters that came into their offices. They also kept track of public opinion as it was expressed in the media, especially the press.

During the nineteenth century various journals began presenting public opinion in a new form known as the "straw poll." Such polls, which tabulated the political preferences of specific communities or groups, were thought to give the press more trustworthy information than could be obtained by interviewing party leaders. Newspapers favored the polls as a means of demonstrating their independence and professionalism. They could support a particular candidate even though news stories showed that the candidate was trailing in the race. By the turn of the twentieth century, straw polls had become a routine practice.[6]

Techniques for predicting election results on the basis of past voting information were introduced in the 1940s, but it was not until the development of computer technology in the early 1960s that polling came into its own. Not only can computers process vast quantities of information, but computerized polling also allows for the use of much more sophisticated methods of analysis. The advent of computers dramatically increased the use and importance of scientific polling.

President Harry Truman holds aloft a copy of the *Chicago Tribune* that confidently announced the election of Governor Thomas Dewey as president in November 1948. Public opinion polls had all predicted a victory by Dewey. The polls were wrong; the *Tribune's* analysis of the early voting returns was in error. Truman had won the election.

Scientific Polling

Today the most important method used to find out about public opinion is **scientific polling,** the use of scientific methodology and mathematical probability to analyze public attitudes toward issues and candidates in electoral campaigns. Scientific polling was first used in the United States in the fields of advertising and market research. Since World War II, it has also become widely used in academic research, politics, journalism, and the media.

One of the earliest polling organizations was the American Institute of Public Opinion, better known as the Gallup Poll. The first organization to attempt a nationwide poll (in 1944) was the University of Chicago's National Opinion Research Center (NORC). Since then a large number of polling organizations have been established. Some of them, such as the Gallup and Harris polls, sell their results to clients. Others are academic research organizations like NORC and the Center for Political Studies at the University of Michigan.

Polling organizations sell their results to candidates, television and radio stations, and newspapers and magazines. Those results, of course, are "news" and are published by the media. Modern media polls are sponsored by all three of the major television networks and by some of the nation's largest newspapers—*The Wall Street Journal* and *The New York Times,* for example—and the national news magazines—*Time, Newsweek, US News and World Report.* Media polling has grown rapidly since the 1970s.

Many of the clients of polling organizations are politicians and candidates for office who want to know what people believe the main issues to be and how they feel about those issues. Candidates also want to know how popular they are compared with other candidates. The results of surveys conducted for candidates often are not made public unless the candidate thinks publication of the findings would benefit his or her campaign.

How Polls Are Conducted

The basic tools of modern scientific polling are the sample and the survey.[7] **Sampling** is the process of choosing a relatively small number of cases to be studied to derive information about the larger population from which they have been selected. (A *population* is any group of people, organizations, objects, or events about which the researcher wants to draw conclusions; a *sample* is any subgroup of a population that is identified for analysis.)

To be of value to the researcher, a sample must be representative; that is, every major attribute of the population from which the sample has been drawn must be present in the sample in roughly the same proportion, or *frequency,* as it is in the larger population. For example, a representative sample of the U.S. population must, among other things, contain the same proportions of blacks, whites, Native Americans, Hispanics, and other groups as the population as a whole.

The method used to choose a representative sample is known as *random sampling.* Although it may involve sophisticated statistical analysis, random sampling is essentially a lottery system; the sample is chosen in such a way that each case (or individual) in the entire population has an equal opportunity to be selected for analysis, just as in a properly run lottery every number has an equal chance of being the winning number.

Once a random sample has been selected, the researcher can carry out the actual study. If the purpose of the study is to find out what people think or how

A representative of a polling organization conducts an interview. Public-opinion polling is relied upon in both politics and commerce.

they act, the best (and sometimes the only) way to find out is to ask them. The method used to do this is known as **survey research.** It may be defined as a method of data collection in which information is obtained directly from individuals who have been selected so as to provide a basis for making inferences about some larger population. The techniques used in survey research include direct questioning through face-to-face or telephone interviews and mailed or self-administered questionnaires.

Survey research can be broken down into a series of steps, beginning with specifying the purpose of the research and ending with reporting the findings. Some key steps in the research process are *instrumentation* (drafting the questions and other items that will appear on the questionnaire or interview guide), *pretesting* (administering the survey instrument to a small sample to ensure that the instructions can be interpreted correctly), *surveying* (administering the survey instrument to the entire sample), *coding* (reducing the data collected to numerical terms), and *analyzing* the data.

TELEPHONE POLLS   As noted earlier, polls conducted by the media have become the most important form of political polling. Media polls use two basic methods: the telephone poll and the exit poll. The findings of polls such as the CBS News/*New York* Times and ABC/*Washington Post* polls are generally based on **telephone polls,** in which telephone numbers are selected through random-digit dialing; up to four callbacks are made to reach the selected respondent. Such a poll usually takes about fifteen or twenty minutes to administer. Some telephone polls are conducted on a quarterly or monthly basis and measure public opinion on such subjects as support for presidential policies or pending legislation. Some are shorter surveys intended to monitor opinion on a particular governmental action or event.

Telephone surveys always include standard demographic questions on such matters as household income, education, and marital status and may include questions about political party identification, participation in past elections, and interest in the current campaign. The data gathered can be weighted to match nationwide population distributions by region, race, sex, age, and education; the resulting figures provide reasonably accurate estimates of public opinion for all adult Americans.

A variant of the telephone survey that has been used by the media since 1984 is the **tracking poll.** Such a poll may include up to 1,000 interviews in a single day and will indicate changes in voter preferences from day to day during the week or so preceding an election.[8]

EXIT POLLS   Another frequently used polling method is the **exit poll,** in which voters are interviewed at the polls on election day. This method was developed in the 1960s but did not become common until the next decade. At first such polls were used to determine voter preferences in a few selected precincts; soon, however, journalists discovered that they could use them to predict the outcome of an election while it was still in progress.

The questionnaires used in exit polls may contain thirty or forty items, but they can be completed in a few minutes. This is important, because the television networks need to obtain the results of the polls within an hour or less after the last interview so that they can be used on the evening news programs.

In an exit poll, the interviewer attempts to question voters leaving the polling place in a systematic way throughout the day. The interviewer may, for example, approach every *n*th voter, with the *n* varying according to the size of the electoral precinct. (The precincts in which the poll is to be conducted are randomly selected.) The voter is asked to fill in the questionnaire and place it in a container; the results are collected several times during the day and are tallied and entered into a computer.

A typical national exit poll collects information from 15,000 or more voters. This total is large enough to contain subgroups (such as Jews, Hispanics, or professional women) whose voting preferences may be compared and analyzed. An even more important feature of exit polls is their immediacy: Voters are interviewed right after they have voted and before the results are known. This has made the exit poll an increasingly popular method for learning about voting patterns as well as for predicting election results. By 1988 there was at least one network exit poll in every state, and all three major networks conducted national exit polls.[9]

Polling organizations allow themselves a margin of error of 3 to 4 percent; that is, if the actual outcome is within 3 or 4 percent of the stated outcome, they consider their analysis to be accurate. As a result, in a close election their prediction of voter intentions can be accurate, given the margin of error they allow themselves, but they may name the wrong candidate as the winner. (The pollsters themselves would not say that they are predicting anything, just that they are determining public opinion at the time of the poll.)

FOCUS GROUPS   Since the early 1980s, candidates have made increasing use of the *focus group,* a technique that has long been used by marketing organizations to gauge the potential popularity of new products. Originally developed by social scientists as the *focused interview,* in which the interviewer probes an individual's response to a specific stimulus, the technique was soon expanded to groups. In a typical focus group, a professional poll taker holds a conversation with about twelve participants. The participants (ordinary citizens who are paid a small fee for their participation) are asked about their views on candidates and issues. Their responses are recorded by hidden microphones and video cameras; later the dialogue is transcribed and analyzed by experts.

Focus groups have become popular among both elected officials and candidates and are a staple of presidential campaigns. In recent presidential elections, most campaign ads have been tested before focus groups before appearing on television. The comments of focus-group participants can have a profound impact, even changing the course of a campaign. President Clinton relied heavily on focus

CLOSE-UP

TELEVISION AND THE 2000 ELECTION IN FLORIDA

At 7 P.M. on November 7, 2000—Election Day evening—the polls closed in the eastern part of Florida. The events that followed would create a storm of controversy and embarrass the national news services, the nation's polling organizations, and many of the country's newspapers.

At 7:50 P.M. the Associated Press and the major television networks began announcing that the Democratic candidate for president, Al Gore, would win the electoral vote in Florida. Gore's purported victory in Florida would, in effect, make him president of the United States, since several other large battleground states—Illinois, Pennsylvania, and Michigan—were also favoring him. The Voter News Service—a consortium of polling organizations that conducted exit polling on Election Day—had provided the information about Gore's Florida victory to the Associated Press and the television networks.

At 9:30 the Republican presidential candidate, George W. Bush, began calling the networks to say that they had made a mistake and that the vote in Florida was too close to call. By 9:50 the networks began retracting their original announcement that Florida had gone for Gore. At about 2:15 on the morning of November 8, the networks announced that Florida had gone to Bush and therefore, he

was the nation's next president. Newspapers all across the country published editions whose front pages boldly announced that Bush had been elected.

At 3 A.M. on November 8, Al Gore called George W. Bush and conceded the election to the Texas governor. But during the next forty-five minutes, Gore received information that Bush's Florida lead was diminishing and that state law required that there be an automatic recount in very close state elections. At 3:45, Gore called Bush again and in a testy conversation between the two men, withdrew his concession. At 4 A.M. the networks altered their stand once again and announced that the Florida election was too close to call. The fight for Florida's key electoral vote would continue for weeks and agitate Americans as no other presidential election had in the nation's history.

In February 2001, CNN released a study of network coverage of the 2000 presidential election. The study, prepared by three well-regarded journalists, concluded that election night coverage of the event was a "debacle." The study stated that the "television news organizations staged a collective drag race on the crowded highway of democracy, recklessly endangering the electoral process, the political life of the nation and their own credibility...."

groups in the months leading up to the 1996 election. The result was a repositioning of his campaign to present a more conservative image. For example, Clinton stressed the need to be tough on crime and drugs, balance the federal budget, and reduce the size of the government; he also signed a major welfare reform law.

The method used to select focus-group participants is a far cry from the scientific techniques employed in survey research. The goal is to find people who will feel comfortable speaking candidly in a group setting. Usually this results in groups whose members are similar in race, sex, and social class. Once group members relax and get to know one another, their comments may become very frank, revealing opinions that are often suppressed in more public settings. Thus, focus groups can be extremely valuable to polling organizations because they provide clues to the feelings and attitudes that determine how people actually vote.

Criticisms of Public-Opinion Polling

Despite its prevalence in modern politics, scientific polling is not universally acclaimed. Critics point to a variety of problems in the way polls are conducted. Those problems are of two main types: problems related to the sample and problems associated with the phrasing of questions. There are also special problems associated with exit polls and polling in primary elections.

PROBLEMS RELATED TO THE SAMPLE A number of problems can arise in the selection of a sample of individuals to be polled. If a polling organization has limited funds, it may include too few people in a sample. Results from a sample of fewer than 1,000 people cannot be generalized to a large population, yet samples of 500 to 700 respondents are not uncommon. Another problem is that the sample may not be representative of the larger population. For example, poll takers sometimes interview registered voters about their preferences for particular candidates, without finding out whether those individuals are actually planning to vote. This is a major problem of preelection telephone polling. In most nonpresidential elections, only about one-third of eligible voters actually vote; a poll that samples the two-thirds who do not vote will obtain misleading information. Most telephone polls do not include procedures for identifying likely voters because of the extra effort and expense involved.[10]

Exit polls, of course, gather information from people who have already voted, but they suffer from a related problem in that the conclusions derived from the data are based on assumptions about the likely voter turnout in each precinct, which in turn are based on past voting patterns. If those patterns change—that is, if turnout increases or declines—the assumptions become misleading.

Unrepresentative samples can result from a variety of other procedural errors, such as using a phone directory for a wealthy community (where many people are likely to have unlisted phone numbers) or calling people at home in the afternoon (when more women than men and more retired people than younger people are likely to be home). Also, poor people and minorities tend to be underrepresented in telephone surveys and surveys taken in shopping malls.

Many people do not want to participate in telephone polls. They receive many calls from salespeople, some of whom pretend to be pollsters, so that they come to view such calls as a nuisance. Thus, refusal rates are high and can contribute to inaccurate poll results.[11]

PROBLEMS ASSOCIATED WITH THE PHRASING OF QUESTIONS
The wording of survey questions is crucial; in fact, writing questions may be the most difficult part of a poll taker's job. Sometimes the findings of a poll can hinge on the connotations of a single word, such as "welfare" as opposed to "assistance to the poor." Unfamiliar words, such as "impeachment," can have similar effects. Even the most carefully worded questions, however, can produce unexpected results, especially when feelings like pride or guilt are involved. For example, most Americans will say that they are environmentalists, simply because it would be embarrassing to say that they are not concerned about this important issue.

A graphic illustration of how the phrasing of questions can influence the result of a poll came early in President George W. Bush's administration. The president had nominated John Ashcroft to be attorney general of the United States. One poll asked: "Do you think Congress should approve Bush's choice of John Ashcroft for attorney general even though his far-right views on issues like abortion, drugs and gun control may make it difficult for him to be an effective attorney general?" "No" answers received 41 percent; "yes," 37 percent. Another national poll conducted at the same time asked: "Bush has nominated John Ashcroft for attorney general. Do you think the U.S. Senate should or should not confirm Ashcroft as attorney general?" Fifty-four percent believed Ashcroft's nomination should be approved; 26 percent said that it should not.

Related to the wording of questions is the form in which they may be answered. Most polls use forced-choice questions in which the respondent must choose among a set of answers such as "Very likely," "Somewhat likely," and "Not likely," or indicate a preference for one of two or three candidates. Questions asked of potential voters may not include a "Don't know" or "Undecided" option. Thus, many polls may compel a respondent to provide an answer, even though the person has no opinion or is undecided on a subject.

SPECIAL PROBLEMS WITH PRIMARY ELECTION AND EXIT POLLS Polling in primary elections (nominating elections—see Chapter 6) poses special problems. Primaries often do not receive as much media coverage as do general elections, and voters may not yet have made up their minds at the time the polls are conducted. But what makes primary polling especially difficult is that voter turnouts for those elections are often very small. A surge of support for one candidate among a relatively few voters can change the outcome and cause the poll results to be inaccurate.

Exit polls also encounter some special problems. Because voters fill out questionnaires and place them in a box, there is no reason for them to lie on an exit poll. However, the problem mentioned earlier—flawed assumptions about precinct turnouts—can skew the results. In addition, many voters do not wish to be polled; in New York City, for example, as many as 40 percent refuse to fill out exit poll questionnaires. Moreover, if poll takers fail to keep track of the sex, race, and apparent age of those who do not participate and weight the responses accordingly, the results of the poll may be misleading.

A further criticism of exit polls is that they have tended to overstate support for the Democratic party, probably because some conservative Republicans refuse to participate in such polls, believing that the media have a liberal bias.[12]

In addition, critics of exit polls have argued that these polls could discourage some people from voting in the belief that the election has already been decided. The low turnout in the 1996 presidential election—less than 50 percent of the eligible voters—may have been caused in part by pollsters' predictions that Clinton was the sure winner. The failure of voters to turn out could affect the results of close elections. There is some evidence that in presidential elections exit polls have contributed to reduced voter turnout in the western states, where voting centers are the last to close because they are located in earlier time zones. Exit polls therefore may well have affected the outcomes of some close congressional and state elections in the West.

Despite their alleged shortcomings, polls have become a central feature of American politics. The number of polls has proliferated; not only the major networks but also at least 40 percent of American newspapers conduct polls. The quality of those polls varies, partly because the demand for polling has grown beyond the supply of trained poll takers and, sometimes, available funds. Accurate or not, polls have an immense impact on the conduct of American politics. They influence the behavior of politicians and journalists, and probably that of the American public as well.[13]

THE NATURE OF THE MEDIA

The media have always played an important role in the American political process. While the nature of this role has changed dramatically since the nation's founding, the ability of the media to influence voters and politicians alike cannot be underestimated. In the eighteenth and nineteenth centuries, the media outlets available to politicians were limited to newspapers and journals. During this time, the editors and owners of major newspapers often used their papers as a forum in which to expound upon their personal political beliefs. It was not uncommon for newspaper owners to emphasize stories that supported their political party and ignore news items that reflected negatively on their personal views. For much of the nineteenth century, most American newspapers were closely identified with a particular political party.

In the late nineteenth century the content of newspapers began to change. As literacy rates increased, newspapers tried to increase the breadth of their appeal. Rather than targeting their messages toward a politically informed and well-educated elite, they took aim at a much larger and less politically interested group. From the early 1850s to the turn of the century, the number of daily newspapers increased from approximately 250 to over 2,200. As the audience changed, the content of the news changed as well. In order to attract the interest of the public, newspapers began to focus their coverage on sensational stories and scandals. This type of news reporting is commonly referred to as **yellow journalism.**

The yellow journalism of the late nineteenth century is best exemplified by the newspapers of William Randolph Hearst. Hearst's papers were infamous for running a story first and checking the facts later. If the story had lots of sex or violence (preferably both), Hearst would run it on the front page to increase sales. Hearst's papers were read throughout the United States, allowing him to influence public opinion on a variety of issues. When Hearst felt that President McKinley was doing nothing during the civil war in Cuba, he ran dozens of front-page stories in his newspapers purporting to show the brutal and senseless acts being perpetrated against the "innocent" Cubans by the "inhuman" Spanish colonists. By constantly attacking McKinley and the Spanish, Hearst managed to sway public opinion toward the Cuban rebels. Although we will never know exactly how many of the stories carried by Hearst's papers were either exaggerations or outright lies, there is little question that Hearst's constant pressure was at least partly responsible for President McKinley's eventual decision to declare war on Spain and send U.S. troops to Cuba to fight against the Spanish colonists.

The newspaper empires of Hearst and others marked the peak of the print media's ability to influence public opinion. By the early 1920s radio broadcasting had become a major player in the competition to disseminate political information. Radio quickly became the dominant source of political news for many Americans and a preferred media outlet for most politicians. Thanks to the immediacy of radio, politicians could now speak directly to the public, circumventing the newspaper editors who generally summarized (and occasionally misrepresented) what the politicians had to say. Radio also brought national and international news to the forefront. In the heyday of the newspapers, most news coverage focused on local and state issues. But since a single radio newscast could be routed to every station in the country, national and international news coverage increased dramatically during the 1920s and 1930s.

The first part of the twentieth century also ushered in many new journalistic standards for both newspapers and radio. The media began to focus on presenting the facts of a story, rather than allowing editors and owners to slant the news to fit their political ideologies. The media emphasized objective, rather than opinionated, news coverage. In most major newspapers the ideological bias of the editors and owners was limited to the editorial pages and left out of the regular news coverage. While yellow journalism still exists, it has generally been relegated to tabloid papers such as those sold in supermarket checkout aisles.

Radio remained a major force in the realm of political information until the 1950s. With the emergence of television, most Americans turned to televised evening news programs to get the political news of the day. The ability to combine audio and visual elements in a constant flow made televised news very appealing to most Americans. Indeed, today television is the source of most of the information the public receives about politics. Over the past five decades the Roper polling organization has asked the public, "Where do you usually get most of your news about what's going on in the world today—from the newspapers or radio or television or magazines . . .?" A large majority of people have always indicated that television provides the most information.

Roles of the Media

Although the media fulfill a wide variety of functions, ranging from socialization to entertainment, there are three roles in which they interact directly with the political sphere: the roles of reporter, agenda-setter, and investigator.

THE MEDIA AS REPORTER   In general, the primary responsibility of the media is to present the news as it happens. The members of the media report the actions of government to the people. Since it is impossible for the public to constantly monitor the actions of government, the public relies on the media to present them with a condensed yet accurate version of the activities of government. The framers of the Constitution saw this as the primary function of the media. They believed that an informed public is critical to the maintenance of democracy. As long as the people are informed about the actions of government, they can make informed decisions in the voting booth as well.

THE MEDIA AS AGENDA-SETTER   Although the primary function of the media is to report what government is doing, it is also important for the media to consider what the government *should* be doing. Part of the task of the media is to identify the current public issues that warrant government action. By bringing such issues to the attention of the public through news coverage, the media can influence the processes of government.

While the ability to help set the public agenda can often force government to address issues that it would otherwise ignore, the power to mobilize the public on a particular issue or set of issues is a double-edged sword. If the media choose to ignore an issue, that issue has little hope of ever entering the public forum. For example, during the late 1990s the broadcast media decided to emphasize the ethnic violence in Kosovo and Serbia rather than the massacres in Rwanda and other African nations. As a consequence of this decision, many more Americans were willing to support sending peacekeeping troops to the Balkans than were willing to endorse sending similar troops into Central Africa. While there is little debate that atrocities were being committed in the Balkans, the level and magnitude of the violence paled in comparison to the enormous numbers of civilians killed during the Central African ethnic cleansings.

This power to narrow the public's focus extends to the political arena. Every time a presidential election rolls around, the media tend to focus on a few candidates. In the prelude to the 2000 election, for example, the media's attention was focused almost exclusively on three Republican candidates, George W. Bush,

Elizabeth Dole, and Senator John McCain. Little mention was made of other potential contenders, despite the fact that some of these candidates were just as qualified to be the president of the United States.

It is worth noting that the media cannot automatically force issues into the public sphere. If the issue the media choose to examine does not strike a sympathetic chord with the public, the coverage carries little weight. Over the past decade numerous media outlets have presented hard-hitting, highly critical exposés of the nursing home industry, yet all of this coverage has generated little public debate about reforms. The media examined the potential problems with health maintenance organizations (HMOs) as early as the late 1980s, yet this issue did not become a matter of significant public concern until large numbers of Americans started joining HMOs in the 1990s.

THE MEDIA AS INVESTIGATOR   In conjunction with the role of reporting facts, the media also serve as an independent check on the behavior of government and government officials. Since it is impossible for the public to keep track of the actions of government officials, they rely on the media to keep tabs on them. During the late nineteenth century, the journalists who exposed the corrupt workings of government and industry were called **muckrakers.** Although this term has been dropped from the lexicon of political discussion, the spirit of the muckrakers lives on in journalism. Investigative reporters for the media try to uncover corruption, abuses of power, scandal, and other unethical or illegal activities by government officials.

Two powerful illustrations of the potential impact of investigative journalism are the investigations of the Watergate break-in during President Nixon's term and the affair between President Clinton and White House intern Monica Lewinsky. In both cases journalists uncovered unethical and possibly illegal activities on the part of the president. In both cases efforts were made by the White House to try to hide the truth from the public, and in both cases the truth was eventually revealed at least partly through the unceasing work of members of the media. As a result of these two investigations, one president (Richard Nixon) was forced to resign based on his involvement in illegal activities, while the other (Bill Clinton) became only the second president in the nation's history to be tried by the Senate on impeachment charges. It is highly unlikely that either of these incidents would have been brought to the attention of the public without the work of investigative journalists.

The Media and Elections

In their search for news about elections, journalists look for something tangible to report; this often causes them to focus on elections as a horse race rather than on the issues and policies being discussed in a campaign. Moreover, most reporters do not analyze or evaluate candidates' policy proposals. Instead, they report on such matters as the candidates' standings in the polls, the amount of money they raise, and the endorsements they attract.

Journalists also have a tendency to focus on incumbents rather than on challengers, and to pay more attention to better-known candidates than to those who are less well known. One reason for this is that it is easier to cover incumbents; many of their official activities are reported anyway, and they have already established a relationship with the media.

There are some significant differences between the print and electronic media in their coverage of political campaigns. For one thing, the electronic media present much less news than the print media. A political story on the network news, for example, receives between thirty seconds and two minutes of coverage. Television reporters rarely give in-depth coverage to candidates and campaigns. In addition, a TV news story must have an interesting visual background if it is to hold viewers' attention. If a campaign event does not take place in interesting surroundings, it is likely to be ignored. The print media do not operate under such pressures.

An estimated $3.9 billion was spent on the 2004 presidential and congressional elections. About $2.5 billion came from contributions made by individuals. The remaining amount was given by various private groups and organizations.[14] Much of the money was spent on television advertisements at the local, not national level. In both the 2000 and 2004 elections advertising rates in some areas soared and some time slots were difficult to purchase. This was especially true of presidential ads in cities located in important competitive states such as Ohio, Florida, and Nevada.

Presidential election campaigns often appear to be managed almost solely for the benefit of television news. Each stop and public appearance is carefully planned and scripted with the evening news programs in mind. The candidates' images are crafted to appeal to viewers, and each day has a theme—the message to be delivered to the voters that evening. Little attention is given to substantive issues, and there is almost no contact with actual voters. In short, "Political operatives are seeking to isolate not just the candidate but the entire campaign from anything resembling spontaneous reality."[15]

A key feature of television coverage of campaigns is the *sound bite*. This technique developed out of the advertising industry's recognition that people are likely to remember short, punchy messages. Coupled with the tendency of politics to become increasingly image conscious, it has resulted in campaign coverage that is dominated by brief, narrowly focused vignettes in which the candidate may speak for only a few seconds. Perhaps reflecting an increasingly fast-paced society, the average length of a sound bite decreased from 42.3 seconds in 1968 to only 9.8 seconds in 1988 and has remained constant since then.[16]

Radio news programs give much more coverage to political events. They often have available time that needs to be filled. Thus, radio stations may even use political press releases in the form in which they were written by a candidate's campaign staff; sometimes they feature comments that have been taped by candidates and offered to radio stations. (The latter are especially desirable, because they sound like news and can easily be included in news programs.) Candidates who have difficulty getting attention from television and newspaper reporters may compensate by taking advantage of the availability of radio air time.

The media devote much more attention to presidential campaigns than to nonpresidential campaigns. Coverage of a presidential campaign begins as long as two years before the election, and by the beginning of the election year the campaign will be the subject of daily reports. In contrast, coverage of gubernatorial races does not begin until Labor Day, and coverage of senatorial races often does not start until a month before the election. Nonpresidential candidates also receive much less media scrutiny than presidential candidates.

Television Advertising

Today it is impossible to run a national political campaign without heavy reliance on television, and it is virtually impossible for a candidate to run for office at the state level without extensive use of television commercials. In fact, TV advertising accounts for about two-thirds of the budget of a typical statewide campaign. The costs of television advertising vary according to the size of the population to be reached, the number of markets in which the candidate must advertise, and the number of exposures desired. (It is generally assumed that between three and five exposures are required for a message to "sink in."[17]) Differences in the size of state populations and the cost of TV advertising in different states play a significant role in a campaign organization's choices about the use of television advertising.

Television is less important in congressional campaigns than in national and statewide campaigns. The use of television in congressional primary contests varies in different regions of the country, depending on cost and on the degree of similarity between the television market and the congressional district. In the Southwest, where TV advertising is still relatively inexpensive, three-quarters of House candidates buy television advertising. On the West Coast the proportion falls to one-quarter; in the Middle Atlantic region fewer than one-fifth of congressional candidates use television. In the general election fewer than half of all House candidates use TV advertising. Various studies have shown that the cost efficiency and market potential of television ads are greater in the midwestern and southern states than in New England and the western states. Television also is generally more effective in rural districts than in urban areas.[18]

Candidates for local offices are less likely to use broadcast advertising. Instead, they rely on direct voter contact, both in person and by direct mail and telephone. These methods are preferred because they can be more readily targeted at district audiences. Direct mail is used extensively in urban congressional districts, where it is used to reinforce intensive personal voter contact.[19]

Recent political campaigns have witnessed a dramatic increase in the frequency of *negative advertising*—ads that attack the opposing candidate. Such ads have become common in campaigns at all levels of government but are espe-

President George W. Bush answers questions at a press conference. Presidential press conferences, which are extensively covered by television and the press, are examples of the free media.

cially prominent in presidential elections. In the 1988 presidential race, one commentator claimed that the candidates used advertising "at least as much to bash the other side as to promote themselves."[20] Perhaps the best-known negative advertisement is the one in which the senior George Bush's Democratic opponent, Michael Dukakis, was attacked for allowing a convicted murderer named Willie Horton to be released from prison, after which he committed another serious crime. Although there are some indications of a backlash against negative advertising, many candidates continue to make extensive use of such ads.

Knowing that many people dislike negative advertising, campaign strategists have devised a variation on the negative ad. They now spend money and energy on attempts to convince the public that a rival's campaign is more negative than it really is. "Candidates and their surrogates are branding as negative comments by their foes that in other campaigns might have been dismissed with a yawn," comments one observer.[21]

Political consultants say that there is a simple explanation for the use of negative advertising: It works. Research has shown that although people often express a dislike for such advertising, they also tend to remember the ads. Positive advertising must be repeated numerous times to have the same impact. Another cause of the increase in negative advertising is the growing cost of paid media. Because negative ads are more likely to be remembered, they are more cost-effective than positive ads. Negative ads cannot be ignored; if the candidate who is attacked by such an ad does not quickly answer the charges, he or she is likely to lose ground in the polls.

The Question of Media Bias

Both liberals and conservatives accuse the news media of being biased against them. Conservatives believe that the media espouse a number of liberal causes that are more in harmony with Democrats than with Republicans. Liberals argue that the media are controlled by large corporate entities that bias the news toward conservative economic and social issues. As with most such political debates, neither view is completely true or completely false.[22]

EDITORS VERSUS REPORTERS   It is difficult to generalize about the political beliefs of members of the media. Some studies have portrayed members of the media as being more liberal than the general public. These studies have been widely cited by conservative columnists throughout the nation. The problem with any generalizations about the media is that such broad statements miss an important distinction. Although a majority of reporters consider themselves liberals, editors and owners are decidedly more conservative.[23] And since owners and editors may choose to influence the overall content of the news, it is possible that any bias in the news would be in favor of conservatives rather than liberals. On the other hand, a number of the nation's major newspapers and weekly news magazines—including *The New York Times, The Washington Post,* and *Time Magazine*—generally side with the policies and candidates of the Democratic party.

MEDIA OWNERSHIP   One of the most controversial aspects of the media bias question is the increasing concentration of news outlets in the hands of a few corporate entities. As fewer and fewer companies control a greater number of media outlets, many critics of the media fear that the result will be homogenized and uncontroversial news. For example, when Disney and ABC merged, the resulting conglomerate controlled radio stations, newspapers, cable television stations,

Republican presidential candidate George W. Bush appears on the Fox News Sunday television show during the New Hampshire primary election, January 2000.

and a major broadcast network. The merger of Time-Warner with Ted Turner's media empire created an organization that owned film studios, news magazines, cable channels, and a widely watched cable news station, Cable News Network (CNN). If one organization can control so many different sources of information at the same time, it becomes much easier for the organization to control the flow of information.

The trend toward concentration of media ownership is more than balanced, however, by other trends in communication. The number of smaller local and national cable stations that provide information to the public has been growing in recent years. Moreover, the Internet and the World Wide Web offer an almost unlimited amount of information that is provided by a vast number of individuals and by tens of thousands of private and public organizations located throughout the world.

The New Media

A striking feature of recent presidential election campaigns has been the frequent appearance of candidates on cable television interview programs. The trend toward greater reliance on cable television accelerated during the 2000 presidential nomination campaigns. While candidates continued to make appearances on Sunday morning network shows such as *Meet the Press,* they looked to cable television as a means of gaining greater exposure to the voting public. This development represented a major change from earlier campaigns, when candidates relied heavily on network news programs. Why has this change occurred?

The main reason for the switch to the new media is the decline in ratings experienced by network news shows. NBC, CBS, and ABC have been losing viewers at an alarming rate as more and more people switch to cable television. While the number of people who watch presidential election campaigns on television has grown, the number who view them on one of the major television networks has fallen sharply; the audience share of network news—that is, the percentage of households that view presidential election campaigns—fell to about 32 percent in 1998-1999 from 40 percent in 1987-1988. During the same period the number of American households that had cable television grew significantly.[24] (See Figure 4.1.) In 2002, about two-thirds (67.8 million) of the approximately 102 million American households had cable television, 4 million more than in 1996. In addition, some 14.5 million households were equipped to receive television broadcasts by satellite, almost three times the number in 1996.[25] The number of cable and satellite subscribers has continued to grow in recent years.

Advances in communications technology will undoubtedly increase the importance of the new media in political campaigns. It is too soon to predict the effects of these changes in any detail, but it is already clear that nontraditional media are profoundly changing the way Americans—including candidates and voters—receive information and communicate with one another. The rapidly growing popularity of the Internet and the World Wide Web is especially likely to affect political communication in the twenty-first century.

The Internet

The use of the Internet in American politics had modest beginnings in the 1996 presidential election campaign. The two major political parties and many candidates for public office posted websites to expound their views on public issues. But the information they offered was often little more than summaries of plat-

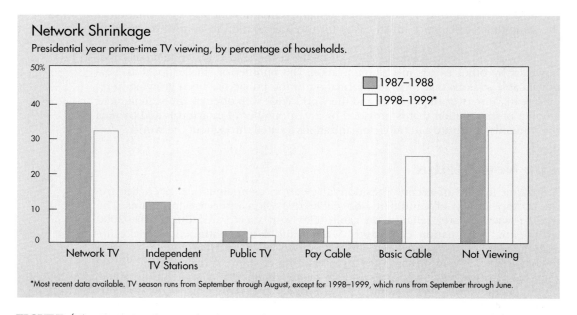

FIGURE 4.1 Viewing of network television declined between 1987 and 1999. During the same period the percentage of households with access to cable television soared.

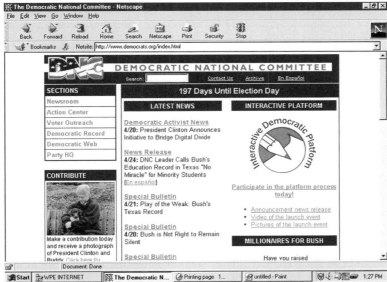

Web pages used by the Democratic and Republican parties during the 2000 presidential campaigns

form positions and campaign speeches. There was little evidence that this new technology had a significant effect on the outcome of the election.

By the 2000 presidential election the use of Web pages by political candidates became fairly common and the sites more sophisticated. Both presidential candidates—Al Gore and George Bush—as well as the national committees of both the Democratic and Republican parties, created websites. These sites were used to set

CLOSE-UP

INTERNET VOTING: IS IT THE WAVE OF THE FUTURE?

In January 2000 a possibly historic event took place: the first voting via the Internet in an American election. It was conducted by the Republican party in three remote districts in Alaska. Party members in those areas were able to cast their vote for one of six Republican presidential candidates in a nonbinding straw poll. (Thirty-five voters cast ballots in the poll.) Two months later the Arizona Democratic party permitted its 800,000 members to vote on the Internet in its binding presidential primary. Each eligible voter was given a number by the party. When they reached the Web address on their computer, they were required to provide some form of identification, such as a Social Security number or date of birth. The voter could then select a candidate and click on his or her name. Two or more clicks locked in the choice.

Some observers view Internet voting as a means of increasing the number of people who vote in elections. Rather than having to travel to a polling place to cast a ballot, the voter can do so in the privacy of his or her home. Internet voting would also be less expensive than the present system, which requires voting machines and the staffing of tens of thousands of polling centers across the nation.

But there are problems with Internet voting. An important problem is that it might discriminate against poor people, especially minorities, who are less likely to have computers and access to the Web. There is also the problem of security. The privacy of a person's vote must be assured, and no one must be able to cast more than one vote. In time Internet voting will probably become common, but its widespread adoption is unlikely until the economic and technological problems just mentioned are solved.

forth the political views of each party's candidate and to criticize the ideas of their opponents. Further, the sites were used to recruit volunteers for campaign work and to sell political merchandise (such as Gore silver-plated cufflinks at $16.00!).

The Internet was also used as an inexpensive means of advertising, suggesting that budgets for television advertising may be sharply reduced in future elections. And some candidates used very sophisticated methods to target specific audiences. McCain and George W. Bush, for example, used *banner ads*—which appear at the top or bottom of the computer screen—to reach specific on-line users based on their voter or party registration.[26]

But fund-raising was probably the most important use made of the Internet during the 2000 elections. Websites permitted the use of credit cards to make contributions, providing an easy way for supporters to give money and an inexpensive way for candidates to raise cash. (One need only list name, profession, employer, credit card number, and the size of the contribution to make a financial gift to a favored candidate.) On the evening of Senator John McCain's victory in the February 1 New Hampshire primary, thousands of people logged on to his website to contribute to his campaign. Money rolled in at the rate of about $20,000 per hour and produced a total of over $2.5 million. McCain also held what was probably the first "cyber fund-raiser," a sixty-minute question-and-answer period with chat room guests who could send e-mail questions to the candidate. Sitting in an office in Charleston, South Carolina, McCain was able to communicate his image to the computer screens of about 500 subscribers and raise $50,000 for his campaign.[27]

The 2000 election also saw the first small experiments with voting by means of the Internet. And it is likely that before very long candidates for public office will go on-line to poll the public about their views on various issues.

The use of e-mail by candidates became important in the 2000 elections. While in 1996 only a small percentage of the public had e-mail, by 2000 the proportion had risen to an estimated two-thirds of the population with access to e-mail either at home or at work. Thus, candidates used e-mail to contact supporters about their campaigns and their stands on issues, and to answer criticisms by other candidates or by the media. The Internet allows candidates to reach a growing portion of the public twenty-four hours a day, at little cost and without reliance on the traditional media.

It is too soon to evaluate the effect the Internet will have on American politics and, perhaps more important, on the nation's democratic political system. Major changes always produce warnings of dire consequences from some observers. But others say that democracy can be advanced only by increasing the amount of information available to the public, and without question, this is the main function the new technology of the Internet will perform for society.

Proposals for Reform

The increasing dependence of political campaigns on the media, especially television, has become a matter of concern to many analysts of American politics. Critics believe that negative advertising has given a nasty tone to many campaigns and that excessive use of sound bites has tended to trivialize important public issues. These observers see much news coverage of political campaigns as superficial, focusing on images rather than issues and providing little of substance for viewers to evaluate in deciding how to vote.

Some newspapers have begun to watch televised political advertising with a critical eye and publish reports on the accuracy of the content and the methods used to create the ads. Some newspapers, for example, reprint the text of new political advertisements, accompanied by an analysis that may challenge, clarify, contradict, or present a context for claims made in the commercial. These so-called "truth boxes" have had some effect on campaign advertising; media consultants have become somewhat more careful about documenting their claims.

But newspaper truth boxes have some drawbacks. For one thing, they are published only once, whereas a commercial may be repeated dozens or even hundreds of times. For another, they focus on literal statements rather than on the visual and aural content of ads. Yet viewers recall video images more effectively than written or spoken statements. "People tend to believe what they see more than what they hear," comments one expert. "You can try to counteract it by explaining what a candidate is trying to do. But people still succumb to the beautiful visuals."[28]

Proposals have been offered to address the problem through legislation. One proposal would attempt to curb negative advertising by requiring candidates to appear in person in their commercials, thereby forcing the candidate to take personal responsibility for the content of the ad. But the constitutionality of this proposal has been questioned, since it could be viewed as interfering with the First Amendment guarantee of freedom of speech. An alternative plan, which has been considered by Congress, would provide public financing in the form of vouchers to purchase TV time in blocks of one to five minutes; the purpose of this proposal is to reduce candidates' dependence on brief television sound bites.

Many media experts do not believe that longer advertisements and news spots would solve the problem of negative advertising. Some scholars and public officials favor an approach in which free TV time would be granted to parties rather than to candidates. This approach is widely used in other democracies. However, most of the countries that currently use it are parliamentary democracies with multiparty systems that are quite different from the candidate-centered, two-party system of the United States. Also, the number of TV stations is much more limited in other countries, making it more likely that viewers will be exposed to political commercials and debate. In the United States, the multiplicity of television stations and cable services results in a fragmentation of the TV audience, with the result that any given message is unlikely to reach a large percentage of viewers.

Even these reforms may not be enough to counteract the superficiality of American political campaigns. That may require more fundamental changes in American culture. As one political scientist has pointed out, "You cannot improve discourse. Lack of education, lack of demands by the public that a certain level of discourse be reached are the problem. That will not change with free time. That is corrected with more and better civic education, starting from kindergarten."[29]

HOW AMERICANS PARTICIPATE

For public opinion to influence government policy, it must be translated into actions; in other words, to have an effect on the political system, people must participate in that system. Voting, of course, is one way to participate. But participation can take many other forms: belonging to a political club, working for a political party or candidate, attending a political rally or meeting, or contributing money to a campaign, for example. Rates of participation for all of these activities are generally below 10 percent. (See Table 4.1.)

TABLE 4.1

PERCENTAGE OF POPULATION INVOLVED IN CAMPAIGN ACTIVITIES IN PRESIDENTIAL ELECTION YEARS: 1980–1996

	1980	1984	1988	1992	1996
Do you belong to any political club or organization?	3	4	4	a	a
Did you give any money or buy tickets or anything to help the campaign of one of the parties or candidates?	8	7	9	11	9
Did you go to any political meetings, rallies, dinners, or things like that?	8	4	7	8	6
Did you do any other work for one of the parties or candidates?	4	4	3	3	3

[a]Question was not asked in 1992 or 1996.
Source: Center for Political Studies, National Election Studies, *General Social Surveys.* Data provided by the Interuniversity Consortium for Political and Social Research.

When participation is examined in terms of social and economic status, a significant pattern emerges. Of those who participate least, a greater percentage are members of lower socioeconomic classes; those who participate most tend to be higher in social and economic status. People with more years of formal schooling are more likely to engage in political activities, as are people with higher incomes. There are also racial and ethnic differences in political participation, with members of minority groups less likely to participate, owing partly to lower levels of educational attainment. As these obstacles are removed and average educational levels increase, we can expect more active participation by racial and ethnic minorities. Participation patterns based on social status, on the other hand, are unlikely to change.[30]

Political participation is likely to result in more favorable action by government officials. Therefore, those who participate often obtain the most benefits from the government—benefits such as favorable tax policies or the protection of Medicare and Social Security benefits, for example. But those who participate less may need such benefits more. A person living in an inner-city neighborhood, struggling to support a family on a small income, is probably too busy even to think much about politics; yet such people need the benefits of participation more than those who do become involved. It is for this reason that activists who want to obtain more benefits for certain groups spend a great deal of energy trying to get members of those groups to vote and to participate more in political activities.[31]

Of course, the most common form of political participation is voting. In fact, for many Americans participation begins and ends with voting. The subject of voting—and nonvoting—by Americans will be discussed in detail in Chapter 6.

CONCLUSION

From the standpoint of public opinion and the media, the two most important developments of the past fifty years are public-opinion research and television coverage of political issues. These two forces have greatly influenced the character of American politics and will continue to affect the political system in the twenty-first century.

As a result of public opinion polling by social scientists, we know a great deal more about what the American public believes with regard to political issues and how people vote in elections. Public-opinion polling has some limitations, however. It does not attempt to explain individual behavior; its conclusions deal with the behavior of groups in society. Moreover, polling is not a precise science. There is a need for greater refinement in the techniques used by public-opinion researchers. The projections made by polls in recent presidential elections were accurate in naming the likely winner but were wide of the mark in stating the margin of victory.

Television's impact on American politics has been even more far-reaching. Americans today learn much of what they know about politics from television news. Candidates at the national and state levels employ television as their primary means of communicating with the public. And as we shall see in Chapters 5 and 6, television has also affected other aspects of the political system. It has, for example, altered the nature of political campaigns, the role of the national convention in nominating presidential candidates, the costs of political campaigns, and the methods used to pay for those costs.

The Internet has the potential to alter American politics in fundamental ways. The presidential nomination campaigns of 2000 saw the first extensive use of the new technology in national politics. The impact of the Internet could be seen in the way in which candidates conducted their campaigns and in the manner in which they raised money from the public. The public also responded to the election in different ways as a consequence of the Internet. It was now possible to contact the candidates at their websites to learn their views on issues and to use e-mail to ask questions and give personal opinions to candidates.

The growing importance of the Internet in American politics was again evident in 2004. Its significance was most striking in the area of fund raising during the presidential nomination period. Several Democratic presidential candidates—especially Vermont Governor Howard Dean—successfully raised large sums of money through the Internet. The Internet has another great advantage: it is cost effective. Unlike other methods of fund raising, the Internet is inexpensive to use.

QUESTIONS FOR THOUGHT

1. What is political socialization, and what are the major factors that affect this process?

2. How are scientific polls conducted?

3. What are exit polls, and how are they conducted?

4. What is meant by the media as reporter? The media as agenda-setter? The media as investigator?

5. In what ways is the Internet important in contemporary American politics?

INTERNET ACTIVITIES

1. *Public Opinion Polls.* Go to the Gallup Organization website at **http://www.gallup.com/** and select "Gallup Poll." Then select "Presidential Approval Ratings" to determine which presidents had the highest and lowest approval ratings from the public. Check out their latest polls at **http://www.gallup.com**.

2. *Highbrow Media for Public Affairs.* Go to the *Atlantic Monthly* at **http://www.theatlantic.com/atlantic/**. Select "Site Guide." Check out "Atlantic Unbound." Review the thematic list of articles. Select one that matches your academic major or interests and write a brief report. The *Atlantic* publishes major articles that intelligently address the major political, economic, and cultural forces in public life. For an informed view on issues like euthanasia, affirmative action, foreign policy, and much more, return here often.

KEY TERMS

exit poll	political socialization	survey research
muckrakers	public opinion	telephone polls
political culture	sampling	tracking poll
political opinion	scientific polling	yellow journalism

SUGGESTED READING

Asher, Herbert. *Polling and the Public,* 5th ed. Washington, DC: Congressional Quarterly Press, 2001.

Davis, Richard. *The Press and American Politics,* 2nd ed. Upper Saddle River, NJ: Prentice Hall, 1996.

———. *The Web of Politics: The Internet's Influence on American Politics.* New York: Oxford University Press, 1999.

Delli Carpini, Michael X., and Scott Keeter. *What Americans Know About Politics and Why It Matters.* New Haven, CT: Yale University Press, 1996.

Lavrakas, Paul S., and Michael W. Traugott. *Election Polls, the News Media, and Democracy.* Upper Saddle River, NJ: Prentice Hall, 1999.

Morone, James A. *The Democratic Wish: Popular Participation and the Limits of American Government,* rev. ed. New Haven, CT: Yale University Press, 1998.

Norrander, Barbara, and Clyde Wilcox. *Understanding Public Opinion,* 2nd ed. Washington, DC: Congressional Quarterly Press, 2001.

Paletz, David L. *The Media in American Politics.* New York: Longman, 1999.

Sabato, Larry J., Mark Stencel, and S. Robert Lichter. *Peepshow: Media and Politics in an Age of Scandal.* Lanham, MD: Rowman & Littlefield, 2001.

West, Darrell. *Air Wars: Television Advertising in Election Campaigns, 1952–2000.* Washington, DC: Congressional Quarterly Press, 2001.

NOTES

1. Herbert McClosky, "Consensus and Ideology in American Politics," *American Political Science Review* 58 (1964): 365. See also Herbert McClosky and John Zaller, *The American Ethos* (Cambridge, MA: Harvard University Press, 1984).

2. William H. Flanigan and Nancy H. Zingale, *Political Behavior of the American Electorate,* 9th ed. (Washington, DC: Congressional Quarterly Press, 1998), p. 8.

3. Flanigan and Zingale, *Political Behavior,* pp. 8–11.

4. David Easton and Jack Dennis, *Children and the Political System: Origins of Political Legitimacy* (New York: McGraw-Hill, 1969), pp. 73–91.

5. Robert D. Hess and Judith U. Torney, *The Development of Political Attitudes in Children* (Garden City, NY: Doubleday/Anchor, 1968), pp. 105–8, 111.

6. Kathleen A. Francovic, "Media Polls: Monitoring Changes in Public Opinion," *ICPSR Bulletin* (Ann Arbor, MI: Interuniversity Consortium for Political and Social Research, February 1990) p. 1.

7. The discussion of sampling and survey research is based on Jarol B. Manheim and Richard C. Rich, *Empirical Political Analysis: Research Methods in Political Science* (White Plains, NY: Longman, 1986), pp. 86–91, 105–7.

8. Frankovic, "Media Polls," pp. 1–2.

9. Ibid.

10. Michael Oreskes, "In Year of Volatile Vote, Polls Can Be Dynamite," *New York Times,* November 2, 1990, p. A19.

11. Everett Carll Ladd, "The Pollsters' Waterloo," *Wall Street Journal,* November 19, 1996, p. A22.

12. Ibid.

13. Oreskes, "Volatile Vote," p. A19.

14. Nicholas Zamiska, "US Elections Are to Set Record for Spending at $3.9 Billion," *Wall Street Journal,* October 21, 2004, p. A4.

15. Gerald F. Seib and Michel McQueen, "A Campaign Becomes a 'Made for TV' Race: A Picture a Day Obviates Thousands of Words," *Wall Street Journal,* September 16, 1988, p. 48.

16. Randall Rothenberg, "Politics on TV: Too Fast, Too Loose?" *New York Times,* July 15, 1990, sec. 4, pp. 1, 4.

17. Jerry Hagstrom and Robert Guskind, "Shopping for Airtime," *National Journal,* February 20, 1988, pp. 462–67.

18. Edie N. Goldenberg and Michael W. Traugott, *Campaigning for Congress* (Washington, DC: Congressional Quarterly Press, 1984), pp. 116–19; John R. Alford and Keith Henry, "TV Markets and Congressional Elections," *Legislative Studies Quarterly* 9 (November 1984): 665–75.

19. Stephen A. Salmore and Barbara G. Salmore, *Candidates, Parties, and Campaigns,* 2nd ed. (Washington, DC: Congressional Quarterly Press, 1989), pp. 143–44.

20. Michael Oreskes, "TV's Role in '88: The Medium Is the Election," *New York Times,* October 30, 1988, p. 1.

21. Peter Marks, "Emphasis on Negativity Isn't New, Just a Different Method of Trying to Tar an Opponent," *New York Times,* January 29, 2000.

22. Public concern with bias in the news media is shown by the popularity of Bernard Goldberg's best selling 2001 book, *Bias: A CBS Insider Exposes How the Media Distort the News* (Washington, DC: Regnery Publishing, 2001).

23. The Roper Center, *The Public Perspective,* October/November 1996, p. 8

24. Bob Davis, "New TV Paradox Presents Challenge for Candidates," *Wall Street Journal,* January 17, 2000, p. A20.

25. Kathy Chen, "In the Race for Presidential Campaign Coverage, Cable Moves into the Lead over Broadcast TV," *Wall Street Journal,* September 20, 2000, p. A28.

26. Glenn R. Simpson, "On-line Political Ads Spawn Variety of Tactics," *Wall Street Journal,* January 17, 2000, p. A20.

27. Don Van Natta, Jr., "Courting Web-Head Cash," *New York Times,* February 13, 2000, sec. 4, p. 4.

28. Doris A. Graber, quoted in Randall Rothenberg, "Newspapers Watch What People Watch in the TV Campaign," *New York Times,* November 4, 1990, sec. 4, pp. 1, 4.

29. Larry J. Sabato, quoted in Rothenberg, "Politics on TV," p. 4.

30. M. Margaret Conway, *Political Participation in the United States,* 2nd ed. (Washington, DC: Congressional Quarterly Press, 1991), pp. 34–35.

31. Sidney Verba and Norman H. Nie, *Participation in America* (New York: Harper and Row, 1972), pp. 118–19.

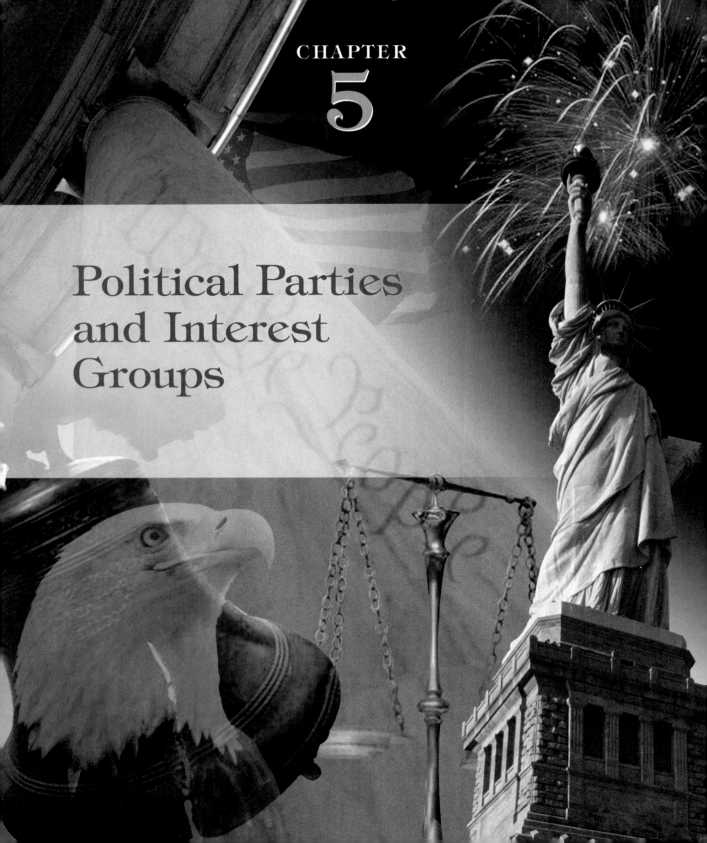

Political Parties and Interest Groups

In his description of factions, James Madison was not referring to political parties and interest groups as we know them today. But he did understand that in a free society people will have different opinions and will try to influence the actions of government in their favor. In these respects, therefore, his definition of a faction fits the modern political party and interest group. Madison's concerns are also relevant today: Political parties and interest groups are unavoidable in a democratic society; they are a natural outgrowth of freedom. But their activities are not always beneficial to society as a whole.

In this chapter we turn our attention to organized political activity—that is, to how groups participate in politics. We will focus on two basic types of groups: political parties and interest groups. *Political parties* try to influence policy primarily by getting their members elected or appointed to government offices. *Interest groups* do not put forward their own candidates for public office. Instead, they seek to influence government indirectly by shaping public opinion, supporting or opposing candidates, and influencing the decisions of government officials. Although the activities of political parties and interest groups overlap, it is possible to separate them for the purpose of analyzing and studying their roles in the political system.

> By a faction, I understand a number of citizens, whether amounting to a majority or a minority of the whole, who are united and actuated by some common impulse or passion, or of interest, adverse to the rights of other citizens or to the permanent aggregate interest of the community.
>
> —James Madison,
> The Federalist, No. 10

POLITICAL PARTIES

Political parties are not mentioned in the Constitution, but there have been parties of various kinds—Federalists, Democratic-Republicans, Whigs, Democrats, Republicans—throughout the nation's history. It seems that "parties and democracy arose together; they have lived and prospered in a closely symbiotic relationship; and if one of them should ever weaken and die, the other would die with it."[1]

Political parties perform a variety of functions. Along with interest groups and the mass media, parties play a role in keeping the public informed about current political issues and helping people form opinions on those issues. The minority political party—the one that does not control Congress or the presidency—serves as a check on the majority party. It examines and criticizes the proposals of the majority party and often suggests alternatives.

The functions of political parties also include the recruitment and selection of leaders, the representation and integration of group interests, and the control and direction of government. Party activities center on the processes of recruiting, electing, and appointing political leaders to office, including administrative and judicial positions. They provide the conditions under which many thousands of elective offices can be filled in an organized manner. By proposing and campaigning for specific lists of candidates, the parties bring a degree of order and predictability to the political process.

The goal of party activities is to obtain the power and other advantages associated with public office. But in pursuing that goal the parties also provide various services to the public: They help educate voters on current issues and simplify the choices voters face on election day. "The parties do what voters cannot do by themselves: from the totality of interests and issues in politics, they choose those that will become 'the agenda of formal public discourse.' "[2]

Another important function of parties is the representation and integration of group interests. The parties' elected officials act as "brokers" among interest groups. They consider the claims of each group, accepting some and modifying or rejecting others in a process of continual bargaining and compromise. The capacity of parties to represent diverse interests and to integrate the claims of competing groups is an important element of a democratic political system.[3]

Finally, political parties recruit candidates and organize campaigns to gain public office and control the government. Since the late 1960s it has been rare for one party to control both the executive and legislative branches of government; the party that has controlled the presidency has not also been able to win control of both houses of Congress. The 1992 and 2002 elections were the few recent exceptions to the pattern of *divided government* that has existed since 1969. In the 1992 election the Democrats won the presidency and majorities in both houses of Congress. But in 1994, 1996, and 1998 the Republicans elected majorities in the House and the Senate, while the Democrats retained control of the presidency.

This pattern was reversed in the 2000 national election. The Republicans won the presidency and held a five vote majority in the House of Representatives. The Senate was split 50–50, thus enabling the Republicans to organize the upper chamber with the vote of the vice president. But a Republican senator from Vermont abandoned the party in 2001 and converted the slim Republican majority in the Senate to a one-vote Democratic majority.

But once again in 2002, one party gained control of all of the elected branches of the federal government. By winning a small majority of seats in the U.S. Senate, the Republicans added to their existing control of the presidency and the House of Representatives. This pattern of Republican control continued in the 2004 election. The party successfully reelected George Bush as president and retained both houses of the legislatures with increased majorities.

Thus, although the parties can be said to organize the government, they do not always fully control governmental decision making. And as we shall see later in the chapter, interest groups compete with parties in seeking to obtain public policies that are favorable to their interests; indeed, sometimes such groups are more powerful than parties.[4]

THE AMERICAN TWO-PARTY SYSTEM

In 1789 and 1793 George Washington was the Electoral College's unanimous choice for president. But during Washington's second term in office, two distinct parties—the Federalists and the Democratic-Republicans—became important political forces. By the time John Adams was elected president in 1796, both parties were operating on a national scale. Since then, two major parties have normally played a dominant role in American elections and politics.

From its inception, the American party system—at least at the national level—has had several notable traits. First, it has been a **two-party system;** almost every election in the nation has been primarily a contest between two political parties. More than two parties nominate candidates for public office in many elections, but only the candidates of the two major parties have had a real chance of winning. (See Figure 5.1, page 102.)

In the twentieth century the one time a third party had a chance of winning a national election was in 1912, when ex-President Theodore Roosevelt deserted the Republican party to run on the Progressive party ticket. He received more than 27 percent of the popular vote and won eighty-eight electoral votes. But with the Republican vote divided between Roosevelt's supporters and those who voted for the Republican candidate, William Howard Taft, the Democratic party's candidate, Woodrow Wilson, was elected president. The second most successful third-party candidate was Ross Perot in 1992. The Texas businessman garnered 19 percent of the popular vote and ran second in several states, but did not win any electoral votes.

Second, at the national level the party system has been marked by long stretches of single-party dominance. One or the other of the two major parties has controlled the presidency for long periods. From 1800 to 1860 the Democrats won twelve out of fifteen elections, and from 1860 to 1932 the Republicans were defeated only four times. The Democrats returned to power in 1932 with the election of Franklin D. Roosevelt and, except for Dwight D. Eisenhower's victories in 1952 and 1956, won every national election until 1968. Since that year, however, the Republican party has won five of the eight national elections: Richard Nixon won in 1968 and 1972, Ronald Reagan in 1980 and 1984, and the first George Bush in 1988. The Democrats were successful in 1976, and again in 1992 and 1996 with Bill Clinton. But the Republicans regained the presidency in the very close and controversial election of 2000 and retained it in 2004 with the reelection of George Bush.

Two-party systems are not found in all democracies; many democratic nations have **multiparty systems,** in which a number of parties compete successfully for elective office. Why, then, does the United States have a two-party system?

Several theories attempt to account for the existence of two dominant parties in the United States. The most widely accepted of these is the *institutional* theory, which holds that the nation's election system, especially the use of single-member districts in choosing members of Congress and of state and local legislatures, creates a two-party system. The single-member system permits only one candidate to win—the one who receives a majority or a plurality of the votes cast. All other candidates, regardless of the size of their vote, receive nothing for

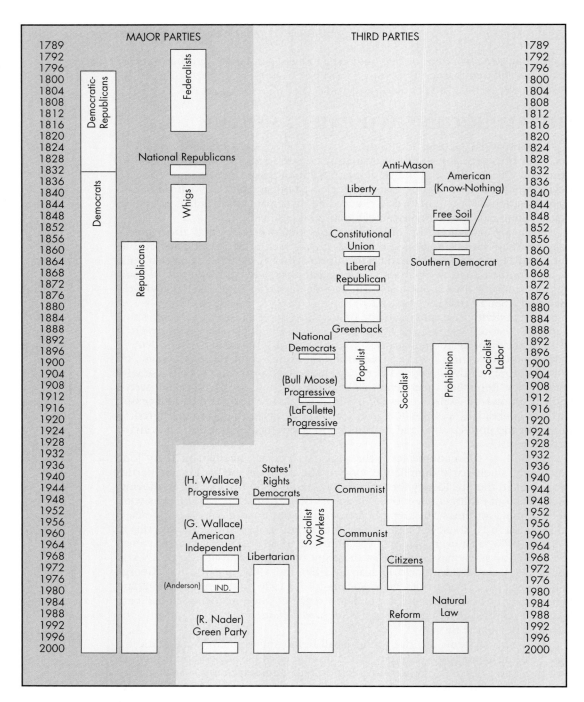

FIGURE 5.1 American Political Parties since 1789. The dates indicate the years in which parties either ran presidential candidates or held national conventions. The lifespan of many political parties can only be approximated because parties existed at the state or local level before they ran candidates in presidential elections, and parties continued to exist at local levels long after they ceased to run presidential candidates.

Source: Center for Political Studies, University of Michigan.

their efforts. Thus, the opposition's best chance of winning lies in uniting to defeat the majority party. The formation of third parties serves only to divide the minority and strengthen the majority party's hold on the elective office.

The effect that an election system can have on political parties is best shown by comparing the single-member-district method with the system of *proportional representation* (PR) used in many democracies. Under proportional representation, legislators are elected from large districts, and the parties are rewarded with seats in the legislature in proportion to the percentage of votes they obtain. Countries that use this system, such as Russia and Israel, have multiparty systems rather than only two major parties.[5] In multiparty systems, parties can be organized on a wide variety of bases. Some of these may represent economic interests such as business or labor, others may be based on religious beliefs, and still others may be based on a strong commitment to protection of the environment.

Another explanation of the development of the American two-party system takes a *historical* perspective. Noting the tendency of human institutions to preserve their initial form, this explanation points to the first political issue faced by the new nation, ratification of the Constitution. This was a yes/no issue that divided Americans into groups based on agricultural interests on the one hand and financial and mercantile interests on the other. This pattern has persisted ever since.

Still another explanation may be described as *cultural.* In this view, different racial, religious, and ethnic groups have been able to find a niche in American society rather than separating themselves from it. Class consciousness also has been less common in the United States than in European nations. Thus, there is less reason for multiparty politics—for example, no party seeking to establish a state religion, no significant support for a socialist or communist government, no party promoting the interests of labor. Instead, there are two major parties, each of which represents a broad range of interests.[6]

Party Competition

There is a high degree of two-party competition in presidential elections. Between 1976 and 2000 only one election was decided with a difference of more than 5 percent in the popular vote of the two major political party candidates. In the 2000 election the difference was less than 0.1

The situation is very different in state and local elections. Historically, there have been some parts of the country—congressional districts, states, cities, and entire regions—where one party has been dominant. The South was for a long time a strong one-party area. The Democratic party almost totally controlled the politics of that region from the decade after the end of the Civil War until the 1960s; however, in a striking turnabout, in recent decades the South has become more Republican. In contrast, New England, which was once generally Republican, has become more Democratic in the past twenty years. Some states are traditional strongholds of one of the two major parties: Rhode Island, Hawaii, and Maryland are predictably Democratic, while Utah, Idaho, and Wyoming are Republican strongholds. And most of the nation's major cities—Chicago, Detroit, and New York, for example—have traditionally favored Democratic party candidates.

An examination of congressional elections reveals that Senate races are generally more competitive than those for House seats. Running as an incumbent is a decided advantage in Senate contests. But when there is no incumbent, competition between the two parties is often very high, and party control of the Senate may be determined by the result of those contests. Races for seats in the House of Representatives are much less competitive. Since the end of World War II at least 90 percent of incumbents have been reelected, and this figure has surpassed 95 percent in many recent congressional elections. Indeed, there are some congressional districts in which candidates are elected without any opposition.

Party competition thus is quite variable; in fact, it is possible to rank states and localities on a scale from noncompetitive to highly competitive. At the bottom of the scale are the one-party states and districts. Farther up the scale are areas where one party almost always elects the public officials, but the minority party has enough support to pose a threat to the dominant party. Above them are areas that lean slightly toward one party or the other, and at the top are areas in which the parties are in active and continual competition.[7]

Why do one-party systems exist within a two-party system? Several reasons for this situation have been suggested. One is that there may be a local basis for party loyalty that overrides any other factor. In the South, Democratic dominance in national, state, and local elections was based on the long-held and deeply felt belief that the Republicans were responsible for the Civil War and the punitive post–Civil War Reconstruction policies. Another explanation of one-party dominance is that the people who live in a given area may be so similar that most of them support the same ideals and the same party. This might, for example, explain the Republican leanings of residents of very wealthy suburban areas and the overwhelming strength of the Democratic party in the poorest areas of the nation's large cities.[8]

Another way of looking at one-party dominance is in terms of party competition itself. One party may be the minority in a given area and unable to change that situation. Suppose, for example, that voters in a certain area have always identified with the Republican party. The Democrats are unable to win elections and become known as the losing party. As such, they are less able to attract financial contributions, campaign workers, and strong candidates to run for office, all of which are needed to win elections. As a result, they continue to lose and the area continues to be dominated by the Republican party.

The Nature of American Political Parties

The most salient characteristic of the American political party system is that it is essentially a two-party system. The system has some other important characteristics, however. One of these is that the parties are highly decentralized. The national parties have historically been weak; the state parties are independent of national control; and within the states, the county and local parties have great influence. State and local parties, for example, are free to nominate candidates and shape party positions on public issues without significant interference by the national party. (The decentralization of power within the major parties will be discussed in more detail later in the chapter.)

Another significant characteristic of the parties is that they are coalitions. Different segments of the population have traditionally supported one or the other major political party. For example, for more than sixty years union families, African Americans, many Catholics, Jews, people with relatively little education, and the poor have strongly supported the Democratic party. The Republicans, on the other hand, have attracted the loyalty of owners of both small and large businesses, farmers, small-town and rural dwellers, whites, Protestants, people with higher incomes and more education, nonunion families, and "old stock" Americans.[9] (Voting behavior is discussed more fully in Chapter 6.)

Related to this characteristic is another important aspect of American political parties: ideological diversity. To win elections and gain power, the parties need to be adaptable—to be able to shape their programs in such a way as to attract individuals and groups with a wide range of views on issues of public policy. As a result, party ideology is not clearly defined; rather, party positions on various issues are usually set forth in very general terms and can be interpreted differently by party members and officeholders.[10]

Ideological diversity tends to produce moderation. Because the parties have to appeal to many diverse groups with different political interests, they tend to avoid taking positions that are too extreme or dogmatic. Although important differences exist between the two major parties, each usually tries to take stands that will alienate as few voters as possible. Another reason that the parties avoid extreme positions is that most Americans hold moderate views on public issues. Party leaders realize that they must appeal to a broad segment of the American people whose political views are generally moderate. Indeed, national elections are won by the party that successfully appeals to this moderate majority.

In sum, the American two-party system is decentralized, and the parties are broad-based coalitions of ideologically different groups and interests. But this does not mean that there is no room for other kinds of parties. Although the nation has operated under a two-party system throughout its history, there has been no shortage of minor political parties that have contested elections at all levels of government.

Minor Parties

Greenbackers, Free Soilers, Bull Moosers, Populists, Socialists, Progressives, Independents, Libertarians—all have nominated candidates for national, state, and local public offices at one time or another, but rarely have those candidates won elections. Such **minor parties,** or "third" parties, exist primarily to oppose the policies and programs of the two major parties and to advance their own ideas. They do not have the popular support or the resources to get their candidates elected. (One minor party did become one of the nation's major political parties when, shortly before the American Civil War, the Republican party replaced the Whigs.)

Some minor parties are organized around a particular political ideology, such as socialism. Or they may form around a specific issue—the Prohibitionist party opposed alcoholic beverages, and the Liberty and Free-Soil parties of the 1840s and 1850s fought against slavery. Still other minor parties fall somewhere between issue and ideology. The Progressives of 1948, for instance, combined a social-reform program with support for a policy of friendship with the Soviet Union. Recently, environmentalists have organized Green parties in a number of states, and Ralph Nader ran as the Green party candidate in the 2000 presidential election.

Minor parties also differ in their origins. The Communist and Socialist Workers parties had their origins in European politics of the early twentieth century. The Populist party, on the other hand, arose out of a protest against the economic hardships suffered by farmers and laborers in late-nineteenth-century America. Other minor parties are "splinter" parties that have broken with one of the major parties. In 1912, for example, Theodore Roosevelt sought the presidency as the candidate of the Progressive party after having been denied the Republican nomination; his was the most successful third-party candidacy in the twentieth century. Similarly, in 1968 the American Independent party was created by Alabama Governor George Wallace to oppose what he believed were the overly liberal policies of the Democratic party. And as has already been said, the most successful recent third-party candidacy was that of Ross Perot in 1992. The Texas businessman campaigned on the need to reduce the federal budget deficit and to save the jobs of American workers from foreign competition. He received 19.7 million popular votes but won no electoral votes.

Most minor parties disappear soon after contesting one or two national elections. Only a few have nominated candidates for national elections for many decades. Perhaps the most important role some minor parties have had is to propose new ideas that later become adopted by one of the major political parties. The function of minor political parties "has not been to win or govern, but to agitate, educate, [and] generate new ideas. . . . When a third party's demands become popular enough, they are appropriated by one or both of the major parties and the third party disappears. . . . [They] are like bees: Once they have stung, they die."[11]

CLOSE-UP

MINOR PARTIES—PAST AND PRESENT

Minor political parties were very active during the 1996 presidential election. In addition to Reform party candidate Ross Perot, twenty other candidates were on the ballot in at least one state. Among the most prominent of these was Ralph Nader of the Green party, who ran on a self-imposed $5,000 budget. He pledged to put an end to "corporate welfare," reform campaign financing, and promote a multiparty system. Other candidates proposed a variety of policies that differed markedly from the major-party platforms. Harry Browne of the Libertarian party called for greater privatization of government services, including eliminating the federal government's role in education, crime control, and health care. John Hagelin of the Natural Law party proposed phasing out nuclear power, adopting a flat tax, and abolishing political action committees; he also favored federally financed transcendental meditation for high blood pressure. Howard Phillips of the U.S. Taxpayers party promised to restore American law "to its biblical premises." The party's platform also called for balancing the federal budget, abolishing the Internal Revenue Service, and ending federal financing for the National Endowment for the Arts.

In most elections minor parties have little or no influence. But there have been a few exceptions. In 1919, for example, the Eighteenth Amendment to the Constitution was ratified—a victory for the Prohibition party, which had struggled for years to outlaw the manufacture and sale of alcoholic beverages. The amendment was repealed in 1933. Only one minor party ever became a major party: the Republican party, which replaced the Whig party between 1856 and 1860. Republican candidates ran on a platform of opposition to slavery and its extension into new U.S. territories—"free soil and free men."

It can be argued that Ralph Nader, the Green Party candidate, caused the defeat of Al Gore in Florida in the 2000 presidential election and thus cost him the presidency. Nader received over 97,000 votes in Florida. If Nader had not been on the Florida ballot, many of his votes would likely have gone to Gore. By winning Florida's electoral votes, Gore would have received a majority of the electoral votes and been elected president.

THE STRUCTURE OF POLITICAL PARTIES

Political parties are not mentioned in the Constitution, but as we have seen, they have existed since the earliest years of the nation's history. The rules for their organization and structure are found in state law and in party rules. In general, "the organizational framework for political parties mirrors the geographic organization of the United States. That is, parties begin at the local level and eventually emerge at the national level."[12] The exceptions to this rule are the many congressional districts that cross city and county boundary lines.

On paper, the national party organizations resemble a pyramid, with the national party organizations at the top and the local units at the base. This image suggests that power flows downward from the top to the bottom of the pyramid. The reality is quite different, however. The state and local units are, in fact, largely independent of the national parties, and most of the authority within the parties is located at the lower levels rather than at the top. As we shall see shortly, the national parties' influence has grown in recent years, but largely in one area: that of supplying financial assistance to state and local party units.

The National Parties

In theory, the **national convention** is the political party's top national authority. In practice, however, it has few real powers. It meets every four years to nominate presidential and vice presidential candidates, and it adopts party rules and a party platform. But it has no voice in the selection of candidates for congressional, state, or local office, nor can it force candidates to support its platform.

Also in theory, the **national committee** of each party is the executive organ of the party during the time between meetings of the national convention. Like the national convention, the national committee does not have much authority. It decides where and when to hold the next party convention, and it raises campaign funds. The **national chair,** formally elected by the national committee but usually chosen by the party's presidential nominee, dominates the national committee with the help of the committee's permanent staff. But it is rare for a national chair to emerge as a strong leader of the party. This is especially true of the national chair of the party that has won the presidential election, since the president is the dominant figure in that party.

The national committees of both parties have become more active in giving financial aid to their local and state organizations. Today they play a prominent role in supplying financial support to state and local parties. A financial relationship of this type would have been unthinkable even as recently as twenty-five years ago.[13]

The State and Local Parties

In the early twentieth century, state party organizations were important features of the American political system. They were often led by powerful U.S. senators. But the adoption in 1913 of the Seventeenth Amendment to the Constitution, which provided for the popular election of senators, ended this era of state party bosses. State party organizations began a long period of decline that did not end until the last decades of the twentieth century.[14]

In more than half the states the members of the state party committees are chosen by local party committees or conventions. The state party chairs, who head the state organizations, are selected either by the state committees or at state conventions.

In many states today, party organizations play an influential role in politics. They are active in fund-raising, mobilizing voters, public opinion polling, recruiting candidates to run for office, and providing money and expertise to party candidates. Much of the revival of state parties is the result of the increasing flow of money from the national party organizations. According to one expert, "State party organizations have grown and developed in recent decades, at least in part from an infusion of funds and influence from the national level."[15]

The most important local party organization in most states is the county committee. The committee is headed by the county chair, who is generally elected by the committee's members. The county chair is active in campaign planning and fund-raising and also participates in the recruitment of candidates for public office and for membership on the precinct committees. In some states there are congressional district party organizations. If the party has elected the district legislator, the organization will attempt to ensure that he or she will be reelected and will also assist in providing services to his or her constituents.

Below the county committee there are also city, township, **ward,** and **precinct** committees, which vary considerably in size and importance. Like other party committees, they focus their efforts on campaigns and elections. The most basic party unit is the precinct committee, which functions within a specific election or voting district. The strength of a precinct committee is directly related to its size; in urban areas a precinct may include as many as 2,000 voters, whereas in very rural areas there may be only a dozen voters in a precinct. Members of precinct committees engage in campaign activities, party organizational work such as recruitment of candidates and campaign workers, and dissemination of political information to voters.[16] (See Figure 5.2.)

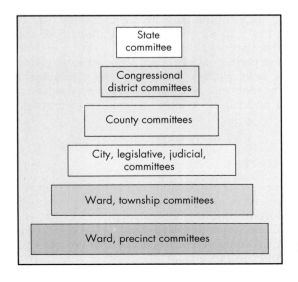

FIGURE 5.2   Typical Pyramid of Party Organization in a State.

Decentralization of Party Power

While the government has become more and more centralized, the power of the political parties has remained in the hands of state and local units. After all, the national parties nominate only two candidates for public office—the president and the vice president—at the party conventions held every four years. All other candidates for public office, including congressional seats, are chosen by the state and local parties.

Even at the local level, however, the parties do not have the power they once had. The party "machines" of the late nineteenth century and the first half of the twentieth century have largely vanished. The classic political machine provided a host of services to the millions of immigrants from eastern and southern Europe who came to the United States and settled in the nation's largest cities. The machine provided help in the form of housing, food, legal services, employment—including government jobs—and other services. The party organization asked for only two things in return: loyalty to the machine and votes at election time.[17]

Although political machines did not develop in every large city, they were a prominent feature of the urban political scene for many decades. The extension of the civil service system in the twentieth century, the growth of government welfare programs, and the spread of economic prosperity in the decades following World War II all contributed to the decline of the big-city political machine.[18]

In contrast to the urban machine of the past, in many localities today party structure is loose and sometimes almost nonexistent. One study of political parties describes this condition as follows:

> In such cases, most of the committee positions in the party's county unit are unfilled or held by completely inactive incumbents. A chairman and a handful of loyal party

Mayor Richard Daley of Chicago at the 1976 Democratic Party National Convention in New York City. Until his death later that year, Mayor Daley was a powerful figure in city, state, and national Democratic party politics. He was one of the last of the big-city "bosses."

officials may meet occasionally to carry out the most essential affairs of the party. Their main activity occurs shortly before the primary elections as they plead with members of the party to become candidates or offer themselves as candidates in order to "fill the party ticket." They are largely without influence or following, for often their party is a chronic minority party. They meet infrequently, raise little money for election campaigns, and create little or no public attention.[19]

Most local party organizations operate somewhere between the two extremes just described—machine politics and disorganization—but it is fair to say that they are somewhat closer to the second than to the first. A typical county or city organization consists of a chair and an executive committee that are most active at election time. These officials are aided by a handful of volunteer activists who generally receive no salary and may not even have an office. The situation is even worse at the precinct level. Many precinct organizations do not have a chair and may not even possess a list of local voters.[20]

PARTIES AND VOTERS: THE DECLINE OF PARTY IDENTIFICATION

During long periods of U.S. history, many Americans identified strongly with one of the two major political parties. In describing the intense loyalty to the Republican party that was characteristic of the late nineteenth century, one author has written:

> Many men were Republicans as they were church elders or lodge brothers. It was as if one belonged to an order. Their loyalties, their faith and pride in party, were often deeper, more vital to their self-respect and sense of worth than they could express. Delegates to Republican national conventions . . . sometimes had their official badges cast in gold and passed them along in their wills as precious relics.[21]

The same intensity could be seen in the devotion of many Americans to the Democratic party during much of the twentieth century, especially after the New Deal policies of the Roosevelt administration helped rescue the nation from the economic crisis of the 1930s. Political scientists use the term **party identification** to refer to the loyalty of voters to a particular party.

From the 1930s until the 1980s, public opinion surveys consistently showed the Democratic party with a wide lead over the Republicans in the number of people who identified with a political party. Only once in this long period (in 1946) did the Republicans reach parity with the Democrats. As recently as 1980, 41 percent of Americans said they were Democrats, whereas only 22 percent indicated that they were Republicans. During the 1980s, when Ronald Reagan was president, the number of people who identified themselves as Republicans grew, and by the end of that decade the Democrats held only a narrow lead.[22] But during most of the 1990s the Democrats increased their lead over the Republicans. In 1990, 39 percent of the electorate identified themselves as Democrats, compared to only 24 percent for the Republicans. In 1994 the split was reduced to 34 percent for the Democrats and 31 percent for the Republicans, but by 1996 the Democratic advantage was 38 percent to 29 percent.[23]

Polls taken since the September 11 terrorist attacks have generally shown gains in the number of Americans who identify themselves as Republicans. While some polls have found that Republican identifiers outnumber Democrats, others still find the Democrats in the lead. Based on surveys taken throughout 2001, the Harris polls show the Democrats with a five point lead—36 percent to 31 percent for Republicans. According to Harris, this Democratic lead is the smallest since it began studying party identification in 1969.[24]

Another significant change in public opinion in the past fifty years has been the increase in the number of people who refer to themselves as **Independents**—individuals who do not identify with any political party. In 1940 only one out of five Americans was an Independent. Since 1970 between 31 and 38 percent of Americans have identified themselves as Independents.[25] The decline in party identification can be seen in Americans of all ages, but it is especially striking among younger voters. In addition, new voters of all ages are increasingly likely to enter the electorate with no party ties. Together, these two groups account for about 75 percent of the decline in partisanship in the American electorate.[26]

Independent voters split their ticket when voting more often than do those who identify with one of the major political parties. They show a moderate degree of interest in government and wait longer in the campaign before deciding on their candidate. But they are also less active politically, less knowledgeable, and less likely to vote than people who identify with a political party.[27]

Scholars have suggested several possible reasons for the general decline in party identification and the increase in the number of independent voters. One theory views the parties as going through a period of "realignment," whereas a second major theory holds that they are in a period of "disintegration" or "dealignment."

According to the realignment theory, voters are in the process of changing their party loyalties, and the result will be a system of new party allegiances.[28] Such a realignment occurred after the national election of 1932. With the election of Franklin D. Roosevelt as president, the Democrats replaced the Republicans as the majority party, and they continued to control both Congress and the presidency for much of the next four decades. There is little evidence in contemporary American politics to support the theory of realignment.

There is more evidence to support the theory of dealignment in American politics. Dealignment stands in sharp contrast to realignment. In realignment, party identification becomes stronger, whereas it weakens in a period of dealignment. New voters are not attached to the politics that brought about a realignment. During such a period, "voters are much more susceptible to the personal appeals of candidates, to local issues, and to other elements that might lead to departures from underlying party loyalty."[29]

There is much evidence to support the theory that parties are in decline. Independent voters make up at least one-third of the electorate, and the number of voters who strongly identify with either the Democratic or Republican party has remained low for some time. The effects of the decline of party identification can be seen in the coverage of elections by television and other media. References to the parties are far less frequent than they once were; at the same time, emphasis on individual candidates has increased dramatically. Indeed, "voting the candidate rather than the party" appears to have become part of the American political culture.[30]

The idea of a political system without parties, or with very weak parties, is a source of concern to many students of American politics. They believe that political parties are the most effective means by which citizens can hold public officials accountable for their actions or inaction. Without parties, responsibility for conduct cannot be placed on the officials of a single party who can be replaced at the next election. If the voters cannot blame the party for policy failures, where can responsibility be placed? Many observers see this as a very serious problem; they believe that strong political parties are essential to the preservation of democratic government.

THE PARTY IN THE LEGISLATURE

At the beginning of the chapter we noted that political parties play a role in organizing and operating the government. By this we mean that parties have influence within the executive, judicial, and legislative branches of government. Thus, understanding the party's role in the executive branch requires an analysis of the president's role as party leader. In the judicial branch, it is important to appreciate the significance of party affiliation in the nomination and appointment of federal judges. In this section, however, we concentrate on perhaps the most important aspect of the political party—its role in the operation of the legislative branch of government.

Critics of the American party system point to the system of party government that prevails in European political systems, especially the British parliamentary system. In that system the major political parties are almost always united either for or against any major issue that comes to a vote in the legislature. It is typical for all the members of one party to vote against all the members of the other.

In a parliamentary system the party with the majority in the legislature actually creates the executive branch, whose continued existence depends on the backing of the legislative majority. Moreover, in most European nations the party organizations have wide-ranging power over members who hold elective offices. This power includes the authority to deny a member the right to run for office under the party's label at the next election.

The American political system differs markedly from those of other Western democracies. Instead of a parliamentary system, we have one based on the separation of powers. The executive branch is independent of the legislative branch and is legally responsible to the electorate, not to Congress. Indeed, the legislative and executive branches may be controlled by different parties—as has been the case during much of the past three decades.

In the United States a party's control over members holding elective office is very weak. In the legislature a party can exercise modest sanctions over members—such as denying a legislator a desired seat on an important congressional committee—but those sanctions are infrequently used. And the parties have little say in the nomination of candidates for Congress. The *direct primary* (which is largely unknown in Europe) places the choice of candidates in the hands of the voting public, not the party. (See Chapter 6 for a discussion of the primary system).

At the start of each Congress, the majority party elects the Speaker of the House and the President Pro Tem of the Senate. After that, the party's power over its members declines. A president seeking to enact a legislative program sometimes must turn to members of the opposition party to obtain a majority in favor of the legislation. In the fall of 1993, an extreme example of this phenomenon occurred. President Clinton gained passage of the North American Free Trade Agreement (NAFTA) by winning the support of 132 out of 175 Republicans in the

House; only 102 of 258 members of his own party voted in support of the president on the issue.

But to say that party discipline in Congress is weak is not to say that it is unimportant. In fact, many studies of voting patterns in Congress have concluded that party affiliation is by far the most important factor in determining the way members vote. But **party unity votes**—those in which a majority of the members of one party vote together on an issue and the majority of the members of the other party vote in opposition—have been very common in recent decades. During much of the 1980s and 1990s the average number of party unity votes by both Democratic and Republican legislators has exceeded 75 percent. This partisan behavior was especially pronounced in 1995, the first year since 1953 in which the Republicans controlled both the House and the Senate.[31]

The influence of the party may be seen in the fact that legislators usually try to support their party's program even when that means going against the wishes of their constituents or their own feelings. In one study of Congress, 94 percent of the Democrats and 96 percent of the Republicans answered yes to the question of whether they generally desired to support their party's position on issues. Indeed, 74 percent of the Democrats and 72 percent of the Republicans said that their party's stand was the first factor that affected their position on issues.[32]

REFORM OR STATUS QUO?

The American two-party system has been criticized for not offering the voter a clear choice. The major-party presidential candidates, it is said, offer few real differences to the electorate. It is also argued that the party has no control over its candidates once they have been elected—that it is impossible to force a candidate to keep campaign promises.

Several proposals for reform of the political party system have been made, including calls for a more centralized and democratic structure, more issue-oriented programs, and greater effort by officeholders to carry out their party's programs. Although there have been some revisions in party organization, the parties have ignored calls for changes that would make them highly centralized, disciplined, and issue oriented.

Discussions about reform of the American political party system may be irrelevant if the parties continue to decline in importance. One observer has warned that parties are "an endangered species" and has called for "a renewed appreciation of what useful things parties—as institutions and not just as labels—are to have around." In this view, "restoring the organized parties to vigorous health . . . should be the [nation's] No. 1 reform objective."[33]

INTEREST GROUPS

The United States is a huge nation with a large and diverse population and economy. Interest groups reflect that diversity. Business, labor, agriculture, and consumers are represented by interest groups. So are social, religious, ethnic, and patriotic groups, and people who are concerned about specific issues such as the environment, abortion, or crime. Moreover, the goals of different groups in society often clash. For example, the goals of conservationists attempting to preserve a forest area to protect wildlife will conflict with those of workers in the area whose livelihood is based on logging. These are the kinds of conflicts that were anticipated by Madison in his comment on factions that appeared at the beginning of this chapter.

An **interest group** may be defined as an assemblage of people who share common attitudes and interests and who try to influence the political system by shaping public opinion, opposing or supporting candidates for public office, and influencing the decisions of government officials. Some interest groups are large and have a national membership; examples include the AFL-CIO and the Chamber of Commerce of the United States. Others, such as a community group, may involve only a small number of people trying to solve a specific local problem, such as the quality of the local schools. Some groups are formal, with a definite structure and a set of regulations; others are informal and tend to dissolve when their goals have been achieved.

Almost all Americans either belong to one or more interest groups or are represented by such groups even though they are not formal members. In this way interest groups are similar to political parties: They represent the opinions and demands of citizens and use their strength to win benefits from the government. In fact, interest groups are a highly significant force in the formulation of public policy in the United States.

The Growth of Interest Groups

Interest groups of various kinds have existed throughout American history, but during the twentieth century their number increased greatly, and ever since the 1970s there has been an explosion in the number of politically active groups.

Lobbyists meet on Capitol Hill. Representing the many interest groups that exist in American society, lobbyists are a prominent feature of government in Washington, DC.

Several factors account for the increase in the number of interest groups. One is the basic structure of American government; federalism and separation of powers encourage group activity. If an interest group is unable to achieve its goals at the state level, for example, it may have more success in Washington. Or if a group cannot influence the legislative branch of the government, it can seek to gain the support of the executive branch or start a lawsuit in the courts to achieve its objectives.

The economic specialization of American society has also increased the number of interest groups that are active. For instance, the development of the computer has created many new businesses. This, in turn, has led to the creation of groups and associations that devote themselves to furthering the interests of the computer industry.

The increase in the number of interest groups is also due partly to the success of many older groups, such as the American Medical Association, the American Association of Retired Persons, and the National Rifle Association. Their many legislative successes over the years have convinced many Americans that interest groups are the best way to influence government.

The Structure of Interest Groups

Some interest groups have constitutions or charters, hold periodic elections, and charge membership dues. Many of the largest groups are organized like the government, with power divided between national and local levels.

The degree to which members take part in interest group activities varies widely. Many group members do not attend meetings or work for the group's goals; they are members in name only. Other members are active in the organization's affairs; they strongly identify with the group's goals and devote their energies to furthering the group's interests.

Like political parties, interest groups depend heavily on their leaders. The leaders of a group control its professional staff and the information available to its members and to the public. Consequently, the more effective its leadership, the more influential the group is likely to be.

Types of Interest Groups

Some interest groups are formed around a single issue and serve no other purpose than to work toward a favorable resolution of that issue. Most, however, are formed to serve their members' interests on a large number of subjects and on a continuing basis. As those interests change, so does the group's program. Various groups have been formed to serve what they consider to be the "public interest" rather than the interests of any particular group. It is, of course, difficult or impossible to obtain agreement on what is meant by the public interest; indeed, some critics question whether there is such a thing as "a" public interest.

In the past most interest groups have had an economic basis—agriculture, business, labor, and so forth. But there are also a variety of noneconomic interest groups based, for example, on racial or religious interests or on issues such as gun control, abortion, or conservation.

ECONOMIC INTEREST GROUPS   Most interest groups are formed to represent their members' economic interests. Agricultural groups, for instance, try to protect their members against the hardships caused by fluctuating farm prices.

The specialized nature of modern farming has led to the formation of groups that are concerned with specific areas of agriculture—the National Apple Institute, for example. There are also a number of larger groups that claim to represent farmers in general. They include the National Grange, the American Farm Bureau Federation, and the National Farmers' Union.

Business interests are represented in the nation's capital by a variety of groups. Some are known as **trade associations** and speak for companies in a particular sector of the economy. The American Bankers Association, for example, represents the interests of banks, and the Automobile Manufacturers Association represents those of automakers. Several large organizations seek to represent business interests in general. The Chamber of Commerce of the United States and the National Association of Manufacturers are the major groups that perform this function in Washington.

Labor as a whole is represented by the AFL-CIO, a federation of over a hundred unions. The AFL-CIO was created in 1955 by the merging of the American Federation of Labor, which is composed of skilled workers such as carpenters, and the Congress of Industrial Organizations, which consists largely of unskilled workers in mass-production industries such as steel. Most of the nation's organized workers are affiliated with the AFL-CIO, which is very active politically and well financed. Membership in the AFL-CIO has declined in past decades, however, largely as a result of the decline in American manufacturing. In 2000 there were about 16.2 million union members in the private sector of the economy, or about 13.5 percent of the nation's private workforce.[34]

Public employees—people employed by federal, state, or local governments—are a fast-growing part of the American labor movement. Historically, governments have opposed the right of their workers to form unions. But since the 1960s this right has increasingly been recognized at all levels of government, though it is generally illegal for the unions to strike. In 2000 there were 7.1 million unionized government workers, accounting for 37.5 percent of the public workforce.[35]

The most important unions of public employees are the American Federation of Teachers (AFT), the American Federation of State, County and Municipal Employees (AFSCME), both of which are connected with the AFL-CIO, and the National Education Association (NEA), an independent union. Not only have these groups pressed hard for increased benefits for their members, but they have also become major interest groups, spending large sums on political campaigns and lobbying on a wide variety of issues.

During the 1996 national election trade unions spent approximately $35 million in an unsuccessful attempt to help the Democrats regain control of both houses of Congress. Unions were again active in the 1998 off-year elections. Although the Republicans maintained control of both houses of Congress, the Democrats did gain seats in the House of Representatives. Union organization and spending played a major role in bringing about this unusual result. (The president's party—the Democrats in 1998—almost always loses seats in Congress in off-year elections.)

Unions were again active in the 2000 national elections. They were unsuccessful in their efforts to have Al Gore elected president and to enable the Democrats to regain control of the House of Representatives. But the Democrats did gain five seats in the United States Senate, creating a temporary 50/50 tie between Democrats and Republicans in that chamber. But, as has already been mentioned, the 2001 defection of one Republican senator from that party allowed the Democrats to organize the Senate.

Professionals such as doctors and lawyers have their own interest groups. Although their membership is not large, these groups are influential because of the wealth and status of their members. **Professional associations** are concerned with licensing requirements in their states—that is, with the standards a person must meet to practice in the state—but they can also be very active on some issues related to government. The American Bar Association (ABA), for example, has long been concerned with the quality of appointees to the federal courts, and since 1945 the ABA has been active in screening and evaluating judicial nominees. The ABA also takes stands on a variety of legal issues that are subjects of public debate, such as abortion and the rights of criminal defendants. For many decades the American Medical Association has been a vigilant opponent of legislative proposals that would give government greater control over physicians and the services they provide. In 1993, for example, its strong opposition to President Clinton's health-care plan was an important factor in the defeat of that proposal.

NONECONOMIC INTEREST GROUPS Some noneconomic interest groups have a religious or moral basis (for example, the U.S. Catholic Conference, the National Council of Churches, the Southern Baptist Christian Life Commission, and the American Jewish Congress). The interests of women are represented by several groups, of which perhaps the best known is the National Organization for Women (NOW), which has been active in eliminating gender-based discrimination, protecting the right to have an abortion, and furthering the interests of women. The interests of African Americans are the concern of groups like the National Association for the Advancement of Colored People (NAACP) and the Urban League. Of the groups that claim to speak for the "public interest," the largest is Common Cause, which was established in 1970. This group has played an especially important role in promoting campaign finance reform.

SINGLE-ISSUE GROUPS An important trend in recent years has been the rise of **single-issue interest groups** that focus entirely on a single issue, such as abortion or gun control. For example, groups such as NARAL Pro-Choice America (formerly known as the National Abortion Rights League) and the National Right to Life Committee spend large amounts of money and effort to persuade the government to accept their views of abortion. The Sierra Club is one of a number of organizations concerned with conservation and environmental problems. Single-issue groups judge candidates and public officials by their views on one issue. In some primary and general elections, the outcome can depend on how much pressure such groups place both on the candidates and on the voters. The result, according to one writer, is the "fragmentation" of American politics and failure to consider the overall public good.[36]

POLITICAL ACTION COMMITTEES Labor unions and corporations are barred by federal law from making direct contributions to political campaigns, and trade unions cannot use members' dues to make contributions to candidates. To escape these prohibitions, many unions and corporations have created independent **political action committees** (PACs). The PACs have been successful in raising and spending large sums of money obtained through contributions by union members and corporate officers, and they have taken positions on a variety of national issues. The 1974 amendments to the Federal Election Campaign Act expressly sanctioned the creation of political action committees, and the number of such organizations has multiplied since then.

In addition to trade unions and corporations, many other types of interest groups have created PACs. The Association of Trial Lawyers of America and the American Federation of State, County, and Municipal Workers have been among the largest political contributors to recent general election campaigns. There are also ideological PACs, which promote either conservative or liberal ideas and candidates. Some PACs take an active interest in issues that affect other nations. For example, several pro-Israel PACs have been active in Washington for many years promoting strong ties between the United States and Israel.

Once an organization has established a political action committee, it can raise money from its members or employees. Federal law permits a PAC to give $5,000 to a candidate in a primary election and an additional $5,000 in the general election. It can also give $15,000 annually to a national party committee. Some PACs also engage in other kinds of political activity: assisting in voter registration, operating telephone banks on election day, distributing campaign literature, and canvassing potential voters. The money spent on these activities does not count toward the $5,000 limit as long as the PAC's activities are kept separate from those of the candidate's personal campaign organization. (Campaign spending laws are discussed more fully in Chapter 6.)

According to the Federal Election Commission, the organization that administers federal campaign spending laws, there were 4,328 PACs in 2002; 1,672 were created by corporations and another 914 by trade associations and health-related groups; 1,257 were established by independent, ideological organizations; only 326 were connected to labor unions.[37]

The influence of PACs on elections has been a source of concern for many Americans during the past several decades. Much of this concern has centered on the ability of PACs to raise large amounts of money to spend on political campaigns. In the fifteen-month period covering part of 2001 and 2002, PAC contributions were almost equally divided between the two major political parties: $66.4 million was given to the Republicans and $64.8 million to the Democrats. Incumbent legislators received 87.6 percent of the money; challengers received only 4.9 percent; open-seat candidates were given the remaining 7.4 percent.[38]

An examination of campaign spending by PACs tends to support the perception held by many people that these groups have a great deal of influence on elections. The amount of spending by PACs has increased in recent years. In 1995 and 1996, PACs spent $217 million on election campaigns. The total amount reached $259.8 million in 1999 and 2000. Of that amount, $91.5 million was expended by corporate PACs, $51.6 million by labor, and $37.3 million by independent groups.[39]

ACTIVITIES OF INTEREST GROUPS   The chief method used by interest groups to influence public policy is **lobbying,** trying to persuade legislators to vote for or against a particular bill or convince members of the executive branch that a particular program is or is not desirable. Those who perform this task are called *lobbyists.* The term was initially used several centuries ago in Great Britain in reference to journalists who waited in the lobbies of the House of Commons to interview legislators. In the United States the term is frequently given a negative connotation.

Individuals employed as lobbyists come from a variety of backgrounds. Many are lawyers and public relations experts affiliated with large Washington firms. A large percentage of lobbyists are former members of Congress and administrators who have worked in the executive branch. Individuals with these backgrounds are in great demand by interest groups because of their personal contacts and their knowledge of how Congress and executive agencies function.

Some interest groups also attempt to achieve their policy goals by bringing lawsuits in the courts or by supporting legal actions begun by other individuals or organizations. Grassroots activity designed to influence public opinion is another frequently used strategy. Finally, many interest groups give financial and other forms of electoral support to candidates for public office.

LOBBYING CONGRESS Lobbying in Congress may be directed at individual legislators and their staffs, but much effort is aimed at the standing committee that deals with the issue of concern to the interest group. Lobbyists for interest groups often testify before congressional committees and submit prepared statements that present the organization's views on proposed legislation. They may also prepare drafts of proposed legislation and submit them to individual members of Congress. These personal appearances and documents enable interest groups to present detailed information about a particular subject to members of Congress—knowledge that they might not be able to obtain from any other source.

Interest groups pay their lobbyists to keep them up to date on developments within the government that could affect their members. Accordingly, lobbyists become experts not only in the subject their interest group is concerned with, but also on the House and Senate committees and subcommittees that deal with that topic. Lobbyists keep an eye on the activities of those House and Senate committees and try to establish close ties with the committee members, especially the chairs.

LOBBYING THE EXECUTIVE BRANCH Most interest groups do not have direct access to the president or his personal staff. Those that do may find that the president is unreceptive to their ideas. This is particularly true in the area of foreign policy. "Presidents and their staffs look at the larger picture. They often have their own ideologies and interests and will not risk being seen as a tool of 'special interests.' Presidents want to be seen as representatives of the entire nation."[40]

But the situation with regard to executive departments and agencies is very different. They are concerned not with the large national picture but with specific aspects of government, and lobbyists have learned how to maximize their influence on the federal bureaucracy. They do this in four basic ways. First, they use the traditional method of direct lobbying. They present their ideas about proposed policies to the agency in written statements and, most important, at the hearings that most agencies hold before making final policy decisions.

Second, lobbyists pressure individual members of Congress to hold a committee hearing about agency policy, to threaten a reduction in funding for the agency in the next budget, or to propose legislation that will deprive an agency of some aspect of its authority.

Third, lobbyists seek to have sympathetic executives appointed to policy-making positions within the bureaucracy. And finally, lobbyists can make personal visits to an agency head and initiate letter-writing campaigns directed at an agency by the interest group's supporters. This type of grassroots mobilization can be an especially effective way to influence agency decisions.[41]

Although the president is less accessible than are other government officials, there are numerous ways in which interest groups can influence decision making in the White House. That influence may be direct—for example, when the president asks representatives of an interest group for information and advice when drawing up a legislative proposal. More often, however, it is indirect, occurring through contacts with members of the president's staff. Lobbyists also seek to influence policy in the executive branch by influencing the decisions of policy-making officials in the departments and agencies of the government. The key to success in the executive branch is knowing precisely which individuals on the White House staff or in the bureaucracy have the greatest influence on policymaking in a particular area.

In attempting to influence legislative decisions, lobbyists also attempt to develop ties with congressional staff members. Staffers are employed both by the standing committees of Congress and by individual legislators, and lobbyists understand their importance in the legislative process. In the words of one scholar,

> Committee staff often play a major role in drafting technical legislation, and they frequently meet with lobbyists who have information to convey. Lobbyists also seek to meet with members' personal staff, who are often involved in meetings to decide key votes or to discuss possible legislative initiatives.[42]

INTEREST GROUPS AND THE COURTS Although the courts are protected by law from all direct lobbying activities, several ways exist by which interest groups can indirectly influence the judiciary. One of those ways is to bring lawsuits in the courts. The best-known example of such action is the series of cases brought by the NAACP to enforce the civil rights of African Americans. The Supreme Court case of *Brown* v. *Board of Education of Topeka* (1954),[43] which made school segregation unconstitutional, was handled by the NAACP and argued by its attorneys. Similarly, the American Civil Liberties Union (ACLU) represents individuals in cases involving issues of civil liberties and civil rights. Since its founding in the 1920s, the ACLU has been especially active in litigating cases involving the Bill of Rights and the equal protection clause of the Fourteenth Amendment.

Interest groups can also file *amicus curiae* ("friend of the court") **briefs.** In such cases the group, although not a party to the actual conflict, can present its views on the issues in question and attempt to convince the court of the merits of its arguments. The NAACP and the ACLU frequently file *amicus curiae* briefs in civil liberties and civil rights cases. But many groups file such briefs with the Supreme Court when cases arise that affect their interests. For example, in the 2003 Supreme Court cases involving two affirmative programs used at the University of Michigan—*Gratz* v. *Bollinger* and *Grutter* v. *Bollinger*—more than sixty *amicus curiae* briefs were filed by a wide variety of groups, the majority in support of the school's policies.[44]

GRASSROOTS ACTIVITIES The primary form of grassroots lobbying "involves using group members (or the general public) to pressure policymakers to support the group's agenda."[45] It usually involves the unstated warning that the members will work to defeat a legislator who opposes their position or the promise of electoral backing if the legislator supports it.

Support from those back home may be expressed in the form of letters, telegrams, faxes, and telephone calls to senators and representatives. In addition, delegations from the home district may make a personal visit to the legislator to express their opinions on an issue, implying that an unfavorable response will result in loss of voter support at election time. But members of Congress can often tell when an inflow of mail has been artificially created. This is obvious when the letters or faxes all arrive about the same time and have similar wording. The member may come to the conclusion that the content of the letters does not represent the majority viewpoint.

Grassroots lobbying is best directed at legislators who are undecided about a particular issue. Lobbying either supporters or opponents of the group's position is generally an unwise use of an organization's financial and human resources. In the case of an opponent, it has the added hazard that the legislator may be motivated to devote more effort to defeating the organization's goals.

Perhaps the most effective lobbying is done by strongly ideological groups such as the National Rifle Association and the NARAL Pro-Choice America. These organizations have the capacity to "mobilize their large and diverse memberships into political action."[46]

Interest groups also use other grassroots tactics to further their policy objectives. Some advertise in newspapers or on television to get their message across to the public. They hope that the public will support their views and will put pressure on the government to adopt the policies they favor. Or they may simply hope that the public will develop a favorable attitude toward the interest group. Some corporations, for example, help finance public television programs and radio broadcasts of cultural events.

Finally, grassroots activities may take the form of public demonstrations. When they are carried out on a large scale, these events are usually planned and organized by coalitions of groups with shared policy goals. During the 1960s and 1970s, for example, civil rights groups and those opposed to the war in Vietnam organized many demonstrations designed to win public support for their views. In recent years several major demonstrations have been held in Washington, DC. In 1996 a coalition of Hispanic, labor, and civil rights groups led a Latino and Immigrants' Rights March, the first such demonstration by Hispanic people. And in May 2000 mothers from across the country demonstrated in the "Million Mom March" in Washington in support of stronger gun control legislation.

In the past several decades many other groups have held demonstrations at both the local and the national levels. At times demonstrations have been so common that their organizers have been unable to obtain media coverage for them. Yet coverage on the evening news shows is of central importance in getting the public to pay attention to the demonstration and the policy objectives of the particular group.

There is always a danger, however, that demonstrations will alienate the public. People may see them as "unruly exercises or as reflecting a narrow, selfish view." Demonstrations may also defeat their purpose if organizers resort to excesses. Finally, demonstrations, regardless of their form, cannot be successful unless they are combined "with other tactics in a sustained lobbying drive."[47]

In recent years lobbyists have made increasing use of the technologies of the electronic age. Some groups have installed banks of fax machines that automatically send faxes requesting group members to ask employees or customers to contact members of Congress on a particular issue. Other lobbyists run TV commercials including a toll-free number that viewers can call; the call is answered by a telemarketing company and transferred directly to the office of the appropriate member of Congress. Still another effective new technology is the use of satellite networks that connect an organization's Washington headquarters to affiliates in every state, thereby allowing the association's leaders to appear on television in the affiliates' offices and rally the membership to action.

Finally, the cyber age has added new dimensions to grassroots activity. Most political organizations have websites and therefore are able to reach their

Protesters against the U.S. war on Iraq gather on the National Mall in Washington, D.C., in January, 2003.

members and the general public directly. Similarly, an increasing number of members of Congress have e-mail addresses and home pages on the Web. Thus, interest groups can have their members and supporters contact legislators and communicate their opinions to them quickly and inexpensively.

ELECTORAL SUPPORT Many interest groups contribute money to political campaigns. The important role of political action committees in financing congressional campaigns has already been mentioned. Besides contributing funds to the candidates they favor, interest groups may offer other forms of electoral support, such as providing political consultants, sponsoring public-opinion polls, organizing campaigns to register voters, and providing workers to staff local campaign organizations. And of course, organizations urge their members to vote for candidates who favor the group's policies and to defeat candidates who oppose them.

Funding of Interest Groups

Interest groups obtain the funds to finance their activities in a variety of ways. Corporations, of course, can simply budget a particular amount for lobbying activities. Noncorporate interest groups generally raise money from several kinds of sources. Most rely on dues paid by members, but the proportion of revenues obtained in this way differs greatly from one group to another. Some groups also obtain gifts and donations from individuals and corporations and grants from foundations.

Another source of organizational income is staff-generated revenues of various kinds. These revenues come from magazines, pamphlets, informational booklets, and the like that are sold to members and to the public, as well as from conferences, seminars, and training sessions. The American Association of Retired

People (AARP) sells insurance, prescription drugs, and other services to its large membership. A few organizations also obtain income from financial investments and endowments; an example is the American Medical Association, which earns several million dollars a year in investment income.[48] (See Table 5.1.)

How Powerful Are Interest Groups?

Power is not evenly distributed among interest groups. Some groups are large and influential, others small and relatively unimportant. The larger groups tend to have more power because they benefit from the support of thousands and sometimes millions of members. Loyalty can also be an important factor. If a group is unified and its members are able to agree on specific goals and work together to achieve those goals, the group will be more influential. In addition, some groups are more powerful because they are better organized and have more financial resources than others.

A recent study by the nonpartisan Center for Responsive Politics (CRP) revealed the large amounts of money spent on lobbying in Washington and the influence some groups have in shaping public policy. The CRP estimated that some $1.42 billion was spent by lobbying groups in 1998, an increase of 13 percent from the previous year. This growth was caused by legislative debates over public health and tobacco regulation. Insurance companies spent the largest amount, $77.2 million. Drug companies spent $73.8 million, and cigarette makers $67.4

TABLE 5.1

TOP TEN PACS BY CONTRIBUTIONS TO CANDIDATES JANUARY 2001–MARCH 2002

Rank	Committee	Type*	Contributions to Candidates
1	Association of Trial Lawyers of America Political Action Committee	T	$1,783,753
2	American Federation of State, County, and Municipal Employees	L	$1,411,500
3	Machinists' Non-Partisan Political League	L	$1,364,750
4	International Brotherhood of Electrical Workers Committee on Political Education	L	$1,360,450
5	Realtors' Political Action Committee	T	$1,183,570
6	Democrat Republican Independent Voter Education	L	$1,178,718
7	Dealers' Election Action Committee of the National Automobile Dealers Association	T	$1,156,250
8	Laborers' Political League-Laborers' International Union of North America	L	$1,097,500
9	Build Political Action Committee of the National Association of Home Builders	T	$1,082,000
10	United Auto Workers Voluntary Community Action Program	L	$1,029,450

*L = Labor
T = Trade/Membership/Health
Source: Federal Election Commission. "PAC Activity Contines to Trail 2000 Levels." Washington, DC. May 28, 2002.

million. The tobacco companies almost doubled their spending and succeeded in defeating regulatory legislation that was being considered in Congress.

The uneven distribution of power among interest groups has been a subject of much criticism. Some groups, it is claimed, are simply too big, too powerful, and too effective. Some are not opposed by other groups, or if they are, the opposition is weak. Another criticism of interest groups is that they represent only a small percentage of the population—a minority with very specific, narrow interests—and that the widely held view that interest groups represent the majority of the population is a myth. The great increase in the number of interest groups in recent decades makes it unlikely that this criticism remains entirely valid today.

Efforts to limit the power of interest groups have centered on controlling the activities of lobbyists. In 1946 Congress passed the Federal Regulation of Lobbying Act, which required lobbyists to register with the government, list their employers and salaries, and file quarterly financial reports with the Senate and the House of Representatives. This legislation was largely ineffective because loopholes in the law made it possible for many lobbyists to avoid registering. Only a small percentage of Washington lobbyists actually complied with the 1946 law.

Over the years, Congress gave halfhearted consideration to proposals to tighten the rules governing lobbyists, but no significant changes were made. Public outrage at the number of scandals involving legislators and lobbyists and the belief that relations between these groups were too close finally led Congress to act. The Lobbying Disclosure Act of 1995 established a variety of new rules governing lobbyists and legislators. The new law defines a lobbyist as "any individual

CLOSE-UP

RULES FOR LOBBYISTS

Elaborate lunches and dinners are out. So are lavish gifts and all-expenses-paid trips to recreational resorts. Lobbyists now must observe the "Toothpick Rule," the "Gravy Rule," and the "Bagel Rule."

In 1995 Congress passed legislation setting forth new rules governing the activities of lobbyists. They were responding to public pressure to reform the existing rules, which had been in effect since 1946. Those rules were full of loopholes that allowed lobbyists to entertain members of Congress and shower them with gifts in the hope of gaining votes for the causes they represent.

In addition to defining *lobbyist*, the 1995 law explains the meaning of the term *lobbying contacts*—telephone calls or letters to lawmakers, government officials, or their aides on practically any subject except sports and the weather.

Many of the new rules center on food. No longer may a lobbyist take a member of Congress to a fancy restaurant for a sit-down meal. Receptions are allowed—hence the "Toothpick Rule," which permits food on the end of a toothpick. Breakfast is also acceptable—hence the "Bagel

Rule." (Of course, lobbyists who are personal friends of members of Congress may take their friends to dinner, but the legislators must pay for the meal themselves.) The new rules favor small, inexpensive gifts such as pens and baseball caps. Expensive gifts are not allowed.

The 1995 regulations favor standing over sitting. "If you stand at a bar and pay for a drink, that's OK," says a lawyer hired by the House of Representatives to explain the rules to lobbyists. "But if you're sitting down, ordering rounds of drinks and hors d'oeuvres, that's beginning to look an awful lot like a meal." The rules also permit finger food (at either receptions or breakfasts), but not food that must be eaten with utensils. That's where the "Gravy Rule" comes in—it bars food covered with gravy, which must be eaten with utensils and therefore is a meal.

Why no meals? Because at a meal a lobbyist can monopolize a lawmaker's time, whereas at a reception everyone is standing and mingling, not to mention trying to balance a plate of finger food, a napkin, and a drink.

employed or retained by a client or organization for financial or other compensation, and whose lobbying activities constitute more than 20 percent of his or her income during a semiannual period."[49]

The 1995 legislation also requires lobbyists to register with the secretary of the Senate and the clerk of the House of Representatives, and to provide information about the lobbyist, the client, the issues, the lobbyist's activities, and the objects of those activities. Another report must be filed every six months containing additional information, including the total income received by the lobbyist, the sources of that income, the specific bills that are the subject of the lobbying, and the executive agencies that were contacted by the lobbyist during the six-month period covered by the report.[50] The law also contains a complex set of regulations dealing with gifts and favors given to legislators by lobbyists.

CONCLUSION

The second half of the twentieth century saw major changes in the American political parties and the role of interest groups in the political system. The political parties have declined in importance and influence, and it seems doubtful that they will regain their former strength and power.

Although political parties have been in decline, both the number and the importance of interest groups have grown, and they have become active in attempting to shape government policy. Of course, some of these groups are not new—a few date back to the nineteenth century. But many were created during the past thirty-five years, including most of the single-issue groups and political action committees.

Perhaps the most important, and in some ways the most disturbing, development of recent years is the tendency for "issue politics" to replace "party politics." A group may form around a particular issue, push for the enactment of a specific law, and keep an eye on the way that law is carried out. Many people find such activity much more satisfying than traditional party politics. For one thing, it can produce visible results—the passage or blocking of legislation, for example. For another, issue politics permits people to choose the problem that concerns them most deeply and concentrate on it. Party politics, by contrast, deals with many public matters, and a citizen may agree with some of the party's policies but not with others.

Many observers contend that interest group activity has resulted in greater participation in the political process. More people today attend meetings, write to members of the legislature, lobby Congress, and collect signatures on petitions. Moreover, many individuals gain a greater sense of purpose than can be obtained from working for a party, and they can be involved year round, not just at election time.

There are drawbacks to issue politics, however. Interest groups sometimes lack the ability to compromise the way the parties can. In this way they make it harder for government officials to reach workable solutions to problems. Moreover, unlike political parties, interest groups are not responsible for the success or failure of government programs. Thus, even though the proliferation of interest groups has resulted in increased participation, it may also have brought about a decrease in accountability and responsibility.

QUESTIONS FOR THOUGHT

1. Why does the United States have a two-party system?

2. Why can American political parties be described as decentralized?

3. What are interest groups? How do they differ from political parties?

4. How do interest groups seek to influence the decisions of government?

5. What are political action committees?

6. What criticisms have been leveled against the role of political action committees?

INTERNET ACTIVITIES

1. *Interest Group Ratings of Politicians.* Go to Voter Information Services (VIS) at **http://www.vis.org/.** Proceed to "VIS Ratings." Review the site, especially the "Key to Groups" and "How to Interpret Ratings." Find the American Conservative Union and the Americans for Democratic Action ratings for your U.S. representative and one of your U.S. senators.

2. *Party Platforms.* Go to one of the following sites for a list of political parties. Choose one of the parties and follow the links to its website. Briefly summarize the party's positions on major policy issues:

   http://www.yahoo.com/Government/Politics/Parties/
   http://www.lib.umich.edu/govdocs/webdirlp.html/#platform

KEY TERMS

amicus curiae briefs
independents
interest group
lobbying
minor party
multiparty system
national chair

national committee
national convention
party identification
party unity vote
political action committee
political party
precinct

professional associations
single-issue interest group
trade associations
two-party system
ward

SUGGESTED READING

Aldrich, John H. *Why Parties?: The Origin and Transformation of Political Parties in America.* Chicago: University of Chicago Press, 1995.

Barone, Michael, Richard E. Cohen, and Charles E. Cook, Jr. *The Almanac of American Politics 2002.* Washington, DC: National Journal, 2002.

Browne, William P. *Interest Groups and U.S. Public Policy.* Washington, DC: Georgetown University Press, 1998.

Cigler, Allan J., and Burdett A. Loomis, eds. *Interest Group Politics.* Washington, DC: Congressional Quarerly Press, 2002.

Glaser, James. *Race, Campaign Politics and Realignment in the South.* New Haven, CT: Yale University Press, 1996.

Green, John C., and Daniel M. Shea. *The State of the Parties: The Changing Role of Contemporary American Parties,* 3nd ed. Lanham, MD: Rowman & Littlefield, 1999.

Hula, Kevin W. *Lobbying Together: Interest Group Coalitions in Legislative Politics.* Washington, DC: Georgetown University Press, 1999.

Mahood, H. R. *Interest Groups in American National Politics.* Upper Saddle River, NJ: Prentice Hall, 2000.

Reichley, A. James. *The Life of the Parties: A History of American Political Parties.* Lanham, MD: Rowman & Littlefield, 2000.

Wolfe, Bruce, and Bertram J. Levine. *Lobbying Congress: How the System Works.* Washington, DC: Congressional Quarterly Press, 1996.

NOTES

1. Clinton Rossiter, *Parties and Politics in America* (Ithaca, NY: Cornell University Press, 1960), p. 67.

2. William J. Keefe, *Parties, Politics, and Public Policy in America,* 8th ed. (Washington, DC: Congressional Quarterly Press, 1998), p. 30.

3. Ibid., pp. 31–32.

4. Ibid., p. 33.

5. See Douglas J. Amy, *Real Choices/New Voices* (New York: Columbia University Press, 1993), for a discussion of the effects of election laws on the party and political systems of nations.

6. John F. Bibby, *Politics, Parties, and Elections in America* (Chicago: Nelson-Hall, 1996), pp. 38–39.

7. Fred I. Greenstein and Frank B. Feigert, *The American Party System and the American People,* 3rd ed. (Englewood Cliffs, NJ: Prentice Hall, 1985), p. 84.

8. Paul Allen Beck and Frank J. Sorauf, *Party Politics in America,* 7th ed. (New York: HarperCollins, 1992), pp. 46–47.

9. Keefe, *Parties, Politics, and Public Policy,* p. 67.

10. Ibid., p. 72.

11. Richard Hofstadter, *The Age of Reform* (New York: Knopf, 1956), p. 97.

12. L. Sandy Maisel, *Parties and Elections in America,* 3rd ed. (Lanham, MD: Rowman & Littlefield, 1999), p. 66.

13. Ibid., p. 67.

14. Ibid., pp. 72–74.

15. Ibid., pp. 77–80.

16. Keefe, *Parties, Politics, and Public Policy,* pp. 26–27.

17. Ruth K. Scott and Ronald J. Hrebenar, *Parties in Crisis,* 2nd ed. (New York: Wiley, 1984), p. 119.

18. Ibid., pp. 120–23.

19. Beck and Sorauf, *Party Politics in America,* p. 83.

20. Ibid., pp. 83–84.

21. David McCullough, *Mornings on Horseback* (New York: Simon & Schuster, 1981), p. 297.

22. Michael Oreskes, "Republicans Show Gains in Loyalty," *New York Times,* January 21, 1990, p. 22.

23. William H. Flanigan and Nancy H. Zingale, *Political Behavior of the American Electorate,* 9th ed. (Washington, DC: Congressional Quarterly Press, 1998), p. 61.

24. "Party Identification: Democrats Still Lead, But Their Lead (5 points) Is as Low as It Has Ever Been," The Harris Poll # 8, February 13, 2002.

25. Flanigan and Zingale, *Political Behavior,* p. 61.

26. Keefe, *Parties, Politics, and Public Policy,* p. 198.

27. Beck and Sorauf, *Party Politics in America,* p. 194.

28. James L. Sundquist, *Dynamics of the Party System* (Washington, DC: Brookings Institution, 1973), pp. 1–2.

29. Flanigan and Zingale, *Political Behavior,* p. 57.

30. Walter Dean Burnham, "Foreword," in Martin P. Wattenberg, *The Decline of American Political Parties, 1952–1984* (Cambridge: Harvard University Press, 1986), p. xii.

31. Maisel, *Parties and Elections,* p. 471.

32. David J. Vogler, *Politics of Congress,* 4th ed. (Boston: Allyn & Bacon, 1983), p. 114.

33. Everett C. Ladd, Jr., *Where Have All the Voters Gone?* 2nd ed. (New York: Norton, 1982), pp. 72–73.

34. U.S. Bureau of the Census, *Statistical Abstract of the United States, 2003,* 123rd ed. (Washington, DC: Government Printing Office, 2003), Table 656, p. 431.

35. Ibid.

36. William J. Crotty, *American Parties in Decline,* 2nd ed. (Boston: Little, Brown, 1984), pp. 142–43.

37. Federal Election Commission, "PAC Activity Continues to Rise," News Release, June 27, 2002.

38. Ibid.

39. *Statistical Abstract 2003,* Table 426, p. 273.

40. Eric M. Uslaner, "Lobbying the President and the Bureaucracy," in Paul S. Herrnson, Ronald G. Shaiko, and Clyde Wilcox, *The Interest Group Connection* (Chatham, NJ: Chatham House, 1998), p. 208.

41. William T. Gormley, Jr., "Interest Group Intervention in the Administrative Process: Conspirators and Co-Conspirators," in Paul S. Herrnson, Ronald G. Shaiko, and Clyde Wilcox, *The Interest Group Connection* (Chatham, MD: Chatham House, 1998), pp. 214–215.

42. Clyde Wilcox, "The Dynamics of Lobbying the Hill," in Paul S. Herrnson, Ronald G. Shaiko, and Clyde Wilcox, *The Interest Group Connection,* p. 91.

43. 347 U.S. 483 (1954).

44. 539 U.S. 244 (2003) and 539 U.S. 306 (2003).

45. Wilcox, "The Dynamics of Lobbying," p. 96.

46. Ibid., p. 97.

47. Jeffrey M. Berry, *The Interest Group Society,* 2nd ed. (New York: HarperCollins, 1989), pp. 110–12.

48. Kay Lehman Scholzman and John T. Tierney, *Organized Interests in American Society* (New York: HarperCollins, 1986), pp. 90–92.

49. Richard G. Shaiko, "Lobbying in Washington: A Contemporary Perspective," in Paul S. Herrnson, Ronald G. Shaiko, and Clyde Wilcox, *The Interest Group Connection* (Chatham, NJ: Chatham House, 1998), p. 14.

50. Ibid.

CHAPTER

6

Nominations
and Elections

In this chapter we discuss several aspects of what James Madison called "the elective mode of obtaining rulers," including nomination and election procedures, campaign strategy, legislation affecting campaign financing, and the Electoral College. Part of the chapter will focus on the complex methods by which presidential candidates are nominated. We begin, however, with a general history of the various methods of nominating public officials at the national, state, and local levels.

> The aim of every political constitution is, or ought to be, first to obtain for rulers men who possess most wisdom to discern, and most virtue to pursue, the common good of the society; and in the next place, to take the most effectual precautions for keeping them virtuous whilst they continue to hold their public trust. The elective mode of obtaining rulers is the characteristic policy of republican government.
>
> —James Madison,
> The Federalist, No. 57

NOMINATION PROCEDURES

In most democratic nations the political parties choose candidates for public office. The United States, however, has not followed that practice. Ever since the early nineteenth century, reformers have successfully argued for the adoption of nomination systems that would be more democratic—that is, would weaken the political parties and give the people greater power to choose candidates.

The earliest means of choosing candidates for public office in the United States was the *legislative caucus*. In Congress and in each state legislature, caucuses composed of the elected legislators of each political party met privately to select their party's candidates. The legislative caucus as it originally operated had an obvious defect: Districts that had elected legislators from one party were not represented in the caucus of the other party. To remedy that defect, the so-called *mixed caucus* was developed. Delegates from districts that were not represented were permitted to join the caucus to make nomination decisions.

But this reform proved to be short-lived, and it was not long before the caucus system was largely abandoned. Andrew Jackson, the popular hero of the War of 1812, and his supporters succeeded in overturning what they called "King Caucus." In the 1824 election the Democratic party caucus failed to pick Jackson, the most popular candidate. Jackson's backers realized that the legislative caucus in Congress would never nominate him for president. They therefore sought to discredit the system by arguing that it was undemocratic.

In place of the caucus, the Jacksonians favored the **convention** system, contending that it would democratize American politics. In the convention system, delegates, who attend party conventions, make decisions. By the 1832 election, the convention was used by both major political parties to nominate candidates for president and vice president. It was gradually adopted by the states to nominate candidates for other national, state, and local public offices and to elect party officials and delegates. Although the convention still permitted party leaders to exercise considerable control over nominations, its adoption was a significant step toward making the nomination system more democratic.

Early in the twentieth century a reform movement known as *progressivism* pressed for the abolition of the convention system and used the same argument that had been used against the caucus by the Jacksonians. Progressives contended that the conventions were not sufficiently democratic because they allowed the political party organizations to exercise too much influence. In place of the convention system, they favored the use of the direct **primary** system, in which the voters in a primary election nominate candidates and officials.

The primary system has been adopted by all of the states and has become by far the most common method of nominating individuals for public office. It is also used in most states to elect party officials, such as state and local committee members and delegates to conventions, especially the national party conventions. A person can have his or her name placed on a primary ballot by means of a petition signed by a required number of registered voters. Thus, there can be a number of candidates in a primary election, though not infrequently there is only one. When this occurs, of course, there is no primary contest for the nomination.

Some states require the use of a **runoff primary** when none of the candidates receives a majority of the votes in a primary election. This system, used in most southern and border states, is a holdover from the time when the Democratic party dominated politics in that part of the country. Since whoever won the Democratic primary would win the general election, many candidates would enter the primary, and frequently no candidate would win a majority of the vote. The runoff primary is held between the two candidates who received the most votes, and the victor becomes the party's nominee in the general election. Although the South is no longer a one-party area, the runoff primary remains a feature of politics in that region even though the frequency of its use has declined.

The primary system has largely replaced the convention, although conventions are still used by a small minority of the states to nominate at least some public officials, and in a few they are still used to nominate candidates for statewide offices. In several states—Connecticut, for example—the losing candidates in a convention can demand that a primary be held if his or her vote in the convention is above a fixed percentage. Some southern states—Virginia, Alabama, Georgia, and South Carolina—permit the parties to use either the convention or the primary system for nominating candidates.

There are two basic types of primaries: closed and open. A majority of states use the **closed primary,** in which only voters who have registered with a particular party may vote. About twenty states use some type of **open primary,** in which the voter does not have to register as a party member before taking part. On primary day the voter can select the ballot of the party in whose primary he or she wants to participate. Three states—Alaska, California, and Washington—go even further and use a so-called **blanket primary,** in which voters do not have to choose a party and are also free to vote in either primary on an office-by-office basis—for example, voting Republican for one office and Democratic for another.

Political parties generally favor the closed primary. Because anyone who is registered can participate in an open primary, it is harder for the party organization to control nominations. Open primaries also encourage "raiding," in which voters who normally support one political party in the general election invade the other's primary and cast their ballots for an insurgent candidate or for a weak or unpopular candidate. If that person wins the primary, the other party's nominee has a better chance of winning the general election.

NOMINATING A PRESIDENTIAL CANDIDATE

The procedures for nominating a presidential candidate differ from those used to nominate other public officials. The national convention system, created by the Jacksonians in the early nineteenth century, has been retained for this purpose. The national conventions of both major parties still formally choose their presidential and vice presidential candidates. But today the real decisions regarding the choice of candidates for national elections take place in the state primaries, where delegates pledged to support particular candidates are chosen.

Choosing the Delegates

PRESIDENTIAL PRIMARIES   First used in Wisconsin in 1905, the **presidential primary** has now been adopted by a large majority of the states. In 1956 nineteen states had primaries. By 1976 the total had reached twenty-nine. In 2004 forty states and the District of Columbia held presidential primaries. A large majority of both Democratic and Republican delegates are chosen in state primaries. Caucuses are still used in the other states to select the remaining delegates.

States rushed to adopt the presidential primary as it became more and more evident that the nominations of the major parties were being decided in the preconvention primary campaigns. Since the early 1960s a majority of the candidates have been chosen in this way. Rather than deny voters the right to influence the selection of presidential candidates, state legislatures have adopted state presidential primary laws. The primary takes the formal selection of delegates out of the control of state party leaders and places it in the hands of the voters.

The exact form of the primary varies, depending on state law and party rules. All primary states provide for the election of convention delegates; some also provide for a preference vote in which voters can indicate their choice of candidate. Delegates are chosen either by statewide voting (at-large delegates) or at the local level (district delegates). The former system is used in smaller, less populous states; the latter is used in larger, more populous ones.

There are other differences in the ways in which the two major parties select delegates. Republican party rules require the use of a *winner-take-all system*—that is, the candidate with the most votes wins all the delegates. Democratic party rules, in contrast, require the use of *proportional representation,* in which candidates receive delegates in proportion to the percentage of the vote they win. A final difference is that the Democratic party provides for so-called "superdelegates." These delegates are not chosen in primaries but serve because of their position as party leaders or elected officials: Democratic governors, senators, representatives, and officials of the Democratic National Committee. 725, or about 6 percent of the delegates to the 2004 Democratic National Convention were superdelegates. (For the first time in 2004 the Republicans created a small group of superdelegates—all members of the Republican National Committee.)

Each party determines the total number of delegates who will attend its national convention. In 2004 there were 4,353 delegates to the Democratic National Convention and 2,509 to the Republican National Convention. These widely divergent figures result from the parties' use of different formulas to assign delegates to each state and territory represented at the convention.

The formulas used by the parties to assign the number of delegates to each state are too complex to be discussed here. The consequences of applying those formulas, however, can be described. The Democratic party's rules emphasize population and therefore favor the most heavily populated states, such as California, New York, and Texas. The Republican party's rules give greater delegate strength to smaller states and to those in the South, Southwest, and West, areas in which the party is politically strong.

CAUCUSES AND CONVENTIONS In states that do not use primaries—Iowa, Maine, and Michigan, for example—**caucuses,** meetings of party members at the local or precinct level, choose delegates to county conventions. The county conventions then select delegates to district or state conventions, which in turn select delegates to the national convention.

Republican presidential candidate George W. Bush campaigns during the 2000 primary campaign, Laconia, New Hampshire, January 13, 2000.

Traditionally, caucuses were controlled by the political parties, which were able to have party regulars chosen as delegates. But in today's presidential nominating campaigns, candidates organize their supporters to attend caucus meetings. Private-interest groups—teachers' unions and environmental groups, for example—which also urge their members to attend caucus meetings and support particular candidates, further their efforts.

The Preconvention Campaign

Before the major party conventions meet, each candidate attempts to win the support of a majority of the delegates. Nowadays candidates concentrate on winning state primaries, starting with the first primary, which usually is held in New Hampshire early in the year. A candidate who can win in the early primaries will gain not only delegate support but also national publicity, the support of delegates from states that use a caucus system, increased financial backing, and greater popularity with voters. A series of primary victories, combined with growing popularity in public-opinion polls, can produce a "bandwagon effect" in which delegates rally to the support of the candidate they believe is likely to win the nomination.

Candidates also organize and campaign in nonprimary states. In recent presidential campaigns, the Iowa local caucuses have become especially important. These meetings, which are held in late January, provide one of the first indications of the popularity of the various candidates. Because of this, many candidates put considerable time and effort into gaining support at the Iowa caucuses.

The 2000 nomination campaign had two unusual features. The first was the emergence of two insurgent candidates who challenged their party's choice of

An Iowa caucus, January 24, 2000 in Des Moines.

presidential candidate. The second was the speed with which the nominations of George W. Bush and Al Gore took place.

Serious contests for the presidential nominations of the two major parties are rare. Most of the challengers to the party favorite do not stand a realistic chance of gaining the nomination. Certainly neither Vice President Gore nor Texas Governor Bush expected to face a serious rival. Gore held the second highest office in the land, had the strong backing of President Clinton and many elected officials in Congress, and was supported by influential groups such as unions. But former New Jersey Senator Bill Bradley ran against the vice president. He raised a substantial amount of money, gained a significant number of enthusiastic supporters, and ran well in the New Hampshire primary. He was never able to win a party caucus or primary, however, and withdrew from the race in mid-March.

Governor Bush's backers included most Republican governors and members of Congress, and he was expected to win the nomination without a serious challenge. But when Senator John McCain of Arizona decided to run for the party's presidential nomination, Bush was faced with a major contest. Senator McCain upset the Texas governor in the New Hampshire primary and later won victories in other New England states. He gained strong backing from independent voters and even from some Democrats who were able to vote in the open primaries that the party had established in a number of states, including New Hampshire. Bush's support among traditional Republicans eventually gained him victories in the southern states and in such delegate-rich states as New York and California. By mid-March McCain also acknowledged defeat, and Bush became the Republican party's presidential nominee.

Normally the presidential nomination season stretches from the time of the Iowa caucuses in late January and the New Hampshire primary in early February to the nominating conventions held in the summer. But many states found that when they scheduled primaries or caucuses late in the season they played no role in the process, since the party's nominees had already been chosen. This caused many states to schedule their primaries early in the nomination season, a process known as **frontloading.** As a result, in 2000 both parties effectively selected their nominee after a nominating campaign that lasted less than two months. By March 15 both the Republican and Democratic nominees had won enough delegates to guarantee their nomination at the summer conventions.

The movement to schedule primaries early in the calendar year will continue in 2004. Democratic Party rules permit Iowa to hold its caucus on January 18, 2004, and New Hampshire its primary on January 27. All other states and territories must schedule their primaries and caucuses between February 3 and June 8, 2004. Missouri and South Carolina have decided to schedule their events for February 3 and it is likely that other states will do the same. Frontloading not only results in the early nomination of presidential candidates by both political parties; it also makes it extremely difficult for relatively unknown candidates to emerge as viable choices for primary voters. Before their names become well known to the voting public, the primary season has ended.

The National Convention

After all the delegates have been selected, the parties prepare to hold their **national conventions.** Several years earlier, the national party committees have selected the cities in which the conventions will be held and the days on which they will meet—usualy sometime in August of the election year. The main task of the convention is to nominate the party's presidential and vice presidential candidates. But the national convention also performs other functions, including the preparation and approval of a party platform.

ADOPTING A PLATFORM The first major task of a national convention is to adopt a **party platform.** This consists of a series of statements of general policy, each of which is called a *plank.* The platform is usually a set of compromises through which the party seeks to unite its diverse supporters; often this requires the writing of vague, general statements about current political issues. If the party is nominating an incumbent president, the platform will reflect his policies, and the opposing party's platform will include criticisms of the president's policies and his conduct in office. Although party platforms are often dismissed as meaningless, a comparison of the platforms of the major political parties can sometimes reveal significant differences over major policy issues. For example, Republican platforms have opposed abortion, whereas Democratic party platforms have endorsed it as a basic constitutional liberty possessed by women.

NOMINATING A PRESIDENTIAL CANDIDATE The nomination procedure begins with a series of nominating and seconding speeches in which the names of the candidates are proposed to the convention. After all the names have been placed before the delegates, an oral roll-call vote of the states is taken and a nominee is chosen.

National party conventions have been held since the early nineteenth century and may continue to exist for many years to come. But their importance has declined during the past several decades. Today the national conventions simply ratify the choice of a presidential nominee that has already been made in the state primaries. Not since the 1952 Democratic convention has more than one roll call been necessary to select a nominee. And only on rare occasions has a close contest been decided by a convention vote; the case of Ronald Reagan and Gerald Ford at the 1976 Republican convention, in which Ford won by a narrow margin, was an exception to the general pattern.

But conventions continue to serve as a means of rallying the party faithful. They are also valuable as a way of obtaining television time to publicize the party, its candidates, and its platform. Indeed, today's conventions are organized and scripted by the parties to appeal to television viewers and seek to avoid any occurrence that would damage the party's image.

The television networks, however, are increasingly unhappy with the presentation of the national conventions. The percentage of viewers watching the conventions has declined steadily over the years, and little news occurs at the conventions to justify three or four days of coverage. (Usually the only major news is the choice of the candidate for vice president, who will serve as the presidential nominee's running mate.) As a result the three major television networks sharply reduced the amount of time given to live coverage of the national party conventions.

NOMINATING A VICE PRESIDENTIAL CANDIDATE It is customary for the presidential nominee to choose his own running mate, and his selection is always approved by the convention. Presidential nominees have traditionally been concerned primarily with "balancing the ticket." The balancing may be based on geography, political philosophy, age, or other considerations. Whereas the president chooses his closest advisers on the basis of personal knowledge and friendships, vice presidents may be strangers selected specifically for the purpose of balancing the ticket. Sometimes they are even political opponents of the nominee. For example, in 1960 John F. Kennedy selected Lyndon B. Johnson as his running mate even though there were important philosophical differences between the two men, and even though Johnson had been Kennedy's rival for the Democratic party's presidential nomination. Most recent presidents have turned away from the use of largely political considerations in making their vice presidential selection and have stressed the qualifications of the candidate. For example, in 2000 George Bush picked Richard Cheney as his running mate even though he came from Wyoming, a solidly Republican state with only three electoral votes. The choice was made because of Cheney's long experience in government. In 2004, John Kerry selected North Carolina Senator John Edwards to be his running mate. Although Edwards had only limited experience in government—he had served only one term in the Senate—he had showed strength in his campaign for the presidential nomination and was very popular with Democratic Party voters.

A NATIONAL PRIMARY?　　Much criticism has been directed at the present system of nominating presidential candidates because of its complex and confusing procedures. The most often proposed alternative is a national primary. The idea of a national primary, in which voters would be able to choose among a number of candidates, is not new. President Woodrow Wilson suggested it as early as 1913. Direct nomination of candidates in national primaries would eliminate national conventions, would simplify the nomination system, and might give the people greater control over the nomination process.

The idea of a national primary has never received strong support; moreover, it has several major weaknesses. Well-known candidates would have a decided advantage in a national primary. Conversely, there would not be enough time for a relatively unknown candidate (such as Jimmy Carter in 1976, Michael Dukakis in 1988, or Bill Clinton in 1992) to gain sufficient support to win such a primary. Moreover, if no candidate won more than 50 percent of the vote in a national primary, it would probably be necessary to hold a runoff primary between the two candidates with the highest percentages of the vote to ensure that the final nominee had the support of a majority of the party's voters. Such a system might be confusing to the average voter and reduce turnout for the second primary.

THE CAMPAIGN

The American presidential election campaign is the world's most closely watched political event. Aided by campaign managers, media consultants, public-opinion pollsters, speechwriters, endless energy, and tireless smiles, the major candidates compete for the chance to govern the nation for the next four years. The winner of the November presidential election will become the most powerful political leader in the world.

The national conventions meet during the summer of a presidential election year, and the campaign officially begins as soon as the two major candidates have been nominated. (In reality, the campaign begins as soon as the primaries select the party nominees. John Kerry had obtained a majority of the Democratic convention delegates by early March of 2004, making the campaign eight months long.) The speech making and banner waving continued until early November—the longest political campaign in any democratic nation.

Today candidates for major political office make extensive use of television advertising, media consultants, focus groups, and polling, all of which are much more expensive than traditional newspaper, leaflet, and magazine advertising. This change has made political campaigning increasingly expensive. The Center for Responsive Politics estimated that a record $3.9 billion was spent on the 2004 presidential and congressional campaigns. This total represented a 30 percent increase over the $3 billion that was spent in 2000. Most of the money—$2.5 billion—came from contributions made by individuals.[1]

Campaign Financing

Throughout American history the major parties have obtained the financial support of a relatively small number of wealthy contributors to meet the costs of campaigns. The Republican party has usually been able to outspend the Democrats in presidential campaigns because more wealthy people support the Republicans. But the Democrats have also derived much of their campaign support from very wealthy contributors—the entertainment industry and trial lawyers, for example. In addition, the Democrats have been helped by large contributions from the political action committees of labor unions.

The increasing use of television starting in the 1950s is largely responsible for the skyrocketing costs of political campaigning. As the expense of campaigns increased, the dependence of the parties on the very wealthy also grew. Big contributors gave even larger amounts of money to pay for the new campaign methods of the television age.

The danger that large contributors could influence the policies of the candidates and parties they support has long been a source of concern to observers of American politics. The 1972 campaign dramatized this problem. In that campaign the Republicans alone spent an estimated $61 million. Later it was discovered that some contributors had violated existing campaign spending laws. Dairy producers, for example, had secretly donated $680,000 to the Nixon campaign and received favorable treatment from his administration. A number of corporate executives also had made illegal contributions. To compound the problem, some of the money had been used to finance the burglary of the Democratic National Committee headquarters at the Watergate apartments in Washington, DC. The demands for reform that followed these revelations led to the passage of new campaign finance legislation in 1974, legislation that greatly changed the way presidential election campaigns are funded.

Campaign Finance Legislation

Before 1971 there had been occasional halfhearted attempts to regulate campaign financing, but none of those early attempts was effective. The first major attempt to regulate campaign finance came in 1971 with the enactment of the Federal Election Campaign Act (FECA). This law set limits on the amount of money that presidential and vice presidential candidates or their families could contribute to their own campaigns. It also required campaign committees and candidates to report the names and addresses of all contributors of amounts over $100. The abuses of the 1972 presidential campaign and the Watergate scandal revealed the inadequacy of this legislation.

THE FEDERAL ELECTION CAMPAIGN ACT OF 1974   In response to the scandals of 1972–1973, Congress enacted the Federal Election Campaign Act of 1974. The new legislation extensively amended the 1971 law. Its main provisions established a system for federal financing of presidential campaigns and set limits on the amount of money that could be raised from other sources. It created special funds for presidential primaries, nominating conventions, and the general election campaign. A candidate seeking nomination in a presidential primary is eligible to receive federal funds if he or she is able to raise a minimum of $5,000 in each of twenty states, counting only the first $250 of each contribution. Candidates who meet this standard will receive funds equal to the amount of private money they have obtained; only the first $250 of each contribution is matched, however. To receive this money, the candidate must accept a ceiling on overall national spending, as well as limits on spending for each state campaign.

Public funds for presidential campaigns are supplied out of tax revenues. A box on the individual income tax return now permits each taxpayer to earmark $3.00 of his or her tax payment for this purpose. (Fewer than 12 percent of tax filers do so, however.) This money is placed in a federal campaign fund, which is used to finance the presidential campaign. A major political party—that is, one that received 25 percent or more of the vote in the most recent election—is eligible to receive federal funding of the costs of its nominating convention. Moreover, each major-party nominee (not the political party) is eligible to receive federal funds to pay for the campaign. Federal funding for both conventions and campaigns is adjusted upward every four years to allow for inflation. The figures for the 2000 conventions and election campaign were approximately $13.3 million and $67 million, respectively.

Both major parties are automatically eligible to receive public money. Minor parties are eligible for retroactive payment of federal funds if they receive at least 5 percent of the total popular vote in the November election. All candidates who take public money must agree not to take additional money from private sources. (Since the system began in 1976 only the third-party presidential candidate, Ross Perot, has declined to take public money.)

The FECA also imposed restrictions on the amount of money that can be spent by individuals and political action committees to support candidates for federal office. For example, the 1974 law limited individual spending to $1,000.00 for each Senate and House candidate in a primary election and a second $1,000.00 for the general election. PACs were limited to $5,000.00 for each candidate for federal office. (The new 2002 federal campaign reform law raises the amounts that can be contributed to candidates after November 5, 2002.)

The FECA contains record-keeping and disclosure provisions. For example, all contributions of $200 or more must be identified and recorded both by candidates and by political organizations. Criminal penalties are provided for violating these sections of the law. Finally, the legislation created a six-person Federal Election Commission to administer the law. The president, with the advice and consent of the Senate, appoints the commission's members. The commission is often criticized for not being sufficiently energetic in enforcing the provisions of the FECA.

In reviewing provisions of the 1974 Federal Election Campaign Act, the Supreme Court established that spending money on political subjects is partly protected by the First Amendment to the Constitution. While the nation's highest court upheld most of the 1974 law, it did invalidate a provision of the legislation that imposed restrictions of the right of individuals to spend personal money on their own campaign for political office.[2]

There is, however, a huge loophole in the laws governing the financing of American elections. This loophole is known as **soft money.** It is based on a 1979 amendment to the FECA that was designed to encourage voluntary involvement in presidential campaigns. The amendment allows national party organizations (but not candidates) to receive unlimited amounts of money from private groups to be used on party-building activities. The law encourages the national party organizations to solicit private money and give it to their state and local affiliates. The difference between soft and **hard money** has been explained as follows:

> Hard money is subject to individual and group limits; soft money is not; hard money can be used by the party to promote its presidential and vice presidential names by name; soft money cannot. Soft money may, however, be used for party-building activities such as issue advocacy, generic advertising, and registering potential supporters and getting them out to vote.[3]

Record amounts of soft money were raised by the two major parties in recent years. The Republicans have usually raised more soft money, but between 1999 and 2000 the parties competed on relatively equal terms. (See Figure 6.1.) Republicans obtain much of their money from business groups, while the greatest support for the Democrats comes from labor unions, trial lawyers, and the entertainment and media industries.

CONGRESSIONAL CAMPAIGNS The campaign finance legislation just described does not provide for public funding of congressional campaigns. The

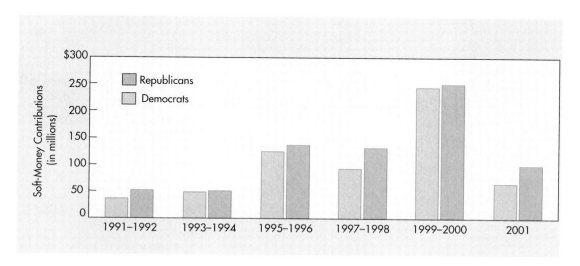

FIGURE 6.1 Pattern of Soft-Money Contributions to the Republican and Democratic Parties, 1991–2001

Source: Federal Election Commission

candidate finances these campaigns, either from his or her own resources or, more frequently, with funds obtained from private contributions. The amount of money spent in congressional campaigns has increased greatly in recent years. Between 1990 and 1998 the average amount spent by House candidates rose from over $259,000 to over $364,000. (The average cost of Senate elections actually declined slightly in the same period.) In House elections, the percentage of money given by individuals rose while that given by PACs declined. In the Senate, individual and PAC giving remained about the same, but the percentage of money contributed by the candidates more than doubled. (See Table 6.1.)

The pattern of contributions to candidates for the House of Representatives strongly favors incumbents—both Democratic and Republican—over challengers. In 1998 House incumbents spent on average more than two and one-half times the amount spent by their opponents. A similar pattern of incumbents outspending challengers is also found in Senate elections, although the differences are not as great as in the House. Spending by major-party candidates for open seats (those for which there is no incumbent candidate) does not show the same large differences.[4]

Between campaigns, legislators devote a considerable portion of their time to raising funds. Fund-raising by House members, who must seek reelection every two years, is almost continuous. Ironically, many House incumbents face only token challengers who are poorly financed and have little chance of winning.

TABLE 6.1

AMOUNTS AND SOURCES OF CONGRESSIONAL FINANCING: AUGUST 2004

House

Party	No. of Cands.	Average Raised	Average Spent	Average Cash on Hand	Average from PACs	Average from Indivs.
All	434	$844,233	$489,223	$652,389	$325,938	$490,939
Dems	205	$763,929	$472,012	$588,447	$300,574	$439,743
Repubs	228	$917,555	$504,911	$709,524	$349,700	$537,022

Senate

Party	No. of Cands.	Average Raised	Average Spent	Average Cash on Hand	Average from PACs	Average from Indivs.
All	99	$1,928,619	$1,028,865	$1,772,084	$399,977	$1,406,775
Dems	47	$2,281,043	$1,082,069	$2,167,000	$413,007	$1,735,393
Repubs	51	$1,573,959	$946,685	$1,409,003	$395,596	$1,065,294

Source: Federal Election Commission, August 2004 News Release.

Often the main purpose of the large sums of money amassed by members of Congress between elections is to scare off opponents; much of the money may never actually be used in campaigns.

The existing system for financing congressional campaigns has been roundly criticized and has become an important political issue in recent years. Much concern is expressed over the high costs of congressional campaigns and the political influence of large contributors. Although donors claim that their contributions give them nothing more than access to legislators, many people believe that their elected representatives are captives of the contributors to their campaigns and that their votes on legislative issues have been purchased by special interests.

The Democratic party's campaign finance problems, which emerged at the close of the 1996 presidential election campaign, added to public concern about this issue. The influence of foreign contributors and the use of questionable fundraising tactics by President Clinton and his aides led to congressional investigations in 1997 and a growing demand for new campaign finance legislation.

After a decade of debate on the subject, Congress finally passed a new campaign finance law early in 2002. The legislation made a number of important changes. First, it raised the legal amounts that could be contributed to candidates for public office and indexed those figures to the rate of inflation. Second, it outlawed soft money contributions to the national political parties. And finally, the law made it a crime for any private organization to run issue-related ads on television within sixty days of a general election that make any reference to a candidate for public office. The campaign finance law went into effect the day after the November 5, 2002 election.

The new legislation raised important First Amendment issues of freedom of speech and press. Aware of this problem, Congress established a procedure for quick review of these questions by the U.S. Supreme Court. Numerous lawsuits were soon filed challenging the constitutionality of the Bipartisan Campaign Finance Law of 2002. The ban on certain types of political speech in the days prior to an election (or primary) was the most controversial part of the new law. But in a 5–4 decision in December 2003, the court upheld all of the major provisions of the legislation.[5]

Campaign Strategy

Candidates for public office must make plans long before the actual campaign begins. They often hire a professional consultant, an opinion research organization, an advertising agency, speechwriters, a direct-mail organization, attorneys, an accounting firm, and similar services. The campaign manager is aided by the consultant, who generally takes care of opinion surveys, fund-raising, budgeting, public relations, advertising, and the like. All these activities have a single purpose: to create and communicate to the public a favorable image of the candidate and his or her policies.

The two major parties usually adopt different campaign strategies. The Democrats have an advantage over the Republicans in the number of registered voters, but those voters are less likely to turn out on election day. The Democrats therefore strive for party unity and stress the importance of voting. The Republicans, by contrast, often try to gain voter support for "the candidate, not the party" in an attempt to gain the votes of Democrats and Independents.

The strategies used by candidates vary from one election to the next. The major issues in the campaign and the personalities of the candidates always shape campaign strategy. Incumbent presidents organize their campaigns differently from nonincumbents. They often seek to use the prestige of the White House to their advantage. They may choose not to respond to attacks by their opponents and to curtail their campaign trips around the country, insisting that the affairs of the nation are too demanding and important for them to engage in ordinary political campaigning. Instead, they engage in activities that are likely to be shown on the nightly television news programs—signing bills and meeting with representatives of foreign governments, for example. President Nixon used this "White House rose garden" approach successfully in his 1972 bid for reelection. But this strategy does not always work; President Carter employed it in his 1980 reelection campaign and was overwhelmingly defeated by Ronald Reagan. Incumbent presidents sometimes pursue a strategy of active public campaigning. In 1996, for example, President Clinton campaigned extensively throughout the nation.

A candidate who is seeking to defeat an incumbent will inevitably attack the incumbent's record. He will criticize the president's general program, his failure to keep campaign promises, and other mistakes. In 1980 Reagan criticized Carter's record in both domestic and foreign policy. He dramatized this criticism by asking voters the simple question, "Are you better off today than four years ago when Mr. Carter became president?"

All candidates, whether incumbent or not, must seek to offset any perceived shortcomings and capitalize on their strong points. In 1976 Jimmy Carter's problem was that he was almost unknown outside his home state of Georgia. Accordingly, his strategy was to attack the corruption and sheer size of the government in Washington while stressing his "down home" character and moral qualities. In both the 1980 and the 1984 elections, Ronald Reagan portrayed himself as the representative of traditional American values—patriotism, the family, and religion. During the 1988 presidential campaign, the senior George Bush stressed his broad background in foreign affairs and the peace and prosperity experienced by the nation during the Reagan administration. He also criticized Michael Dukakis for being soft on crime and too liberal on other issues. In 1992 Bill Clinton campaigned as a Washington outsider who would end "gridlock" and bring about economic prosperity.

Candidates for the presidency go to great lengths to make themselves attractive to voters, but they do not attempt to woo the entire voting population. The operation of the Electoral College system (discussed later in this chapter) requires that a candidate devote much energy to the states with the largest populations and, hence, the greatest number of electoral votes. The candidate's goal is to win a *plurality*—a larger number of votes than the number received by the nearest rival—of the popular vote in enough states that his total electoral vote will be 270 or more.

Presidential elections are won or lost in the most populous states: California, Texas, New York, Pennsylvania, Florida, Illinois, Ohio, and Michigan. The 2004 election was no exception. It was clear from the start that some of these states would be safe for one of the candidates: Texas would vote for President Bush; California, New York, and Illinois were certain to support John Kerry. As a result, both candidates concentrated much of their time and effort on Pennsylvania, Michigan, Ohio, and Florida. Kerry won the first two states, but Bush took Florida and Ohio and was reelected president.

TELEVISION DEBATES

Despite the use of television in presidential campaigns since the 1950s, it took a long time for televised debates between candidates to become an accepted practice. No federal law requires candidates to debate, and for many years presidential nominees refused to do so. In 1960 Vice President Richard Nixon appeared in a series of four debates with his Democratic rival, Massachusetts Senator John F. Kennedy. No other debates took place until 1976, when Gerald R. Ford and Jimmy Carter made three joint TV appearances, and their running mates also debated. That marked the first time an incumbent president (Ford) faced an opponent on television. Debates have been held in each presidential election campaign since then. In 2004 the presidential candidates held three debates and the vice presidential nominees held one.

Some observers have criticized the presidential debates on the ground that they are more like press conferences than true debates. One often-used format consists of reporters asking questions of the candidates, the candidates' responses to those questions, and a closing statement by each participant. Despite the shortcomings of such debates, the appearance of presidential candidates on television provides a unique opportunity for millions of Americans to see the candidates and evaluate their personalities, knowledge of the issues, and ability to handle a difficult situation.

Televised debates are now an important feature of every presidential election. The public expects such debates to occur, and it is highly unlikely that any candidate would refuse to participate in such an event.

The first television debate by presidential candidates George W. Bush and Al Gore, fall 2000.

THE ELECTION

The election of the president, the vice president, and most other national, state, and local officials takes place on the first Tuesday after the first Monday in November. The procedures used in elections include registration of voters, voting by secret ballot, and counting of the ballots. Election of the president and the vice president involves the constitutionally required procedure for counting electoral votes, a process that occurs in mid-December and early January.

Registration

Registration is a procedure in which a person who wants to vote presents an election official with proof that he or she meets all the legal requirements for voting in the upcoming election. Individuals who have registered do not have to reregister unless they change their name or address or have not voted for a specified number of years. The states adopted registration systems in the early years of the twentieth century to reduce voting fraud—for example, to prevent people from voting more than once on election day. This system remains in place today except in a few less populous states, which permit citizens to appear at the place of voting on election day and cast their ballot.

Critics have argued that the registration system contributes to the relatively low voter turnout in the United States. Registration usually occurs only at certain times of the year and only at designated locations. Many people simply do not know how to go about registering to vote.

In 1993, in an effort to simplify registration and increase voter turnout, Congress enacted the National Voter Registration Act (the so-called Motor Voter law). This law allows citizens to register to vote at the same time that they renew their automobile registration and requires that registration materials be available at various state offices. The law seems to be less effective than its supporters hoped.

Balloting

The secret **ballot** used in the United States was developed in Australia in the mid-nineteenth century and was designed to prevent fraud in elections. The government prints the ballot, which lists all the candidates, and appoints officials to distribute the ballots at specified polling places on election day.

The ballot may be organized in either of two ways. The *office-block* or *Massachusetts ballot* lists all the candidates according to the office for which they are running; the first block may list all the candidates for U.S. senator, the second all the candidates for governor, and so on. This approach encourages split-ticket and Independent voting, but the voter may get tired and ignore the blocks of candidates at the bottom of the ballot.

The more common *party-column* or *Indiana ballot* lists candidates for all offices in columns according to party. In some states a person can vote a "straight ticket" by marking a box next to the name of the party or, where voting machines are used, by pulling a lever at the top of the party column. In other states the voter must choose a candidate for each office separately. In either case the party-column ballot encourages the voter to vote along party lines rather than to consider the merits of each candidate.

In October 2002, Congress enacted legislation designed to improve the methods of voting used in the United States. The stimulus was, of course, the problems revealed in Florida during the 2002 presidential election. The law appropriated $3.9 billion over three years to help states purchase new voting systems or to upgrade existing punch card or lever machines. It also permits persons whose names do not appear on registration records to vote provisionally; their names must later be checked by registration officials. The most controversial part of the new law provides for the creation of statewide registration lists based on the last four digits of a voter's Social Security number or driver's license. Some critics have argued that the identification system is discriminatory and will create new restrictions on voting.

Electing the President and Vice President: The Electoral College

Thomas Jefferson called it "the most dangerous blot on our Constitution," yet it has been a fixture of American politics since the nation's earliest years. In Article II (as modified by the Twelfth, Twentieth, and Twenty-third Amendments), the U.S. Constitution provides for the election of the president and the vice president by an **Electoral College.** As mentioned in Chapter 2, this system was devised by the Constitutional Convention as a compromise between the delegates who favored direct popular election of the president and those who wanted Congress to select the president. Under the Electoral College system, the voters actually cast their ballots not for the presidential and vice presidential nominees themselves but for slates of electors chosen by the state political parties. Because the position of elector is basically an honorary one, each party normally awards it to people who have been loyal party members.

Each state may select a number of electors equal to its total number of U.S. senators and representatives. In addition, the Twenty-third Amendment, adopted in 1961, gave residents of the District of Columbia the right to choose at least three electors. The party slate that wins the largest number of popular votes is elected in that state. To be elected president by the Electoral College, a candidate must receive a majority (270) of the total number of electoral votes (538). This can be achieved by winning a plurality of the vote in any combination of states whose electoral vote totals at least 270.

The members of the Electoral College are elected every four years under procedures established by the legislatures of each state. Early in the nation's history some states provided for the choice of electors by the state legislators, but that system was eventually replaced by one in which electors are selected by popular election. Every state now provides for the popular election of presidential electors. Forty-eight states require the use of a winner-take-all system, in which the presidential candidate who wins the largest number of popular votes in a state gains the state's entire electoral vote.[6]

The winner-take-all system has important consequences. As we have seen, it favors the states with the largest populations. Most presidential candidates concentrate their campaign efforts in the dozen or so most populous states. They

CLOSE-UP

THE ELECTORAL COLLEGE

Sometimes viewed as an anachronism, the Electoral College is alive and well. Every four years, about a month after the presidential election, each state's electors meet to cast their ballots for president and vice president. The electors assemble at noon in the state capital, are sworn to "faithfully perform the duties of the office of elector," and mark a paper ballot with an X to indicate the candidate of their choice. On December 18, 2000, a total of 538 electors performed this brief ceremony in the capitals of the fifty states and in the District of Columbia.

Electors are chosen in the same vote that elects the presidential and vice presidential candidates. Although they are pledged to vote for the winner in their state, they are legally free to vote for the candidate they prefer. However, it is extremely rare for an elector to exercise an independent choice. One example occurred in 1988, when a West Virginia elector cast her presidential vote for the Democratic party's vice presidential candidate as a protest against what she considered the foolishness of the Electoral College system.

The rewards of being an elector are not great. Alabama pays its electors $8.00 for expenses and 20 cents a mile for travel. New York is somewhat more generous. It treats its electors to lunch at a French restaurant, gives them a pewter plate as a memento, and reimburses them for the costs of travel to the state capital. The total cost to New York State is under $10,000.

understand that by winning those states—even by the smallest popular-vote margins—they will gain large blocks of electoral votes and are likely to win the presidency. (See Figure 6.2.)

By law the electors meet in the capital of their state on the first Monday after the second Wednesday in December to cast separate ballots for their party's presidential and vice presidential candidates. The results of the voting in each state are sent to the president of the U.S. Senate (the vice president of the United States). Before a joint session of Congress in early January, the vice president opens the certificates, the electoral votes are counted, and the president and the vice president are formally elected.

If no candidate receives a majority of the electoral votes for president, the chief executive is chosen by the House of Representatives. The Twelfth Amendment sets forth the revised procedure that must be followed in such a case. Voting by states, with each state having one vote, the House must select from among the candidates with the three highest electoral-vote totals. It is necessary to obtain a majority of the votes of the fifty states to be elected president.

If no vice presidential candidate receives a majority of the electoral vote, the Senate elects the vice president. It must choose between the two candidates with the largest number of electoral votes. The person who gets a majority of the votes in the Senate is elected vice president.

PROBLEMS WITH THE ELECTORAL COLLEGE   The Electoral College has the potential to produce results that go against the spirit of a democratic society. Under this system, for example, it is possible for a person to win the presidency even though he has received fewer popular votes than his opponent. Four presidents have been elected in this fashion: John Quincy Adams (1824), Rutherford B. Hayes (1876), Benjamin Harrison (1888), and George W. Bush (2000). This situation came very close to occurring in 1976. Jimmy Carter received about 1.7 million more

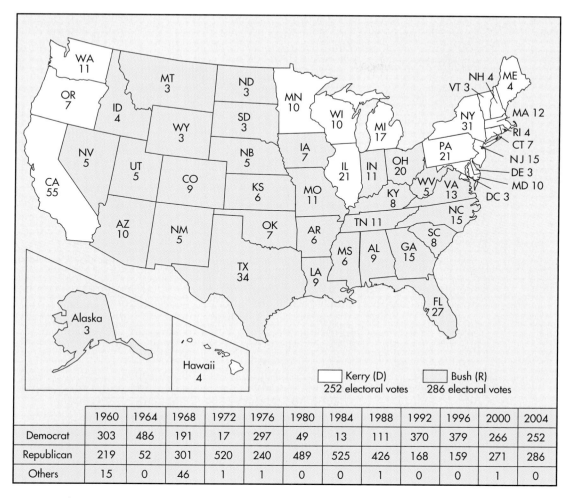

	1960	1964	1968	1972	1976	1980	1984	1988	1992	1996	2000	2004
Democrat	303	486	191	17	297	49	13	111	370	379	266	252
Republican	219	52	301	520	240	489	525	426	168	159	271	286
Others	15	0	46	1	1	0	0	1	0	0	1	0

FIGURE 6.2 The 2004 Presidential Election.

popular votes than Gerald R. Ford, but a switch of about 4,000 votes in Hawaii and 3,500 votes in Ohio would have given Ford the majority of the electoral votes.

An additional problem with the system arises when no candidate receives a majority of the electoral votes. Under this system, created by the Constitution, it is possible for a minority of the House members to elect the president, since voting is by state and not by individual. For example, if the majority of a state's legislators are Democrats, they would vote together and cast their state's vote for the Democratic presidential candidate. Critics contend that this system is undemocratic and should be changed. It should be noted, however, that only twice in the nation's history—1801 and 1825—and under highly unusual circumstances, has the House been called upon to elect the president.

REFORM OR ABOLITION? Because of the problems associated with the Electoral College system, a variety of proposals have been suggested for changing or abolishing the system. Some require only a change in law by the state legislatures. The electors could be eliminated with the electoral-vote system remaining in place. This would eliminate the possibility of the "faithless elector" who votes for a candidate other than the person who received the most popular votes in his or her state.

Another proposal that requires only legislative action has already been adopted by Maine and Nebraska. The so-called *single-member district plan* provides for the election of two electors on a statewide basis; the remaining electors would be chosen individually from the districts used for the election of members of the House of Representatives.

Other proposals for change require the adoption of a constitutional amendment. Most recent proposals call for replacing the Electoral College system with direct popular election. These plans usually provide that if no presidential candidate received 50 percent of the popular vote (some plans use 40 percent), a runoff election would be held between the two candidates with the highest percentages of the vote. The winner of this runoff election would become president.

Despite its shortcomings, there is much support for the Electoral College system, and strong arguments can be made in its defense. It maintains the role of the states in a vital political decision. With only a few exceptions in the nineteenth century and the 2000 presidential election, the electoral-vote system has always selected the candidate with the plurality or majority of the popular vote. Moreover, the Electoral College serves to maintain the stability of the two-party system. It is almost impossible for third parties to have any success in national elections because it is very difficult for them to win electoral votes under the winner-take-all system used by almost all the states.

The reform that is discussed most often—direct popular election—would encourage the growth of minor political parties, since they could hope to have more influence under such a system. Direct election might make it difficult for either of the two major parties to win a majority of the popular vote, thus requiring a runoff election. Minor parties could draw off enough votes to prevent either major party from receiving the proportion of the popular vote required to elect its candidates. The minor parties would then be in a position to bargain with the Democratic and Republican candidates for their backing and to obtain promises of support for some of their policies.

It is impossible to discuss in abstract terms the merits or demerits of the Electoral College or of any proposal designed to alter the method of choosing the president. Each system distributes political advantages to different groups. The present method, for example, generally favors the most populous states. The direct-election scheme would eliminate the role of the states in selecting the president; each candidate would seek individual votes without regard to state boundaries. A vote received in a small state would have the same value as one obtained in a very populous state.

The 2000 presidential election revealed the shortcomings of the Electoral College system. For the first time in more than one hundred years, a president was elected by a slim majority in the Electoral College but had fewer popular votes than his opponent. Further, the chaos in counting the vote in Florida might well have created a situation in which no president was chosen by the Electoral College, and the selection of the nation's chief executive would have been made by the House of Representatives. Only the decision by the U.S. Supreme Court to halt the vote count in Florida prevented this from occurring. Despite these developments, no effort was made to modify or change the Electoral College system. Apparently, the Electoral College has become an unchangeable part of this nation's political system.

Congressional Elections

The 435 seats in the House of Representatives, plus one-third of the 100 Senate seats, are up for election every two years. For many candidates for seats in the House of Representatives, obtaining their party's nomination in effect means victory in the general election. This is because many representatives are elected from one-party districts—usually defined as areas in which one political party always wins at least 55 percent of the vote and the other never obtains more than 45 percent.

The competitiveness of House races declined through much of the twentieth century. In 1936 some 137 House seats were decided by 55 percent of the vote or less. By 1988 the number had declined to only 37 seats; the average margin of victory for House contests was almost 73 percent. The reelection rate for the House of Representatives reached 90 percent in 1980 and 98 percent in 1990. However, in the same period Senate elections were far more competitive; an average of 41 percent of Senate races were decided by majorities of 55 percent or less.[7]

The reelection rate for incumbents dropped during most of the 1990s. In 1992, for example, 13 new senators and 110 new representatives were elected, a result of many retirements of Democratic members and the impact of the redistricting that took place after the 1990 census. This pattern was repeated in 1994, when the Republicans gained a majority in the House for the first time in forty years and defeated many Democratic incumbents. But by the end of the decade the reelection rate for incumbents again reached 98 percent, a figure that was repeated in both the 2002 and 2004 House elections.

Incumbent members of the House have several built-in advantages over their challengers. They are usually better known in their districts, have established a history of providing services to their constituents, and have numerous supporters who can be called upon to work during the campaign. And the *franking privilege* of members of Congress enables them to mail information about their activities to constituents at no cost.

But two other factors provide even more important reasons for the success rates of House members. Many House districts have been *gerrymandered,* meaning that their boundaries have been drawn in a highly irregular way so as to give one political party an advantage over the opposition party in elections (see Chapter 7). And as we have already seen, legislative incumbents receive far more financial support from the public than do their opponents. Without adequate financial backing, the parties find it very difficult to attract strong candidates to run against entrenched incumbents.

One consequence of the high reelection rate of House members was the emergence of a movement to limit the number of terms that national legislators may serve, as many states have done for their own state legislators. The most frequently suggested limit for national legislators was twelve years—two terms for senators and six for representatives. Opponents of this change argued that limiting the number of terms a person may serve in Congress is both unwise and unconstitutional. Proponents contended that the change would make legislators more accountable to the people and that Article I, Section 4, of the Constitution permits the states to regulate the manner by which members of the House and Senate are chosen.

Arkansas's national term-limit law was challenged in the courts, and in 1995 the United States Supreme Court decided by a 5 to 4 vote that states may not impose term limits on national legislators. Such a change, the Court declared, can only be accomplished by the adoption of a constitutional amendment.[8]

In congressional districts and states that are competitive, the presence of a popular president or presidential candidate on the ballot may influence the outcome of legislative elections. This is often referred to as the **coattail effect.** A popular presidential candidate may help House and Senate candidates who are running on the same party ballot get elected. The 1980 election illustrates this effect. Ronald Reagan's triumph in the presidential election helped produce a net gain of thirty-three Republicans in the House of Representatives and twelve in the Senate.

But the effect of a popular presidential candidate does not always help his party in congressional elections. Although Reagan captured 525 of a possible 538 Electoral College votes in the 1984 election, the Republican party gained only 16 seats in the House of Representatives and actually lost two in the Senate. In 1988 George Bush, the father of the nation's current president, won the electoral votes of forty states, but the Republican party lost a small number of seats in both houses of Congress. It was the first time in twenty-eight years that the party that captured the presidency had suffered such a loss in the House of Representatives. Similarly, in 1992 Bill Clinton was elected president, but his party lost nine seats in the House of Representatives. In 1996, although President Clinton was reelected with a large electoral-vote majority, his party was able to gain only nine seats in the House of Representatives and actually lost two seats in the Senate.

If congressional candidates believe that their party's presidential candidate will not run a strong race, they avoid identifying their campaign with that of their party's presidential nominee. Instead, they stress their own achievements or the shortcomings of their opponents. In the 1984 and 1988 elections, for example, many Democratic candidates for the House and Senate avoided tying their campaigns to those of their party's presidential candidates, who were believed to have little chance of winning the election.

In a midterm election candidates in competitive districts cannot ride the coattails of a presidential candidate. Even a popular president normally is unable to transfer that popularity to legislative candidates when his name is not on the ballot. The general rule is that the president's party will lose seats in the off-year election. In 1994, for example, with a new Democratic president in office, the party lost fifty-two seats and the majority it had held in that chamber since 1954.

Only three times since the American Civil War has this electoral phenomenon not occurred. In 1934, during the Great Depression, the Democrats sharply increased their numbers in both houses of Congress in that off-year election. In 1998 the Democrats gained a handful of seats in the House of Representatives despite the fact that President Clinton was enmeshed in scandal and was about to be impeached by the House of Representatives.

The 2002 midterm election produced very surprising results. In the two weeks prior to the November election, President Bush actively campaigned in states where important Senate and House elections were being held. Many observers believed that the president was making a mistake and that he had little chance of influencing the outcome of these elections. But the critics were wrong.

Most of the Republican candidates President Bush campaigned for won their elections. Not since 1934 had the president's party gained seats in both houses of Congress in an off-year, and not since 1954 had the Republicans controlled both the executive and legislative branches of government.

HOW AMERICANS VOTE (AND DON'T VOTE)

Voting is the only form of political activity that is engaged in by a majority (or close to a majority) of adult Americans. This final section of the chapter will be devoted to a discussion of who actually votes and why they vote the way they do.

Who Votes?

"The act of voting requires the citizen to make not a single choice but two: He must choose between rival parties or candidates. He must decide also whether to vote at all."[9] Apparently many Americans make only one choice—they choose not to vote.

Voter turnout (the percentage of eligible voters who actually vote) in presidential elections has varied during different periods of American history. It was high—over 70 percent—in the nineteenth century, but between the 1860s and the 1920s it declined considerably, reaching a low of about 45 percent in 1924. After that the turnout rate rose again until 1940, when it was about 63 percent. But then it dropped sharply, rose briefly to an estimated 63 percent in 1960, and again began a decline to 50 percent in 1988. The figure rose to 54 percent in 1992 but then slipped to only 49 percent in 1996, the lowest turnout in a presidential election since 1924. The Bush-Kerry contest of 2004 saw a sharp upward turnout in participation when 59 percent of eligible voters cast ballots. (See Figure 6.3.)

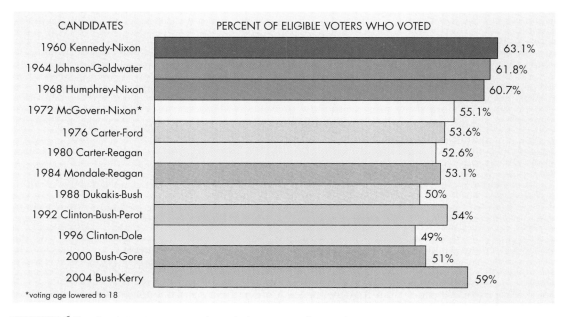

FIGURE 6.3 Participation in Presidential Elections, 1960–2004.

Public opinion polls consistently find that large numbers of Americans pay no attention to presidential elections. One analyst of American voting behavior has commented that more than 50 percent of American children grow up in households in which neither parent votes.[10]

Participation in midterm congressional elections has traditionally been lower than in presidential elections. In 1990 only about 36 percent of the eligible American voters cast ballots for members of Congress. This figure was about the same as in 1986, the year in which the smallest off-year election turnout occurred since the end of World War II. In the 1994 midterm election, however, the turnout rose to 39 percent. That was the year in which the Republicans scored major victories in the House of Representatives. But by 1998 the figure had returned to the 36 percent level.

Participation in primary elections has seen almost a steady decline over the past forty years. In 1966 participation in primary elections peaked at 35.3 of the voting-age population. By 1998 the figure had descended to 17 percent and remained at this level in the thirty-seven states that held statewide primaries in 2002.[11]

Voter turnout in the United States is often compared unfavorably with that in European democracies, where turnout percentages are often considerably higher. These comparisons are somewhat misleading, however. Rates in European nations are based on the names of all adult citizens, who are automatically able to vote. But such comparisons do not take into consideration state registration requirements in the United States.[12] In almost all states Americans must register to vote by a certain date before the election in order to qualify to vote. Registration requires a certain amount of effort, and millions of eligible voters do not make this effort.[13]

Regardless of how voter turnout is calculated, it is still true that many Americans do not vote. Leaving aside the need to register and the other legal requirement for voting—residency in the state and county (federal law limits this to no more than thirty days in national elections)—the basic explanation for low turnout is lack of interest, information, and political involvement on the part of citizens. People who are interested in election campaigns and who identify with a political party, for example, are more likely to vote than those who are not.

Many studies have attempted to determine which groups in American society contribute most to the low turnouts for U.S. elections. Their conclusions have identified people with low income (which is strongly associated with less education) and young people as those who are least likely to vote. In recent elections, for example, only 40 percent of people who earned less than $10,000 a year voted, compared with 80 percent of those who earned more than $50,000. Similarly, only 20 percent of people under age twenty-five voted, while over 60 percent of those over sixty-five went to the polls.

But patterns of nonvoting are not static, and significant changes have taken place in the behavior of some groups. Thus, although whites still vote in somewhat greater proportions than do African Americans, the difference has narrowed in recent presidential and congressional elections. The elimination of discriminatory barriers to voting during the 1960s and 1970s, the growth of a better-educated, more prosperous black middle class, and the increase in the number of black candidates for high public office help explain the growing number of blacks who register and vote.

Similarly, women traditionally voted less than men. This was true from 1920, when the Nineteenth Amendment granting women the vote was passed, until the 1980s. The women's movement, increased education, and greater prosperity have altered the political behavior of women. The gender difference in voter turnout decreased steadily during the 1970s and early 1980s. In 1984 the Census Bureau reported that for the first time the percentage of women voters surpassed that of men. Since 1984 more women than men have voted in presidential elections.

Those Americans who are concerned about low voter turnout have concentrated on reforms that will make it easier for citizens to register to vote. A few states allow individuals to appear at the polling place on election day and qualify at that time. Turnout has increased in those states, but because of the possibility of fraud, this system has failed to gain widespread acceptance. As mentioned earlier, in 1993 Congress passed the National Voter Registration Act to make registration easier and thus increase voter turnout.

It is ironic that voter turnout in the United States remains low despite the fact that the legal barriers to voting have fallen and registration procedures have been simplified. This has led some observers to conclude that the nation has entered a "postelectoral" political era. Increasing numbers of voters believe that elections are no longer important. The traditional significance of elections has been replaced by a system in which major decisions are made by congressional investigating committees and the courts, and through revelations in the media.[14]

How Do Americans Vote?

Social scientists have devoted considerable attention to analyzing the types of Americans who support the two major political parties. Of course, not all Americans are supporters of either the Democratic or the Republican party. Close to one-third are independents who do not identify with a political party. It is difficult to make fully accurate generalizations on this subject, given the immense size and diversity of the voting-age population and its increasing independence. But studies of American voting behavior have identified a number of important factors that influence party support. The most important of these factors are education, income, place of residence, race, religion, and sex.

Education and income are closely related. Education usually determines a person's occupation and income and, hence, his or her social class. And there is a direct correlation between higher social class and voting for Republican candidates. Conversely, individuals with less education and lower incomes are more likely to vote Democratic. In the 2004 election the greatest support for the Republican candidate, George Bush, came from people earning $100,000 or more, whereas Democrat John Kerry received 63 percent of the vote of persons earning less than $15,000.

Place of residence also has an effect on voting behavior. The Republican party was organized in the 1850s, shortly before the outbreak of the Civil War. It has traditionally been the party of the North, especially farmers and residents of small towns in that region. After the end of World War II, it also gained strong support in the suburbs of large cities and more recently in the southern states.

From the end of the Civil War until recent decades, the Democratic party could count on the support of the so-called "Solid South". For almost 100 years the Republican party hardly existed in the states of the old Confederacy. Since the

1950s, however, the Republicans have gained increasing support among white voters in the South and are now the dominant party in a majority of the southern states. On the other hand, traditionally Republican New England has grown increasingly Democratic. Massachusetts and Vermont, for example, are among the most Democratic states in the nation today.

Place of residence influences voting patterns in other ways as well. Ever since the election of Franklin D. Roosevelt to the presidency in 1932, the Democratic party has received strong backing from voters in large cities in the North. Cities like Boston, New York, Philadelphia, Detroit, and Chicago have long given overwhelming support to Democratic candidates.

Race is another factor that affects voting behavior. From the Civil War until the 1930s, blacks who were able to vote supported the Republicans, the party of Abraham Lincoln. But during the 1930s President Roosevelt's New Deal benefited many poor blacks, who switched their allegiance to the Democratic party. Indeed, blacks today are more strongly associated with the Democratic party than any other group in American society. In all recent presidential elections, blacks have strongly supported Democratic candidates. In the 2004 presidential election an estimated 88 percent of African-Americans cast their ballots for the Democratic candidate, John Kerry. (See Table 6.2).

Hispanic voters have also been strong supporters of the Democratic party: 67 percent voted for Al Gore in the 2000 national election. The largest minority group in the United States and the most rapidly growing part of the nation's population, Hispanics are not easy to categorize. They come from many different nations; some are native born while others were born outside this country. On social issues such as abortion and divorce, many tend to take a conservative stand, especially those Hispanics who are not native born. Sixty percent of Hispanics are registered Democrats, while 20 percent are Republican and 19 percent Independents. But some Republican candidates have received a significant amount of support from Hispanic voters.[15] President Bush, for example, received 44 percent of their vote in 2004.

Religion is also a factor that influences voting. Catholics and Jews have a long tradition of support for the Democratic party. Between 1880 and 1920 many Catholics and Jews came to the United States as poor immigrants and settled in the large cities. It was usually the Democratic party that provided them with jobs and various social services and gained their political loyalty. President Roosevelt's New Deal served to reinforce their ties to the Democratic party. The Republican party has made inroads on the Catholic vote, however, especially in presidential elections and among more affluent and better-educated Catholics. Ronald Reagan was especially successful in gaining the support of Catholic voters during his 1980 and 1984 presidential campaigns. But Catholic voters supported the Democratic candidate, Bill Clinton, in both 1992 and 1996. Jewish support for Democratic candidates has always been very strong; 74 percent of Jewish voters supported John Kerry in 2004.

The influence of religion on voting can also be seen in the support many white Protestants have given to the Republican party. Since the mid–nineteenth century, Protestants outside the South have tended to vote Republican. And as we have already seen, in recent presidential elections the Republican party has sharply increased its support among the largely Protestant white voters in the South. In the 2004 election George W. Bush received 59 percent of the Protestant vote and 78 percent of the white evangelical Christian vote.

Women march in Brooklyn, New York, in 1919 demanding the right to vote. The Nineteenth Amendment of the Constitution was ratified a year later in response to demonstrations of this type.

In recent years there has been considerable discussion of the so-called *gender gap*—the tendency of women to see political issues differently than men do, and to vote differently. On some issues, public-opinion polls have revealed significant differences between the views of women and men. Women, for example, are much less likely than men to back the use of military force in international affairs. With regard to voting, women have been more likely to support the Democratic party; at the same time men have become increasingly more likely to vote Republican.

The gender gap is to be found among older women voters because issues related to Social Security and Medicare are important concerns for them. It is also present among single women who are, on average, less affluent than married women. Many are single mothers who benefit from various government programs that have traditionally been supported by the Democratic party. Republican candidates, on the other hand, receive support from a majority of married women.

In sum, the Democratic and Republican parties can best be understood as loose *coalitions,* or alliances of voters from a variety of backgrounds. Republicans tend to be white, Protestant, and better educated, have higher incomes, and live on farms, in small towns, or in the suburbs of large cities and in the western part of the United States or in the South. The Democratic coalition includes women, blacks, Hispanics, many Catholics, Jews, members of labor unions, the less well educated, and the poor.

TABLE 6.2

PORTRAIT OF THE ELECTORATE, 2000

	Percentage of Total Voters	Gore	Bush	Nader
Men	48%	42	53	3
Women	52%	54	43	2
White	82%	42	54	3
Black	10%	90	8	1
Hispanic	4%	67	31	2
Asian	2%	54	41	4
Married	65%	44	53	2
Unmarried	35%	57	38	4
18–29 year olds	17%	48	46	5
30–44 year olds	33%	48	49	2
45–59 year olds	28%	48	49	2
60 and older	22%	51	47	2
Not a high school graduate	5%	59	39	1
High school graduate	21%	48	49	1
Some college education	32%	45	51	3
College graduate or more	42%	48	48	3
College graduate	24%	45	51	3
Post-graduate education	18%	52	44	3
From the East	23%	56	39	3
From the Midwest	26%	48	49	2
From the South	31%	43	55	1
From the West	21%	48	46	4
White Protestant	47%	34	63	2
Catholic	26%	49	47	2
Jewish	4%	79	19	1
Family income under $15,000	7%	57	37	4
$15,000–$29,999	16%	54	41	3
$30,000–$49,999	24%	49	48	2
Over $50,000	53%	45	52	2
Over $75,000	28%	44	53	2
Over $100,000	15%	43	54	2
Total Vote		**48**	**48**	**2**

Data collected by Voter News Service based on 13,279 voters leaving 300 polling places on Election Day, 2000.
Source: The New York Times, November 12, 2000, p. 4. Copyright © 2000 by The New York Times Company. Reprinted by permission.

CONCLUSION

Much of American politics is traditional. Long campaigns, speeches, demonstrations, and the like have characterized the nation's political scene ever since its early years. And the national convention has been in continual use since the 1830s.

But much has also changed, especially in the twentieth century. Instead of trains, jet planes transport candidates around the country. First radio and now television have reduced the importance of personal appearances as the chief means by which candidates communicate with the public.

Since the 1960s other changes have occurred in the American election system that are less obvious but have had a profound effect on national politics. Among them are the importance of the direct primary in the selection of presidential candidates and the reduction of the role of the party convention to that of ratifying choices already made in the primaries, and the reform of campaign finance laws for presidential nomination and election campaigns.

The campaign finance laws enacted during the 1970s have also had important effects on presidential election campaigns. For one thing, because federal money is available, some candidates who might not have been able to afford to enter and compete in the primaries can now do so. For another, the law encourages candidates to seek relatively small contributions from many voters and rely less on large contributions from a few very wealthy individuals. The legislation has also stimulated the rapid growth of political action committees, a development that has had a number of unforeseen and undesirable consequences. In addition, the use of soft money in campaigns has greatly reduced the effectiveness of the campaign finance law.

The congressional campaign finance system has been subjected to some strong criticism. It is claimed that congressional candidates have become more dependent on contributions from interest groups and PACs and that this makes such groups more powerful than ever. Indeed, PAC money has contributed to the high reelection rates of House members, since most of the money is given to incumbents rather than to challengers. It is also argued that far from making campaign financing more open, the law has given rise to some questionable practices because corporations, unions, and other organizations have sought ways to get around the limits set by existing legislation, especially through the use of unregulated soft money contributions to party organizations. Moreover, the Federal Election Commission does not have enough power to enforce the law effectively.

After many years of discussion, Congress finally responded to these criticisms. In 2002 it enacted campaign reform legislation that, among other things, sought to outlaw soft money in national politics. The law became effective with the 2004 national election. It is too early to evaluate the full consequences of the legislation. But it is apparent that the reform law did stop the rapidly growing cost of national campaigns nor prevent private groups from raising and spending large sums of money on both presidential and congressional primaries and elections.

QUESTIONS FOR THOUGHT

1. What is a presidential primary? A caucus?

2. How are presidential campaigns financed?

3. What is the Electoral College, and how does it function?

4. Should the Electoral College be abolished? If so, what should take its place?

5. What groups in the U.S. population tend not to vote?

6. Which groups in American society tend to support the Democratic party? Which groups tend to support the Republican party?

INTERNET ACTIVITIES

1. *Campaign Finances.* Go to **http://www.tray.com/fecinfo/** or **http://www.fec.gov/** and find the amount of money contributed to candidates for either your U.S. Representative or one of your U.S. Senators.

2. *Electoral College Results.* Review the Electoral College maps for the U.S. presidential elections from 1980 to 1996 at the U. of Virginia Geography site at **http://fisher.lib.virginia.edu/elections/maps** Identify any voting patterns you see. Which states/regions tend to vote Republican or Democratic? Which states are more competitive? How will these patterns affect the presidential campaign strategies used by Republican and Democratic candidates?

KEY TERMS

ballot	frontloading	primary
blanket primary	hard money	registration
caucus	Independent	runoff primary
closed primary	national convention	soft money
coattail effect	open primary	voter turnout
convention	party platform	
Electoral College	presidential primary	

SUGGESTED READING

Bush, Andrew and James Ceaser. *The Perfect Tie: The True Story of the 2000 Presidential Election.* Lanham, MD: Rowman & Littlefield, 2001.

DiClerico, Robert, ed. *Campaigns and Elections in America.* Upper Saddle River, NJ: Prentice Hall, 2000.

Dudley, Robert, and Alan Gitelson. *American Elections: The Rules Matter.* New York: Longman, 2002.

Gainborough, Juliet F. *Fenced Off: The Suburbanization of American Politics.* Washington, DC: Georgetown University Press, 2001.

Jacobson, Gary C. *The Politics of Congressional Elections,* 5th ed. New York: Longman, 2001

Kahn, Kim Fridkin. *The Political Consequences of Being a Woman.* New York: Columbia University Press, 1996.

Layman, Geoffrey. *The Great Divide: Religious and Cultural Conflict in American Party Politics.* New York: Columbia University Press, 2001.

Longley, Lawrence D., and Neil R. Pierce. *The Electoral College Primer 2000.* New Haven, CT: Yale University Press, 1999.

Manza, Jeff, and Clem Brooks. *Social Cleavages and Political Change: Voter Alignment and U.S. Party Coalitions.* New York: Oxford University Press, 1999.

Mayer, William G., ed. *In Pursuit of the White House 2000: How We Choose Our Presidential Nominees.* New York: Chatham House, 2000.

Menefee-Libey, David. *The Triumph of Campaign-Centered Politics.* New York: Chatham House, 2000.

NOTES

1. Nicholas Zamiska, "U.S. Elections Are to Set Record for Spending at $3.9 Billion," *Wall Street Journal,* October 21, 2004, p. A4.

2. *Buckley* v. *Valeo,* 424 U.S. 1 (1976).

3. Stephen J. Wayne, *The Road to the White House 2000* (Boston/New York: Bedford/St. Martin's Press, 2000), pp. 34–35, 45.

4. William H. Flanigan and Nancy H. Zingale, *Political Behavior in Midterm Elections* (Washington, DC: Congressional Quarterly Press, 2000), p. 40.

5. Floyd Abrams, "Congress Turns Political Speech into a Crime," *Wall Street Journal,* March 27th, 2002, p. A18.

6. Since 1972 Maine has used a district plan for choosing electors in which two electors are chosen on a statewide basis and one is chosen from each of the state's congressional districts. Nebraska employed this system for the first time in 1992. In each of the elections contested under this system, the electoral votes have gone to a single candidate.

7. David E. Rosenbaum, "It's a House of the Same Representatives," *New York Times,* September 25, 1988,

sec. 4, p. 1; Warren Weaver, Jr., "More and More House Races Aren't Races But Runaways," *New York Times,* June 15, 1987, pp. A1, B10.

8. *U.S. Term Limits* v. *Thornton,* 514 U.S. 779 (1995).

9. Angus Campbell, Philip E. Converse, Warren E. Miller, and Donald E. Stokes, *The American Voter* (New York: Wiley, 1960), p. 49.

10. Adam Clymer, "The Body Politic," *New York Times,* January 2, 2000, p. 1.

11. Richard A. Oppel, Jr., "Despite Big Issues, Primaries Prompted Only 17% to Vote," *New York Times,* September 28, 2002, p. A14.

12. Ronald C. Moe, "Myth of the Non-Voting American," *Wall Street Journal,* November 4, 1980, p. 28.

13. Stanley Kelley, Jr., Richard E. Ayres, and William G. Brown, "Registration and Voting: Putting First Things First," *American Political Science Review* 61 (June 1967): 359–80. In a few democratic countries, such as Australia and Belgium, citizens are fined for not voting. Turnout in those nations is consequently very high.

14. Benjamin Ginsberg and Martin Shefter, *Politics by Other Means* (New York: Basic Books, 1990).

15. Lizette Alvarez, "Hispanic Voters Hard to Profile, Poll Finds," *New York Times.* October 4, 2002, p. A20.

Congress

Woodrow Wilson was a 29-year-old graduate student in political science at Johns Hopkins University when he wrote *Congressional Government.* Thirty years later, after serving as president of Princeton University and governor of New Jersey, he was elected president of the United States. Wilson admitted that he had overstated the importance of Congress and underestimated that of the president. But his basic point remains accurate: The governmental system of the United States cannot be understood without a thorough understanding of Congress.

   This chapter will concentrate on the organization and structure of Congress and describe some of the procedures it uses to conduct its work.

THE FUNCTIONS OF CONGRESS

When we speak of Congress, we are really referring to two Congresses: the Congress that enacts legislation for the nation as a whole and the Congress that represents the people of all the states and localities in the nation. Congress, in other words, has a dual nature—it is at the same time a legislative and a representative body. Its main function, of course, is to enact laws, operating primarily on the basis of its expressed (or enumerated) powers under Article I, Section 8, of the Constitution. But it is not simply a lawmaking body. It is a collection of 535 senators and representatives whose positions depend on the support of voters in San Diego, Kalamazoo, Orlando, Bangor, and thousands of other communities throughout the United States. We therefore begin this chapter with a discussion of these two basic functions of Congress—legislation and representation.

> As the House of Commons is the central object of examination in every study of the English Constitution, so should Congress be in every study of our own. Anyone who is unfamiliar with what Congress actually does and how it does it . . . is very far from a knowledge of the constitutional system under which we live.
>
> —Woodrow Wilson, *Congressional Government* (1885)

A photo of the Capitol taken about 1846.

Legislative Functions: Expressed Powers

TAXING AND SPENDING   Congress passes *tax laws,* which raise money for the government, and *appropriations laws,* which determine how the money is spent. Taxes are used both to raise money and to regulate the economy. The Constitution requires that all tax bills originate in the House of Representatives, where they are handled by the Ways and Means Committee. After they have been passed by that committee, tax measures must be approved by the entire House of Representatives. In the Senate, the Finance Committee handles tax legislation. When it completes its work, the bill is sent to the full Senate for final consideration.

Congress also has the constitutional power to make decisions regarding the spending of tax revenues. It does this through a two-step process involving authorizations and appropriations. **Authorizations** establish specific programs and set limits on the amounts that may be spent on them by the executive branch; **appropriations** provide the money itself. The amount appropriated may be less than the amount authorized. (See Figure 7.1)

THE BUDGET PROCESS   In 1974 Congress passed the Budget and Impoundment Control Act. This legislation was intended to create a new procedure for establishing the annual federal budget. The legislation was motivated by fear of *inflation,* rapid increases in federal spending and the national debt, and the belief that the executive branch had acquired too much power over government spending.

The 1974 law created budget committees in both houses of Congress, established the Congressional Budget Office to provide Congress with economic information, limited the president's power to *impound* (not spend) funds appropriated by Congress, and changed the beginning of the federal fiscal year from July 1 to October 1 so as to give Congress more time to consider the budget proposals made by the president in January of each year. The Budget and Impoundment Control Act also established a schedule for the enactment of all tax, authorization, and appropriations legislation. The procedure begins in the spring of each year and is supposed to be completed by October 1.

The Office of Management and Budget (OMB) is the staff agency that assists the president in the preparation of the budget. It examines the budget of each

Congress of the United States,

BEGUN and held at the City of NEW-YORK,
On Wednesday the fourth of March, one thousand
seven hundred and eighty-nine

An ACT *making* Appropriations *for the service of the present* Year.

Sec. I.   **B**E *it enacted by the Senate and House of Representatives of the United States of America in Congress assembled,* That there be appropriated for the service of the present year, to be paid out of the monies which arise, either from the requisitions heretofore made upon the several states, or from the duties on impost and tonnage, the following sums, viz. A sum not exceeding two hundred and sixteen thousand dollars for defraying the expenses of the civil list, under the late and present government; a sum not exceeding one hundred and thirty-seven thousand dollars for defraying the expenses of the department of war; a sum not exceeding one hundred and ninety thousand dollars for discharging the warrants issued by the late board of treasury, and remaining unsatisfied: and a sum not exceeding ninety-six thousand dollars for paying the pensions to invalids.

FREDERICK AUGUSTUS MUHLENBERG,
Speaker of the House of Representatives.
JOHN ADAMS, *Vice-President of the United States,*
and President of the Senate.

APPROVED September the 29th, 1789.
GEORGE WASHINGTON, *President of the United States.*

FIGURE 7.1   The first appropriations bill passed by the First Congress of the United States, September 29, 1789. It was also the shortest of its kind in the nation's history. The First Congress appropriated a total of $2,154,344.20 for the first three years of the government. The proposed 2003 federal budget was $2.1 trillion.

government agency and adjusts it in accordance with the general policies established by the president. The director of the OMB then presents the president with estimates of total revenues and expenditures. The president may make final changes in these figures. In January the president presents his budget to Congress, along with a budget message.

The period from late winter to early fall is a time of heated debate between the legislative and executive branches over the final version of the budget. Congress considers the budget not as a single document but in the form of thirteen spending bills dealing with the basic areas of government activity: defense, agriculture, foreign operations, and so forth. Although all spending bills are supposed to be enacted by October 1, they rarely are, and Congress usually adopts *continuing resolutions,* or stopgap spending bills, that keep the federal agencies running.

For many years budget deficits were the main financial problem confronting the government. From 1982 to 1990 the yearly deficits ranged from $128 billion to $212 billion, reaching almost $235 billion in 1994. These sizable annual deficits forced the government to borrow heavily. The situation changed dramatically in the late 1990s. Cuts in defense spending and in some domestic programs helped to reduce the deficits, but more important, tax revenues grew rapidly as a result of the economic prosperity that marked President Clinton's second term.

This increase in federal revenue altered the federal government's financial situation. President Clinton and the Republican Congress agreed in principle that the government would produce a balanced budget by fiscal year 2002. Then it became clear that the federal budget would actually produce a surplus for the first time in more than thirty years. In the last years of the Clinton presidency and during the 2000 presidential election campaign, a key issue was what to do with the surpluses projected for the early years of the new century.

But this issue quickly became moot when the nation's economy began to decline. The boom times of the 1990s came to a dramatic stop and the economy slowed during the first years of the twenty-first century. Unemployment increased only modestly, but the stock market suffered a serious decline. The September 11 terrorist attack on the United States further injured the country's economy. Declining tax revenue caused by the struggling economy and sharp increases in military spending to meet defense needs brought about a return to budget deficits. In 2004 the federal budget reached a record $422 billion. (See Table 7.1.)

INTERSTATE COMMERCE Another major domestic power of Congress granted by Article I, Section 8, of the Constitution is the authority to regulate interstate commerce. The U.S. Supreme Court has adopted a very broad view of this congressional power. The commerce clause provides the constitutional basis for much of the legislation Congress has passed to control and regulate the American economy. For example, the laws that deal with air traffic, railroads and trucking, radio and television broadcasting, labor-management relations, and the stock and commodity exchanges are all based on the commerce clause.

The scope of the commerce clause is not limited to economic issues, however. Major provisions of the federal criminal code that make certain interstate acts illegal (such as using interstate telephone lines to commit fraud) are based on the commerce clause of the Constitution. This provision has also been used to deal with the problem of racial discrimination. The 1964 Civil Rights Act made it a crime for businesses that provide accommodations to interstate travelers (hotels, motels, and many restaurants) to practice racial discrimination.

FOREIGN AFFAIRS AND TREATIES Although the Constitution gives the president the primary role in foreign affairs, Congress also has significant powers in this area. In Article I, Section 8, the Constitution gives the legislature the power to tax and spend for the defense of the nation, regulate foreign commerce, create uniform rules for the naturalization of immigrants, punish piracy, declare war, and raise and support both an army and a navy. Congress's power over the appropria-

TABLE 7.1

PRESIDENT BUSH'S 2002 AND 2003 FISCAL YEAR BUDGETS AND PROJECTIONS FOR FISCAL YEARS 2004, 2005, 2006, AND 2007 (IN BILLIONS OF DOLLARS)

	Actual		Projected			
Outlays	**2002**	**2003**	**2004**	**2005**	**2006**	**2007**
Discretionary						
Defense	332	371	388	408	423	437
Nondefense	379	399	413	418	424	432
Subtotal, discretionary	**711**	**771**	**801**	**826**	**847**	**870**
Emergency response fund	**36**	**17**	**8**	**3**	**2**	**1**
Mandatory						
Social Security	453	473	494	515	538	566
Medicare	223	232	242	260	282	307
Medicaid	147	161	173	188	205	223
Other mandatory	291	305	302	307	319	323
Subtotal, mandatory	**1,114**	**1,171**	**1,212**	**1,270**	**1,345**	**1,419**
Net interest	**171**	**180**	**196**	**198**	**197**	**194**
Total outlays	**2,032**	**2,138**	**2,217**	**2,298**	**2,390**	**2,483**
Receipts	**1,867**	**2,029**	**2,169**	**2,351**	**2,451**	**2,567**
Surplus [Deficit]	**−165**	**− 109**	**− 48**	**53**	**60**	**84**

Source: U.S. Office of Management and Budget, "President Bush's 2002 and 2003 Fiscal Year Budgets and Projections for Fiscal Years 2004, 2005, 2006, and 2007," 2002.

tion of funds is an especially important source of authority to influence the nation's foreign policy.

Article II, Section 2, of the Constitution requires that all treaties made by the president with foreign nations receive the "advice and consent" of two-thirds of the Senate before they can become effective. The Senate has rejected only about twenty treaties since the nation's founding. But it can also require the president to make changes in proposed treaties or attach reservations to them, and it has exercised that authority on many occasions.

The American constitutional historian Edward S. Corwin described the provisions of the Constitution as "an invitation to struggle for the privilege of directing American foreign policy."[1] Throughout most of American history, this struggle was won by the president. However, in the early 1970s, as the Vietnam War drew to a close, Congress asserted its constitutional powers. The War Powers Resolution of 1973 was the most important attempt to project Congress's authority in foreign and military affairs. The resolution sought to limit the president's freedom to use military forces in combat situations without obtaining the approval of Congress. It requires that the president end the use of military force within sixty days unless Congress declares war or agrees to the continued employment of the nation's armed forces; the president can, if necessary, extend the period for an additional thirty days. (See Chapter 8 for a fuller discussion of this legislation.)

Presidents Reagan, George H. W. Bush, and Clinton all asserted the power of their office in foreign affairs, and Congress retreated from the more assertive position it had established in the 1970s. During the 1980s Democrats in Congress criticized President Reagan's support of the Contras (opponents of the leftist government in power in Nicaragua at the time), and Congress passed legislation that imposed restrictions on the use of federal money to support these groups. But Reagan's decisions to invade the Caribbean island of Grenada in 1983 and to bomb Libya in 1986 were carried out without advance consultation with Congress. Similarly, the senior President Bush invaded Panama in December 1989 without first consulting with congressional leaders. And in August 1990, in response to Iraq's invasion of Kuwait, Bush sent a massive American military force into the Middle East to defend against a threatened Iraqi invasion of Saudi Arabia. This was the largest such American buildup since the Vietnam War. It occurred while Congress was on its summer recess, and President Bush did not consult with congressional leaders before acting.

The president continued to add to the number of military personnel in the Persian Gulf during the last months of 1990. Although some members of the legislature opposed this policy, Congress took no action to stop the president. Finally, on January 12, 1991, after a debate, both houses of Congress voted to give the president the right to go to war against Iraq. The vote, however, was quite close. The resolution passed the Senate 52 to 47, with all but two of the no votes cast by Democrats.

During his first administration President Clinton sent American military personnel to both Haiti and Bosnia and conducted a sustained bombing attack on Serbia during 1999. In all three instances there was only minor congressional opposition to the president's military decisions.

Within a few days after the September 11 attack on the United States, Congress overwhelmingly adopted a joint resolution authorizing President George W. Bush "to use all necessary and appropriate force against those nations, organizations or persons, he determines planned, authorized, committed, or aided the terrorist attacks that occurred on September 11, 2001, or harbored such organizations or persons, in order to prevent any future acts of international terrorism against the United States by such nations, organizations or persons." The successful war that was conducted in Afghanistan in 2001–2002 against the Taliban and Al Qaeda was based on this grant of power to the nation's chief executive.

In October 2002 President Bush again received the support of the Congress to use American military force. This time the congressional resolution was directed at Iraq. The vote in the House of Representative was 296 to 133, and in the Senate 77 to 23. Almost all the negative votes were cast by Democrats. On March 19, 2003, President Bush ordered the start of military action against Iraq. In less than three months, the U.S. military, with the assistance of British, Australian, and Polish troops, successfully destroyed Saddam Hussein's government and began the liberation of Iraq.

Legislative Functions: Implied Powers

After enumerating the powers granted to Congress, Article I, Section 8, of the Constitution concludes by giving the legislature **implied powers:** Congress has the right "to make all Laws which shall be necessary and proper for carrying into

Execution the foregoing Powers, and all other Powers vested by this Constitution in the Government of the United States, or in any Department or Officer thereof."

This provision gives Congress a broad range of choices in selecting the means to carry out its expressed powers, as long as the means selected are constitutional. The "necessary and proper" clause thus adds significantly to the authority of Congress to act in both the domestic and the international spheres.

Representation

Another important function of members of Congress is to represent the people of their particular district or state. This representation takes two basic forms: policy representation and service. *Policy representation* is concerned mainly with attempting to pass legislation that is in the best interests of a senator or representative's constituents. *Service* consists of nonlegislative activities that benefit individuals or groups in the home district or state.

Most members of Congress find that they lack the time to fulfill all the responsibilities of representation. They are required to perform what amounts to a juggling act: Tuesday through Thursday they are busy on Capitol Hill, and they spend the remaining days responding to the demands of constituents.[2]

Senators and representatives often find that they must choose between meeting the demands of constituents and carrying out their legislative responsibilities. In a survey of House members, representatives were asked about the differences between how they actually spend their time and how they would spend it under ideal circumstances. More than half the respondents stated that they felt that solving constituents' problems interferes with lawmaking and other congressional duties.[3]

Social Security pensions, Medicare claims, veterans' allowances, naturalization problems, tardy tax refunds, payment to companies that do business with the

---

CLOSE-UP

JEANNETTE RANKIN

The first woman elected to Congress, Jeannette Rankin, was actually elected twice: first in 1916 and again in 1940. In 1916 the Nineteenth Amendment, which gave women the right to vote, had not yet been ratified. But in the western states, including Rankin's home state of Montana, women were permitted to vote under state law. During her first term in the House of Representatives Ms. Rankin drafted and lobbied for a constitutional amendment to grant women the right to vote.

An ardent activist, Rankin worked for numerous causes, including woman suffrage, children's rights, international peace, and prohibition. Her unconventional views on these and other issues contributed to her defeat in 1919. For the next twenty-five years, she continued to lobby for peace and work with consumer groups, and in 1940 she was reelected to Congress.

Rankin was the only woman to vote against U.S. entry into both world wars. In fact, hers was the only vote against entry into World War II, and it ended her political career. Bystanders were so outraged by her action that the Capitol police were called upon to protect her as she returned to her offices after the vote.

Although she was forced to leave politics, Rankin did not abandon her antiwar activities. In 1968 she led a demonstration of several thousand women on the steps of the Capitol protesting America's involvement in the Vietnam War.

government—the range of constituent requests is as broad as the functions government performs. Some studies of Congress have concluded that **casework** tasks consume too much of lawmakers' time, to the detriment of their responsibilities as legislators. But performing services for constituents is necessary to build support and goodwill. When one member of Congress was asked how important casework is, he declared: "About second to breathing."[4]

New legislators are often surprised by the great number of demands made by their constituents. They find that the public often seems more interested in personal services than in current issues or how their representative voted on a major bill. As one member of Congress commented, "I thought I was going to be Daniel Webster and I found that most of my work consisted of personal work for constituents."[5]

The new congressman or congresswoman who fails to appreciate the importance of casework is likely to have a short career as a Washington legislator. Indeed, because reelection is a primary concern of members of Congress, they are strongly motivated to perform these personal services for voters. This is especially true during the first few terms of a new House member who is trying to build support in his or her district.

Other Constitutional Functions

In addition to its lawmaking authority, Congress performs a variety of nonlawmaking functions that have been assigned to it by the Constitution. Among these are the following:

WATCHDOG AND OVERSIGHT FUNCTIONS   Congress is responsible for overseeing the executive branch of the government and thereby keeping the president and his administration accountable to the people. Although it is not expressly mentioned in the Constitution, this is a major function of Congress. Its purpose is to ensure that the laws passed by Congress are being administered effectively and to obtain information necessary to enact new legislation. The **oversight** function is carried out by the committees of Congress, which may conduct investigations of specific government programs and policies. During the fall of 2002, for example, the joint intelligence committees of Congress conducted an investigation into the terrorist threat to the security of the United States at which the directors of the FBI and the CIA testified. Congress can also compel testimony by private individuals who may have relevant knowledge of subjects under investigation. It can subpoena witnesses and hold in contempt individuals who refuse to cooperate with a lawful investigation. While upholding Congress's broad power to investigate, the Supreme Court has declared that there is "no power to investigate for the sake of investigating." It must be related to some legitimate legislative purpose.

APPOINTMENTS   According to Article II, Section 2, of the Constitution, presidential nominations of ambassadors, Supreme Court justices, and all "officers of the United States"—such as department heads—must receive the "advice and consent" of the Senate. Twenty-eight times in the nation's history the Senate has refused to confirm nominees to the United States Supreme Court. But it is rare for the Senate to reject the president's choice for a position within the executive branch; only two nominees for cabinet positions have been rejected by the Senate in more than four decades. However, although formal rejections are unusual, it is not uncommon for nominations to be withdrawn because of Senate opposition. In 1993, for example, three of President Clinton's nominations to positions in the Justice Department (including two for attorney general) were withdrawn when it appeared that they could not win the necessary majority in the Senate. And in 1997 opposition developed in the Senate to President Clinton's nominee to the position of director of the Central Intelligence Agency, and the name was withdrawn by the president. Between 2001 and 2004 President Bush's first nominee to be secretary of labor did not receive Senate approval, several judicial nominees were rejected, and another dozen were never voted on.

ELECTORAL FUNCTIONS   As mentioned in Chapter 6, if no presidential candidate receives a majority of the electoral votes in the general election, the House of Representatives has the power to elect the president from among the three candidates with the most electoral votes. (In such a situation it votes by states, with each state having one vote.) Similarly, the Constitution assigns the Senate the power to choose the vice president from the two candidates with the most electoral votes if no candidate obtains a majority of those votes. In addition, the president of the Senate (that is, the vice president of the United States) has the ceremonial duty of counting the electoral votes sent to Congress by the states and announcing the results.[6]

VICE PRESIDENTIAL NOMINATIONS AND PRESIDENTIAL DIS-ABILITY   The Twenty-fifth Amendment to the Constitution assigns Congress a major role when the office of the vice president becomes vacant and during times of presidential disability. When a president nominates someone to fill the office of vice president, both houses of Congress must confirm the nomination by a majority vote. This occurred twice during the early 1970s. When Vice President Spiro Agnew resigned, President Nixon's nomination of Gerald Ford to the office was confirmed by Congress. In 1974, when Ford became president after the resignation of President Nixon, he nominated Nelson Rockefeller to become vice president, and the nomination was confirmed by Congress.

The Twenty-fifth Amendment also gives Congress a role in deciding whether the president is disabled and therefore unable to perform the duties of the office, as well as deciding when the president is well enough to resume office. This provision has not been used since the amendment was adopted in 1967.

IMPEACHMENT   Congress also plays a role in the **impeachment,** conviction, and removal of the president, the vice president, federal judges, and other civil officers of the United States if it believes those individuals to be guilty of treason, bribery, or other high crimes and misdemeanors. The House of Representatives decides whether to levy formal charges against the official (to impeach), and it does this by a majority vote. The Senate, after a trial, then determines by a two-thirds vote whether to convict and remove the person from office. The power to impeach has rarely been used; there have been only seventeen impeachment trials in the nation's history. The Senate has conducted thirteen trials of federal judges; one Supreme Court justice was impeached but not convicted, and unsuccessful impeachment proceedings were brought against a member of Congress, a cabinet official, and Presidents Andrew Johnson and Bill Clinton.

AMENDMENTS TO THE CONSTITUTION   Chapter 2 discussed the procedure set forth by Article V for amending the Constitution. Congress has the power to propose amendments by a two-thirds vote, and it also has the authority to determine whether ratification of the proposed amendment shall be by a three-fourths majority of the state legislatures or by special state conventions. (With one exception, it has always chosen the former method.)

DISCIPLINING AND EXPELLING MEMBERS Article I, Section 5, of the Constitution declares "each House [of Congress] shall be the judge of the Elections, Returns, and Qualifications of its own Members." This clause gives to the Senate and the House of Representatives the power to prevent a newly elected member from taking his or her seat in Congress. The Supreme Court has ruled, however, that this power applies only to the exclusion of individuals who do not meet the constitutional requirements for membership. A representative must be at least 25 years old, have been a citizen of the United States for at least seven years, and be a resident of the state from which he or she is elected; a senator must be at least 30 years old, have been a citizen at least nine years, and be a resident of the state from which he or she is elected. Exclusion cannot be based on any other ground.[7]

Article I, Section 5, goes on to state that "each House may . . . punish its Members for disorderly Behavior, and, with the Concurrence of two thirds, expel a Member." This is the basis for the authority to censure or expel members of Congress who are guilty of misconduct. The Constitution does not specify the kinds of misconduct to which this power may be applied [8]; indeed, Congress has rarely exercised this power. Only fifteen senators have been expelled, none of them since the Civil War, when several were expelled for supporting the rebellion. Only five members of the House of Representatives have been expelled; of these, three were expelled during the Civil War. The most recent use of this constitutional power came in July 2002, when Representative James A. Traficant, an Ohio Democrat, was expelled by the House of Representatives after he had been convicted in federal court on ten counts of racketeering, corruption, and bribery. Votes to censure have also been relatively rare and have occurred in response to various forms of misconduct.

THE CONGRESSIONAL DISTRICT

Article I, Section 2, of the Constitution provides that House seats shall be assigned to the states on the basis of population. This task—**reapportionment**—is performed every ten years, when the population of the United States is counted by the Census Bureau. Each state gets at least one seat, but after each census the other seats are apportioned among the states according to population. States whose populations have grown relative to those of other states gain new seats; those that have lost population relative to others have seats taken away from them. Since 1929 the total membership of the House has been limited to 435 (except for a brief period during the late 1950s following the admission of Alaska and Hawaii as states, when the figure was 437).

In almost all states, the legislature determines the boundaries of its congressional districts as well as those of its state legislative districts. Boundaries must be changed after each census to reflect population shifts that occurred during the preceding ten years. Until the 1960s, state legislatures were controlled by rural and small-town interests. Following World War II, large numbers of people moved to cities and suburbs, but state legislatures failed to redraw district boundaries to reflect this huge population shift. As a result, individuals who lived in urban areas were underrepresented in the House of Representatives and in most state legislatures.

The issue of unequal representation reached the Supreme Court in 1964 in a case involving congressional districts in Georgia.[9] The Court ruled that the Constitution requires that the populations of congressional districts be substantially equal. It applied the "one person, one vote" principal to congressional elections and held that "as nearly as is practicable one [person's] vote in a congressional election is to be worth as much as another's". Under the 2000 census each congressional district must contain 654,361 persons. (The "one person, one vote" principle does not apply to the Senate because the framers of the Constitution created that chamber on the principle that each state should have an equal vote.)

State legislatures can draw district boundaries for House seats in such a way as to give a particular political party an advantage. This practice, known as **gerrymandering,**[10] involves the division of territory into voting districts that give an advantage to the majority party. To maximize its chances of winning elections, the majority party can create legislative districts that contain sufficient numbers of its supporters to guarantee victory in the election.

The Supreme Court has generally avoided cases involving gerrymandering, unless it can be shown that the boundaries of a legislative district were drawn with the intent of discriminating against voters of a particular race. In the years following the 1990 census the Supreme Court invalidated a number of proposed congressional district lines because they unconstitutionally used race as a basis for the districting. White voters successfully argued that the lines were drawn in order to guarantee the election of African American legislators.[11]

In the spring of 1999, however, the Supreme Court issued a unanimous ruling that seemed more accepting of congressional district lines that had been

CLOSE-UP

POLITICS AND THE CENSUS

The importance of the ten-year census cannot be questioned. The census determines the allocation of seats in the House of Representatives and is the basis for drawing the boundaries of congressional districts as well as those of the state legislatures. The population information is also used by Congress as the primary basis for distributing federal funds to states and localities. Thus, it is little wonder that partisan politics are a major feature of the redistricting process that occurs in most states. In all but four states, party control of the legislature and the governor's office affects the district boundaries that are created. (New Jersey, Idaho, Washington, and Hawaii bypass the legislature and allow commissions and the state courts to draw district boundaries.)

Before the 2000 census, even the method of counting to be used by the Census Bureau became a subject of partisan politics. It is generally agreed that the population is undercounted in poorer areas, especially minority neighborhoods in major cities. A more accurate count would benefit the Democratic party, since the poor generally support its candidates. President Clinton therefore proposed that the Census Bureau supplement its usual method of counting—mail, followed by personal interviews for those who do not respond—with a statistical sampling method that would estimate the undercounted population. Some states and localities, as well as some House Republicans, objected to the use of sampling and challenged Clinton's proposal in the courts. The Supreme Court agreed and held that the census legislation enacted by Congress over the years required the use of an "actual enumeration" of the population for the purposes of legislative apportionment.

drawn to favor African American candidates. While the Court did not reject its prior decisions on the subject, it stated that such a district might not be automatically unconstitutional so long as the motivation for it was primarily political rather than racial. "A jurisdiction may engage in constitutional gerrymandering, even if it so happens that the most loyal Democrats happen to be black and even if the state were *conscious* of that fact," Justice Thomas wrote. [12]

The 2000 census population figures led to changes in the number of seats held by eighteen states. The apportionment of the 108th Congress saw eight states gain and ten lose seats in the House of Representatives. In general, states in the South and West benefited from the 2000 census, while those in the East and Midwest suffered declines. (See Table 7.2.)

The Two Houses: Similarities and Differences

The two houses of Congress are equal partners in the lawmaking process. Each must approve a bill before it can become law. In each house, the majority party elects the leader of that house (the Speaker of the House and the President Pro Tempore of the Senate). In addition, in both houses' committees are controlled by the majority party, and the important committee chairs are always members of the majority party.

However, certain significant differences exist between the House and the Senate. The most obvious difference, of course, is size: The Senate has 100 members and the House 435. This factor leads to differences in style. Perhaps the most

TABLE 7.2

SHIFTING POLITICAL POWER AMONG THE STATES, 2002–2011

State	Number of Seats	Change
Arizona	8	+2
California	53	+1
Colorado	7	+1
Connecticut	5	−1
Florida	25	+2
Georgia	13	+2
Illinois	19	−1
Indiana	9	−1
Michigan	15	−1
Mississippi	4	−1
Nevada	3	+1
New York	29	−2
North Carolina	13	+1
Ohio	18	−1
Oklahoma	5	−1
Pennsylvania	19	−2
Texas	32	+2
Wisconsin	8	−1

CLOSE-UP

THE FIRST BLACK SENATOR

Hiram Revels of Mississippi, the first black member of the United States Senate, gained his seat by a 48-to-8 vote held in the Senate on February 25, 1870. The vote followed an emotional debate in which the Democrats questioned the legality of the state government of Mississippi that had been created during the post–Civil War Reconstruction period, and the Republicans claimed that the Democrats were "hiding their anti-Negro sentiments behind a mask of technicalities." Despite strong opposition by senators from some southern states, the majority voted to seat Revels.

From today's perspective it is surprising that anyone would attempt to challenge Hiram Revels's credentials. A college graduate and an ordained minister in the African Methodist Episcopal Church, Revels had helped organize black regiments during the Civil War and had served as a chaplain in the Union Army, an alderman in Natchez, Mississippi, and a Mississippi state senator.

During the year he served in the U.S. Senate, Revels spoke in defense of freedmen's rights and enforcement of federal election laws, and in opposition to school segregation. After leaving the Senate, he went on to become secretary of state of Mississippi and president of Alcorn Agricultural College.

striking difference noticed by most visitors to the Capitol is the apparent formality and impersonality in the House chamber as contrasted with the relatively informal atmosphere in the Senate.[13] Size also influences the procedures followed by the House and the Senate. Senate rules are short and relatively simple; House rules are many and complex. House rules, for example, sharply limit the time in which a member may speak during a debate, whereas senators are subject to few time limits.

Another difference between the two houses of Congress derives from the different terms of office of their members (two years in the House, six years in the Senate). This means that representatives are campaigning almost all the time, whereas senators have more time before they must seek reelection. As a result, senators can pay more attention to aspects of legislation that do not directly affect their chances of winning or losing voter support.[14]

A further major difference between the two houses of Congress is the political outlook of their members. Senators have statewide constituencies. As a result, they must keep in mind the interests of a variety of groups. Most representatives have smaller constituencies; each speaks for the residents of a particular district. A representative's concerns, therefore, are often limited to more local issues that are of interest to fewer groups.

THE MEMBERS OF CONGRESS

William Mosley ("Fishbait") Miller, the longtime doorkeeper of the House of Representatives, once described the members of Congress as "535 high school class presidents with a few prom queens thrown in."[15] In a more serious vein, one observer admitted that Congress "has its quota of knaves and fools" but added that "it has its fair share of knights. And sandwiched between these upper and nether crusts is a broad and representative slice of upper-middle-class America."[16]

Most members of Congress have a college degree and are either lawyers or people who have had careers in business, banking, or education. Although the number of lawyers in Congress is quite large, the total has actually declined in

Representative Nancy Pelosi (D., Calif.) speaks at a press conference in San Francisco, November 2002. She had just been chosen to be her party's leader, the first woman to hold this position in either the House or Senate.

recent years. The number of legislators with backgrounds in business and banking, on the other hand, has grown rapidly in past decades. Recently there has also been a sharp increase in the proportion of members with backgrounds in politics or public service. On the other hand, very few members of Congress are members of trade unions or scientists or clergymen. (See Table 7.3.)

Although women constitute slightly more than 50 percent of the nation's population, relatively few have served in Congress. Their numbers have, however, increased in recent elections: A record forty-seven women were elected to the House of Representatives in 1992, compared with twenty-nine in 1990. In the 2004 elections, sixty-five women were elected to seats in the House. A similar pattern of growth can be seen in the Senate. Whereas only two women served in the Senate during the 1980s and early 1990s, the number grew to thirteen in the 108th and 109th Congresses.

Minority groups have also made gains in House membership (though less in the Senate), making that institution more diverse than it has ever been. The number of African Americans in the House increased from twenty-six in 1991 to forty in the 109th Congress. During the same period the number of Hispanic members rose from eleven to twenty-three. Three Asian-Americans were elected to the House in the November 2004 national elections. One African-American and two Hispanics were elected to the Senate in the 2004 elections.

Congressional Leadership

Leadership posts in the two houses of Congress are positions of power. This power is not as great today as it has been in some periods in the past, but it is still very significant. Congressional leaders, who are elected by their fellow members, often have a major effect on the legislation passed by Congress.

TABLE 7.3

MEMBERS' OCCUPATIONS 108TH CONGRESS

	House			Senate			Congress
	Democrat	Republican	Total	Democrat	Republican	Total	Total
Actor/Entertainer		2	2				2
Aeronautics		2	2	1		1	3
Agriculture	8	18	26		5	5	31
Artistic/Creative		1	2*				2*
Business/Banking	56	109	165	9	16	25	190
Clergy	1	1	2				2
Education	50	37	88*	7	5	12	100*
Engineering	1	7	8		1	1	9
Health Care	4	1	5				5
Homemaker/Domestic	2	2	4				4
Journalism	3	7	11*	1	5	6	17*
Labor	5	2	7		2	2	9
Law	86	75	161	29	30	60	221**
Law Enforcement	6	3	9				9
Medicine	5	11	16		3	3	19
Military		3	3		1	1	4
Professional Sports		1	1		1	1	2
Public Service/Politics	77	68	145	17	13	30	175
Real Estate	3	27	30	2	1	3	33
Secretarial/Clerical		2	2				2
Technical/Trade	1	3	4				4
Miscellaneous	1	3	4				4

*Total includes independent Bernard Sanders of Vermont. **Total includes independent James M. Jeffords of Vermont.
Note: Some members have more than one occupation.
Source: Congressional Quarterly Weekly, January 25, 2003, p. 193.

THE SPEAKER OF THE HOUSE The Constitution provides that the **Speaker of the House**—the presiding officer of the House of Representatives—shall be elected by the entire House. In practice, this means that the candidate of the majority party wins the election and becomes the Speaker. The authority of the Speaker has changed over the course of American history. During much of the nineteenth century the Speaker's powers were shared with the chairs of major standing committees. The office grew in importance, however, and by the turn of the century the Speaker played a dominant role in the House. The Speaker's authority reached its zenith in the years between 1903 and 1910, when Joseph Cannon held the office. Cannon's often-arbitrary rule led to a reaction by the members of the House, and new rules were adopted under which the Speaker lost the right to sit on the House Rules Committee and the power to appoint committee members and chairs.

Today the Speaker's position is a powerful one, though not what it was during the Cannon era. The Speaker has the traditional rights of a presiding officer: the right to recognize members for the purpose of speaking and the authority to interpret the rules of the House. With the aid of the parliamentarian, the Speaker assigns new bills to specific committees. The assignment of a bill can be crucial;

giving a bill to a friendly or a hostile committee can determine its fate. The Speaker's power in this area is limited, however, because the jurisdiction of the various committees is set forth in House rules.

The Speaker's formal powers also include the right to make appointments to special committees, including the conference committees that attempt to resolve differences between the versions of a bill passed by the two houses of Congress. In fact, however, the Speaker usually appoints the candidates whose names have been sent to him by the chair of the committee that considered the legislation.

After the 1994 congressional elections, the newly elected Speaker, Newt Gingrich of Georgia, attempted to use the powers of the office to become an equal of the president in domestic affairs. For more than a year he succeeded in doing so. Press and public attention focused on the Speaker and at times overshadowed even that given to the president. While serving as the Republican minority leader, Gingrich had organized the drive to make the Republicans the majority party in the House. During the 1994 election he and other Republicans campaigned on a program of reforming the rules of the House of Representatives and carrying out an extensive set of political and social reforms embodied in the so-called Contract with America. The "contract" set forth a ten-part program of reform that included a constitutional amendment requiring a balanced budget, a line item veto for the president, welfare reform, tax cuts for families, a rollback of government regulations, legal reform, and congressional term limits. As part of the contract, the Republicans promised that a vote would be taken on each of the proposals within the first 100 days of the new Congress.

Once in power, the Republicans moved quickly to make significant changes in House rules. Three standing committees were eliminated; committee staffs were cut; most committee and subcommittee hearings were opened to the public; and House members were limited to serving on two standing committees and four subcommittees. In addition, term limits were instituted for the Speaker and committee and subcommittee chairs; the Speaker may serve no more than four consecutive terms, and committee and subcommittee chairs no more than three terms. (The Senate adopted a similar term-limit rule for the chairs of its committees.) Further, a three-fifths majority of the House is now required to pass any bill that would raise taxes. (Term limits for the Speaker were ended in 2003.)

But the Republicans were less successful in gaining passage of all parts of the program set forth in the Contract with America. Although a major overhaul of the nation's welfare system was enacted in 1996, and the president was granted the line-item veto power, other features of the contract—including the balanced budget amendment, legal reform, and congressional term limits—either did not pass in the House or were defeated in the Senate.

Speaker Gingrich's attempt to shift power from the president to Congress also was ultimately unsuccessful. In the system of separation of powers, the nation's chief executive is given a degree of authority that makes it almost impossible for Congress to become the dominant branch of government. President Clinton's use (and threatened use) of the veto power blocked passage of major parts of the Republican program. Lacking a two-thirds majority in either chamber of Congress, the Republicans were unable to override the president's vetoes. Further, Clinton was able to use his position as the only nationally elected political official to counter the Republican program with his own agenda. By the second year of the 104th Congress, the Republicans were in disarray, and Clinton had greatly strengthened his position and that of his party—only a year after the Democratic defeat in the 1994 election.

President Clinton was reelected in 1996, but the Republicans retained control of both houses of Congress. Gingrich was reelected Speaker in January 1997, but his power was significantly reduced. Public-opinion polls showed that his approval rating was very low. Moreover, Gingrich had enemies within his own party. Although an attempt to replace him as Speaker in early 1997 failed, a growing number of House Republicans had become disenchanted with his leadership. His position was further weakened when the House voted to rebuke the Speaker for violating a House rule that prohibited the use of a tax-exempt organization for political purposes.

The results of the November 1998 House elections sealed Gingrich's fate. With few exceptions in American history, the president's party has always lost seats in off-year elections. The Speaker campaigned actively for his party's candidates and predicted a significant gain in the number of House Republicans. The results, however, went counter to historical trends and the Speaker's predictions: The Democrats picked up five seats in the House, reducing the Republican majority to five. Faced with this loss and the strong possibility that his party would not reelect him as Speaker, Gingrich announced his intention to resign his seat in the House. Within the short period of four years, Gingrich had risen to the apex of power in Washington—for a time the equal of the president—only to see that power slip away and, along with it, his career in the House of Representatives. (See Table 7.4 for the recent history of party control of the House and Senate.)

Senate Leadership

The Constitution makes the vice president of the United States the presiding officer of the Senate. As **President of the Senate** he may vote in order to break a tie, but aside from that function he has no significant legislative duties. He is not even permitted to engage in floor debate. The majority party also nominates a **President Pro Tempore** ("for the time being") to help preside over the Senate. (By custom this position is filled by the member of the majority party with the longest record of continuous service in the Senate.) The vice president rarely attends Senate sessions, and the President Pro Tempore rarely presides; neither is a position of great importance in the Senate. The job of presiding over the Senate is usually shared by junior members. Although the presiding officer of the Senate has many of the formal powers of the Speaker of the House—such as the right to recognize members who wish to speak and the right to interpret rules—he or she has little real power or influence.

THE MAJORITY LEADERS The **Senate majority leader** is chosen by the majority party in the Senate. This role consists of scheduling bills for consideration by the Senate, a task that the majority leader performs together with the minority leader. The majority leader also plays an important role in working out compromises when divisions exist on proposed legislation either within the majority party or between the two parties, as well as between the two houses or between the Senate and the president.

Senate majority leaders have rarely been as powerful as the Speaker of the House. Only in the case of Texas Senator Lyndon Johnson, who dominated the Senate during much of the 1950s, has a majority leader been powerful enough to be considered the equal of the Speaker. The relative weakness of the majority leader is partly due to senators' strong sense of independence. But more important, the rules of the Senate do not favor strong leaders. As we shall see later in the chapter, the majority leader does not have the power to end debate on any

TABLE 7.4

COMPOSITION OF CONGRESS BY POLITICAL PARTY, 1973–2003

Year	Party and President	Congress	House			Senate		
			Majority party	Minority Party	Other	Majority Party	Minority Party	Other
1973[1][2]	R (Nixon)	93d	D-239	R-192	1	D-56	R-42	2
1975[3]	R (Ford)	94th	D-291	R-144	-	D-60	R-37	2
1977[4]	D (Carter)	95th	D-292	R-143	-	D-61	R-38	1
1979[4]	D (Carter)	96th	D-276	R-157	-	D-58	R-41	1
1981[4]	R (Reagan)	97th	D-243	R-192	-	R-53	D-46	1
1983	R (Reagan)	98th	D-269	R-165	-	R-54	D-46	-
1985	R (Reagan)	99th	D-252	R-182	-	R-53	D-47	-
1987	R (Reagan)	100th	D-258	R-177	-	D-55	R-45	-
1989	R (Bush)	101st	D-259	R-174	-	D-55	R-45	-
1991[5]	R (Bush)	102d	D-267	R-167	1	D-56	R-44	-
1993[5]	D (Clinton)	103d	D-258	R-176	1	D-57	R-43	-
1995[5]	D (Clinton)	104th	R-230	D-204	1	R-52	D-48	-
1996[5]	D (Clinton)	104th	R-236	D-197	1	R-53	D-46	-
1997[5][6]	D (Clinton)	105th	R-226	D-207	2	R-55	D-45	-
1999	D (Clinton)	106th	R-222	D-212	-	R-54	D-45	1
2001	R (Bush)	107th	R-221	D-210	2	D-50	R-49	1
2003	R (Bush)	108th	R-229	D-205	1	R-51	D-48	1
2005	R (Bush)	109th	R231	D-201	1	R-55	D-44	1

[D=Democratic, R=Republican. Data for beginning of first session of each Congress (as of January 3), except as noted. Excludes vacancies at beginning of session]

*Represents zero.

[1]Senate had one Independent and one Conservative-Republican.

[2]House had one Independent-Democrat.

[3]Senate had one Independent, one Conservative-Republican, and one undecided (New Hampshire).

[4]Senate had one Independent.

[5]House had one Independent-Socialist.

[6]As of beginning of second session.

[7]Three seats not decided as of November 2004.

Source: U.S. Census Bureau, *Statistical Abstract of the United States, 2001*, Table 387, p. 243. Updated to include 2004 election results.

bill under consideration. Each senator has the right to unlimited debate, which can be limited only by a vote of three-fifths (sixty) of the members.

The **House majority leader** is second in importance to the Speaker. This position, too, is chosen by the majority party, but unlike the Speaker, the House majority leader is responsible only to his or her party and is not an officer of the entire House. The job of the majority leader, both in the House and in the Senate, is defined by tradition rather than by congressional or party rules. It consists primarily of serving as the party's principal spokesman. In addition, majority leaders plan legislative agendas, consult with the president about legislative proposals, and attempt to influence colleagues to support or defeat particular measures.[17]

MINORITY LEADERS AND FLOOR WHIPS The House and Senate **minority leaders** are elected by the minority party in each house. They plan their party's strategy and are expected to examine and criticize the majority party's arguments. The majority and minority leaders are aided by assistant floor leaders, or **whips,**[18] who round up the votes of party members by giving them information for or against a bill that is coming to a vote and persuading them to be present when their votes are needed. The whips thus serve as a liaison between the party leader and the members.

THE COMMITTEE SYSTEM

Woodrow Wilson once wrote that "Congress in session is Congress on public exhibition, while Congress in its committee rooms is Congress at work."[19] Although floor debates are necessary in some cases, most of the actual work of Congress is done in committees and subcommittees. These committees are very important to the individual members of Congress. In committee a member can have a direct effect on the shaping of legislation. Moreover, a member's committee assignments can determine his or her effectiveness. A senator from a rural state, for example, can better serve the interests of his or her constituents as a member of the Agriculture Committee than as a member of the Banking, Housing and Urban Affairs Committee.

Types of Committees

The most important committees in Congress are the permanent or **standing committees.** These committees do most of the work on legislative proposals. (Each standing committee specializes in particular areas and deals only with bills related to those areas.) Thus, they can decide the fate of proposed legislation. Only a minority of the bills that are introduced are acted on by the committees. Those that are approved by committees are "reported" to the full House or Senate.

The majority party always holds a majority of the seats on a standing committee, and the chair of the committee is always a member of the majority party. The House of Representatives now has nineteen standing committees; the Senate has seventeen. Legislators serve on a number of committees, but each senator is limited to membership on two major committees, such as Appropriations or Foreign Relations. In the House, a member must serve on at least one major committee.

Most standing committees are divided into subcommittees that deal with specialized areas of the parent committee's jurisdiction and are created at the discretion of that committee. For example, the House Committee on International Relations has five subcommittees that deal with different areas of the world: Europe, the Western Hemisphere, Africa, East Asia and the Pacific, and the Near East and South Asia. Subcommittees have progressively become more numerous as the concerns of the government have expanded, and their importance has also increased. In the 107th Congress there are approximately ninety-one subcommittees in the House of Representatives and seventy subcommittes in the Senate. (See Table 7.5.)

In addition to the standing committees, there are three other types of congressional committees: select committees, joint committees, and conference committees. **Select committees** are formed to examine particular issues. For example, in response to the September 11, 2001 attacks on the United States, the House of Representatives created the Select Committee on Homeland Security.

TABLE 7.5

STANDING COMMITTEES IN THE SENATE AND HOUSE OF REPRESENTATIVES: 108TH CONGRESS (2003–2005)

Senate	House of Representatives
Agriculture (4)*	Agriculture (5)
Appropriations (13)	Appropriations (13)
Armed Services (6)	Armed Services (6)
Banking, Housing and Urban Affairs (5)	Budget (none)
Budget (none)	Education and the Workforce (5)
Commerce, Science, and Transportation (7)	Energy and Commerce (6)
Energy and Natural Resources (4)	Financial Services (5)
Environment and Public Works (4)	Government Reform (7)
Finance (5)	House Administration (none)
Foreign Relations (7)	International Relations (6)
Government Affairs (3)	Judiciary (5)
Health, Education, Labor and Pensions (5)	Resources (5)
Indian Affairs (none)	Rules (none)
Judiciary (6)	Science (4)
Rules and Administration (none)	Small Business (4)
Small Business and Entrepreneurship (none)	Standards of Official Conduct (none)
Veterans' Affairs (none)	Transportation and Infrastructure (6)
	Veterans' Affairs (3)
	Ways and Means (6)
Total: 17 standing committee; 69 subcommittees	*Total:* 19 standing committees; 86 subcommittees

* Numbers in parentheses represent the number of subcommittees.

Select committees have the same powers as standing committees, except that they cannot receive bills or report legislation to the floor of the House or the Senate. Select committees are often used for oversight purposes. For example, there is a House Permanent Select Committee on Intelligence and a Senate Select Committee on Intelligence.

Joint committees are formed by the House and Senate to deal with issues that Congress believes require coordinated action by the two houses. Such committees include members of both houses and are permanent, but they are rarely given the right to bring legislation to the floor of either house, only to investigate and make recommendations. They are normally used for oversight purposes (for example, the Joint Committee on Taxation) or for housekeeping (for example, the Joint Committee on Printing). Joint committees offer the advantage of coordinating and simplifying congressional procedures, but Congress is reluctant to use this approach. Political rivalries and the fear that they will encroach on the jurisdiction of standing committees are among the factors that make joint committees unpopular. House members are especially fearful of Senate domination of such committees.

Conference committees are joint committees formed to work out a compromise when different versions of a bill have been passed by the House and the Senate. (Bills must pass both houses in exactly the same form before they can be sent to the president.) Conference committees are normally used with major pieces of legislation; differences over less significant legislation are usually resolved without sending a bill to conference.

A conference committee may have from three to nine members; occasionally a larger committee is formed. Members—called managers or conferees—are drawn from both parties. They are appointed by the Speaker of the House and the presiding officer of the Senate on the basis of suggestions of the chairs and ranking minority members of the committees that reported the measure, and they are usually members of those committees. Only members who voted for the bill are selected. Both houses normally ask the committee chair and the ranking majority and minority members of the committee to serve on the conference committee.

Differences are ironed out by bargaining over each section of the legislation. The members of the committee vote as representatives of the House and Senate, not as individuals. A majority of the managers from each house must approve a compromise before it can be adopted. If a final agreement is reached by the conference committee, the *conference report* will be sent to the floor of each house. There it cannot be amended, only adopted or rejected. If both houses approve the work of the conference committee, the bill is sent to the president, but if the conference report is rejected by either house, the bill dies. It is possible, however, for the full House and Senate to direct the conference committee to make a further effort to reach an agreement.

Under congressional rules, conference committees are not permitted to make any significant changes in the bill being considered. In practice, however, conference committees possess some discretion to add new provisions and sometimes even to "write an entire new measure."[20] Because most important legislation goes to conference committees and the reports of those committees are usually accepted by Congress, it is evident that a small number of legislators often have considerable influence on the passage of laws.

Committee Assignments

Members of all standing committees are elected by the full House or the full Senate, but these elections are merely ratifications of the choices made by the parties. The balance of party members on the standing committees is decided by the majority party leadership in the House and by agreement between the majority and minority leaders in the Senate. It is customary for party representation on a committee to be approximately the same as the percentage of party members in the chamber as a whole.

The Republican Committee on Committees makes its party's assignments to House committees. Since 1910 this committee has consisted of one member from each state that has Republican members in the House. Before 1975 the Democrats' committee assignments were made by the Democratic members of the Ways and Means Committee. In 1975 this power was given to the Steering and Policy Committee of the Democratic Caucus.

In the Senate, Republican committee assignments are also made by a Republican Committee on Committees, whose members are appointed by the chair of the Senate Republican Conference (the equivalent of the Democratic Caucus). Democratic committee assignments are made by the Democratic Steering Committee, whose members are appointed by the party leaders. (In both the Senate and the House the Democratic Caucus has the final power to approve decisions of the steering committees.)

After each legislative election many changes occur in the membership of committees. Vacancies occur because of retirements or the defeat of an incumbent. New members of Congress must be given places; others seek to change their assignments. There is great demand for assignments to the most important and prestigious committees, and both parties now attempt to appoint newer members of Congress to some of these positions.

Important changes occurred in committee assignments for the 107th Congress (2001–2003). Women received appointments to a number of the most important committees in the Senate. These assignments reflected the election of thirteen women to the Senate—ten Democrats and three Republicans—the largest number to serve in the history of the chamber. Five were selected to be members of the Appropriations Committee and four to the Commerce Committee. One first-term senator, Blanche Lincoln (D., Arkansas) received an appointment to the Finance Committee by her party. Included in the committee's jurisdiction is the major issue of Social Security. "Women live seven years longer than men and ought to have a say in Social Security," Senator Lincoln declared following her selection.[21]

Committee Chairs

Until the 1970s the chairs of standing committees had broad power over their committees. They could create and abolish subcommittees, hire the committee's professional staff, and decide when the committee would meet and hold hearings on a bill. A new member of Congress once described this influence as follows:

> I knew committee chairmen were powerful, but I didn't realize the extent of the power or its arbitrary nature. Recently, when my chairman announced he planned to proceed in a particular way, I challenged him to indicate under what rule he was operating. "My rules," he said. That was it.[22]

A series of reforms during the early 1970s changed that situation, reducing the power of committee chairs and increasing the authority of committee members. Committee chairs still hire the staff, but the time for meetings is set by a vote of the entire committee in consultation with the chair.

In other reforms carried out between 1971 and 1975, the House of Representatives adopted a number of rules that increased the independence and importance of its subcommittees and reduced the authority of committee chairs over subcommittees. Other reforms further decentralized power within the House by bringing more representatives into positions of authority.

In 1973 Congress also modified the **seniority system,** under which the position of committee chair automatically went to the majority party member with the longest continuous service on that committee. In each house, committee chairs are now chosen by the party caucus. And as we have seen, since 1995 committee chairs in both houses are limited to serving three consecutive terms.

Although seniority is still a significant factor in deciding the choice of committee chairs, it is no longer the sole controlling force. During the 1990s both parties bypassed senior legislators on committees and appointed more junior members. In 1995 the Republicans replaced the chairs of three committees in this way. More important, if the two houses of Congress retain the present rules regarding term limits for committee chairs, the seniority system will effectively be ended in the early years of this century.

In the Senate, party rules provide that the Republican members of each committee shall elect its chair, subject to the approval of the Republican Conference. Democratic senators select committee chairs by secret ballot when one-fifth of the Democrats in the Senate request this procedure. To date, neither party has used these procedures to deny a committee chair position to a senator who would have received the position under the seniority rule.

As a result of the weakening of the seniority system and other reforms instituted during the 1970s, it is possible for new members of Congress to influence the legislative process to a much greater extent than in earlier years. In the past, so-called "backbenchers" had to serve for a decade or more before they could have a significant effect on legislation. Today it is possible for newly elected members to make a difference within a few years. As one member put it, "You don't have to wait around to have influence. Entrepreneurs do very well."[23]

The Major Committees

Key committees in the Senate include: the Appropriations Committee, which considers government expenditures for all programs administered by the departments and agencies of the federal government; the Foreign Relations Committee, which deals with all aspects of American foreign policy; the Finance Committee, which reviews proposals having to do with taxes, tariffs, Social Security, veterans' pensions, and foreign-trade agreements; the Armed Services Committee, which deals with military and defense policy; and the Senate Budget Committee, which lists the annual revenues and spending of the federal government.

The major committees in the House of Representatives are Rules, Ways and Means, Appropriations, and Budget. The Rules Committee is important because it determines the order in which all major legislation (except money bills) will be considered by the House as a whole. By granting a special order, or rule, that stipulates when and under what conditions a bill will be debated on the House floor, it controls the flow of legislation. By refusing to issue a rule, the Rules Committee can prevent legislation from coming to a vote.

The Ways and Means Committee deals with taxation, tariffs, Social Security programs, and trade agreements with foreign nations. Unlike other committees, it can report a bill directly to the floor without going through the Rules Committee. The Appropriations Committee recommends specific appropriations for the programs provided for in the federal budget. The House Budget Committee, like its Senate counterpart, obtains budget information and creates a resolution concerned with annual federal revenues and spending.

Despite criticism that the committees and subcommittees of Congress are too large, their membership has not been reduced. This is especially true in the House. The House Transportation and Infrastructure Committee has seventy-three members, and the Appropriations Committee sixty. The average size of the standing committees is about forty members. Each member of the House serves on an average of five committees and subcommittees.[24]

The Senate has had greater success in limiting the size of its committees and particularly that of its subcommittees. Still, the Appropriations Committee has twenty-eight members, and at least four other committees have twenty members. The average size of Senate committees is about eighteen members, and each senator serves on an average of ten committees and subcommittees.[25]

The Legislative Bureaucracy

Members of Congress are assisted by numerous staff aides. These aides mobilize public opinion, advise legislators on how to vote, respond to requests from constituents, and negotiate with lobbyists. Congressional committees also have staff aides. But unlike members' personal staffs, which are concerned primarily with the individual member's reelection, committee staffs focus on legislative policy.[26]

Each House member is entitled to hire no more than eighteen full-time and four part-time employees. The average House member's staff totals about fifteen. There is no official limit on the number of personal staff aides that a senator may hire. Senators' personal staffs range in size from thirteen to seventy-one members; the average is about thirty-one.

Some observers of Congress have expressed concern about the influence of congressional staff aides, who are hired, not elected. They feel that these individuals often undercut the lawmaking role of senators and representatives. Often it is staff aides, rather than the members of Congress themselves, who meet to discuss issues and negotiate the content of bills. In such situations it is the aides, rather than the elected officials, who determine government policy.[27]

As is true of most bureaucracies, the number of employees in the legislative branch has shown a marked tendency to grow. Between 1972 and 1994 the personal staff of House members increased from 5,280 to 7,537; in the Senate the number rose from 2,426 to 5,366. The number of committee staff members showed a similar pattern of increase. By 1990 there was general agreement in Congress that staffs should be decreased, especially staffs that served the various legislative committees. When the Republicans gained control of the House after the November 1994 election, they promised to reduce congressional staffs. In the next two years the size of committee staffs was cut by 45 percent (the number of personal staff members was reduced by only 7.5 percent). Smaller declines—about 10 percent—occurred in the Senate.[28]

THE LEGISLATIVE PROCESS

The legislative process actually begins long before a bill is introduced in the House or the Senate. The starting point of legislation is awareness of public problems. As such problems become more prominent, they are increasingly likely to be placed on the **policy agenda,** "the list of subjects to which government officials and those around them are paying serious attention."[29]

Once an issue becomes part of the policy agenda, one or more members of Congress may introduce a bill designed to resolve it. The bill must pass through the legislative process to become law. It is difficult to speak of a "typical" procedure that a bill must follow on the path to either adoption or defeat, although there are certain definite stages. Each of these presents an obstacle that could cause the death of the bill. (See Figure 7.2.)

The Introduction of a Bill

Any senator or representative can introduce a bill. A senator can do so by sending the bill to the Senate desk; a representative can do so by depositing the proposal in the "hopper" located on the floor of the House. To coordinate legislative efforts, a senator and a representative may agree to introduce identical legislation. The

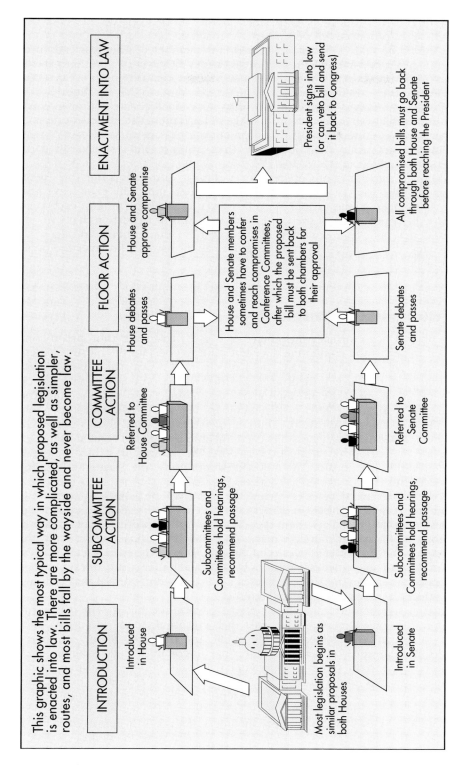

This graphic shows the most typical way in which proposed legislation is enacted into law. There are more complicated, as well as simpler, routes, and most bills fall by the wayside and never become law.

INTRODUCTION	SUBCOMMITTEE ACTION	COMMITTEE ACTION	FLOOR ACTION	ENACTMENT INTO LAW

Introduced in House

Subcommittees and Committees hold hearings, recommend passage

Referred to House Committee

House debates and passes

House and Senate approve compromise

President signs into law (or can veto bill and send it back to Congress)

Most legislation begins as similar proposals in both Houses

Introduced in Senate

Subcommittees and Committees hold hearings, recommend passage

Referred to Senate Committee

Senate debates and passes

House and Senate members sometimes have to confer and reach compromises in Conference Committees, after which the proposed bill must be sent back to both chambers for their approval

All compromised bills must go back through both House and Senate before reaching the President

FIGURE 7.2 How a Bill Becomes a Law.

number of bills introduced is very large; in the 106th Congress (1999–2001) 9,158 bills were proposed but only 604 were enacted.[30]

It should be understood that although any member of Congress can introduce a bill, not every member has an equal chance of having legislation passed. Because Congress is a partisan body, members of the minority party—especially in the House of Representatives—have little or no chance of having their version of a bill enacted into law. Even in the majority party, members are not on an equal footing in the ability to influence the passage of legislation. The leaders of the majority party can use their authority to promote the passage of some party members' bills; by not using their influence, they can prevent less favored party members from achieving their goals.

Although a member of Congress must actually introduce a bill, the executive branch is the source of most major items of legislation. The president's program is announced in the various speeches given at the beginning of each year, especially the annual State of the Union address. Drafts of legislation that embody the president's policies are written in the executive departments and agencies and introduced in Congress by representatives and senators who favor the president's policies.

The Committee Stage

Once a bill has been formally introduced, it is assigned to the appropriate committee for review. If the committee does not want to consider the bill, it is tabled, or put aside, and considered dead. This happens to the vast majority of all proposed bills. In the House, a **discharge petition** is the only device that can be used to take a bill out of the jurisdiction of a committee. The petition requires the signatures of a majority (218) of the members of the House. Once this is obtained, the House must approve the motion to discharge. Although this procedure is rarely employed, it was successfully used in February 2002 to bring a campaign finance law to the floor of the House for a vote. The bill was passed by the entire House and ultimately became law following adoption by the Senate and signing by President Bush.

If the committee decides to review the bill, it will be assigned to one of its subcommittees. Subcommittee members often develop considerable knowledge of their subject, and this gives them the ability to study a proposed law in depth. On important bills, a subcommittee may hold **public hearings** at which individuals testify on the merits or demerits of the bill. These witnesses—technical experts, officials of executive agencies, lobbyists, and others—are questioned by members of the committee. In some cases a bill is so controversial that hearings on the subject last for weeks or even months.

After a subcommittee has completed its work, the bill is sent to the full committee for consideration. In the past this was usually done in an executive session—a meeting that is closed to the public and attended only by committee members. But current House rules require that all committee and subcommittee hearings be open to the public except when national security or sensitive law enforcement issues are under consideration. The committee examines the bill item by item and it is revised, or "marked up." A report explaining the legislation is prepared by the committee. Should there be opposition to the legislation, the report may contain the views of the minority members. If a majority approve the bill, it is "reported out" of the committee. If the majority votes against reporting the bill, the bill dies.

If the standing committee approves the proposal, it is sent to the full House or the full Senate, where the committee chair manages the debate on the bill. If it is necessary to iron out differences between the versions of a bill passed by the two houses, the chair of the committee that considered the legislation will suggest to the presiding officer of the chamber which members of the committee should serve on the conference committee.

The Calendar

When a bill is reported out of the standing committee, it is placed on a **calendar** in the Senate or the House. The Senate has one calendar that is used for all pending legislation. Routine bills are considered in the order in which they appear on the calendar. In the case of controversial legislation, a time for debate is arranged by the majority leader in consultation with the minority leader, the chair of the committee that considered the bill, and senators who have a special interest in the proposed legislation.

A bill reported to the House is put on one of three major calendars: the Union Calendar for appropriations and tax legislation, the House Calendar for all other public bills, and the Private Calendar for bills dealing with specific individuals, corporations, or localities. In addition, the Consent Calendar is used for bills that require little or no debate.

The House has special methods for scheduling major bills for floor debate. Bills are not necessarily taken from the two major calendars—the Union and House Calendars—in the order in which they are listed. In the case of money bills on the Union Calendar, the Appropriations Committee can claim priority in floor debate and will arrange a time for debate with the leaders of the House, that is, the Speaker and the majority leader. In the case of nonmoney bills, the House Rules Committee plays a central role in determining the order of debate. When a bill is reported out of committee and placed on the House Calendar, the chair of the committee will request that the Rules Committee assign the bill a **rule.** The rule takes the bill from the calendar and fixes the time at which it will be considered by the entire House.

Floor Procedure

IN THE HOUSE   When a bill comes up for debate in the House of Representatives, the House usually transforms itself into a Committee of the Whole so that it can operate under more flexible rules of procedure. Only 100 members need be present for the Committee of the Whole to have a quorum, rather than the 218 required under the rules controlling procedure for the House of Representatives. The Committee of the Whole may either reject or approve amendments to the bill, but any amendments it adopts must receive the consent of the entire House.

IN THE SENATE   Mainly because of its smaller size, the Senate operates under much simpler rules than those governing the House. For example, as already noted, bills are considered on the floor of the Senate either in the order in which they appear on the Senate Calendar or, in the case of more controversial bills, under **unanimous consent agreements.** These agreements are worked out by the Senate leadership and set the terms for consideration of the bill by placing limits on motions, amendments, and debate.

FILIBUSTERS   A distinctive feature of Senate procedure is the broad right of each member to speak—a right that is sharply restricted under the procedures of the House of Representatives. This makes possible the Senate **filibuster,** in which one or more senators speak continuously in an effort to prevent a bill from coming to a vote. Filibusters can be especially useful in preventing the passage of legislation during the closing weeks of a session of Congress. But a unified minority can employ this device effectively at any time.

A filibuster can be ended only by a **cloture vote.** The Senate adopted its first cloture rule (Rule 22) in 1917. It required a two-thirds vote of the entire Senate membership. In 1959 the rule was changed to two-thirds of those present, and in 1975 it was changed to its present form: Cloture occurs when three-fifths of the entire Senate (sixty members) vote to end debate on an issue. After cloture has been voted, the rules of the Senate require that a final vote be taken after no more than thirty hours of debate. Present Senate practice also permits other legislation to be considered while the filibuster continues. As a result, marathon filibusters with continuous round-the-clock oratory no longer occur.

Before the 1975 rule change, successful cloture votes in the Senate were rare. Between 1917 and 1975 the Senate voted to limit debate on only twenty-one occasions. Filibustering has become more common in the past several decades.

CLOSE-UP

THE FILIBUSTER

The Senate rule that permits unlimited debate on an issue makes possible one of the most interesting features of politics in the United States—the Senate filibuster.

The right of unlimited debate in the Senate has produced episodes of both high drama and humor. In 1850 Henry Foote of Mississippi drew a pistol on Thomas Benton of Missouri during a filibuster. In 1908 Robert M. LaFollette, Sr., of Wisconsin spoke for more than eighteen hours against a currency bill that he claimed was a giveaway to the rich. His speech was interrupted when he was given a glass of milk that contained ptomaine poison. (Fortunately, he recovered.) In 1935 Huey Long of Louisiana spoke for sixteen hours against one of President Roosevelt's legislative reforms. The high point of the filibuster came when Long provided recipes for Louisiana-style cooking. The record for the longest one-man filibuster is held by Senator J. Strom Thurmond of South Carolina. In 1957 Thurman spoke for twenty-four hours in an unsuccessful attempt to stop passage of a civil rights bill. (Thurmond retired from the Senate in 2003 at the age of 100 after serving almost half a century in that chamber. He was the oldest person ever to serve in the U.S. Senate.)

When a 1917 filibuster was successful in preventing the arming of American merchant ships just before the nation's entry into World War I, a frustrated Woodrow Wilson described the Senate speakers as a "little group of willful men" whose actions made the government "helpless and contemptible." This event led to the adoption of Rule 22, the first rule to impose some limits on debate in the Senate.

But ever since the adoption of the 1975 rule, cloture votes have also become common, and the Senate has acted to restrict debate far more frequently.

Presidential Approval or Disapproval

If a bill is passed by both houses of Congress, it is signed by the Speaker of the House and the President of the Senate and sent to the president of the United States for signature. The president may sign the bill, in which case it becomes law, or he can **veto** the bill by returning it with his objections to the house in which it originated. Congress may **override** the presidential veto by a two-thirds vote in each house. Because such a vote is hard to achieve, it is relatively rare for a bill to become law over a presidential veto. (See Chapter 8 for a fuller discussion of the veto power.)

CONCLUSION

In 1994 control of Congress changed in a most dramatic manner. From 1954 to 1994 the Democratic party had controlled the Senate for all but six years (1981–1987). After the 1994 election, what had been a fourteen-seat Democratic majority became a six-seat Republican majority.

The effect of the 1994 election on the House of Representatives was even more astonishing. In the period from 1930 to 1994 the House had been controlled by the Democrats for all but four years (1947–1949 and 1953–1955). That the Democrats would hold a majority of seats in the House was an accepted feature of American government, as certain as the sun rising in the east each morning. But in the 1994 election the Republicans became the majority party in the House for the first time in forty years.

In the wake of the change, scholars and journalists debated whether the new Republican majority was a temporary phenomenon or the beginning of a long-term trend in American politics. The 1996 election provided some support for the latter view. Although President Clinton handily won reelection, his party failed to regain control of the House and actually lost two Senate seats to the Republicans. For the first time since the 1920s, the Republicans kept control of the House for a second consecutive two-year period. But the Democrats gained seats in the 1998 off-year elections, contradicting the rule that the president's party usually loses seats in off-year elections. Although the Republicans narrowly won the 2000 national election, they lost control of the Senate and saw their majority in the House of Representatives reduced.

Divided government—in which Congress and the president are controlled by different political parties—has been a common feature of American government in recent decades. Divided government brings with it the image of "gridlock," a government that is unable to agree on important policy issues confronting the nation. But divided government need not mean paralysis. The United States has experienced divided government for more than half of the past fifty years, yet studies have shown that there is little difference in legislative productivity between periods when the White House and Congress are controlled by the same party and periods when they are controlled by different parties.

The 2002 elections brought an end to divided government. The Republicans were able to overcome the tradition that the president's party loses congressional seats in the off-year elections; they regained control of the Senate and increased their majority in the House. For the first time in half a century, the Republican party controlled all elected branches of the federal government. Whether this is the start of a new era in American government will largely depend on the success the Republicans have in conducting the nation's foreign and domestic policies.

QUESTIONS FOR THOUGHT

1. What are the major nonlegislative functions of Congress?

2. What constitutional requirements must be met by the states in drawing the boundaries of congressional districts?

3. Who are the constitutional officers of the United States Congress? Who are the main political officers?

4. What are the major types of congressional committees?

5. Why is the committee system central to the operation of Congress?

6. What are the main steps in the process by which legislation is adopted by Congress?

INTERNET ACTIVITIES

1. *Representation.* Go to the U.S. Census Bureau site at **http://quickfacts. census.gov/qfd**. Select your home state. See profiles of your home district and "Browse more data sets" and follow links to Congressional Districts. How do the characteristics of the district affect the kind of politics that exists there? What kinds of issues are important? Does the U.S. representative embody the character of the district?

2. *How Did They Vote?* Go to Project Vote Smart at **http://www. votesmart.org/index.phtm** and check out this marvelous political site. Select "Congress Track." Follow links to any of the four or five organizations tracking voting records to find how your representative and the senators from your state voted on the last federal budget.

KEY TERMS

appropriations	implied powers	select committees
authorization	joint committees	Senate majority leader
calendar	minority leaders	seniority system
casework	override	Speaker of the House
cloture vote	oversight	standing committees
conference committees	policy agenda	unanimous consent
discharge petition	President of the Senate	agreements
filibuster	President *Pro Tempore*	veto
gerrymandering	public hearings	whips
House majority leader	reapportionment	
impeachment	rule	

SUGGESTED READING

Binder, Sarah, and Steven S. Smith. *Politics or Principle? Filibustering in the United States Senate.* Washington, DC: Brookings Institution Press, 1996.

Campbell, Colton C., and Nicol C. Rae. *The Contentious Senate: Partisanship, Ideology and the Myth of Cool Judgement.* Lanham, MD: Rowman & Littlefield, 2000.

Deering, Christopher, and Steven S. Smith. *Committees in Congress,* 3rd ed. Washington, DC: Congressional Quarterly Press, 1997.

Dewhirst, Robert. *Rites of Passage: Congress Makes Law.* Upper Saddle River, NJ: Prentice Hall, 1997.

Lee, Frances E., and Bruce I. Oppenheimer. *Sizing Up the Senate: The Unequal Consequences of Equal Representation.* Chicago: University of Chicago Press, 1999.

Lindsey, James M. *Congress and the Politics of U.S. Foreign Policy.* Baltimore: Johns Hopkins University Press, 1994.

Mayhew, David R. *America's Congress.* New Haven, CT: Yale University Press, 2000.

Peters, Ronald M., Jr. *The American Speakership: The Office in Historical Perspective,* 2nd ed. Baltimore: Johns Hopkins University Press, 1997.

Shea, Daniel, and Kelly D. Patterson, eds. *Contemplating the People's Branch.* Upper Saddle River, NJ: Prentice Hall, 2000.

Uslaner, Eric M. *The Movers and the Shirkers: Representatives and Ideologues in the Senate.* Ann Arbor: University of Michigan Press, 2000.

NOTES

1. Edward S. Corwin, *The President: Office and Powers,* 4th rev. ed. (New York: New York University Press, 1957), p. 171.

2. Richard F. Fenno, Jr., *Home Style: House Members in their Districts* (Boston: Little, Brown, 1978), p. 35.

3. House Committee on Administrative Review, *Final Report,* 2 vols., H. Doc. 95-272, 95th Cong., 1st sess., December 31, 1977, 2:875.

4. Representative Gary Ackerman (D., NY), quoted in Irwin Ross, "Congressmen as Local Ombudsmen," *New York Times,* February 2, 1992, sec. 12, p. 1.

5. Quoted in Charles L. Clapp, *The Congressman: His Work as He Sees It* (Garden City, NY: Doubleday, 1964), pp. 51-53.

6. In 1961, Richard M. Nixon, then President of the Senate and the Republican presidential candidate, announced to Congress the victory of his Democratic opponent, John F. Kennedy. In 1969, the defeated Democratic presidential candidate, Vice President Hubert H. Humphrey, declared the victory of his Republican rival, Richard M. Nixon. And in 1989, then Vice President George Bush announced his own election as president.

7. *Powell v. McCormack,* 395 U.S. 486 (1969).

8. Over the course of American history, unsuccessful attempts have been made to expel members on many charges, including dueling and being a Mormon.

9. *Wesberry v. Sanders,* 376 U.S. 1 (1964). The Court also applied the "one person, one vote" principle to the state legislatures. See *Reynolds v. Sims,* 377 U.S. 533 (1964).

10. *Gerrymandering* was named for Elbridge Gerry (1744-1814), diplomat, governor of Massachusetts, and vice president of the United States. While serving as governor, Gerry arranged to have state election districts drawn so as to favor his political party. Because one district's irregular shape resembled that of a salamander, it was dubbed a gerrymander.

11. See, for example, *Shaw v. Reno,* 509 U.S. 630 (1993).

12. *Hunt v. Cromartie,* 526 U.S. 541 (1999).

13. Lewis A. Froman, Jr., *The Congressional Process: Strategies, Rules and Procedures* (Boston: Little, Brown, 1967), p. 7.

14. David J. Vogler, *The Politics of Congress,* 4th ed. (Boston: Allyn & Bacon, 1983), p. 204.

15. William Miller, *Fishbait* (New York: Warner Books, 1977), p. 13.

16. Quoted in Committee on House Administration, *History of the United States House of Representatives* (Washington, DC: Government Printing Office, 1962), p. 35.

17. Roger H. Davidson and Walter J. Oleszek, *Congress and Its Members,* 3rd ed. (Washington, DC: Congressional Quarterly Press, 1990), p. 165.

18. The term *whip* is derived from fox hunting. The *whipper-in* keeps the hounds from straying from the pack while chasing the fox.

19. Woodrow Wilson, *Congressional Government* (Boston: Houghton Mifflin, 1885). This book was published almost thirty years before Wilson was elected president of the United States.

20. Edward V. Schneier and Bertram Gross, *Congress Today* (New York: St. Martin's Press, 1993), pp. 448-49.

21. David Rogers, "Female Senators Win Coveted Positions on Influential, Formerly Male Panels," *Wall Street Journal,* January 12, 2001.

22. Quoted in Clapp, *The Congressman,* p. 252.

23. Jeffrey H. Birnbaum, "Backbenchers Like Schumer Leap to the Fore in House Where Seniority Is Sovereign No More," *Wall Street Journal,* June 19, 1987, p. 54.

24. Nicol C. Rae and Colton C. Campbell, eds., *New Majority or Old Majority: The Impact of Republicans on Congress* (Lanham, MD: Rowman Littlefield, 1999), pp. 83-84.

25. Ibid.

26. Davidson and Oleszek, *Congress and Its Members,* p. 219.

27. Ibid.

28. Roger Davidson, "Building the Republican Regime: Leaders and Committees," in Rae and Campbell, pp. 86-87.

29. John W. Kingdon, *Agendas, Alternatives, and Public Policies* (Boston: Little, Brown, 1984), p. 3.

30. U.S. Bureau of the Census, *Statistical Abstract of the United States, 2001,* 121st ed. (Washington: DC: Government Printing Office, 2001), Table 391, p. 246.

The Chief Executive

Alexander Hamilton's oft-stated view of the presidency has been accepted by most presidents since the beginning of the twentieth century. This view has coincided with an immense growth of executive power, a development that has been fueled by wars—especially World Wars I and II and the Vietnam War—and by international tensions and domestic economic problems.

Expansions of executive power have occurred when chief executives have used the general language in Article II of the Constitution, such as the statement that makes the president "Commander in Chief of the Army and Navy of the United States," to justify actions that earlier presidents would not have taken. The precedents established in this way have then served as a basis for similar actions by later chief executives. Each such precedent thus creates "an institutional legacy that . . . [leaves] the office more powerful than before."[1]

Since the nation's founding, forty-two individuals have been elected president of the United States. A newly elected president is inaugurated at noon on January 20 in the year following the election. At that time the president recites the oath of office: "I do solemnly swear that I will faithfully execute the office of President of the United States and will to the best of my ability preserve, protect, and defend the Constitution of the United States." George Washington, the first president, added the phrase "so help me God," perhaps because he recognized the awesome powers and duties of the presidency.

Article II of the Constitution begins by stating that "the Executive Power shall be vested in a President of the United States." With these words it created an office that was unknown under the Articles of Confederation and had few historical precedents. In a few general statements, the Constitution gave the president certain basic powers. Yet the president's power is also limited by the restraints imposed by the Constitution and by political forces

> Energy in the Executive is a leading character in the definition of good government. . . . A feeble Executive implies a feeble execution of the government . . . [A] government ill executed, whatever it may be in theory, must be, in practice, a bad government.
>
> —*Alexander Hamilton, The Federalist No. 70*

CLOSE-UP

A President by Any Other Name . . .

In an era when presidents of the United States are routinely referred to as Jimmy, Ron, George, or Bill, it may be hard to imagine the intensity of the debate that occurred in the First Congress on the issue of how to address the nation's chief executive.

The Senate began considering the issue on April 22, 1789, and took a full three weeks to resolve it. Vice President John Adams called for a form of address that would command respect both from the American people and from foreign nations (many of which were monarchies). He was vehemently opposed by Senator William Maclay of Pennsylvania, who expressed concern that "from these small beginnings we shall follow on, nor cease, until we have reached the summit of court etiquette and all the frivolities, fopperies and expenses practiced in European governments."

The matter was referred to a joint committee of the House and Senate, which decided that no titles other than president and vice president of the United States should be used in addressing these officials. The House agreed with this proposal, but the Senate rejected it and appointed a special committee on titles to consider the matter further. On May 14 this committee proposed that the president be addressed as "His Highness the President of the United States of America, and Protector of Their Liberties."

Senator Maclay was quick to react. "Let us read the Constitution," he said. "'No title of nobility shall be granted by the United States.' . . . The appellations and terms given to nobility in the Old World are contraband language in the United States."

Although Adams remained convinced that titles were essential, saying that he feared "the Contempt, the Scorn and the Derision of all Europe," Maclay and other critics prevailed. As a result, throughout the nation's history the chief executive has been referred to as the president of the United States and addressed, even on the most formal occasions, simply as "Mr. [or, someday, Ms.] President."

outside the Constitution, as well as by the president's own philosophy, skill, and character and by historical events.

In this chapter we examine the office of the president, its powers, and the limits on that power. But any study of the American presidency requires an examination not only of the nature of the office itself but also of the people who have served as the nation's chief executive. More than Congress and the courts, the presidency is a product of the individuals who have held the office and the manner in which they have exercised its powers.

SELECTION AND REMOVAL OF THE PRESIDENT

Who May Become President?

Under Article II, Section 1, of the Constitution, "no person except a natural born Citizen . . . shall be eligible to the office of President." It is not clear what the framers intended by the phrase "natural born." The phrase certainly excludes naturalized citizens—those who were born in another nation but have become American citizens according to the provisions of an act of Congress. However, it is not entirely clear whether the phrase "natural born" includes only people born in this country or also people born abroad of parents who are U.S. citizens. Most scholars think it applies to both groups.

The Constitution also states that the candidate must have lived in this country at least fourteen years and must be at least 35 years old. Only a few presidents—

Theodore Roosevelt, John F. Kennedy, and Bill Clinton, for example—were less than 50 years old when they took office. Roosevelt, who became president at the age of 42, was the youngest president in the nation's history. Ronald Reagan, the oldest, was almost 70 when he was inaugurated for his first term in January 1981.

In addition to meeting these few legal requirements, a presidential candidate must satisfy political requirements that are far more significant than the constitutional ones. Among those requirements are holding political offices such as state governor or United States senator, possessing nationwide popular appeal, and being able to successfully navigate the complex presidential nomination and election system.

Succession and Disability

Recognizing the unique and important role of the president, the authors of the Constitution included a provision for the transfer of presidential duties if that need should arise. Article II states that "in case of the removal of the President from office, or of his death, resignation or inability to discharge the powers and duties of said office, the same shall devolve on the Vice President." At first it was uncertain whether the vice president became only the "acting president" or whether he actually became president. Vice President John Tyler, the first person to acquire the office upon the death of a president (William Henry Harrison in 1841), resolved the matter by insisting that he was legally entitled to the full powers of the president.

More difficult problems arise when a president becomes physically or mentally disabled. In 1919 President Woodrow Wilson suffered a stroke and was disabled for more than a year. He remained in office because at the time the Constitution had no provision for declaring a president disabled and hence unable to govern.

George W. Bush is given the oath of office by Chief Justice William H. Rehnquist to become the nation's forty-third persident, January 20, 2001.

The Twenty-fifth Amendment, ratified in 1967, was designed to solve the difficult problems of presidential succession and disability. It contains detailed provisions for the transfer of power: "The Vice President shall become President" in the event of the "removal of the President from office or of his death or resignation." The amendment also provides for the appointment of a vice president when that office becomes vacant. The president nominates a vice president, but the appointment must be confirmed by a majority vote of both houses of Congress. This provision was used only six years after the adoption of the amendment, when Vice President Spiro Agnew resigned and President Richard Nixon nominated Gerald Ford as vice president. It was used again in 1974, when Ford became president upon Nixon's resignation and Ford nominated Nelson Rockefeller as vice president. As a result, between August 1974 and January 1977 the United States had both a president and a vice president who had not been chosen in a national election.

The Twenty-fifth Amendment also provides that if the president becomes disabled he may submit to the Speaker of the House and the president *pro tempore* of the Senate a written declaration that he can no longer fulfill his duties as president. The vice president then becomes acting president. In 1985, for example, President Reagan wrote to the officers of Congress to inform them that he was to undergo surgery and would be incapacitated for a brief period. During that time the vice president, George Bush, served as acting president.

Two provisions of the Twenty-fifth Amendment have not yet been employed. One provides that if the president cannot fulfill the duties of the office adequately but is unwilling or unable to submit such a declaration, the vice president and a majority of the members of either the cabinet or an agency estab-

The United States Senate votes on the articles of impeachment adopted by the House of Representatives against President Clinton, February 1999.

lished by Congress (a panel of doctors, for example) can submit to Congress a written statement declaring that the president is disabled. In such a case the vice president immediately becomes acting president.

The second unused provision of the amendment establishes a method by which the president can regain the office after a period of disability. He reassumes the powers and duties of the presidency upon transmitting to Congress a written statement that the disability no longer exists. But the president's claim can be challenged by the vice president and a majority of the members of either the cabinet or a special body created by Congress. Congress must then resolve the conflict. The president regains the office unless Congress decides by a two-thirds vote that he is still unable to perform the duties of the office. If a two-thirds vote is obtained, the vice president remains acting president.

Impeachment and Removal

The Constitution gives the House of Representatives the power of **impeachment,** that is, the power to indict or formally accuse an official of wrongdoing. This authority applies to the president, the vice president, federal judges, and other civil officers of the United States and must be based on charges of "Treason, Bribery, or other high Crimes and Misdemeanors." First, the House hears evidence about the alleged offenses. If it believes that the evidence warrants the action, it will draft "articles of impeachment" listing the charges. If the articles are adopted by a majority of the House, the named person is impeached. The Senate then sits as a court and conducts a trial of the case. A two-thirds vote of all the senators present is required for conviction and removal from office. The Chief Justice of the United States presides in a trial of the president.

Only two presidents, Andrew Johnson in 1868 and Bill Clinton in 1999, have ever been impeached by the House, and neither of them was convicted by the Senate. President Nixon was not formally impeached for his involvement in the

CLOSE-UP

A PRESIDENT IMPEACHED . . . BUT NOT CONVICTED

On December 19, 1998, for only the second time in American history, a president was impeached by the House of Representatives. The House approved two articles of impeachment against President William Jefferson Clinton. The first charged the president with perjury before a federal grand jury and was adopted by a vote of 228 to 206. The article alleged that President Clinton had made false statements regarding a civil case brought against him by Paula Jones for sexual harassment. (The alleged statements concerned the nature of his relationship with Monica Lewinsky, a White House intern.) The second article accused the president of obstructing justice by attempting to cover up the existence of evidence related to the Paula Jones case; it was approved by a vote of 221 to 212. Two other articles of impeachment did not receive the required majority vote.

The two charges against the president were tried before the Senate in February 1999. As required by the Constitution, the Chief Justice of the United States, William Rehnquist, presided over the trial. A committee of House managers presented the case for removing the president from office; attorneys for the president presented arguments against removal. The Senate vote on both articles of impeachment failed to achieve the constitutionally required two-thirds majority, and President Clinton was therefore acquitted of the charges brought against him by the House of Representatives.

President Richard Nixon as he appeared on national television to announce his resignation as president, August 8, 1974.

Watergate scandal, but it is very likely that he would have been impeached and probably also convicted had he not resigned from office in August 1974.

THE PRESIDENT'S ROLES AND POWERS

"From outside or below, a President is many men or one man wearing many 'hats,' or playing many 'roles.' . . . The President himself plays every 'role,' wears every 'hat' at once."[2] The president's roles are a mixture of constitutional tasks—chief of state and commander-in-chief, for example—and several roles that are not included in the Constitution but are derived from congressional legislation and precedents set by earlier chief executives. Among these are the roles of party head, public-opinion leader, and manager of the economy. In this section we examine each of the president's roles separately, but it should be kept in mind that these functions are related and often overlap.

Chief of State

The United States is represented by the president, whether in Washington, traveling in the United States or abroad, or relaxing at home away from the nation's capital. This fact reflects the president's constitutional role as chief of state—the symbolic center of the national government. As the spokesman for more than 285 million Americans, the president represents the nation as a whole. In this role the president is expected to stand "above politics" and to unify the country. Thus, in the role as chief of state, the president serves a function similar to that of the king or queen in a monarchy.

One of the president's duties as chief of state is to serve as the nation's ceremonial head. Whether greeting a group of students on the White House lawn, meeting the head of a foreign nation, or laying a wreath on the Tomb of the Unknowns, the president is serving as a symbol of American government.

Because ceremonial duties are numerous and time-consuming, presidents assign many ceremonial tasks to the vice president. (The first President Bush, who served two terms as President Reagan's vice president, jokingly declared that he had attended more funerals than any other person in history.) But all presidents still devote some time to performing this role. They recognize that, when properly used, the president's role as chief of state can be a source of power and influence. However, the president is not merely the symbolic head of the nation; he is also the country's only nationally elected official, one who possesses broad constitutional and political authority.

Roles Related to Foreign Affairs

The Constitution makes the president the main authority in foreign relations, although as we saw in Chapter 7, it also assigns Congress important powers in this area. Article II gives the president several specific powers related to foreign affairs.

CHIEF DIPLOMAT   The Constitution empowers the president to appoint all U.S. ambassadors and other diplomats with the advice and consent of the Senate (Article II, Section 2) and gives him the sole authority to receive "Ambassadors and other public Ministers" from foreign nations.

A dramatic example of the president's authority as the nation's chief diplomat was President Nixon's trip to the People's Republic of China in 1972. Founded in 1949, the People's Republic had had no direct diplomatic contacts with the United States for almost a quarter of a century. Nixon's visit to China and his meetings with its political leaders changed that situation. After the trip, diplomatic, commercial, and cultural exchanges between the two countries were begun. It was not until 1979, however, that President Jimmy Carter formally recognized the People's Republic of China through his constitutional power to "receive Ambassadors and other public Ministers" from foreign nations.

The president's power to send and receive ambassadors is an important aspect of his authority in foreign affairs. By agreeing to exchange ambassadors with another nation, the president grants *diplomatic recognition* to that country. This action means that the two nations are prepared to deal directly with each other through normal and accepted channels of diplomacy. Following the breakup of the Soviet Union in 1989, for example, President Bush extended diplomatic recognition to many of the new nations in Eastern Europe and Central Asia that had been created as a result of that event. During President Clinton's first term in office, he agreed to exchange ambassadors with Vietnam—some twenty years after the two nations had been enemies in war. The United States still does not have diplomatic relations with some nations, such as Iran, North Korea, and Cuba.

TREATIES AND EXECUTIVE AGREEMENTS   Agreements between the United States and other nations can take several forms. The most important of these are treaties and executive agreements. A **treaty** is negotiated by representatives of the president. When negotiations are completed, the Constitution requires that the proposed treaty receive the advice and consent of two-thirds of the Senate before it can be signed by the president and go into effect.

The requirement that the Senate give its advice and consent to treaties represents a significant limitation on executive power. Although the Senate usually approves treaties that have been negotiated by the president, it sometimes takes other actions. The Senate can accept the treaty with stated reservations, or it can attach amendments to a treaty, in effect requiring that the president renegotiate the agreement. The Senate can also take no action on a proposed treaty, thereby preventing the agreement from taking effect.

The vast majority of treaties are approved by the Senate. Only about twenty treaties have been rejected by the Senate since the Constitution was ratified. The most famous example is the Treaty of Versailles, which ended World War I. President Wilson had personally taken part in the negotiation of the treaty, which was intended to settle the problems created by the war. Its most controversial provision called for the creation of a League of Nations. The treaty failed to win the required two-thirds vote of the Senate, largely because of opposition to U.S. membership in the League. The most recent rejection of a treaty occurred in late 1999, when the Senate voted against a comprehensive nuclear test ban treaty that had been strongly supported by President Clinton.

The Constitution says nothing about how treaties can be terminated, and the Supreme Court has never clearly resolved this problem. Throughout American history presidents have claimed that the right to terminate a treaty is an executive one that does not require the advice and consent of two-thirds of the Senate, and the Senate has generally allowed presidents to exercise this authority. In late 2001, for example, President Bush withdrew from a 1972 anti-ballistic missile treaty with the former Soviet Union.

Executive agreements, though they are not expressly mentioned in the Constitution, are often used by presidents. Executive agreements have been especially common since the end of World War II. They are, in fact, far more common than treaties. From 1746 to 1997, the United States adopted about 11,000 executive agreements, more than eleven times the number of treaties negotiated during the same period.

An **executive agreement** is an understanding between the president and the chief executive of a foreign nation that does not require the advice and consent of the Senate. In 1937 the Supreme Court clarified the status of executive agreements by holding that they have the same legal force as treaties. Both are the supreme law of the land under the supremacy clause of Article VI of the Constitution.[3]

The decision to use an executive agreement or a treaty is the president's alone. That choice will be based largely on the nature and relative importance of the agreement. Major commitments, such as membership in the United Nations (1945), turning over control of the Panama Canal to Panama (1978), or the 1988 treaty with the Soviet Union eliminating two classes of nuclear missiles, demand a treaty with Senate approval.

An agreement involving less important matters will usually take the form of an executive agreement; tariff reductions are an example. Major exceptions to this pattern include the 1940 Lend-Lease Agreement between President Franklin D. Roosevelt and Great Britain (in which the president signed over fifty destroyers in exchange for ninety-nine-year leases on certain British naval bases in the Caribbean), as well as the post–World War II executive agreements made at Yalta and Potsdam by Presidents Roosevelt and Truman. In January 1981, only days before leaving office, President Jimmy Carter signed an executive agreement with the Islamic Republic of Iran that provided for the release of fifty-two American hostages seized by Iran in 1979 and created a method for resolving financial claims between the two nations. (The executive agreement was subsequently approved by Carter's successor, President Reagan.) The Supreme Court upheld the legality of the agreement on the grounds that it was justified by existing laws and by a long history of presidential settlement of claims against foreign nations.[4]

A modern example of the use of an executive agreement as the basis for a major change in American international policy came in 1992 when the leaders of Canada, Mexico, and the United States signed the North American Free Trade Agreement (NAFTA). The agreement provides for the gradual elimination of tariffs on most goods sold in North America by the three countries.

There has been some criticism of the use of executive agreements when they commit the United States to important international policies. Many senators view executive agreements as a means of bypassing the Senate's constitutional right to give its advice and consent to international agreements. More important, they prevent the Senate from making amendments and reservations that would require new negotiations by the president.

FORMULATION OF FOREIGN POLICY The scope of foreign policy ranges from recognizing foreign governments and making treaties and agreements with them to sending military forces into combat situations. Presidents are continually called upon to make important foreign-policy decisions. In performing this task the president can draw upon information gathered by American embassies and consulates overseas, the Departments of State and Defense, White House Staff agencies (the National Security Council), the Central Intelligence Agency, and other executive agencies that are concerned with foreign affairs. (See Chapter 9 for a fuller discussion of this subject.)

The secretary of state is the president's link with the Department of State, but the role of the secretary varies from one administration to another. Some presidents have given the secretary of state broad authority to conduct foreign policy. Others have downgraded the secretary's role and relied instead on close advisers in the White House, especially the national security adviser, who is the executive head of the National Security Council.

During the Nixon administration the president's national security adviser, Henry Kissinger, not only advised him on international issues but also was given broad authority to conduct foreign policy. President Reagan also gave his White House advisers the power to make policy decisions. But this arrangement led to a major scandal involving a secret attempt by members of the White House staff to sell arms to Iran and use the proceeds to support opponents of the leftist government that was in power in Nicaragua at the time. In George W. Bush's administration both his secretary of state, Colin Powell, and his national security adviser, Condoleezza Rice, have played important roles in the formulation and execution of American foreign policy.

Modern presidents have increasingly become involved in the actual conduct of foreign policy by negotiating with the heads of foreign governments. The ease of international communication and travel has contributed to the growth of this so-called "personal diplomacy", especially in the Middle East. President Carter brought the leaders of Egypt and Israel together and helped produce a settlement of the major differences between these nations. Through his two terms in office

President Clinton attempted to broker a peace agreement between the leaders of Israel and the Palestinian Liberation Organization. Unlike President Carter, however, his attempts ended in failure.

WORLD LEADER Some observers view the president as not only the chief diplomat of the United States but also the leader of the democratic world. This role may be looked upon as an extension of the president's constitutional powers as chief of state, commander-in-chief, and chief diplomat. During the almost half century of the cold war, American presidents led the free world against the Soviet Union and its communist allies. Since the September 11 attack on the United States President Bush has assumed the role of world leader in the war against international terrorism. Today no other nation's chief executive can claim to speak with the same authority as the president of the United States.

Commander-in-Chief

According to Article II, Section 2, of the Constitution, "The President shall be Commander in Chief of the Army and Navy of the United States, and of the Militia of the several States, when called into the actual service of the United States." The president thus has final responsibility for the conduct of American military policy. Congress, however, shares with the president the responsibility for determining the nature of that policy. It does so, for example, through its power to declare war and to appropriate money for military purposes.

The president appoints military officers and plans policy with the secretary of state, the secretary of defense, the National Security Council, and other foreign and military policy advisers. The day-to-day operations of the armed forces are left to the secretary of defense, the service secretaries in the Defense Department, and the Joint Chiefs of Staff (the appointed heads of each of the military services).

The authority of the president and the secretary of defense over the top officers of the Army and Navy guarantees civilian control of the military. A dramatic example of the principle of civilian control occurred in April 1951, during the Korean War, when President Truman fired General Douglas MacArthur, the commanding officer of the American and Allied forces in Korea. MacArthur was popular in the United States, but his public statements about military policy in Korea were at odds with presidential strategy, and the president dismissed him.

Article I, Section 8, of the Constitution gives Congress the power to declare war, and Congress has exercised this power on only five different occasions (the War of 1812, the Mexican War, the Spanish American War, and World Wars I and II). But on more than 200 occasions the president has taken military action without an official declaration of war by Congress. In about one-third of those situations, Congress specifically authorized the president's action by either appropriating funds to support the military action or passing resolutions backing the conduct of the chief executive. But in all the other situations, the president has taken military action without a statement of congressional support. Modern examples include President Reagan's invasion of the Caribbean island of Grenada in 1983 and his bombing of Libya in 1986, the first President Bush's invasion of Panama in 1989, and President Clinton's decisions to send military personnel to Haiti in 1994 and Bosnia in 1995 and to bomb Serbia in 1999.

Many of the military actions undertaken by presidents were of short duration and involved the protection of American citizens and their property. But a

United States soldiers from the 5th Corps gather for a briefing at an air base in Germany prior to leaving for Kuwait, November 2002.

number of major conflicts were fought without a declaration of war, including the American Civil War, the war in Korea during the early 1950s, and the war in Vietnam during the 1960s and early 1970s. In each of those situations the president claimed that he had a constitutional right as commander-in-chief to commit American military forces to combat. (Although Congress never formally declared war on Vietnam, in 1964 it did adopt a resolution that authorized the president to use military force in southeast Asia.)

A major commitment of military personnel by an American president came in August 1990, when the first President Bush placed a large American military force in the Middle East to protect Saudi Arabia from a threatened invasion by Iraq. This followed Iraq's invasion and occupation of Kuwait. By the end of 1990, half a million troops from the United States and its allies had been assembled in the area, with the capability to mount an offensive against Iraq. The United Nations approved the use of force against Iraq beginning any time after January 15, 1991, if Iraq did not voluntarily withdraw its forces from Kuwait.

President Bush maintained that as commander-in-chief, and with the backing of the United Nations, he had the legal authority to commit the nation's military forces to a war with Iraq without the consent of Congress. But any potential constitutional conflict between the president and Congress was avoided when both houses of the legislature, in a divided vote (52 to 47 in the Senate), authorized the chief executive to wage war on Iraq. This step, although not a formal declaration of war, was the equivalent of such an action. The war began on January 16, 1991, with the president's authorization of a massive air attack on military targets in Iraq. This was quickly followed by the authorization of ground forces, which liberated Kuwait, destroyed a significant portion of the Iraqi army, and soon brought an end to the war.

Following the September 11 attack on the United States, President Bush, acting as commander-in-chief, sent military personnel and equipment to Afghanistan in the fall of 2001 to destroy the Taliban government of that nation and the Al Qaeda terrorists that it allowed to operate there. The president's actions had received the prior approval of Congress (though it could be contended that he needed no such authority since the nation had been attacked). In a joint resolution adopted on September 14, 2001, the Congress declared in part:

> [T]he President is authorized to use all necessary and appropriate force against those nations, organizations, or persons he determines planned, authorized, committed, or aided the terrorist attacks that occurred on September 11, 2001, or harbored such organizations or persons, in order to prevent any future acts of international terrorism against the United States by such nations, organizations or persons.

Another joint resolution was adopted by Congress in the fall of 2002 that gave President Bush the authority to conduct a war against the Middle Eastern nation of Iraq. This step was taken by Congress following the unanimous approval of the United Nations Security Council to take action against Iraq if Saddam Hussein did not allow UN inspectors to enter the country and determine whether it had destroyed all of its weapons of mass destruction. Following these steps a military build-up of U.S. and allied forces took place in the Middle East. At the same time UN inspectors were permitted to enter Iraq to determine if that nation did, in fact, possess nuclear, biological, or chemical weapons.

Inspectors were allowed to enter Iraq but their numbers were limited and the Iraqi government placed restrictions on their movement within the nation. After three months of unsuccessful inspections, President Bush attempted to obtain a second UN resolution authorizing the use of military force against Iraq. However, French, German, and Russian opposition made it impossible to obtain passage of such a resolution.

On March 19, 2003, President Bush with the backing of more than thirty nations began military action against Iraq. In less than three months the American and British military destroyed the Iraqi army and brought to an end the more than thirty year dictatorship of Saddam Hussein.

Some critics argue that the president lacks the authority to take military action without a formal declaration of war by Congress. The United States Supreme Court has never clearly decided this question. Several attempts were made during the Vietnam War to obtain a judicial answer to the question, but the Supreme Court refused to hear the cases in which the issue was raised. As we shall see later in the chapter, in 1973 Congress adopted the War Powers Resolution, which attempted to set limits on the president's ability to conduct military operations without its approval.

Chief Administrator

Article II, Section 2, of the Constitution gives the president the right to make appointments to the executive branch of government with the advice and consent of the Senate.[5] In addition, his executive powers have been interpreted by the

CLOSE-UP

THE USA PATRIOTS ACT OF 2001

In October 2001, in response to the September 11 terrorist attack on the United States, the Congress enacted the USA Patriots Act of 2001. This lengthy statute grants broad new powers to the executive branch of government to combat domestic and international terrorism. Some of its provisions raise important issues of civil liberties that will be tested in the federal courts and ultimately decided by the U.S. Supreme Court. The major features of the law deal with three subjects: surveillance, immigration, and money laundering.

The surveillance provisions cover a variety of situations. Information gained by federal grand juries can be given to law enforcement, immigration, and intelligence agencies. Secret government searches can be conducted and notice given to the owner after a reasonable period of time. The government is empowered to tap telephones, retrieve voice mail, track Web surfing, and trace e-mail of suspected terrorists with reduced judicial oversight, and to monitor computer trespasses on Web service providers such as AOL. These last provisions automatically expire on December 31, 2005 unless Congress reenacts them.

The law permits the government to detain aliens suspected of terrorism for up to seven days without a hearing and to detain aliens who have been shown to be a danger to national security. Further, the law permits the deportation of aliens who engage in fund-raising for terrorist groups.

The money laundering sections of the law require foreign banks under some circumstances to reveal the names of their customers and transactions and American banks to monitor some private accounts of aliens.

Supreme Court as including a broad, exclusive right to remove executive officers of the federal government.[6] These powers guarantee that a president can maintain in high executive positions only individuals who are willing to carry out the policies of his administration. Thus, in December 2002, President Bush dismissed both his secretary of the treasury and director of the National Economic Council.

As chief administrator of the executive branch, the president is responsible for managing the wide variety of departments and agencies that interpret and carry out legislation passed by Congress. This authority looks simple on paper, but in reality it is an extremely difficult one for the nation's chief executive. The president is in office for a few years, but the agencies are staffed by career civil servants whose primary loyalty is to their organization and its programs. Conflict, therefore, is almost inevitable, and although the president is responsible for the activities of the executive branch, he is rarely in full control of them.

Most modern presidents have complained about the difficulty of serving as the nation's chief administrator. Indeed, some people believe it is impossible for one person to handle this job. The problem is mainly one of numbers; the executive branch has almost 2.6 million civilian employees. The president cannot control all the activities of this huge bureaucracy, nor can he know very much about its day-to-day functioning. (The federal bureaucracy will be discussed in more detail in Chapter 9.)

Because of these limitations, the president's appointments to high-level positions within the executive branch are extremely important: "The appointment of the right people as cabinet [and subcabinet] members is fundamental to management control." Appointments should not be made in order to represent the various groups that have supported the president. Rather, it is important to select administrative officials who are "philosophically in tune with the President. . . . Making the right appointments at the outset of a new government is one of the keys for a President in getting a managerial grip on the office."[7] Often, however,

President Bush meets with the prime ministers of Portugal, Great Britain, and Spain in the Azores on March 16, 2003. The meeting was held to discuss the crisis in Iraq.

presidents do not look primarily to philosophy and instead appoint friends, political associates, and individuals who have the backing of important groups that have supported the president.

Chief Legislator

The president's role as chief legislator has developed out of the constitutional power to sign or veto legislation (Article I, Section 7) and the power to advise Congress on the State of the Union (Article II, Section 3). It can also be traced to the fact that the president is the only government official who is elected by the nation as a whole. The 535 members of Congress represent people in different geographic areas, some covering no more than a few square miles. The president, by contrast, represents the entire country. Many presidents use this fact to gain public support for their legislative programs. Through television speeches and press conferences, presidents attempt to influence public opinion in the hope that popular support for their policies will persuade senators and representatives to back them.

The president has access to all the information gathered by the executive branch and can use that knowledge in proposing policies for the nation. Thus, part of the president's job is to design a legislative program. Indeed, when presidents do not propose legislative programs dealing with major public issues, many people complain that they have failed to carry out their duties as president. This is in sharp contrast to the view that prevailed in the nineteenth century, when the separation of powers was seen in more absolute terms, and presidents did not play a major role in setting the legislative agenda for Congress.

Modern presidents present their legislative programs through public speeches and written communications. The three main presidential communications concerned with legislative matters are the State of the Union address, which is called for by the Constitution and consists of a general statement of policy that for almost a century has usually been delivered in person to a joint session of Congress; the National Budget message, in which the president describes the condition of the economy, his domestic-policy goals, and the major expenditures required in the coming year; and the Annual Economic Report (required under the Employment Act of 1946), in which the president discusses current economic trends and problems affecting the American economy. The last two messages are usually delivered in the form of written statements sent to Congress. In addition to these messages, presidents send many written communications to Congress. These state the president's major concerns and are often followed by detailed legislative proposals prepared by legal experts on the president's staff.

Presidents naturally hope to have Congress approve their legislative agenda. They realize, however, that merely announcing a program and having bills introduced in the legislature will not accomplish their goals. The president can usually rely on a core of supporters in Congress drawn largely from his own political party. But creating a legislative majority requires convincing doubtful members of his party and reaching out to potential backers in the opposition party.

Presidents use a number of methods to create the needed majority in both houses of Congress. They have traditionally used promises of *patronage*—such as judicial appointments, federal construction projects, campaign support, and favors of various kinds. In addition, presidents since John F. Kennedy have created a staff position in the White House whose purpose is to serve as a liaison with Congress and to oversee the chief executive's legislative program.

Informal contacts with legislators are another means of gaining support for the president's policies. Private meetings, parties, and telephone calls have been used successfully by some presidents; Lyndon Johnson and Ronald Reagan were especially good at using these techniques. Other presidents, including Richard Nixon and Jimmy Carter, lacked the personal and political skills to employ these techniques successfully.

A president who is faced with opposition in Congress can go over the heads of the legislators and speak directly to the American people. By means of a televised speech, the president can attempt to persuade individuals and interest groups to put pressure on their legislators to vote for his policies.[8]

The separation-of-powers system was intended to create conflict between the executive and legislative branches of government. Presidents must confront this reality in attempting to have their domestic policies adopted. (Presidents have generally been more successful in achieving their foreign-policy objectives.) Normally presidents achieve their greatest legislative success during their first years in office. The president's popularity is at its peak in those years, and Congress often finds it difficult to oppose him.

In sum, no president can be a successful legislative leader unless he is a successful politician. He cannot get his programs through Congress without using all his political skills. This means that the president and his major advisers in the executive branch must spend a great deal of time persuading legislators, not commanding them. Over the course of American history, the balance of power between the president and Congress has alternated between the two elected branches of the government.

THE VETO POWER   In Article I, Section 7, the Constitution assigns the president a "qualified negative" over acts of Congress in the form of the **veto** power. When a bill is passed by Congress, it is sent to the president for signature. If it is signed, the bill becomes law. If the president does not approve of a particular bill, the Constitution permits him to take one of the following steps:

1. Keep a bill ten days and not act on it. After ten days, provided that Congress remains in session, an unsigned bill becomes law. This passive form of disapproval is rarely used, however.
2. Veto a bill by sending it back to Congress without signature. The unsigned bill is accompanied by a statement of the president's objections to it. A veto can be overridden by a two-thirds vote of both houses of Congress, but because such a majority is hard to obtain, overrides of presidential vetoes are infrequent. (See Table 8.1.)
3. Use the so-called **pocket veto.** If the president does not act on a bill sent to him within ten days of the adjournment of Congress, the proposal dies. By figuratively "putting the bill in his pocket," the president vetoes the measure without giving Congress an opportunity to override the veto. Pocket vetoes occur fairly frequently because many bills are passed in the days just before Congress adjourns.

In addition to the veto power almost all state governors have the right to use a **line item veto.** The line item veto allows a chief executive to veto specific provisions of an appropriations or tax bill while accepting the remaining provisions of the law. American presidents have no such authority. They must choose between accepting or rejecting the entire proposal. The latter choice would mean

TABLE 8.1

CONGRESSIONAL BILLS VETOED, 1913–2003

Period	President	Total	Vetoes Sustained	Bills Passed over Veto
1913–1921	Wilson	44	38	6
1921–1923	Harding	6	6	0
1923–1929	Coolidge	50	46	4
1929–1933	Hoover	37	34	3
1933–1945	F. Roosevelt	635	626	9
1945–1953	Truman	250	238	12
1953–1961	Eisenhower	181	179	2
1961–1963	Kennedy	21	21	0
1963–1969	Johnson	30	30	0
1969–1974[a]	Nixon	42	36	6
1974–1977	Ford	72	60	12
1977–1981	Carter	31	29	2
1981–1989	Reagan	78	69	9
1989–1993	G.H.W. Bush	46	45	1
1993–2001	Clinton	36	35	1
2001–2005	G.W. Bush	0	-	-

[a]Nixon resignation effective August 8, 1974.
Source: U.S. Bureau of the Census, *Statistical Abstract of the United States, 1999,* 119th ed. (Washington, DC: Government Printing Office, 1999), Table 475, p. 294. Updated to include 2001–2005.

shutting down parts of the government, and presidents have been unwilling to take this step. Thus, presidents sign money and tax bills even though they may contain provisions that are objectionable to them.

Many presidents have asked Congress to grant them the power to use a line item veto. Most such requests were not even considered by Congress, since the line item veto would expand the power of the president and reduce that of the legislative branch. But in 1996 a Republican Congress passed legislation that provided for a presidential line item veto. Republicans had included support for this idea in their 1994 election campaigns, expecting that it would help reduce government spending and assuming that it would be exercised by Republican presidents. However, President Clinton, who signed the legislation, was reelected to the presidency in 1996. Within a few months he exercised the line item veto on a number of spending provisions in appropriations bills.

But the president's line item veto power was to have a very short history. It was soon challenged in the federal courts, and the Supreme Court found the legislation unconstitutional. The Court contended that the Constitution establishes the president's veto power and that Congress cannot alter this system through the exercise of its ordinary legislative power.[9]

THE PARDON POWER Article II, Section 2, of the Constitution grants the president "the Power to grant Reprieves and Pardons for Offences against the United States, except in Cases of Impeachment." The pardon power is not subject to congressional control. This authority is derived from a power long held by British monarchs: the right to exercise mercy. It is held by all state governors as well as by the president, and also includes the authority to issue amnesty to groups. (The power to issue amnesty was exercised by President Jimmy Carter on behalf of individuals who had evaded the draft during the Vietnam War.)

Most presidential uses of the pardon power cause little or no controversy. Pardons are frequently given to aged or ill federal prisoners during the holiday season at the end of the year. But pardons are occasionally used in situations that create much political controversy. Three examples occurred in the recent past. In the fall of 1974, President Ford issued an unconditional pardon to Richard Nixon, who had only recently resigned as president. Near the end of his term in office, the first President Bush issued pardons to six former officials in President Reagan's administration who had been implicated in the Iran–Contra scandal that occurred during Reagan's second term. In September 1999 President Clinton issued pardons to fourteen imprisoned Puerto Rican nationalists who had been convicted of crimes such as armed robbery and weapons possession. Controversy also surrounded the pardons issued in the closing weeks of his presidency, which included a convicted major drug dealer and an alleged financial swindler who had fled the United States to avoid prosecution. (Note that the pardon power can be used by a president before an individual is tried and convicted of a crime. President Nixon had not been charged with any crime when President Ford issued his pardon. And the first President Bush pardoned former Secretary of Defense Caspar Weinberger after he had been indicted but before he had been tried for his alleged criminal acts.)

Party Leader

The candidate who wins his or her party's presidential nomination is called upon to act as the party's main spokesperson. Upon taking office, the winning candidate will be the party's national leader. This role is not mentioned in the Constitution, but it is a source of real political power for the president.

As party leader, the president is expected to appear at party fund-raising events, speak at party meetings and rallies, and try to maintain party unity. In the role of party leader, he is expected to appoint party members to important diplomatic, administrative, and judicial positions. He is often asked to campaign for his party's candidates for office. During a presidential election year, a popular presidential candidate can attract added support for national, state, and local party candidates and thus help some of them win election. In off-year elections, however, presidents are rarely able to transfer their popularity to their party's candidates, although President Bush was able to use his popularity in the November 2002 elections to increase the number of Republicans in both houses of Congress.

The president's control over his party stems from the fact that the party needs him to present its platform to the nation, to raise funds, to get its members elected or appointed, and to push its bills through Congress. The president's influence on Congress is based in part on his role as party leader. In this role, he uses the techniques of persuasion and patronage to gain congressional support. For example, in return for support of his program, the president can give his backing to a local project that a senator or a representative is anxious to obtain.

It should be noted, however, that party members often hold conflicting views that cannot always be changed by the president. The decentralized and varied nature of American parties tends to produce party members who will disagree with some aspects of the president's program. Even the most strenuous efforts by the president may not be enough to persuade such a legislator to change his or her mind.

National Opinion Leader

The president's impact on public opinion depends to a great extent on his skill in communicating with the American public. His almost unlimited access to the media—to the press and television—gives him great potential influence. But he

President John F. Kennedy at a press conference, April 3, 1963. Kennedy was a master of such meetings and used them to strengthen his position as national-opinion leader.

must use the media carefully. Too much exposure can be harmful to the president's image and may even reduce his influence. But if he uses the media wisely and comes across as an effective leader, he can work wonders. As President Wilson put it, "[The president's] is the only national voice in affairs. Let him once win the admiration and confidence of the country, and no other single force can withstand him, no combination of forces will easily overpower him. His position takes the imagination of the country."[10]

One of the earliest channels used by the president to communicate directly with the public was the White House press conference. President Theodore Roosevelt is said to have invented this technique when he invited reporters to the White House and discussed the issues of the day while having his morning shave. President Wilson made the press conference more formal by scheduling weekly meetings with reporters. Since Wilson's time, the number of Washington press correspondents has increased dramatically. With the advent of radio and, later, television, the press conference became a nationwide broadcast, with millions of Americans able to listen to or view its live coverage.

Presidents have used the press conference with varying frequency. President Kennedy used it often; President Nixon, by contrast, tried to avoid meeting with reporters and abandoned the use of press conferences during his last troubled years in office. Similarly, President Clinton made limited use of press conferences in his last years as president in the wake of the scandal surrounding his affair with White House intern Monica Lewinsky.

The mass media have also been used to gain public support for the president's actions. In his famous "fireside chats" during the Great Depression of the 1930s, President Franklin D. Roosevelt tried to give hope and confidence to radio listeners. Today television gives the president even greater ability to reach the public. Among recent presidents, Reagan and Clinton were perhaps the most skillful in using TV to communicate to the American people about their political programs. Indeed, Reagan was often referred to as "the great communicator." Reagan's background as a motion picture and television actor enabled him to use this medium very effectively. Although he often performed poorly at press conferences, his televised speeches were remarkable for their ability to present both his ideas and his personality to the American public. Clinton's personal magnetism, on the other hand, made him a very effective campaigner both in person and on television.

On other occasions, presidents have been less successful in their attempts to use television. For example, during the Vietnam War, President Johnson used television in his efforts to persuade Americans that U.S. military activity in Vietnam was justified. Similarly, President Nixon used television to defend his actions in relation to the Watergate affair. Both presidents failed in those attempts to sway public opinion.

To sum up, in the role of national opinion leader, the president has the ability to reach many millions of Americans through radio and television. Effective use of the media is essential to strong leadership. But if the president seeks to "sell" an unpopular position, even the most skillful use of the mass media will not necessarily bring success.

Manager of the Economy

Ever since passage of the Employment Act of 1946, the president has been formally responsible for managing the economy, but even before that time he was expected to keep it running smoothly and prevent economic downturns. Today fiscal policy, inflation, unemployment, the stability of the dollar, foreign trade, and

President Franklin D. Roosevelt delivering one of his famous "fireside chats" to the nation. Roosevelt was the first president to use radio as an effective method of communicating his policies to the American public.

other economic matters are among the president's major concerns, and many people judge him primarily by how well he can cope with these issues.

Managing the economy is not an easy task. Most economic decisions are made by private individuals and companies, and the president cannot simply tell them what to do. Within the government, some departments are more responsive to the president's directives than others. As we shall see in Chapter 9, an important set of agencies—the independent regulatory commissions—are not subject to the president's control. One such agency, the Federal Reserve Board, has the primary responsibility for determining monetary policy (for example, raising or lowering interest rates). In short, the president's economic powers do not match the economic responsibilities.

Economic conditions can make or break a president. Whenever the economy slows down, the president is under pressure from business, unions, farmers, and the general public to take action. Failure to handle an economic recession adequately can sharply reduce a president's popularity and lead to losses for his party's candidates in the next election. President Bush's defeat in 1992 was caused in large part by the economic recession that occurred while he was in office. Bush was defeated despite the great popularity he had gained as a result of his successful conduct of the Persian Gulf War early in his administration. In contrast, prosperity generally leads to personal and electoral success both for the president and for his party. President Clinton's reelection in 1996 can be attributed largely to the good economic conditions of that year: low inflation and unemployment, a booming stock market, and general economic prosperity.

LIMITS ON THE PRESIDENT'S POWERS

The powers granted to the president by the Constitution have served as the basis for the development of the modern presidency. In the twentieth century, especially since the 1930s, the office of the president steadily gained influence in both domestic and international matters. The Vietnam War, however, demonstrated to the American public the great dangers that come with excessive and unrestrained authority.

The framers of the Constitution understood that uncontrolled political power poses a threat both to individual liberties and to a stable political order. Thus, although they created a strong, independent president, the framers never intended that authority to be unlimited. In this section we review the most important limitations on the president's powers.

Judicial Review

The judicial branch of the government is one source of control over the president. The United States Supreme Court has the right to exercise judicial review over all presidential actions. The Court has been reluctant to declare any president's wartime actions illegal, however. During this nation's three largest wars—the Civil War and the two world wars—the Supreme Court did not declare any step taken by the president unconstitutional. Moreover, it has never been willing to decide on the constitutionality of undeclared wars such as the Korean and Vietnam conflicts, which were based in large part on the president's power as commander-in-chief.

Nevertheless, in several significant cases the Supreme Court has curbed presidential authority. Soon after the end of both the Civil War and World War II, the Supreme Court voided a wartime policy of the president.[11] In 1952 the Court ruled against President Harry Truman's seizure of the nation's steel industry during a labor-management dispute that occurred while the United States was involved in the Korean War. By a 6-to-3 vote, the Court held that Truman had exceeded his powers under Article II of the Constitution, and he was ordered to return the steel mills to their owners.[12]

President Nixon was dealt several setbacks by the Supreme Court. His attempt to prevent the publication by major newspapers of a government study of the Vietnam War—the *Pentagon Papers*—was rejected by the Court.[13] In 1974, during the Watergate scandal, the Supreme Court ordered Nixon to turn over to the courts tape recordings of conversations between him and his assistants that were relevant to criminal trials that were pending against several of his major advisers. The Court rejected Nixon's claim that the tapes were privileged executive materials.[14] This decision led directly to the resignation of the president in August 1974. President Clinton was handed a major defeat in 1997, when the Supreme Court unanimously held that he could be sued for sexual harassment while serving as president.[15]

The War Powers Resolution

Throughout most of American history Congress has limited the president in the domestic sphere while giving him very broad freedom to act in foreign and military matters. This surrender of power in foreign affairs allowed Presidents Kennedy, Johnson, and Nixon to wage a large-scale war in Southeast Asia. Congressional opposition to the conflict grew slowly, and only in the early 1970s did it gain sufficient strength to gain passage of provisions in defense appropriations bills that denied the president the right to use federal money to conduct war in Laos and Cambodia.

The War Powers Resolution of 1973 was the most significant piece of legislation passed in that period. The law sought to regulate the future use of American

CLOSE-UP

THE WATERGATE SCANDAL

The only resignation of a president in American history occurred as a result of the Watergate scandal of the early 1970s. Unlike most political scandals, however, Watergate did not involve money. It was about power—specifically, about making sure President Richard Nixon would win reelection in 1972. Ironically, the 1972 election was a landslide victory for Nixon; there never was any real chance that his opponent, George McGovern, would win.

The scandal began with an unsuccessful burglary. On June 17, 1972, five men were caught going through files in the Democratic National Committee's headquarters in the Watergate Hotel in Washington, DC. One of them, James W. McCord, Jr., was the security director of the Committee to Re-Elect the President. They were indicted on charges of burglary and pleaded guilty, but in a letter to the judge, McCord claimed that the defendants had been pressured to make the guilty plea and that others were involved in the affair.

In the spring of 1973 the Senate formed a committee to investigate the scandal, and on June 25 John Dean, who had been fired from his position as President Nixon's lawyer, testified that the Watergate break-in was part of a program of political espionage that involved the president. Shortly afterward a presidential aide disclosed that conversations in the Oval Office had been tape-recorded. The president refused to release the tapes, but the Senate Watergate Committee obtained subpoenas for several of the taped conversations.

On October 20, 1973, in an episode known as the Saturday Night Massacre, the special Watergate prosecutor, Archibald Cox, was fired by the acting attorney general. (The attorney general and the deputy attorney general had both refused to fire Cox and had resigned.) President Nixon appointed a new special prosecutor, Leon Jaworski. Jaworski continued to request that the president turn over the tapes, but he refused on the ground that the tapes were protected by a constitutional privilege granted to the nation's chief executive.

On March 1, 1974, seven former presidential aides were indicted for conspiring to cover up the Watergate affair, and President Nixon was named as an unindicted co-conspirator. On May 9 the House Judiciary Committee began impeachment proceedings, and on July 24 the Supreme Court ruled, in *United States v. Nixon,* that the president must turn over the subpoenaed tapes to the special prosecutor. The House Judiciary Committee then approved three articles of impeachment against the president.

On August 5 the president released transcripts of three conversations he had had with an aide just after the Watergate break-in. The tapes revealed that Nixon had ordered a halt to the FBI's investigation of the break-in to prevent discovery that his reelection committee was involved. (There was no proof that Nixon had been involved in planning the burglary.) As demands for his removal increased, Nixon announced that he would resign. On August 9, 1974, President Nixon resigned and Vice President Gerald Ford was sworn in as president.

---

military forces by the president when war has not been declared by Congress. It attempted to curb the ability of the president to wage war on the basis of his power as commander-in-chief of the armed forces and his authority to conduct foreign affairs.

The War Powers Resolution requires the president to consult with Congress before American troops are introduced into hostile situations and to continue this consultation as long as they are engaged in such situations. But the resolution goes beyond this requirement and tries to establish specific controls on the president's use of American military forces. In the absence of a declaration of war by Congress, the president must send a written report to Congress within forty-eight hours after American troops have been sent into threatened or actual war situations. Within sixty days after the report has been submitted, the president must end the use of American armed forces unless Congress declares war or approves the military action. Congress can extend this period for an additional thirty days if necessary for the safe withdrawal of the troops. The law also provides that Congress can halt the use of the troops before the end of the sixty-day period by adopting a concurrent resolution.

The provisions of the War Powers Resolution have come into play on a number of occasions since the law was enacted. All presidents who have held office since the adoption of the resolution have sent American military forces into combat or near-combat situations or have used them on rescue missions. On these occasions, the president and Congress have responded in different ways to the requirements of the resolution, as can be seen in the following examples:

- Early in 1980 President Carter informed Congress of the failed attempt to rescue the fifty-two American hostages being held in Iran. He made no attempt at prior consultation, nor did he inform the legislature of his action until several days after the mission had been aborted.

- American Marines were sent into Lebanon in the fall of 1983 to serve as a peacekeeping force. In September 1983 Congress invoked the War Powers Resolution and set an eighteen-month timetable for their withdrawal. However, President Reagan removed the Marines before the expiration of the time set by Congress.

- The invasion of Grenada by American troops on October 25, 1983 was carried out without prior consultation with Congress. Legislative leaders were not informed of the military action until two hours after Reagan had ordered the landing. The fighting ended quickly, and American forces were withdrawn before the sixty-day period available to the president had expired. President Reagan maintained that the provisions of the War Powers Resolution did not apply to this situation. Similarly, Reagan informed Congress of his bombing of Libya while the planes were airborne.

- The most extensive deployment of American military power since the Vietnam War came in the summer of 1990, when President Bush sent some 150,000 American military personnel, together with ships, planes, and tanks, to Saudi Arabia and the Persian Gulf to defend those areas from a possible attack by Iraq. The president contended that the American troops had been placed in the region for defensive purposes only and that there were no existing hostilities and no threat of "imminent" hostilities. Bush therefore contended that the War Powers Resolution did not apply. The president did notify congressional leaders on the day troops were dispatched to the Persian Gulf area and later held meetings with other members of Congress. But he maintained that these steps were taken because he believed in consulting with Congress, not because he was under any legal obligation to do so. Congress did eventually vote to approve the military action to remove the Iraqi invaders from Kuwait. But this occurred only days before the attack began and after American and allied military forces in the area had been increased to half a million men and women.

- In 1995 President Clinton sent American troops to Bosnia with the goal of separating the warring Serbian and Bosnian forces and preparing the way for free elections in the area. And during the summer of 1999 President Clinton began an extensive bombing campaign against Serbia. The provisions of the War Powers Resolution were not raised by the president or Congress in either instance.

Critics have argued that the War Powers Resolution represents an unwise interference with the president's freedom to act in a crisis and an unconstitutional limitation on his role as commander-in-chief of the armed forces. (Presidents since 1973 have maintained that the central provisions of the law are unconstitutional.) During outbreaks of hostility, the president would be stripped of his constitutional authority as commander-in-chief unless Congress approved the continued use of American military power.[16]

One observer summarized the overall effect of the War Powers Resolution as follows: "Since 1973, presidents of both parties have acted in ways that effectively nullify the resolution. . . . What the War Powers Resolution has achieved, however, is a bit more interbranch consultation over the president's deployment of troops abroad."[17]

The Budget and Impoundment Control Act

Some modern presidents have claimed the authority to refuse to spend money that has been appropriated by Congress, a power known as *impoundment*. Although the Constitution does not actually grant the president this authority, since the end of World War II several presidents have impounded funds on the basis of their power as chief executive. During the early 1970s, President Nixon used the power of impoundment as a form of veto, claiming that it was necessary to keep down the rate of inflation. Congress objected strongly, arguing that appropriations are laws and that the president is required to put them into effect.

In 1974 Congress passed the Budget and Impoundment Control Act, which was designed to limit this executive practice. The law provides that a president may delay a spending program temporarily unless either house of Congress passes a resolution forbidding that action. If the president wants to cancel a spending program permanently, he must receive the consent of both the House and the Senate within forty-five days. If either house refuses its consent, the president must release the money at the end of the forty-five-day period.

The Bureaucracy

Although this may not have been intended by the nation's founders, the executive bureaucracy also places limits on presidential power. The built-in bureaucratic resistance to change, which can be seen in any large organization, frequently frustrates a president's goals and policies. President Dwight D. Eisenhower, for example, came to the presidency after a long military career, including many years as a general. He had become accustomed to giving orders and having them carried out. Eisenhower discovered that being president was different. He issued orders and, he sadly commented, "Nothing happened."

Earlier it was stated that the departments and agencies of the executive branch are not always responsive to the president. This has become a major problem for presidents as the federal bureaucracy has grown. This does not mean, however, that the bureaucracy is constantly opposed to the president. Bureaucrats are reasonable people; like the president, they believe their actions are in the best interests of the nation. Thus, even though the bureaucracy and the president may define the national interest differently, both definitions may be reasonable. A president who understands this has a better chance of winning the cooperation of officials in the executive branch.[18]

The Oval Office of the president, the White House, Washington, DC.

The Media

The news media—newspapers, magazines, radio, and television—generally serve as a restraint on the power of government. They perform this function by exposing and publicizing facts about the operation of the political system. The authors of the Constitution understood the importance of a free press as a control on government. The First Amendment provides a specific guarantee of freedom of the press to protect it against any attempt by government to regulate and control its operations.

The president and the executive branch are continually under examination by the news media. The information published by the media ranges from the trivial to significant facts about major policies and wrongdoing in government. The Watergate scandal of the early 1970s showed how the media could help unearth and publicize facts about illegal conduct in the executive branch—including the presidential office. During 1986 and 1987, the media played an important role in publicizing President Reagan's failed policy of selling arms to Iran and then using the anticipated profits to aid the Nicaraguan rebels. The media also played a significant role in publicizing the facts surrounding the Monica Lewinsky scandal that engulfed President Clinton in 1998.

Public Opinion

A final check on the president's power is an informed, alert public. A president who lacks public support may refrain from unwise or unpopular policies. Some presidents have tried to ignore public opinion, but with little success.

Studies of public attitudes toward the president have found that presidents are blamed for problems that are beyond their control, whereas a good performance may go unrecognized. Also, public approval of the president tends to decline throughout his years in office. There is a "honeymoon" during the first months in office, but then the opposition party and other groups begin criticizing the president's actions and proposing alternative policies. Thus, the president's ability to implement his program normally decreases over time.

The president is also limited by the public's *issue attention cycle*—the fact that the public's attention rarely stays focused on any one issue for very long.[19] More difficult for the president are the times when he is forced to act on an issue on which the public is sharply divided. Whatever he does, he is bound to make enemies; but even when he does not act, he is likely to be criticized by some disappointed supporters.

THE PERSONAL DIMENSION

We have seen that the powers of the presidency are limited not only by the checks and balances contained in the Constitution but also by such factors as judicial review and public opinion. What we have not discussed, however, is the role of the president's character and beliefs and their effect on his conduct in office. The powers of the presidency are not the only factors that determine the effectiveness of any president.

The nation's founders created the presidency as a one-person office, and despite the expansion of the executive branch in the twentieth century, in effect, it remains just that. Since George Washington's inauguration in 1789, forty-two men have served as president of the United States. Each has brought a unique set of beliefs, motivations, and political skills to the office, as well as his own distinct character. These qualities have had important and far-reaching effects on how each man has approached his duties as president and how he has used the power of the office.

Beliefs, Motivations, Skills

One way to analyze American presidents is to divide them into two groups: weak and strong. "Weak" presidents are those who consciously limit their authority; "strong" ones are those who extend their power as far as they feel is necessary, limited only by what the system of checks and balances will permit. Note that weak and strong are relative terms, not absolute ones—some presidents are stronger (or weaker) than others.

The argument for limited presidential power was best stated by President William Howard Taft:

> The true view of the Executive function is, as I conceive it, that the President can exercise no power which cannot be fairly and reasonably traced to some specific grant of power or justly implied and included within such express grant as proper and necessary to its exercise. . . . There is no undefined residuum of power which he can exercise because it seems to him in the public interest.[20]

Taft believed that the president could exercise only the specific powers granted to him by the Constitution or by Congress. This view was shared by Presidents Calvin Coolidge, Herbert Hoover, and to some extent Dwight Eisenhower. None of these presidents felt that he should expand the use of executive powers. Eisenhower, for example, believed that

> the principle of separation of powers required the President actually to impose restraints on himself because of the overwhelming power that the Presidency has acquired; and . . . a belief that the incidental influences flowing from the Presidency itself should not be exploited to promote causes beyond those assigned to the President by the Constitution.[21]

Such presidents, in short, believe that the chief executive should play a less active role within the system of separation of powers.

Theodore Roosevelt was the first twentieth-century president to be generally considered "strong." Roosevelt felt that it was his job to do all he could for the American people—that he was a steward of the people. "I did not usurp power," he declared,

> but I did greatly broaden the use of executive power. In other words, I acted for the public welfare. I acted for the common well-being of all our people, whenever and in whatever manner was necessary, unless prevented by direct constitutional or legislative prohibition. I did not care a rap for the mere form and show of power; I cared immensely for the use that could be made of the substance.[22]

Most modern presidents may be classified as strong. International problems, as well as domestic economic problems, demand strong executive leadership. Weak presidents were more common in the nineteenth and early twentieth centuries, and it seems unlikely that any president today would advocate such a restricted view of the powers of the nation's chief executive.

Strong and weak presidents differ not only in their beliefs about the presidency itself but also in the motivations that lead them to seek the office of president. Most strong presidents have been active in their efforts to win leadership positions and have had the goal of the presidency in mind throughout their political careers. Once in power, they have enjoyed the exercise of that power. Weak presidents, by contrast, have not been strongly motivated by the desire to be a

Theodore Roosevelt served as president from 1901 to 1909 and was one of the first presidents to advocate a theory of strong executive powers.

political leader. Some have been successful in nonpolitical careers (for example, Taft in law, Herbert Hoover as an engineer) before entering politics.[23]

As might be expected, the differences between weak and strong presidents are expressed in the political skills they bring to the presidency and in the way they put those skills to work. Here the relationship between the president and Congress is all-important. The president must be able to persuade others that his program is desirable, that his actions are justified, and that he deserves their support. A president with the skills and the desire to persuade others to support his goals can accomplish much.[24]

Strong presidents often have impressive political skills. Lyndon Johnson, for example, was famous for his ability to convince members of Congress that things should be done his way. In his first years in office, Johnson was highly successful in getting Congress to adopt much of his domestic reform program in such areas as health care, education, and civil rights. But political skills alone do not make a great president. Johnson's clever use of power on domestic issues was not enough to win widespread support for his Vietnam policies. Nor could Richard Nixon avoid the consequences of his misdeeds in office, although he managed to fend off the threat of impeachment for more than a year. Bill Clinton was a skilled politician who was popular with much of the American public, but he could not prevent his impeachment by Congress for misdeeds in office. Political skills, to be effective, must go hand-in-hand with moral leadership, and morality is an aspect of individual character.

Presidential Character

Some political scientists, historians, and psychologists have tried to analyze the relationship between character, or personality, and politics. This relationship is of particular interest with respect to the president, not only because of the fascination of the office itself, but also because the president is the most powerful political figure in the world today.

The late Duke University political science professor James David Barber developed a theory of presidential character based on two broad dimensions: active-passive and positive-negative. The first has to do with the amount of energy a person puts into being president; the second deals with how he feels about being president. Using this approach, Barber has devised four categories of presidential character: active-positive, active-negative, passive-positive, and passive-negative. He has summarized these general categories as follows:

> The "active-positive" type tends to show confidence, flexibility, and a focus on producing results through rational mastery. The "active-negative" tends to emphasize ambitious striving, aggressiveness, and a focus on the struggle for power against a hostile environment. "Passive-positive" types come through as receptive, compliant, other-directed persons whose superficial hopefulness masks much inner doubt. The "passive-negative" character tends to withdraw from conflict and uncertainty, to think in terms of vague principles of duty and regular procedure.[25]

Among the presidents whom Barber has classified as active-positive are Franklin D. Roosevelt, Harry Truman, and John F. Kennedy. Active-negatives include Woodrow Wilson, Herbert Hoover, Lyndon Johnson, and Richard Nixon. William Howard Taft, Warren Harding, and Ronald Reagan were passive-positives, and Calvin Coolidge and Dwight Eisenhower were passive-negatives.

Many of the nation's greatest presidents can be classified as active-positive. This is because, in Barber's words,

> Active-positive presidents are more open to evidence because they have less need to deny and distort their perceptions for protective purposes. Their approach is experimental rather than deductive, which allows them to try something else when an experiment fails to pan out, rather than escalate the rhetoric or pursue the villains responsible. Flexibility in style and a world view containing a variety of probabilities are congruent with a character ready for trial and error and furnish the imagination with a wide range of alternatives.[26]

If there is a lesson to be learned from Barber's analysis of presidential character, it is "Beware the active-negative." Active-negatives are often strong leaders with great political ability, but they are motivated by a desire for personal power. They are aggressive but have difficulty managing their aggressive feelings. For the active-negative, life is a battle "to achieve and hold power, hampered by the condemnations of a perfectionist conscience."[27]

Individuals with active-negative personalities are dangerous because they become inflexible when challenged. The clearest illustrations of this pattern are President Lyndon Johnson's refusal to change his policies on the Vietnam War despite enormous public pressure to do so, and President Richard Nixon's stubborn persistence in attempting to cover up the Watergate scandal—a stubbornness that ended in his resignation from the presidency.

Barber's approach has attracted the attention of politicians as well as some political scientists and has been both praised and criticized. Some have been influenced by his ideas and credit him with developing a useful analytical tool. Others, however, believe that Barber's predictions are vague, that his methods are unscientific, and that the character of any individual is too complex for analysis. Barber's critics also dislike the concept of character analysis, which, they point out, can easily turn into character assassination.[28]

Whatever the drawbacks of Barber's theory, it has served to focus attention on the personal dimension of the presidency. Both the style and the character of the person who is elected president are important factors in determining how that person will conduct himself in office. These factors are as significant as the legal powers and limitations of the office. It is therefore important that the American public consider the beliefs of candidates for the presidency. These factors may be as significant as candidates' views on political issues.

THE VICE PRESIDENT

The framers of the Constitution created the office of vice president as an afterthought; almost no discussion was devoted to this subject during the Constitutional Convention. The Constitution simply provides that a vice president shall be chosen by the Electoral College; that he shall be acting president when a president is temporarily disabled; that he shall assume the office and duties of the president upon the death, resignation, or removal of the president; and that he shall be the president of the Senate, voting only to break a tie on the rare occasions when this occurs. The vice president, in other words, has little to do as long as the president remains in office. It is for this reason that John Adams, the nation's first vice president, wrote that "my country has in its wisdom created for me the most insignificant office that ever the invention of man contrived."

Charles G. Dawes, vice president under President Calvin Coolidge, described the position as "the easiest job in the world." He had only two responsibilities, Dawes declared: to sit and listen to the speeches of senators and to examine the morning papers for information about the health of the president! However, nine vice presidents have assumed the office of president after the death or resignation of the president; collectively, they have gone on to serve as president for a total of twenty-six years. And four of those who succeeded to the presidency were later elected to that office. Thus, again quoting Adams, "I am Vice President of the United States. In this I am nothing, but I may be everything."

Vice presidential candidates are formally chosen by each party's national convention. But the selection is entirely in the hands of the party's presidential nominee; the conventions merely ratify that choice. Vice presidential running mates have traditionally been chosen by the presidential nominee to balance a ticket. Thus, geography, political philosophy, and age have been the bases for selection, not friendship or qualification for the presidency. (Both presidents Clinton and Bush in their selection of Al Gore and Dick Cheney rejected historic practice and chose men whom they knew personally and who had wide experience in government.)

In the past, presidents have tended to keep the vice president isolated from decision making, reflecting the fact that their relationship was based largely on political considerations. The vice president's isolation and lack of influence was perhaps best illustrated by the fact that President Franklin D. Roosevelt, who died in office in 1945, never informed Vice President Harry Truman that the atomic bomb was being developed.

Traditionally, the vice president has acted as a substitute for the president in performing various ceremonial functions, thereby relieving the president of these time-consuming duties. Recent presidents have attempted to give their vice presidents more important assignments, such as chairing cabinet committees or White House conferences and making diplomatic trips abroad. They have also sought to keep them better informed about both domestic and foreign-policy matters. President Bush has made Vice President Cheney a central figure in policy making in his administration, elevating the office to an importance it has never had in American history. Thus, while the office of the vice president remains a weak and ambiguous one, the vice president is still the person who may one day become "everything."

CONCLUSION

Article II of the Constitution was written in such a way as to permit the presidency to expand to meet the needs of a changing and growing nation. But the nation's founders could not have foreseen how important the presidency would become in response to the demands of modern society.

The growth of the presidency has been caused in part by the actions of "strong" presidents, but the economic and social problems of an industrial society have also played a major role in the expansion of presidential powers. The public's expectation that the president will maintain economic growth and avoid recession has increased markedly in the past half century. The public has also come to expect a high level of service from the national government, and it holds the president largely responsible when its expectations are not met.

Probably the greatest force contributing to the expansion of the president's power has been war. In the twentieth century the two world wars and the conflicts in Korea and Vietnam greatly increased the scope of presidential power. The current war on terrorism produced a sharp increase in presidential power as President Bush responded to the danger posed to the United States and its allies by international terrorism. Congress also responded to this threat by enacting legislation designed to support the president in both his domestic and international policies against terrorism.

Aside from the impact of war, the emergence of the United States as a world power has strengthened the office of the president. In the years since the outbreak of World War II, the United States has become involved in a complex web of foreign alliances and commitments, which have had the effect of increasing the power of the president.

The framers of the Constitution gave both the president and Congress a role in foreign affairs. But there are areas in which the Constitution is either silent or ambiguous. And it is in this twilight zone that the contest between the president and Congress has been fought. For the most part, the courts have stayed out of this debate. They have viewed the conflict as political, not judicial, and have left the problem to be resolved by the elected branches of the government.

A return to the nineteenth-century system of weak presidents dominated by the legislative branch is not possible in today's world. But no president can be allowed to function above the law. The system of separation of powers that the nation's founders created two centuries ago provides adequate safeguards against an "imperial" presidency, and strong presidents can function within the boundaries set by the Constitution and legislative acts. As Supreme Court Justice Robert Jackson wrote in 1952, "With all its defects, delays, and inconveniences, men have discovered no technique for long preserving free government except that the Executive be under the law, and that the law be made by parliamentary deliberations."[29]

QUESTIONS FOR THOUGHT

1. What is meant by the "problem of presidential succession," and how does the Twenty-fifth Amendment to the Constitution attempt to solve it?

2. What are the similarities and differences between a treaty and an executive agreement?

3. Describe the veto power given to the president by the Constitution.

4. How does the War Powers Resolution attempt to limit presidential power?

5. Summarize James David Barber's theory of presidential character.

INTERNET ACTIVITIES

1. *Popularity.* Go to the Gallup Poll site at **http://www.gallup.com,** and select "Presidential Approval Ratings." Which president had the highest and lowest approval ratings? What is George W. Bush's current rating? What impact does popularity have on the ability of the president to lead the nation?

2. *Flexible Power.* Go to the White House site at **http://www.whitehouse.gov/WH/Welcome.html**. From "NEWS" go to "Executive Orders." Do a search for an executive order on a topic of your choice ("Bosnia," for example). Briefly summarize the order and indicate the specific code(s) or constitutional power(s) cited by the president that he believes authorizes him to take this action. Should the president have this kind of power granted to him? Review other executive orders. Why is presidential power this flexible?

KEY TERMS

executive agreement   line item veto   treaty

impeachment   pocket veto   veto

SUGGESTED READING

Cronin, Thomas E. *The Paradoxes of the American Presidency.* New York: Oxford University Press, 1998.

DiClerico, Robert E. *The American President,* 5th ed. Upper Saddle River, NJ: Prentice Hall, 2000.

Ellis, Richard J., ed. *Founding the American Presidency.* Lanham, MD: Rowman & Littlefield, 1999.

Genovese, Michael A. *The Power of the American Presidency, 1789-2000.* New York: Oxford University Press, 2000.

Henderson, Phillip G. *The Presidency: Then and Now.* Lanham, MD: Rowman & Littlefield, 2000.

Jones, Charles O. *Passages to the Presidency: From Campaigning to Governing.* Washington, DC: Brookings Institution Press, 1998.

Mayer, Kenneth R. *With the Stroke of a Pen: Executive Orders and Presidential Power.* Princeton, NJ: Princeton University Press, 2001.

Milkis, Sidney M., and Michael Nelson. *The American Presidency: Origins and Development, 1776-1998,* 3rd ed. Washington, DC: Congressional Quarterly Press, 1999.

Nelson, Michael, ed. *The Presidency and the Political System,* 6th ed. Washington, DC: Congressional Quarterly Press, 2000.

Preston, Thomas. *The President and His Inner Circle.* New York: Columbia University Press, 2001.

Rozell, Mark J. *Executive Privilege: Presidential Power, Secrecy and Accountability,* 2nd ed. Lawrence, KS: University Press of Kansas, 2002.

NOTES

1. Norman C. Thomas, Joseph A. Pika, and Richard A. Watson, *The Politics of the Presidency,* rev. 3rd ed. (Washington, DC: Congressional Quarterly Press, 1994), p. 23.

2. Richard E. Neustadt, *Presidential Power* (New York: Wiley, 1960), p. viii.

3. *United States v. Belmont,* 301 U.S. 324 (1937).

4. *Dames & Moore v. Regan,* 453 U.S. 654 (1981).

5. For a study of presidential appointments, see James W. Riddelsperger, Jr., and James D. King, "Presidential Appointments to the Cabinet, Executive Office, and White House Staff," *Presidential Studies Quarterly* 16 (Fall 1986): 691-99.

6. *Myers v. United States,* 272 U.S. 52 (1926).

7. Richard P. Nathan, *The Administrative Presidency* (New York: Wiley, 1983), pp. 88-90.

8. Roger H. Davidson and Walter J. Oleszek, *Congress and Its Members,* 3rd ed. (Washington, DC: Congressional Quarterly Press, 1990), pp. 241-42, 245-48.

9. *Clinton* v. *City of New York,* 524 U.S. 417 (1998).

10. Woodrow Wilson, *Constitutional Government in the United States* (New York: Columbia University Press, 1908), p. 68.

11. *Ex parte Milligan, 4 Wall.* 2 (1866); *Duncan v. Kahanamoku,* 327 U.S. 304 (1946).

12. *Youngstown Sheet and Tube Co. v. Sawyer,* 343 U.S. 579 (1952).

13. *The New York Times Co. v. United States,* 403 U.S. 713 (1971).

14. *United States v. Nixon,* 418 U.S. 683 (1974).

15. *Clinton v. Jones,* 520 U.S. 681 (1997).

16. Eugene V. Rostow, "Repeal the War Powers Resolution," *Wall Street Journal,* June 27, 1984, p. 34; Rep. Robert K. Dornan (R., Ca.), letter, *Wall Street Journal,* November 17, 1987, p. 39.

17. Terry Eastland, "War Powers Resolution Redux," *Wall Street Journal,* November 17, 1993, p. A23.

18. Thomas E. Cronin, *The State of the Presidency,* 2nd ed. (Boston: Little, Brown, 1980), p. 168.

19. Ibid., p. 330.

20. William Howard Taft, *Our Chief Magistrate and His Powers* (New York: Columbia University Press, 1925), p. 138.

21. Quoted in Arthur Larsen, *Eisenhower: The President Nobody Knew* (New York: Scribner's, 1968), p. 12.

22. *Theodore Roosevelt, An Autobiography* (New York: Scribner's, 1913), p. 357.

23. Erwin C. Hargrove and Roy Hoopes, *The Presidency: A Question of Power* (Boston: Little, Brown, 1975), pp. 142-43.

24. For an excellent discussion and analysis of this subject, see the influential study by Neustadt, *Presidential Power.*

25. James David Barber, "Analyzing Presidents," *Washington Monthly,* October 1969, p. 34.

26. James David Barber, *The Presidential Character,* 4th ed. (Englewood Cliffs, NJ: Prentice Hall, 1992), p. 490. See also Stanley A. Renshon, *The Psychological Assessment of Presidential Candidates* (New York: New York University Press, 1996).

27. Barber, *The Presidential Character,* p. 9.

28. Anthony Ramirez, "Is Ronald Reagan Similar to Coolidge? Should You Care?" *Wall Street Journal,* September 17, 1980, p. 19.

29. *Youngstown Sheet and Tube Co. v. Sawyer,* 343 U.S. 579 (1952).

CHAPTER

9

The Federal
Bureaucracy

When we think of the federal bureaucracy, what usually comes to mind is its darker side: miles of red tape, being "given the runaround," dealing with people who are unsympathetic to our needs. All these things make it seem impossible to get a reasonable response from an agency of the government. In reality, though, **bureaucracy** is simply a way of organizing people to achieve a specific goal, that is, to get work done. Ideally, a bureaucracy is efficient and effective. But as James Q. Wilson points out, there is a continual struggle for power over the federal bureaucracy, and that struggle results in the problems of red tape and unresponsiveness that have given bureaucracy in general, and the federal bureaucracy in particular, a bad name.

From time to time studies are done to find out how the federal bureaucracy functions and what could be done to improve it. One such study was conducted by Al Gore while he was serving as vice president. Generally known as the Gore Report, its official title is *Creating a Government That Works Better and Costs Less.* The report included several criticisms of the federal bureaucracy, among them the size and wastefulness of many government organizations; their preoccupation with standard operating procedures; the lack of incentive for them to innovate or improve; and the relative lack of penalties for poor performance by their employees.

The Gore Report itself has come in for some criticism. James Q. Wilson, the perceptive observer of bureaucracy whose remarks are quoted at the beginning of the chapter, believes that the report's goals, however worthwhile, are practically impossible to achieve. The Gore Report calls for a reduction in red tape, greater emphasis on customer service, more power for lower-level employees, and cuts in spending. But as Wilson notes, it is not in the interest of Congress or the executive branch to carry out these reforms. They seek to respond to the demands of their constituents—for example, the demand that the government "finish the highway system." Efforts to do that, far from reducing red tape

Our government features red tape, complex procedures, divided authority and hamstrung employees because these are the ways by which the struggle for the control of the bureaucracy is waged by the three institutional contenders for power over it—the presidency, Congress and the courts. . . . To reform the bureaucracy would require persuading these institutional contenders to reduce their power and thus their ability to serve important constituencies—a daunting task.

—*James Q. Wilson*[1]

and cutting costs, will require more than twenty new goals and constraints, including the following:

> preserve historic sites, reduce erosion, encourage the use of seat belts, control outdoor advertising, hire Indians, reduce drunken driving, use recycled rubber in making asphalt, give 10 percent of the construction money to businesses owned by women or other "disadvantaged" individuals, buy iron and steel from American suppliers, require metropolitan area planning, and limit the use of calcium acetate in performing seismic retrofits on bridges.[2]

This chapter focuses first on the structure and organization of the federal bureaucracy. It then discusses some of the characteristics pointed out by Professor Wilson: the powers of the bureaucracy and the limitations on its exercise of authority.

THE ORGANIZATION OF THE EXECUTIVE BRANCH

Within any bureaucracy each unit of organization (department, agency) falls into one of two broad categories: line and staff. **Line agencies** are those that carry out government policies and provide various types of services. **Staff agencies,** by contrast, neither execute policies nor provide services. Instead, they gather information and make it available to the chief executive officer whenever it is needed. The line agencies of the federal government are the executive departments, the various government agencies and corporations, the independent regulatory commissions, and certain central services and control agencies. The main staff agencies are the cabinet and the Executive Office of the President.

Line Agencies

THE EXECUTIVE DEPARTMENTS   The organization of the executive branch is based on the principle of division of labor. The basic units are the fifteen executive or cabinet **departments:** State, Treasury, Defense, Justice, Interior, Agriculture, Commerce, Labor, Health and Human Services, Housing and Urban Development, Transportation, Energy, Education, Veterans Affairs and Homeland Security. (The newest department, Homeland Security, was created in November 2002, in response to the problem of domestic security created by the terrorist attacks on the United States. It will be the third largest department after Defense and Veterans Affairs.) Each department is headed by a secretary, who is a member of the president's cabinet. Below the secretary are a deputy secretary, perhaps an undersecretary, and one or more assistant secretaries. Each of these officials is appointed by the president with the advice and consent of the Senate and can be removed at the chief executive's discretion. (See Figure 9.1.)

Although all the departments are organized along the same general lines, they differ greatly in their size and functions. In 2002 the Department of Defense had a civilian workforce of 670,166, whereas the Department of Education had only 4,647 employees. There are other differences, too. Four of the departments—State, Defense, Treasury, and Justice—perform basic governmental functions. The others are geared toward particular segments of society, such as farmers or workers. This factor, together with size, affects the relative importance of the various

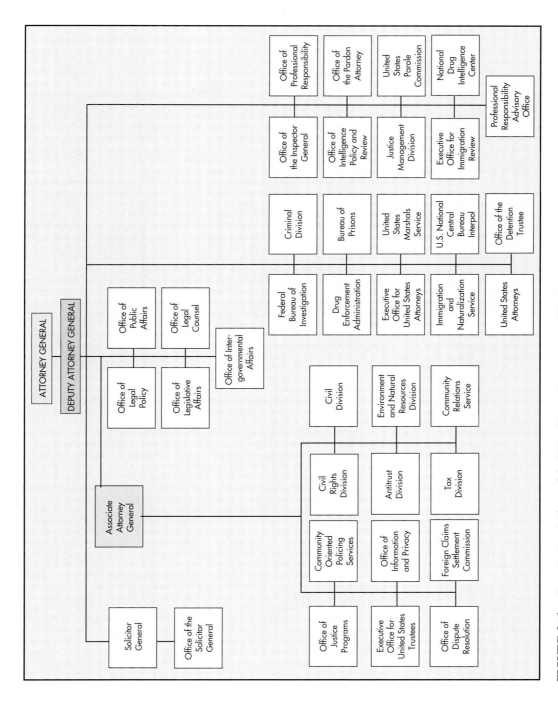

FIGURE 9–1 Organizational Chart of the United States Department of Justice.

Source: The U.S. Department of Justice Accountability Report F4 2001, Appendix B 2001.

229

departments. Thus, Defense and State are considered much more important than, say, Energy or Education. Indeed, some Republicans—including President Reagan and some members of Congress—have advocated eliminating these departments, but their attempts to do so have been unsuccessful.

Departments are generally divided into **bureaus,** which are headed by bureau chiefs. The bureaus, like the departments, differ widely in their functions. They may be organized according to whom they serve (for example, the Bureau of Indian Affairs in the Interior Department), what they do (the Federal Bureau of Investigation in the Justice Department), or the geographic area they serve (the African Affairs Bureau in the Department of State).

Most federal bureaus have central offices located in Washington, DC. These offices often have relatively small staffs and are concerned with setting policy. The majority of a bureau's employees are located in field offices scattered across the nation and in foreign countries. These **field services,** in turn, consist of hundreds of subunits that are responsible for specialized tasks. Examples of field offices include the local Social Security and Internal Revenue Service offices.

AGENCIES   Federal **agencies** are separate from the cabinet departments but are still under upper-level executive control. The major officials of the forty or so federal agencies are also appointed by the president with the advice and consent of the Senate and can be removed by the president at will. Examples of federal agencies include the Environmental Protection Agency, the National Aeronautics and Space Administration, and the Small Business Administration. In general, agencies are formed when a governmental function is too limited to warrant department status.

CORPORATIONS   The Federal Deposit Insurance Corporation (FDIC), Amtrak, the Tennessee Valley Authority (TVA), and the U.S. Postal Service are examples of **government corporations.** These organizations combine certain aspects of private businesses with characteristics of government agencies. They are especially useful when the government is providing a service, such as bank deposit insurance in the case of the FDIC or electric power in the case of the TVA, that can best be run by a corporation that is free from excessive interference by the president and Congress but is still subject to general policies established by the legislature.

Each government corporation has a governing board, whose members are appointed by the president with the advice and consent of the Senate and serve for a fixed period. The corporations are intended to be financially self-sustaining. Their income is derived from the services they render to the public (such as the selling of power by the TVA and the sale of postage by the Postal Service). But some government corporations, most notably Amtrak, are in fact subsidized by congressional appropriations. These features make the corporations quite different from the departments and the agencies, which are subject to greater control by both Congress and the president.

INDEPENDENT REGULATORY COMMISSIONS   About a dozen major **independent regulatory commissions** have been created by Congress and given broad authority to regulate a particular area of the nation's economy. Each regulatory body is headed by a number of commissioners—five is typical—who are appointed by the president with the advice and consent of the Senate. The members serve for fixed but staggered terms of office. Some laws that create commissions also set limits on the number of commissioners who may be members of the same political party.

CLOSE-UP

THE HOMELAND SECURITY DEPARTMENT

In November 2002 Congress enacted the most far-reaching reorganization of the executive branch of government in more than half a century when it created a new Homeland Security Department. President Bush had initiated the proposal earlier in the year in response to the security failures that allowed the September 11 attacks on the United States to take place and to the continuing terrorist threat to this nation.

When the Homeland Security Department is completely organized it will contain agencies drawn from twenty-two existing organizations and will be the third largest of the fifteen government departments. It will employ almost 180,000 people; its 2004 budget was $29.1 billion. Among the agencies moved to the Homeland Security Department are: the enforcement tasks of the Immigration and Naturalization Service (Justice Department); the Customs Service and the Secret Service (Treasury Department); the Coast Guard (Transportation Department); and the Federal Emergency Management Agency (an independent organization).

The two most important anti-terrorist organizations—the Central Intelligence Agency and the Federal Bureau of Investigation—will not become part of the Homeland Security Department. But it will have a new intelligence section that will analyze the domestic threats that concern both the CIA and the FBI.

The commissions are independent in the sense that their members cannot be removed by the president merely because they disagree with his policies. They can be removed only for causes set forth in law, such as criminal conduct or neglect of duties. These commissions often exercise more power than that possessed by the cabinet departments and their secretaries.

The Federal Communications Commission, the Federal Trade Commission, the Federal Reserve Board, the Securities and Exchange Commission, and the National Labor Relations Board are examples of independent regulatory commissions. They make important decisions in the areas of the economy that they regulate. The Federal Communications Commission, for example, assigns valuable radio and television licenses to private applicants, and the Federal Trade Commission decides whether companies have engaged in unfair business practices.

Many of the independent commissions were created by Congress during the 1930s, the period of President Franklin D. Roosevelt's New Deal. The purpose of these commissions was to free Congress from the task of legislating on complex aspects of the American economy. The independent commissions were to be expert regulators that would put into effect the general policy objectives established by Congress.

The independent regulatory commissions are said to exercise all three powers of government—executive, legislative, and judicial. Not only do they enforce the laws passed by Congress, but they also have broad power to establish regulatory policies. In addition, they perform a judicial function in that they settle disputes that arise under their interpretation of the law—subject to review in the federal courts. For this and other reasons, the independent agencies have been subject to criticism. One study, for example, concluded that the "independent agency is a constitutional sport, an anomalous institution created without regard to the basic principle of separation of powers upon which our government was founded."[3]

Others have pointed to the close relationship that sometimes develops between the commissions and private interests. It has been argued that some of the independent commissions tend to identify the well-being of the public with that

CLOSE-UP

THE FEDERAL RESERVE SYSTEM

Created by Congress in 1914, the Federal Reserve System is the central bank for the nation. It is the banker for both the federal government and the nation's private banks. It issues the nation's money, regulates private banks, and determines monetary policy. The system is composed of twelve district Federal Reserve Banks and the Board of Governors, which has its offices in Washington, DC.

Much of the power of the Federal Reserve is centered in the Board of Governors, whose seven members are appointed by the president with the advice and consent of the Senate for fourteen-year terms. This organization prevents any president from dominating the Board with his appointees. Moreover, the president has no power to remove members of the Board except for causes set in law—for example, malfeasance in office; he cannot dismiss a Board member because of disagreement over policy.

A major function of the Federal Reserve Board is the setting of the nation's monetary policy. Its power to raise or lower interest rates is one of the principal ways in which the Board carries out this power. Thus, when the nation's economy is slow-

ing, the Federal Reserve Board can lower interest rates to encourage businesses to borrow to expand their activities, and consumers to purchase large-ticket items such as cars and homes. Conversely, when the Board believes that the economy is overheating and there is a danger of inflation, it can raise interest rates to make it more expensive for both companies and consumers to borrow money.

Thus, during the late 1990s, when the American economy was very strong, the Federal Reserve raised interest rates. At the end of 2000 rates reached a high of 6.50 percent. But during 2001 the nation's economy began to weaken dramatically. The September 11 terrorist attacks contributed to the worsening economic condition of the country. The Federal Reserve responded to this situation by reducing interest rates. By March 2004 the federal funds rate stood at 1 percent, the lowest it had been in more than four decades. A growing concern with inflationary pressures in the economy finally caused the Federal Reserve Board to reverse the direction of interest rates. In June, August, and September of 2004 the Board raised interest rates by .25 percent, bringing the federal funds rate to 1.75 percent.

of the industry or area they are supposed to regulate. The result, according to some critics, is that the regulatory commission is itself "regulated" or controlled by special interests and that the voice of other groups and of the public is not adequately heard. This criticism may be valid in some cases, but there is considerable variation in the extent to which regulatory commissions are influenced by special-interest groups.

The policies of a regulatory commission depend in part on the views of the people appointed by the president to serve on that commission. Although presidents cannot fire commissioners because of differences of opinion, they can shape the philosophy of a commission through their appointments.

INDEPENDENT CENTRAL SERVICES AND CONTROL AGENCIES

A final set of line agencies handle some of the functions required to keep the government running. Among these agencies are the Office of Personnel Management, which administers the **civil service** (civilian employees of the federal government), and the General Services Administration, which oversees federal buildings and transportation, purchases supplies, and operates institutions such as the National Archives and Records Service.

Staff Agencies

You will recall that staff agencies do not carry out policy but are concerned with gathering information and providing advice. In the executive branch this function is performed partly by the cabinet but mainly by the Executive Office of the President.

THE CABINET The president's **cabinet** is made up of the heads of the fifteen executive departments plus a few other top officials, such as the ambassador to the United Nations. Each of these individuals plays a dual role: He or she is in charge of implementing the president's program in a particular area and at the same time may attempt to influence the president's policies in that area.

The cabinet can be seen as being divided into an "outer" and an "inner" cabinet. The inner cabinet consists of the secretaries of state, defense, and treasury and the attorney general. Holders of these positions play a "counseling" role in relation to the president. For example, the president's foreign-policy decisions are a product of frequent and close consultation with the secretary of state. The same can be said for major defense and economic policies. Members of the outer cabinet—the secretaries of labor, agriculture, education, and so forth—have what have been described as "advocacy" positions: They represent a specific group of citizens and are involved mainly in carrying out policy and providing services for that sector of society.[4]

In the early years of the nation's history, the cabinet played a major role in governmental decision making. Cabinet meetings were held regularly (as often as twice a week), and all areas of government policy were discussed by everyone present. The cabinet served as an important adviser to the president. By the twentieth century the cabinet had become much less important as an advisory body. Presidents have found it to be too large and unwieldy to be of much value as a source of guidance. A few presidents have attempted to revive the advisory function of the cabinet, but with little success; the president's personal advisers in the Executive Office of the President have played a far more significant role than the cabinet in shaping policy decisions.

This is not to say that cabinet members are unimportant. As individuals, they play a valuable role as advisers in specific policy areas. Each heads a large

President Bush attends the opening session of the NATO summit in Prague, November, 2002. Also present were, from left to right, British Prime Minister Tony Blair, National Security Advisor Condoleezza Rice, Secretary of Defense Donald Rumsfeld, and Secretary of State Colin Powell.

bureaucracy with extensive resources for gathering and analyzing information. Individual cabinet members thus serve as "the contact points between the President and bureaucracy."[5]

THE EXECUTIVE OFFICE OF THE PRESIDENT. The Executive Office of the President was created in 1939 after a committee formed to study the administrative role of the president came to the conclusion that "the President needs help." The Executive Office actually consists of several agencies that provide staff assistance to the president: the White House Office, the Office of Management and Budget, the Council of Economic Advisers, the National Security Council, and several smaller units. Every new president makes some changes in the structure of the Executive Office, but the major units remain unchanged.

The White House Office At least since the 1950s, as the influence of the cabinet as a source of advice to the president has declined, that of the White House Office has grown. The White House Office includes a large number of clerical workers and, most important, the president's personal staff. Presidents rely heavily on these assistants for advice and services. Each chief executive organizes his personal staff in a different manner, so it is difficult to generalize about this group. Presidents normally appoint a *chief of staff,* who heads the White House Office and controls access to the chief executive. They also appoint a variety of assistants and deputy assistants for domestic, national security, economic, and managerial affairs. In addition, there are speechwriters, a legal adviser, liaison officers to deal with Congress, and a press secretary who meets with the news media.

All these assistants share a single purpose: to make the president's job easier. Since the various appointees to the White House Office directly serve the president, their selection does not require the advice and consent of the Senate, and the president can remove them as he sees fit. They tend to be people whom the president trusts and whose loyalty can be counted on.

The White House Office grew dramatically in the twentieth century. In the early decades of the century, President Theodore Roosevelt's White House staff consisted of thirty-five people. Just before World War II, President Franklin Roosevelt's staff employed only about fifty. The number of people in the White House Office reached its peak in the early 1970s and then decreased; it has remained at about 400 or a little less since the 1980s.[6]

Different presidents have organized the White House Office in different ways. As one scholar has written,

> A White House staff reflects the organizational preferences and personality of the President it serves. Some White House offices have been highly unstructured, with presidential assistants functioning virtually as personal extensions of the President. Others, however, have been structured as tightly as a military command post, with rigid lines of authority linking the President to assistants. . . . Several staffs fell in between these two extremes, with a mix of both structured and free-wheeling relationships between the President and assistants.[7]

The two most recent presidents have employed sharply different organizational styles. The second President Bush adopted a structured approach to organizing the White House Office; President Clinton, on the other hand, followed a much more fluid organizational style. Clinton attempted to be personally involved in the details of governmental policy and relied on the advice of his wife, Hillary Rodham Clinton, and friends who held positions in the White House Office and elsewhere in the government.

Many observers of the White House during the early years of Clinton's presidency criticized it for its lack of structure and the president's freewheeling style of governing. At the end of his first term, however, Clinton made changes in the operations of the White House Office that resulted in greater discipline in its structure and functioning.

The Office of Management and Budget   The most important unit within the Executive Office is the Office of Management and Budget (OMB). The director of the OMB, who is nominated by the president with the advice and consent of the Senate, has been a key figure in most recent administrations. The OMB performs several functions, including reviewing the budgets and legislative proposals of all the federal departments and agencies. It uses this information to prepare the president's annual budget proposals.

Before 1921, cabinet departments and executive agencies submitted their budget requirements to Congress annually. The House Appropriations Committee analyzed those requests, but it was very difficult for the committee to judge whether the amounts requested were justified. Moreover, the president had no way of making up an executive budget or knowing how money was spent,

CLOSE-UP

THE "EAST WING"

There is no reference to the First Lady in the United States Constitution, nor is there any other official recognition of the role of the president's wife in the federal government. Yet throughout American history First Ladies have often participated in their husbands' administrations. Their activities have varied greatly over the years, depending on their personalities and interests as well as on the customs of the time. During the War of 1812 Dolley Madison remained in the White House as long as possible, finally packing the original drafts of the Constitution and the Declaration of Independence and departing as the British drew near. Sarah Polk served as her husband's personal secretary, and Helen Taft attended cabinet meetings. Edith Wilson could be said to have served as acting president after Woodrow Wilson suffered a stroke in 1919. She handled all correspondence addressed to the president from the Senate, the cabinet, and the public.

Although no subsequent First Lady has played as powerful a role as Mrs. Wilson, several have created important positions for themselves in their husbands' administrations. Of these, perhaps the most famous is Eleanor Roosevelt, who represented the president on numerous public occasions and also traveled throughout the country to report to him on the conditions of Americans during the Great Depression of the 1930s and World War II. Hillary Rodham Clinton also played a very influential policy role in the Clinton administration, especially during her husband's first years in office, when she helped formulate a far-reaching plan to alter the nation's health care system. (Congress refused to approve the proposal.)

In recent decades the First Lady's office, sometimes called the East Wing, has developed into an unofficial, but very real, part of the federal government. The First Lady's staff consists of about twenty-five people, with offices in the White House and salaries that are part of the federal payroll. They include press secretaries, speechwriters, social secretaries, schedulers, and project directors. The First Lady is also protected by the Secret Service. In sum, the East Wing is an active, functioning part of all administrations, and one that can, on occasion, affect national policy.

although under the Constitution he is responsible for the operation of the executive branch of the government. With the passage of the Budget and Accounting Act of 1921, which established the first executive budget office, it became possible to create a more effective executive budget. In recent decades the OMB has become "the most highly developed administrative coordinating and program review unit in the Executive Office; it provides the central institutional mechanism for imprinting . . . presidential will over the government."[8]

The OMB's task of serving as a control on the bureaucracy puts it in a peculiar position. On the one hand, it is supposed to be a neutral administrative agency, using its technical expertise in the interests of the nation as a whole. On the other hand, it is almost as important as the White House Office in shaping and implementing the president's policies. On some occasions these roles have come into conflict, and it has been extremely difficult for the OMB to maintain a neutral stance.

The Council of Economic Advisers   The Council of Economic Advisers (CEA), created in 1946, consists of a chair and two other economists appointed by the president, and a permanent staff of about twenty economists who provide technical support. The council's job is to review the state of the economy and advise the president on ways of dealing with such problems as unemployment, inflation, or slow economic growth. The council also prepares the annual *Economic Report of the President* and recommends adjustments in government spending and taxation.

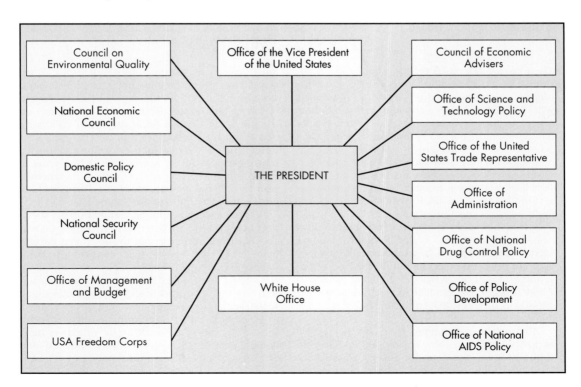

FIGURE 9–2   Organizational Chart of the Executive Office of the President.

In the first twenty-five years of its existence, the council was influential in shaping the government's economic policy; presidents relied heavily on its advice. For example, the council played an important role in developing President Lyndon Johnson's Great Society program in the mid-1960s. The importance of the council declined in subsequent decades; presidents increasingly turned to the director of the OMB and the secretary of the treasury for economic advice.[9] Although the first President Bush relied heavily on the council, especially its chair, for economic advice, President Clinton paid greater attention to the advice provided by the secretary of the treasury.

The National Security Council The National Security Council (NSC) was created in 1947 to advise the president on matters related to national security. It coordinates domestic, foreign, and military policies, drawing upon experts in the military and civilian bureaucracies. The council consists of the president, the vice president, the secretaries of state and defense, a member of the White House staff (who serves as its director), and the director of the Office of Emergency Preparedness. Its meetings are often expanded to include the chairman of the Joint Chiefs of Staff, the ambassador to the United Nations, the director of the CIA, and other cabinet officials and members of the White House staff who may be concerned with a particular issue.

Since the 1960s the NSC has become less important as a collective body. At the same time, the *national security adviser,* who heads the NSC, has strongly influenced, and sometimes dominated, the formulation of foreign policy. This top adviser, backed by the permanent staff of the NSC, has become a significant rival to the secretary of state in influence on presidential decision making. The confused and competitive relationship between the National Security Council and the Department of State has led some observers to suggest that the lines of responsibility between these agencies should be spelled out more clearly.

Figure 9.2 is an organization chart of the Executive Office. On the chart, the various parts of the Executive Office look neat and orderly, but the reality is anything but orderly. As one observer commented: "Instead, there is considerable confusion and intermingling of economic, social, budgetary, defense, foreign policy, political, and personal staffs, all of which are engaged in palace intrigues and court politics."[10]

THE FEDERAL BUREAUCRATS
The Size of the Bureaucracy

"When George Washington's first administration was inaugurated in 1790," one scholar has written,

> it functioned with nine simple executive units and approximately 1,000 employees. A century later, the 1891 census recorded that over 150,000 civilians were working in the Harrison administration. During its first 100 years the American government had grown nearly 10 times as fast as the population. By 1979 the executive branch employed over 2,800,000 civil servants, divided among 12 cabinet departments, 59 independent agencies, and the several bureaus of the White House Executive Office.[11]

The number of civilian employees of the federal government has actually decreased since the late 1980s, mostly as a result of cuts in the Department of Defense after the end of the cold war. In 2000, 2.6 million people were employed in the executive branch of the government, a decline of 1.6 percent since 1990. (This total excludes employees of the Central Intelligence Agency, the National Security Agency, and the Defense Intelligence Agency.)[12]

Who Are the Bureaucrats?

We tend to think of government bureaucrats as a uniform mass of people sitting behind desks in Washington, DC, but in reality they are a varied group. Federal government employees include not only administrators and clerks but also lawyers, mechanics, nurses, cooks, economists, wildlife managers, and many other kinds of workers. Only about one out of fourteen federal government employees works in Washington; the rest are in other parts of the United States and the world. A government employee may be a receptionist at the Kalamazoo, Michigan, Social Security office; a rural development specialist in Nairobi, Kenya; a member of the foreign service in Bangkok, Thailand; an agricultural extension worker in Iowa; or a computer programmer in California. What most of these employees have in common is a view of government or civil service as a career.

THE SPOILS SYSTEM Civil service has not always been considered a career. In the first few decades of the nation's history, government jobs were prizes that were awarded to friends and supporters of each new president when he took office. This practice (which is often linked with President Andrew Jackson, although he was not the first to use it) is known as the **spoils system**—from the saying "to the winner go the spoils," in this case government jobs. It had the virtue of bringing people from many parts of the country and many different backgrounds into government. At the state and local levels the spoils system served as the basis for building and maintaining the political parties.

The practice of rewarding loyal supporters with government jobs was defended by George Washington Plunkitt, head of the New York County Democratic party around the turn of the nineteenth century: "First, this great and glorious country was built up by political parties; second, parties can't hold together if their workers don't get offices when they win; third, if the parties go to pieces, the government they built up must go to pieces, too; fourth, then there'll be hell to pay."[13]

The most serious fault of the spoils system was that it encouraged the creation of new, sometimes unnecessary jobs and too often led to the hiring of unqualified people. Much effort was spent in training a new workforce after every change of administrations, and there was a tendency for government officials to exploit their positions for personal gain.[14]

The spoils system came under fire in the late nineteenth century as part of the general reform movement that swept the country at the time. The goal of the reformers was to replace the spoils system with a merit system, in which people would compete for jobs in the government and would be hired on the basis of ability, not party membership.

The Pendleton Act of 1883 brought an end to the spoils system in the federal government and replaced it with a merit system. Today the federal government has relatively few patronage positions. (The spoils system still remains common, however, in some states, including Indiana, Ohio, and Pennsylvania.)

Fewer than 6,000 positions in the federal government are not covered by the merit system. About one-fifth of them are high-level policy-making positions for which civil service would be inappropriate. The remaining positions are part-time or honorific in nature or require special skills such as those of scientists, doctors, and lawyers; examinations for these positions are viewed as unnecessary.

THE MERIT SYSTEM   The most important feature of the **merit system** is the use of standardized written tests. When people are hired on the basis of test scores, competition is not limited and hiring is related to ability rather than to political beliefs. The civil service tests also serve to weed out unqualified candidates and are easily administered by those who do the hiring.

Standardized tests have some drawbacks, however. They may eliminate a few candidates who could do certain jobs but are not good at taking tests, and they may result in the hiring of people who are overqualified for their positions. They have also been criticized for discriminating against minority groups. The tests, it is claimed, require the kinds of knowledge that are typically possessed by white middle-class Americans and thus discriminate against black and Hispanic candidates. While minorities hold a high percentage of positions within the federal civil service, they are still underrepresented at the highest levels of employment.

Merit system examinations have been modified in response to these criticisms. Some changes have come as a result of court decisions that require both

The Pentagon, home of the Department of Defense. On September 11, 2001, a plane hijacked by terrorists was crashed into the Pentagon, causing many deaths and extensive damage to the building.

public and private employers to prove that their tests are valid indicators of an applicant's ability to handle the job in question. Also, if the racial, ethnic, or gender makeup of a government agency is very different from that of the labor market in which it hires its employees, it will be called upon to prove that its tests are not discriminatory.

CLASSIFICATION   The Classification Act of 1949 assigned many federal jobs to a general schedule (GS) containing eighteen classes based on job title, duties, and qualifications. The salaries of government employees are related to those classes. Thus, under the salary schedule in effect in September 2002, a person with a GS grade from 1 to 4 would earn between $13,870 and $24,833 a year; someone in the top grades of 13 to 15 would earn between $55,837 and $100,897 annually.

In 1978 Congress created a new category of government employees, the Senior Executive Service (SES). This category consists of about 13,000 top administrators. Instead of receiving automatic pay raises based on the length of time they have been in the civil service, members of the SES receive cash bonuses for good performance. Job tenure is also governed by the quality of the individual's work. The main goals of the SES are to reward excellence and to encourage the most able employees to remain in the civil service.

There are some problems with the Senior Executive Service, however. These career civil servants may hold top positions in the federal government through several administrations, performing valuable functions such as supervising cancer research or the collection of economic data. The problems arise when a president from one party is replaced by a president from the other. The incoming president may view career civil servants who worked for the previous administration as obstacles to the implementation of proposed new policies. He may therefore attempt to remove those workers or shift them to less important positions. The law is supposed to protect civil servants against such actions, but these transfers nonetheless occur.

POLITICAL EXECUTIVES   As noted earlier, fewer than 6,000 government employees are not part of the civil service system. Of this number, approximately 1,100 are **political executives** who hold important policy-making positions in government. This category includes department secretaries, undersecretaries and assistant secretaries, agency heads, ambassadors, U.S. attorneys and marshals in the ninety-four judicial districts of the country, and the commissioners of the various independent regulatory agencies. All require the approval of the Senate.

Presidents take the appointment of political executives very seriously. They seek people who are both qualified for the positions to which they will be appointed and loyal to the chief executive. A newly elected president has numerous appointments, and these choices must be made in the relatively short period between election day and the first few months of the president's administration. Under these conditions it is not easy to find the right people for the many vacant positions. Inevitably, some of the individuals selected are unsuited to their jobs or have opinions and values that are so similar to the president's that they provide little critical appraisal of the chief executive's policies.

Another obstacle that each president must overcome is obtaining the advice and consent of the Senate. The Senate holds hearings on all major nominations; it is concerned with such issues as whether there are any personal financial misdeeds in the nominee's record or whether the choice entails any *conflict of*

The United States Embassy in Vienna, Austria.

interest (in the form of a close financial connection between a nominee to a regulatory agency and the industry he or she will be regulating).

It is rare for the Senate actually to reject a presidential nominee. One modern example of such a rejection took place in March 1989, when the Senate defeated the first President Bush's nomination of former Texas senator John Tower as secretary of defense. It was the first Senate rejection of a cabinet nomination in thirty years. However, it is more common for a president to withdraw a nomination because of Senate opposition to a candidate. In the opening months of the second Bush administration, the president's nomination for the position of Secretary of Labor was withdrawn because of Senate opposition to the nominee.

To avoid the possibility of a withdrawal or actual rejection of a nominee, presidents often consult privately with Senate leaders about the acceptability of a candidate before making the name public. Thus, even though the power to give advice and consent to executive nominations is infrequently used to defeat a president's choice, it must be considered in selecting individuals to fill important positions in the executive branch.

If a president is elected to a second term in office, there are numerous personnel changes at high levels of the executive branch. Most leave office for personal reasons; a few are quietly asked to leave by the president. Thus, soon after President Clinton was reelected in November 1996, half of his fourteen-member cabinet resigned and were replaced by new appointees.

SOURCES OF BUREAUCRATIC POWER

Size

It has become commonplace to refer to the federal bureaucracy as the "fourth branch" of the government—and with good reason. As the part of the government that is responsible for carrying out policies and programs, the bureaucracy has a great deal of power. This power stems from several sources, of which the most obvious is sheer size. The bureaucracy is in charge of administering federal spending—$2.3 trillion for fiscal year 2004—and directing programs that affect all Americans in one way or another. It is difficult, if not impossible, to control the approximately 2.6 million civilian employees in the executive branch. The president, as the head of the federal executive bureaucracy, cannot be sure that his directives will be carried out.

Expertise

A second source of bureaucratic power is expertise. As we have seen, one of the features of a bureaucracy is specialization or division of labor. Not only is the executive branch divided into departments and agencies that specialize in major areas such as agriculture or commerce, but also within each unit of the government there are subunits that are even more specialized, each of which employs experts in various fields for which it is responsible. Thus, the Department of the Interior includes the National Park Service. Forest rangers, wildlife managers, and other experts are employed by the Park Service to work in the many public parks that are owned and operated by the federal government.

As the complexity of the federal bureaucracy has increased with the creation of more and more specialized units and the funding of increasing numbers of federal programs, its expertise has also grown. As a result, when new programs and policies are being considered, Congress and the president are more likely to listen to experts from the bureau or agency involved than to get information from other sources. In this way the bureaucrats can have an important influence on the programs they will be carrying out.

The Agency/Committee/Interest Group Triangle

Another important but less well-understood source of bureaucratic power is the close three-way relationship that often develops among members of the executive agency administering a program, the congressional committees and subcommittees that appropriate money to it and oversee its operations, and the special-interest groups affected by the agency's activities. These relationships are often referred to as "iron triangles."

To understand the agency/committee/interest group triangle, it is necessary to appreciate the fact that each member of the triangle benefits from the relationship. From the standpoint of the agency, the benefit is more influence. An executive agency with a large and vocal clientele has much more clout with Congress and the White House. If it also has friendly ties with a congressional subcommittee, it has a greater chance of getting its programs approved and funded. The members of the committee benefit from this arrangement by gaining influence over the creation of public policy. For their part, the interest groups gain a greater voice in setting policy through their association with the agency and the subcommittee.

Perhaps the best way to understand the impact of these three-way relationships is through an example. Beginning in the 1930s the government operated a system for protecting the market price of major agricultural products such as wheat, corn, peanuts, and tobacco. For many decades the growers of these crops, their elected representatives who served on the congressional agriculture committees, and the Department of Agriculture worked together to guarantee the continued existence of the price support system.

Delegation of Power by Congress

Until the early twentieth century, Congress dominated the federal government. Not only did it make the laws but it also controlled how they were carried out. This was possible in an earlier, simpler time, before the government grew into the large, complex organization it is today. Congress now has great difficulty dealing with all the matters in which the government is involved.

But it was not only the complexity of modern government that caused Congress to loosen its hold on the reins of government. Beginning in the late nineteenth century, reformers called for an end to legislative "meddling" with the affairs of the executive branch. And in the early twentieth century, more and more people were viewing public administration as a career, demanding greater freedom from congressional control.

As a result of those forces, Congress has delegated broad powers to the executive branch of government and the independent regulatory commissions. Much of the legislation enacted by Congress contains very general language that gives agencies the authority to assign specific meaning to the statutes they administer. Congress also gives many agencies the power to make rules that have the same force as congressional laws. Thus, there now exists a large body of agency rules, known as *administrative law,* which has been created by the administrative agencies rather than by Congress. The multivolume regulations issued over the years by the U.S. Internal Revenue Service are probably the most famous (or infamous) example of administrative rule-making.

RESTRAINTS ON THE BUREAUCRACY

To hear some people talk—businesspeople complaining about government "over-regulation," liberals who distrust the Central Intelligence Agency—the federal bureaucracy exercises too much power. At the same time, there is a common stereotype of bureaucrats as "timid, unimaginative, and reluctant to make decisions" and "paralyzed with indecision when confronted with an opportunity to exercise authority."[15] Neither of these views is accurate. Bureaucrats are not powerless, but their power is not absolute. There are important restraints on the bureaucracy.

Some of the limitations on the bureaucracy are constitutional and legal. These include the powers of the president, Congress, and the courts. Other limitations are more informal. One example is the fact that the bureaucracy must share power and compete with Congress and with private groups. Often, intense pressure is placed on governmental agencies by these private organizations. The media also play a role in limiting the power of the bureaucracy, as do the internal restraints that the bureaucracy places on itself. In this section we discuss both the constitutional and legal checks on the bureaucracy and the more informal restraints on its authority.

The Powers of the President

Because the president is the constitutional head of the executive branch, he is responsible for the bureaucracy. As we have seen, however, it is extremely difficult to control the sprawling organization that the federal bureaucracy has become today. Still, every president makes some attempt at controlling the bureaucracy. This effort begins with the president's appointment power; the more new people (who are loyal to him) the president can bring into the bureaucracy, the greater his chance of gaining some control over its operations.

APPOINTMENT POWER   The Constitution gives the president the authority to appoint all higher-level members of the executive branch, subject to the advice and consent of the Senate. However, the Constitution (Article II, Section 2) also permits Congress to grant the president the power to appoint lower executive officials alone (or to vest such appointments in the courts of law or in the heads of the government departments). The president's appointment power extends to all policy-making positions, including all heads of executive departments and agencies and all undersecretaries and assistant secretaries, but it does not apply to the civil service. It allows the president to select men and women who are in basic agreement with his views on important issues of public policy.

As mentioned earlier, the Senate rarely interferes with the hiring of upper-level executive officials. Its examination of a nominee for such a position is usually brief, and it almost never rejects a candidate suggested by the president. But the president's power to appoint federal officials who function solely within a state, as opposed to regional or national officials, is limited by **senatorial courtesy.** Under this unwritten rule the president must clear his nominations with the senior senator of the president's party from the state in question. If the senator declares a particular nominee "personally obnoxious," the Senate will reject the nomination. If neither of the senators from the state in question is a member of the president's party, the president can seek advice from members of his party in the House of Representatives or party leaders in the state.

REMOVAL POWERS   In addition to the power of appointment, the president has certain **removal powers.** These powers are not mentioned in the Constitution, but the Supreme Court has stated that the president has the power to remove any executive official and that Congress cannot limit this authority. According to the Court, this power is part of the president's power as chief executive, and any attempt by Congress to limit it is unconstitutional.[16] (This power, like the power of appointment, does not apply to civil service positions.) But the Supreme Court has also ruled that members of the independent regulatory commissions may be removed by the president only for causes specified by Congress, because these agencies are not purely executive but have judicial functions and serve chiefly as agents of the legislature.[17]

In removing a member of the executive branch, the president usually acts with care so as to avoid political embarrassment. A top-level official will probably be asked to resign to avoid adverse publicity. Rarely is a high government official actually fired by the president.

POWER TO REORGANIZE   Historically, any significant change in the organization of the federal government required the passage of legislation by Congress. Beginning in the 1930s, however, Congress delegated to the president the right to make changes in the structure of the executive branch, subject to rejection by either branch of the legislature within sixty days of the time the proposal was made. This procedure applies to all administrative changes except minor ones such as the name of an agency. (Departments cannot be created or abolished without an act of Congress.)

THE PRESIDENT'S LEADERSHIP ROLE   The president can use the prestige of his office, plus his own leadership ability, to guide the bureaucracy and keep it within certain bounds. The president can set budget and hiring limits and make policy statements, and in many cases the bureaucracy will fall into line. Of course, the effectiveness of presidential leadership will vary, depending on the character and skills of the president, and there will always be resistance. As a former State Department official has pointed out, the president and the bureaucrats have a different sense of time: The bureaucrats "will be around long after the new wave has fallen back exhausted from their shore."[18] They are not motivated to change the nature of their work—which is, after all, their career—with the coming of each new administration.

The Powers of Congress

Congress has several important lawmaking powers that serve to set limits on what the bureaucracy can do. Its power to appropriate money is a basic control: To reduce an agency's budget is to limit its ability to function. Congress has the power to delegate to executive agencies and independent commissions specific authority to regulate and administer programs. And it can, of course, take away or alter that authority. In 1978, for example, Congress deregulated the interstate railroad and trucking industries and thus deprived the Interstate Commerce Commission of powers it had long exercised.

Congress can also eliminate an agency, although it is more difficult to terminate an agency than to end a program, since a single agency may administer a number of programs. Organizations are often able to survive long after their usefulness has ended or their popularity has declined.

Elimination of agencies is rare, but it does occur. On January 1, 1985, the Civil Aeronautics Board went out of existence as a result of congressional action. For many decades the CAB had regulated the fares and flying schedules of the nation's commercial airlines. When Congress deregulated the airline industry in 1978, it also provided for the termination of the CAB. But it took another six years to agree on a specific plan to assign the remaining functions of the CAB to the Department of Transportation and to end the board's existence.

Finally, Congress can pass laws that change the decisions of administrative agencies. It rarely does so, however, mainly because it simply does not have the time. The number of regulations issued by the federal bureaucracy is so great that even if it did nothing else, Congress would be unable to examine them all. Moreover, Congress is more concerned with attempting to solve new problems than with dealing with the consequences of actions it has taken in the past.

In addition to using these powers, Congress has passed specific legislation designed to control the executive branch of the government. That legislation includes the Freedom of Information Act of 1966 and the Congressional Budget and Impoundment Control Act of 1974. Congress also possesses the basic right to supervise the activities of the federal bureaucracy through its constitutional power of legislative oversight.

THE FREEDOM OF INFORMATION ACT OF 1966 In 1966, to the dismay of some federal agencies, Congress enacted a law that requires them to open their files to any person who requests specific documents. The purpose of the Freedom of Information Act is to make available to public scrutiny the decision-making processes of federal agencies. The act contains some significant exceptions, however. Government agencies do not have to make public those records that are concerned with national defense and foreign policy; statutes that specifically bar disclosure, such as the 1974 Federal Privacy Act; trade secrets and commercial and financial information obtained on the basis of confidentiality; personnel practices and rules; or the medical and personnel files of federal employees.

BUDGET ACT CONTROLS We mentioned earlier that Congress delegated a large degree of control over the budgetary process to the executive branch in the Budget and Accounting Act of 1921. In 1974, however, it regained a major role in that process with the passage of the Congressional Budget and Impoundment Control Act. This act set up a means by which Congress could deal with the budget as a whole instead of one appropriation at a time. As discussed in Chapter 7, it also created the Congressional Budget Office, whose purpose is to keep watch over the national budget and to report its findings to Congress.

Chapter 8 described the action taken by Congress to stop the **impoundment** of funds by the president. This legislation, part of the 1974 act just mentioned, also serves as a restraint on the bureaucracy in that it gives Congress the final say on the spending of federal money.

LEGISLATIVE OVERSIGHT **Oversight** (the term here means "supervision," not "failure to notice") of bureaucratic activities is an important constitutional power of Congress. It is an aspect of the system of checks and balances, a method by which Congress exercises control over the executive branch.

In general, members of Congress have been reluctant to exercise their oversight function very aggressively. They have been more concerned with two other goals: staying in office and affecting government policy through new legislation.[19] Moreover, to be effective as watchdogs over agency activities, members of Congress have to become experts in the areas in which the agencies are active. In some cases this does happen. As a result of long service on a specific committee, a member of Congress may develop a great deal of expertise in the committee's area of interest. But the three-way relationship described earlier often takes over, making the legislator unwilling to upset the applecart by scrutinizing the bureaucrats too closely.

There are times, however, when Congress becomes eager to investigate executive units. In 1987 a joint committee of Congress conducted an investigation of the Reagan administration's secret sales of military equipment to Iran and its related policy of using the proceeds from those sales to aid rebel forces in Nicaragua. In the early 1990s Congress exercised this power with respect to the banking scandal that rocked the nation's savings and loan institutions. The investment activities of President Clinton and his wife—known as the Whitewater affair—were also investigated by Congress in 1995 and 1996. In 2002 a joint committee of Congress investigated the security failures that led to the September 11 terrorist attacks on the United States.

At a humbler level, members of Congress engage in what is known as *casework,* that is, helping their constituents deal with government agencies like the Internal Revenue Service or the Social Security Administration. Casework also serves as a check on the bureaucracy and can prevent injury and injustice in individual situations, but its effect is limited. This kind of "meddling" is insignificant compared with the flood of bureaucratic activity that goes largely unsupervised by Congress.

JUDICIAL REVIEW The federal courts have the ultimate power to control the decisions and actions of executive agencies and independent regulatory commissions. Legal challenges to the decisions of these bodies can be taken to the federal courts. For example, many organizations concerned with environmental

Attorney General John Ashcroft, Secretary of Homeland Security Tom Ridge, and FBI Director Robert Mueller testify before a Senate Judiciary Committee on the progress of the war on terrorism, March 2003.

issues have brought lawsuits in federal courts seeking to overturn decisions of the Department of the Interior and the Environmental Protection Agency. And in 1996 the nation's tobacco companies challenged the rules issued by the Food and Drug Administration to regulate tobacco advertising and promotions aimed at young people. But legal actions begun in the courts are not the only reason for the importance of judicial review. The mere existence of judicial review serves as a deterrent to arbitrary acts by government agencies.

Although judicial review is a significant check on the illegal use of bureaucratic power, its availability and scope are limited. Normally, federal courts will not hear a case until the challenging party has exhausted all avenues of appeal within the agency itself. The courts also place considerable weight on the agency's interpretation of federal law and will uphold it as long as it is not unreasonable.

Whistleblowers

Another important limitation on the bureaucracy is provided by **whistleblowers**—employees who "blow the whistle" on waste, fraud, and abuse. Corporate and government employees who reveal the mistakes or misdeeds of their employers may be dealt with harshly; they may be reprimanded, fired, or demoted. An example is the case of Lynn Bruner, a civil servant who became a district director in the Equal Employment Opportunity Commission in 1986. When she arrived at her new position, she noticed that there was a large backlog of age-discrimination cases (which must be investigated within two years or they become invalid). She soon reached the conclusion that such cases were intentionally allowed to lapse, and she made a statement on the matter to a major newspaper. She was promptly given a negative job rating and informed that she would be demoted and transferred.[20]

In 1989 Congress acted to protect whistleblowers against arbitrary actions by employers. As one member of the House described it, the Whistleblowers Protection Act is designed to allow employees to "confidently carry out their responsibilities without fear of retribution, of ruined careers, lost jobs, and destroyed families, hopes and dreams." The act provides that a federal agency accused of penalizing a whistleblower must provide "clear and convincing" evidence that the action in question did not stem from the worker's whistleblowing.[21]

Other Restraints

In addition to the powers of Congress, the president, and the courts, there are several other significant restraints on the bureaucracy. The news media play an important role in controlling bureaucratic authority. Because the media both influence and reflect public opinion, executive officials pay attention to the views expressed in the media, especially in major newspapers like *The Washington Post* and *The New York Times,* news magazines such as *Time* and *Newsweek,* and the major television networks and cable stations. Reporters and correspondents gather information and present it to readers and viewers, who then may question the government's policies.

The media also keep bureaucrats on their toes through the threat of exposure. Not only do reporters make public the personal wrongdoings of bureaucrats, they can also publish information that government agencies might prefer to conceal. A classic example of the latter is the publication by *The New York Times* and *The Washington Post* of the Defense Department's study of the Vietnam War, the so-called *Pentagon Papers,* in 1971, an action that was vigorously opposed by the Nixon administration in the federal courts. In addition, the media can sometimes serve as a channel through which executive agencies communicate with the public. Reporters are always looking for news, and the agencies are willing to supply information that will make them look good. There is little danger that the media will become a tool of the bureaucracy, however, for "the news that reporters commonly seek is information that agencies are reluctant to divulge."[22]

In addition to the media, other outside groups can serve to limit the actions of the bureaucracy. In some cases a private group is an almost permanent opponent of a government agency. Some business associations, for example, do all they can to limit the powers of regulatory commissions. In other cases the relationship between an agency and a private group (for example, between the Department of Agriculture and farm groups) is a friendly one. Even in these cases, however, the private group limits the bureaucracy in that its views have some influence on what the agency does.

Another set of limitations on bureaucratic power is provided by the bureaucracy itself. For one thing, there is competition within the bureaucracy: Various agencies compete for funds, programs, and influence. A good example is the competition among the branches of the armed forces for funding in general and control over the development of weapons systems in particular. Competition also exists within executive agencies as different groups of experts present competing solutions to problems such as the budget deficit.

A basic restraint on the bureaucracy is provided by the values of bureaucrats. If bureaucrats believe that their role is that of a public servant and that their power must be used for the public good and not for personal gain, abuses of bureaucratic power are less likely. Values like these are taught in the schools and constantly expressed in the media and elsewhere. Thus, bureaucrats are always reminded of their proper role in a democratic government. Although self-restraint alone cannot be depended on to keep the bureaucracy in line, it must be counted among the factors that prevent bureaucrats from becoming lawbreakers.

Finally, the power of some bureaucratic agencies has been diminished since the 1970s as a result of **deregulation.** Banking, transportation, and communication are among the areas in which Congress has repealed regulatory legislation. A recent example of deregulation occurred when Congress enacted the Telecommunication Act of 1996. This law eliminated many federal regulations affecting the telecommunications industry and made the states responsible for the remaining operations.

CONCLUSION

Many people are concerned about the exercise of power by government officials. They believe that there are insufficient restraints on the power of bureaucrats to regulate the American people. In reality, however, the power of the bureaucracy is often exaggerated. Government agencies are not free to do whatever they like.

They compete with one another; they are limited by Congress, the courts, and private groups; and deregulation has occurred in major areas of the economy.

It can be argued that the federal bureaucracy has more power than is acceptable in a democratic political system. There is no doubt that the bureaucracy is very large and that its decisions have a significant impact on the lives of citizens. The great size of the bureaucracy is due largely to the actions of Congress. Legislation is drafted in very general terms and must be translated into a functioning program by some government agency—either one that already exists or a new one established to carry out the new policy.

When citizens are frustrated by the activities of the bureaucracy (or its lack of activity), they turn to their representatives in Congress for help, not recognizing that Congress was the source of the problem in the first place. As one observer has described the situation, "The bureaucracy serves as a convenient lightning rod for public frustration and a convenient whipping boy for congressmen."[23]

Despite the often misplaced public resentment of the bureaucracy, the powerful, if not absolute, role of the federal bureaucracy is unlikely to be challenged in the foreseeable future. Although there has been much talk about "reinventing" and "downsizing" government, relatively little has changed. And little will change as long as members of Congress satisfy voters by continuing existing programs and establishing new ones.

QUESTIONS FOR THOUGHT

1. What are the differences between line and staff organizations?
2. How are the independent regulatory commissions organized, and what function do they perform?
3. What organizations make up the Executive Office of the President?
4. In what ways can Congress exercise control over the federal bureaucracy?

INTERNET ACTIVITIES

1. *Federal Reserve System.* Go to **http://www.federalreserve.gov/general.html**. Write a synopsis of the functions of the FRS. Summarize the selection process. What background characteristics do the members share?
2. *Iron Triangle.* Go to **http://www.tray.com/fecinfo/**. Go to "Candidate $ Leaders." Select "list them" and click on a candidate to find contributions to that candidate. Go to **http://congress.org/** to find that individual's committee assignment in Congress. Repeat this process for another PAC and individual. Record the data as you go. What pattern for contributions emerges?

KEY TERMS

agencies	field services	oversight
bureaus	government corporations	political executives
bureaucracy	impoundment	removal powers
cabinet	independent regulatory	senatorial courtesy
civil service	commissions	spoils system
departments	line agencies	staff agencies
deregulation	merit system	whistleblowers

SUGGESTED READING

Bozeman, Barry. *Bureaucracy and Red Tape.* Upper Saddle River, NJ: Prentice Hall, 2000.

Bardach, Eugene, and Robert A. Kagen. *Going by the Book: The Problem of Regulatory Unreasonableness.* Somerset, NJ: Transaction, 2002.

Donahue, John D., ed. *Making Washington Work.* Washington, DC: Brookings Institution Press, 1999.

Fesler, James W., and Donald F. Kettl. *The Politics of the Administrative Process,* 2nd ed. New York: Chatham House, 1996.

Gawthrop, Louis C. *Public Service and Democracy: Ethical Imperatives for the 21st Century.* New York: Chatham House, 1998.

Golden, Marissa Martino. *Bureaucratic Behavior in a Political Setting.* New York: Columbia University Press, 2000.

Heinrich, Carolyn J., and Laurence E. Lynn, Jr., eds. *Governance and Performance.* Washington, DC: Georgetown University Press, 2000.

Kerwin, Cornelius M. *Rule Making: How Government Agencies Write Law and Make Policy,* 2nd ed. Washington, DC: Congressional Quarterly Press, 1999.

Light, Paul C. *The New Public Service.* Washington, DC: Brookings Institution Press, 1999.

Rouse, John E., and George E. Berkley. *The Craft of Public Administration,* 8th ed. New York: McGraw-Hill, 2000.

NOTES

1. "Mr. Clinton, Meet Mr. Gore," *Wall Street Journal,* October 28, 1993, p. A22.

2. Ibid.

3. Godfrey P. Miller, "Independent Agencies," in Philip B. Kurland et al., eds., *The Supreme Court Review, 1986* (Chicago: University of Chicago Press, 1987), pp. 96–97.

4. Thomas E. Cronin, *The State of the Presidency,* 2nd ed. (Boston: Little, Brown, 1980), p. 276.

5. Benjamin I. Page and Mark P. Petracca, *The American Presidency* (New York: McGraw-Hill, 1983), p. 193.

6. U.S. Bureau of the Census, *Statistical Abstract of the United States, 1995,* 115th ed. (Washington, DC: Government Printing Office, 1995), Table 540, p. 350.

7. Harold M. Barger, *The Impossible Presidency: Illusions and Realities of Executive Power* (Glenview, IL: Scott, Foresman, 1984), p. 205.

8. Larry Berman, *The New American Presidency* (Boston: Little, Brown, 1987), p. 118.

9. Barger, *Impossible Presidency,* p. 198.

10. Ibid., p. 195.

11. Bruce D. Porter, "Parkinson's Law: War and the Growth of American Government," *Public Interest* (Summer 1980), p. 50.

12. U.S. Bureau of the Census, *Statistical Abstract of the United States, 2003,* 123rd ed. (Washington, DC: Government Printing Office, 2003), Table 500, p. 337.

13. William L. Riordan, ed., *Plunkitt of Tammany Hall* (New York: Dutton, 1963), p. 13.

14. Herbert Kaufman, "The Growth of the Federal Personnel System," in Wallace S. Sayre, ed., *The Federal Government Service* (Englewood Cliffs, NJ: Prentice Hall, 1965), pp. 29, 31.

15. Francis E. Rourke, *Bureaucracy, Politics, and Public Policy,* 2nd ed. (Boston: Little, Brown, 1976), p. 166.

16. *Myers v. United States,* 272 U.S. 52 (1926); *Bowsher v. Synar,* 478 U.S. 714 (1986).

17. *Humphrey's Executor v. United States,* 295 U.S. 602 (1935).

18. Hodding Carter, III, "The Unequal Bureaucratic Contest," *Wall Street Journal,* January 8, 1981, p. 19.

19. Fred A. Kramer, *Dynamics of Public Bureaucracy: An Introduction to Public Management,* 2nd ed. (Cambridge, MA: Winthrop, 1981), p. 369.

20. Gillian Sandford, "Reprisals Related by EEOC Worker," *Congressional Quarterly,* March 25, 1989, pp. 643–44.

21. Rep. Gerry Sikorski (D., Minn.), quoted in Macon Morehouse, "'Whistleblower' Protection Bill Cleared Easily by House," *Congressional Quarterly,* March 25, 1989, p. 643.

22. Rourke, *Bureaucracy,* p. 173.

23. Francis E. Rourke, ed., *Bureaucratic Power in National Policy-Making,* 4th ed. (Boston: Little, Brown, 1986), p. 230.

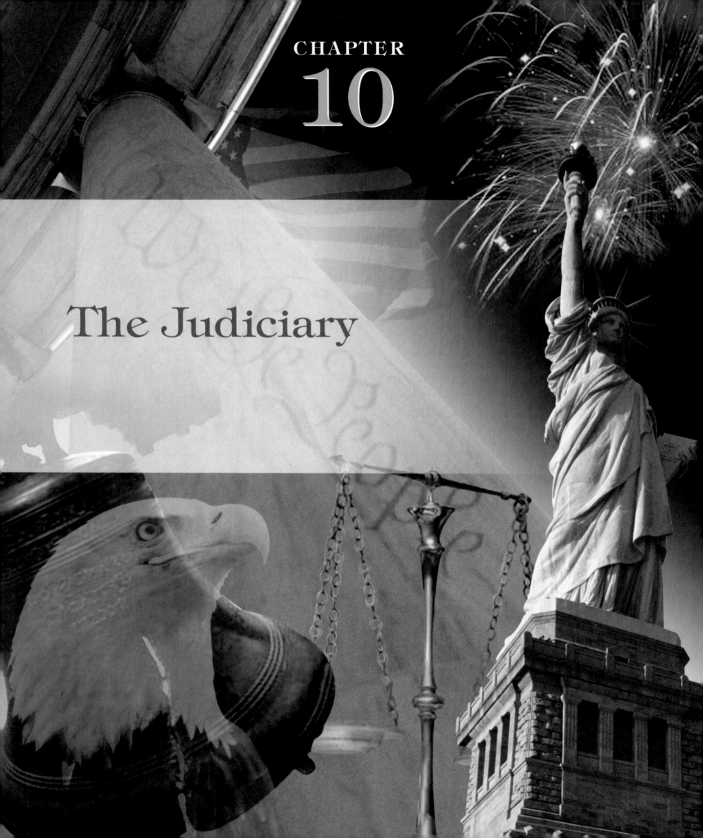

The Judiciary

Time has shown that Madison was correct in his view of the attitude of the American public toward the judicial branch of government. Throughout the nation's history the American public has generally held the federal courts, and especially the Supreme Court, in high esteem. Although the courts have occasionally made rulings that aroused controversy and criticism, Americans have rarely questioned the usefulness and importance of an independent judiciary.

Federal courts deal with all aspects of federal law. They frequently are asked to interpret the meaning of laws enacted by Congress, but it is in its role of interpreter of the Constitution that the judiciary takes on its greatest importance. And the fact that the United States Supreme Court is the final interpreter of the Constitution places the Court at the center of the nation's governmental system.

This chapter focuses on the meaning of the term *law* and the role of the courts in American society. It describes the nation's dual court system, with special attention to the Supreme Court, and it examines the means by which federal judges and Supreme Court justices are selected. It also explores a major function of the judiciary—judicial review—in which the courts review the acts of state and national governments and measure them against the supreme law of the land, the U.S. Constitution.

In his *Federalist,* No. 78 essay, Alexander Hamilton wrote that the judiciary would be the least powerful branch of the federal government since the only authority it had was judgment. But we shall see in Chapters 11 and 12 that the exercise of judgment by the Supreme Court has a very important impact on the formation of public policy for this nation.

> It may always be expected that the judicial branch, when happily filled, will most engage the respect and reliance of the people as the surest expositor of the Constitution.
>
> —James Madison (1834)

THE LAW

Before we can discuss the courts and how they operate, we need to understand the nature of the law. For our purposes, **law** may be defined as the principles and regulations established by a government, applicable to a people, and enforced by the government. There are five basic types of law: common law, equity, statutory law, constitutional law, and administrative law.

Common law, often called "judge-made" law, is a set of rules that have been created by judges in the course of rendering decisions on court cases. Common law dates from medieval times in England, when the king gave certain officials the authority to travel around the country and settle legal disputes. The decisions of these judges were based on good sense and custom, and depended on the facts of the case. Once a rule had been generally accepted by the English judges, it was applied to similar situations that arose in the future. These rules accumulated until they formed a body of judicial rulings that became known as the common law.

Precedents are important in our legal system because in most situations courts will apply the principle of *stare decisis.* This legal rule requires courts to apply existing precedents to cases involving similar facts. *Stare decisis* is not an absolute rule; courts may change existing precedents when they believe that the circumstances require a change. But such changes are the exception rather than the rule. Because of *stare decisis,* the law is both stable and predictable, and similar legal problems will have the same legal rules applied to them.

The English colonists brought the common law with them to the New World. As new rules were added and old rules changed, American common law evolved. In the United States today judicial practice is guided by common-law rules in every state except Louisiana, whose legal system is based on French law.

Common law had some limitations, however. It did not provide a way of dealing with a wrongful act that had not yet occurred. It could not be applied until the act had been committed and the case had been brought to court. Moreover, its remedies were confined to awarding money damages to an injured party. **Equity** evolved in response to those weaknesses in the common law. Like common law, equity was based on previous judicial decisions. But it was different in that one of the king's officers, the chancellor, was given the power to prevent an illegal act and to grant remedies other than awards of money. The chancellor's office developed into a separate court—an equity or chancery court—that could issue a court order requiring a person or company to refrain from a particular act.

Consider the following example. Assume that *A* owns a piece of land on which he is carefully growing his favorite tree. *A* finds out that *B* is planning to build a road on *B*'s nearby property that will result in the death of his tree. Under common law, *A* must wait until this act has occurred before suing *B* for money damages. But under equity, *A* may be able to obtain a court order, called an **injunction,** that requires *B* to refrain from building the road. If *B* violates the injunction, she can be punished for contempt of court.

There are no separate equity courts in the federal court system; equity matters are handled by the regular federal courts. Most states also have an integrated court system in which common-law and equity cases are administered by the same courts. A few states (Delaware, for example) maintain separate equity courts.

Statutory law differs from both common law and equity. A *statute* is a law that has been formally declared by a legislature, in contrast to "judge-made" law. The twentieth century saw a shift toward more statutory law; many areas of law that were once governed by common law are now covered by statutes.

On some occasions **treaties** may also be included in the domestic law of the United States. Because the Constitution makes treaties the supreme law of the land (Article VI, Section 2), some provisions of these international agreements can be enforced in U.S. courts. Thus, for example, a citizen of another country may inherit property in the United States if a treaty between the United States and that country provides for such a right.

Constitutional law results from the interpretation and application of a national or state constitution. It includes all the statements made by both federal and state courts in interpreting constitutional provisions. Through its decisions, the United States Supreme Court plays an especially important role in defining the meaning of constitutional provisions for the nation as a whole.

Finally, there is a body of law called **administrative law,** which consists of the regulations that have been issued by administrative agencies. During the twentieth century executive agencies grew rapidly in both number and power. This occurred largely as a result of increased regulation of the nation's economic and social life by the government. Thus, there is now an extensive set of rules, collectively known as administrative law, issued by agencies of the federal, state, and local governments. The United States Internal Revenue Service, for example, has issued countless regulations based on its interpretation of the tax laws enacted by Congress.

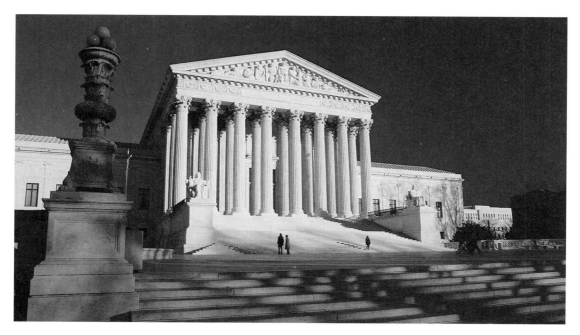

The United States Supreme Court building, Washington, DC.

Criminal and Civil Law

The law may be divided into two broad areas: criminal and civil. **Criminal law,** which today is almost entirely statutory, deals with acts that endanger the public welfare. Because the government—state and federal—alone enforces criminal law, the government is the **plaintiff** (the party that brings the case to court) in all criminal trials; the party accused of the crime is the **defendant.**

Crimes are usually classified as either misdemeanors or felonies. These terms are defined differently in the laws of the various states and in federal law. As a general rule, **misdemeanors** are less serious acts for which punishment may consist of a jail term of up to one year. **Felonies** are more serious acts for which punishment may involve a jail sentence of one year or more (or death, in states that have the death penalty for murder). Some crimes (for example, violation of national tax laws) are covered by federal law, but most are defined by state laws. Some acts may violate both federal and state law (kidnapping).

States enact criminal laws as part of their general reserve powers; criminal laws passed by Congress are based on its enumerated powers. For example, the crime of failing to pay federal taxes on tobacco products is based on Congress's power to tax; the crime of using the mails for fraudulent purposes is based on Congress's power to establish a postal system.

Throughout American history most criminal laws have been enacted by the state legislatures and prosecuted at the county level by elected district attorneys. Criminal laws passed by Congress are enforced by the United States Attorneys. There is a U.S. Attorney's office in each of the districts served by a federal district court. The office is headed by a U.S. Attorney, appointed by the president with the advice and consent of the Senate, who directs a staff of lawyers who handle all criminal or civil cases involving the U.S. government that arise in that district. While Congress has enacted an increasing number of federal criminal laws in recent years, the vast majority of criminal cases are still handled by the state judicial systems.

Civil law deals primarily with disputes between private individuals or corporations and defines the rights of the parties in the dispute. A divorce suit is a civil case; so is a negligence case in which an accident has caused injury to a person or to property. Sometimes the government is involved in a civil case. Under the Sherman Antitrust Act, for example, the government can seek money damages from a corporation that enters into any "contract, combination, or conspiracy in restraint of trade." A civil case may also arise when a person or a group sues the government, as when an individual is wrongfully injured by a law enforcement agent of the government.

The Adversary System

Unlike the executive and legislative branches of government, the judiciary is largely passive. The courts must wait for cases to be brought to them before they can settle disputes. When a case comes to court, it takes the form of a conflict between parties on each side of the dispute. Each side attempts to present a view of the facts that is favorable to its case. Thus, the American legal system is often referred to as an **adversary system** because it is based on the assumption that truth will emerge from the clash of opposing interests.

The Role of the Courts

Under Article III of the Constitution, the federal courts may hear only "cases and controversies"; that is, there must be a real conflict of interest—criminal or civil— between the parties. The Supreme Court interpreted the phrase "cases and controversies" as follows: "The term implies the existence of present or possible adverse parties, whose contentions are submitted to the court for adjudication."[1] Moreover, the party bringing a federal suit must demonstrate some form of personal injury, not a general wrong that is shared by the public at large. The party "must distinguish himself from the general citizenry, by showing a personal stake, a particular concrete injury, something more than 'generalized grievances.' "[2]

These principles have a number of important consequences. The federal courts generally will not hear cases brought by individuals solely on the basis of their status as federal taxpayers. Moreover, they will not give **advisory opinions.** Neither Congress, the president, nor a private citizen can seek an opinion from the courts on whether a proposed governmental action is constitutional or not; a case must be brought to a federal court before the court will consider the issue. (In some states, such as Massachusetts and Colorado, the courts are permitted to give advisory opinions.)

The Role of the Judge

The judge is the presiding officer of the court and the expert on all issues of law that arise in court. In a trial court the function of the judge is to maintain a "legal atmosphere," one in which arguments and evidence can be presented according to the rules of judicial procedure. The judge also instructs the jury regarding the law that applies in the case and discusses the possible verdicts it may reach. Finally, the judge pronounces a judgment or a sentence based on the jury's verdict or, in the case of a non-jury trial, on the basis of his or her analysis of the facts.

Laws are written in general terms and are intended to apply to a large number of cases. But the cases to which they apply may be very different. The judge often must decide which law should apply in a given case and then determine the meaning of the legal rule. This occurs at all levels of the judiciary. A local judge must define the meaning of negligence in a personal-injury case, whereas the Supreme Court will be called upon to clarify the concept of freedom of speech under the First Amendment.

Thus, it is clear that judges do not simply match the law to the case. If they did, the outcome would always be predictable. The need to interpret the law has the effect of giving judges a degree of discretion in the application of the law.

THE DUAL COURT SYSTEM

Having described the general features of the American legal system, we turn our attention to the courts themselves and how they operate. First, however, it should be noted that as a consequence of its federal form of government, the United States has a *dual court* system: a federal court system and fifty state court systems. (The District of Columbia, Puerto Rico, and the U.S. territories also have federal as well as local courts.) The state systems are separated geographically, of course, but the federal and state courts overlap. The structure of these many systems is established by the constitutions and statutes of the federal government and the fifty states.

The concept of *jurisdiction* is basic to understanding the American court system. **Jurisdiction** is the right of a court to hear a particular type of case. This right is granted either by a constitution or by a legislative statute. Without jurisdiction, a court has no authority to decide a dispute. The jurisdiction of state courts is very broad; that of the federal courts is much more limited. In a few situations the state and federal courts share jurisdiction and the plaintiff can choose to sue in either court system.

Article III, Section 2, of the Constitution sets forth the jurisdiction of the federal courts. Jurisdiction may be based on either the subject matter or the nature of the parties in a particular case. Jurisdiction based on subject matter consists of all cases arising under the U.S. Constitution, federal laws, and treaties, as well as admiralty and maritime cases. Jurisdiction based on the nature of the parties can include several types of situations, such as the following:

1. Cases affecting ambassadors, other public ministers, and consuls
2. Cases in which the United States is a party
3. Disputes between two or more states
4. Disputes between citizens of different states

A legal dispute must fall within one of these provisions to be heard in the federal courts. Not all such cases are heard in federal courts, however; Congress has set certain additional limits on federal jurisdiction. For example, in disputes between citizens of different states—a frequent basis for federal court jurisdiction—the amount involved must be over $75,000. Cases involving smaller amounts must be heard in state courts.

A court's jurisdiction may be original or appellate. Courts that have **original jurisdiction** are trial courts; they determine the facts of the case as well as the law that applies to them. Courts with **appellate jurisdiction** handle appeals; they review the decisions of lower courts to determine whether they applied the correct rule of law. The United States Supreme Court, for example, has both original and appellate jurisdiction. Only rarely, however, does the Supreme Court exercise its original jurisdiction, which is limited to cases affecting ambassadors, other public ministers, and consuls and those in which states are the parties. In all other cases the Supreme Court has appellate jurisdiction. Appeals generally go from a federal district court to a court of appeals and then to the Supreme Court. In a case involving the U.S. Constitution, a treaty, or congressional law, an appeal may go directly to the Supreme Court from the highest state court with jurisdiction over the case.

It is important to understand that each court system has the right to make the final interpretation of the law in the cases over which it has jurisdiction. Thus, the highest court in each state is the final interpreter of the laws of that state, and the United States Supreme Court is the final interpreter of federal law. If a question of federal law arises in a state court—for example, if a person who has been arrested claims that his or her Fourth Amendment rights have been violated—the United States Supreme Court has the final power to rule on the issue.

CLOSE-UP

THE SUPREME COURT AS A TRIAL COURT

Ellis Island, point of entry for the immigrant fore-bears of four out of ten Americans, originally consisted of three acres of rock in the middle of New York Harbor. Since 1904, however, twenty-four acres of landfill have been added to it. The island now extends into the western half of the harbor, which is controlled by New Jersey. So who owns the landfill portion of the island, New York or New Jersey?

This dispute had been simmering for decades, but in 1993 New Jersey finally sued New York over the issue. The case was tried in the United States Supreme Court, which acted as a trial court under the original jurisdiction granted to it by the U.S. Constitution.

Cases like the Ellis Island dispute are rare. In its entire history the Court has decided only about 129 cases under its original jurisdiction; most of them have involved boundary disputes. In the Ellis Island case, New York claimed sole ownership of the island, while New Jersey claimed that it owned the landfill portion of the island under an 1834 agreement giving it control of the underwater portions of the western half of the harbor. Thus, whereas New York viewed the matter as an issue of property, New Jersey saw it as a dispute over boundaries.

When the Supreme Court must decide a case based on its original jurisdiction, it usually appoints a special "master"—usually a former jurist—to hear the facts and prepare a report. The master in the Ellis Island case visited the island and listened to a series of witnesses, including surveyors and state and federal officials. The case was then heard in a meeting room in the Supreme Court Building. Although the justices did not hear the case themselves, they received a recommendation from the master. In 1998 the Court accepted the recommendation of the master and awarded the disputed territory to New Jersey.

The State Courts

The various state court systems are organized in different ways, making it hard to present a brief description of the state courts. A few generalizations can be made, however. In some states, the lowest level of the court system is the justice of the peace or police court. In many other states, county, district, or municipal courts are found at the lowest level. (In large cities the local trial courts may be organized in a different—and more complex—way.) In most states the most important trial court is a *superior or circuit court*. Most of the states have an appellate court between the trial courts and the highest court in the state. All states have an appellate court of last resort, usually called the supreme court (in New York it is called the Court of Appeals and in Maine and Massachusetts the Supreme Judicial Court). Almost all states have special courts that deal with family problems (called domestic relations or family courts) and courts that deal with wills and estates (called probate or surrogate's courts).

The vast majority of both civil and criminal cases are brought in state courts, which therefore must handle a huge volume of cases. It is difficult to provide fully accurate information on the number of new cases filed each year in state courts. The judicial systems of the fifty states are too large and too decentralized to allow for the collection of accurate data. But what evidence does exist strongly indicates that there has been an increase in the number of state cases.

In many state court systems long delays are common, partly because of their heavy workload and partly because of their loose structure. Some states have attempted to centralize their court systems so as to increase their efficiency. Even

A typical New England courthouse located on the village green. Most civil and criminal cases are heard in state and local, not federal, courts.

so, in large cities and metropolitan areas there typically is a large backlog of cases awaiting trial.

Judges who serve on the major federal courts are appointed by the president with the advice and consent of the Senate and hold office for life—or, as the Constitution expresses it, during "good behavior." The system for selecting state judges and their terms of office are very different. During the era of Jacksonian democracy (1825–1845), many states changed their method of selecting judges from appointment to direct election by the voters with specified terms of office. This system is still in common use in the states for filling both trial and appellate judges. But in the twentieth century a growing number of states abandoned the election method of selecting judges and reverted to appointment by the governor or mayor. Some states have established systems that combine appointment and election. The governor makes the initial appointment, and then, after a set period of time, the public votes on whether to allow the judge to remain in office.

The Federal Courts

There are two types of federal courts: constitutional and legislative. The **constitutional courts** are established by Congress under the provisions of Article III, Section 1, of the Constitution, which declares that "the Judicial power of the United States shall be vested in one supreme Court, and in such inferior Courts as the Congress may from time to time ordain and establish."

The principal constitutional courts are the United States district courts, the United States courts of appeals, and the United States Supreme Court. Several other constitutional courts deal with specialized subjects. The Court of International Trade decides disputes arising under the nation's tariff laws (whether the government has imposed the correct levy on a product imported from another country). The Court of Customs and Patent Appeals reviews decisions of the U.S. Patent Office and some rulings of the U.S. Tariff Commission and the Court of International Trade. In 1982 Congress created the United States Court of Appeals for the Federal Circuit, which hears appeals from the U.S. Court of Customs and Patent Appeals and from the United States Claims Court. The decisions of these special courts can be appealed to the Supreme Court.

The **legislative courts** are created by Congress under its power in Article I, Section 8, to "constitute tribunals inferior to the Supreme Court" and its various expressed powers to legislate in specific areas. The principal legislative courts are the United States Court of Military Appeals, which reviews the decisions of military courts-martial; the United States Tax Court, which settles disputes between taxpayers and the Commissioner of Internal Revenue; the United States Court of Veterans Appeals; and the federal territorial courts, which handle cases in Guam, Puerto Rico, the American Virgin Islands, and the Northern Mariana Islands. The United States Court of Claims is a trial court that hears financial claims against the federal government.

Judges who serve on the legislative courts are appointed in the same way as members of the constitutional courts: They are nominated by the president, and their appointments require the advice and consent of the Senate. But the two types of courts differ in one significant way. Judges on constitutional courts have life tenure. In contrast, the length of service of judges on legislative courts is determined by Congress and varies from one court to another. For example, the three civilian judges who serve on the United States Court of Veterans Appeals and on the United States Court of Military Appeals are appointed for fifteen-year terms.

The most important federal constitutional courts are the district courts, the courts of appeals, and the Supreme Court. In the remainder of this section we examine each of these types of courts.

UNITED STATES DISTRICT COURTS   There are eighty-nine district courts in the fifty states, plus one each in the District of Columbia, the Commonwealth of Puerto Rico, and the territories of the United States. The number of cases heard by these courts increased during the first half of the 1990s, then stabilized and began a slow decline. Between 2000 and 2001, for example, new civil case filings dropped from 259,517 to 250,907; criminal filings also declined but only by a very small amount—from 62,745 to 62,708.[3] The drop would have been sharper except for an increase in drug, weapon, robbery, and sex-offense cases.[4]

The district courts are the trial courts of the federal judicial system; they hear both civil and criminal cases. However, they have only original jurisdiction; that is, they never hear cases on appeal. Each state has at least one federal district court. The boundary lines for a district never cross state lines, but a state may be divided into two, three, or even four districts (as in California, Texas, and New York), depending on such factors as population and the number of cases that must be handled. Congress has authorized the appointment of 665 federal district court judges. Each state has at least two district court judges, but the number of judges serving in a district ranges from two (in Alaska, for example) to as many as twenty-eight (in the Southern District of New York, which includes two New York

City counties and several suburban counties to the north). One observer has described the district courts as follows:

> [They] . . . are the basic trial courts of the federal judiciary. In that role they are the busiest of the three court layers. From some points of view the work of the trial court is both more interesting and more creative than that found in the two appellate tiers. The battle of the opposing platoons of counsel . . . takes place here. And it is here that we find the jury, that intriguing, albeit controversial, institution of citizen participation in the judicial process.[5]

UNITED STATES COURTS OF APPEALS   The thirteen courts of appeals are exclusively appellate courts. Eleven of these courts are regional, covering three or more states. A twelfth court is located in the District of Columbia; the thirteenth, the Court of Appeals for the Federal Circuit, is a national court that primarily hears cases involving patents and tariffs. (See Figure 10.1.) Except for this last court, the courts of appeals hear both civil and criminal cases. The appeals come from federal district courts located within the appellate court's circuit. In addition, about 12 percent of the work of these courts involves appeals from decisions of bankruptcy courts and of the federal regulatory agencies, such as the Federal Communications Commission and the Federal Trade Commission; most of

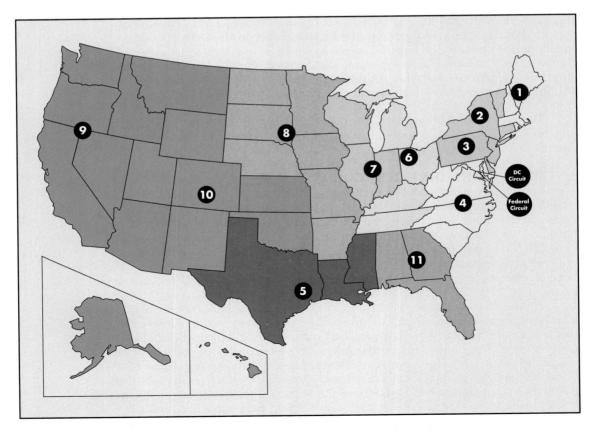

FIGURE 10–1   Geographical Boundaries of the United States Courts of Appeals.

these agency appeals come to the circuit court of appeals that sits in the District of Columbia.

Less than 25 percent of cases are appealed. Even so, the appellate courts have experienced an increase in cases that parallels the increase in cases filed in the district courts. Appeals to the U.S. courts of appeals (not including the U.S. Court of Appeals for the Federal Circuit) increased in each of the seven years between 1995 and 2001. In the 12-month period ending in September 2001, the number of new civil appeals rose from 25,259 to 35,064, and criminal appeals grew from 10,216 to 11,105.[6]

There are 179 judges on the thirteen federal courts of appeals. The number of judgeships for each circuit generally depends on the number of cases heard in that court. Thus the federal appeal courts have from six judges (the First Circuit) to twenty-eight (the Ninth Circuit). Each case that comes to a court of appeals is normally heard by a panel of three judges. The attorneys for the opposing parties present written arguments, or **briefs,** to the court. They are also allowed a limited time in which to present oral arguments. After hearing these presentations and studying the briefs and the trial records of the case, the judges confer privately before announcing their decision.

The courts of appeals have no choice regarding which cases they will hear. In most situations the losing party in the district court or regulatory agency has a right to appeal. The main exception to this rule is that the government may not appeal a loss in a criminal case; such appeals are barred by the Fifth Amendment prohibition against double jeopardy.

The decisions of the courts of appeal are often of great importance. As we shall see, the United States Supreme Court decides only between 75 and 80 cases during its October to June term. This means that many of the rulings of the courts of appeal will not be reviewed by the nation's highest court and will, therefore, be the law of the land in the geographic areas covered by each of these courts.

THE SUPREME COURT

The United States Supreme Court is the nation's highest court and the only one that was actually created by the Constitution (Article III, Section 1). The Supreme Court is the final interpreter of the law on all matters involving the U.S. Constitution, federal laws, and treaties, whether the case began in a federal court or a state court. As such, it has enormous power to shape federal law—including constitutional law, since many of its cases are concerned with constitutional issues.

The Supreme Court is in session from early October until late June or early July each year. It usually hears oral arguments from Monday to Thursday for two weeks of each month. Fridays are devoted to conferences at which cases are discussed and voted upon and requests for appellate review are considered. The remaining two weeks of each month are devoted to examining the cases and writing opinions.

Oral Arguments

The attorneys for the parties in a case that the Supreme Court has agreed to hear submit carefully written, detailed briefs so that the justices can become familiar with the facts and issues of the dispute. In cases in which the Court allows oral arguments, attorneys may present their views in person. The justices may, and often do, interrupt the attorneys. In the early nineteenth century it was not un-common for the Court to hear several days of argument on a single case. Today, however, its heavy workload no longer permits such a luxury; each case usually receives one hour (half an hour for the attorney for each side in the dispute). This time restriction is strictly enforced, even if an attorney's presentation must be halted in the middle of a sentence. A system of lights on the lectern signals the attorney twice—when there are five minutes remaining and when the time has expired.

The justices may interrupt oral arguments at any time to ask questions, or they may wait until the end of the presentation. In either case this procedure demands a good deal of poise and skill on the part of the lawyer. Some justices are gentle in questioning attorneys; others ask difficult and probing questions and seem to enjoy putting lawyers on the spot.

Conferences

After studying the briefs and hearing oral arguments for several cases, the justices debate the cases in their secret Friday conferences. The doors of the conference room are locked; no one other than the nine justices is present, and no record of the discussion is kept. The justices are seated around a large, rectangular conference table. The chief justice presents his own view of a case first, followed by the other justices in descending order of seniority. A final vote may then be taken, but this is not usually done, since the justices have already made known their views on the case.[7]

Opinions

The writer of the Court's **majority opinion** faces a difficult task: He or she must not only declare the decision of the Court but also create a statement that will satisfy all the justices who voted with the majority. Often justices reach the same decision for somewhat different reasons; such differences must be reconciled in the opinion.

The assignment of majority opinions is handled in the following manner: When the chief justice is part of the majority, he either writes the opinion himself (the usual procedure for very important cases) or assigns the case to another justice who has voted with the majority. The assignment may be based on any of a number of factors, including the legal expertise and philosophy of the individual justices and the desire to equalize the justices' workloads. If the chief justice is not part of the majority, the task of making the assignment falls to the member of the majority with the most seniority on the Court.

Besides the majority opinion, two other kinds of opinions may be written: concurring and dissenting opinions. When justices who voted with the majority feel that the majority opinion does not adequately explain why they voted as they did, they may write **concurring opinions** stating that they agree with the decision on the case but not for the reasons set forth in the majority opinion. A **dissenting opinion** may be written by any justice who voted with the minority. Even though it may have no immediate effect, it serves as a record that may be referred to in the future. As former Chief Justice Charles Evans Hughes once stated:

CLOSE-UP

DISSENTING OPINIONS

The practice of filing dissenting opinions began shortly after the formation of the Supreme Court in 1789. But throughout much of the Court's history such opinions were the exception rather than the rule. In the early decades of the twentieth century, perhaps 85 percent of the justices' decisions were unanimous. But since the 1930s dissenting opinions have become very common; in many recent terms of the Court dissents were filed in about two-thirds of the cases that were decided.

Most dissenting opinions have little lasting effect. They are quickly forgotten or, at best, are recorded in casebooks on American constitutional law. In the latter setting they become useful educational tools; they require students to consider other possible reasoning besides that found in the majority opinion. A few dissenting opinions have, however, had profound and lasting consequences. For example, in the years after World War I, Justices Oliver Wendell Holmes, Jr., and Louis Brandeis became famous for their dissenting opinions upholding freedom of speech for political radicals.

Perhaps the most famous—and significant—dissent in American constitutional history was written by Justice John Marshall Harlan in the case of *Plessy v. Ferguson*. The Supreme Court had ruled that racial segregation did not violate the equal protection clause of the Fourteenth Amendment as long as the government provided "separate but equal" facilities for whites and blacks. Justice Harlan, a Kentuckian by birth and a former slave owner, condemned the Court's decision and foreshadowed the position it would take six decades later in *Brown v. Board of Education* (1954).

In view of the Constitution, in the eye of the law, there is in this country no superior, dominant, ruling class of citizens. There is no caste here. Our Constitution is color-blind, and neither knows nor tolerates classes among citizens. The humblest is the peer of the most powerful. The law regards man as man, and takes no account of his surroundings or of his color when his civil rights as guaranteed by the supreme law of the land are involved. It is, therefore, to be regretted that this high tribunal, the final expositor of the fundamental law of the land, has reached the conclusion that it is competent for a State to regulate the enjoyment by citizens of their civil rights solely upon the basis of race.

A dissent in a court of last resort is an appeal to the brooding spirit of the law, to the intelligence of a future day, when a later decision may possibly correct the error into which the dissenting judges believe the court to have been betrayed.[8]

On several days of each month in which the High Court is in session—usually Mondays and Tuesdays—decisions are announced. Printed copies of Court opinions are made available to the public and the press. These written opinions are the primary means by which the Supreme Court communicates its ideas to the judiciary, the legal profession, and the public.

The Role of the Chief Justice

The chief justice is "first among equals." Like the eight other justices, he has only one vote, but his power to assign the writing of the opinion (if he votes with the majority) gives him some extra authority. Moreover, his presentation of a case to the other justices in the Friday conference could influence the other members of the Court. The chief justice presides over the Court when it is in session and performs certain administrative tasks connected with the federal courts. Finally, the Constitution provides that when a president is impeached by the House of

Representatives, the chief justice presides over the trial in the Senate. Thus, Chief Justice William Rehnquist presided over the Senate trial of President Clinton on charges of perjury and obstruction of justice in early 1999.

Chief justices have had varying degrees of influence on their colleagues. During the early decades of the nineteenth century, Chief Justice John Marshall dominated the Court with his strong personality and intellect. Charles Evans Hughes in the 1930s and Earl Warren in the 1950s and 1960s were highly respected and very influential. The present chief justice, William H. Rehnquist, has received praise for increasing the efficiency of the Court and for the genial way in which he deals with his colleagues. (See Table 10.1.)

Bringing a Case before the Court

Almost all the cases heard by the Supreme Court fall within its appellate jurisdiction; that is, they are appeals from lower-court decisions. These cases reach the Court primarily by means of a writ of *certiorari*. A **writ of *certiorari*** is an order directing a lower court to send the record of a case to the Supreme Court for review. It is a discretionary writ; it enables the Court to decide which cases are important enough for it to consider. The procedure begins when the losing party in a federal court of appeals, or the highest state court with jurisdiction over the case, petitions the Supreme Court for a writ of *certiorari*. If at least four of the justices agree that "there are special and important reasons" for the Court to hear the case, the writ will be issued; this is known as "the rule of four." Congress has

TABLE 10.1

CHIEF JUSTICES OF THE UNITED STATES

Chief Justices	Place of Birth	Year of Birth	Appointed by	Date Oath Taken	Date Service Ended
John Jay	New York	1745	Washington	Oct. 1789	June 1795
John Rutledge[a]	South Carolina	1739	Washington	[b]	
Oliver Ellsworth	Connecticut	1745	Washington	Mar. 1796	Dec. 1800
John Marshall	Virginia	1755	Adams	Feb. 1801	July 1835
Roger Brooke Taney	Maryland	1777	Jackson	Mar. 1836	Oct. 1864
Salmon Portland Chase	New Hampshire	1808	Lincoln	Dec. 1864	May 1873
Morrison Remick Waite	Connecticut	1816	Grant	Mar. 1874	Mar. 1888
Melville Weston Fuller	Maine	1833	Cleveland	Oct. 1888	July 1910
Edward Douglass White[a]	Louisiana	1845	Taft	Dec. 1910	May 1921
William Howard Taft	Ohio	1857	Harding	July 1921	Feb. 1930
Charles Evans Hughes[a]	New York	1862	Hoover	Feb. 1930	June 1941
Harlan Fiske Stone[a]	New Hampshire	1872	F. Roosevelt	July 1941	Apr. 1946
Frederick Moore Vinson	Kentucky	1890	Truman	June 1946	Sept. 1953
Earl Warren	California	1891	Eisenhower	Oct. 1953	June 1969
Warren Earl Burger	Minnesota	1907	Nixon	June 1969	June 1986
William H. Rehnquist[a]	Arizona	1924	Reagan	Oct. 1986	—

[a] Also served as an Associate Justice of the Supreme Court.
[b] Rutledge served a 4-month recess appointment. The Senate refused to approve his nomination.

expanded the Court's discretionary power to choose its cases so that today, with very few exceptions, almost all appeals come to the Court on writs of *certiorari.*

The Court's Workload

The number of *certiorari* petitions has grown steadily over the years. In 1980 it was 5,144. The figure rose to 6,316 in 1990 and to almost 9,000 during the 2000 term of the Supreme Court.[9] Many petitions are sent by prisoners in federal and state penitentiaries; a large majority concern issues of civil liberties and civil rights. (See Chapters 11 and 12.) However, the Court accepts only a very small percentage of the petitions it receives.

The number of cases decided by the Supreme Court with full written opinions has decreased dramatically in recent years. During its 1985–1986 term, the Court issued 146 signed opinions. In both its 2000 and 2001 terms it decided only 79 cases and in the 2003 term the total declined to only 73 opinions. Part of the explanation for the decrease is Chief Justice Rehnquist's belief that the Court was deciding too many cases and that the quality of its work had suffered as a result.

SELECTION OF FEDERAL JUDGES

Choosing federal judges is one of the most important responsibilities of the president. The president's power to appoint federal judges enables him to shape the character of the judiciary. Because they serve during "good behavior," the individuals selected will continue to influence the American legal system for years, perhaps decades, after the president has left office. Presidential appointments to the courts of appeals and the Supreme Court are particularly important. These courts resolve disputes over legal rules found in statutes and in the Constitution. For example, what is the meaning of the First Amendment statement that Congress shall not establish religion? The answers to such questions have a major effect on public policy.

Selecting Judges for Lower Federal Courts

Although Articles I and II of the Constitution set forth some minimum age and citizenship requirements for serving in Congress or as president, there are absolutely no constitutional requirements for serving in the federal courts—not even that the nominee be an attorney or that Supreme Court judges have prior judicial experience. In fact, however, presidents have always chosen lawyers for judicial posts, and in recent decades candidates for the Supreme Court have had some prior experience in either a federal or a state appeals court.

Lower-court judges are formally nominated by the president with the advice and consent of the Senate.[10] Although the president has the constitutional power to make judicial nominations, he does not usually participate directly in this process. Such participation would not be practical because of the large number of vacancies at any given time, and therefore much of the work is usually performed by officials in the Justice Department. Moreover, in practice, under the long-established tradition of **senatorial courtesy,** the judges in a particular state are selected jointly by the president and the senior senator from that state who belongs to the president's party. Thus, during a Democratic administration candidates for lower-court judgeships are approved by the Democratic senator from the state in which the judge is to serve. If there are no Democratic senators, the president is free to consult with Democratic representatives from that state, with the state governor (if he or she is a Democrat), or with state party officials.

Senatorial courtesy plays a much more limited role in the selection of appeals court judges; its primary use is in connection with appointments to the district courts.[11] Senators of the president's party usually play an active role in the selection of judges for their states; they often actually designate the person to be nominated. Some simply submit a list of acceptable candidates to the Justice Department, leaving the choice to the president's staff. The candidates are then investigated by the FBI, and officials in the Justice Department review the FBI's report. Traditionally, a committee of the American Bar Association evaluates all judicial nominees and rates their qualifications. But upon taking office in 2001, President Bush announced that his administration would not consider these recommendations in making decisions about the appointment of federal judges.

The Senate Judiciary Committee plays a major role in the nomination process. Although most choices are routinely approved, the committee occasionally holds hearings at which supporters and opponents of a particular candidate present arguments for and against the nomination. The Judiciary Committee can also delay approval of the president's choices by slowing the pace of nomination hearings.

Judicial Appointments, 1980–2004

During his two terms in office, Ronald Reagan appointed four Supreme Court justices and filled about half of all lower-court judgeships—more than any other president since Franklin Roosevelt. Like those of other presidents, Reagan's appointments were partisan in nature; but Reagan went further and chose Republicans who were generally conservative in their legal philosophy. This approach was continued by the first President Bush, who appointed 187 judges between 1989 and 1993.

The judges appointed by Reagan and the first President Bush were predominantly young white males who had already established a reputation for legal conservatism. Few women, African Americans, or members of other minority groups were appointed. (President Bush, however, did appoint Clarence Thomas, a black Republican, to the Supreme Court.)[12]

President Clinton appointed 377 federal judges during his two terms in office. This figure represents more than 40 percent of the total number of seats on the U.S. district and appellate courts. One study of President Clinton's judicial nominees found that he had chosen more women and African Americans for the federal bench than had Presidents Reagan and Bush combined. His selections tended to be political moderates, a fact that disappointed many Democratic liberals.[13]

During most of his first two years as president, the younger George Bush confronted a Senate controlled by the Democrats. In July 2000—more than a year and a half into his administration—only fifty-seven of his nominees had been confirmed by the Senate; fifty other nominees to fill ninety-three vacancies on the lower federal courts were still pending. The Senate Judiciary Committee had not even held hearings on many of these nominations. (Two of the president's nominees to the U.S. courts of appeals were actually rejected by the Judiciary Committee.) But the election of a Republican-controlled Senate in November 2002 changed this situation; the president was now in a stronger position to have his judicial nominees approved.

Appointing Supreme Court Justices

Next to sending American military forces into combat, the appointment of a Supreme Court justice is the most important decision an American president may make. Because justices have life tenure, the appointee will most likely serve on the Court for many years after the president has left office. For that reason, presidents give careful thought to the task of filling a vacancy on the Supreme Court.

Presidents take into account a wide variety of factors in selecting a Supreme Court justice. Among those factors are age, religion, race, place of residence, political party, judicial experience, and judicial philosophy. No African American served on the Court until 1967, when President Lyndon Johnson appointed Thurgood Marshall, and no woman served on the Court until 1981, when President Reagan appointed Sandra Day O'Connor. Justice Antonin Scalia was the first Italian American appointed to the Court (1986). (See Table 10.2 for the occupations of Supreme Court justices at the time of their appointment.)

The nominee's political party and judicial beliefs are especially important in the appointment of a Supreme Court justice. The president will almost always appoint a member of his own party whose judicial philosophy matches his own. Thus, all the justices appointed by President Reagan—Sandra Day O'Connor in 1981, William H. Rehnquist and Antonin Scalia in 1986, and Anthony M. Kennedy

Sandra Day O'Connor, Associate Justice of the United States Supreme Court. The first woman to serve on the nation's highest court, Justice O'Connor was appointed by President Reagan in 1981.

TABLE 10.2

OCCUPATIONS[a] OF SUPREME COURT DESIGNEES AT TIME OF APPOINTMENT[b]

Federal officeholder in executive branch	22
Judge of inferior federal court	28
Judge of state court	22
Private practice of law	18
U.S. senator	8
U.S. representative	4
State governor	3
Professor of law	3
Associate Justice of U.S. Supreme Court[c]	3
Justice of the Permanent Court of International Justice	1

[a] Many of the appointees held a variety of federal or state offices, or even both, prior to their selection.

[b] In general, the appointments from state office are clustered at the beginning of the Court's existence; those from federal office are more recent.

[c] Justices White, Stone, and Rehnquist were promoted to the Chief Justiceship in 1910, 1930, and 1986, respectively.

Source: From *The Judicial Process: An Introductory Analysis of the Courts of the United States* by Henry J. Abraham. Copyright © 1993 by Henry J. Abraham. Used by permission of Oxford University Press, Inc. Updated to include the appointment of Justice Stephen G. Breyer in 1994.

in 1988—were Republicans with generally conservative judicial views. This was the case, for example, with the first President Bush's appointments of Clarence Thomas and David Souter (both Republicans) and President Clinton's appointment of Ruth Bader Ginsburg and Stephen G. Breyer (both Democrats). (See Table 10.3.)

The appointment of Justice Breyer to the Supreme Court in 1994 was the most recent change in the composition of the nation's highest court. Not since the early nineteenth century has there been such a long period without a change in the membership of the court. The next appointments—whenever those vacancies occur—will be especially important. The present Supreme Court has decided a number of major issues related to civil liberties and civil rights by vote of 5 to 4. The president who makes these nominations will help shape the direction the Court will take during the coming years.

Confirmation and Tenure

The same basic procedure is followed in confirming nominations to the Supreme Court as in confirming appointments to the lower federal courts. The primary difference is that senatorial courtesy does not apply; the president is entirely free to make the initial selection of a nominee. Once that choice has been made, the nomination is sent to the Senate, which must approve the candidate by a majority vote.

Twenty-eight presidential nominees—almost 20 percent of the total—have been denied Senate confirmation since the nation's founding. One of the most

TABLE 10.3

MEMBERS OF THE UNITED STATES SUPREME COURT, 2002–2003 TERM

	Home State	Year of Birth	Year of Appointment (President Who Appointed)
Chief Justice			
William H. Rehnquist	AZ	1924	1986 (Reagan)
Associate Justices			
John Paul Stevens	IL	1920	1975 (Ford)
Sandra Day O'Connor	AZ	1930	1981 (Reagan)
Antonin Scalia	NJ	1936	1986 (Reagan)
Anthony M. Kennedy	CA	1936	1988 (Reagan)
David H. Souter	NH	1939	1990 (Bush)
Clarence Thomas	GA	1948	1991 (Bush)
Ruth Bader Ginsburg	NY	1933	1993 (Clinton)
Stephen G. Breyer	CA	1938	1994 (Clinton)

important factors governing confirmations is timing. About 90 percent of nominations made during a president's first three years in office were confirmed. But less than 66 percent of the choices made in the last year of a president's term have received the consent of the Senate.[14] Senators who are not members of the president's political party have often voted against the nominee in the hope that their party's candidate will win the upcoming election and thus be able to fill the vacancy on the court.

In the past several decades the Senate has once again asserted its power over appointments to the Supreme Court; it has blocked five presidential nominations. In 1968 President Johnson attempted to elevate Associate Justice Abe Fortas to the position of chief justice. The nomination was withdrawn when it became clear that Fortas lacked sufficient support in the Senate. In 1969 and 1970, two successive nominees selected by President Nixon were rejected by the Senate. President Reagan's nomination of Robert Bork in 1987 was also voted down, making Bork the twenty-seventh person to be denied Senate confirmation. (Soon afterward, Douglas Ginsberg became the twenty-eighth, when President Reagan withdrew his name because it was clear that the Senate would not confirm the choice—largely because it became known that Ginsberg had smoked marijuana earlier in his life.)

The Senate Judiciary Committee plays a key role in considering presidential nominees to the Supreme Court. Its practices have varied over the years. Many choices have been approved rapidly, with as little as a single day spent on hearings. But the process is likely to be more prolonged when a president selects controversial candidates. In 1916 the Judiciary Committee held hearings over a four-month period before approving President Wilson's choice of Louis Brandeis. During the 1987 hearings on the nomination of Robert Bork,

Supreme Court nominee Clarence Thomas testifies before the Senate Judiciary Committee, October 1991. He categorically denied all allegations of improper conduct and was narrowly confirmed by the Senate.

committee members questioned the candidate for five days. And in the fall of 1991, the nomination of Clarence Thomas extended over a period of twelve days before he was narrowly approved by the Senate. Part of the Senate Judiciary hearings dealt with charges made by Anita Hill, a professor at the University of Oklahoma Law School. The hearings on this issue took place before a national television audience, and the sensational charges included discussions of alleged sexual improprieties by the nominee.

On the other hand, President Clinton's nominations of Ruth Bader Ginsburg in 1993 and Stephen G. Breyer in 1994 were quickly approved by the Senate with almost no opposition. The moderate views and outstanding legal credentials of the two candidates produced broad bipartisan support.

THE FUNCTIONS OF THE JUDICIARY

The main functions of the judiciary in general and the Supreme Court in particular are the interpretation of statutes and constitutional provisions and the exercise of judicial review. *Statutory interpretation* involves deciding the meaning and intent of a statute enacted by the legislature. Courts are also called upon to determine the meaning of various provisions of the Constitution, such as "due process of law" in the Fifth and Fourteenth Amendments and "interstate commerce" in Article I, Section 8. The United States Supreme Court is primarily a constitutional court, but each term it decides a significant number of cases inloving the interpretation of statutes. Only occasionally do courts exercise their ultimate power—the power of judicial review—to declare a law unconstitutional.

Judicial Review

The American judiciary has the power to decide whether the acts of the executive and legislative branches of government are in conflict with the Constitution and, if so, to declare them void. This is the power of **judicial review,** and its existence makes the courts, especially the Supreme Court, important actors in the American governmental system.

The legal basis of the Supreme Court's authority to review the decisions of state courts is Article VI of the Constitution. Not only does this article state that the Constitution and all federal statutes and treaties "shall be the supreme law of the land," it also declares that "judges in every state shall be bound thereby, any Thing in the Constitution or laws of any State to the contrary notwithstanding."

The power to exercise judicial review over acts of Congress or the president is not expressly stated in the Constitution. It is based primarily on the Supreme Court's ruling in the case of *Marbury v. Madison* (1803).[15] Chief Justice John Marshall's opinion in that case established the precedent under which the federal courts could use the power of judicial review to declare an act of Congress unconstitutional.

Marbury v. Madison arose out of an unusual situation. The Federalist party had been defeated in the election of 1800. Eager to maintain its influence in the federal judiciary, the Federalist-controlled Congress enacted legislation to create a number of new judicial positions. The outgoing president, John Adams, appointed loyal members of the Federalist party to fill those offices. William Marbury, one of the new appointees, was to become a justice of the peace for the District of Columbia. His appointment had been approved, and his commission to hold office had been prepared and signed. But the commission had not yet been delivered to him when Adams's term expired and the new Republican president, Thomas Jefferson, took office.

The new secretary of state, James Madison, acting on instructions from Jefferson, refused to deliver the commission to Marbury. Marbury began a legal action in the United States Supreme Court to have the Court compel the delivery of the document by issuing a **writ of *mandamus***—a court order to a public official to perform an act that is legally required.

The immediate issue in the case was the authority of the Supreme Court to issue a writ of *mandamus.* Chief Justice Marshall began his opinion by agreeing with Marbury that he had a legal right to the judicial office in question and that *mandamus* was the proper remedy for the wrong he had suffered. But the chief justice went on to declare that the Supreme Court could not issue the writ. He ruled unconstitutional a provision of the Judiciary Act of 1789 that permitted cases involving *mandamus* to be heard by the federal courts. According to Marshall, it violated Article III, Section 2, of the Constitution, which restricts the original jurisdiction of the Supreme Court to several specific types of cases, not including disputes involving writs of *mandamus.*

Marbury v. Madison contains a closely reasoned argument defending the Supreme Court's right to declare acts of Congress unconstitutional. Briefly,

Marshall contended that written constitutions are adopted to define and limit the power of government and are intended to serve as the fundamental law of the nation. If an act of the legislature could violate this basic law, written constitutions would serve no meaningful purpose. They can be significant only if their provisions control legislative acts. Marshall went on to conclude that it is the duty of the judicial branch of government to decide issues involving conflicts between the U.S. Constitution and the laws passed by Congress:

> It is emphatically the province and duty of the Judicial department to say what the law is. Those who apply the rule to particular cases must, of necessity, expound and interpret that rule. If two laws conflict with each other, the courts must decide on the operation of each.
>
> So if a law be in opposition to the Constitution; if both the law and the Constitution apply to a particular case, so that the court must either decide that case conformably to the law, disregarding the Constitution; or conformably to the Constitution, disregarding the law; the court must determine which of these conflicting rules governs the case. This is of the very essence of judicial duty.
>
> If, then, the courts are to regard the Constitution, and the Constitution is superior to any ordinary act of the legislature, the Constitution, and not such ordinary act, must govern the case to which they both apply.

Over the course of American history, some observers of the American governmental system have criticized the use of judicial review by the federal courts. These critics have based their arguments on several grounds: (1) the Constitution did not expressly assign this power to the courts; (2) the mistakes of the legislative and executive branches of the government are best corrected by those two branches themselves, and if they are not, the people will replace the officials involved at election time; and (3) judicial review violates the principle of majority rule because it puts supreme power over the Constitution and official acts in the hands of nine justices who are appointed for life.

These arguments have not been sufficient to overturn the principle established in *Marbury,* and the American governmental system has operated under this principle for almost two centuries. One writer offered the following explanation of the significance of the case:

> The Marshall opinion denying Marbury his commission covers seventeen pages in the official reports of the Supreme Court. But its breadth cannot be measured in pages. It must be admired for its assertion that all men, even Presidents, must adhere to the law. . . . It must be admired primarily, however, for establishing a rule of law, a procedure for settling disputes without the sword.[16]

Despite the significance of *Marbury,* judges are generally reluctant to exercise the power of judicial review, especially to acts of Congress. By the end of 2001, only about 160 federal statutes had been declared unconstitutional. Indeed, between 1803, when *Marbury* was decided, and 1857, no federal law was declared unconstitutional by the Supreme Court. (In 1857, in the infamous Dred Scott decision,[17] the Court upheld the legality of slavery.) In 1995, for example, the Court struck down the Gun-Free School Zones Act of 1990, which made it illegal to possess a firearm within 1,000 feet of a private or public school. The Court held that the law exceeded the power of Congress to regulate interstate commerce.[18]

Judicial review has become more common in the twentieth century, but it is still unusual for acts of the Congress and the president to be pronounced void. The power of judicial review is exercised far more frequently against state laws and practices (approximately 1,200 since the nation's founding). Thus, judicial review is more significant as a control on the states than as a control on Congress and the president.

Restrictions on the Court

The Constitution places some restrictions on the power of the Supreme Court and the federal judiciary. Once appointed, a federal judge who sits on a constitutional court serves for life, and his or her salary cannot be reduced. A judge may be removed only by means of **impeachment** and conviction for "Treason, Bribery or other high Crimes and Misdemeanors" (Article II, Section 4); however, Congress has rarely invoked this power.

But Congress has other legal powers over the courts. It can, in theory, alter or abolish all of the Supreme Court's appellate jurisdiction,[19] change the jurisdiction of all other federal courts, reduce the pay of future federal judges, cut appropriations to pay for the operation of the courts, and increase the number of federal judges, including those on the Supreme Court.

CLOSE-UP

IMPEACHMENT OF FEDERAL JUDGES

As is the case for presidents, vice presidents, and other civil officers of the United States, federal judges are subject to the ultimate constitutional check: They can be impeached by the House of Representatives and removed from office if convicted by a two-thirds majority of the Senate.

To date, only one Supreme Court justice has been impeached—Samuel Chase in 1804—and he was not convicted by the Senate. (Chase, a staunch opponent of President Jefferson, may not have had a proper judicial temperament, but he had not committed any impeachable offenses.) However, twelve impeachment proceedings have been conducted against other federal judges, and ten of them went to trial. As a result of those trials, three judges were acquitted and seven convicted and removed from office. Two judges resigned before the Senate could bring them to trial.

Three of the convictions just mentioned occurred in the late 1980s. They resulted in the re-

moval from office of Harry Claiborne, a district court judge from Nevada (1986); Alcee L. Hastings, a district court judge from Florida (1989); and Walter L. Nixon, Jr., a district court judge from Mississippi (1989).

Hastings's career in the federal government did not end with his impeachment and removal from the bench. He first won a seat in the Florida House of Representatives in 1992, and a year later he was elected to the U.S. House of Representatives. His service in the House raised a new constitutional question. Article I, Section 3, declares that officials who have been impeached and removed from office are ineligible to "hold and enjoy any Office of Honor, Trust or Profit under the United States." It is not clear whether this statement applies to service in Congress, but Congress never took any action to deprive him of his seat, and he has been repeatedly reelected to the House.

During the early 1980s various bills were introduced to prevent the federal courts from hearing cases concerning such issues as abortion and prayer in public schools. Other bills were introduced that would have denied the Supreme Court the right to hear appeals in cases involving these controversial issues. However, none of these proposals were passed by Congress. Even though Congress possesses broad power to shape the federal judiciary, it has almost never used it for the purpose of restricting or punishing the courts. When Congress has changed the jurisdiction of the courts or increased the number of judges, for example, it has done so to increase the efficiency of the federal courts.

Another restriction on the authority of the Supreme Court arises when it makes a decision on a highly controversial issue. The Court's decisions do not enforce themselves; their effectiveness depends on the public's willingness to accept them. On a few occasions there has been significant resistance to Supreme Court rulings. A well-known example is the Court's ruling in *Brown v. Board of Education of Topeka* (1954)[20] that public schools must be desegregated. There was much public opposition to that decision in the South, and in several instances federal troops had to be used to enforce court orders to desegregate public schools in the region. There has also been considerable resistance to the Court's rulings in the early 1960s concerning prayer in public schools. Some communities still have not complied with those decisions, which held that government-authorized prayers and Bible reading in public schools are in violation of the First Amendment.[21]

Decisions of the Supreme Court can be changed by legislation or constitutional amendment. If the Court decides a case involving a federal law on statutory grounds, Congress can overturn the ruling by passing new legislation. When it decides a case on a constitutional basis, however, only an amendment to the Constitution can reverse the ruling. A few constitutional amendments have changed Supreme Court rulings; they include the Eleventh Amendment, Section 1 of the Fourteenth Amendment, and the Sixteenth, Twenty-fourth, and Twenty-sixth Amendments. There have been many attempts to reverse unpopular decisions by constitutional amendment, but most have been unsuccessful.

It should also be understood that courts are *passive* entities. Unlike Congress, which can consider an issue whenever it chooses to do so, federal courts must wait for lawsuits to arise. Even then the Supreme Court may deny a writ of *certiorari,* preferring to wait for a later case dealing with the issue. The abortion issue, for example, had been brought to the Court on several occasions prior to its 1973 decision in *Roe v. Wade.*

Judicial philosophy may also play a role in restricting the power of judges and courts. The philosophy of **judicial self-restraint** also serves to place limits on the Court. This principle holds that judges should exercise great self-control in using their judicial power and should generally defer to the policies of the elected branches of the government. The doctrine of judicial self-restraint is accepted in varying degrees by different justices.

Some justices, however, reject a limited role for the judiciary and favor a policy of **judicial activism.** Advocates of this philosophy are more likely to declare actions of the other branches unconstitutional and are more inclined to have the courts set policy for the nation.

Justice Antonin Scalia opposes both judges who seek to find the intent of the drafters of the Constitution and those who would interpret constitutional language according to its current meaning. He believes that judges should apply an

CLOSE-UP

FDR'S "COURT-PACKING" PLAN

One of the most celebrated events in the history of the Supreme Court occurred in 1937, when President Franklin D. Roosevelt proposed the so-called "court-packing" bill. Roosevelt faced a hostile, conservative Supreme Court that had declared major portions of his New Deal program unconstitutional. He therefore asked Congress to pass a law providing for the addition to the Supreme Court of one new appointee for every sitting justice over the age of seventy, up to a maximum of fifteen. Had the legislation passed, the president would have gained the right to appoint six people who were sympathetic to the New Deal and would then vote to support his legislative policies.* During the spring of 1937, while Congress was debating Roosevelt's plan, several members of the Court began to take a different view of the government's power to regulate the economy. As a result, in a series of narrowly decided cases the Court sustained the right of the national and state governments to enact regulatory measures.**

The legislation proposed by FDR was within the constitutional power of Congress, but it represented unwise political interference with the independence of the Supreme Court. Largely for that reason, the heavily Democratic Congress, which usually favored Roosevelt's proposals, refused to adopt the court-packing plan. Still, the incident illustrates the fact that congressional laws can be used to control judicial power.

*Congress has changed the number of Supreme Court justices several times. The original Court consisted of six justices. In 1801 the number was reduced to five; from 1807 to 1837 there were seven; from 1837 to 1863, nine; from 1863 to 1866, ten; and from 1866 to 1869, seven. Since 1869 the Court has consisted of nine justices.

**Alfred H. Kelley, Winfred A. Harbison, and Herman Belz, *The American Constitution,* 6th ed. (New York: W. W. Norton, 1983), pp. 500–502.

approach that he terms **textualism.** They should interpret constitutional provisions according to the meaning of the language at the time that the document was written.[22] In contrast, some judicial activists believe in an approach that is often referred to as the "**living Constitution.**" For example, the late Justice William Brennan believed that the Constitution must be kept up to date and that judges are responsible for performing this task. Thus, in interpreting the Eighth Amendment's ban on "cruel and unusual punishment," Brennan believed that the objective of the provision was to protect human dignity. He therefore concluded that the death penalty was always unconstitutional, since it denies human dignity. He held to this view despite the fact that in several places the Constitution specifically permits the use of capital punishment. In setting forth his philosophy, Justice Brennan declared:

> We current Justices read the Constitution in the only way that we can: as Twentieth Century Americans. We look to the history of the time of the framers and to the intervening history of interpretation. But the ultimate question must be, what do the words of the text mean in our time?[23]

It is important to note that the difference between restrainers and activists is not absolute. The activists do believe in some limits, and those who favor self-restraint do use their judicial power in some situations. The difference between the activists and the self-restrainers is basically a disagreement over when the Court should say no.[24]

THE SUPREME COURT: A BRIEF HISTORY

Under the Articles of Confederation there had been no national court system. Although the Supreme Court was created by the Constitution, it was by no means a foregone conclusion that the Court would play a significant role in the operation of the new government. During the first years of its existence (1789–1801), the Court had relatively few cases on its docket, and no chief justice served longer than a few years.

With the appointment of John Marshall as chief justice in 1801, the Court's fortunes began to change. Marshall served for thirty-four years, during which time he established the Supreme Court as an independent force within the governmental system. His powerful intellect dominated the Court, and his interpretation of important clauses in the Constitution provided the precedents that shaped the course of American constitutional development. As we have seen, it was Marshall's opinion in *Marbury v. Madison* that established the principle of judicial review. It was also the Marshall Court that provided a broad interpretation of the power of Congress under Article I, Section 8, of the Constitution.

The history of the Supreme Court can be divided into three periods. From 1800 until the end of the Civil War in 1865, the Court was concerned primarily with issues related to federalism—with finding the proper balance between the powers of the national government and those of the states. Chief Justice Marshall emphasized national powers at the expense of the states, but his successor, Roger Brooke Taney (1835–1864), sought to reverse that trend, stressing the importance of state authority. With the North's victory in the Civil War, the nationalist view of the Constitution prevailed.

The second period in the Court's history extended from the close of the Civil War until about 1938. This was a period of great industrial growth, and with that growth came the problems of an industrial society. Popular support for reform legislation led to the enactment of laws dealing with child labor, minimum wages and maximum hours, and the right to form labor unions. The Supreme Court invalidated many of those laws on constitutional grounds.

The conflict between the Court and the other branches of government came to a head during the Great Depression of the 1930s. During President Franklin D. Roosevelt's first term (1933–1937), the Court held much of his New Deal program unconstitutional. Although Roosevelt's attempt to "pack" the Court failed (see Close-Up, FDR's "Court-Packing" Scheme), in 1937 the Court altered its position and began to issue rulings upholding the legality of social and economic reform legislation. In the late 1930s resignations from the Court gave Roosevelt an opportunity to appoint new justices who strongly supported the New Deal. The government's power to regulate the economy had been established.

In the late 1930s the Supreme Court entered the third stage in its history—an era in which it would focus predominantly on issues of civil liberties and civil rights. The majority of the cases decided by the Court since 1940 have involved questions of freedom of speech and religion, the rights of the criminally accused, and issues of race and gender discrimination. The consequences of this shift were especially dramatic during the years that Earl Warren served as chief justice (1953–1969). As we shall see in the next two chapters, far-reaching changes in constitutional policy occurred under Warren's leadership.

CONCLUSION

American courts play an important role in the governmental system largely because they possess the power of judicial review. Courts in nations in which judicial review does not exist resolve legal disputes between parties, but they do not possess the power to declare actions of the executive or legislature branches unconstitutional.

The United States Supreme Court is the most important judicial body in this country because it has the final authority to interpret the national constitution. In recent decades the Supreme Court has devoted much of its time to defining the meaning of the various provisions of the Bill of Rights and the Fourteenth Amendment. These decisions have a major impact on the people of this nation, for they make clear the extent of their freedom from illegal and arbitrary governmental actions. This function is particularly important today, when the nation is at war with international terrorism. During times of war the power of government tends to expand both abroad and at home. This expansion inevitably creates conflicts with the civil liberties of Americans. The importance of the nation's judiciary will be magnified as the courts attempt to resolve these disputes between the power of government and the rights of individuals.

The next two chapters analyze the role of the courts, and especially of the United States Supreme Court, in defining the liberties and rights of Americans.

QUESTIONS FOR THOUGHT

1. Name and describe the five types of law.
2. Name the main federal courts and their jurisdiction.
3. What is a **writ of *certiorari*,** and what is its importance?
4. What role does the U.S. Senate play in the confirmation of judicial nominees?
5. What is meant by judicial review?
6. Describe the principal theories of constitutional interpretation.

INTERNET ACTIVITIES

1. *U.S. Supreme Court.* Go to Cornell Law at **http://supct.law.cornell.edu/ supct/justices/fullcourt.html**. For each member of the Supreme Court find the following information: law school attended, who appointed, year appointed and length of service, and a recent decision.

2. *Judicial Threat to Liberty?* Go to **http://www.memory.loc.gov/const/fed/ fed_78.html** where you will read *Federalist Paper* No. 78. Answer the following questions based on your reading: Why did Hamilton see the court as the branch of government that is least likely to threaten the liberty or property interests of the citizens. What are the two great advantages of having an appointed rather than an elected court system?

KEY TERMS

administrative law
adversary system
advisory opinions
appellate jurisdiction
briefs
civil law
common law
concurring opinions
constitutional courts
constitutional law
criminal law
defendant

dissenting opinions
equity
felonies
impeachment
injunction
judicial activism
judicial review
judicial self-restraint
jurisdiction
law
legislative courts
"living Constitution"

majority opinion
misdemeanors
original jurisdiction
plaintiff
senatorial courtesy
stare decisis
statutory law
textualism
treaties
writ of *certiorari*
writ of *mandamus*

SUGGESTED READING

Abraham, Henry J. *Justices and Presidents: A Political History of Appointments to the Supreme Court,* 4th ed. New York: Oxford University Press, 1999.

Belsky, Martin H. *The Rehnquist Court.* New York: Oxford University Press, 2002.

Bork, Robert. *The Tempting of America: The Political Seduction of the Law.* New York: Free Press, 1990.

Franck, Matthew J. *Against the Imperial Judiciary: The Supreme Court vs. The Sovereignty of the People.* Lawrence, KS: University Press of Kansas, 1996.

Leuchtenburg, William E. *The Supreme Court Reborn: The Constitutional Revolution in the Age of Roosevelt.* New York: Oxford University Press, 1995.

Maltese, J.A. *The Selling of Supreme Court Nominees.* Baltimore: Johns Hopkins University Press, 1995.

Nelson, William E. *Marbury v. Madison: The Origins and Legacy of Judicial Review.* Lawrence, KS: Univesity Press of Kansas, 2000.

O'Brien, David. *Storm Center: The Supreme Court in American Politics,* 5th ed. New York; Norton, 1999.

Perry, Barbara A. *The Priestly Tribe: The Supreme Court's Image in the American Mind.* Westport, CT: Greenwood, 2000.

Tarr, G. Alan. *Judicial Process and Judicial Policymaking,* 2nd ed. Belmont, CA: West/Wadsworth, 1999.

NOTES

1. *Muskrat v. United States,* 219 U.S. 346 (1911).

2. *Schlesinger v. Reservists Committee to Stop the War,* 418 U.S. 208 (1974).

3. Administrative Office of the U.S. Courts, *U.S. District Courts—Civil Cases Filed by Origin During the 12-Month Periods Ending September 30, 1997 Through 2001,* Table S-7, p. 44 (2001).

4. Administrative Office of the U.S. Courts, *2001 Caseload Highlights* (2001).

5. Henry J. Abraham, *The Judiciary: The Supreme Court in the Governmental Process,* 9th ed. (Madison, WI: Brown & Benchmark, 1994), p. 12.

6. Administrative Office of the U.S. Courts, *2001 Caseload.* See also: *U.S. Courts of Appeals, Appeals Commenced, Terminated, and Pending, by Nature of Suit or Offense, in Appeals from the U.S. District Courts During the 12-Month Period Ending September 30, 2001,* Table B-1A, p. 79 (2001).

7. William H. Rehnquist, *The Supreme Court* (New York: Morrow, 1987), pp. 289–90, 293.

8. Charles E. Hughes, *The Supreme Court of the United States* (New York: Columbia University Press, 1928), p. 68.

9. Bureau of the Census, *Statistical Abstract of the United States,* 1998, Table 365, p. 224. (Updated to include figures for the 2000 term of the court).

10. This discussion is based on Stephen L. Wasby, *The Supreme Court in the Federal Judicial System,* 4th ed. (Chicago: Nelson-Hall, 1993), pp. 97–110.

11. Since appeals courts serve several states, it is more difficult to determine which senator should suggest a candidate for any given state. Here again, tradition plays a major role, with certain vacancies "belonging" to particular states.

12. David M. O'Brien, "The Reagan Judges: His Most Enduring Legacy?" in Charles O. Jones, ed., *The Reagan*

Legacy: Promise and Performance (Chatham, NJ: Chatham House, 1988), pp. 60, 75–78.

13. Paul M. Barrett, "More Minorities, Women Named to U.S. Courts," *Wall Street Journal,* December 23, 1993, p. B1.

14. Wasby, *The Supreme Court in the Federal Judicial System,* p. 127.

15. I Cranch 137 (1803).

16. Leonard Baker, *John Marshall: A Life in Law* (New York: Macmillan, 1974), pp. 408–9.

17. *Dred Scott v. Sandford,* 19 Howard 393 (1857).

18. *United States v. Lopez,* 115 S.Ct. 1624 (1995).

19. "The Supreme Court shall have appellate Jurisdiction, both as to Law and Fact, with such Exceptions and under such Regulations as the Congress shall make" (Article III, Section 2).

20. 347 U.S. 483.

21. See Chapter 11 for further discussion of *Engel v. Vitale,* 370 U.S. 421 (1962), and *Abington School District v. Schempp,* 374 U.S. 203 (1963).

22. Antonin Scalia, *A Matter of Interpretation* (Princeton, NJ: Princeton University Press, 1998), pp. 37–38.

23. William J. Brennan, "The Constitution of the United States: Contemporary Ratification." Speech presented at the Text and Teaching Symposium, Georgetown University Law School, Washington, DC, October 12, 1985.

24. Abraham, *The Judiciary,* p. 78.

CHAPTER

11

Civil Liberties

CHAPTER OUTLINE

The rights enumerated in the Bill of Rights were designed to limit the power of government over the individual. They were derived from the framers' knowledge of history, especially the struggles against arbitrary government actions in Great Britain and in the American colonies. Hence, the Bill of Rights is, in effect, a charter of civil liberties. Its guarantees include freedom of speech, press, and assembly, as well as protection against arbitrary procedures in criminal prosecutions.

Civil liberties may be defined as the individual rights that are guaranteed by the Constitution, especially in the Bill of Rights and the **due process clause** of the Fourteenth Amendment. Civil liberties are not the same as civil rights, which are concerned with protection against discrimination and are derived largely from the equal protection clause of the Fourteenth Amendment and from statutes passed by federal or state legislatures. (Civil rights are discussed in Chapter 12.)

The courts, especially the United States Supreme Court, have the task of interpreting civil liberties and civil rights—that is, defining the rights of the individual that are protected against the power of government. Ever since the end of World War II, civil liberties and civil rights have been by far the most important areas of concern for the Supreme Court. During these years, the Court has significantly expanded the scope of individual liberties in this nation. It has done so by extending most of the provisions of the Bill of Rights to the states and by expanding the interpretation given to many of the provisions in the Bill of Rights.

"If there be any fixed star in our constitutional constellation, it is that no official, high or petty, can prescribe what shall be orthodox in politics, nationalism, religion, or other matters of opinion or force citizens to confess by word or act their faith therein."

—*Justice Robert Jackson,*
West Virginia Board of
Education v. Barnette
(1943)

APPLYING THE BILL OF RIGHTS TO THE STATES

In 1833 the Supreme Court held that the limitations on government set forth in the Bill of Rights applied only to the national government and not to the states.[1] Its ruling was based on the view that the Bill of Rights had been added to the Constitution because the people feared the power of the national government and that it was not intended to apply to the actions of the states.

This decision has never been changed, but under the due process clause of the Fourteenth Amendment, ratified in 1868, nearly all the limitations contained in the Bill of Rights have been extended to the states. The Fourteenth Amendment declares that no state shall "deprive any person of life, liberty or property without due process of law." The Supreme Court has used the Bill of Rights as a standard in defining the "liberty" that the Fourteenth Amendment protects against infringement by state governments. Beginning in the 1920s, the Supreme Court began including particular provisions of the Bill of Rights within the protection of the Fourteenth Amendment. This process, generally known as **selective incorporation,** was completed during the 1960s when the Court added most of the protections of the accused contained in the Fourth, Fifth, and Sixth Amendments to the list of rights guaranteed to the individual against the power of state and local governments. (It should be noted that the Bill of Rights does not limit the actions of private individuals, only those of government and its agents.)

Today the constitutional rights of individuals are practically uniform throughout the nation. Only a few guarantees contained in the Bill of Rights have not been applied to the states by the Supreme Court; the Fifth Amendment guarantee of indictment by a grand jury is the major exception. The important problems facing the Court today center on the specific meaning of the various protections of individual liberties found in the Bill of Rights. The Supreme Court is often faced with cases that raise difficult and often highly controversial issues concerning the nature and extent of the liberties enjoyed by American citizens.

FREEDOM OF RELIGION

Religion is the first subject considered in the Bill of Rights. The First Amendment states: "Congress shall make no law respecting an establishment of religion or prohibiting the free exercise thereof." This statement puts two limitations on government with respect to religion. The first, the **establishment clause,** prohibits many forms of association between church and state. The second, the **free exercise clause,** bars the government from limiting the right to hold and express religious beliefs and engage in almost all religious practices.

The Free Exercise Clause

In a large number of cases going back to the 1930s, the United States Supreme Court has interpreted the First Amendment to protect the right to express religious ideas and to bar the government from restricting these ideas. Many of these cases were brought by the Jehovah's Witnesses, a religious group that promotes its ideas by publishing and distributing printed materials. The most recent case on this topic was decided by the Supreme Court in June of 2002. The small village of Stratton, Ohio, adopted an ordinance that prohibited canvassers from "going in and upon" private residential property to further any cause without first register-ing with the mayor's office and obtaining a permit. The Court found that distri-buting religious tracts is an age-old practice and that the city ordinance unconstitutionally violated the Jehovah's Witnesses' right to freedom of religion, speech, and press.[2]

In interpreting the free exercise clause, the Supreme Court has held that al-though religious beliefs are not subject to government control, certain religious practices may be forbidden. The first major case to deal with freedom of religion was *Reynolds v. United States* in 1878.[3] Reynolds, a Mormon, had violated a con-gressional statute that outlawed bigamy. The Supreme Court upheld the convic-tion of Reynolds and the constitutionality of the statute, even though polygamy was permitted at the time under Mormon religious doctrine. The Court decided that although religious freedom includes the right to believe anything, it does not include the right to commit unlawful acts. It refined that opinion in the 1890 case of *Davis v. Beason,* noting that religious freedom is allowed, "provided always the laws of society, designed to secure its peace and prosperity, and the morals of its people are not interfered with."[4]

In recent decades, however, the Court has extended the free exercise clause to most forms of religious conduct that conflict with governmental policy. In these cases the Court considers the claim of religious freedom and examines it against the interest claimed by the government. Only if government can show a **compelling interest,** and no other type of regulation would serve its purpose, will the claim of religious freedom be rejected. This approach makes it difficult for the government to sustain its position. Thus, for example, the Supreme Court

Religious and political speech are basic freedoms protected by the First and Fourteenth Amend-ments. Here young church mis-sionaries go door to door seeking to spread their religious beliefs.

upheld the right of a member of the Seventh Day Adventist Church to receive state unemployment benefits after she had been dismissed from her job for refusing to work on Friday evenings and Saturdays. The state of Florida had failed to show a compelling interest sufficient to overcome the free exercise claim of the church member.[5]

But in a 1990 case, a majority of the members of the Court abandoned the compelling interest test and adopted an approach that was more favorable to the government. Two Native Americans were employed as drug counselors for the state of Oregon. They were dismissed from their jobs because of evidence that they used peyote, a drug that was illegal under state law. They were denied unemployment benefits even though the use of the peyote had occurred as part of a religious ceremony conducted by the Native American church. The Oregon Supreme Court reversed this decision and the State of Oregon appealed to the United States Supreme Court. The Supreme Court held that the free exercise rights of the Native Americans had not been denied. The state policy criminalizing the use of peyote was constitutional since it was applied neutrally to all residents of Oregon and did not discriminate against religion.[6]

The Establishment Clause

The establishment clause has been a subject of more heated and continual debate than has the free exercise clause. This debate has centered on three major issues: aid to religious or parochial schools, prayers and Bible reading in public schools, and religious displays on public property.

AID TO PAROCHIAL SCHOOLS When the issue of aid to parochial schools first arose during the 1940s, the Supreme Court interpreted the establish-

A group prays on the Mall in Washington, DC, in support of religious freedom.

ment clause as requiring a "wall of separation" between church and state. This test seemed to create an absolute standard that would permit no contact between religion and government. However, the Court soon began making exceptions: It allowed some forms of public aid to parochial schools, such as paying the costs of transporting children to such schools.[7]

Pressure to expand the amount and kind of state aid to parochial schools grew during the 1960s as the cost of operating those schools—most of which are Roman Catholic—rose sharply. Some state legislatures responded by passing laws that paid for teachers' salaries and special educational programs, covered the cost of some administrative and construction expenses, and gave tax credits and deductions and tuition reimbursements to parents whose children attended private schools.

In the 1971 case of *Lemon v. Kurtzman,* the Supreme Court developed a three-part test to determine whether a law violates the establishment clause. First, the law must have a secular purpose. Second, the primary effect of the program must not be either to promote or to interfere with religion. Third, the government's policy must not result in "excessive entanglement" of church and state.[8]

During the next several decades the Court used the *Lemon* tests to rule most forms of public aid to religious schools unconstitutional. It declared unconstitutional a law that provided loans of maps, films, and laboratory equipment to church-related schools.[9] Similarly, it invalidated a New York State law that created a school district for a single religious group and then provided state funds to pay for the cost of educating disabled children.[10]

Conservatives on the Court had long been critical of the *Lemon* case. In 1997 they achieved a stunning success when the Court reversed a major establishment clause case that it had decided less than fifteen years earlier.[11] In 1985, by a 5-to-4 vote, the Court had used the *Lemon* test to bar public school teachers from traveling to parochial schools to teach federally funded remedial classes.[12]

The 1997 decision was especially important in light of a controversial establishment clause issue that came to the Court during the 2001–2002 term. That issue is the constitutionality of school voucher programs that have been adopted by a small number of states and cities. Voucher programs provide public money to the parents of schoolchildren who attend failing public schools. The parents may then use the money to pay their children's tuition at any private school they choose, even if it is affiliated with a church. Teachers unions and many civil rights organizations have vigorously opposed the creation of such programs.

In what was probably the most important establishment clause case in four decades, a 5-to-4 Court majority upheld the Ohio program that operated in the Cleveland school district. "[W]here a government aid program is neutral with respect to religion, and provides assistance directly to a broad class of citizens who, in turn, direct government aid to religious schools wholly as a result of their own genuine and independent private choice, the program is not readily subject to challenge under the Establishment Clause," Chief Justice Rehnquist wrote.[13]

With the federal constitutionality of school choice programs now settled, the conflict between supporters and opponents will turn to the state legislatures and to state courts. Opponents will seek to block the passage of any new programs, and they will also challenge the constitutionality of school vouchers under provisions of state constitutions, many of which are very specific about prohibiting public money being used to assist churches.

SCHOOL PRAYER   In 1962 a storm of controversy arose over the Supreme Court's decision in *Engel v. Vitale.* This case dealt with the constitutionality of

New York State's so-called "Regents' prayer," a short nondenominational prayer that had been approved by the New York State Board of Regents. In a 6-to-1 decision the Court ruled that the prayer was an unconstitutional establishment of religion because the government (the Board of Regents) had authorized a religious practice on public school property.[14] The Court has also held that Bible reading in public schools is unconstitutional.[15]

A few states have adopted legislation designed to avoid the Court's original school prayer decisions, but these efforts have not been successful. For example, an Alabama law that authorized a period of silence in public schools "for meditation or voluntary prayer" was found to be an unconstitutional establishment of religion because its main purpose was to promote religious observance.[16] The Court has also invalidated a school-sponsored prayer at a graduation ceremony and a student-led prayer said before home football games at a Texas high school. Both were found to involve illegal government endorsement of religion.[17]

RELIGIOUS DISPLAYS ON PUBLIC PROPERTY The Supreme Court has decided a number of cases involving the display of religious symbols on public property. It is difficult to summarize the Court's actions in this area because the facts of each case have been quite different. In 1989, for example, the Court held that it was unconstitutional for the government to display a nativity scene that included the Latin words for "Glory to God in the Highest." Such a display had been placed on the main staircase of the county courthouse in Pittsburgh, Pennsylvania. The Court found that the display violated the establishment clause because it clearly endorsed the crèche's religious message. On the other hand, the Court upheld the display on public property of a Chanukah menorah that had been placed next to a large Christmas tree with a sign stating that they were part of the city's salute to liberty. In this case the Court reasoned that the presence of the menorah was simply a way of showing that Christmas is not the only way to celebrate the winter holiday. Moreover, the sign linking the tree and the menorah to liberty emphasized the secular purpose of the display.[18]

Sometimes situations arise in which claims of freedom of religion and freedom of speech come into conflict with the establishment clause. One such situation arose in the 1995 case of *Rosenberg v. The Rector of the University of Virginia.*[19] The editor of *Wide Awake,* a Christian student magazine, sued the university over its policy of denying the magazine a share of student activity fees. The university claimed that *Wide Awake* was a sectarian religious publication and that giving it financial support would violate the establishment clause of the First Amendment. The editor claimed that the school's policy violated his rights to freedom of religion and speech. In a 5-to-4 vote the Supreme Court held that the university had violated the First Amendment by discriminating against religious viewpoints.

FREEDOM OF SPEECH, PRESS, ASSEMBLY, AND PETITION

The First Amendment states: "Congress shall make no law abridging the freedom of speech, or of the press." But the Supreme Court has never interpreted this freedom as absolute. It has held that in certain very limited circumstances the government does have a right to restrict freedom of speech. In holding that government could punish the use of "fighting words"—words that when said directly to another person are likely to cause a breach of the peace—the Court set forth some of the general limits on freedom of expression:

> There are certain well-defined and narrowly limited classes of speech, the prevention and punishment of which have never been thought to raise any Constitutional problem. These include the lewd and obscene, the profane, the libelous, and the insulting or "fighting" words—those which by their very utterance inflict injury or tend to incite an immediate breach of the peace. It has been well observed that such utterances are no essential part of any exposition of ideas, and are of such slight social value as a step to truth that any benefit that may be derived from them is clearly outweighed by the social interest in order and morality.[20]

In this section we examine these exceptions as well as other First Amendment issues that have been considered by the Court. Although we deal separately with issues related to freedom of speech, press, assembly, and petition, it is important to note that the boundaries among these different rights are not always clear in practice. The right to hold a rally and make speeches in front of a public building, for example, involves the guarantees of speech, assembly, and petition.

Censorship: The Rule Against Prior Restraint

The concept of **prior restraint** is basic to the interpretation of the First Amendment. Prior restraint means preventing or censoring material before it is spoken or published. The Supreme Court has prohibited all forms of prior restraint on the ground that government censorship in advance of publication constitutes an especially serious threat to First Amendment guarantees because it denies the public total access to ideas and information.

The prior restraint doctrine was first stated in U.S. constitutional law in the case of *Near v. Minnesota* (1931). The Supreme Court declared unconstitutional a state law that allowed police officials to prevent the publication of newspapers containing "malicious, scandalous or defamatory" statements. In ruling on the case, Chief Justice Hughes wrote "liberty of the press has meant . . . immunity from previous restraints or censorship."[21]

Perhaps the most important Supreme Court case involving prior restraint was the "Pentagon Papers" dispute of 1971. Formally titled *History of the U.S. Decision-making Process on Viet Nam Policy,* the "Pentagon Papers" consisted of a "classified" or secret government study of the Vietnam War. When two newspapers began to print parts of this classified material, which they had secretly obtained, President Richard Nixon sought a court injunction to halt further publication. The case—*The New York Times Co. v. United States*—came before the Supreme Court, which ruled that the prior restraint sought by the government was unjustified and upheld the newspapers' right to publish the papers. In a short opinion six members of the Court agreed that

> any system of prior restraints of expression comes to this Court bearing a heavy presumption against its constitutional validity; the Government thus carries a heavy burden of showing justification for imposition of such a restraint. The district court . . . held that the Government had not met that burden. We agree.[22]

Sedition: Advocacy of Illegal Acts

Sedition may be defined as speech or writing that advocates or incites discontent or rebellion against government. The First Amendment places no restraint on the authority of government to regulate overt acts directed against public institutions, but it does restrict the power to punish the expression of seditious ideas. Only a few national sedition laws have been adopted since the nation's founding. In 1798 Congress passed the first such law, but it was repealed within a few years. Congress did not pass another sedition law until 1918. That law was used to convict political dissenters for seditious speaking and writing during and just after World War I. The third national sedition law, the Smith Act, was passed shortly before the United States entered World War II. Under that act, advocating violent overthrow of the government, organizing any group with such intentions, or conspiring to do either of these was defined as a crime.

Dennis v. United States (1951) was the first major test of the Smith Act. The Supreme Court found the law constitutional and ruled that the leaders of the American Communist party could be convicted under its provisions. The Court interpreted the statute as prohibiting only "advocacy, not discussion" and held that the convictions of the Communist party leaders could be upheld even though there was no evidence that the defendants had made any specific plans to overthrow the government.[23]

In *Brandenburg v. Ohio* the Supreme Court set forth its present standard for deciding on the constitutionality of prosecutions for sedition, which narrowed the power of government in this area. Under the *Dennis* decision, only abstract advocacy of forcible action was protected by the First Amendment; a demand for revolutionary change, even in the distant future, was not protected. In *Brandenburg* the Court held that the First Amendment requires the showing of imminent danger and the likelihood that the danger will actually occur:

> The constitutional guarantees of free speech and free press do not permit a State to forbid or proscribe advocacy of the use of force or of law violation except where such advocacy is directed to inciting imminent lawless action and is likely to incite or produce such action.[24]

CLOSE-UP

CAN RACIST SPEECH BE PROHIBITED?

In 1984, St. Paul, Minnesota, passed a local ordinance that made it a crime to engage in speech or behavior likely to arouse "anger or alarm" on the grounds of "race, color, religion or gender." Similar laws have since been adopted in many communities.

St. Paul prosecuted and convicted a white teenager under the ordinance for allegedly burning a crudely made cross on the lawn of a black family. The conviction was appealed to the United States Supreme Court, and it unanimously found that the ordinance violated the First Amendment.

Writing for five members of the High Court, Justice Scalia stated that the Constitution barred government from "silencing speech on the basis of its content." In this instance, St. Paul had made illegal only those fighting words that "communicate messages of racial, gender or religious intolerance." "Selectivity of this sort," Justice Scalia wrote, "creates the possibility that the city is seeking to handicap the expression of particular ideas."*

R.A.V. v. St. Paul, 112 S.Ct. 2538 (1992).

Protecting Public Order: The First Amendment in Public Places

Various problems arise in connection with the right of individuals and groups to use public places to hold political rallies, distribute literature, and the like. The right to use public forums—public streets and parks, for example—to express political views is very broad. But limitations on First Amendment use of public property may be made when a place is dedicated to a particular use. Government may, for example, prohibit demonstrations near schools during class hours if they interfere or threaten to interfere with school activities.[25] And it may prevent groups from blocking the entrance to public buildings and by so doing interfering with the lawful functioning of that structure.

Government may make reasonable regulations regarding the time, place, and manner of public meetings. It can, for example, restrict the time they are held so that rallies do not disturb the people in a residential area from sleeping, or it may prohibit demonstrations on bridges or main streets of a city that might interfere with the flow of traffic and create safety problems for the general public. But the government may not discriminate in the application of a policy to favor one group over another based on the content of their ideas.[26]

A recent example of the problem of government regulation of the use of public streets came in the 1999 case of *Chicago v. Morales*. A number of cities have passed anti-loitering ordinances whose purpose is to give police the power to deal with the problem of street gangs. A Chicago law made it a criminal act to "remain in one place with no apparent purpose" when in the presence of a suspected gang member and ordered to move on by a police officer. In a 6-to-3 opinion the Supreme Court invalidated the ordinance on the ground that it was unconstitutionally vague. Writing for the majority, Justice Stevens stated, "The entire ordinance fails to give the ordinary citizen adequate notice of what is forbidden and what is permitted." It also failed to give the police officer adequate guidance in deciding whether a citizen's presence on the street has no apparent purpose. "It matters not whether the reason that a gang member and his father,

The First Amendment protects the freedom of speech of persons with unpopular, controversial political ideas. Here the Reverend Louis Farrakhan, who has been accused of making anti-Semitic and racist statements, speaks to a group of his followers.

for example, might loiter near Wrigley Park to rob an unsuspecting fan or just to get a glimpse of Sammy Sosa leaving the ball park."[27]

Protecting Public Morals: Obscenity

Another controversial area involving the First Amendment concerns material that is alleged to be obscene. It is difficult to establish a clear definition of obscenity, however, for what is obscene to one person might not be to another, and moral standards change over time and differ from one community to another.

Ever since the 1950s the Supreme Court has attempted to set standards for judging whether a film, book, play, or other published material is obscene. In *Roth v. United States* (1957) it held that sex and obscenity are not synonymous: "The portrayal of sex . . . in art, literature, and scientific works, is not itself sufficient reason to deny material the constitutional protection of freedom of speech and press." Obscenity, on the other hand, "is not protected by the freedom of speech and press." The Court also established a test for determining whether a particular work is obscene. An item was to be judged obscene if "to the average person, applying contemporary community standards, the dominant theme of the material taken as a whole appeals to the prurient interest."[28] The key terms in this test are *average person* (which excludes children and other highly susceptible people) and *dominant theme* (which requires that the item be judged in its entirety; thus, a book cannot be declared obscene because of a few scattered passages).

In 1973, after more than a decade of legal confusion over the meaning of obscenity, the Supreme Court made another attempt to clarify the law in this area. In *Miller v. California* the Court defined the basic tests for obscenity:

(a) whether . . . the average person, applying "contemporary community standards," would find that the material, taken as a whole, appeals to the prurient interest . . .; (b) whether the work depicts or describes, in a patently offensive way, sexual conduct specifically defined by the applicable state law; and (c) whether the work, taken as a whole, lacks serious literary, artistic, political, or scientific value.

The Court made it clear that in applying the community standard test, a jury need not consider a national standard but is free to consult local tastes.[29]

The *Miller* case has not completely resolved the problem of defining obscenity. And despite this restatement of the law, which appeared to increase the ability of government to punish those who publish and sell obscene materials, prosecutors still find it very difficult to obtain convictions in obscenity cases.[30] The Supreme Court has, however, upheld the right of communities to use their zoning power to regulate the location of businesses that show or sell sexually explicit materials.[31] Further, the Court has held that the standards used to define obscenity do not apply to the sale or distribution of sexually oriented materials to minors[32] and that child pornography is not protected by the First Amendment.[33]

The Supreme Court has also ruled that the First Amendment protects the right of an individual to possess obscene material for private use in the home. But in 1990 the Court modified its position on this subject. It held that a state may make it a crime to possess in one's home pornographic pictures of children.[34] This ruling places in jeopardy the Supreme Court's earlier decision upholding the right of adults to possess obscene material in one's home so long as the possession is not for commercial purposes.

CLOSE-UP

FREE SPEECH AND THE INTERNET

The rapid growth of the Internet raises difficult issues related to freedom of speech. Each day millions of people seek information and "speak" to each other by means of their computer screens. Often the "speakers" are anonymous. Should the providers of on-line Internet services, such as Earthlink and America Online, be held responsible for the speech of people who use their services? That would be like holding telephone companies responsible for the speech of people who make obscene phone calls.

Some observers question whether the traditional rules of free speech can be applied to the Internet. They believe that there is a need for new rules to deal with special situations, such as the possibility that children will gain access to indecent material. In 1996 Congress responded to these concerns by passing the Communications Decency Act, which attempts to regulate the availability of sexually explicit material on the Internet.

In *Reno* v. *American Civil Liberties Union* (1997)* the Supreme Court declared unconstitutional a provision of the Communications Decency Law that made it illegal to "knowingly" transmit "obscene or indecent" messages to any person under the age of 18. It found that the word *indecent* was unconstitutionally vague and that the effect of the law was to deny adults materials that are protected under the First Amendment. "Regardless of the strength of the government's interest" in protecting children, "the level of discourse reaching a mailbox simply cannot be limited to that which would be suitable for a sandbox," the Court declared.

The Supreme Court has continued to oppose other attempts to regulate the content of Internet transmissions. In *Ascroft* v. *Free Speech Coalition* (2002)** the Court declared unconstitutional a provision of the Child Pornography Prevention Act of 1996 that made it a crime to create, distribute, possess, advertise, or promote "virtual" child pornography—material that used computer-derived images of youngsters, not actual children. But in 2004 the nation's highest court upheld a law requiring public libraries to install anti-pornography filters on computers with Internet connections as a condition for receiving federal financial grants.***

*521 S.Ct. 2329 (1997).

**April 16, 2002

***March 2, 2004.

Libel and Slander

Although the First Amendment's protection of freedom of speech and press has been interpreted broadly, it does not guarantee the freedom to use defamatory speech or language. **Defamation** includes both slander and libel. **Slander** refers to spoken words that are false and hold an individual up to public ridicule and contempt; **libel** refers to defamation by written word. Defamation law applies only to a statement of fact; an expression of opinion can never be the basis for a lawsuit.

The Supreme Court has made it very difficult for a public official to sue successfully for defamation. In the famous case of *The New York Times Co. v. Sullivan* (1964), it ruled that under its then existing law, Alabama could not hold *The New York Times* liable for publishing an advertisement that contained false statements of fact regarding the treatment of blacks by officials of Birmingham, Alabama. The Court held that for a statement about a public official to be considered libelous, the plaintiff must prove that the statement was made with actual malice, "that is, with the knowledge that it was false or with reckless disregard of whether it was false or not."[35]

The Court soon extended the actual-malice rule of the *Sullivan* case to individuals who have become "public figures," such as show business and sports celebrities. But the Court has generally defined this category quite narrowly. It has held, for example, that an attorney in a publicized lawsuit was not a public figure and therefore did not have to prove actual malice to win a libel case. He had "not accepted public office or assumed an 'influential role in ordering society.'"[36]

The Supreme Court has said that the Constitution grants greater protection to private individuals against defamatory statements than is granted to public figures because private individuals have not voluntarily surrendered their privacy and have less access to the media to respond to criticism. Private individuals, therefore, only have to prove some degree of fault by the defendant—for example, that the statement in question was made negligently—and that they have sustained some type of injury, such as, the loss of a job or friends, as a result of the statement. Private persons, unlike public ones, do not need to prove actual malice to be successful in a libel case.

The number of libel suits brought against newspapers, magazines, and television stations increased greatly after the *Sullivan* case but has leveled off in recent years. Many cases are either dismissed or settled before they go to trial. Plaintiffs do win a very high percentage of cases that are actually tried, and juries often award large sums of money in damages. However, many cases are reversed on appeal, or the amount of money awarded by the jury is substantially reduced by an appellate court.

The First Amendment and Campaign Spending

In 1974 Congress enacted the first major law that regulated campaign spending in federal elections. Many of its provisions were challenged in the federal courts on the grounds that they violated the First Amendment's guarantee of freedom of speech. The Supreme Court decided these issues in the 1976 case of *Buckley v. Valeo*.[37]

In the *Buckley* case the Court upheld important parts of the law, including limitations on the amounts of money individuals and groups could spend on political campaigns. It found that First Amendment interests were outweighed by the important governmental purpose of eliminating political corruption. But the Court found several other parts of the law to be unconstitutional—specifically, those that placed limits on the amount candidates could spend on campaigns and on the amount of personal money a candidate could spend in promoting his or her own candidacy.

The Supreme Court again considered the constitutionality of federal campaign spending legislation in December 2003. The Bipartisan Campaign Reform Act of 2002 outlawed the spending of soft money by national political parties and placed restrictions on advertising that specifically mentions political candidates within thirty days of a primary election and sixty days of a general election. The legislation was challenged in the courts as a violation of the First Amendment. In order that these important issues be quickly resolved, the law contained a provision that guaranteed an expedited appeal to the nation's highest court. On December 10, 2003 the Supreme Court upheld the constitutionality of the major provisions of the law.[38]

The Right of Association

The right of association is not expressly stated in the Constitution, but the Supreme Court has held that it is derived from the freedoms of the First Amendment. The Court formally recognized this right for the first time in the case of

NAACP v. Alabama (1958), which arose during the period of civil rights protests in the South. The Court ruled that the National Association for the Advancement of Colored People could not be required to give its membership lists to the state of Alabama. Making public the names of members of the NAACP could subject those individuals to physical and economic harassment and thus interfere with their right to join together in an association designed to express their beliefs.[39]

The Court has also held that the right of association includes the right of individuals to join together in a nonviolent economic boycott of businesses that practice racial discrimination.[40] And in a controversial decision in 2000, the Court upheld the First Amendment right of the Boys Scouts of America to bar persons who are known to be gay from leadership positions in the organization.[41]

Commercial Speech

Until the 1970s courts in the United States refused to apply any First Amendment protections to **commercial speech.** Then, in a series of groundbreaking opinions, the Court held that the First Amendment provided some protection for commercial speech. It held, for example, that states cannot make it illegal for lawyers, doctors, and other professionals to advertise fees charged for basic services.[42] Such advertising provides the public with important information to use in making decisions.

Recent decisions by the Supreme Court show that it strongly supports the application of the First Amendment to commercial speech. In a 1996 case the Court held that Rhode Island could not prohibit retailers from advertising the prices of liquor, nor could it bar newspapers and other media from publishing ads for these products.[43] And in 1999 the Court unanimously struck down a federal ban on radio and television advertising of private casino gambling in states where such gambling was legal.[44]

These decisions suggested that the Supreme Court would restrict states from regulating tobacco advertising beyond the present requirements imposed by federal law that require warning labels on cigarette packages and bar cigarette ads on television. The Court dealt with this issue in a case that raised constitutional questions about a Massachusetts law that imposed broad new limitations on tobacco advertising in the Commonwealth. In a unanimous decision the nation's highest court struck down those parts of the law that outlawed tobacco advertisements on outdoor signs. At the same time, the Court upheld Massachusetts's rules that limited indoor displays of tobacco ads.[45]

It is important to note that the Supreme Court has repeatedly stated that the First Amendment's protection is not as broad in the case of commercial speech as it is in the case of noncommercial speech. Commercial speech can be restricted, for example, if it is false or misleading or if it promotes unlawful conduct.

Symbolic Speech

Freedom of speech is not confined to words; it includes some forms of expressive conduct that are referred to as *symbolic speech.* This is conduct that dramatizes a person's beliefs, such as flying a banner or wearing an armband. Not all symbolic activity is protected by the First Amendment, however. In 1984, for example, the Supreme Court held that the right to engage in some forms of symbolic speech did not include the right of demonstrators to sleep in Lafayette Park and the Mall in Washington, D.C., in an effort to call public attention to the plight of homeless people. The High Court upheld the right of the National Park Service to prohibit camping in these public places.[46]

Perhaps the most controversial free-speech issue in recent times has been whether the First Amendment protects the right to burn or deface an American flag. In 1989 the Supreme Court, by a 5-to-4 vote, declared unconstitutional a Texas law that punished desecration of the flag.[47] In the wake of that decision, Congress quickly enacted a law that made it a federal crime to burn or deface the American flag. In the 1990 case of *United States v. Eichman,* the Court, again by a 5-to-4 vote, invalidated this legislation.[48] In both cases the Court found that the government was engaged in illegal content regulation; it was singling out specific ideas for prohibition while allowing other ideas to be expressed.

Free Press and a Fair Trial

A few situations arise in which certain provisions of the Bill of Rights come into conflict. The most important of these is the clash between the First Amendment guarantee of freedom of the press and the Sixth Amendment right of a person accused of a crime to a fair trial and an impartial jury. Sixth Amendment rights are threatened when the news media give extensive coverage to a crime. This is not a problem in the vast majority of cases, which receive little or no press coverage. The difficulty arises in the relatively few sensational cases that receive widespread media attention that may be prejudicial to the accused person.

Several procedures can be used to deal with this problem. In a landmark 1966 case, *Sheppard v. Maxwell,* the Supreme Court held that it is mandatory for a trial judge to control the effects of pretrial publicity by either changing the location of the trial, postponing the trial, instructing the jury to ignore press reports about the case, or even sequestering (confining) the jury during the trial. The Court has also held that the trial judge may control the flow of information to the news media by using the contempt-of-court power to restrict statements made by parties, witnesses, lawyers, and court officials connected with the case.[49] But the courts may not prohibit the press from publishing information regarding a criminal trial—so-called "gag orders."

The Supreme Court has also held that the right of the press and the public to attend criminal trials is protected by the First Amendment and that a trial judge may not exclude the press from such proceedings.[50] Similarly, the press and the public have the right of access to a court when jurors are being selected for a criminal case.[51]

The First Amendment does not give television stations the right to have cameras in courtrooms, but government may, if it chooses, grant that right. Today almost all states permit cameras in courtrooms. The trial judge has the power to decide whether cameras are to be permitted in the courtroom and to impose regulations regarding their use to protect the due process rights of the defendant. The federal courts, however, do not permit television coverage of trials.

THE RIGHTS OF THE CRIMINALLY ACCUSED

Films and TV shows about crime and criminals are commonplace. Crimes and arrests of criminals make headlines in newspapers and are featured on local television news programs. Widespread concern about crime has made it one of the most important public issues, and government has responded by passing new criminal laws and by increasing the severity of punishments for those found guilty of criminal conduct. But despite all the attention given to crime, criminal-justice procedures are not generally understood by Americans, nor are the constitutional rights of accused persons.

The Constitution contains several provisions limiting the powers of the government in relation to people accused of crimes. For example, it bars both the national and the state governments from passing *ex post facto* laws. These are laws that impose a penalty for committing an act that was not considered criminal when it was committed or that increase the punishment for a crime after it has been committed. This is a fundamental protection of individual rights that has rarely, if ever, been violated.

The Constitution also prohibits the enactment of bills of attainder. A *bill of attainder* is an act of a legislature that singles out specific people or groups and orders that they be punished without judicial trial. Only a few legislative acts have been struck down by the Supreme Court as bills of attainder. In 1965, for example, the Court declared void an act of Congress that made it a crime for a member of the American Communist party to be an employee or an officer of a trade union.[52]

But most of the constitutional rights of the criminally accused are contained in the Bill of Rights. They were intended to protect citizens against certain types of conduct by law enforcement authorities and judges. Their purpose was to prevent innocent people from being wrongly convicted, even though a few guilty ones might go free. We will now discuss the major rights of the criminally accused under the Fourth, Fifth, Sixth, and Eighth Amendments and the due process clause of the Fourteenth Amendment.

Search and Seizure

The Fourth Amendment declares that

> The right of the people to be secure in their persons, houses, papers and effects, against unreasonable searches and seizures, shall not be violated, and no warrants shall issue, but upon probable cause, supported by oath or affirmation, and particularly describing the place to be searched, and the persons or things to be seized.

This provision reflects the common-law rule that "a man's home is his castle," and it imposes important restrictions on government. In attempting to make an arrest or obtain evidence of criminal acts, the government must follow certain procedures. The general rule set forth by the Fourth Amendment is that searches and seizures may be conducted only after a search warrant has been issued by a judge or a magistrate. To justify the warrant, the law enforcement officer must show the judge, in a written affidavit, sufficient information to establish "probable cause." The affidavit must also specifically describe the place to be searched and the person or things to be seized. This requirement was intended to prevent general searches of homes and neighborhoods and general seizures of people and property, practices used by British colonial officials prior to the American Revolutionary War.

The Fourth Amendment does not require that all searches and seizures be based on warrants. In fact, many arrests and seizures occur without warrants. The language of the Fourth Amendment indicates that the nation's founders understood this fact; it recognizes that in some situations warrantless searches and seizures are reasonable and therefore valid.

Police search an automobile for illegal drugs. The courts have held that warrantless searches of automobiles are constitutional if based on probable cause.

The courts have created a growing number of exceptions to the warrant requirement of the Fourth Amendment. Among these are searches based on voluntary consent, searches incident to a lawful arrest, seizure of evidence that is in "plain view" of a police officer, and "stop and frisk" situations that involve detention short of actual arrest. Also, because of their mobility, automobiles can be searched without warrants as long as there is probable cause to believe that the automobile contains contraband.[53]

The search of automobiles has presented many difficult problems for the Supreme Court. The Court has generally upheld broad, though not unlimited, police power to search automobiles. The police may not, for example, randomly stop automobiles unless they have some suspicion of criminal activity.[54] But it is permissible for the police to stop automobiles at fixed checkpoints in the absence of any individualized suspicion.[55]

Automobile searches without warrants are constitutional, but there must be probable cause to conduct the search.[56] If there is reasonable cause, a warrantless search may extend to luggage and containers.[57] Finally, in conducting a warrantless search of an automobile, it is lawful to expand the search to include passengers[58] and the property of passengers.[59]

The Exclusionary Rule

Under the common law a court could permit the use of any item of evidence at a trial, regardless of the methods used by the police to obtain it. In 1914, however, the Supreme Court ruled that evidence obtained as a result of illegal search and seizure could not be used against the accused in a federal criminal case.[60] This rule, the so-called **exclusionary rule of evidence,** is intended to deter illegal searches and seizures by the police. The rule was not binding on the states until the 1961 decision of the Supreme Court in *Mapp v. Ohio.* The majority opinion for the court declared: "We hold that all evidence obtained by searches and seizures in violation of the Constitution is, by that same authority, inadmissible in a state court."[61]

The exclusionary rule, unique to the law of this country, has been the subject of much criticism. Opponents have contended that the exclusionary rule permits people who have committed crimes to go free because trial juries are denied access to reliable evidence of an incriminating nature. Opponents of the exclusionary rule have called for its abolition. Others would modify the rule, allowing illegally obtained evidence to be introduced in criminal trials under certain conditions.

The Supreme Court has accepted some of these criticisms and has created several exceptions to the exclusionary rule. In *Nix v. Williams,* for example, it held that illegally obtained evidence is admissible in a criminal trial if the government can establish that the evidence would "inevitably" have been found by the police through the use of lawful methods. In this case, the evidence was the body of a murdered child that had been buried in snow by the murderer.[62] And in *United States v. Leon* the Court ruled that evidence obtained by the police is admissible when they have acted in "good faith" reliance on a warrant issued by a magistrate, even if that warrant was later found to be defective.[63]

In the important 1995 case of *Arizona v. Evans,* the Court again found an exception to the exclusionary rule. The police had stopped Evans for a routine traffic violation. Using a computer terminal in his patrol car, the officer determined that there was an outstanding arrest warrant for Evans on a misdemeanor charge. The officer arrested Evans and searched his car. During the search he found illegal drugs. It later turned out that the arrest warrant had been canceled but had not been removed from the police department's computer files. The Supreme Court upheld Evans's claim that his Fourth Amendment rights had been violated because there was no valid warrant either for his arrest or for the seizure of the marijuana, and that the only evidence against him—the marijuana—should be excluded from his trial.

The purpose of the exclusionary rule, Chief Justice Rehnquist contended, is to deter the police from illegal conduct. If the evidence were excluded in this case, it would have no deterrent effect on the behavior of the police. Returning to the exception the Court had created more than a decade earlier in *Leon,* the chief justice argued that the police officer had acted in "good faith" on the information in the police computer files. The evidence therefore could be used against the defendant.[64]

Electronic and Other Forms of Surveillance

Another challenge to the Fourth Amendment has arisen as a result of technological advances. When the Fourth Amendment was adopted in 1791, its authors could not have foreseen the development of electronic listening devices, which make it unnecessary to enter a home or a place of business to conduct a search. The development of increasingly sophisticated methods of electronic surveillance has forced the courts to reexamine the Fourth Amendment. Initially, the Supreme Court refused to apply the warrant requirements of the Fourth Amendment to telephone tapping and other electronic listening devices. It was not until 1967, in *Katz v. United States,* that the Court extended the scope of the Fourth Amendment to include electronic eavesdropping. The Fourth Amendment protects "people, not places," the Court declared. It extends to situations in which a person has a "reasonable expectation of privacy."

> What a person knowingly exposes to the public, even in his own home or office, is not a subject of Fourth Amendment protection. . . . But what he seeks to preserve as private, even in an area accessible to the public, may be constitutionally protected.[65]

In 1968, after many years of considering such legislation, Congress passed the Omnibus Crime Control and Safe Streets Act. This act legalized electronic surveillance by federal, state, and local police, but it placed them under the limitations of the Fourth Amendment. The law requires that police officers obtain a warrant from a magistrate when they intend to use a wiretap.

As noted earlier, the Supreme Court's 1967 decision in *Katz v. United States* established that the warrant requirement of the Fourth Amendment applied to situations in which a person "has a reasonable expectation of privacy." The Court has periodically been called upon to interpret this phrase in reference to particular situations. It has held that a person can reasonably expect privacy while talking to someone in a home or a place of business. In 1999 the Supreme Court unanimously ruled that residential privacy was violated when police took photographers and reporters into a home to witness a search or arrest.[66] And most recently, the court held that the police may not employ a heat-sensing device to look inside a person's home to obtain evidence of criminal conduct without first obtaining a search warrant.[67] But the right of privacy does not extend to garbage placed in front of a home for collection.[68] Nor can a person who is in a home only temporarily to conduct business challenge the validity of a search of that home, since he or she has no "legitimate expectation of privacy" in that place.[69]

Freedom from Self-Incrimination

The Fifth Amendment provides that no person "shall be compelled in any criminal case to be a witness against himself." In a criminal case, therefore, the government must establish the guilt of a person by presenting evidence obtained from sources other than the accused person. This protection applies not only to people who are actually suspected of criminal wrongdoing but also to those who testify before investigatory bodies such as grand juries and congressional committees. Although this protection against **self-incrimination** has always limited the federal government, it was not made fully binding on the states until 1964, when the Supreme Court ruled that "the Fourteenth Amendment secures against state invasion the same privilege that the Fifth Amendment guarantees against federal infringement—the right of a person to remain silent."[70]

The Fifth Amendment requires that the silence of an accused person not be interpreted as an indication of guilt. Thus, when defendants in criminal trials choose not to take the stand in their own defense, the jury must be warned by the judge not to interpret that decision as evidence of guilt.

Indictment by a Grand Jury

The Fifth Amendment declares that "no person shall be held to answer for a capital, or otherwise infamous, crime unless on a presentment or indictment of a Grand Jury." A capital crime is one that is punishable by death. An "infamous" crime refers to serious violations of the law, or felonies.

Unlike a trial, or *petit,* jury, a **grand jury** does not render a verdict of guilty or not guilty. Rather, it determines whether the government, represented by the prosecuting attorney, has sufficient evidence to warrant a criminal trial on the charges made against the accused person. If the grand jury believes that the government has enough evidence, it returns an **indictment,** or true bill. Although the main purpose of the grand jury is to protect persons from unjustified criminal trials, in practice grand juries return indictments in more than 90 percent of the cases they hear.

Indictment by a grand jury is one of the few procedural guarantees of the Bill of Rights that is not binding on the states. Thus, although some states (mostly in the eastern half of the nation) use the grand jury because of their own constitutions and laws, a majority do not. Instead, they employ the **bill of information** in felony cases. This is a written affidavit filed by a prosecutor and presented to a court to show that there is enough evidence to justify a trial. The same device is used by governments throughout the United States to charge individuals with misdemeanor crimes.

Double Jeopardy

Protection against **double jeopardy** is guaranteed by the Fifth Amendment: "Nor shall any person be subject for the same offense to be twice put in jeopardy of life or limb." In 1969 the Supreme Court held that the guarantee against double jeopardy applied to the states under the Fourteenth Amendment.[71]

The protection against double jeopardy basically means that once a person has been tried for a particular crime and the trial has ended in a verdict of not guilty, the government cannot appeal that decision nor can that person be tried again for the same crime. The double jeopardy provision does not, however, prevent a defendant from being tried again for the same offense if the jury cannot arrive at a verdict or if there is a mistrial. Moreover, if the defendant has been convicted but the verdict has been set aside after a successful appeal, the government may retry that defendant for the same offense.

The Right to Counsel

"In all criminal prosecutions, the accused shall enjoy the right. . . . to have the Assistance of Counsel for his defense." This Sixth Amendment guarantee was designed to ensure that accused people are represented by a lawyer, someone who understands the law and court procedures. The right to counsel becomes an issue in cases involving defendants who cannot afford to hire a lawyer.

In *Powell v. Alabama* (1932) the right to counsel was applied to the states through the Fourteenth Amendment in cases involving the death penalty,[72] and since 1938 the Supreme Court has applied an absolute rule requiring that attorneys be appointed for all indigent defendants in federal cases. This right, Justice Black wrote, "is necessary to insure fundamental human rights of life and liberty."[73]

The Scottsboro Boys case was a major criminal trial that attracted worldwide attention. In this 1933 photo four of the nine young, poorly educated black defendants, who were accused of raping two white women, are marched to the courthouse. Their convictions were later overturned by the United States Supreme Court because of constitutional violations, including denial of counsel in a capital case.

It was not until 1963, in *Gideon v. Wainwright,* that the right to counsel was applied to the states in cases that do not involve the death penalty. In this decision the Court held that the Sixth Amendment right to have an attorney applies to all state felony trials.[74] In 1972 it extended the *Gideon* ruling to include misdemeanor cases in which a person might be imprisoned.[75]

The *Gideon* case left unanswered the question of the precise point in the criminal process at which a person's right to counsel begins. That question was answered in *Escobedo v. Illinois* (1964). Escobedo had repeatedly requested an attorney while he was being questioned by police, but none was provided. Statements he had made during the questioning were later used to convict Escobedo of murder. The Supreme Court reversed the conviction, holding that the right to counsel begins when police conduct is no longer investigatory but accusatory. In this case, the police activity had centered on Escobedo, and the questions had been designed to produce a confession from him. At this point the presence of an attorney is critical. "No system of criminal justice can, or should, survive if it comes to depend for its continued effectiveness on the citizens' abdication through unawareness of their constitutional rights."[76]

The Right to an Impartial Jury

The Sixth Amendment guarantees an impartial jury for those accused of crimes. An important issue related to this protection is jury selection. The examination of prospective jurors (the ***voir dire***) is the principal means by which the goal of impartiality is sought. Questioning by the attorneys for both sides of the lawsuit (and sometimes by the presiding judge) seeks to discover the existence of bias that would prevent the person from deciding the case solely on the basis of the facts presented in the courtroom. Because of the importance of obtaining impartial jurors, attorneys are able to exercise an unlimited right to reject jurors for cause.

But attorneys can also use so-called *peremptory challenges* to reject jurors. These are always limited in number and can be used without explanation. Attorneys use peremptory challenges as a means to create a jury that they believe will be more favorable to their client.

The issue of peremptory challenges has been considered by the Supreme Court on a number of occasions. In 1986 the Court held that the use of peremptory challenges to exclude blacks from a jury constitutes a violation of the equal protection clause of the Fourteenth Amendment.[77] And in 1994 the Court held that systematically excluding persons from a jury because of their gender is also an illegal form of discrimination.[78]

Ironically, these decisions of the Court may make it harder for minorities and women to prevail in some court cases. For example, prosecuting attorneys in sex-crime cases usually prefer to have women on juries on the theory that they will be more sympathetic to the victim. But attorneys will no longer be able to use peremptory challenges to exclude men from serving on juries in this type of case.

The rights to counsel, a jury trial, and cross-examination of witnesses are guaranteed by the Sixth Amendment to the Constitution. Here an attorney speaks to a jury during a trial.

Confessions

The use of confessions in criminal cases raises two important constitutional questions. One is whether statements obtained by the police from people accused of crimes violate the Fifth Amendment protection against self-incrimination. The other is whether an accused person should have a Sixth Amendment right to counsel when being questioned by the police.

The police view confessions as a vital and speedy method of solving crimes. But confessions can be obtained through coercion and are subject to abuse by law enforcement officials. Since the 1930s the Supreme Court has heard many cases involving confessions and has formulated standards designed to reconcile the interests of the police and the rights of the accused. The first test used by the Court in such cases was whether the confession had been given voluntarily, but ever since 1966 the Court has imposed more specific controls on the police.

In *Miranda v. Arizona* (1966) the Supreme Court set forth the procedural rules that police must follow before anyone may be questioned. The Miranda rules require that detainees be warned prior to any questioning that they have the right to remain silent, that anything they say can be used against them in a court of law, that they have the right to the presence of an attorney, and that if they cannot afford an attorney one will be appointed for them prior to any questioning if they so desire. Opportunity to exercise these rights must be afforded throughout the interrogation. After such warnings have been given, and such opportunity been made available, the individual may knowingly and intelligently waive these

---

CLOSE-UP

SILENCE AND SELF-INCRIMINATION

"You do not have to say anything unless you wish to do so, but what you say may be given in evidence."

"You do not have to say anything. But if you do not mention now something which you later use in your defense, the court may decide that your failure to mention it now strengthens the case against you."

In 1995 Great Britain changed this warning that the police must give to individuals who have been taken into custody. It is radically different from the *Miranda* warning that is required in the United States. The first version above was in use before 1995; the second is a new version that was passed by Parliament as part of a major anticrime bill. Both versions give accused persons the right to remain silent, but the second version warns them that their silence might be used against them in court.

The new version is an outgrowth of public concern about the rising crime rate in Britain. That concern led Parliament to modify the law to make it easier for the government to convict criminals.

According to a spokesman for the British government, the warning "is based on the proposition that, if an innocent person has an explanation to give, he can usually be expected to give it at the first opportunity, not store it up for use when the proceedings have developed as far as a trial." The government contends that the warning does not abolish the right to silence or curtail the presumption of innocence. It is intended only to discourage professional criminals from exploiting the legal system.

Under the new law, judges and juries will be allowed to draw inferences about a defendant's refusal to answer questions or explain his or her actions—including the inference that the suspect was using silence to conceal guilt. In the United States, such an inference would violate the defendant's rights under the Fifth Amendment. In Great Britain, however, there is no written Constitution or Bill of Rights, and Parliament has the authority to define the rights of citizens through legislation.

A police officer reads an arrested man the *Miranda* warnings, which inform him of his protection against self-incrimination and his right to an attorney.

rights and agree to answer questions or make a statement. But unless and until such warnings and waiver are demonstrated by the prosecution at trial, no evidence obtained as a result of interrogation can be used against a person.[79]

These constitutional rules apply when a person has been taken into custody or otherwise significantly deprived of freedom of movement by the police. They are necessary, in the view of the Court, to guarantee the Fifth Amendment protection against self-incrimination. Without these rules, there is too much danger that the police may obtain statements and confessions that are not truly voluntary.

The *Miranda* decision has never been overruled by the Supreme Court, and its basic principles still govern in-custody interrogations by the police. But the Court has refused to extend *Miranda* to related situations, and it has created some exceptions to its application. It has held, for example, that a witness before a grand jury need not be informed of his constitutional rights even though he is suspected of criminal wrongdoing.[80] It has also created a "public safety" exception to the *Miranda* rules. In *New York v. Quarles* the police had pursued a suspected rapist who was thought to be armed. The man was found in a supermarket, but no gun was discovered. Without giving him the *Miranda* warning, the officer asked him where the gun was, and the suspect pointed toward a carton. The Supreme Court ruled that the evidence was admissible, holding that public safety was threatened by the existence of the concealed gun and that the protection of the public superseded the need for strict application of the *Miranda* rules.[81]

"Cruel and Unusual Punishment" and the Death Penalty

The Eighth Amendment prohibits the use of "cruel and unusual punishments." Throughout most of this nation's history this provision was rarely used as a basis for challenging acts of government. But since the 1970s it has been raised on a large number of occasions to question the constitutionality of the death penalty. Since 1972 the Supreme Court has said that the death penalty is not in itself a cruel and inhuman punishment when applied to someone who has been convicted of murder (though it may not be imposed for other crimes). Nevertheless, it has held that the Eighth and Fourteenth Amendments require that state death penalty laws meet certain standards. For example, the determination of guilt or innocence and the sentencing of a guilty person in a capital case must take place in separate proceedings. The Court has also held that in making the decision as to whether to impose the death penalty, the sentencing court must be able to consider both mitigating and aggravating factors. The death penalty cannot be imposed automatically once a defendant has been convicted, nor can a court be allowed to use uncontrolled discretion in making this decision. The court must be able to consider specific mitigating factors, such as the age of the defendant, prior convictions, and whether the crime was committed under the influence of drugs or alcohol. It must also be able to consider aggravating factors such as the amount and type of violence used in the killing.[82]

In a case decided in June 2002, the Court determined that juries, not judges must decide the factual issues about whether to impose the death penalty.[83] The decision affected the laws of nine states and nearly 800 death row prisoners in those states.

The present Supreme Court has generally upheld state death penalty laws against various constitutional challenges, though usually by narrow 5-to-4 votes. In this area of law, the Court has shown great deference to the judgments of state governments. It has, for example, rejected a claim that statistical evidence shows that the death penalty is applied disproportionately to black defendants. The Court found that such evidence is not sufficient to establish unconstitutional discrimination. A defendant "must prove that the decision makers in his case acted with discriminatory purpose."[84] The Supreme Court has also upheld the right of a state to execute youths who were from 16 to 17 years of age at the time that they committed murder. And it has held that the Eighth Amendment does not in and of itself prohibit the execution of a mentally retarded person.[85]

At the close if its 2001–2002 term, the Supreme Court retreated from a position it had taken in 1989 that had permitted the execution of a retarded person. In *Atkins v. Virginia*, the Court invalidated the laws of eighteen states that allowed such punishments. In support of its new position, the Court cited a new "national consensus" against executing the retarded.[86]

Capital punishment was once quite common in the United States, reaching a peak during the 1930s and 1940s, when over 100 people were executed annually. Public support for the death penalty declined during the 1950s, and many states repealed their death sentence laws. Between 1967 and 1977 no executions occurred in the United States. But a dramatic increase in crime throughout the nation led to renewed public support for capital punishment, and the Supreme Court's decisions on the death sentence gave constitutional support to public demands for reinstatement of this form of punishment. Today thirty-eight states have laws providing for capital punishment in cases of aggravated murder.

An average of 290 persons were sentenced to death in the states during the 1990s. But the numbers have sharply declined in recent years. In the first four years of this century the average dropped to 174, and in 2003 only 143 death penalties were imposed.[87]

Since 1988 Congress has enacted legislation applying the death penalty to a variety of criminal acts. Federal prosecutors can ask for the death penalty for individuals accused of murder in connection with drug trafficking, most murders involving the use of a gun, deaths resulting from civil rights violations, carjacking, mail bombs, acts of terrorism, and causing a train wreck that results in death. Thus far, only one federal prisoner has been executed: Timothy McVeigh was convicted of the April 19, 1995, bombing of the federal courthouse in Oklahoma City that killed 168 Americans and was put to death in June 2001.

CONCLUSION

The positions taken by the Supreme Court are influenced by the personal philosophies of the justices. During the 1960s the Court handed down many decisions based on a broad interpretation of the individual liberties guaranteed by the Bill of Rights. But from the 1970s to the present, the nation's highest court has become more conservative on some issues of individual rights, largely as a result of the appointment of more conservative justices by Republican presidents Ronald Reagan and George H. W. Bush.

The present Supreme Court's more conservative orientation is not generally reflected in issues related to the First Amendment protections of freedom of speech and press. The Court has continued to define these liberties broadly. But the conservatism can be seen in the new rules dealing with both freedom of religion and the establishment of religion that have been created by the Court in recent years.

The conservatism of the Supreme Court is most conspicuous in the area of criminal procedure. Although it has not actually overruled any

of the landmark decisions from the 1960s, it has narrowed their application and created new rules that generally favor the government. During each term of the Court, the government, not the defendant, wins most of the victories on issues of criminal procedure.

The September 11 terrorist attack on the United States has created new issues of civil liberties. The USA Patriots Act of 2001 significantly increased the power of the president and of the executive branch of government with regard to private banking, the surveillance of telephone conversations, voice mail, e-mail and web surfing, and the detention and deportation of aliens who are suspected of terrorist activities. (A fuller discussion of the law can be found in Chapter 8.) The constitutionality of various actions of the federal government to deal with terrorism has been raised in the federal courts, and in June 2004 the Supreme Court issued its first rulings on the government's power to detain enemy combatants.[88]

QUESTIONS FOR THOUGHT

1. What is the relationship of the Bill of Rights to the states?

2. What are the major exceptions to the First Amendment's guarantees of freedom of speech and the press?

3. What is the meaning and importance of the doctrine of no prior restraint?

4. What constitutional rights did *Miranda v. Arizona* establish for persons in police custody?

5. What is meant by the exclusionary rule of evidence?

INTERNET ACTIVITY

Review a Landmark Case. Go to **http://supct.law.cornell.edu/supct/** where you will find links to current and historic cases in constitutional law arranged by name and by topic. Select a case to analyze. Write a summary that outlines the essential facts of the case and sets forth the basic constitutional issues in question. What was the impact of this case on the exercise of liberty? Try **http://www.aclu.org/** for additional resources.

KEY TERMS

bill of information
civil liberties
commercial speech
compelling interest
defamation
double jeopardy
due process clause

establishment clause
exclusionary rule of evidence
free exercise clause
grand jury
indictment
libel
prior restraint

sedition
selective incorporation
self-incrimination
slander
voir dire

SUGGESTED READING

Cookson, Catherine. *Regulating Freedom: The Courts and the Free Exercise Clause.* New York: Oxford University Press, 2000.

Gedicks, Frederick Mark. *The Rhetoric of Church and State.* Durham, NC: Duke University Press, 1995.

Goldstein, Robert Justin. *Burning the Flag: The Great 1989–1990 American Flag Desecration Controversy.* Kent, OH: Kent State University Press, 1996.

Johnson, John W. *The Struggle for Student Rights: Tinker v. Des Moines and the 1960s.* Lawrence: University Press of Kansas, 1997.

Anthony Lewis. *Make No Law: The Sullivan Case and the First Amendment.* New York: Random House, 1991.

Perry, Michael J. *We the People: The Fourteenth Amendment and the Supreme Court.* New York: Oxford University Press, 1999.

Rothwax, Harold. *Guilty: The Concept of Criminal Justice.* New York: Random House, 1996.

Rudenstein, David. *The Day the Presses Stopped: A History of the Pentagon Papers Case.* Berkeley: University of California Press, 1996.

Shiffrin, Steven H. *Dissent, Injustice and the Meanings of America.* Princeton, NJ: Princeton University Press, 2000.

Smolla, Rodney. *Free Speech in an Open Society.* New York: Knopf, 1993.

NOTES

1. *Barron v. Baltimore,* 7 Peters 243 (1833).
2. *Watchtower Bible & Tract Society v. Village of Stratton,* (June 17, 2002)
3. 98 U.S. 145 (1878).
4. 133 U.S. 33 (1890).
5. *Hobbie v. Unemployment Appeals Commission of Florida,* 480 U.S. 136 (1987).
6. *Employment Division of Oregon v. Smith,* 495 U.S. 872 (1990)

7. *Everson v. Board of Education of the Township of Ewing,* 330 U.S. 1 (1947).
8. 403 U.S. 602 (1971).
9. *Meek v. Pittenger,* 421 U.S. 349 (1975).
10. *Kiryas Joel v. Grumet,* 512 U.S. 687 (1994).
11. *Agostini v. Felton,* 521 U.S. 203 (1997).
12. *Aguilar v. Felton,* 473 U.S. 402 (1985).
13. *Zelmann v. Simmons-Harris,* (June 27, 2002).

14. 370 U.S. 421 (1962). The Regents' prayer was: "Almighty God, we acknowledge our dependence upon Thee, and we beg Thy blessings upon us, our parents, our teachers and our country."

15. *Abington School District v. Schempp*, 374 U.S. 203 (1963).

16. *Wallace v. Jaffree*, 472 U.S. 38 (1985).

17. *Weisman v. Lee*, 505 U.S. 577 (1992); *Sante Fe Independent School District v. Doe*, 530 U.S. 290 (2000).

18. *Allegheny County v. ACLU*, 492 U.S. 573 (1989).

19. 515 U.S. 819 (1995).

20. *Chaplinsky v. New Hampshire*, 315 U.S. 568 (1942).

21. 283 U.S. 697 (1931).

22. 403 U.S. 713 (1971).

23. 341 U.S. 494 (1951).

24. 395 U.S. 44 (1969).

25. *Grayned v. City of Rockford*, 408 U.S. 104 (1972).

26. For a recent example of a case on this subject, see *Thomas v. Chicago Park District* (January 15, 2002).

27. 527 U.S. 41 (1999).

28. 354 U.S. 476 (1957).

29. 413 U.S. 15 (1973).

30. See *Jenkins v. Georgia*, 418 U.S. 153 (1974).

31. *Young v. American Mini Theatres, Inc.*, 427 U.S. 50 (1976); *Renton v. Playtime Theatres, Inc.*, 475 U.S. 41 (1986).

32. *Ginsberg v. New York*, 390 U.S. 629 (1968).

33. *New York v. Ferber*, 458 U.S. 747 (1982).

34. *Stanley v. Georgia*, 394 U.S. 557 (1969); *Osborne v. Ohio*, 495 U.S. 103 (1990).

35. 376 U.S. 254 (1964).

36. *Gertz v. Robert Welch, Inc.*, 418 U.S. 323 (1974).

37. 424 U.S. 1 (1976).

38. *McConnell v. Federal Election Commission*, 540 U.S. 93 (2003).

39. 357 U.S. 449 (1958).

40. *NAACP v. Claiborne Hardware Co.*, 458 U.S. 886 (1982).

41. *Boy Scouts of America v. Dale*, 530 U.S. 640 (2000).

42. *Bates v. State Bar of Arizona*, 433 U.S. 350 (1977).

43. *Liquor Mart v. Rhode Island*, 517 U.S. 484 (1996).

44. *Greater New Orleans Broadcasting Association, Inc. v. United States*, 527 U.S. 173 (1999).

45. *Lorillard Tobacco v. Reilly*, 533 U.S. 525 (2001).

46. *Clark v. Community for Creative Non-Violence*, 468 U.S. 288 (1984).

47. *Texas v. Johnson*, 491 U.S. 397 (1989).

48. *United States v. Eichman*, 496 U.S. 310 (1990).

49. 384 U.S. 333 (1966).

50. *Richmond Newspapers, Inc. v. Virginia*, 448 U.S. 555 (1980).

51. *Press-Enterprise Co. v. Superior Court*, 464 U.S. 501 (1984).

52. *United States v. Brown*, 381 U.S. 437 (1965).

53. *Carroll v. United States*, 267 U.S. 132 (1925).

54. *Delaware v. Prouse*, 440 U.S. 648 (1979).

55. *Michigan Department of State Police v. Sitz*, 496 U.S. 444 (1990).

56. *Almeida-Sanchez v. United States*, 413, U.S. 266 (1973).

57. *California v. Acevado*, 500 U.S. 565 (1991); *United States v. Ross*, 456 U.S. 798 (1982).

58. *Ybarra v. Illinois*, 444 U.S. 85 (1979).

59. *Wyoming v. Houghton*, 525 U.S. 295 (1999).

60. *Weeks v. United States*, 232 U.S. 383 (1914).

61. 367 U.S. 643 (1961).

62. 467 U.S. 431 (1984).

63. 468 U.S. 897 (1984).

64. 514 U.S. 1 (1995).

65. 389 U.S. 347 (1967).

66. *Wilson v. Layne*, 526 U.S. 603 (1999).

67. *Kyllo v. United States*, 533 U.S. 27 (2001).

68. *California v. Greenwood*, 468 U.S. 35 (1988).

69. *Minnesota v. Carter*, 525 U.S. 83 (1998).

70. *Malloy v. Hogan*, 378 U.S. 1 (1964).

71. *Benton v. Maryland*, 395 U.S. 784 (1969).

72. 287 U.S. 45 (1932).

73. *Johnson v. Zerbst*, 304 U.S. 458 (1938).

74. 372 U.S. 335 (1963).

75. *Argersinger v. Hamlin*, 407 U.S. 25 (1972).

76. 378 U.S. 478 (1964).

77. *Batson v. Kentucky*, 476 U.S. 79 (1986).

78. *J.E.B v. Alabama*, 511 U.S. 127 (1994).

79. 384 U.S. 436 (1966).

80. *United States v. Mandujano*, 425 U.S. 564 (1976).

81. 467 U.S. 649 (1984).

82. *Gregg v. Georgia*, 428 U.S. 153 (1976); *Roberts v. Louisiana*, 428 U.S. 325 (1976); *Woodson v. North Carolina*, 428 U.S. 280 (1976).

83. *Ring v. Arizona* (June 25, 2002).

84. *McClesky v. Kemp*, 481 U.S. 279 (1987).

85. *Stanford v. Kentucky and Wilkens v. Missouri*, 492 U.S. 361 (1989).

86. *Atkins v. Virginia*, (June 20, 2002).

87. Adam Liptak, "Fewer Death Sentences Being Imposed in the United States," *New York Times* September 15, 2004, p. A16.

88. *Hamdi v. Rumsfeld, Rumsfeld v. Padilla*, and *Rasul v. Bush* (June 28, 2004).

Civil Rights

The concept of equal rights for all is one that goes back to the founding of this nation. The Declaration of Independence declared that "all men are created equal." A number of provisions of the United States Constitution also sought to further the goal of equality. The Reverend Martin Luther King, Jr., speaks to this moral and legal commitment in the statement that begins this chapter.

Unfortunately, the United States has too often not lived up to the ideal of equality. Slavery and the long history of racial discrimination in this nation are only the most obvious examples of this failure. Women have been denied important legal rights. Ever since the late 1970s, in response to the persistent and organized activities of the women's movement, issues of gender equality have risen to an important position on the public-policy agenda. Questions of equal rights for members of other groups within the American population—ethnic and racial minorities, the disabled, and gay men and women, among others—have also become prominent. These questions—questions about equality and freedom from discrimination, collectively known as *civil rights*—are the subject of this chapter.

Civil rights are not the same as civil liberties. Civil rights are often confused with the Bill of Rights. As we have seen, however, the Bill of Rights is basically a list of civil liberties. When we speak of the **civil rights** of a particular group, such as Hispanics or the disabled, we are not referring to their First Amendment freedoms to believe what they choose or to express unpopular opinions. We are referring to their right not to be discriminated against because of some characteristic, such as national origin or disability.

Various provisions of the Constitution provide a basis for the protection of civil rights: the equal protection clause of the Fourteenth Amendment; the Thirteenth, Fifteenth, Nineteenth, and Twenty-fourth Amendments; the due process clause of the Fifth Amendment; and, as will be seen, the power of Congress to pass civil rights legislation, which is based on its power to regulate interstate commerce and to enforce the various constitutional amendments that are concerned with discrimination.

In this chapter we explore the past and present application of these sections of the Constitution, focusing on the problem of

> Our Constitution and our national conscience demand that every American be accorded dignity and respect, receive the same treatment under the law, and enjoy equal opportunity.
>
> —*The Rev. Martin Luther King, Jr.*

discrimination against black and Hispanic Americans, discrimination based on sex, and the rights of the disabled. We also discuss the problem of voting rights and consider significant court decisions having to do with civil rights.

The problem of civil rights for black Americans has been a major issue in the domestic life of this nation for most of its history; the question of civil rights for women, Hispanic Americans and other ethnic groups, gay and lesbian Americans, and the disabled is of more recent origin. Governments at all levels as well as the private sector have been forced to reexamine and change their policies toward these and other groups in American society.

THE RIGHTS OF AFRICAN AMERICANS

Racial prejudice in America began in the seventeenth century, when Native Americans and Europeans first met. The Native Americans were driven from their lands and denied access to European culture as it was taking root in American soil. Forced ever westward by the Europeans' quest for new land on which to settle, the Native Americans were gradually evicted from their tribal lands; by 1890 all the remaining free tribes in the West had been forced to settle on reservations.

Race relations in the colonies were further complicated by the arrival of captive African blacks. At first slavery was not confined to the South. Black slaves were brought to the northern colonies, but the smaller northern farms did not require a large workforce and had nothing for slaves to do during the long winters. The southern plantations, by contrast, depended on slavery. By the first half of the nineteenth century, slavery was well established in the United States, and even free blacks were often deprived of their civil rights. As time went by, the difference between the South and the North became more and more pronounced, and the issue of slavery became an explosive one.

As the new nation expanded westward, the question of whether slavery should be permitted in the new territories served as a focus for the differences between Northerners and Southerners. The matter first arose in 1819, when a bill to admit Missouri to the Union came before the House of Representatives. To the surprise and indignation of southern members, Representative James Tallmadge of New York proposed an amendment banning the further entry of slaves into Missouri. The amendment passed in the House but was defeated in the Senate. When Congress again took up the question in January 1820, a compromise was reached. Missouri was admitted as a slaveholding state, but slavery was not permitted in U.S. territories north of Missouri's southern boundary.

For a generation the Missouri Compromise resolved the legal issue of whether slavery would be permitted in the territories and new states of the American West. It did not, however, deal with the moral issue of whether it was right for one person to own another. Abolitionists—people who sought to have slavery abolished—continued to speak out against slavery and to agitate for an end to the practice. One of the leading abolitionists was a New England minister, William Ellery Channing, who wrote:

> [A man] cannot be property in the sight of God and justice, because he is a Rational, Moral, Immortal Being; because created in God's image, and therefore in the highest sense his child; because created to unfold godlike faculties, and to govern himself by a Divine Law written on his heart, and republished in God's Word. His whole nature

forbids that he should be seized as property. From his very nature it follows, that so to seize him is to offer an insult to his Maker and to inflict aggravated social wrong.[1]

In 1857 the United States Supreme Court attempted to resolve the slavery issue, but its efforts only served to anger large segments of American society and to aggravate existing tensions. In the infamous *Dred Scott* decision, the Supreme Court sided with the supporters of slavery by ruling that slaves were not citizens, upholding the right of slave owners to possess human property, and declaring the Missouri Compromise unconstitutional.[2]

The slavery issue was finally decided on the battlefields of the Civil War in the early 1860s. The Emancipation Proclamation of 1863 freed the slaves in the states that had taken part in the rebellion against the United States, and in 1865 the Thirteenth Amendment permanently outlawed slavery. After the war the Fourteenth and Fifteenth Amendments were passed in an attempt to give the freed slaves the full rights of citizenship.

During the decade of Reconstruction following the Civil War, Congress enacted a number of civil rights laws designed to enforce the principles set forth in the Civil War amendments. But after the presidential election of 1876, support for extending civil rights to black Americans declined quickly, and by the close of the nineteenth century the South was a racially segregated society.

The movement away from racial equality was clearly reflected in two major decisions by the United States Supreme Court during the last decades of the nineteenth century: the *Civil Rights Cases* and *Plessy v. Ferguson*. In the *Civil Rights Cases* of 1883, the Court declared unconstitutional the main provisions of the Civil Rights Act of 1875. This law had made it both a crime and a civil wrong for any person to deny another "the full and equal enjoyment of any of the accommodations, advantages, facilities and privileges of inns, public conveyances on land or water, theaters, and other places of public amusement." The Court took a narrow view of the Fourteenth Amendment, holding that because the amendment bars only discrimination by government, Congress could remedy only governmental,

Frederick Douglass (1817–1895). After escaping from slavery in 1838, Douglass became a leader in the abolitionist movement. He lectured on the subject, published an abolitionist newspaper, and aided fugitive slaves. During the Civil War he recruited blacks into the Union army. Douglass backed Congress's post–Civil War Reconstruction policies and was an active supporter of the Republican party; he was also an early champion of women's rights. Toward the end of his life he held several federal appointments, including that of Minister to Haiti.

not private, acts of discrimination. "It is state action of a particular character that is prohibited. Individual invasion of individual rights is not the subject-matter of the Amendment," the Court declared.[3]

The Court's decision in *Plessy v. Ferguson* (1896) was the next step in the movement away from racial equality. This decision established the **separate-but-equal doctrine** as a valid interpretation of the Fourteenth Amendment's statement that "No state shall deprive any person within its jurisdiction the equal protection of the laws." The case involved a Louisiana statute requiring whites and nonwhites to occupy separate railway cars. The law was challenged on the ground that the state had violated the equal protection clause of the Fourteenth Amendment. The Supreme Court ruled that as long as facilities for whites and nonwhites were equal, the Fourteenth Amendment had not been violated even though the facilities were separate.[4] The Court thus gave constitutional protection to a wide variety of so-called **Jim Crow laws,** which segregated people of different races in most public and private institutions and facilities in the southern states and made little or no attempt to make these facilities equal to those provided for whites.[5]

But the problem of racial inequality was not unique to the South. Before World War I the vast majority of blacks lived in the South, although even in the nineteenth century many northern cities had small black communities. America's entry into World War I in 1917 resulted in a significant migration of blacks to northern industrial centers such as New York, Philadelphia, and Chicago. World War II produced an even larger movement of blacks in search of the jobs created by the war. During the 1950s and 1960s the migration of rural blacks to the large northern and western cities continued at a rapid pace. The growing use of machinery in southern agriculture eliminated the need for much farm labor, which had been the main source of employment for rural blacks.

By the 1960s Hispanic people, who had left Mexico, Puerto Rico, the Caribbean islands, and the countries of Central and South America, came to the United States in large numbers. Together with African Americans they made up a large percentage of the population of America's major cities, where they faced discrimination in employment, housing, and other areas of social life. Most

Segregation extended to all phases of life in the South before the 1960s— even bathrooms and drinking fountains.

> ## CLOSE-UP
>
> ### ASIANS IN THE UNITED STATES: THE EARLY YEARS
>
> The first significant movement of Asians into the United States occurred in the mid–nineteenth century, when Chinese laborers came to California to meet the demands for cheap labor, especially to build the western railroads. An 1868 treaty allowed immigration from China but barred Chinese from becoming U.S. citizens.
>
> Anti-Chinese prejudice and the competition for jobs led to riots in San Francisco in 1877 and the subsequent passage of the Chinese Exclusion Act of 1882. Beginning with this law, all legal immigration from China was ended for more than six decades. In 1943 Congress extended citizenship rights to Chinese Americans and established an annual quota for immigration from China. The quota was 105! This quota system remained in effect until 1965, when all such immigration quotas were eliminated.
>
> The experience of Japanese immigrants was similar, although the number of Japanese immigrants to America was always much smaller than the number arriving from China. The industriousness of the Japanese in agriculture and labor soon produced the same sentiments that confronted the Chinese immigrants. Bowing to pressure from the Asiatic Exclusion League, which was formed in
>
> 1905, San Francisco adopted a policy of segregating white and Asian students in the public schools. In 1907 a "gentleman's agreement" was entered into by Japan and the United States in which Japan agreed not to grant passports to workers who desired to immigrate to the United States.
>
> Japanese Americans were subjected to harsh discrimination by the U.S. government beginning several months after Japan attacked the American naval base at Pearl Harbor, Hawaii, on December 7, 1941. Some 125,000 people of Japanese descent who lived on the West Coast of the United States were forced to enter internment camps, where they were held for most of the war. As commander-in-chief of the armed forces, President Franklin D. Roosevelt ordered the action on the theory that it was necessary to protect the security of the West Coast. The Supreme Court upheld the internment as a valid exercise of the president's constitutional powers. Many of the interned individuals were American citizens, either by birth or through naturalization. It was not until 1989 that Congress passed legislation that apologized to the Japanese Americans and made payments of $20,000 to each survivor of the camps.

recently this flow of immigration was augmented by the arrival of people from the Middle East and from China, Korea, India, and other Asian countries. The new immigrants settled in major cities such as Los Angeles, San Francisco, and New York and also experienced various forms of discrimination.

One response to discrimination is the creation of organizations designed to protect and advance the interests of minority groups. As we have already seen, the first important organization of this kind, the National Association for the Advancement of Colored People (NAACP) was founded by W.E.B. DuBois and other prominent African American civil rights leaders. The NAACP is not only the oldest but also the largest of the organizations dedicated to achieving civil rights for minority groups. Although it engages in a wide variety of activities, its greatest successes have come through the many court actions that it has brought in an effort to achieve racial equality and justice.

African Americans have also organized other groups dedicated to furthering civil rights. These range from the moderate Urban League to more militant black nationalist groups such as that led by the Reverend Louis Farrakhan. Many of these organizations have worked to strengthen racial consciousness. As a result, African Americans have developed great interest and pride in their history. Self-help groups at the community level have been organized to address such

Demonstrators in Detroit, Michigan, show their support for the University of Michigan's affirmative action program, March 2003.

problems as poor housing, drugs, lack of education, and unemployment, which affect many black Americans.

Other minority groups, such as Puerto Ricans and Hispanic Americans, have also organized and become more vocal in their demands for equality. The Puerto Rican Legal Defense and Education Fund and the League of United Latin American Citizens are two examples of this type of civil rights organization.

The first civil rights issue we examine is school desegregation. We continue with a discussion of equality in public facilities and employment.

School Desegregation and *Brown v. Board of Education*

As we have seen, beginning in 1896 the Supreme Court used the principle of "separate but equal" as the rule for interpreting the Fourteenth Amendment. The doctrine was originally employed in cases involving transportation, but in the early twentieth century it was extended to public education. During the 1930s the NAACP developed a legal strategy to challenge the separate-but-equal doctrine in the federal courts. The organization would first bring lawsuits attacking the doctrine in public professional schools in the South. Then it would challenge the rule in public colleges and universities. Finally, the legal attack would be made on segregation in public elementary and secondary schools.

The NAACP's strategy was successful. Beginning in the late 1930s, the Supreme Court undermined the separate-but-equal doctrine by ruling that state educational institutions had not provided equal treatment for black Americans.

The victorious attorneys in *Brown v. Board of Education* celebrate in front of the Supreme Court building in Washington, D.C., May 17, 1954. The attorneys are, from left to right, E.C. Hayes, Thurgood Marshall, and James M. Nabrit.

For example, in *Sweatt v. Painter* (1950) the University of Texas Law School had refused admission to a qualified black man on the grounds that a separate state law school had been created for blacks. The Supreme Court declared the system unconstitutional on the ground that the state had not provided truly equal facilities for black students. It found that the two law schools were unequal in such factors as library facilities and the quality of faculty, as well as in such intangible factors as reputation and prestige.[6]

But it was not until the historic case of *Brown v. Board of Education of Topeka* (1954) that the separate-but-equal doctrine was rejected by the Supreme Court as the governing principle in cases involving public education. The case began when Oliver Brown sued the Board of Education of Topeka, Kansas, to allow his daughter to attend a public school near his home instead of a black school farther away. The case attracted intense national interest when it and several similar suits were accepted for decision by the Supreme Court. The Court's ruling would affect more than 3 million black children in segregated schools across the nation. The Court listened to arguments on the case during both its 1952–1953 and 1953–1954 terms. The attorney for the appellants in the *Brown* case was Thurgood Marshall, then counsel for the NAACP and later a justice of the U.S. Supreme Court. On May 17, 1954, the Court announced its decision. Again it had examined intangible factors—this time the harmful psychological effect of segregation on black children:

Does segregation of children in public schools solely on the basis of race, even though the physical facilities and other "tangible" factors may be equal, deprive the children of the minority group of the equal educational opportunities? We believe that it does.

We conclude that in the field of public education the doctrine of "separate but equal" has no place. Separate educational facilities are inherently unequal. Therefore, we hold that the plaintiffs and others similarly situated for whom the actions have been brought are, by reason of the segregation complained of, deprived of the equal protection of the laws guaranteed by the Fourteenth Amendment.[7]

In a companion case decided on the same day, the Court also declared that it was unconstitutional for the federal government to segregate children in the public schools of the District of Columbia. Although the Constitution contains no equal protection clause that applies to the national government, the Court held that the due process clause of the Fifth Amendment places similar restrictions on the exercise of federal power and thus bars segregation in education.[8]

A year later the Supreme Court issued an order setting forth standards for desegregating public schools. It declared that local public school districts must end segregation "with all deliberate speed." The task of supervising this process was assigned to the federal district courts in the affected areas.[9]

School desegregation took place relatively quickly in border states such as Maryland and Delaware and in the District of Columbia. But it moved at a snail's pace in the Deep South. Frequently, local school boards either did nothing or proposed plans that required only minimal changes in the existing system. When lawsuits were brought to achieve desegregation, the federal district courts—staffed by judges from the area—often frustrated the objectives of the *Brown* decision.

A major crisis in the battle for school desegregation was the 1957 confrontation between Governor Orville Faubus of Arkansas and President Dwight Eisenhower. When the governor used the Arkansas National Guard to bar black youngsters from entering a Little Rock school, the president sent U.S. troops to enforce the federal court order requiring the desegregation of the city's public schools. In response to the claim that state officials could nullify a federal court order, the Supreme Court stated that

. . . the constitutional rights of children not to be discriminated against in school admission on grounds of race or color. . . can neither be nullified openly and directly by state legislators or state executive or judicial officers, nor nullified indirectly by them through evasive schemes. . . . Article 6 of the Constitution makes the Constitution the supreme law of the land. . . . The federal judiciary is supreme in the exposition of the law of the Constitution. . . . No state legislator or executive or judicial officer can war against the Constitution without violating his undertaking to support it.[10]

The situation in the South did not change significantly until Congress passed the Civil Rights Act of 1964. Title VI of that act permitted the executive branch of the government to cut off federal financial aid to local and state governments that discriminated on the basis of race. The following year Congress enacted the first major law that provided federal financial aid for public education. Southern communities that badly needed this assistance would lose funds if they continued to practice segregation in their schools. The results were dramatic. In 1963 fully 98 percent of black students in the South attended schools whose enrollments were entirely black. In 1968 the figure had fallen to 68 percent, and in 1972 it was 9 percent.[11]

In the North, segregation of African Americans and other minority groups has most often taken the form of ***de facto*** ("in fact") **segregation** that has resulted largely from housing patterns and the decisions of private citizens. Segregation resulting from the actions of government is known as ***de jure*** ("by law") **segregation.** *De facto* segregation is especially prevalent in the nation's public schools. Children normally attend schools that are located in their neighborhoods, regardless of the makeup of the school. The result is that schools in neighborhoods where blacks predominate have mostly black students. The Supreme Court has held that *de facto* segregation does not violate the Fourteenth Amendment. It must be proven that the government helped create the segregated situation.

The problem of ending legal segregation in education is great, especially in large school districts. School buildings cannot be moved, neighborhood housing patterns are already established, and the number of school-age youngsters may be very large. During the 1960s and 1970s the Supreme Court authorized the federal district courts to use a variety of devices to desegregate such schools. They could change the attendance zones of schools within the district. Racial quotas could be used; for example, if 50 percent of the students in the district were white and 50 percent were black, the courts could use those figures as goals for integrating each school in the district. Finally, the courts could order the busing of children from their neighborhood to a school in another part of the district. However, the use of busing as a remedy for *de jure* segregation was especially controversial. Busing was adopted voluntarily by some school districts; in others it was imposed by court order after a finding that the local public schools had been illegally segregated.

With the approval of the Supreme Court, court-ordered busing was put into effect in many areas of the nation. It remained a feature of American education for several decades. But in 1991 the Supreme Court held that busing should be ended when all vestiges of illegal segregation had been eliminated.[12] In recent years, therefore, busing has been ended in such cities as Wilmington, Cleveland, Denver, Nashville, and Oklahoma City. And in 1999 it was ended in the Charlotte-Mecklenburg school district in North Carolina—the area in which the Supreme Court had first accepted court-ordered busing in 1971.

The task of desegregating the public schools in many northern cities is particularly difficult, if not impossible. The majority of students in cities such as New York and Detroit are not white. Many white families have moved outside the central cities and into other school districts, and school enrollments in those areas are likely to be mostly white. Some proponents of school integration have argued that the courts should ignore the political boundary lines between city and suburban school districts and exchange students among those districts. But the Supreme Court has held that such plans are illegal unless it can be shown that racial discrimination was practiced by the state government or by suburban officials as well as by the inner-city government.[13]

A 2001 study by the Civil Rights Project at Harvard University concluded that there was an increase in segregated classrooms during the decade of the 1990s. It found that 76 percent of all African American students and 70 percent of Latino students attended predominantly minority schools. These figures represented an increase over the figures for a decade earlier. The report, "Schools More Separate: Consequences of a Decade of Resegregation," offered a number of reasons for these developments: housing segregation, demographic factors, a drop in federal backing for desegregation, and judicial decisions limiting or removing orders to desegregate schools.[14]

These trends have caused some observers to wonder about the value of further efforts to integrate schools. Black members of school boards in several major cities have questioned whether requiring white and black children to mix is actually necessary for achieving equal academic opportunities. Although supporters of integration argue that it allows children of all races and ethnicities to become familiar with the cultures of other groups, some black educators are not convinced that black children benefit academically from such contact. They believe that instead of attempting to force integration on unwilling school districts, a greater effort should be made to enhance institutions that are predominantly black—a proposal that resembles the long-discredited separate-but-equal doctrine. As one observer wrote,

> A mixture of white resistance to integration, population shifts, an increasingly conservative judiciary and black impatience and political empowerment seem to be converting separate but equal from a dead dragon into a rising phoenix. The once discredited doctrine is making a comeback, embraced in varying degrees by such divergent figures as Louis Farrakhan, the head of the Denver school board and Supreme Court Justice Clarence Thomas.[15]

The Civil Rights Act of 1964

Equal access to public facilities such as restaurants, buses, theaters, hospitals, and parks was another major goal of the civil rights movement. Segregation in public facilities was not seriously challenged until 1955, when blacks in Montgomery, Alabama, led by the Reverend Martin Luther King, Jr., boycotted the local bus company for a year. The company lost much of its business and was forced to cut back schedules, lay off drivers, and raise fares. Finally, the two sides reached a settlement: The bus company agreed not only to end segregation on the buses but also to hire black drivers. This breakthrough led to others. The Interstate Commerce Commission banned segregation of interstate passengers, and the Supreme Court ordered that restaurants in a bus terminal serving interstate travelers be desegregated.[16]

Protests against other forms of racial discrimination followed the Montgomery victory. The first lunch counter sit-in took place in Greensboro, North Carolina, on February 1, 1960. By 1963 *sit-ins* had become the most popular and often the most effective means of protesting racial discrimination in public facilities. In that year the Supreme Court reversed the convictions of black protesters in Greenville, South Carolina, who had refused to leave an all-white lunch counter. It ruled that a Greenville city ordinance requiring segregated eating facilities violated the equal protection clause of the Fourteenth Amendment.[17]

Demonstrations, marches, sit-ins, violence against blacks and civil rights supporters in the South, and perhaps most important, the huge 1963 civil rights march on Washington—all led to the passage of the Civil Rights Act of 1964. The law is composed of a number of titles (sections) that a are concerned with different areas of discrimination.

TITLE II: EQUALITY IN PUBLIC PLACES Title II of the 1964 civil rights law forbids discrimination in public facilities because of race, color, religion, or national origin. The act applies to such facilities as motels, hotels, and restaurants that engage in interstate business, and the U.S. Justice Department has the power to enforce the law. The 1964 law was based on Article I, Section 8, of the

President Lyndon Johnson signs into law the 1964 Civil Rights Act, one of several major civil rights laws enacted during his presidency.

Constitution, which gives Congress the power to regulate interstate commerce. Congress contended that it was exercising this power to remove a burden on interstate commerce—the burden of segregation, which discouraged African Americans from traveling because of the difficulty of finding restaurant and hotel accommodations.

In *Heart of Atlanta Motel v. United States,*[18] the Supreme Court found that there was sufficient evidence that racial discrimination placed a burden on interstate commerce to justify the enactment of Title II of the 1964 Civil Rights Act by Congress. It rejected the argument that since the motel was only a local business, Congress had no authority to regulate it. The power to regulate interstate commerce, the Court declared, included local activities that had ". . . a substantial and harmful effect upon . . . commerce."

The Civil Rights Act of 1964 was extremely successful. Within a relatively short period accommodations in hotels and restaurants became generally available without regard to race. The fierce opposition to desegregation that had prevailed until the 1960s gradually gave way to a spirit of acceptance and tolerance.

TITLE VII: EQUALITY IN EMPLOYMENT Equal opportunity for all people to obtain jobs that offer self-respect and a decent wage did not become a major issue in Congress until the early 1960s. Title VII of the 1964 Civil Rights Act

CLOSE-UP

LANDMARK VICTORIES FOR GAYS

In a controversial ruling with major implications for the gay-rights movement, the Supreme Court in 1996 struck down an amendment to the Colorado constitution that would have banned state and local laws protecting homosexuals against discrimination. The Colorado case, *Romer v. Evans*, marked the Court's first opportunity to rule on the merits of such legislation. In this case the constitutional amendment would have eliminated existing state policies and local ordinances that prohibited discrimination based on sexual orientation.

In the majority opinion Justice Anthony Kennedy stated that the Colorado provision violated the guarantee of equal protection set forth in the Fourteenth Amendment to the U.S. Constitution. Comparing the case to major race-based cases, Justice Kennedy characterized the Colorado measure as legislation based on prejudice. However, the actual scope of the *Romer* decision is narrow: The Court did not apply the most demanding level of judicial review—"strict scrutiny"—to the case, but instead applied the "rational basis" test in overturning the Colorado amendment. The Court was not willing to classify homosexuals as "an independently iden-

tifiable group" whose rights deserve protection to the same extent as those of racial minorities.

The Court's ruling protects antibias provisions contained in state and local laws that serve to protect gays and lesbians. Some twenty states and the District of Columbia and approximately 165 cities and counties make it illegal for the government and/or private employers to engage in employment discrimination based on sexual orientation. And some 19 states have hate crime laws that cover acts motivated by sexual orientation. (There are no federal antidiscrimination or hate crime laws that protect homosexuals).

The most recent victory for gay Americans came in the spring of 2004 when the Supreme Court invalidated a Texas sodomy law that made it a crime for two persons of the same sex to engage in certain defined sexual acts. The high court held that the law violated the liberty of adults to participate in private conduct that is protected by the due process clause of the Fourteenth Amendment.*

Lawrence v. Texas, 539 U.S. 558 (2004).. ˆ

forbids discrimination in employment on the basis of race, color, religion, sex, or national origin. The law established the Equal Employment Opportunity Commission (EEOC), which has the power to investigate complaints of discrimination and to resolve disputes through conciliation. If that is not effective, the EEOC can bring lawsuits in the federal courts against private employers. The Justice Department is also authorized to enforce Title VII against governmental agencies that discriminate. People who feel that they have been discriminated against can sue for the wrong done to them personally; they may also bring **class action** suits. These are legal actions brought by one or more individuals as representatives of a group of similarly situated people. For example, an employee can sue a company on behalf of other workers who have allegedly also been victims of discriminatory hiring or promotion policies by that employer. Unlike other types of lawsuits, a class action suit requires approval of the court before it can be started. Similarly, settlement of the case also requires the consent of the court. This condition is intended to ensure that the settlement is fair to all members of the class, not beneficial just to the representatives.

All intentional acts of employment discrimination are illegal under Title VII of the Civil Rights Act of 1964. The question soon arose as to whether the law also applies to situations in which there is no proof that the employer acted intentionally, yet a particular business practice such as an educational requirement had the effect of preventing qualified members of minority groups or women from

Antidiscrimination laws and affirmative action plans have enabled women to obtain employment positions that previously were almost always held by men. Law enforcement is one occupation in which the number of women has increased in recent years.

obtaining employment. In 1971 the Supreme Court held that Title VII applies not only to intentional forms of discrimination but also to "practices that are fair in form, but discriminatory in operation."[19]

TITLE IX: EQUALITY IN EDUCATION   Title IX makes it illegal for any educational institution receiving federal financial assistance (almost all do) to discriminate on the basis of race or gender. Sexual harassment is considered discriminatory if it occurs within a school, and schools are liable for the sexual harassment of students by teachers or administrators. Further, the Supreme Court recently held that a school can be held liable for sexual harassment of one student by another. For the institution to be liable, the harassment must be pervasive, and school officials must have knowledge of the situation and be deliberately indifferent to it.[20]

Under the provisions of Title IX, schools must provide equal educational opportunities for all students. One result is that schools have had to equalize the amounts of money they spend on athletic programs for men and women. This has led to a significant expansion of athletic programs for women—basketball, soccer, and lacrosse, for example.

Title IX of the 1964 Civil Rights Act requires that schools provide equal educational opportunities for all students. One major result of the law has been a dramatic increase in athletic programs available to women.

WOMEN'S RIGHTS

The women's rights movement has a long history in the United States. Its formal beginnings can be traced to a convention held in Seneca Falls, New York, in 1848. Under the leadership of Elizabeth Cady Stanton and Lucretia Mott, the convention adopted resolutions that called for equality of rights for women regarding property, contracts, marriage, and business. The Seneca Falls Convention also took the then-controversial step of supporting the right of women to vote.

Women were also active in the antislavery movement before the American Civil War and in a variety of other reform causes. But the right to vote became the main objective at the end of the nineteenth century. In 1890 the National American Suffrage Association was formed under the leadership of Carrie Chapman Catt and Anna Howard Shaw. By 1900 four states—Colorado, Idaho, Utah, and Wyoming—had granted females the right to vote. By 1914 seven more states were added to the list.

Change was occurring but at too slow a pace for many supporters of women's suffrage. The more militant suffragists turned their attention to Washington, DC, and away from the states. The Congressional Union was formed, and under the leadership of Alice Paul its members paraded through the streets of the nation's capital and demonstrated in front of the White House. President Woodrow Wilson finally gave his backing to the cause, and in 1916 both political parties endorsed the right to vote for women. In 1919 Congress passed the women's suffrage amendment. It was quickly ratified by the required number of states and in 1920 became the Nineteenth Amendment to the Constitution.

The modern women's movement had its historic origins in the struggle for women's suffrage that took place during the first two decades of the twentieth century. But it was the civil rights movement of the 1960s that provided the spark that led to the present-day movement to gain equal rights for women.

Leaders of the women's movement point out that women have been discriminated against, given inferior roles in society, and denied educational and employment opportunities equal to those enjoyed by men. For example, on average, women who work outside the home generally earn about 75 percent of what men earn, regardless of whether they are factory or clerical workers or are employed in management or professional positions.

For many generations single women have worked to support themselves, but since the 1970s there has been a sharp rise in the number of married women in the labor force. The increased cost of living and the desire for greater personal fulfillment have been the main causes of this trend. Many working women have small children, and a majority of women with school-age youngsters work outside the home, usually full-time. In addition, in recent years there has been a rapid increase in the number of unmarried and divorced women with children to support. These developments have made such issues as employment discrimination, job opportunities, and availability of child-care facilities the major focus of the women's movement.

Spurred by the success of the civil rights movement, women have organized to fight for their civil rights. One of the oldest and most influential women's rights groups is the National Organization for Women (NOW). In 1967 it held the first national conference on women's rights in Washington, DC. At that conference it listed its demands in the form of a Bill of Rights for women. Included in the document were "demands for the development of child-care centers to facilitate the entrance of women into the labor force and to allow for increased education; the extension of maternity leaves, Social Security benefits, and tax deductions for child-care expenses as a means for encouraging women to stay in the labor force; and the availability of birth control and abortion on demand to allow women to control their reproductive lives and to decide when and if they want to assume parental responsibilities."[21]

NOW and other women's rights groups have continued to promote this agenda through public-education programs and by lobbying at all levels of government. They have also called for the enactment and enforcement of laws intended to outlaw discrimination based on sex. In addition, women have instituted many lawsuits against both public and private organizations that discriminate against females in employment, education, and other areas of social life.

As we shall see shortly, women have won many legal and political battles since the movement began in the late 1960s. But there was one major defeat: The states were unwilling to ratify a constitutional amendment that would have guaranteed equal rights for members of both sexes. The main provision of the proposed Equal Rights Amendment (ERA) declared that "equality of rights under the law shall not be denied or abridged by the United States or by any State on account of sex."

The ERA was approved by the necessary two-thirds vote of both houses of Congress in 1972 and was forwarded to the states for ratification. The original deadline for ratification was March 22, 1979, but this date was extended by

Congress to June 30, 1982. By that time only thirty-five of the states had ratified the amendment—three short of the three-fourths required for it to become part of the Constitution.

Equality in Employment

The political activities of the women's movement, together with its intensive efforts to educate and inform the public, have produced significant legislative victories. Many state and local governments have enacted legislation that forbids discrimination against women. Several federal laws also deal with this problem. As noted earlier, Title VII of the Civil Rights Act of 1964, as amended by the Equal Employment Opportunities Act of 1972, prohibits discrimination in employment based on sex. Title VII permits only bona fide occupational qualifications to serve as an exception to the prohibition against sex-based discrimination in employment. This narrow exception would apply, for example, in cases in which privacy requires a member of a particular sex, as in the hiring of a restroom attendant, or in which authenticity requires a member of a particular sex, as in the hiring of a fashion model.

A new form of employment discrimination that has been recognized by the Equal Employment Opportunities Commission (EEOC) and by the courts is *sexual harassment*. Sexual harassment can take two basic forms. In one, sexual favors are sought in return for some positive employment decision by the employer—a job, promotion, or raise in salary, for example. A more complex form of sexual harassment occurs when an employer creates or allows to exist a sexually hostile work environment. In this form of sexual harassment, no request or demand is made for sexual favors. The Supreme Court has ruled that a hostile work environment is one in which discrimination, ridicule, or intimidation is severe or pervasive. The test for these conditions is whether "a reasonable person" would find the situation abusive or hostile and detrimental to job performance. However, there is still a good deal of uncertainty about this part of sexual harassment law.

The Constitution and Women's Rights

ABORTION RIGHTS Women's rights groups have been active in the courts in cases of alleged denial of women's rights. A major constitutional victory of the women's movement was the Supreme Court's decision in the case of *Roe v. Wade* (1973). In this ruling the Court declared a Texas abortion law unconstitutional on the ground that it violated a liberty protected by the due process clause of the Fourteenth Amendment—the liberty to make a decision about the ending of a pregnancy. The Texas law was typical of abortion statutes that existed at the time in more than forty states in that it made abortion illegal except to save the life of the mother. According to the Court, such laws failed to balance the constitutional rights of the individual against the interests of society. It summarized its decision as follows:

> A state criminal abortion statute of the current Texas type, that excepts from criminality only a *life saving* procedure on behalf of the mother, without regard to pregnancy stage and without recognition of the other interests involved, is violative of the Due Process Clause of the Fourteenth Amendment. (a) For the stage prior to approximately the end of the first trimester, the abortion decision and its effectua-

tion must be left to the medical judgment of the pregnant woman's attending physician. (b) For the stage subsequent to approximately the end of the first trimester, the State, in promoting its interest in the health of the mother, may, if it chooses, regulate the abortion procedure in ways that are reasonably related to maternal health. (c) For the stage subsequent to viability, the State, in promoting its interest in the potentiality of human life, may, if it chooses, regulate, and even proscribe, abortion except where it is necessary, in appropriate medical judgment, for the preservation of the life or health of the mother.[22]

The *Roe* decision has been both applauded and denounced, and in the almost thirty years since the Court's ruling, abortion has been perhaps the most controversial domestic issue in the United States. Supporters of the *Roe* decision have praised it as a recognition of the constitutional right of women to control their own bodies; opponents have denounced it for its failure to recognize the right to life of the unborn fetus and have criticized the decision as an abuse of the Court's judicial power.

In the years between 1973 and 1989, opponents of the *Roe* decision made many, largely unsuccessful, attempts to overturn or modify the decision. A proposed constitutional amendment to permit the states to restrict abortions never obtained the necessary two-thirds vote in Congress. Some states passed legislation designed to limit the scope of the *Roe* ruling, and a few such laws were upheld by the Supreme Court. For example, the Court accepted a Virginia law requiring that second-trimester abortions be performed only in licensed clinics.[23] But during the 1970s and 1980s laws that would have had a more direct effect on the rules set forth in the *Roe* decision were found unconstitutional.

During the 1980s, however, the membership of the Supreme Court changed. Retiring justices—some of whom had supported the original *Roe* decision—were replaced by more conservative jurists. In the 1989 case of *Webster v. Reproductive Health Services,* the Court, by a 5-to-4 vote, upheld a Missouri law that imposed a number of restrictions on a woman's right to have an abortion. For the first time, the Court indicated that it was willing to give the states greater freedom to control access to abortions.[24]

That willingness was shown even more clearly three years later in the case of *Planned Parenthood v. Casey.*[25] In that case, the Supreme Court upheld a so-called "informed consent" law adopted by Pennsylvania. The law requires that all women seeking an abortion first be given literature produced by the state enumerating alternatives to abortion and then wait a minimum of twenty-four hours before the abortion is performed. The state law also requires young women under 18 to obtain written consent for the abortion from a parent or guardian. Today a majority of states have such consent laws.

The *Casey* decision did not actually overrule *Roe,* but it modified some of the central features of that case. In *Roe* the Court made it clear that it would subject to strict scrutiny any restrictions on the right of a woman to have an abortion before the third trimester of pregnancy. In place of that high standard, in *Casey* the Court declared that it would now ask whether the restriction placed "an undue burden" on women seeking to have an abortion. In applying this new approach and upholding the Pennsylvania law, the Supreme Court overruled a number of earlier decisions that had struck down similar state statutes.

SEX-BASED DISCRIMINATION Unlike *Roe* and other abortion-related cases, which involve the meaning of the due process clause of the Fourteenth Amendment, most court challenges to sex-based discrimination have been brought under the equal protection clause of that amendment. In 1971 the Supreme Court, for the first time, declared unconstitutional on equal protection grounds a state law that discriminated against women. The case of *Reed v. Reed*[26] was a simple one: A young child died and left a small estate. Both parents petitioned an Idaho court to be selected as the administrator of the estate. The father was selected because Idaho law required that in such a situation the court must automatically appoint the father. The Supreme Court unanimously held that the law was arbitrary and irrational and therefore violated the equal protection clause of the Fourteenth Amendment.

Since 1971 the Supreme Court has heard a large number of cases involving claims of illegal sex-based discrimination. The unanimity shown in the *Reed* case quickly disappeared, however, and the Court has been divided over the proper standard to use in cases involving claims of sex discrimination. Some members of the Court want to consider laws based on sex classifications as suspect, which would place them in the same category as laws that discriminate on the basis of race. The concept of a *suspect category* evolved from the post–World War II series of Supreme Court cases dealing with laws based on race. In those cases the Court abandoned its traditional test of the equal protection clause, which was to ask whether the law in question was reasonable (the **reasonableness test**). It placed race-based laws in a "suspect" category and subjected them to **strict scrutiny.** It did not make the usual assumption that the law in question was constitutional, and it demanded a very high standard of proof—demonstration of "a compelling governmental interest"—to justify laws based on race. Using this approach, the Court has found all such laws to be unconstitutional.

Thus far, however, a majority of the Supreme Court justices have refused to place laws based on sex in the suspect category, while also declining to apply the traditional test of reasonableness. Instead, the Court created an intermediate standard, the **substantiality test:** "To withstand constitutional challenge . . . classifications by gender must serve important governmental objectives and must be substantially related to achievement of those objectives."[27]

The Court has found most laws that discriminate against women unconstitutional. For example, women cannot be barred from employment because of arbitrary weight or height standards.[28] Nor can an employer pay women lower retirement benefits than men, even though on the average women live longer than men.[29] The Court has also declared unconstitutional some laws that discriminate against men. It ruled, for example, that a state-supported nursing school denied a male applicant the equal protection of the law when it refused to admit him because of his sex.[30] On the other hand, the Court has upheld a federal law that requires military draft registration for men but not for women[31] and a state law that punishes males, but not females, for the crime of statutory rape.[32]

In 1996 the Supreme Court decided one of the most important discrimination cases of recent years. It held that the state-supported Virginia Military Institute's 157-year-old history of admitting only males violated the equal protection clause of the Constitution. In making the decision the Court raised the standard that government must meet to justify policies that treat men and women differently. Justice Ginsburg described the new standard as **skeptical scrutiny,** referring to a level of analysis that falls somewhere between the tests of substantiality and strict scrutiny. One of the most interesting features of the case—*United States v. Virginia*[33]—was the Court's refusal to accept the state's creation of a military program for women at a nearby women's college. The Court found that the alternative program was an inadequate substitute for attending the Virginia Military Institute.

The Court has also upheld the right of the states to legislate against sex discrimination. Thus, a state may make it illegal for a private club to exclude women from membership.[34] And in a case of great significance both to employers and to working women, the Court upheld the right of the state of California to require companies to give up to four months of unpaid leave to employees who are unable to work because of pregnancy, childbirth, or related medical problems.[35]

THE CIVIL RIGHTS OF THE DISABLED

Until fairly recently the disabled were largely excluded from the mainstream of society, both by overt discrimination and by physical barriers such as steps, curbs, and narrow doorways. However, like women, African Americans, and other minority groups, the disabled have organized to put pressure on public and private agencies to grant them equal treatment with other groups in society and to improve their access to public facilities. In response to such pressure, Congress passed the Rehabilitation Act of 1973, which bars discrimination against the disabled by the federal government and by contractors receiving federal funds. The Education for All Handicapped Children Act of 1974 requires that handicapped youngsters be provided with a "free appropriate public education" in the least restrictive environment suitable to their needs.

But the most far-reaching legislation affecting people with physical and mental disabilities is the Americans with Disabilities Act of 1990. The act defines a disability as a condition that "substantially limits" a "major life activity" such as walking or reading. People suffering from AIDS are covered, as are recovering alcoholics and drug abusers; in fact, the act affects over 45 million Americans.

The 1990 act may be compared to the Civil Rights Act of 1964 in its scope; it bars discrimination against the disabled in employment, transportation, public accommodations, and telecommunications. The law applies to all employers with fifteen or more employees, as well as to employment agencies and labor organizations. Employers must make reasonable accommodations to the disabilities of those individuals; that is, they must make facilities physically accessible, restructure job duties and modify work schedules, purchase or modify equipment, and provide readers, interpreters, or other support services. Businesses that can demonstrate that such changes would present an "undue hardship" may be exempted from these requirements. In addition, public accommodations must be made accessible to people in wheelchairs, and telephone companies must provide relay services allowing hearing- or voice-impaired people to place and receive calls.

An important area affected by the 1990 law is transportation. The act requires operators of railroads, intercity and intracity bus lines, mass transit systems, and school bus companies to ensure that all new vehicles are accessible to people with physical disabilities. All trains and subways must have at least one car that is accessible to the disabled. Public mass transit systems must provide alternative transportation for people who cannot board buses or subways. Key subway and railway stations must be modified so as to be accessible to the disabled.

The ADA defines disability as "a physical or mental impairment that substantially limits . . . [a] major life activity." In 1998 the Supreme Court gave its first interpretation of this provision of the law. It found that symptomatic HIV

A disabled man works at an office computer. The 1990 Americans with Disabilities Act outlaws employment discrimination against the disabled and requires employers to make reasonable accommodations to the disabilities of their workers.

is a covered disability because it "substantially limits" the "life activity of procreation."[36]

But in a series of decisions a year later, the Court held that the ADA does not apply to conditions that are correctable. These include eyesight conditions that can be improved by wearing eyeglasses, and illness such as diabetes and high blood pressure, which can be controlled with medication.[37] And in a unanimous decision in 2002, the Supreme Court further restricted the meaning of the term *disability* by requiring not only proof that the individual suffered from substantial limitations to work-related activities but also to those that are "central to daily life."[38]

AFFIRMATIVE ACTION

A procedure designed to improve the situation of minority groups and women in employment and in other areas of social life such as college and professional-school admissions is known as affirmative action. **Affirmative action** refers to a variety of policies and programs that seek to advance the position of minorities and women. Since the late 1960s many affirmative action programs have been adopted by national, state, and local governments, by public institutions such as state colleges and universities, and by many private employers and organizations.

Originally these programs involved attempts to increase the number of women and minority-group members attending college or employed by business and government. They took the form of increased recruitment activity or special training and education programs. Other programs used *quotas,* reserving a fixed percentage of total admissions, hirings, or promotions for members of minority groups.

Affirmative action programs using quota systems have been extremely controversial. Supporters of such programs maintain that they are necessary to reverse the economic, educational, and psychological effects of past discrimination. Moreover, it is argued that the nation's economic and social life will be advanced by improving the condition of minority groups and that quotas do not violate the Constitution.

Opponents of quota-based affirmative action plans contend that these plans tend to aid members of minority groups who are able to advance on their own ability while doing little to help those who are most in need of assistance. It is argued that there is also a danger, in professions such as medicine and law, that less qualified individuals will be providing important services to the public. Opponents also maintain that quotas are psychologically damaging to members of minority groups because they know that other people doubt their qualifications for particular positions and because they feel that they have not attained success as a result of their own talents. Finally, opponents argue that all governmental quotas based on race, nationality, or sex constitute a form of illegal discrimination.

The Supreme Court first ruled on the constitutionality of affirmative action programs in 1978 in the case of *Regents of the University of California v. Bakke*.[39] Allan Bakke, a white male, had applied to the University of California Medical School at Davis. His application was rejected twice. During the same period, the school accepted a specific number of Mexican American and African American students whose qualifications were lower than Bakke's. The school set aside a quota of sixteen out of one hundred places for minority students and considered their applications separately. Bakke argued that this procedure denied him the equal protection of the laws guaranteed by the Fourteenth Amendment.

In a 5-to-4 decision the Supreme Court ordered that Bakke be admitted to the Davis Medical School. The Court held that it was illegal for a public university to use a quota-based admissions policy, at least in the absence of evidence that the school had engaged in discriminatory practices in the past. But the Court upheld the right of a university to consider race as one factor in its admissions program. Such consideration was valid because it served the legitimate purpose of creating diversity in the student body.

The affirmative action issue has continued to divide the Supreme Court ever since the *Bakke* decision. Many of the Court's rulings in these cases have involved votes of 5 to 4 or 6 to 3. In the years immediately following the *Bakke* decision, a majority of the justices accepted some affirmative action programs. For example, the Court upheld the legality of a voluntary affirmative action program that was the product of an agreement between an employer and a trade union.[40] But the justices appointed by Presidents Reagan and Bush between 1981 and 1991 created a new majority that has been unsympathetic to government-sponsored affirmative action programs.

In the 1989 case of *City of Richmond v. J.A. Croson Co.*,[41] the Supreme Court declared unconstitutional a program requiring that 30 percent of all money appropriated for public works in the city be set aside for minority-owned construction companies. By a 6-to-3 vote, the Court held that the law violated the constitutional right of white businessmen and women to the equal protection of the laws. As a result of this case, many cities have eliminated affirmative action plans that favored women and minorities. Further, when legal challenges have been brought against such programs, courts have uniformly ruled against them as violating the Fourteenth Amendment's equal protection clause.

In an important 1995 decision the Supreme Court, by a 5-to-4 vote, invalidated an affirmative action program created by Congress requiring that "not less than 10 percent" of funds appropriated to the Department of Transportation be spent on contracts awarded to small businesses "owned and controlled by socially and economically disadvantaged individuals." In this case—*Adarand Constructors v. Pena*—the Supreme Court, for the first time, applied the standard of strict scrutiny to federal affirmative action programs, a standard that it had previously applied only to race-conscious policies of state and local governments. Under this approach, the federal government now has to establish that an affirmative action program serves a "compelling interest" and is "narrowly tailored" to achieve this purpose.[42]

In 1996 the Supreme Court declined to consider a decision of a federal appeals court in Texas that struck down a University of Texas Law School admissions policy that sought to increase the number of African American and Hispanic students admitted to the school. The appeals court held that the state school could not use race as a basis for admitting students.[43]

Since the *Bakke* decision in 1978, there has been much uncertainty over whether race could be used as a standard in admitting students to public colleges and universities. In recent years college administrators have stressed the need for diversity in admitting students. They have contended that diversity in the student body is a necessary condition for quality education. Ultimately the U.S. Supreme Court would have to decide whether these arguments were consistent with the equal protection clause of the Fourteen Amendment.

In early December 2002, the Supreme Court agreed to hear two cases involving the admissions policy of the University of Michigan. One case involved the law school, the second the university's undergraduate college. In both cases—*Grutter v. Bollinger*[44] and *Gratz v. Bollinger*[45]—white students were denied admission to the programs while minority students with either similar or lower academic credentials were admitted.

The Michigan cases raised identical Fourteenth Amendment equal protection questions. Is diversity a compelling state interest that permits the university to consider race in its admissions program? If so, is the program "narrowly tailored" to achieve its goals without unduly damaging other legal interests?

The Supreme Court upheld the law school's admissions policy. It ruled that the program was narrowly tailored to achieve the government's compelling interest in creating a diverse student body. Michigan's undergraduate policy, however, was declared unconstitutional. The Court held that the school's policy of awarding twenty points to minority students toward the necessary one hundred to be admitted was the functional equivalent of an illegal quota.

THE RIGHT TO VOTE

The basic right to vote is derived from state law and not from the Constitution. However, the Constitution imposes some important restrictions on the freedom of the states to establish standards for voting.

One of those restrictions is the Fifteenth Amendment. Adopted in 1870, five years after the end of the Civil War, the amendment states that "the right of citizens of the United States to vote shall not be denied or abridged by the United States or by any State on account of race, color, or previous condition of servitude."

Despite the clear principle established by the amendment, the struggle of African American citizens to exercise the right to vote was a long and difficult one. The barriers they faced were not effectively removed until the late 1960s.

After the Civil War the southern states used a series of devices to avoid the mandate set forth in the Fifteenth Amendment. Combined with intimidation and violence, these schemes disenfranchised most blacks in the South and kept southern politics almost entirely in the hands of whites.

The first major barrier was the **grandfather clause,** under which a person who had voted before 1866 or was descended from someone who had voted before 1866 was not required to meet various other requirements for voting. Anyone else—meaning blacks—had to pass discriminatory literacy, educational, or "good character" tests. Another device, used by the Democratic party in the South until it was declared unconstitutional in 1944, was the **white primary.** In the largely one-party South of the time, nomination in the Democratic primary was a guarantee of electoral victory on election day. To maintain white control of the nomination system, for many decades blacks were barred from voting in Democratic party primaries.

Poll taxes were a major obstacle to millions of poor voters, both white and black, in some southern states. In those states that had poll taxes, each voter was required to pay a small tax as a prerequisite to voting. In 1964, with the ratification of the Twenty-fourth Amendment, poll taxes were abolished in national elections. State poll taxes were declared unconstitutional by the Supreme Court in 1966.

After the white primary, poll taxes, and other devices had been declared unconstitutional, there remained one last, and very effective, barrier to be overcome before blacks could vote: the **literacy test.** The use of literacy tests as a requirement for voting began in the mid–nineteenth century. At first the tests simply required the would-be voter to demonstrate some basic knowledge of reading and writing. Later they were used in the South as a means of preventing blacks from voting. By requiring that voters be able to read, understand, and interpret the state and national constitutions, the southern states were able to deny the vote to a large portion of their black population.

Literacy tests continued to be used in the South until the 1960s and were administered in a discriminatory fashion by white registrars. It was a simple matter for these officials to allow even illiterate whites to pass the tests while failing blacks who were educated and obviously literate. It took federal legislation, especially the Civil Rights Acts of 1965, 1970, and 1975, to eliminate the literacy test once and for all.

The Voting Rights Act of 1965

In 1964, three million African Americans of voting age were not registered to vote in the eleven states of the South. Only 32 percent were registered in Louisiana, 23 percent in Alabama, and 6.7 percent in Mississippi.[46] The literacy test remained the greatest barrier to black voting, especially in the rural areas of the South. In response to civil rights protests across the nation, Congress passed the Voting Rights Act of 1965. Through this legislation the use of literacy tests or other such devices was to be suspended in any state or county of the nation in which less than 50 percent of the voting-age population had been registered on November 1, 1964, or had voted in the presidential election of November 1964. In those districts, local registrars were required to register voters without regard to their literacy. The executive branch of government was given the power to appoint federal examiners to register voters should local officials refuse to do so.

Section 5 of the Voting Rights Act applies to most of the southern states and to portions of seven other states that have had low voter turnout at elections (including three boroughs of New York City). It requires state and local governments seeking to change their election laws in any way to obtain clearance from the Justice Department or the Federal District Court in Washington, DC, to ensure that the changes have neither a discriminatory motive nor a discriminatory effect. Another part of the law applies to the entire country and makes it illegal to pass any measure relating to voting that has a discriminatory purpose.

In 1970 Congress enacted legislation that completely outlawed the use of literacy tests by the states. And in 1975 it expanded the Voting Rights Act to protect "language minorities," that is, groups whose members neither speak nor write English. The law now provides that any state or political subdivision in which at least 5 percent of the population cannot speak or understand English well enough to participate in elections must print ballots and other voting materials in both English and the second language. (The most widely used second language is Spanish, particularly in the southwestern states and in large cities such as Los Angeles and New York.) Several states and several hundred counties in various parts of the nation must now conduct elections using bilingual ballots and instructions.

In 1982 Congress amended the Voting Rights Act to make it easier for civil rights groups to prove that a state or local government has engaged in discriminatory practices. A violation of the voting rights law can be established by showing that the *result* of a particular practice or procedure is discriminatory; it is no longer necessary to establish that the government *intended* to discriminate.

The Voting Rights Act of 1965 had an enormous impact on the political life of the South. The protection provided by the federal law led to huge voter registration drives by African Americans during the late 1960s and early 1970s. More than four million blacks were registered to vote during the decade following the passage of the 1965 law. Open appeals to race and support for segregation rapidly disappeared from southern politics. The example of Mississippi is illustrative. With the largest black population of any state, it had the lowest percentage of voting by black citizens. It also experienced perhaps the worst turmoil over the issue of voting rights; the head of the state chapter of the NAACP was killed in 1963, and three civil rights workers were murdered in 1964 while attempting to encourage registration to vote by blacks. Today many blacks have been elected to state and local offices in Mississippi, and blacks register and vote in approximately the same percentages as whites.

CONCLUSION

In the past three decades much progress has been made toward guaranteeing the civil rights of all Americans. Race relations in the United States have changed greatly since the Supreme Court decided the case of *Brown v. Board of Education* in 1954. The system of separate and unequal treatment of African Americans that existed in the South for generations has been ended. The legal rights of African Americans and other minority groups have been made more secure by subsequent Court decisions and by legislative and executive actions. Long denied the right to vote, African Americans have become more politically active and are a force in American politics. Despite these gains, however, major difficulties still confront African Americans. Unemployment, substandard housing, poor education and job skills, teenage pregnancy, crime and drugs are far more serious problems for these groups than they are for white Americans. And they are much more difficult to solve than the problem of legal discrimination.

Significant progress has been made toward achieving greater equality between the sexes. Women's rights advocates have won many notable legal and political successes during the past quarter century. However, the constitutional right of a woman to obtain an abortion, which was established in *Roe v. Wade* in 1973, has been modified by the Supreme Court. Its 1992 decision in the *Casey* case extended powers to the states to regulate abortions.

With respect to the civil rights of the disabled, the United States has made a major commitment to ensuring equal rights for this group. The passage of the 1990 Disability Act is already producing the expected far-reaching changes in American society. Employment practices have changed, and newly designed facilities to aid the disabled are altering the appearance of commercial centers and places of public accommodation.

QUESTIONS FOR THOUGHT

1. What are the major provisions of the Civil Rights Act of 1964? Of the 1965 Voting Rights Act?

2. What test does the Supreme Court use to decide whether a law based on gender is unconstitutional?

3. What rules regarding a woman's right to obtain an abortion were established in the case of *Roe v. Wade?* In what respects has *Roe* been modified by subsequent Supreme Court decisions?

4. What are the main arguments for and against affirmative action plans?

5. What are the main provisions of the Americans with Disabilities Act of 1990?

INTERNET ACTIVITIES

1. *Is Affirmative Action Fair?* Go to **http://www.yahoo.com/**. Do a search on "affirmative action." Find documents and supporting materials about the history of affirmative action, including landmark court cases. What should be done about affirmative action today? Defend your position with reason and facts. Additional resources: can be found at **http://www.aclu.org**.

2. *Civil Rights and You.* Go to the Civil Rights Division of the Department of Justice at **http://usdoj.gov/crt**. Select "Division Overview." Review this document. Choose two areas for which the Civil Rights Division has specific responsibility. Indicate the exact titles of the laws that empower the division to act in these areas. Summarize any recent actions the division has taken in defense of civil rights in these two areas.

KEY TERMS

affirmative action	grandfather clause	separate-but-equal doctrine
civil rights	Jim Crow laws	skeptical scrutiny
class action	literacy test	strict scrutiny
de facto segregation	poll tax	substantiality test
de jure segregation	reasonableness test	white primary

SUGGESTED READING

Cushman, Clare, ed. *Supreme Court Decisions and Women's Rights.* Washington, DC: Congressional Quarterly Press, 2000.

Garrow, David J. *Liberty and Sexuality: The Right to Privacy and the Making of Roe v. Wade.* New York: Macmillan, 1994.

Graham, Hugh Davis. *The Civil Rights Era: Origins and Development of National Policy, 1960-1972.* New York: Oxford University Press, 1990.

Kluger, Richard. *Simple Justice: The History of Brown v. Board of Education and Black America's Struggle for Equality.* New York: Knopf, 1976.

Kull, Andrew. *The Color Blind Constitution.* Cambridge: Harvard University Press, 1992.

Nieman, Donald G. *Promises to Keep: African Americans and the Constitutional Order, 1776 to the Present.* New York: Oxford University Press, 1990.

Orfield, Gary. *Dismantling Desegregation.* New York: Norton, 1996.

Paterson, James T. *Brown v. Board of Education: A Civil Rights Milestone and Its Troubled Legacy.* New York: Oxford University Press, 2001.

Skerry, Peter. *Mexican Americans: The Ambivalent Minority.* New York: Free Press, 1993.

Skrentny, John David. *Color Lines: Affirmative Action, Immigration, and Civil Rights Options for America.* Chicago: University of Chicago Press, 2001.

NOTES

1. William Ellery Channing, *Works* (Boston: George G. Channing, 1849), pp. 26-27.

2. *Dred Scott v. Sandford,* 19 Howard 393 (1857).

3. 109 U.S. 3 (1883).

4. 163 U.S. 537 (1896).

5. The term *Jim Crow* originated with an eighteenth-century Kentucky dance. In the early nineteenth century it became associated with African Americans, and by 1840 the segregated black car on railroads became known as the Jim Crow. Eventually the term was applied to all forms of racial segregation.

6. 339 U.S. 629 (1950).

7. 347 U.S. 483 (1954).

8. *Bolling v. Sharpe,* 347 U.S. 497 (1954).

9. *Brown v. Board of Education of Topeka, Kansas,* 349 U.S. 294 (1955).

10. *Cooper v. Aaron,* 358 U.S. 1 (1958).

11. Harrell R. Rodgers, Jr., "The Supreme Court and School Desegregation: Twenty Years Later," *Political Science Quarterly* 89 (1974): 751, 753.

12. *Board of Education of Oklahoma City v. Dowell,* 498 U.S. 237 (1991).

13. *Milliken v. Bradley,* 418 U.S. 717 (1974).

14. Diana Jean Schemo, "U.S. Schools Turn More Segregated, a Study Finds," *New York Times,* July 20, 2001, p. 1.

15. Steven A. Holmes, "Look Who's Saying Separate Is Equal," *New York Times,* October 1, 1995, p. 4-1.

16. *Boynton v. Virginia,* 364 U.S. 454 (1960).

17. *Peterson v. City of Greenville,* 373 U.S. 244 (1963).

18. 379 U.S. 241 (1964).

19. *Griggs v. Duke Power Co.,* 401 U.S. 424 (1971).

20. *Davis v. Monroe County Board of Education,* 526 U.S. 629 (1999).

21. Quoted in Ethel Klein, *Gender Politics* (Cambridge: Harvard University Press, 1984), p. 47.

22. 410 U.S. 113 (1973).

23. *Simopoulos v. Virginia,* 462 U.S. 506 (1983).

24. 492 U.S. 490 (1989).

25. 505 U.S. 833 (1992).

26. 404 U.S. 71 (1971).

27. *Craig v. Boren,* 429 U.S. 190 (1976).

28. *Dothard v. Rawlinson,* 433 U.S. 321 (1977).

29. *Arizona Governing Committee v. Norris,* 463 U.S. 1073 (1983).

30. *Mississippi University for Women v. Hogan,* 458 U.S. 718 (1982).

31. *Rostker v. Goldberg,* 453 U.S. 57 (1981).

32. *Michael M. v. Superior Court,* 450 U.S. 464 (1981).

33. 518 U.S. 839 (1996).

34. *Board of Directors of Rotary International v. Rotary Club of Duarte,* 481 U.S. 537 (1987).

35. *California Federal Savings and Loan v. Guerra,* 479 U.S. 272 (1987).

36. *Bragdon v. Abbott,* 524 U.S. 624 (1998).

37. *Sutton and Hinton v. United Air Lines, Inc.,* 527 U.S. 471 (1999); *Albertson, Inc. v. Kirkingburg,* 527 U.S. 555 (1999).

38. *Toyota Motor Manufacturing v. Williams,* 534 U.S. 164 (2002). See also: *US Airways v. Barnett* (April 29, 2002).

39. 438 U.S. 265 (1978).

40. *United States Steel Workers v. Weber,* 443 U.S. 193 (1979). No constitutional issue was raised in this case

because the plan concerned two private organizations and did not involve the government.

41. 488 U.S. 469 (1989).

42. *Adarand Constructors, Inc. v. Pena,* 515 U.S. 200 (1995).

43. *Hopwood v. Texas* 78 F.3d 932 (5th cir.), cert. denied, 518 S.Ct. 2581 (1996).

44. 539 U.S. 306 (2003).

45. 539 U.S. 244 (2003).

46. U.S. Commission on Civil Rights, *Political Participation* (Washington, DC: Government Printing Office, 1968), pp. 227, 243, 246.

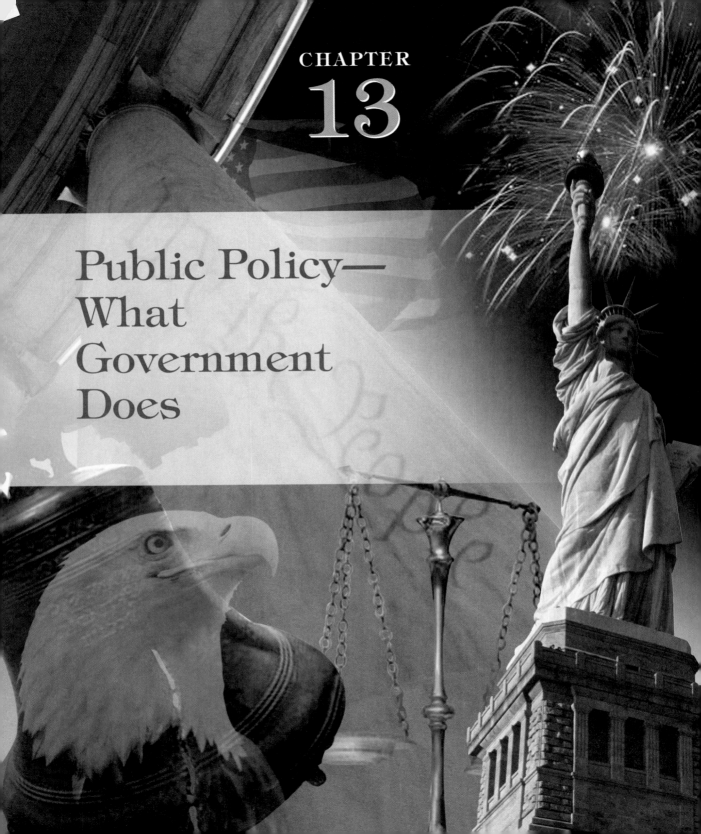

Public Policy—What Government Does

In earlier chapters we examined the institutional structure of American government—that is, what government is. In this chapter we look at what government does. We will see that what government does is to make public policy in response to problems that exist or arise in society. To understand the policies established by government at any time, we must first have some idea of what public policy is and what policy making entails. The chapter will then examine three specific domestic policy areas: fiscal policy, monetary policy, and social welfare. In the final chapter of the book—Chapter 14—we will consider foreign policy: what it has been, what it is at present, and how foreign policy is made.

> Politics is who gets, what, when and how.
>
> —Harold D. Lasswell (1936)

WHAT IS PUBLIC POLICY?

The term *public policy* is not a clearly understood term whose meaning is generally accepted by scholars. Different students of the subject have defined public policy in different ways. One definition declares that public policies "are purposeful decisions made by authoritative actors in a political system, recognized because of their formal positions, as having the responsibility for making binding choices among goals and alternatives for the society." The decisions seek to change private goals into public commitments.[1]

There are a number of characteristics of public policy that should be understood. Policy decisions may involve either positive acts to establish a public commitment or decisions not to act at all.[2] Such negative choices may be as important as positive acts that governments may perform. A choice not to build a road between two isolated communities within a state, for example, will likely hinder the economic development of that area.

While public policy may primarily involve governmental actors such as the legislative and executive branches of government, informal actors such as private organizations and groups also play a significant role. Nor is policy making limited to legislation, executive orders, and administrative rules; the decisions of courts can also determine public policy. Finally, policies can be both short-term and long-term. They may be intended to solve an immediate problem such as that wrought be a hurricane or tornado. Or they may be designed to deal with a problem that will affect the future for decades, such as improvement of the public education system.

In summary, **public policy** is purposeful, goal-oriented action that is taken by government to deal with problems, real or perceived, that arise in a society. Public policy generally does one or more of the following: reconcile conflicting claims made on scarce resources, create incentives for collective action, prohibit morally unacceptable behavior, protect the rights and activities of individuals and groups, and provide direct benefits to individuals.

Who Makes Public Policy?

Various models have been proposed to explain how the public policy process operates and, most important, who controls and benefits from it. We look at four such models: group theory, elite theory, corporatism, and the idea of subgovernments.

The first model, **group theory** (and a version of it known as **pluralism**) holds that public policy is a product of competition among groups.[3] The central argument of group theorists is that societies are made of a large number of social, ethnic, religious, and economic groups that are more or less organized. These groups put pressure on government to make policies that favor their interests. Groups with more power and influence are usually more successful in shaping policies that further their goals. Each area of public policy involves a distinct set of problems and a separate set of political actors and forces. In this model of policy making there are multiple centers of power, and public policy emerges from the political struggle among groups with competing demands.

The second model, **elite theory,** believes that public policies are made by a relatively small group of highly influential leaders who share common outlooks and goals.[4] Policy is not a product of group conflict and demands as the group theorist contend. Rather, it is determined by the preferences of the *power elite,* or ruling class. Policymakers adopt the preferences of the elite; public policies reflect their values and serve their interest. Public policy is not shaped by the majority but by a minority with great political and economic power.

A third model, **corporatism,** assumes that interests do not merely attempt to influence policy but seek to become part of the policy-making and implementation system.[5] When they are successful in becoming part of the decision-making system, the groups—through their control over their membership—make society more manageable for government. Thus, for example, professional organizations of physicians and lawyers establish licensing standards for their fields, a power that is delegated to these groups by state government.

The last model used to explain public policy making is that of **subgovernments,** sometimes referred to as "iron triangles." (We encountered this idea in Chapter 9 in the discussion of the relationships among government agencies, congressional committees, and interest groups.) Supporters of this model claim that the government does not make policy choices on its own but endorses decisions made by sections of the government in alliance with interest groups. These subgovernments are coalitions of members of Congress, the federal bureaucracy, and interest groups.[6] They form around particular policy areas and involve the relevant legislators, bureaucrats, and interest groups, all of which have similar interests. They are especially likely to be found in specialized areas of policy making about which there is little public awareness, such as the use of public lands by ranchers and mining interests. In recent years this model has lost favor among political scientists who argue that there are many more actors in the policy-making process than the three groups included in the subgovernment theory.[7] One scholar, for example, believes that "issue networks," networks of people who have expertise in a particular policy area, dominate the process.[8]

Types of Public Policy

Since President Roosevelt's New Deal of the 1930s, most Americans have come to accept the presence of the federal, state, and local governments in the day-to-day functioning of the nation. As a consequence, there has been rapid expansion of the number of public policies designed to deal with the wide range of problems that arise in the complex society of the United States. Political scientists have developed several models to classify and analyze public policies.

One model classifies policies on the basis of their impact on the society and the relationships among those involved in policy formulation.[9] In this scheme, policies may be regulatory, distributive, or redistributionist in nature. **Regulatory policy** embodies rules of conduct with sanctions. Many government agencies perform a regulatory function. The Environmental Protection Agency enforces federal law intended to guarantee that Americans have healthy air to breathe and pure water to drink. Similarly, the Securities and Exchange Commission regulates the stock exchanges of this country in order to protect the investing public from deception and fraud.

Distributive policy provides tangible benefits to individuals and groups in a noncompetitive manner. Such governmental programs as Social Security, unemployment insurance, Medicaid, and Medicare are examples of major national distributive policies. Finally, **redistributive policy** reallocates resources between groups in society. The use of tax revenues to provide welfare benefits of various kinds to the poor is an example of this type of public policy.

A second model of public policy views policy as being either material or symbolic.[10] **Material policies** provide tangible resources or power to their beneficiaries; they may also impose costs on other groups. **Symbolic policies,** on the other hand, have little or no material impact and no tangible advantages or disadvantages. Instead, symbolic policies appeal to widely held *values* such as equality, liberty, and patriotism. Government may use this type of policy to divert public attention from more important issues or to satisfy the public's demands without actually providing any substantive benefits.

A third model classifies public policy as either substantive or procedural.[11] **Substantive policies** are plans of action. They give advantages and disadvantages to members of the society and have benefits and costs. In contrast, **procedural policies** are concerned with the way in which something will be done and who will perform the task. The procedures used in courts and the steps that must be followed by administrative agencies in establishing rules are examples of procedural policies.

Because of the political nature of policy making, policies may be classified as either liberal or conservative.[12] *Liberal* policies seek government intervention to bring about some type of social or economic gain, whereas *conservative* policies oppose intervention and favor private, nongovernmental solutions to problems. Many feel, however, that this distinction has become blurred in recent years; for both liberals and conservatives, the question is not whether government should intervene but in what areas, in what form, and on whose behalf.

Finally, policy may be categorized as either domestic or foreign. *Domestic policy* deals with problems or situations existing in the United States, while *foreign policy* is concerned with the interests of the nation in the global arena. Today, however, domestic policies increasingly have an international dimension, making the distinction between the two types of policies less clear. Economic policy, for example, must be concerned with the impact of the world economy on economic conditions in this country. An increase in trade with foreign nations, for example, may cost jobs for some American workers.

THE POLICY-MAKING PROCESS

Stages of the Process

Political scientists have developed a framework for studying the policy-making process that consists of several sequential stages.

1. *Issue identification and agenda setting.* In this stage the attention of policymakers is drawn to a problem that might require governmental action. If the subject is a legitimate one, it becomes an **issue.** If the issue is considered serious enough, it gains a place on the policy-making agenda.
2. *Policy formulation.* Proposals are then developed for dealing with the issue.
3. *Policy adoption.* Efforts are made to gain enough public support for a proposal to make it part of the government's public policy.
4. *Policy implementation.* The policy is converted into a public program. If it is a federal domestic policy, it may be administered entirely at the national level or by cooperative efforts with state and local governments.
5. *Policy evaluation.* The consequences of the policy are examined to determine the degree of its effectiveness in handling the problem it was meant to solve.

The policy-making process must be viewed as a dynamic, ongoing series of events and not as a set of separate steps. Considering the policy-making process by stages provides a convenient method of study, but it should not be taken as a statement of the often-complex reality of this subject.

ISSUE IDENTIFICATION AND AGENDA SETTING Where do issues come from? Why are some problems ignored? How does an issue get on the policy agenda? These are among the questions that must be answered when consideration is given to the early stages of the policy-making process. Before turning to that subject, however, we must understand what is meant by the term *agenda.*

The policy **agenda** is the list of issues that government and nongovernmental actors are giving serious attention to at any given time.[13] (*Agenda* is a Latin word meaning "things to be done.") Agenda setting is the process through which the full range of issues that could be addressed is narrowed down to the specific few that policymakers will focus on. Agendas can be general, such as the list of issues that gain the attention of the president, or highly specialized, such as the agenda of a congressional subcommittee.

One study of this subject asserts that there are two main types of agendas.[14] The *systematic agenda* covers all issues that are generally recognized as deserving public attention and are within the legitimate jurisdiction of government;

CLOSE-UP

GETTING SOCIAL SECURITY REFORM ON THE POLICY AGENDA

Social Security has often been referred to as "the third rail" of American politics. Any American politician who raised the issue of changing the retirement system would be rewarded by defeat in the next election. Large numbers of senior citizens who either were recipients of Social Security benefits or who would soon be recipients would turn out on election day to vote against any person who dared to question the Social Security system. Further, senior citizens not only voted in large numbers but they were part of one of the most powerful interest groups in Washington—the American Association of Retired People (AARP).

It was not that criticism of the Social Security system did not exist outside of government. Indeed, many who paid the payroll tax that provides the financial basis for Social Security understood that it was a poor investment; the average return upon retirement was less that 2 percent. Investment of the money in any other way would most certainly produce greater benefits, but the government has never allowed the taxpayer any choice over whether to participate in the Social Security system.

Further, financial experts have periodically warned that Social Security was built on an unsound basis; that it had to pay out more than it was receiving in payroll taxes. When this situation became clear, Congress responded by raising payroll taxes and/or increasing the amount of earned income that was taxed. (Benefits have never been lowered, only raised. To cut benefits was to touch the third rail, and no politician would ever make this proposal.)

During the 1990s it was generally recognized both inside and outside of government that the Social Security system would be facing a major financial crisis early in the twenty-first century. The "baby boom" generation—those Americans who were born in the fifteen or so years after the end of World War II—would reach retirement age beginning around 2010. The baby boomers represent a very large group within the population, and the demands on the Social Security system would be very great. The working Americans who were born

later in the twentieth century were smaller in number, and their payroll taxes would not support the financial payouts to the baby boomers.

Presidential candidates during the 1990s spoke vaguely about reforming Social Security but offered no plans. Most legislators avoided the issue or also spoke in general terms. During his second term in office, President Clinton appointed a commission to study the problem and report to him about possible solutions. When the commission made its report, President Clinton rejected its suggestions for moderate reform of the system.

For the first time since the Social Security legislation was enacted, reform of the system became part of the nation's public agenda during the 2000 presidential election. The Republican candidate, George W. Bush, proposed the partial privatization of Social Security. Each participant would be permitted to invest 2 percent of the payroll tax in stocks, certificates of deposits, government or corporate bonds, or other investment vehicles. Bush's proposal would not affect current recipients of Social Security nor those who are about to receive benefits, but it would allow workers to create retirement money outside of the government-sponsored program. The Democratic candidate, Al Gore, squarely opposed the suggested changes and contended that they were "too risky."

The 2002 senatorial elections also proved that political candidates could run successfully for national office on a program that included reform of the nation's Social Security system. Four Republican senatorial candidates did so in 2002, and each won their election.

The first two elections of the twenty-first century made clear that the issue of Social Security reform had finally become part of the public agenda. They showed that candidates who proposed fundamental changes in the system could run for office and be elected; Social Security was no longer "the third rail" of American politics. Discussion of this subject is certain to continue in the near future, and changes in the nation's public pension system are very likely to be enacted into law.

public education is an example. The *institutional agenda* covers all issues that are being seriously considered by policymakers, such as bills actually before the Congress. The institutional agenda is narrower in scope and less abstract than the systematic agenda, and its priorities may differ considerably from those of the systematic agenda. The president might, for example, propose sweeping reforms of public education, whereas the bills before Congress may focus on specific issues, such as placing computers in all schools or setting national standards for academic achievement.

Why do some issues gain a place on the policy agenda while others are ignored? The chance that an issue will reach the policy agenda depends on how it is perceived within the government. When an issue is viewed by the public as a crisis, is advocated by a strong and visible interest group, or is supported by the governmental bureaucracy, there is a good chance that it will move onto the agenda. Such perceptions act as triggers for policy making.[15]

The September 11 terrorist attack on the United States is a striking example of how a crisis can propel an issue to the top of the government's policy agenda. The public, many private groups, and the legislative and executive branches of government were united in seeing international terrorism as the main issue confronting the nation. Fighting terrorism throughout the world and making the United States safe from other attacks almost completely dominated the nation's policy agenda. The war in Iraq further increased the difficulty that proponents of various domestic policy proposals had in getting public attention for these issues.

POLICY FORMULATION AND ADOPTION Policy formulation is the process of creating relevant and supportable courses of action for dealing with specific problems. It does not, however, necessarily lead to the adoption of the policy.[16] The government will not necessarily act to solve an issue simply because the issue has reached the policy agenda. Various actors are involved in policy formulation, including legislators, the president and his advisers, agencies of the executive branch of government, and interest groups—and they may likely disagree about the best solution to the problem.[17]

Policy formulation is a two-step process. First, a decision must be made regarding what, if anything, should be done with a particular problem. Second, if something is to be done, a policy has to be drafted that, if adopted, will achieve the desired objective. For policy formulation to be successful, policy proposals must be acceptable not only to those who make policy within the government, but also to the private participants. Thus, certain provisions may have to be included and others dropped depending upon what will gain the necessary support for the proposed policy. It follows that the more numerous the participants who are involved in the process, the more difficult it will be to arrive at an acceptable proposal. The process of building support for a proposed policy is known as *policy legitimation.*[18]

POLICY IMPLEMENTATION Implementation starts after the decision to adopt a particular policy has been made and ends when the goals of the policy have been achieved. Thus, policy **implementation** can be defined as the directed change that occurs over time following the adoption of a new policy. Often the public views a decision by government to "do something" as the end of the matter. In practice, however, the decision that emerges from the formulation and adoption stages sets in motion a long and complex chain of events—the implementation process—in which any of a large number of things can go wrong. For example, implementation may be hampered by judicial constraints, public apathy, or resistance by those who must alter their behavior to conform to the new policy.[19]

Furthermore, there is a tendency for implementation to become highly bureaucratic and burdened with numerous rules and regulations.[20] In fact, the main actor in the implementation of a policy is the bureaucracy. Indeed, implementation can be viewed as the bureaucratization of policy. It is not uncommon, therefore, for the original policy to become altered and for bureaucrats to substitute their own objectives for those of the elected officials who enacted the basic policy. In the 1970s, for example, various government agencies formulated affirmative action policies and quotas based on race, even though it was clear from the legislative record that Congress had not favored such plans when it enacted civil rights laws a decade earlier.

POLICY EVALUATION From the discussion so far, it should be clear that policy does not always achieve its intended objectives and at times may even have unintended consequences. There are a number of reasons for these developments aside from those that have already been mentioned including: unclear goals, the inability to determine how to achieve the goals, the presence of adversarial conditions within government, and ambiguous criteria for success. These realities dictate that policies must be evaluated periodically in order to determine how they are working. It should be noted that evaluation does not have to wait until a policy has actually been implemented; it can occur throughout the policy-making process.

Evaluation is not solely the domain of government officials. Nongovernmental actors such as the media, academics, and interest groups can also engage in policy evaluation. Although there are many possible approaches to evaluation,[21] there are basically two distinct but interrelated types of evaluation. **Process evaluation** examines the extent to which a policy is implemented according to its stated guidelines, whereas **impact evaluation** is concerned with the extent to which a policy causes a change in the situation it is designed to address. The former type of evaluation measures change against an ideal standard of achievement; the latter deals with the actual nature of the changes that have occurred.

The Context of Policy Making

Like so many other aspects of politics, the process of policy making cannot be separated from the context in which it occurs. In fact, the context may be crucial to understanding why certain policies prevail over others. The overall context of present day public policy is made up of a number of components, including the following major factors.

The first component is the history of *past policies*. The history of policy in a specific area sets limits to new policy options. The existence of laws that regulate safety in the workplace, for example, makes it highly unlikely that those rules will be repealed. If changes are made, they will probably involve small modifications of existing rules.

Environmental factors provide a second aspect of the context of policy making. These include cultural, social, and ideological considerations. The values and beliefs of the public shape its demands for policy action. If those factors are widely shared, policymakers can gain greater public acceptance of policies that incorporate these values. Public opinion sets the boundaries and direction of public policy, and social factors generate demands for particular types of policy. Thus, while health care and the availability of prescription drugs at reasonable prices are important issues of public policy today, widespread public opposition to solutions that are based on extensive or total governmental control and regulation excludes this as a public policy option.

Another environmental factor is the *ideological conflict* between liberals and conservatives over the nature of governmental action. Liberals generally favor governmental solutions to problems; conservatives are more likely to look to private, market-based answers. This debate affects all public discussion of public policy, as the previous example of health care illustrates. Also important is the interaction between the political and economic worlds. Those who possess economic resources also possess political power. This makes it likely that these individuals and groups will have great influence on the formulation of public policy.

The *budgetary process* is also a key component of the policy context, since few policies of any significance can be implemented without public expenditure of money. Such costs cannot be incurred unless government is able to obtain revenues through either taxation or borrowing. This fact of life is the basis for the complicated political process of resource allocation, or budgeting. This, in turn, gives rise to an equally complex process of bargaining and compromise between government and different groups in society. The many groups that exist in society continually place pressure on government to spend more money in their particular area of concern. The unions that represent public school teachers, for example, seek higher salaries for teachers and more spending for school construction. The demand for government spending never ceases, though the public's willingness to pay for this demand through taxes always has limits.

The budgetary process is a highly political one in which bargains are struck, exceptions made, and goals met or not met. Large numbers of actors are usually involved in the process, which is heavily influenced by the need to restrict tax increases, manage government borrowing, and avoid creating excessive budgetary deficits.[22]

The Structure of Policy Making

Political scientists disagree about the structure of policy making—that is, over the nature of how decisions are actually made. Some hold that policies are the product of rational choice, while others believe that policy making is an incremental process that is not primarily rational.

In the *rational choice* model, issues and problems are approached in a well-ordered sequence. Problems are identified, as are the values and objectives that should be incorporated into the policies intended to address them. Next, various alternative solutions are formulated and ranked by how well they satisfy the values and the objectives identified earlier. Finally, decision makers choose the policy that is the most appropriate means of achieving the desired goal.[23]

Those who believe in *incrementalism* see policy making very differently. One proponent of this theory has described policy making as "the Science of Muddling Through."[24] Rather than being largely rational in character, policy making is oriented toward the present and is often remedial in nature. It focuses on making necessary changes and adaptations in existing practices. Incrementalism, therefore, can be seen as the fine-tuning of an existing policy in which numerous actors with competing values make decisions in small or incremental steps. It is perhaps a more realistic view of policy making that than proposed in the rational-choice model.

Our discussion thus far has outlined the process, the context, and the structure of contemporary policy making. This process should be viewed as one of struggle, bargaining, accommodation, and compromise. These characteristics will be evident in the remainder of the chapter as we discuss in some detail two aspects of economic policy—fiscal and monetary policy—and social welfare policy.

ECONOMIC POLICY

From the close of World War II in 1945, economic and foreign policy dominated the policy agenda of this nation. (After the end of the cold war in 1989, economic policy briefly became the number one issue in the United States.) The condition of this nation's economy is of vital importance not only to the well-being of Americans, but also to citizens of other countries of the world. Because of the sheer size of the American economy, its health or weakness directly affects the economies of other nations.

Understanding economic policy requires knowledge not only of the economic issues and problems facing this nation, but also the tools the government uses to manage the economy. In this section we explore a number of such instruments, including fiscal and monetary policy.

Tools and Strategies for Managing the Economy

Since the 1930s two major strategies have guided economic policymakers in government: *Keynesian economics,* which stresses the role of fiscal policy,[25] and *monetarism,* which emphasizes control of the money supply and is closely associated with monetary policy.

FISCAL POLICY **Fiscal policy** operates mainly through the raising and lowering of tax rates and controlling the level of government spending. It uses the government's taxing and spending power to influence economic productivity and the business cycle and to control inflation and unemployment. In so doing,

John Maynard Keynes (1883–1946), a British economist whose ideas influenced the policies of many governments during the Great Depression of the 1930s and the decades following the end of World War II.

Keynesian economic policy also seeks to control the size of the government's budget deficit or surplus.

Keynesian economics is derived from the work of the British economist John Maynard Keynes. Keynes believed that during times of economic depression or recession the government should intentionally spend more and accept an increase in its budget deficit. As a result of this policy the government will temporarily collect less in taxes than necessary to pay for the programs of government. It should then finance its expenditures in part by increased borrowing. These policies will inject new demand—that is, money—into the economy, which will in turn increase consumer spending and reduce unemployment.

Increased consumer spending, however, may lead to inflation, as higher demand stimulates higher prices. Keynesian economics maintains that if the rate of inflation rises, the government should increase taxes. Higher taxes means less spending power, which will result in a slowing of consumer demand and a reduction in inflation. At the same time, the amount the government will have to borrow to cover its expenditures will also decline. The effect will be to further reduce consumption.

One major problem with fiscal policy is that it easily goes awry because predictions about how an economy will respond are not entirely reliable. Because of such problems, by the mid-1970s many economists and policymakers began to move away from Keynesian fiscal policy as a primary tool of economic management. They argued that this approach did not have the impact and effects that it had promised. Many viewed the theory as a failure of liberal government, claiming that fiscal policy represented an unacceptable level of government intervention in the economy.

MONETARY POLICY **Monetary policy** is most closely associated with the work of the Department of Economics of the University of Chicago and with the economist Milton Friedman. It emphasizes the importance of controlling inflation through control of the money supply. (By *money supply* we mean the amount of money in its various forms that is circulating in the economy at any time.) The consequence of reducing the money supply is to reduce the rate of inflation.

The Federal Reserve Board plays a central role in this area of public policy through its power to raise and lower interest rates. Supporters of monetary theory contend that the way to control the money supply is not to raise taxes as the Keynesians would advise, but to increase interest rates, cut government expenditures, or both. Monetarists also insist that the government should play a very limited role in the life of the nation's economy and should allow market forces to make most decisions.

With the election of Ronald Reagan to the presidency in 1980, monetarism in the form of supply-side economics strongly influenced decision making by the new administration. *Supply-side economics* is based on the idea that reducing taxes has the effect of benefiting society as a whole. If taxes are lowered, more funds are available to be reinvested in the nation's economy, thereby increasing jobs, productivity, and ultimately, government tax revenues.

The validity of supply-side economics is still very much an issue. Critics point to the great increase in the federal deficit that took place during the 1980s as proof of the theory's basic weakness. Supporters still use the theory as justification for the lowering of taxes and claim that the unprecedented economic expansion of the 1990s was largely the result of the tax-cutting policies of the Reagan years. Further, they contend that during the 1980s the Democratic

Congress refused to make significant long-term reductions in government spending—a second major goal of supply-side theory.

OTHER ECONOMIC POLICY TOOLS The government also employs other economic instruments to promote the noninflationary growth of the American economy. All recent American presidents—Reagan, Clinton, and both presidents Bush—have strongly supported the lowering of tariffs and the removal of other trade restrictions that hinder the ability of the United States to trade with other nations. Although there has been significant vocal opposition to these policies—the trade unions, for example, argue that free trade means the loss of jobs for Americans—the United States has slowly moved in the direction of free trade.

The dismal character of the American economy in the 1970s—a period of high inflation and very low economic growth—explains the adoption of supply-side economics in the 1980s and the movement toward the reduction of tariffs. It also serves to explain another economic tool that has been used by government in the past several decades—the *deregulation* of the American economy.

CLOSE-UP

PENSION REFORM: A GLOBAL VIEW

The United States is not alone in facing the problems of how to fund a government-operated pension system. Other advanced industrial nations—Japan, Great Britain, France, Germany, and other Western European nations—have similar difficulties. Each has a growing population of persons over the age of 65. In Japan, this part of the population stands at about 17 percent; it will rise to 30 percent by the year 2050. In Western Europe during the same fifty-year period, the number of people over the age of 65 will grow from 16 percent to about 28.

Further, the number of workers who are contributing to the government's pension program is declining relative to the number of retirees. Today there are approximately four workers paying into the pension fund that supports each retiree; the ratio in thirty years will likely drop to two to one. People also live longer and tend to retire sooner. In at least one way, the situation in Europe is more difficult to solve than in the United States. The nations of Europe spend twice a much on pensions and a larger percentage of their gross domestic product than does the United States.

The difference between the amount of money paid into the state-run pension systems in Europe and the amount paid to retired workers is increasing rapidly. Some European governments already have dipped into general tax revenues to keep their systems solvent.

At issue is the ability of governments in the industrialized nations to maintain the living standards of future retirees while at the same time maintaining the soundness of their financial systems. The choices that can be made by government are all fraught with political danger. Taxes can be raised and pensions reduced. But these policies are politically unpopular and face the opposition of strong trade unions. Another choice that government can make is to increase the age of retirement—a decision that reflects the reality that people live longer in the industrialized world. This change alone would have a significant beneficial effect on the viability of government pension systems.

The idea of partially privatizing pensions has been raised in Western Europe just as it has been in the United States. Proposals to allow individuals to create private savings accounts have been made in both France and Germany. Such plans run counter to the strong European belief that the government alone should provide for the welfare of its citizens. But the idea of partial privatization is growing in popularity with younger workers and may well represent the wave of the future in the world's industrialized nations.

Source: Geoff Winestock, "Social Security Reform Rocks the World," *Wall Street Journal*, October 30, 2000, p.A21.

Government regulations were criticized for doing the opposite of their intended purpose; instead of protecting the public, the regulations often served the interests of those being regulated. It meant, for example, that consumers suffered because companies could charge higher prices for goods and services.

The move to loosen regulatory control by government began in 1978 with legislation that phased out the Civil Aeronautics Board and deregulated airline fares. Further deregulation occurred during the Reagan years and has continued, though at a slower pace, since that time. The result of this process is that today there are many fewer governmental restrictions on major sectors of the nation's economy, such as banking, trucking, electric and gas utilities, and radio and television.

The decade of the 1990s had a variety of economic developments and governmental policies. There was a mild recession at the beginning of the decade and a period of unprecedented economic growth and prosperity in the second half of the period. The first President Bush, who had vowed never to raise taxes, raised them anyway (and probably lost reelection to a second term as a consequence). His successor, Democrat Bill Clinton, raised taxes still further in 1993. Clinton's tax bill passed by a single vote in both houses of the legislature. Top income tax rates were lifted from 31 percent to almost 40 percent. Gasoline taxes were raised by more than 4 cents a gallon, and payroll taxes on Social Security were increased. The justification for the increases was to bring down the huge federal deficit that had reached over $290 billion in 1992.

Between 1993 and 1997 the nation's annual budget deficit steadily declined. By the close of the 1990s, not only had the annual budget deficit vanished but also the government budget produced a surplus—the first budget surplus since the late 1960s, and President Clinton rightly claimed political credit for the prosperity that marked his second term in office and for the creation of a budget surplus.

The nation's prosperity was not entirely due to the policies of President Clinton, however. The emergence of a new information economy based on computers, new forms of communication, and the Internet produced new levels of wealth in the country. The election of a Republican Congress in 1994 brought an

Federal Reserve Chairman Alan Greenspan testifies before Congress on the condition of the U.S. economy.

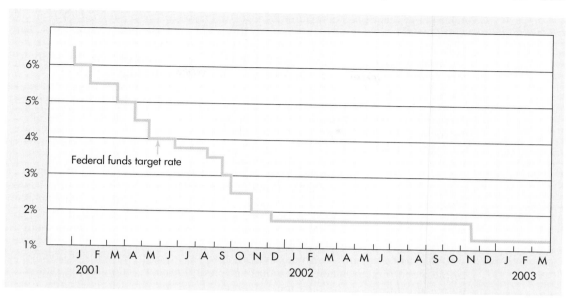

FIGURE 13.1   Short-Term Interest Rates: January 2001–March 2003.

end to further tax increases and imposed restraints on the president's spending programs. Further, the policies of the Federal Reserve Board under Chairman Alan Greenspan kept interest rates throughout most of President Clinton's second term at a level that encouraged economic expansion without producing significant inflation in the American economy. The combination of these forces produced sustained economic growth, low inflation, almost full employment, and a budget surplus. It was almost the perfect economy.

But it was not to last. An economic turndown began in 2000 and continued into 2001. The September 11 terrorist attack on the United States further damaged the American economy. Stock prices fell sharply, unemployment rose, and consumer confidence in the nation's economy declined. Both fiscal and monetary policy were used by the government to counter the downward trend of the economy. In 2001 President Bush was successful in gaining congressional approval for a program of tax reduction, and the Federal Reserve Board began to cut interest rates. Starting in 2001 short-term interest rates were gradually reduced from about 6 percent to 1 percent. (See Figure 13.1.) As the rate of economic recovery grew in the early months of 2004 the Federal Reserve Board became concerned about the threat of inflation. Between June and September 2004 it raised interest rates three times by .25 percent.

SOCIAL WELFARE POLICY

Throughout the century that has just past, providing for the well-being of citizens has been a central concern of government in the United States and Western Europe and in such non-Western democracies as Japan. These nations are often referred to as *welfare states* because of the large number of programs they have adopted that are intended to provide protection for people in times of distress.[26] **Welfare** is a relatively new idea that covers a wide range of social and economic programs of government. Providing education, health care, public housing, unemployment and retirement insurance, and assistance to the poor are only some examples of many types of welfare policies that have been established by government.

Some Americans think of welfare as consisting mostly of handouts to the underprivileged. In fact, many government programs primarily benefit the middle class: Social Security, Medicare, and unemployment insurance are examples of major programs that provide protection for a broad cross section of Americans. Further, government provides a wide variety of benefits to corporate America in the form of special tax treatment and subsidies.

The United States government has created such programs because a large majority of Americans believe that government has a responsibility to protect the residents of this nation in time of personal or national crisis. If a family cannot afford basic housing, government should either provide public housing or subsidize family income so that families are able to pay the cost of private housing. Similarly, when an economic recession occurs and people are put out of work, government should assume the responsibility of providing unemployment benefits paid from a program of unemployment insurance.

Nations vary in the extent of their social services. In Western Europe, for example, government policies provide paid parenting leave, month-long paid vacations, and almost unlimited unemployment benefits. The United States, to the contrary, generally provides fewer, and less extensive, welfare benefits.

Indeed, welfare policies in the United States differ in a number of important ways from those of European nations. First, welfare programs began earlier in Europe than in the United States. Germany adopted both pension and disability programs in the 1880s, and Great Britain in 1887 and 1908 respectively; the United States did not pass legislation on these subjects until the 1930s. The reasons for this difference are twofold: first, the United States has long had a tradition of individualism and a suspicion of government power; second, the United States Supreme Court during the first decades of the twentieth century declared unconstitutional a number of attempts by government to adopt welfare legislation.[27] It was not until the late 1930s that the Supreme Court altered its views on this subject.[28]

The American welfare state also differs from that of most European democracies in that it does not provide universal health coverage, requires a much smaller contribution by private employers to welfare programs, and spends a smaller part of its gross domestic product (GDP)—the total amount of goods and services produced by a nation—on welfare. While the United States has been much criticized for its limited social welfare program—especially by European commentators—many European countries have paid an economic price for their costly welfare policies. The high cost of these programs has acted as a heavy weight on economic growth in these nations. Unemployment in France and Germany, for example, has been over 10 percent for some time; it has been less than 6 percent in the United States during most of the past ten years.

Welfare policies fall into two broad categories: policies that benefit the poor and those that help the general public. The first category includes general assistance programs that give money, food, housing, or health care directly to qualifying individuals. It also includes work assistance programs that provide jobs and job training for the unemployed and categorical assistance programs that target low-income individuals for particular types of assistance.

General assistance programs provide some type of social insurance. Such insurance is designed to shield individuals from lost income resulting from illness, unemployment, or retirement. There are also regulatory agencies and programs that protect persons from some of the problems associated with our complex economic system. They include various types of protections afforded consumers as well as workplace safety regulations.

The federal government has taken several approaches to providing social welfare.[29] The *preventive approach* tries to ensure that people do not become poor, whereas the *alleviative approach* deals with persons who are already poor and attempts to improve their situation. Until recently these approaches have served as the foundation of the welfare policy of this country. A third approach to welfare is the *punitive* one. It is based on the assumption that individuals are poor because of their own moral and character defects. Under this view, government policy should be designed to discourage them from being idle by making it difficult for them to obtain public assistance. When such assistance is provided, it should be limited both in time and amount.

A fourth approach to welfare is *curative* in nature. Advocates of this position contend that the conditions that cause poverty, such as lack of education or job skills, should be remedied. The curative approach is often used when the object of a government policy is to give the poor greater control over the institutions that affect their communities; thus, community organizations may be encouraged by the policy. A final approach is the *incomes approach* in which individuals are asked to work while they receive government assistance. As their job-related income increases, their welfare benefits decline. The assumption behind such policies is that persons gain self-esteem and independence from work and that dependence on government has an adverse effect on individuals.

To obtain a better view of how some of these approaches have been applied, let us take a closer look at welfare policy in the United States, especially from the time of the enactment of the Social Security Act of 1935 until the present.

President Franklin D. Roosevelt signs the Social Security Act of 1935. The legislation created a national pension program for retirees and committed the national government to providing financial assistance for poor families in the country.

Throughout much of American history welfare was considered to be a private, not a governmental, problem. Families, churches, and charitable organizations bore the responsibility for caring for those in distress. It was not until the 1930s that government began to assume significant portions of the responsibility for individuals and families who were not able to provide for their basic needs. President Roosevelt's New Deal established a variety of welfare programs: Social Security for retirees, unemployment insurance for those who could not find work, and child labor laws that outlawed the exploitation of minors. Some of these programs were entirely national in nature, such as the retirement benefits provided for in the Social Security Act of 1935. But most were jointly funded by the national and state governments and administered at the state level. Thirty years later other major welfare programs were created as part of President Lyndon Johnson's Great Society program; they included food stamps and medical care for the poor (Medicaid) and for the elderly (Medicare).

Although most of these programs have had widespread public support, a few have been the subject of criticism. Much of this criticism centered on the core welfare programs for the poor and especially the Aid to Families with Dependent Children (AFDC) program. This general assistance program had been created in 1935 as part of the New Deal and provided money grants to poor families with children. Over time AFDC grew in size and cost. By the mid-1990s almost 13 million people received benefits from the program. One out of five families with children in the United States were covered under the program at a cost of about $23 billion annually.

AFDC and other welfare programs for the poor became part of the national policy agenda during the 1980s and 1990s. In the 1992 presidential campaign Bill Clinton promised that he would reform welfare if he were elected as the nation's chief executive. Welfare reform was also one of the items in the Republican Contract With America in the 1994 congressional elections, and it took center stage as an issue during the next two years.

On two occasions in 1995 the new Republican-controlled Congress passed welfare reform bills, only to have President Clinton veto both. But the president signed the third bill that Congress passed in August 1996. Three years after the Personal Responsibility and Work Opportunity Act went into effect, 4.7 million people had moved from the welfare rolls to economic independence and by 2003 there had been a 54 percent decline in the number of Americans receiving welfare. The law made major changes in the welfare system of the United States. Its most significant provisions included:

1. Public welfare was made a state, not a federal, responsibility.
2. All adult recipients of welfare must find work within a two-year period.
3. Families are limited to five years of benefits in a lifetime, though states are permitted to establish a shorter time limit.
4. The federal government provides block grants to help states finance their welfare programs.
5. Childless adults aged 18 to 50 are limited to three months of food stamps during a three-year period.
6. Unmarried teenaged parents are eligible for welfare benefits only if they live with an adult and remain in school.
7. Present legal immigrants are denied most welfare benefits until a residency period has been met; future legal immigrants are denied welfare benefits, including Medicaid, during their first five years in the United States.

President Clinton signs the welfare reform law, August 1996. The new legislation ended sixty years of federal control of this subject and turned over to the states much of the authority to set policy in this area.

What made such sweeping changes politically possible was the widespread unhappiness with a welfare system that many Americans saw as a symbol of big government that had gone bad, costing taxpayers billions of dollars, demeaning beneficiaries, contributing to the breakdown of the family, and encouraging illegitimacy. Supporters of the reform saw the new system as a way to eliminate these undesirable characteristics. Critics, on the other hand, feared the consequences of eliminating the "safety net" that had long been provided by the federal government. They warned that poverty would increase in the United States and that more than a million children would be placed in jeopardy by the new legislation.

Faced with the end of a major federal program, states had to act quickly to meet the responsibilities that the new law imposed on them. They created a variety of new programs designed to move people from welfare to work. Job training, education, and the creation of child-care centers were among the more traditional approaches used by the states. Other states used more innovative schemes. Kentucky, for example, paid welfare families $900 to relocate from areas in which job opportunities were very limited to areas in which opportunities were greater.

The results of the first five years under the new welfare laws were decidedly positive. The number of persons on welfare rolls dropped sharply all across the United States. Most mothers had found work and their incomes had risen.[30] They were receiving more of their income from earnings and less from welfare benefits. The U.S. Census Bureau reported that the number of persons receiving welfare had declined by 56 percent between 1993 and 1999 from 5.1 million families to 2.4 million. And child poverty had dropped from 22.7 to 16.9 percent.[31]

The positive results that were produced by welfare reform may be in part attributable to the economic times in which the changes were made. The late 1990s were times of unprecedented prosperity in the nation and were marked by very low unemployment. Demand for entry-level workers was very high in most parts of the nation. It was an ideal time for people leaving welfare to find jobs in the American economy.

The economic slowdown that began in 2000 tested the ability of the new welfare system to continue the positive trends of the previous decade. Some disquieting signs quickly became evident. In a growing number of welfare households the only benefits given by government were to "child only" cases. These are cases in which the only member of the household eligible to receive welfare benefits is a child. In some situations the children's parents were disabled and unable to work. In others, the children's immigrant parents were ineligible to receive benefits under the 1996 legislation. But a majority of the children do not live with their parents but with relatives, especially grandparents, who have no legal responsibilities for the youngsters. It has been estimated that over a million children fell into the "child only" welfare cases in 2000.[32]

Despite the economic recession of 2000–2002, welfare rolls did not increase during these years. The economy began a slow recovery after 2002, but even though the recovery was slow, welfare rolls dropped slightly. In early 2004 the number of people receiving welfare was approximately 2 million, more than half the total in 1996—the year the welfare reform law was enacted.[33]

Environmental Protection Agency (EPA) workers wearing protective gear inspect rusty drums suspected of containing toxic waste. This is an example of regulatory policy.

CONCLUSION

Policy-making and fiscal, monetary, and social policy are aspects of the social sciences that are studied and analyzed by scholars. Those who work in the social sciences seek to apply the methods of the natural sciences to this area of study. But neither the objectivity nor the methodology of the natural sciences can be fully duplicated by social scientists. It is likely that any field of study whose subject is an aspect of human behavior must inevitably fall short of being truly scientific. Human behavior is too unpredictable to submit completely to the rigors of the scientific method.

Having mentioned these limitations, it must also be said that as a result of the work of social scientists, we now know much more about how public policy is made and the consequences of particular public policies. Most of our knowledge is relatively new—the product of the last half-century or so. For example, we have a better understanding of how different governmental policies regarding taxing, spending, and interest rates affect an economic system such as that of the United States. The ongoing work of today's social scientists can only add to our knowledge of how government policy is made and the consequences it will have on society.

QUESTIONS FOR THOUGHT

1. What are the major policy issues that are currently on the congressional agenda?

2. State and briefly explain the main stages of the policy-making process.

3. Explain the main differences between fiscal and monetary policy.

4. What are the major provisions of the 1996 Personal Responsibility and Work Opportunity Act? In what ways did it change prior welfare policy?

5. What policies has your state adopted to deal with welfare now that most of the responsibilities for administering welfare have been transferred from the federal government to the states?

INTERNET ACTIVITIES

1. *National Center for Public Policy Research.* Go to **http://www.national center.org/**. Select a topic and article that interests you and write about how this may or may not affect your life.

2. *Policy Agenda Online.* Go to **http://www.publicagenda.org/**. Examine the "New on the Agenda" section and select one current issue and write about your feelings and ideas compared to the overall public opinion, as noted on the site.

KEY TERMS

agenda	implementation	public policy
corporatism	issue	redistributive policy
distributive policy	material policies	regulatory policy
elite theory	monetary policy	subgovernments
fiscal policy	pluralism	substantive policies
group theory	procedural policies	symbolic policies
impact evaluation	process evaluation	welfare

SUGGESTED READING

Aaron, Henry J., and Robert D. Reischauer. *Countdown to Reform: The Great Social Security Debate,* rev. ed. Washington, DC: Brookings Institution Press, 2001.

Blank, Rebecca M., and Ron Haskins, eds. *The New World of Welfare.* Washington, DC: Brookings Institution Press, 2001.

Dye, Thomas R. *Top Down Policymaking.* New York: Chatham House, 2001.

Gillon, Steven M. *That's Not What We Meant to Do.* New York: Norton, 2000.

Glazer, Nathan. *The Limits of Social Policy.* Cambridge, MA: Harvard University Press, 1988.

Kingdon, John W. *Agendas, Alternatives, and Public Policies,* 2nd ed. New York: Longmans, 1995.

Noble, Charles. *Welfare as We Know It: A Political History of the American Welfare State,* 4th ed. New York: Oxford University Press, 1997.

Weaver, R. Kent. *Ending Welfare As We Know It.* Washington, DC: Brookings Institution Press, 2000.

Wells, Donald T., and Chris R. Hamilton. *The Policy Puzzle: Finding Solutions in the Diverse American System.* Upper Saddle River, NJ: Prentice Hall, 1996.

Winston, Pamela. *Welfare Policymaking in the States.* Washington, DC: Georgetown University Press, 2002.

NOTES

1. Charles L. Cochran and Eloise F. Malone, *Public Policy: Perspectives and Choices* (New York: McGraw-Hill, 1995), p.11.

2. Ibid.

3. See Robert Dahl, *Pluralist Democracy in the United States* (Chicago: Rand-McNally, 1967), and David B. Truman, *The Governmental Process,* 2nd ed. (New York: Knopf, 1971).

4. Ralph Miliband, *The State in Capitalist Society* (New York: Basic Books, 1969); C. Wright Mills, *The Power Elite* (Oxford, England: Oxford University Press, 1984).

5. Philippe Schmitter and G. Lehmbruch, eds., *Trends Toward Corporatist Intermediation* (Beverly Hills, CA: Sage Publications, 1979).

6. J. Leiper Freeman, *The Political Process: Executive Bureau-Legislative Committee Relations* (New York: W.W. Norton, 1979); T. L. Gais, M. Peterson, and J. Walker, "Interest Groups, Iron Triangles and Representative Institutions in American National Government," *British Journal of Political Science* 14 (2) (April 1984): 161-86; A. G. Jordan, "Iron Triangles, Woolly Corporatism and Elastic Nets: Images of the Policy Process," *Journal of Public Policy* 1 (1) (February 1981): 95-123.

7. Jack Walker, *Mobilizing Interest Groups in America* (Ann Arbor: University of Michigan Press, 1991).

8. Hugh Heclo, "Issue Networks and the Executive Establishment," in Anthony King, ed., *The New American Political System* (Washington, DC: American Enterprise Institute, 1978), pp. 87-124.

9. See Theodore J. Lowi, "American Business, Public Policy Case Studies and Political Theory," in *World Politics* 16 (July 1964): 677-715.

10. See Murray Edelman, *The Symbolic Uses of Politics* (Urbana: University of Illinois Press, 1964).

11. James E. Anderson, *Public Policy-Making* (New York: Praeger Publishers, 1975), p. 10.

12. Theodore J. Lowi, *The End of Liberalism,* 2nd ed. (New York: W.W. Norton, 1979).

13. Lawrence G. Brewster, *The Public Agenda* (New York: St. Martin's Press, 1984).

14. See Roger J. Cobb and Charles D. Elder, *Participation in American Politics: The Dynamics of Agenda Building* (Baltimore: Johns Hopkins University Press, 1983).

15. Ibid.

16. Anderson, *Public Policy-Making,* p. 93.

17. B. Guy Peters, *American Public Policy: Promise and Performance,* 3rd ed. (Chatham, NJ: Chatham House, 1993).

18. Ibid., ch. 4.

19. L. A. Gunn, "Why Is Implementation So Difficult?" *Management Services in Government* 33 (November 1978): 169-76.

20. Anthony Downs, *Inside Bureaucracy* (Boston: Little, Brown, 1967).

21. Michael Quinn Patton, *Creative Evaluation* (Newbury Park, CA: Sage Publications, 1981).

22. Irene S. Rubin, *The Politics of Public Budgeting,* 2nd ed. (Chatham, NJ: Chatham House, 1993), pp. 1-6, 10-20.

23. Paul R. Schulman, "Nonincremental Policy Making," *American Political Science Review* 69 (1975): 1354-70.

24. Charles E. Lindblom, "The Science of Muddling Through," *Public Administration Review* 19 (1959): 79-88.

25. The theoretical basis for fiscal policy was set forth in a 1936 work by the British economist John Maynard Keynes, *The General Theory of Employment, Interest, and Money.*

26. Norman Ginsburg, *Division of Welfare* (Newbury, Park, CA: Sage Publications), 1993.

27. See for example, *Lochner v. New York,* 198 U.S.45 (1905).

28. See for example, *United States v. Darby,* 312 U.S. 100 (1941).

29. Mark E. Rushefsky, *Public Policy in the United States,* 2nd ed. (Belmont, CA: Wadsworth, 1996).

30. Nancy L. Johnson, "The Results Are In: Welfare Reform Works," *Wall Street Journal,* August 24, 1999, p.A18.

31. Ron Haskins, "The Verdict on Welfare Reform: Work Works," *The Weekly Standard,* November 13, 2000, pp. 20-21.

32. Nina Bernstein, "Child Only Cases Grow in Welfare," *New York Times,* August 14, 2002, p.A1

33. Robert Pear, "Despite Sluggish Economy, Welfare Rolls Actually Fell," *New York Times,* March 22, 2004, p.A21.

CHAPTER
14

Foreign Policy

Why do nations behave the way they do in the international environment? No single factor is likely to account completely for a country's foreign policy decisions let alone its long-term international behavior. Any investigation of the sources of a nation's foreign policy must assess a number of potential determinants or influences. These may be broadly classified as external (or "systemic") and internal (or "domestic"). External sources are found in the international environment. They may take the form of military, economic, or political pressures. One school of thought in political science, known as *realism*, argues that nations are "socialized" by the rough-and-tumble and decentralized (or "anarchic") nature of the international environment and tend to respond to similar pressures in similar ways. Most important, according to this view, are the distribution of power and the interaction of nations in the international system.[1]

By contrast, internal sources of foreign policy reflect the pressure and influence exerted by forces within the nation itself—that is, domestic forces. Among these factors are the political structure of the nation (the relationship between the nation and society), the nature of domestic politics, and the foreign policy preferences of contending political elites. In pluralist democratic societies, another important set of factors consists of "actors" such as business firms, labor unions, and public interest groups that seek to influence the content and direction of the nation's foreign policy.

It is useful to think of a nation's government as a pivot on which external and internal pressures turn. Middle-sized and weak nations obviously are more vulnerable to the pressures of international competition. By contrast, great powers with large internal markets and substantial financial, economic, and military capabilities are buffered against external pressures. Instead of having to adjust their domestic arrangements to these changing forces, the most powerful nations generally seek to shape the international environment according to their own preferences.[2] As a superpower, the United States even has the luxury of projecting its domestic politics into its foreign affairs and thus is better able to achieve its goals than most countries.

> "[America's] glory is not *dominion*, but *liberty*. Her march is the march of the mind. She has a spear and a shield; but the motto upon her shield is, *Freedom, Independence, Peace*. This has been her Declaration; this has been, as far as her necessary intercourse with the rest of mankind would permit, her practice."
>
> —*President John Quincy Adams (1821)*

361

This chapter begins by examining two broad theories of international relations—realism and liberalism—that attempt to explain the behavior of nations by investigating the sources of competition, conflict, and cooperation among them. The second section turns to domestic factors and the role of domestic actors in the formulation of U.S. foreign policy.

COMPETING THEORIES OF INTERNATIONAL RELATIONS

Most Americans would agree that success in foreign policy depends on the ability of political leaders to set sensible and proper goals for their country. The choice of goals, however, depends not only on the preferences of political leaders but also on a broad array of political, economic, and societal interests. Every country has some fundamental national interests that rarely change (such as ensuring the survival of the nation), but other interests are defined and redefined by various domestic actors. What interests have guided American foreign policy over the last two centuries? Two broad theories of international relations—realism and liberalism—help us understand the sources of America's international conduct. In brief, **realism** maintains that cooperation among nations is limited by the competitive strategies that they must adopt in an international environment that lacks institutions capable of enforcing good behavior. By contrast, **liberalism** maintains that capitalism and democracy, as well as international institutions, can lead to enduring cooperation among nations.

REALISM

At the core of realism is the concept of **anarchy.** For realists, international politics, like all politics, is a struggle for power and security. However, there is an important difference between most domestic politics and international politics. Realists argue that the behavior of nations is guided by the fact that there is no supreme political authority or centralized cluster of institutions in the international arena. That is, there is no institution that can establish universal rules of good conduct and punish nations that break those rules. In this decentralized or anarchic international system, nations are free to act according to their interests as they define them.

This condition is in stark contrast to domestic politics in a stable, legitimate nation. Such nations are characterized by a hierarchy of political power and authority—political institutions that have both the means and the perceived right to set rules and enforce behavior. For example, the U.S. government, by virtue of the Constitution, has both the power and the authority to collect taxes from American citizens. Most Americans assume that the Internal Revenue Service, an agency of the U.S. government, has the right to collect taxes. And for those who choose to break the rules and avoid paying taxes, the IRS has legitimate means to force these citizens into correct behavior, including threats of lawful imprisonment.

In the international environment, such all-encompassing institutions are lacking. The United Nations, which has been the premier international organization in world affairs since 1945, is a good example. For years the United States was embroiled in disputes with the United Nations over a number of issues, including the sharing of costs and whether the UN should sponsor programs that assist citizens of member countries in obtaining abortions. As a protest against such programs, the United States has at times refused to pay its full dues (or "taxes") to the United Nations. Unlike the example of tax collection within the United States, where most citizens feel obligated to pay their taxes, the U.S. government (more specifically, the U.S. Congress) did not feel obligated to pay its UN dues. Moreover, the United Nations does not have the power to compel the United States to pay its "taxes."

For a realist, the simple example of nonpayment of UN dues points to a much larger problem in the international environment: the fact that neither the United Nations nor any other international organization can reliably prevent aggression or threatening behavior by nations that seek to change the established arrangements, or "status quo." The UN lacks a world army, and its members therefore must choose whether to act on their own or form coalitions to deal with aggressors.

In the absence of any hierarchical authority to enforce proper conduct, nations must rely on self-help strategies that involve the pursuit of power and advantage. Nations want to prevent other nations from taking advantage of them, but they may also look for opportunities to exploit on their own. The international environment is a competitive arena in which fear and insecurity create a compulsion to maximize power, and violence is an ever-present possibility. Even states concerned primarily with self-preservation may act "aggressively"—building up their military arsenals, for example—because anarchy encourages them to provide for their own security.[3] Some states are driven (often as a result of particular ideologies or powerful interests) by a quest for dominance. Rising powers

The United Nations Building, New York City.

typically become the most dissatisfied with the status quo and seek to revise it. Realists stress that all-around satisfaction with the status quo is not likely to be a common or persistent condition. In the end, power determines whose claims prevail, and if wars happen, it is usually because states are prepared to use armed force to pursue their conflicting aims and calculate that the expected benefits exceed the costs.[4]

Finally, realists emphasize that the distribution of resources and capabilities has a major influence on foreign policy. The most powerful nations have a disproportionate impact on the processes of interaction in the international system. In short, power matters, and the strongest nations have strong incentives to compete for power in the military, economic, and political arenas.[5] The competition for power does not necessarily create a threatening situation for less powerful nations, as evidenced by the fact that Canada does not fear the superior power of its neighbor, the United States. However, when such threats do arise, nations are motivated to take steps to ensure their security, often by "balancing" (building up their military capabilities and/or forming alliances) against the threatening nation or coalition of nations. Thus, over the longer run, aggressive nations that aspire to a position of dominance tend to encourage the rise of countervailing forces to oppose them.[6] In this manner, **a balance of power,** or rough equilibrium, may result because nations will work to increase their armaments and to create alliances to block the aggressive attempts of other nations to dominate the international system. However, dominant powers that do not pose threats to the security of other countries may attract allies rather than repel them, given the potential for joint benefits. Throughout the nation's history, American foreign policy has tended to promote either a stable balance of power or American dominance.

Realism and American Foreign Policy

Although the historical behavior of the United States in world affairs can largely be explained by the realist perspective, many Americans would reject such an explanation. When the United States was founded, Americans believed that they were escaping from the treacherous world of European power politics. From the beginning, they have been convinced of the uniqueness of their experiment in democratic politics and of what was widely considered a morally superior foreign policy.[7] American citizens, in the words of one early American leader, reside in the "city on the hill."

Such lofty self-assessments have allowed Americans to rationalize and disguise the pursuit of national self-interest, defined in terms of power and security. For example, Americans viewed the expansion of the United States during the nineteenth century as a civilizing act rather than as the aggressive conquest of the Indian nations or Mexican territory. They therefore considered the behavior of the United States to be morally superior to the imperialistic behavior of other powers. Never mind that the immense difference in capabilities between the opponents masked the use of power and force, or that other expansionist ventures, such as those of the British and French, were similarly justified as intended to "civilize" lesser peoples. From the realist perspective, these examples demonstrate that power determines whose view of morality prevails.

THE MONROE DOCTRINE Although Americans have often disagreed on the proper role of the United States in world politics, there has been a broad and durable consensus on the core national interests of the United States.[8] Most

CLOSE-UP

THE MONROE DOCTRINE

James Monroe (1758–1831) served two terms as president of the United States (1817–1825). His years as president were marked by a number of important accomplishments, including the purchase of Florida from Spain. But it was the Monroe Doctrine that brought him lasting fame. In 1822 the United States became the first country to accord recognition to the newly independent nations that had been established in Latin America: Mexico, Colombia, Peru, Chile, and Argentina. There was, however, great fear that one or more of the European nations would invade these countries and end their independence. It was against this background of events that President Monroe announced his famous doctrine in his annual message to Congress on December 2, 1823:

> We owe it . . . to candor and to the amicable relations existing between the United States and those European powers, to declare that we should consider any attempt on their part to extend their system to any portion of this hemisphere as dangerous to our peace and safety. With the existing colonies or dependencies of any European power we have not interfered and shall not interfere. But with the Governments who have declared their independence . . . and whose independence . . . we have acknowledged, we could not view any interposition . . . by any European power in any other light than as a manifestation of an unfriendly disposition toward the United States. . . .

> Our policy in regard to Europe . . . is not to interfere in the internal concerns of any of its powers, [but] to cultivate friendly relations with it, submitting to injuries from none.

notably, the United States has always sought to be the dominant power in the Western Hemisphere. Given that American dominance was unlikely to be challenged by any nation or group of nations acting without support from outside the hemisphere, the United States insisted, in the **Monroe Doctrine** (1823) and related policies, that no non-American nation might interfere in the affairs of the Western Hemisphere. In a message to Congress in 1823, President James Monroe sought to safeguard America's position by declaring the Western Hemisphere off limits to European encroachment and colonization.[9]

Monroe and his successors as president understood that the greatest challenges to American dominance in the Western Hemisphere came from Europe. As a result, we have always attempted to prevent the emergence of a major European power that, having conquered or dominated other nations on the continent, could turn its attention across the Atlantic and menace the United States. To this end, the United States has almost always opposed whatever European power—Britain, France, Germany, or Russia—was likely to establish dominance in Europe and thereby threaten the security and independence of the United States.

Even Thomas Jefferson, long an admirer of France because the French Revolution promised freedom from the tyranny of European monarchs, gradually adopted a more "realist" perspective during the Napoleonic era, when France threatened to upset the balance of power in Europe. In 1812 Jefferson looked to Britain, whose political institutions and class privileges he had long deplored, as a counterweight to French power. He wrote:

> It is for the general interest that she [Britain] should be a sensible and independent weight in the scale of nations, and be able to contribute, when a favorable moment presents itself, to reduce under the same order, her great rival. . . . We especially ought

James Monroe (1758–1831). Revolutionary War officer, Virginia politician, delegate to the Virginia Constitutional Convention, U.S. senator, diplomat, secretary of state and war, fifth president of the United States, and originator of the Monroe Doctrine.

to pray that the powers of Europe may be so poised and counterpoised among themselves, that their own security may require the presence of all their forces at home, leaving the other quarters of the globe in undisturbed tranquility.[10]

THE EMERGENCE OF THE UNITED STATES AS A GLOBAL POWER

During Jefferson's time, and for most of the nineteenth century, the United States did not play an active role in the European balance of power. American foreign policy during much of this period is sometimes described as **isolationism,** or disengagement from the rest of the world. However, it is more accurate to describe it in terms of **unilateralism,** meaning acting without the approval or cooperation of other nations. Although the United States remained relatively isolated from European power politics, it became more deeply involved in the affairs of the Western Hemisphere, and its growth as an industrial power, particularly after the American Civil War, gave teeth to the Monroe Doctrine. By 1900 the United States could legitimately defend its role as **hegemon** (the dominant state) of the Western Hemisphere, tolerating no interference in its affairs by European powers.

At the same time, the United States sought to extend its global reach, acting to open trade with Japan in the 1850s. Like other rising nations, the United States had long adopted **mercantilism**—that is, policies based on the idea that wealth and power go together and that the nation therefore should pursue policies designed to increase its wealth. One of the nation's founders, Alexander Hamilton, was an early advocate of such policies, arguing that successful industrialization required subsidies for domestic industries and infrastructure as well as protectionist trade policies.[11] In the nineteenth century, the United States, like Germany, challenged Great Britain's virtual monopoly of world trade.

By the end of the nineteenth century, with American industrial power surging, U.S. foreign policy increasingly resembled that of a European great power. Under President McKinley, the United States went through an imperialist phase when it defeated Spain in the Spanish-American War (1898), a conflict sparked by Spain's attempts to suppress an armed struggle by Cubans for independence. This "splendid little war" gave the United States control over the Philippines, Puerto Rico, and Guam. After McKinley was assassinated in 1901, Vice President Theodore Roosevelt became president. More than any of his predecessors, Roosevelt embraced European *realpolitik,* the harsh and unsentimental pursuit of national interests, as his guiding philosophy in foreign policy.

What this meant in practice was greater assertion of America's presence abroad and frequent intervention in Latin America. This philosophy was expressed in the **Roosevelt Corollary** to the Monroe Doctrine, which justified American intervention in the domestic politics of Latin American nations. The United States occupied Cuba, took control of the national finances of Haiti and the Dominican Republic, and provoked an uprising in Colombia to secure land rights for a canal across the Isthmus of Panama. In December 1907 President Roosevelt demonstrated to the nations of the world the new power of the United States by sending sixteen American battleships on a fourteen-month, 46,000 mile trip around the world.

The Roosevelt era demonstrated that American noninterventionism was giving way to active involvement in international affairs. The United States was now

President Theodore Roosevelt observes the construction of the Panama Canal on November 15, 1906.

CLOSE-UP

PRESIDENT WASHINGTON'S FAREWELL ADDRESS

After serving two terms as the first president of the United States (1789–1797), George Washington decided not to run for reelection for a third term. He announced his decision to the American people in his farewell address, given at the close of eight years in office. At the end of his speech, Washington counseled his countrymen about the dangers of entanglements with foreign nations. This early statement of isolationism influenced American foreign policy until well into the twentieth century.

The great rule of conduct for us in regard to foreign nations is, in extending our commercial relations, to have with them as little political connections as possible. . . .

Europe has a set of primary interests which to us have none or a very remote relation. Hence she must be engaged in frequent controversies, the causes of which are essentially foreign to our concerns. Hence, therefore, it must be unwise in us to implicate ourselves by artificial ties in the ordinary vicissitudes of her politics or the ordinary combinations and collisions of her friendships or enmities. . . .

It is our true policy to steer clear of permanent alliances with any portion of the foreign world. . . .

---

an emerging global player, having transformed itself into a continental power with an effective national government, a strong industrial base, far-flung commercial interests, and an impressive navy. Unlike the great powers in Europe, however, the United States still lacked large ground forces, not only because of the American tradition of opposition to standing armies but also because the United States had no pressing need for them.

WORLD WARS I AND II   U.S. strengths and military weaknesses were evident in World War I. Woodrow Wilson had been elected president on a policy of neutrality in the conflict between the alliances led by France and Russia, on one side, and the German Empire and Austria-Hungary, on the other. The American policy of neutrality was shattered in 1915 when the Germans began submarine attacks on American vessels. In April 1917, with the urging of President Wilson, Congress formally declared war on Germany. But the U.S. expeditionary force required almost a year of training before it was ready for combat, and even then the Americans relied heavily on the Allies (Great Britain and France) for weapons. Although when the United States entered the war Wilson claimed not to be pursuing *realpolitik,* the effect of the American intervention was the maintenance of a balance of power in Europe.

The United States slipped back into isolationism after World War I, only to intervene once more in European politics twenty years later in World War II. Again, the United States entered after the war had started. In December 1941, the Japanese destroyed many American ships when they attacked the U.S. naval base at Pearl Harbor in Hawaii. The United States immediately declared war on Japan and a few days later on Germany and Italy after those nations had joined Japan in its war against this country. This time the United States decisively tilted the balance against Nazi Germany and its attempt to subjugate Europe. After World War II the United States emerged as the most powerful country in the world and assumed many global responsibilities, including the role of permanent "balancer" in Europe. In doing so, it was abandoning a long tradition, first stated by President Washington in his Farewell Address of 1796, of avoiding attachments with other countries, particularly "entangling alliances." The dominant position held by the United States in world affairs after 1945 created a strong American stake in promoting its interests and maintaining the status quo.[12]

THE COLD WAR The United States not only promoted the reconstruction of the Western European and Japanese economies devastated by the war, but also played the critical role in founding the North Atlantic Treaty Organization (NATO, 1949–1950) and other regional security pacts. The purpose of these treaties was to contain the threat posed by the Soviet Union and the spread of communism. Thus, Europe was divided by two hostile alliances: NATO, a voluntary coalition of like-minded democracies, and the Warsaw Pact, a Soviet-controlled alliance of its "satellites," including East Germany, Hungary, Czechoslovakia, Poland, and others. Despite years of tense and often volatile relations known as the "Cold War," a "hot" war between the United States and the Soviet Union never broke out because fear of a nuclear world war induced restraint on both sides.[13]

The United States was not deterred, however, from continuing its policy of intervention in the Western Hemisphere. It supported a coup in Guatemala in 1954 and promoted governments more favorable to U.S. interests in countries such as Panama and the Dominican Republic. In fact, the Monroe Doctrine became part of the justification for preventing the emergence of regimes in places such as El Salvador and Nicaragua that might pursue goals more favorable to Soviet interests than to those of the United States.

The first test of the policy of **containment** of communism was the Korean War (1950–1953). Although the war ended in stalemate and the division of the Korean peninsula, it had a major impact on American policy during the Cold War. Most important, Korea led to a sharp increase in the U.S. defense budget and the strengthening of NATO, including the rearmament of West Germany. The Korean

CLOSE-UP

THE ROOSEVELT COROLLARY TO THE MONROE DOCTRINE

In his December 1904 annual message to Congress, President Theodore Roosevelt set forth his ideas on intervention in the affairs of Latin American nations. His thoughts came to be known as the Roosevelt Corollary to the Monroe Doctrine:

If a nation shows that it knows how to act with reasonable efficiency and decency in social and political matters, if it keeps order and pays its obligations, it need fear no interference from the United States. Chronic wrongdoing, or an impotence which results in a general loosening of the ties of civilized

society, may in America, as elsewhere, ultimately require intervention by some civilized nation, and in the Western Hemisphere the adherence of the United States to the Monroe Doctrine may force the United States, however reluctantly, in flagrant cases of such wrongdoing or impotence, to the exercise of an international police power.

It was on the basis of the Roosevelt Corollary that American presidents sent military forces to occupy nations such as Nicaragua and Haiti during the first decades of the twentieth century.

War also convinced American foreign policymakers of the need to maintain large armed forces and to take action against communist or left-wing forces wherever they appeared. What followed were American interventions in Iran and Lebanon, in addition to those in Latin America that have already been mentioned.

Overshadowing all else was the American involvement in Vietnam, which began at the end of World War II and lasted thirty years, spanning six administrations between 1945 and 1975. It was President Johnson who dramatically expanded U.S. involvement in the 1960s with the decision to send in combat forces. However, the American people did not fully support the war, whereas the North Vietnamese stake was strong and enduring. The defeat of U.S. forces in Southeast Asia led to greater reluctance to commit U.S. military power abroad, as well as to a more favorable attitude toward normalization of relations with the Soviet Union, a policy known as **detente**.[14]

The Cold War finally ended after the last Soviet leader, Mikhail Gorbachev, jettisoned Marxist-Leninist doctrine and permitted the expression of political ideas that challenged the legitimacy of Soviet rule. But once again the United States emerged from a major confrontation stronger than ever. Its renewed strength and growing technological power allowed it to promote its interests either unilaterally or in cooperation with other states. The United States has acted in both ways, but nowhere more boldly than in promoting the preservation and enlargement of NATO. Thanks in large part to a continuing strong U.S. commitment, the alliance survived the end of the Cold War and has now been expanded to include most of the nations of Eastern Europe that had once been part of the Soviet empire. In March 1999 the Czech Republic, Hungary and Poland joined NATO. Seven other Eastern European nations—Bulgaria, Romania, Slovenia, Slovakia, Estonia, Latvia, and Lithuania—were invited to join the Alliance at the November 2000 NATO summit meeting in Prague. They became full members of NATO in May 2004.

In Asia the United States has pursued similar policies that reflect enduring U.S. political, economic, and security interests, including a stable balance of power. Thus, America's insistence on the "open door" principle, which demanded equal access to China's markets in the late nineteenth and early twentieth centuries, stemmed not only from commercial interests but also from a desire to prevent other nations, notably Japan, from dominating China militarily and politically. As in Europe, a hegemon, or dominant nation, in Asia—whether Japan, China, or a combination of powers—might be capable of threatening the security of the United States. After a communist revolution in 1949 transformed China from an ally of the United States into its adversary, the United States confronted this challenge to its security (and to that of its Asian allies) by surrounding both Communist China and the Soviet Union with military and political alliances. The normalization of relations with the People's Republic of China since the early 1970s has promoted greater economic interdependence between the two countries, but without eliminating many of the root causes of fear and confrontation that divide them.

LIBERALISM

Since the nation's founding, liberalism has competed with *realpolitik,* or political realism, as the philosophical mainspring of American foreign policy. As used here, *liberalism* refers to the philosophical tradition that emphasizes the central importance of individual political and economic liberty as positive values shaping the character of a polity. Classical liberalism, which is derived from the works of such diverse thinkers as Emmanuel Kant, John Locke, Adam Smith, and Thomas Jefferson, has been a core component of American political ideology.[15]

President Wilson and World War I

At only one point in American history—the United States' entry into World War I and President Wilson's attempt to shape the postwar world—has American foreign policy been unambiguously driven by ideal liberal tenets. For utopian liberals or idealists like Wilson, the pursuit of national interest created a host of ills, from secret treaties that put weak states at a disadvantage to bloody struggles among the great powers to divide and redivide Africa and Asia into colonies. Wilson believed that European realpolitik was not only immoral but also ineffective at preventing war among great powers. He believed that human nature was innately good and that human potential would be released if bad political institutions were reformed or eliminated. For Wilson, what *ought* to exist in international relations was indistinguishable from what *could* be achieved.

The lynchpin of Wilson's philosophy was commitment to **collective security.**[16] For Wilson and his fellow liberals, the security of nations would be achieved through membership in an international organization dedicated to

President Woodrow Wilson campaigning for public support of the Versailles Treaty during the League of Nations tour, 1919. The proposed treaty was defeated in the U.S. Senate.

maintaining order and cooperation. Peace would be ensured by the commitment of member nations to launch a unified and overwhelming response to any act of aggression against a member nation. Potential aggressors would be deterred because they could expect an unacceptably costly retaliatory blow. Wilson placed his hopes in the collective security principles espoused by the League of Nations created after the end of World War I, but his scheme foundered when the U.S. Senate voted down U.S. entry into the fledgling international organization.

The idea of an international community of nations was, of course, a rejection of balance-of-power politics. It also rejected the realist assumption that in an anarchic international environment nations could not trust one another, and self-help was the only sure way to guarantee survival. Realists such as E. H. Carr, a British historian and journalist, condemned utopian liberalism for promoting the very outcome—war—that Wilson had sought to prevent. According to Carr, the naive supporters of such ideas had blinded Europe to the rising threat of Hitler's Germany by spreading the belief that nations could be induced to value peace, order, and cooperation.[17] Although the idea of collective security enjoyed a brief resurgence at the end of the Cold War, contemporary realists still find little reason to expect nations to honor commitments to collective security when their own interests are not directly threatened; nor, in many cases, would it be easy for third parties to determine which side in a war is the aggressor.[18]

Contemporary Liberalism

In comparison to Wilson's utopian liberalism, contemporary liberals are more pragmatic. They acknowledge many of the insights of the realist perspective, particularly those concerning the competitive aspects of international politics. However, liberals believe that international anarchy does not bar common interests, civility, or order.[19] Moreover, the increased interdependence of societies and economic globalization have reduced the utility of force in international relations while enlarging the sphere of common interests that can be pursued through cooperative endeavors. An example is trade and the international economy. Liberals believe that the growing interdependence of nations in the global economy, based largely on the increased flow of trade, encourages them to value the mutual benefits of economic linkages and therefore to view war—which would destroy such connections—as an unsatisfactory method for pursuing national interests.[20]

Liberals also point to the importance of domestic structures and values as determinants of cooperation in world politics. Here the assumption is that liberal democracies (that is, those with representative institutions and market economies) rarely, if ever, fight wars with one another.[21] Democratic institutions embody the norms of compromise and dialogue, and these values foster cooperation among like-minded nations. Democracies also value public opinion, which may serve as a powerful check on national leaders who favor aggressive foreign behavior. The division of power among different branches of government also serves to check precipitous and/or aggressive actions by national leaders.

A group of liberals called "neo-liberal institutionalists" believe that international institutions or regimes also promote cooperation on important global issues, such as international security, economic development, and protecting the environment. They do so by creating mechanisms for *conflict resolution*, providing information on whether participating nations are meeting their obligations under the rules of the institution, facilitating reciprocity, and perhaps most important, fostering the belief that sustained cooperation among nations is valuable and the expectation that cooperation is durable.[22] Thus, over time nations may become socialized to certain patterns of behavior and learn the value of cooperation. In this sense, international regimes or institutions can be more than simply tall buildings with staffs that coordinate various international arrangements; they involve norms, values, and mechanisms that may become embedded in decision-makers' expectations about the future—for example, the post–World War II American strategy of promoting an open multilateral trading system coupled with the expectation of domestic policies to buffer the adverse effects of global competition.[23]

Liberal international regimes tend to be fostered by a global hegemon, a nation that is dominant in terms of military, economic, institutional, and ideological strength. The hegemon promotes cooperation by constructing institutional arrangements that favor its interests and ideologies. In the post–World War II era, the United States has played the role of global hegemon, creating and supporting global monetary and trade systems (buttressed by institutions such as the World Trade Organization, the World Bank, and the International Monetary Fund) that promote an international economy based on liberal, free-market principles.[24]

Selective Engagement

Although many realists agree that American hegemony serves U.S. interests well, others worry about the possible overextension of American power. They favor a strategy of selective engagement.[25] **Selective engagement** involves the use of U.S. military power in the prevention of major threats to American security, especially in helping to prevent wars from breaking out among the great powers of the world (China, Russia, Japan, and Germany). The policy also seeks to halt the spread of weapons of mass destruction to threatening regimes such as those in Iran and North Korea. On the other hand, the adoption of the policy of selective engagement would lead the U.S. to ignore conflicts and humanitarian disasters (in Somalia, Rwanda, and Haiti) that do not threaten its core interest in maintaining peace among the world's great powers. Overall, realists warn against basing American foreign policy wholly on a liberal foundation. They contend that cooperation does not eliminate competition and creates an environment in which there are winners and losers. Even when all gain, as in a free-trade arrangement, some parties may gain more than others. In the realist view, nations worry about the *relative* distribution of payoffs from international cooperation, not simply whether they are gaining in absolute terms as liberals emphasize. Thus, if nations perceive that the benefits they derive from economic interaction are significantly less than those derived by others, they may restrict or terminate the relationship for fear that it is strengthening potential rivals.[26]

Realists are similarly skeptical about whether the United States should actively promote the spread of democracy as a way to improve the prospects for peace in the international system. Until recently the number of democracies has been relatively small, and geographic distance usually made the possibility of war relatively remote. Moreover, realists point out that peace among democracies may be traced to other causes, such as the side benefits of cooperation with allies.[27] A more reliable method of ensuring American security, in the view of many, is to continue to rely on nuclear deterrence, a strategy that benefits great powers seeking to maintain the status quo.[28]

Liberalism and Realism as Enduring Perspectives

Liberalism remains a powerful force in American foreign policy, competing with realist perspectives for predominance. This dualism is understandable because American foreign policy has always been shaped by two basic objectives: to ensure national security and to serve as a model for other states. It is also understandable that these competing objectives have often produced contradictory foreign policies that sometimes appeared hypocritical. During the Cold War the United States framed this conflict in terms of two antithetical political and socioeconomic systems. The repression in the totalitarian communist system was contrasted with the political and economic freedoms enjoyed by American citizens. Yet when circumstances required, the United States supported repressive regimes in the interest of forging anticommunist alliances. Somoza in Nicaragua, the Shah of Iran, and Mobuto in Zaire were brutal dictators who received American support in exchange for alignment with the United States. One of the lessons of the Cold War was that national interests trump national values when the security of nations is threatened.

THE POST–COLD WAR PERIOD

The end of the Cold War prompted a wave of self-congratulation in the West, eliciting the opinion that the "end of history" was at hand with the triumph of Western liberal economic and democratic values.[29] This assessment was certainly overly optimistic, given the survival of global conflict and tension that has existed since this statement was made in 1992. But it is also true that the United States is now the sole global superpower, a hegemon dedicated to liberal economic and democratic values.

Within this context, realism and liberalism continue to reflect the goals of American foreign policy. This is also true because the world is divided into two groups, or "tiers" of nations that differ substantially in their level of prosperity and degree of commitment to democratic values.[30] The first tier comprises the advanced industrial democracies of North America, Western Europe, and Japan. Although disputes and tensions among these nations persist, their shared democratic culture and similar economic interests have made armed conflict among them highly improbable. The second tier is another matter. This group of nations, accounting for roughly six-sevenths of the world's population, is extremely diverse. Nevertheless, all the nations of the second tier lack institutionalized democracy or advanced market relations. Partly as a result of these conditions, conflict and warfare are frequent.

A salient question of the post–Cold War period is how the United States should behave in the international arena. More specifically, how should it treat the turbulent second tier? Operation Desert Storm, which turned back Iraq's invasion of Kuwait (1990) demonstrated that the United States was willing to use military force to protect its vital national interests in the second tier. In this case, that interest was the flow of oil from the Middle East.

But the United States has also shown itself willing to pursue **multilateralism** in support of human rights and humanitarian values. Indeed, its enviable global position has allowed it to act more freely in promoting such norms while avoiding the effects of commitment to other international norms, such as environmental protection. The decision in 1999 to use NATO forces, led by the United States, to punish Yugoslavia for its ethnic cleansing of Kosovo is a case in point.

A more traditional liberal foreign policy agenda was evident during the administrations of President Clinton, which pursued a policy of spreading democracy and market capitalism in the wake of the collapse of the Soviet Union. Administration efforts focused on the former communist satellites of East Central Europe and the nations created after the collapse of the Soviet Union, most notably Russia. As with previous efforts to reform its conquered foes, the United States is driven by the belief that market democracies are reliable, peaceful partners. Similarly, the Clinton administration supported the entry of China into the World Trade Organization (WTO) on the assumption that economic interdependence will foster political liberalization in China.

Although social-scientific research provides some support for the belief that market democracies help promote international peace, studies have found that democracies are more than willing to wage war against nondemocratic states. Furthermore, the path to market democracy is often rocky. Weak, unstable democracies may be more likely to disturb the international peace than stable authoritarian regimes.[31]

The United States' efforts to smooth the transition to market democracy in the former communist nations have had mixed results. In Russia the transition has been severely hampered by inability to create the necessary political and institutional conditions for market capitalism. In addition, the United States' aid and loan programs, as well as those of multilateral institutions such as the IMF and the World Bank, have not been managed effectively.[32] But the United States and its European allies can take some credit for helping transitional countries such as Hungary, Romania, and Estonia avoid being derailed by the ethnic conflicts that ravaged the former Yugoslavia. The March 2003 destruction of the brutal dictatorship of Saddam Hussein in Iraq again showed that the United States was strongly committed to the promotion of democracy abroad.

THE RISE OF INTERNATIONAL TERRORISM

Terrorism is defined in American law as "premeditated, politically motivated violence against noncombatant targets by subnational groups." Although the United Nations has not been able to agree on a definition of terrorism, it has adopted a number of conventions intended to suppress hostage taking, the financing of terrorism, and terrorist bombing and assassination.[33]

Terrorist activities—motivated by different political ideologies—have been a feature of the contemporary world. In recent decades countries in Europe, South Asia, Africa, the Middle East, and Latin and Central America have struggled to contain terrorist movements. Except for the first attack on New York City's World Trade Center in February 1993, the United States had not been directly affected by international terrorism. It was not until the September 11 attacks on the World Trade Center and the Pentagon that this country was the target of terrorism conducted by Islamic fundamentalists.

But events that occurred during the 1990s showed that Al Qaeda and other Islamic terrorist groups were becoming increasing bolder in confronting the United States. American embassies were attacked in Kenya and Tanzania on August 7, 1998, with 224 persons killed and thousands injured. And the American destroyer *Cole* was dynamited in Yemen in October 2000, with the loss of seventeen American sailors.

The September 11 attacks on the United States—the first such action on the mainland of the United States since the British bombing of Washington, DC, during the War of 1812—showed that this country's geographic situation could not alone provide protection from international terrorism. Other policies were clearly necessary in order to deal with this new threat to the domestic security of the Untied States.

The war against Al Qaeda and Taliban terrorists in Afghanistan that began in the fall of 2001 provided the first expression of U.S. foreign and military policy in the post–September 11 era. During 2002 President Bush turned the nation's attention to Iraq, one of the three countries of the world he described as part of "the axis of evil" along with Iran and North Korea. In October 2002 Congress approved the use of military force against Iraq if that country failed to eliminate its *weapons of mass destruction* (WMD)—those with nuclear, biological, or chemical capabilities.

During this same period, President Bush also attempted to gain support of various allies and of the United Nations in pursuing this nation's policy against Iraq. He had substantial success in achieving the first of these goals. Great Britain gave its full support to the president, including a commitment of military force to oust Saddam Hussein from power. Spain, Italy, Poland, Australia and more than a score of other nations also backed President Bush's policy.

Initially the United Nations gave its support to the president's Middle Eastern policy. In November 2002, the international organization approved a

U.S. Marines in southern Iraq, March 2003. Smoke from a burning oil field appears in the background.

United Nations inspectors search a research center in Baghdad, Iraq, for evidence of weapons of mass destruction, January 2003.

resolution requiring Saddam Hussein to allow UN inspectors to enter Iraq and search for weapons of mass destruction. The resolution also threatened Iraq with "serious consequences" if it failed to cooperate and alluded to the potential use of military action against the nation.

United Nations inspectors were allowed into Iraq but restraints on their movement and the limited number of inspectors made it impossible for them to conduct a careful examination of a country as large as California. After three months of inspections that failed to unearth hidden weapons of mass destruction, President Bush attempted to obtain a second UN resolution supporting the use of force against Iraq. But French, Russian, and German opposition prevented its passage.

On March 19, 2003, the United States, with the support of its allies, began military action against Iraq. In less than a month the Iraqi army had been destroyed and Saddam Hussein's regime was removed from power.

Was the invasion of Iraq a more or less random act by President Bush or was it an expression of a long-term, strategic policy to deal with international terrorism? The president had provided an answer to this question in several statements made during 2002.

The Preemption Doctrine

In a June 2002 speech at the United States Military Academy at West Point, President Bush set forth a new strategic policy for dealing with international terrorism. Known as **preemption,** the plan was the product of months of effort by the

Bush administration following the September 11 attacks on the United States. In his speech to the West Point cadets, President Bush declared: "If we wait for threats to materialize, we will have waited too long". Instead the United States will employ "preemptive action when necessary to defend our liberty and our lives."

President Bush's speech also argued that the policies used so successfully during the Cold War with the Soviet Union—deterrence and containment—were not adequate to deal successfully with terrorism. "The new dangers require new thinking, . . . Deterrence—the promise of massive retaliation against nations—means nothing against shadowy terrorist networks with no nation or citizens to defend. Containment is not possible when unbalanced dictators with weapons of mass destruction can deliver those weapons on missiles or secretly provide them to terrorist allies."[34]

The preemption doctrine was developed in greater detail in a September 2002 policy statement issued by the White House. The document—*The National Security Strategy of the United States*—restated the strategic policy first stated by the president at West Point: "While the United States will consistently strive to enlist the support of the international community, we will not hesitate to act alone, if necessary, to exercise our right to self-defense by acting preemptively against . . . terrorists to prevent them doing harm against our people and our country . . ."[35]

Critics have contended that President Bush's preemption doctrine is an unwise and dangerous strategic policy. Further, opponents of the new policy view it as providing justification for aggressive acts by the United States against sovereign nations.

It remains to be seen whether the preemption doctrine can or will be used successfully against groups that employ terrorism as a policy and those nations that support such groups. The fall 2001 war against terrorist groups in Afghanistan and the defeat of Iraq in the spring of 2003 provide some evidence that preemptive military force can be used successfully. But there remain other nations that present threats to the security of the United States. President Bush has also identified Iran and North Korea as part of the "axis of evil" in the contemporary world. The coming years will test whether the preemption policy provides a workable method for controlling international terrorism.

AMERICAN FOREIGN POLICY: THE DOMESTIC CONTEXT

The United States is different from most other nations in the degree to which domestic factors shape the policy process. By virtue of its enormous and unequaled power in the post–Cold War world, the United States is less sensitive to international pressures and less vulnerable to external threats. Yet participation in the world economy and active involvement in world affairs tends to produce benefits for some groups while being harmful to others. As a result, many domestic actors seek to influence the content of American foreign policy. For many foreign policy issues, therefore, we need to go beyond the realist view of nations as acting rationally to further their own interests. In fact, domestic politics matters in how most nations define their interests, and domestic actors are constantly striving to achieve their competing policy preferences.[36]

Thus, American businesses with a stake in promoting markets abroad, from computer companies like IBM and aerospace firms like Boeing to the film industry in Hollywood, will aggressively lobby U.S. government officials to promote policies that advance their interests (even if those same policies expose other American firms and domestic groups to tougher international competition). At the same time, these same international corporations will actively push foreign governments to abide by international commercial norms that favor trade in these sectors. In this section, therefore, we turn to domestic sources of American foreign policy, which may be grouped into two broad categories: governmental and societal.[37]

Governmental Sources

THE PRESIDENT   The president is the central governmental source of U.S. foreign policy. This is due in part to the powers granted to the president by the Constitution. The president has the power to make treaties and to appoint and receive ambassadors. The president is also designated as commander-in-chief of the armed forces. But while these powers are important, they do not fully explain the enormous influence of the chief executive over foreign policy making.

A crucial factor in the growth of presidential power is the interpretation of the president's role in foreign policy making—by Congress, the Supreme Court, influential political elites, and the American public—which has steadily expanded the prerogatives of the office. This development was particularly pronounced after the United States emerged as a superpower at the end of World War II. It reflected the perception that assertive leadership was necessary if the United States was to act effectively in an international environment made increasingly dangerous by the Cold War.

THE EXECUTIVE BRANCH   The president's dominant role in foreign policy is also due to the growth of executive institutions. The National Security Act, passed by Congress in 1947, was instrumental in expanding the foreign policy bureaucracy under the president's control. The act created the Central Intelligence Agency (CIA), which was given the responsibility for collecting and assessing foreign information. It also created the National Security Council (NSC), composed of the president, the vice president, the secretary of state, the secretary of defense, and other advisers appointed by the president, for the purpose of providing advice on foreign policy. Significantly, the 1947 act reorganized the military forces under the National Military Establishment (renamed the Department of Defense in 1949). A civilian secretary of defense serves as the head of the national military establishment, and the Joint Chiefs of Staff functions as an advisory body to the secretary.

These bureaucracies have aided the president in making timely and informed decisions on foreign policy. In terms of bureaucratic politics, they also undercut the influence and resources of the Department of State, which was created in 1789 to help the president frame and implement the nation's foreign policy. Today, still other departments in the executive branch compete aggressively for the president's attention and for congressional funding, weakening not only the State Department but also the national security bureaucracies, particularly the Department of Defense. Noteworthy is the growing influence of the economic bureaucracies, particularly the Department of the Treasury, due primarily to the increasing economic interdependence of nations and to the impact financial matters have on the health of the American economy and on the nation's international power. Other "economic" agencies and bureaucracies that struggle for a role in the foreign policy process are the Office of the United States Trade Representative, the Department of Commerce, and the Department of Agriculture.

CONGRESS   Congress is the second important player in foreign policy. The powers formally granted to Congress in the Constitution rival those of the president. They include the rights to regulate international commerce, to tax and spend for the common defense, and to declare war. Although Congress has historically deferred to the president in foreign policy, by the late 1960s Congress and important segments of the American public, reacting in part to the human and material losses in the Vietnam War, became concerned that too much power over foreign policy was concentrated in what many called an "imperial" presidency. Increasingly alarmed by the erosion of its prerogatives, Congress moved to correct the imbalance in political power within the foreign policy arena. Over the course of several years it passed a number of measures designed to rein in the presidency. Among them was the War Powers Resolution (1973), which attempted to prevent presidents from initiating and waging war without a significant congressional role.

While Congress as an institution has sought to regain some of the ground it lost to the president in the field of foreign policy, often it is partisan politics, rather than separation of powers, that is responsible for the struggle between the two branches of government. For example, in 1990 some Democrats in Congress brought suit against the first President Bush for allegedly violating the Constitution by initiating military operations against Iraq without a congressional declaration of war.

Whatever the reasons for the clash between Congress and the president, the federal courts have almost always refused to decide these conflicts. Indeed, both the Supreme Court and federal inferior courts have turned away suits by members of Congress as nonjudicial *political questions* and thus beyond the scope of the judiciary. Under these conditions, it is unlikely that control over foreign policy will shift significantly in favor of Congress.

As noted earlier, the president has enormous resources at his disposal. Despite its interest in exercising more control over foreign policy, Congress is much more concerned with domestic politics. The tight rhythm of the electoral cycle (all members of the House of Representatives are elected every two years, as is one-third of the Senate) means that incumbents are interested primarily in satisfying the concerns of their constituents in order to win reelection.

Given these realities, it is difficult to maintain a national perspective in policy making. For example, legislators often view military procurement issues in terms of pork-barrel politics and relations with specific countries in terms of domestic ethnic politics. Inevitably, Congress is strongly influenced by public opinion, which can be volatile and uninformed on foreign policy issues. By contrast, the president is less influenced by the parochialism that grips Congress. The chief executive's perspective and interests are shaped by the fact that he holds office for four years and has a national constituency. For the president, advancing the national interest offers the greatest electoral rewards. Thus, the structure of incentives is quite different for Congress and for the president in terms of the attention and interest each is willing to muster for foreign policy questions.

Congress is also weak in terms of foreign policy due to low levels of power and authority. Its size makes consensus and discipline difficult to achieve. Power is also fragmented in Congress due to the public nature of congressional debate, the pressures of the electoral cycle, and the realities of partisan politics. The

CLOSE-UP

THE SUPREME COURT AND FOREIGN AFFAIRS

The U.S. Supreme Court has decided relatively few cases involving foreign affairs and has played a relatively minor role in this area. One such occasion came in 1936, when the Court decided *United States v. Curtiss-Wright Export Co.** In the first part of the opinion, written by Justice Sutherland, the Court emphasized that foreign affairs are exclusively the concern of the national government and that the states are barred from dealing with other nations. The opinion then proceeded to state that the president is the primary actor in issues of an international nature:

In this vast external realm with its important, complicated, delicate and manifold problems, the President alone has the power to speak or listen as a representative of the nation....

It is important to bear in mind that we are here dealing not alone with an authority vested in the President by an exercise of legislative power, but such an authority plus the

very delicate, plenary and exclusive power of the President as the sole organ of the federal government in the field of international relations.... Moreover, he, not Congress, has the better opportunity of knowing the conditions which prevail in foreign countries, and especially is this true in times of war. He has his confidential sources of information. He has his agents in the form of diplomatic, consular and other officials....

American presidents have frequently cited the *Curtiss-Wright* case as a legal justification for actions they have taken in foreign affairs. Since the Vietnam War, however, Congress has questioned this constitutional theory of presidential power. The adoption of the War Powers Resolution in 1973 is one example of a different view of international relations held by many members of Congress.

*299 U.S. 304 (1936).

reforms of the 1970s that weakened the principle of committee leadership made it even less likely that Congress would be able to speak with authority and unity on foreign policy questions. Finally, Congress is plagued by lack of expertise. While some members have developed considerable expertise in foreign policy matters, aided by intelligence data from the executive branch, Congress as a whole suffers from a lack of expertise that enables the chief executive to take the lead in formulating and implementing foreign policy.

It would be wrong, however, to assume that Congress has little influence on foreign policy.[38] It has an important weapon that it has wielded on several occasions over the past three decades: eliminating or restricting funding for foreign policy. In 1973, as American involvement in the Vietnam War wound down, Congress stopped all funding for U.S. military operations in Vietnam, Laos, and Cambodia. On two occasions between 1982 to 1986, Congress passed legislation designed to prevent the funding of President Reagan's efforts to aid the Nicaraguan *Contras* anticommunist guerrillas who sought to overthrow the leftist, pro–Soviet Sandinista government.

Further, the United States Senate must approve by a two-thirds vote all treaties negotiated by the executive branch of government. Although this power is infrequently exercised, it was recently used on one important occasion. In November 1999 the U.S. Senate used this constitutional power to reject the Comprehensive Nuclear Test Ban Treaty, a multilateral agreement that President Clinton had vigorously supported.

Societal Sources

Domestic *societal* forces that influence foreign policy include a diverse array of interests, such as ethnic groups, unions, manufacturers' associations, and the media.[39] More generally, public opinion as a whole exerts pressure on the formulation and implementation of foreign policy. Although it is difficult to determine exactly how much influence these societal forces have on foreign policy, it is clear that in a democratic political system, nongovernmental pressures on foreign policy—in the form of mobilized interest groups, the media, and elections—are important. Moreover, the American political system is more decentralized than most other advanced industrial democracies, whose governments can more directly regulate the behavior of labor and capital and thus reduce societal pressures on the foreign policy process. In the absence of formal linkages between government and society in the United States, the government is less able to control the foreign policy process.[40]

INTEREST GROUPS What role do interest groups play in shaping U.S. foreign policy? Studies of interest groups and their relationship to the foreign policy-making process point to the following conclusions:[41]

- The influence of interest groups varies from one issue to another; less important issues tend to be subject to more group influence.
- Single-issue groups are usually more successful than large, multi-issue organizations.
- Interest groups have only a limited ability to shape public opinion on foreign policy.
- Interest group activity and influence tends to increase during the electoral season.
- It is difficult for interest groups to gain access to the president and easier for them to wield power over policy making in Congress.

Of the thousands of interest groups that seek to influence policy, economic or business groups appear to have the most influence. Specifically, large corporations, which have significant financial resources, are in the best position to influence the policy process, primarily through campaign contributions.[42] Scholars and analysts are divided over precisely how much influence business groups—and interest groups in general—have on the foreign policy process. Nevertheless, it is generally agreed that interest groups have more policy clout today than in the past. However, although studies have documented the important role of economic groups in setting the agenda, they still find that broad domestic political goals and international pressures tend to have a greater impact on policy choices.[43]

But the terrorist attacks of September 11 drastically altered the influence of interest groups in the formulation of foreign policy that had characterized American government in recent decades. The power of the president always increases during wartime. At the same time Congress gives greater deference to the nation's chief executive, and the influence of interest groups declines.

The first years of America's war on terrorism exhibited each of these tendencies. Shortly after the September 11 attack, Congress passed legislation granting the executive branch of government new powers to deal with domestic terrorism. In the fall of 2002, it delegated to the president the right to use force against the regime of Saddam Hussein in Iraq if that nation did not eliminate its weapons of mass destruction. Although there was considerable domestic opposition to beginning a war on Iraq, in March 2003 President Bush authorized military action against this nation that resulted in the rapid destruction of Saddam Hussein's government.

THE MEDIA   The importance of the media in the U.S. foreign policy process is well documented.[44] Policymakers and **policy influentials,** individuals with expertise and access to the governmental decision-making process, rely on the media for information and advice, even in times of crisis. They are especially dependent on what is known as the "prestige press", a select group of media organs that includes *The New York Times, The Washington Post,* and the *Wall Street Journal.*

The media influence foreign policy in a number of ways. They frame the policy agenda by emphasizing certain stories and ignoring others. Policymakers, in turn, sometimes feel pressured to respond to the issues that attract the most media attention.

The increasingly rapid media coverage of global events—largely a function of technological advances—has also forced the process of making foreign policy into a much shorter time frame. The images of dead American soldiers in Iraq and of captured and beheaded civilian workers in that country put pressure on policymakers to respond rapidly. Reflecting the interaction of the media and democratic governance, these constraints create important obstacles to effective policy making.

CONCLUSION

This brief exploration of the intellectual foundations of U.S. foreign policy underlines the complex pressures that influence America's relations with the world. While the Cold War brought clarity to U.S. foreign policy it also placed important limits on American behavior abroad. Victory in the Cold War established the United States as the only superpower in the world. Fewer constraints existed on our behavior, but there was also less certainty about our role in this new international environment. Partly as a response to this situation, the United States turned its attention away from international problems and toward personal and domestic matters.

The September 11 terrorist attacks on the United States brought an abrupt end to the general indifference of Americans to issues of foreign policy that had characterized the 1990s. The nation was forced to confront a new and different type of international enemy and to formulate new policies to combat the threat of Islamic terrorism. These new policies produced a number of significant successes. In less than two years following the attacks on the United States, two hostile regimes had been replaced through military action: the Taliban in Afghanistan and Saddam Hussein's government in Iraq. Many terrorists had been arrested and charged with criminal conduct both in the United States and in many nations of the world. And while terrorist attacks have continued to occur in other parts of the world, none has yet taken place on U.S. soil.

QUESTIONS FOR THOUGHT

1. What are the main beliefs of those who favor realism as a theory of international relations?
2. What are the main beliefs of those who favor liberalism as a theory of international relations?
3. What is the Monroe Doctrine? The Roosevelt Corollary?
4. How was the policy of containment applied by the United States during the Cold War with the former Soviet Union?
5. What are the main constitutional powers of the president and Congress in foreign policy?
6. What is the preemption doctrine?

INTERNET ACTIVITIES

1. *Foreign Policy Association.* Go to **www.fpa.org**. Go to "Resource Library" and choose an issue. Write an essay about one of the Great Decisions issues found on the site.
2. *American Foreign Policy Council.* Go to **www.afpc.org**. Examine the issues and articles, and write an essay on your feelings about one of the topics.

KEY TERMS

anarchy
balance of power
collective security
containment
detente
hegemon
isolationism

liberalism
mercantilism
Monroe Doctrine
multilateralism
policy influentials
preemption
realism

realpolitik
Roosevelt Corollary
selective engagement
terrorism
unilateralism

SUGGESTED READING

Adler, David Gray, and Larry N. George, eds. *The Constitution and the Conduct of American Foreign Policy.* Lawrence, KS: The University Press of Kansas, 1996.

Allison, Graham T., and Gregory Treverton, eds. *Rethinking American Security: Beyond Cold War to New World Order.* New York: Norton, 1992.

Caraley, Demetrious James, ed. *The New American Interventionism.* New York: Columbia University Press, 1999.

Haass, Richard N. *The Reluctant Sheriff: The United States After the Cold War.* New York: Council on Foreign Relations Press, 1997.

Huntington, Samuel P. *The Clash of Civilizations and the Remaking of World Order.* New York: Simon & Schuster, 1996.

Ikenberry, G. John, ed. *American Foreign Policy: Theoretical Essays,* 2nd ed. New York: HarperCollins, 1996.

Khalilzad, Zalmay. *From Containment to Global Leadership? America and the World After the Cold War.* Santa Monica, CA: The Rand Corporation, 1995.

McDougall, Walter A. *Promised Land, Crusader State: The American Encounter with the World Since 1776.* New York: Houghton Mifflin, 1997.

Nye, Joseph S., Jr. *Bound to Lead: The Changing Nature of American Power.* New York: Basic Books, 1990.

Schulzinger, Robert D. *A Time for War: The United States and Vietnam, 1941–1975.* New York: Oxford University Press, 1997.

NOTES

1. Kenneth N. Waltz, *Theory of International Politics* (Reading, MA:Addison-Wesley, 1979).

2. See Peter J. Katzenstein, ed., *Between Power and Plenty: Foreign Economic Policies of Advanced Industrial States* (Madison: University of Wisconsin Press, 1978); and Idem, *Small States in World Markets: Industrial Policy in Europe* (Ithaca: Cornell University Press, 1985).

3. Robert Jervis, "Cooperation Under the Security Dilemma," *World Politics* 30 (2) (January 1978): 167-214.

4. On these points, see especially, Arnold Wolfers, *Discord and Collaboration. Essays on International Politics* (Baltimore: Johns Hopkins University Press, 1965); Geoffrey Blainey, *The Causes of War* (New York: Free Press, 1988); Robert Gilpin, *War and Change in World Politics* (New York: Cambridge University Press, 1983); Hans J. Morgenthau, *Politics Among Nations: The Struggle for Power and Peace,* 6th ed. (New York: McGraw-Hill, 1988); and Waltz, *Theory of International Politics.* For useful compilations of excerpted texts, see Richard K. Betts, ed., *Conflict After the Cold War: Arguments on Causes of War and Peace* (New York: Macmillan, 1994); and Michael E. Brown, Sean M. Lynn-Jones, and Steven E. Miller, eds., *The Perils of Anarchy: Contemporary Realism and International Security* (Cambridge: MIT Press, 1995).

5. Waltz, *Theory of International Politics.*

6. Ibid; and Stephen M. Walt, *The Origins of Alliances* (Ithaca: Cornell University Press, 1990).

7. Seymour Martin Lipset, *The First New Nation* (Garden City, NY: Anchor Books, 1967).

8. See especially, Hans J. Morgenthau, *In Defense of the National Interest* (New York: Knopf, 1951).

9. See Dexter Perkins, *Hands Off: A History of the Monroe Doctrine* (Boston: Little, Brown, 1941).

10. Cited in Morgenthau, *In Defense of the National Interest,* p. 20.

11. Edward Mead Earle, "Adam Smith, Alexander Hamilton, Friedrich List: The Economic Foundations of Military Power," in Peter Paret, ed., *Makers of Modern Strategy: From Machiavelli to the Nuclear Age* (Princeton, NJ: Princeton University Press, 1986), pp. 217-61.

12. Generally on this period, see Stephen E. Ambrose, *Rise to Globalism: American Foreign Policy 1938-1976* (New York: Penguin, 1976); and John Spanier, *American Foreign Policy Since WWII,* 9th ed. (Holt, Rinehart & Winston, 1982).

13. On the Cold War, see for example: John Lewis Gaddis, *The United States and the Origins of the Cold War 1941-1947* (New York: Columbia University Press, 1972); Idem, *Strategies of Containment* (New York: Oxford University Press, 1982); Idem, *The Long Peace: Inquiries into the History of the Cold War* (New York: Oxford University Press, 1987); Idem, *We Now Know: Rethinking Cold War History* (New York: Oxford,

1997); Raymond L. Garthoff, *Detente and Confrontation: American-Soviet Relations from Nixon to Reagan,* 2nd ed. (Washington, DC: Brookings Institution, 1989). On the nuclear dimension, see McGeorge Bundy, *Danger and Survival: Choices About the Bomb in the First Fifty Years* (New York: Random House, 1988); and Lawrence Freedman, *The Evolution of Nuclear Strategy* (New York: St. Martin's Press, 1994).

14. George C. Herring, *America's Longest War: The United States and Vietnam* (New York: Knopf, 1986); Leslie Gelb with Richard K. Betts, *The Irony of Vietnam: The System Worked* (Washington, DC: Brookings Institution, 1979); and Timothy J. Lomperis, *The War Everyone Lost—and Won* (Washington, DC: Congressional Quarterly Press, 1984).

15. For a useful discussion of liberalism as an ideology, see Michael W. Doyle, *Ways of War and Peace: Realism, Liberalism, and Socialism* (New York: Norton, 1987).

16. See Inis Claude, *Swords into Plowshares: The Problems and Process of International Organization* (New York: McGraw Hill, 1984).

17. E.H. Carr, *The Twenty Years Crisis, 1919-1939,* 2nd ed. (London: Macmillan, 1946).

18. Richard K. Betts, "Systems for Peace or Causes of War? Collective Security, Arms Control, and the New Europe," *International Security* 17 (1) (Summer 1992).

19. The classic treatment of this perspective is Hedley Bull, *The Anarchical Society* (New York: Columbia University Press, 1977).

20. Robert Keohane and Joseph Nye, *Power and Interdependence,* 2nd ed. (Boston: Little, Brown, 1989).

21. See Bruce Russett, *Grasping the Democratic Peace: Principles for a Post-Cold War World* (Princeton, NJ: Princeton University Press, 1993).

22. Robert Keohane, *After Hegemony: Cooperation and Discord in the World Political Economy* (Princeton: Princeton University Press, 1984); Idem, "Neoliberal Institutionalism: A Perspective on World Politics," *International Institutionalism: Essays in International Relations Theory* (Boulder, CO: Westview Press, 1989), pp. 1-11.

23. See for example, John Gerard Ruggie, "Multilateralism: The Anatomy of an Institution," *International Organization* 46 (Fall 1992).

24. See Robert Gilpin, *The Political Economy of International Relations* (Princeton: Princeton University Press, 1987), pp. 72-80; and Keohane, *After Hegemony,* pp. 31-46; 88-103.

25. For the debate, see the useful compilation of articles in Michael E. Brown, et al., eds., *America's Strategic Choices* (Cambridge, MA: MIT Press, 1998).

26. On these points, see especially the chapters by Joseph Grieco, Stephen Krasner, and Michael Mastanduno in David A. Baldwin, ed., *Neorealism and Neoliberalism* (New York: Columbia University Press, 1993).

27. See Henry S. Farber and Joanne Gowa, "Polities and Peace," *International Security* 20 (2) (Fall 1995): 123–46; and Christopher Layne, "Kant or Cant: The Myth of the Democratic Peace," *International Security* 19 (2) (Fall 1994): 5–49.

28. See, for example, the argument in John J. Mearsheimer, "Back to the Future: Instability in Europe after the Cold War," *International Security* 14 (Summer 1990): 5–56.

29. Francis Fukuyama, *The End of History and the Last Man* (New York: Free Press, 1992).

30. See Robert Jervis, "The Future of World Politics," *International Security* 16 (3) (Winter 1991/92); also Donald M. Snow, *National Security: Defense Policy for a New International Order* (New York: St. Martins Press, 1995).

31. Edward Mansfield and Jack Snyder, "Democratization and War," *Foreign Affairs* 74 (May/June 1995): 79–97.

32. On these issues, see Cynthia Roberts and Thomas Sherlock, "Bringing the Russian State Back In: Explanations for the Derailed Transition to a Market Democracy," *Comparative Politics* (July 1999): 477–498.

33. Joseph N. Nye, Jr. *Understanding International Conflicts,* 4th ed. (New York: Longmans, 2003), p. 226.

34. *www.whitehouse.gov/news/releases/2002/06/20020601-3.html.*

35. *www.whitehouse.gov/NSC/NSSALL.html*

36. See Helen V. Milner, *Interests, Institutions, and Information: Domestic Politics and International Relations* (Princeton, NJ: Princeton University Press, 1997); Robert D. Putnam, "Diplomacy and Domestic Politics: The Logic of Two-Level Games," *International Organization* 42 (Summer 1988): 427–60.

37. See the classic work, Louis Henkin, *Foreign Affairs and the Constitution* (Mineola, NY: The Foundation Press, 1972). See also Michael J. Glennon, *Constitutional Diplomacy* (Princeton, NJ: Princeton University Press, 1990). For recent, general examinations of the American foreign policy process, see James M. McCormick, *American Foreign Policy and Process* (Itasca, IL: F.E. Peacock, 1998); and Charles Keg-

ley and Eugene Wittkopf, *American Foreign Policy: Pattern and Process* (New York: St. Martins Press, 1996).

38. See Thomas M. Franck and Edward Weisband, *Foreign Policy by Congress* (New York: Oxford University Press, 1979); and Thomas E. Mann, ed., *A Question of Balance* (Washington, DC: Brookings Institution, 1990).

39. See Chapter 5 for a more complete examination of interest groups.

40. See Thomas Risse-Kappen, "Public Opinion, Domestic Structure, and Foreign Policy in Liberal Democracies," *World Politics* 43 (July 1991): 479–512; and Idem, *Cooperation Among Democracies: The European Influence on U.S. Foreign Policy* (Princeton, NJ: Princeton University Press, 1995).

41. Lester Milbrath, "Interest Groups and Foreign Policy," in James N. Rosenau, ed., *Domestic Sources of Foreign Policy* (New York: Free Press, 1967), pp. 231–52. For a general discussion of interest groups and the foreign policy process, see L. Harmon Ziegler and G. Wayne Peak, *Interest Groups in American Society* (Englewood Cliffs, NJ: Prentice Hall, 1972); and Norman J. Ornstein and Shirley Elder, *Interest Groups, Lobbying, and Policy-Making* (Washington, DC: Congressional Quarterly Press, 1978). See also Kegley and Wittkopf, *American Foreign Policy,* pp. 312–313.

42. For an influential statement, see Charles Lindblom, *Politics and Markets: The World's Political and Economic Systems* (New York: Basic Books, 1977).

43. See John W. Dietrich, "Interest Groups and Foreign Policy: Clinton and the China MFN Debates," *Presidential Studies Quarterly* 29 (2) (June 1999): 280–96; and B. Dan Wood and Jeffrey S. Peake, "The Dynamics of Foreign Policy Agenda Setting," *American Political Science Review* 92 (1) (March 1998): 173–84.

44. On the media in the American foreign policy process, see Bernard Cohen, *The Press and Foreign Policy* (Princeton: Princeton University Press, 1963); and Nicholas O. Berry, *Foreign Policy and the Press* (Westport, CT: Greenwood Press, 1990).

Appendix A

THE DECLARATION OF INDEPENDENCE

When in the course of human events, it becomes necessary for one people to dissolve the political bands which have connected them with another, and to assume among the Powers of the earth, the separate and equal station to which the Laws of Nature and of Nature's God entitle them, a decent respect to the opinions of mankind requires that they should declare the causes which impel them to the separation.

We hold these truths to be self-evident, that all men are created equal, that they are endowed by their Creator with certain unalienable Rights, that among these are Life, Liberty and the pursuit of Happiness.—That to secure these rights, Governments are instituted among Men, deriving their just powers from the consent of the governed. That whenever any Form of Government becomes destructive of these ends, it is the Right of the People to alter or to abolish it, and to institute new Government, laying its foundation on such principles and organizing its powers in such form, as to them shall seem most likely to effect their Safety and Happiness. Prudence, indeed, will dictate that Governments long established should not be changed for light and transient causes; and accordingly all experience hath shown that mankind are more disposed to suffer, while evils are sufferable, than to right themselves by abolishing the forms to which they are accustomed. But when a long train of abuses and usurpations, pursuing invariably the same Object, evinces a design to reduce them under absolute Despotism, it is their right, it is their duty, to throw off such Government, and to provide new Guards for their future security.—Such has been the patient sufferance of these Colonies; and such is now the necessity which constrains them to alter their former Systems of Government. The history of the present King of Great Britain is a history of repeated injuries and usurpations, all having in direct object the establishment of an absolute Tyranny over these States. To prove this, let Facts be submitted to a candid world.

He has refused his Assent to Laws, the most wholesome and necessary for the public good.

He has forbidden his Governors to pass Laws of immediate and pressing importance, unless suspended in their operation till his Assent should be obtained; and when so suspended, he has utterly neglected to attend to them.

He has refused to pass other Laws for the accommodation of large districts of people, unless those people would relinquish the right of Representation in the Legislature, a right inestimable to them and formidable to tyrants only.

He has called together legislative bodies at places unusual, uncomfortable, and distant from the depository of their Public Records, for the sole purpose of fatiguing them into compliance with his measures.

He has dissolved Representative Houses repeatedly, for opposing with manly firmness his invasions on the rights of the people.

He has refused for a long time, after such dissolutions, to cause others to be elected; whereby the Legislative Powers, incapable of Annihilation, have returned to the People at large for their exercise; the State remaining in the mean time exposed to all the dangers of invasion from without, and convulsions within.

He has endeavoured to prevent the population of these States; for that purpose obstructing the Laws of Naturalization of Foreigners, refusing to pass others to encourage their migration hither, and raising the conditions of new Appropriations of Lands.

He has obstructed the Administration of Justice, by refusing his Assent to Laws for establishing Judiciary Powers.

He has made Judges dependent on his Will alone, for the tenure of their offices, and the amount and payment of their salaries.

He has erected a multitude of New Offices, and sent hither swarms of Officers to harass our People, and eat out their substance.

He has kept among us, in times of peace, Standing Armies without the Consent of our legislature.

He has affected to render the Military independent of and superior to the Civil Power.

He has combined with others to subject us to a jurisdiction foreign to our constitution, and unacknowledged by our laws giving his Assent to their acts of pretended legislation:

For quartering large bodies of armed troops among us:

For protecting them, by a mock Trial, from Punishment for any Murders which they should commit on the inhabitants of these States:

For cutting off our Trade with all parts of the world:

For imposing taxes on us without our Consent:

For depriving us in many cases, of the benefits of Trial by Jury:

For transporting us beyond Seas to be tried for pretended offences:

For abolishing the free System of English Laws in a neighboring Province, establishing therein an Arbitrary government, and enlarging its Boundaries so as to render it at once an example and fit instrument for introducing the same absolute rule into these Colonies:

For taking away our Charters, abolishing our most valuable Laws, and altering fundamentally the Forms of our Governments:

For suspending our own Legislature, and declaring themselves invested with Power to legislate for us in all cases whatsoever.

He has abdicated Government here, by declaring us out of his Protection and waging War against us.

He has plundered our seas, ravaged our Coasts, burnt our towns, and destroyed the lives of our people.

He is at this time transporting large armies of foreign mercenaries to compleat the works of death, desolation and tyranny, already begun with circumstances of Cruelty & perfidy scarcely paralleled in the most barbarous ages, and totally unworthy the Head of a civilized nation.

He has constrained our fellow Citizens taken Captive on the high Seas to bear Arms against their Country, to become the executioners of their friends and Brethren, or to fall themselves by their Hands.

He has excited domestic insurrections amongst us, and has endeavoured to bring on the inhabitants of our frontiers, the merciless Indian Savages, whose known rule of warfare, is an undistinguished destruction of all ages, sexes and conditions.

In every stage of these Oppressions We have Petitioned for Redress in the most humble terms: Our repeated Petitions have been answered only by repeated injury. A Prince, whose character is thus marked by every act which may define a Tyrant, is unfit to be the ruler of a free People.

Nor have We been wanting in attention to our British brethren. We have warned them from time to time of attempts by their legislature to extend an unwarrantable jurisdiction over us. We have reminded them of the circumstances of our emigration and settlement here. We have appealed to their native justice and magnanimity, and we have conjured them by the ties of our common kindred to disavow these usurpations, which, would inevitably interrupt our connections and correspondence. They too have been deaf to the voice of justice and of consanguinity. We must, therefore, acquiesce in the necessity, which denounces our Separation, and hold them, as we hold the rest of mankind, Enemies in War, in Peace, Friends.

We, therefore, the Representatives of the united States of America, in General Congress, Assembled, appealing to the Supreme Judge of the world for the rectitude of our intentions, do, in the Name, and by Authority of the good People of these Colonies, solemnly publish and declare, that these United Colonies are, and of Right ought to be Free and Independent States; that they are Absolved from all allegiance to the British Crown, and that all political connection between them and the State of Great Britain, is and ought to be totally dissolved; and that as Free and Independent States, they have full Power to levy War, conclude Peace, contract Alliances, establish Commerce, and to do all other Acts and Things which Independent States may of right do. And for the support of this Declaration, with a firm reliance on the Protection of Divine Providence, we mutually pledge to each other our Lives, our Fortunes and our sacred Honor.

Appendix B

THE ARTICLES OF CONFEDERATION

To all to whom these Presents shall come, we the under signed Delegates of the States affixed to our Names send greeting. Whereas the Delegates of the United States of America in Congress assembled did on the fifteenth day of November in the Year of our Lord One Thousand Seven Hundred and Seventy seven, and in the Second Year of the Independence of America agree to certain articles of Confederation and perpetual Union between the States of Newhampshire, Massachusetts-bay, Rhode Island and Providence Plantations, Connecticut, New York, New Jersey, Pennsylvania, Delaware, Maryland, Virginia, North-Carolina, South-Carolina and Georgia in the Words following, viz, "Articles of Confederation and perpetual Union between the States of Newhampshire, Massachusetts-bay, Rhode Island and Providence Plantations, Connecticut, New-York, New-Jersey, Pennsylvania, Delaware, Maryland, Virginia, North-Carolina, South-Carolina and Georgia."

Article I. The Stile of this confederacy shall be "The United States of America."

Article II. Each state retains its sovereignty, freedom and independence, and every Power, Jurisdiction and right, which is not by this confederation expressly delegated to the United States, in Congress assembled.

Article III. The said states hereby severally enter into a firm league of friendship with each other, for their common defence, the security of their Liberties, and their mutual and general welfare, binding themselves to assist each other, against all force offered to, or attacks made upon them, or any of them, on account of religion, sovereignty, trade, or any other pretence whatever.

Article IV. The better to secure and perpetuate mutual friendship and intercourse among the people of the different states in this union, the free inhabitants of each of these states, paupers, vagabonds and fugitives from Justice excepted, shall be entitled to all privileges and immunities of free citizens in the several states; and the people of each state shall have free ingress and regress to and from any other state, and shall enjoy therein all the privileges of trade and commerce, subject to the same duties, impositions and restrictions as the inhabitants thereof respectively, provided that such restriction shall not extend so far as to prevent the removal of property imported into any state, to any other state of which the Owner is an inhabitant; provided also that no imposition, duties or restriction shall be laid by any state, on the property of the united states, or either of them.

If any Person guilty of, or charged with treason, felony, or other high misdemeanor in any state, shall flee from Justice, and be found in any of the united states, he shall upon demand of the Governor or executive power, of the state from which he fled, be delivered up and removed to the state having jurisdiction of his offence.

Full faith and credit shall be given in each of these states to the records, acts and judicial proceedings of the courts and magistrates of every other state.

Article V. For the more convenient management of the general interests of the united states, delegates shall be annually appointed in such manner as the legislature of each state shall direct, to meet in Congress on the first Monday in November, in every year, with a power reserved to each state, to recal its delegates, or any of them, at any time within the year, and to send others in their stead, for the remainder of the Year.

No state shall be represented in Congress by less than two, nor by more than seven Members; and no person shall be capable of being a delegate for more than three years in any term of six years; nor shall any person, being a delegate, be capable of holding any office under the united states, for which he, or another for his benefit receives any salary, fees or emolument of any kind.

Each state shall maintain its own delegates in a meeting of the states, and while they act as members of the committee of the states.

In determining questions in the united states, in Congress assembled, each state shall have one vote.

Freedom of speech and debate in Congress shall not be impeached or questioned in any Court, or place out of Congress, and the members of congress shall be protected in their persons from arrests and imprisonments, during the time of their going to and from, and attendance on congress, except for treason, felony, or breach of the peace.

Article VI. No state without the Consent of the united states in congress assembled, shall send any embassy to, or receive any embassy from, or enter into any conference, agreement, alliance or treaty with any King prince or state; nor shall any person holding any office of profit or trust under the united states, or any of them, accept of any present, emolument, office or title of any kind whatever from any king, prince or foreign state; nor shall the united states in congress assembled, or any of them, grant any title of nobility.

No two or more states shall enter into any treaty, confederation or alliance whatever between them, without the consent of the united states in congress assembled, specifying accurately the purposes for which the same is to be entered into, and how long it shall continue.

No state shall lay any imposts or duties, which may interfere with any stipulations in treaties, entered into by the united states in congress assembled, with any king, prince or state, in pursuance of any treaties already proposed by congress, to the courts of France and Spain.

No vessels of war shall be kept up in time of peace by any state, except such number only, as shall be deemed necessary by the united states in congress assembled, for the defence of such state, or its trade; nor shall any body of forces be kept up by any state, in time of peace, except such number only, as in the judgment of the united states, in congress assem-bled, shall be deemed requisite to garrison the forts necessary for the defence of such state; but every state shall always keep up a well regulated and disci-plined militia, sufficiently armed and accoutred, and shall provide and constantly have ready for use, in public stores, a due number of field pieces and tents, and a proper quantity of arms, ammunition and camp equipage.

No state shall engage in any war without the con-sent of the united states in congress assembled, unless such state be actually invaded by enemies, or shall have received certain advice of a resolution being formed by some nation of Indians to invade such state, and the danger is so imminent as not to admit of a delay, till the united states in congress assembled can be consulted: nor shall any state grant commis-sions to any ships or vessels of war, nor letters of mar-que or reprisal, except it be after a declaration of war by the united states in congress, assembled, and then only against the kingdom or state and the subjects thereof, against which war has been so declared, and under such regulations as shall be established by the united states in congress assembled, unless such state be infested by pirates, in which case vessels of war may be fitted out for that occasion, and kept so long as the danger shall continue, or until the united states in congress assembled shall determine otherwise.

Article VII. When land-forces are raised by any state for the common defence, all officers of or under the rank of colonel, shall be appointed by the legisla-ture of each state respectively by whom such forces shall be raised, or in such manner as such state shall direct, and all vacancies shall be filled up by the state which first made the appointment.

Article VIII. All charges of war, and all other ex-pences that shall be incurred for the common de-fence or general welfare, and allowed by the united states in congress assembled, shall be defrayed out of a common treasury, which shall be supplied by the several states, in proportion to the value of all land within each state, granted to or surveyed for any Person, as such land and the buildings and improve-ments thereon shall be estimated according to such mode as the united states in congress assembled, shall from time to time direct and appoint. The taxes for paying that proportion shall be laid and levied by the authority and direction of the legislatures of the sev-eral states within the time agreed upon by the united states in congress assembled.

Article IX. The united states in congress assembled, shall have the sole and exclusive right and power of determining on peace and war, except in the cases mentioned in the sixth article—of sending and receiving ambassadors—entering into treaties and alliances, provided that no treaty of commerce shall be made whereby the legislative power of the respective states shall be restrained from imposing such imposts and duties on foreigners, as their own people are subjected to, or from prohibiting the exportation or importation of any species of goods or commodities whatsoever—of establishing rules for deciding in all cases, what captures on land or water shall be legal, and in what manner prizes taken by land or naval forces in the service of the united states shall be divided or appropriated—of granting letters of marque and reprisal in times of peace—appointing courts for the trial of piracies and felonies committed on the high seas and establishing courts for receiving and determining finally appeals in all cases of captures, provided that no member of congress shall be appointed a judge of any of the said courts.

The united states in congress assembled shall also be the last resort on appeal in all disputes and differences now subsisting or that hereafter may arise between two or more states concerning boundary, jurisdiction or any other cause whatever; which authority shall always be exercised in the manner following. Whenever the legislative or executive authority or lawful agent of any state in controversy with another shall present a petition to congress stating the matter in question and praying for a hearing, notice thereof shall be given by order of congress to the legislative or executive authority of the other state in controversy, and a day assigned for the appearance of the parties by their lawful agents, who shall then be directed to appoint by joint consent, commissioners or judges to constitute a court for hearing and determining the matter in question: but if they cannot agree, congress shall name three persons out of each of the united states, and from the list of such persons each party shall alternately strike out one, the petitioners beginning, until the number shall be reduced to thirteen; and from that number no less than seven, nor more than nine names as congress shall direct, shall in the presence of congress be drawn out by lot, and the persons whose names shall be so drawn or any five of them, shall be commissioners or judges, to hear and finally determine the controversy, so always as a major part of the judges who shall hear the cause shall agree in the determi-

nation: and if either party shall neglect to attend at the day appointed, without shewing reasons, which congress shall judge sufficient, or being present shall refuse to strike, the congress shall proceed to nominate three persons out of each state, and the secretary of congress shall strike in behalf of such party absent or refusing; and the judgment and sentence of the court to be appointed, in the manner before prescribed, shall be final and conclusive; and if any of the parties shall refuse to submit to the authority of such court, or to appear or defend their claim or cause, the court shall nevertheless proceed to pronounce sentence, or judgment, which shall in like manner be final and decisive the judgment or sentence and other proceedings being in either case transmitted to congress, and lodged among the acts of congress for the security of the parties concerned: provided that every commissioner, before he sits in judgment, shall take an oath to be administered by one of the judges of the supreme or superior court of the state, where the cause shall be tried, "well and truly to hear and determine the matter in question, according to the best of his judgment, without favour, affection or hope of reward:" provided also that no state shall be deprived of territory for the benefit of the united states.

All controversies concerning the private right of soil claimed under different grants of two or more states, whose jurisdictions as they may respect such lands, and the states which passed such grants are adjusted, the said grants or either of them being at the same time claimed to have originated antecedent to such settlement of jurisdiction, shall on the petition of either party to the congress of the united states, be finally determined as near as maybe in the same manner as is before prescribed for deciding disputes respecting territorial jurisdiction between different states.

The united states in congress assembled shall also have the sole and exclusive right and power of regulating the alloy and value of coin struck by their own authority, or by that of the respective states—fixing the standard of weights and measures throughout the united states—regulating the trade and managing all affairs with the Indians, not members of any of the states, provided that the legislative right of any state within its own limits be not infringed or violated—establishing and regulating post-offices from one state to another, throughout all the united states, and exacting such postage on the papers passing thro' the same as may be requisite to defray the expences of the said office—appointing all officers of the land forces, in the service of the united states, excepting regimental officers—appointing all the officers of the naval forces, and commissioning all officers whatever in the service of the united states—making rules for the government and regulation of the said land and naval forces, and directing their operations.

The united states in congress assembled shall have authority to appoint a committee, to sit in the recess of congress, to be denominated "A Committee of the States," and to consist of one delegate from each state; and to appoint such other committees and civil officers as may be necessary for managing the general affairs of the united states under their direction—to appoint one of their number to preside, provided that no person be allowed to serve in the office of president more than one year in any term of three years; to ascertain the necessary sums of Money to be raised for the service of the united states, and to appropriate and apply the same for defraying the public expences—to borrow money, or emit bills on the credit of the united states, transmitting every half year to the respective states an account of the sums of money so borrowed or emitted,—to build and equip a navy—to agree upon the number of land forces, and to make requisitions from each state for its quota, in proportion to the number of white inhabitants in such state; which requisition shall be binding, and there-upon the legislature of each state shall appoint the regimental officers, raise the men and cloath, arm and equip them in a soldier like manner, at the expence of the united states, and the officers and men so cloathed, armed and equipped shall march to the place appointed, and within the time agreed on by the united states in congress assembled: But if the united states in congress assembled shall, on consideration of circumstances judge proper that any state should not raise men, or should raise a smaller number than its quota, and that any other state should raise a greater number of men than the quota thereof, such extra number shall be raised, officered, cloathed, armed and equipped in the same manner as the quota of such state, unless the legislature of such state shall judge that such extra number cannot be safely spared out of the same, in which case they shall raise, officer, cloath, arm and equip as many of such extra number as the judge can be safely spared. And the officers and men so cloathed, armed and equipped, shall march to the place appointed, and within the time agreed on by the united states in congress assembled.

The united states in congress assembled shall never engage in a war, nor grant letters of marque and reprisal in time of peace, nor enter into any treaties or alliances, nor coin money, nor regulate the value thereof, nor ascertain the sums and expences necessary for the defence and welfare of the united states, or any of them, nor emit bills, nor borrow money on the credit of the united states, nor appropriate money, nor agree upon the number of vessels of war, to be built or purchased, or the number of land or sea forces to be raised, nor appoint a commander in chief of the army or navy, unless nine states assent to the same: nor shall a question on any other point, except for adjourning from day to day be determined, unless by the votes of a majority of the united states in congress assembled.

The congress of the united states shall have power to adjourn to any time within the year, and to any place within the united states, so that no period of adjournment be for a longer duration than the space of six Months, and shall publish the Journal of their proceedings monthly, except such parts thereof relating to treaties, alliances or military operations, as in their judgment require secresy; and the yeas and nays of the delegates of each state on any question shall be entered on the Journal, when it is desired by any delegate; and the delegates of a state, or any of them, at his or their request shall be furnished with a transcript of the said Journal, except such parts as are above excepted, to lay before the legislatures of the several states.

Article X. The committee of the states, or any nine of them, shall be authorized to execute, in the recess of congress, such of the powers of congress as the united states in congress assembled, by the consent of nine states, shall from time to time think expedient to vest them with; provided that no power be delegated to the said committee, for the exercise of which, by the articles of confederation, the voice of nine states in congress of the united states assembled is requisite.

Article XI. Canada acceding to this confederation, and joining in the measures of the united states, shall be admitted into, and entitled to all the advantages of this union: but no other colony shall be admitted into the same, unless such admission be agreed to by nine states.

Article XII. All bills of credit emitted, monies borrowed and debts contracted by, or under the authority of congress, before the assembling of the united states, in pursuance of the present confederation, shall be deemed and considered as a charge against the united states, for payment and satisfaction whereof the said united states, and the public faith are hereby solemnly pledged.

Article XIII. Every state shall abide by the determinations of the united states in congress assembled, on all questions which by this confederation are submitted to them. And the Articles of this confederation shall be inviolably observed by every state, and the union shall be perpetual; nor shall any alteration at any time hereafter be made in any of them; unless such alteration be agreed to in a congress of the united states, and be afterwards confirmed by the legislatures of every state.

And Whereas it hath pleased the Great Governor of the World to incline the hearts of the legislatures we respectively represent in congress, to approve of, and to authorize us to ratify the said articles of con-federation and perpetual union. Know Ye that we the undersigned delegates, by virtue of the power and authority to us given for that purpose, do by these presents, in the name and in behalf of our respective constituents, fully and entirely ratify and confirm each and every of the said articles of confederation and perpetual union, and all and singular the matters and things therein contained: And we do further solemnly plight and engage the faith of our respective constituents, that they shall abide by the determinations of the united states in congress assembled, on all questions, which by the said confederation are submitted to them. And that the articles thereof shall be inviolably observed by the states we respectively represent, and that the union shall be perpetual. In Witness whereof we have hereunto set our hands in Congress. Done at Philadelphia in the state of Pennsylvania the ninth Day of July in the Year of our Lord one Thousand seven Hundred and Seventy-eight, and in the third year of the independence of America.

Appendix C

THE ANTIFEDERALISTS

STATEMENT BY GEORGE MASON
TO THE PHILADELPHIA CONVENTION

George Mason, a delegate from Virginia to the Philadelphia Convention, was one of only three delegates who refused to sign the completed draft of the proposed constitution. The other two were Elbridge Gerry of Massachusetts and Edmund Randolph, also of Virginia. A statement summarizing the views of the three men and written by Mason was presented to the Convention on September 15, 1787, just two days before that body met for the last time.

There is no Declaration of Rights, and the laws of the general government being paramount to the laws and constitution of the several States, the Declarations of Rights in the separate States are no security. Nor are the people secured even in the enjoyment of the benefit of the common law.

In the House of Representatives there is not the substance but the shadow only of representation; which can never produce proper information in the legislature, or inspire confidence in the people; the laws will therefore be generally made by men little concerned in, and unacquainted with their effects and consequences.

The Senate have the power of altering all money bills, and of originating appropriations of money, and the salaries of the officers of their own appointment, in conjunction with the president of the United States, although they are not the representatives of the people or amenable to them.

These with their other great powers, viz.: their power in the appointment of ambassadors and all public officers, in making treaties, and in trying all impeachments, their influence upon and connection with the supreme Executive from these causes, their duration of office and their being a constantly existing body, almost continually sitting, joined with their being one complete branch of the legislature, will destroy any balance in the government, and enable them to accomplish what usurpations they please upon the rights and liberties of the people.

The Judiciary of the United States is so constructed and extended, as to absorb and destroy the judiciaries of the several States; thereby rendering law as tedious, intricate and expensive, and justice as unattainable, by a great part of the community, as in England, and enabling the rich to oppress and ruin the poor.

The President of the United States has no Constitutional Council, a thing unknown in any safe and regular government. He will therefore be unsupported by proper information and advice, and will generally be directed by minions and favorites; or he will become a tool to the Senate—or a Council of State will grow out of the principal officers of the great departments; the worst and most dangerous of all ingredients for such a council in a free country; From this fatal defect has arisen the improper power of the Senate in the appointment of public officers, and the alarming dependence and connection between that branch of the legislature and the supreme Executive.

Hence also sprung that unnecessary officer the vice president, who for want of other employment is made president of the Senate, thereby dangerously blending the executive and legislative powers, besides always giving to some one of the States an unnecessary and unjust pre-eminence over the others.

The President of the United States has the unrestrained power of granting pardons for treason, which may be sometimes exercised to screen from punishment those whom he had secretly instigated to commit the crime, and thereby prevent a discovery of his own guilt.

By declaring all treaties supreme laws of the land, the Executive and the Senate have, in many cases, an exclusive power of legislation; which might have been avoided by proper distinctions with respect to treaties, and requiring the assent of the House of Representatives, where it could be done with safety.

By requiring only a majority to make all commercial and navigation laws, the five Southern States, whose produce and circumstances are totally different from that of the eight Northern and Eastern States, may be ruined, for such rigid and premature regulations may be made as will enable the merchants of the Northern and Eastern States not only to demand an exhorbitant freight, but to monopolize the purchase of the commodities at their own price, for many years, to the great injury of the landed interest, and impoverishment of the people; and the danger is the greater as the gain on one side will be in proportion to the loss on the other. Whereas requiring two-thirds of the members present in both Houses would have produced mutual moderation, promoted the general interest, and removed an insuperable objection to the adoption of this government.

Under their own construction of the general clause, at the end of the enumerated powers, the Congress may grant monopolies in trade and commerce, constitute new crimes, inflict unusual and severe punishments, and extend their powers as far as they shall think proper; so that the State legislatures have no security for the powers now presumed to remain to them, or the people for their rights.

There is no declaration of any kind, for preserving the liberty of the press, or the trial by jury in civil causes; nor against the danger of standing armies in time of peace.

The State legislatures are restrained from laying export duties on their own produce.

Both the general legislature and the State legislature are expressly prohibited making *ex post facto* laws; though there never was nor can be a legislature but must and will make such laws, when necessity and the public safety require them; which will hereafter be a breach of all the constitutions in the Union, and afford precedents for other innovations.

This government will set out a moderate aristocracy: it is at present impossible to foresee whether it will, in its operation, produce a monarchy, or a corrupt, tyrannical aristocracy; it will most probably vi-brate some years between the two, and then terminate in the one or the other.

The general legislature is restrained from prohibiting the further importation of slaves for twenty odd years; though such importations render the United States weaker, more vulnerable, and less capable of defence.

"BRUTUS": ESSAY NO. 1

During the debates over the ratification of the Constitution, the opponents of the document produced a large body of printed works. They ranged in quality from hysterical to serious. Perhaps the most carefully reasoned essays opposing the adoption of the Constitution were those that appeared between October 1787 and April 1788 in the New York Journal under the pseudonym "Brutus." "Brutus" was probably Robert Yates, a New York judge and a delegate to the Philadelphia Convention. His Essay No. 1, excerpted here, attacks the idea of a large consolidated republic, which he believed would be created by the Constitution.

The first question that presents itself on the subject is, whether a confederated government be the best for the United States or not? Or in other words, whether the thirteen United States should be reduced to one great republic, governed by one legislature, and under the direction of one executive and judicial; or whether they should continue thirteen confederated republics, under the direction and control of a supreme federal head for certain defined national purposes only?

This enquiry is important, because, although the government reported by the convention does not go to a perfect and entire consolidation, yet it approaches so near to it, that it must, if executed, certainly and infallibly terminate in it.

This government is to possess absolute and uncontrolable power, legislative, executive and judicial, with respect to every object to which it extends, for by the last clause of section 8th, article 1st, it is declared "that the Congress shall have power to make all laws which shall be necessary and proper for carrying into execution the foregoing powers, and all other powers vested by this constitution, in the government of the United States; or in any department or office thereof." And by the 6th article, it is declared "that this constitution, and the laws of the United States, which shall be made in pursuance thereof, and the treaties made, or which shall be made, under the authority of the United States, shall be the supreme law of the land; and the judges in every state shall be bound thereby, any thing in the constitution, or law of any state to the contrary notwithstanding." It appears from these articles that there is no need of any intervention of the state governments, between the Congress and the people, to execute any one power vested in the general government, and that the constitution and laws of every state are nullified and declared void, so far as they are or shall be inconsistent with this constitution, or the laws made in pursuance of it, or with treaties made under the authority of the United States.—The government then, so far as it extends, is a complete one and not a confederation. It is as much one complete government as that of New York or Massachusetts, has as absolute and perfect powers to make and execute all laws, to appoint officers, institute courts, declare offences, and annex penalties, with respect to every object to which it extends, as any other in the world. So far therefore as its powers reach, all ideas of confederation are given up and lost. It is true this government is limited to certain objects, or to speak more properly, some small degree of power is still left to the states, but a little attention to the powers vested in the general government, will convince every candid man, that if it is capable of being executed, all that is reserved for the individual states must very soon be annihilated, except so far as they are barely necessary to the organization of the general government. The powers of the general legislature extend to every case that is of the least importance—there is nothing valuable to human nature, nothing dear to free men, but what is within its power. It has authority to make laws which will affect the lives, the liberty, and property of every man in the United States; nor can the constitution or laws of any state, in any way prevent or impede the full and complete execution of every power given. The legislative power is competent to lay taxes, duties, imposts, and excises—there is no limitation to this power, unless it be said that the clause which directs the use to which those taxes, and duties shall be applied, may be said to be a limitation: but this is no restriction of the power at all, for by this clause they are to be applied to pay the debts and provide for the common defence and general welfare of the United States; but the legislature have authority to contract debts at their discretion; they are the sole judges of what is necessary to provide for the common defence, and they only are to determine what is for the general welfare; this power

therefore is neither more nor less, than a power to lay and collect taxes, imposts, and excises, at their pleasure; not only [is] the power to lay taxes unlimited, as to the amount they may require, but it is perfect and absolute to raise them in any mode they please. No state legislature, or any power in the state governments, have any more to do in carrying this into effect, than the authority of one state has to do with that of another. In the business therefore of laying and collecting taxes, the idea of confederation is totally lost, and that of one entire republic is embraced. It is proper here to remark, that the authority to lay and collect taxes is the most important of any power that can be granted; it connects with it almost all other powers, or at least will in process of time draw all other after it; it is the great means of protection, security, and defence, in a good government, and the great engine of oppression and tyranny in a bad one. This cannot fail of being the case, if we consider the contracted limits which are set by this constitution, to the late [state?] governments, on this article of raising money. No state can emit paper money—lay any duties, or imposts, on imports, or exports, but by consent of the Congress; and then the net produce shall be for the benefit of the United States: the only mean therefore left, for any state to support its government and discharge its debts, is by direct taxation; and the United States have also power to lay and collect taxes, in any way they please. Every one who has thought on the subject, must be convinced that but small sums of money can be collected in any country, by direct taxes, when the federal government begins to exercise the right of taxation in all its parts, the legislatures of the several states will find it impossible to raise monies to support their governments. Without money they cannot be supported, and they must dwindle away, and, as before observed, their powers absorbed in that of the general government.

It might be here shown, that the power in the federal legislative, to raise and support armies at pleasure, as well in peace as in war, and their control over the militia, tend, not only to a consolidation of the government, but the destruction of liberty—I shall not, however, dwell upon these, as a few observations upon the judicial power of this government, in addition to the preceding, will fully evince the truth of the position.

The judicial power of the United States is to be vested in a supreme court, and in such inferior courts as Congress may from time to time ordain and establish. The powers of these courts are very extensive;

their jurisdiction comprehends all civil causes, except such as arise between citizens of the same state; and it extends to all cases in law and equity arising under the constitution. One inferior court must be established, I presume, in each state, at least, with the necessary executive officers appendant thereto. It is easy to see, that in the common course of things, these courts will eclipse the dignity, and take away from the respectability, of the state courts. These courts will be, in themselves, totally independent of the states, deriving their authority from the United States, and receiving from them fixed salaries; and in the course of human events it is to be expected, that they will swallow up all the powers of the courts in the respective states.

Appendix D

THE FEDERALIST

Number 10

THE SIZE AND VARIETY OF THE UNION AS A CHECK ON FACTION

To the People of the State of New York:

Among the numerous advantages promised by a well-constructed Union, none deserves to be more accurately developed than its tendency to break and control the violence of faction. The friend of popular governments never finds himself so much alarmed for their character and fate, as when he contemplates their propensity to this dangerous vice. He will not fail, therefore, to set a due value on any plan which, without violating the principles to which he is attached, provides a proper cure for it. The instability, injustice, and confusion introduced into the public councils, have, in truth, been the mortal diseases under which popular governments have everywhere perished; as they continue to be the favorite and fruitful topics from which the adversaries to liberty derive their most specious declamations. The valuable improvements made by the American constitutions on the popular models, both ancient and modern, cannot certainly be too much admired; but it would be an unwarrantable partiality, to contend that they have as effectually obviated the danger on this side, as was wished and expected. Complaints are everywhere heard from our most considerate and virtuous citizens, equally the friends of public and private faith, and of public and personal liberty, that our governments are too unstable, that the public good is disregarded in the conflicts of rival parties, and that measures are too often decided, not according to the rules of justice and the rights of the minor party, but by the superior force of an interested and overbearing majority. However anxiously we may wish that these complaints had no foundation, the evidence of known facts will not permit us to deny that they are in some degree true. It will be found, indeed, on a candid review of our situation, that some of the distresses under which we labor have been erroneously charged on the operation of our governments; but it will be found, at the same time, that other causes will not alone account for many of our heaviest misfortunes; and, particularly, for that prevailing and increasing distrust of public engagements, and alarm for private rights, which are echoed from one end of the continent to the other. These must be chiefly, if not wholly, effects of the unsteadiness and injustice with which a factious spirit has tainted our public administrations.

By a faction, I understand a number of citizens, whether amounting to a majority or minority of the whole, who are united and actuated by some common impulse of passion, or of interest, adverse to the rights of other citizens, or to the permanent and aggregate interests of the community.

There are two methods of curing the mischiefs of faction: the one, by removing its causes; the other, by controlling its effects.

There are again two methods of removing the causes of faction: the one, by destroying the liberty which is essential to its existence; the other, by giving to every citizen the same opinions, the same passions, and the same interests.

It could never be more truly said than of the first remedy, that it was worse than the disease. Liberty is to faction what air is to fire, an aliment without which it instantly expires. But it could not be less folly to abolish liberty, which is essential to political life, because it nourishes faction, than it would be to wish the annihilation of air, which is essential to animal life, because it imparts to fire its destructive agency.

The second expedient is as impracticable as the first would be unwise. As long as the reason of man continues fallible, and he is at liberty to exercise it, different opinions will be formed. As long as the connection subsists between his reason and his self-love, his opinions and his passions will have a reciprocal influence on each other: and the former will be objects to which the latter will attach themselves.

The diversity in the faculties of men, from which the rights of property originate, is not less an insuperable obstacle to a uniformity of interests. The protection of these faculties is the first object of government. From the protection of different and unequal faculties of acquiring property, the possession of different degrees and kinds of property immediately results; and from the influence of these on the sentiments and views of the respective proprietors, ensues a division of the society into different interests and parties.

The latent causes of faction are thus sown in the nature of man; and we see them everywhere brought into different degrees of activity, according to the different circumstances of civil society. A zeal for different opinions concerning religion, concerning government, and many other points, as well of speculation as of practice; an attachment to different leaders ambitiously contending for preeminence and power; or to persons of other descriptions 'whose fortunes have been interesting to the human passions, have, in turn, divided mankind into parties, inflamed them with mutual animosity, and rendered them much more disposed to vex and oppress each other than to co-operate for their common good. So strong is this propensity of mankind to fall into mutual animosities, that where no substantial occasion presents itself, the most frivolous and fanciful distinctions have been sufficient to kindle their unfriendly passions and excite their most violent conflicts. But the most common and durable source of factions has been the various and unequal distribution of property. Those who hold and those who are without property have ever formed distinct interests in society. Those who are creditors, and those who are debtors, fall under a like discrimination. A landed interest, a manufacturing interest, a mercantile interest, a moneyed interest, with many lesser interests, grow up of necessity in civilized nations, and divide them into different classes, actu-ated by different sentiments and views. The regulation of these various and interfering interests forms the principal task of modern legislation, and involves the spirit of party and faction in the necessary and ordinary operations of the government.

No man is allowed to be a judge in his own cause, because his interest would certainly bias his judgment, and, not improbably, corrupt his integrity. With equal, nay with greater reason, a body of men are unfit to be both judges and parties at the same time; yet what are many of the most important acts of legislation, but so many judicial determinations, not indeed concerning the rights of single persons, but concerning the rights of large bodies of citizens? And what are the different classes of legislators but advocates and parties to the causes which they determine? Is a law proposed concerning private debts? It is a question to which the creditors are parties on one side and the debtors on the other. Justice ought to hold the balance between them. Yet the parties are, and must be, themselves the judges; and the most numerous party, or, in other words, the most powerful faction must be expected to prevail. Shall domestic manufactures be encouraged, and in what degree, by restrictions on foreign manufactures? are questions which would be differently decided by the landed and the manufacturing classes, and probably by neither with a sole regard to justice and the public good. The apportionment of taxes on the various descriptions of property is an act which seems to require the most exact impartiality; yet there is, perhaps, no legislative act in which greater opportunity and temptation are given to a predominant party to trample on the rules of justice. Every shilling with which they overburden the inferior number is a shilling saved to their own pockets.

It is in vain to say that enlightened statesmen will be able to adjust these clashing interests, and render them all subservient to the public good. Enlightened statesmen will not always be at the helm. Nor, in many cases, can such an adjustment be made at all without taking into view indirect and remote considerations, which will rarely prevail over the immediate interests which one party may find in disregarding the rights of another or the good of the whole.

The inference to which we are brought is, that the *causes* of faction cannot be removed, and that relief is only to be sought in the means of controlling its *effects*.

If a faction consists of less than a majority, relief is supplied by the republican principle, which enables the majority to defeat its sinister views by regular vote. It may clog the administration, it may convulse the society; but it will be unable to execute and mask its violence under the forms of the Constitution. When a majority is included in a faction, the form of popular government, on the other hand, enables it to sacrifice to its ruling passion or interest both the public good and the rights of other citizens. To secure the public good and private rights against the danger of such a faction, and at the same time to preserve the spirit and the form of popular government, is then the great object to which our inquiries are directed. Let me add that it is the great desideratum by which this form of government can be rescued from the opprobrium under which it has so long labored, and be recommended to the esteem and adoption of mankind.

By what means is this object attainable? Evidently by one of two only. Either the existence of the same passion or interest in a majority at the same time must be prevented, or the majority, having such coexistent passion or interest, must be rendered, by their number and local situation, unable to concert and carry into effect schemes of oppression. If the impulse and the opportunity be suffered to coincide, we well know that neither moral nor religious motives can be relied on as an adequate control. They are not found to be such on the injustice and violence of individuals, and lose their efficacy in proportion to the number combined together, that is, in proportion as their efficacy becomes needful.

From this view of the subject it may be concluded that a pure democracy, by which I mean a society consisting of a small number of citizens, who assemble and administer the government in person, can admit of no cure for the mischiefs of faction. A common passion or interest will, in almost every case, be felt by a majority of the whole; a communication and concert result from the form of government itself; and there is nothing to check the inducements to sacrifice the weaker party or an obnoxious individual. Hence it is that such democracies have ever been spectacles of turbulence and contention; have ever been found incompatible with personal security or the rights of property; and have in general been as short in their lives as they have been violent in their deaths. Theoretic politicians, who have patronized this species of government, have erroneously supposed that by reducing mankind to a perfect equality in their political rights, they would, at the same time, be perfectly equalized and assimilated in their possessions, their opinions, and their passions.

A republic, by which I mean a government in which the scheme of representation takes place, opens a different prospect, and promises the cure for which we are seeking. Let us examine the points in which it varies from pure democracy, and we shall comprehend both the nature of the cure and the efficacy which it must derive from the Union.

The two great points of difference between a democracy and a republic are: first, the delegation of the government, in the latter, to a small number of citizens elected by the rest; secondly, the greater number of citizens, and greater sphere of country, over which the latter may be extended.

The effect of the first difference is, on the one hand, to refine and enlarge the public views, by passing them through the medium of a chosen body of citizens, whose wisdom may best discern the true interest of their country, and whose patriotism and love of justice will be least likely to sacrifice it to temporary or partial considerations. Under such a regulation, it may well happen that the public voice, pronounced by the representatives of the people, will be more consonant to the public good than if pronounced by the people themselves, convened for the purpose. On the other hand, the effect may be inverted. Men of factious tempers, of local prejudices, or of sinister designs, may, by intrigue, by corruption, or by other means, first obtain the suffrages, and then betray the interests, of the people. The question resulting is, whether small or extensive republics are more favorable to the election of proper guardians of the public weal; and it is clearly decided in favor of the latter by two obvious considerations:

In the first place, it is to be remarked that, however small the republic may be, the representatives must be raised to a certain number, in order to guard against the cabals of a few; and that, however large it may be, they must be limited to a certain number, in order to guard against the confusion of a multitude. Hence, the number of representatives in the two cases not being in proportion to that of the two constituents, and being proportionally greater in the small republic, it follows that, if the proportion of fit characters be not less in the large than in the small republic, the former will present a greater option, and consequently a greater probability of a fit choice.

In the next place, as each representative will be chosen by a greater number of citizens in the large than in the small republic, it will be more difficult for unworthy candidates to practise with success the vicious arts by which elections are too often carried; and the suffrages of the people being more free, will be more likely to centre in men who possess the most attractive merit and the most diffusive and established characters.

It must be confessed that in this, as in most other cases, there is a mean, on both sides of which inconveniences will be found to lie. By enlarging too much the number of electors, you render the representative too little acquainted with all their local circumstances and lesser interests; as by reducing it too much, you render him unduly attached to these, and too little fit to comprehend and pursue great and national objects. The federal Constitution forms a happy combination in this respect; the great and aggregate interests being referred to the national, the local and particular to the State legislatures.

The other point of difference is, the greater number of citizens and extent of territory which may be brought within the compass of republican than of democratic government; and it is this circumstance principally which renders factious combinations less to be dreaded in the former than in the latter. The smaller the society, the fewer probably will be the distinct parties and interests composing it; the fewer the distinct parties and interests, the more frequently will a majority be found of the same party; and the smaller the number of individuals composing a majority, and the smaller the compass within which they are placed, the most easily will they concert and execute their plans of oppression. Extend the sphere, and you take in a greater variety of parties and interests; you make it less probable that a majority of the whole will have a common motive to invade the rights of other citizens; or if such a common motive exists, it will be more difficult for all who feel it to discover their own strength, and to act in unison with each other. Besides other impediments, it may be remarked that, where there is a consciousness of unjust or dishonorable purposes, communication is always checked by distrust in proportion to the number whose concurrence is necessary.

Hence, it clearly appears, that the same advantage which a republic has over a democracy, in controlling the effects of faction, is enjoyed by a large over a small republic,—is enjoyed by the Union over the States composing it. Does the advantage consist in the substitution of representatives whose enlightened views and virtuous sentiments render them superior to local prejudices and to schemes of injustice? It will not be denied that the representation of the Union will be most likely to possess these requisite endowments. Does it consist in the greater security afforded by a greater variety of parties, against the event of any one party being able to outnumber and oppress the rest? In an equal degree does the increased variety of parties comprised within the Union, increase this security. Does it, in fine, consist in the greater obstacles opposed to the concert and accomplishments of the secret wishes of an unjust and interested majority? Here, again, the extent of the Union gives it the most palpable advantage.

The influence of factious leaders may kindle a flame within their particular States, but will be unable to spread a general conflagration through the other States. A religious sect may degenerate into a political faction in a part of the Confederacy; but the variety of sects dispersed over the entire face of it must secure the national councils against any danger from that source. A rage for paper money, for an abolition of debts, for an equal division of property, or for any other improper or wicked project, will be less apt to pervade the whole body of the Union than a particular member of it; in the same proportion as such a malady is more likely to taint a particular county or district, than an entire State.

In the extent and proper structure of the Union, therefore, we behold a republican remedy for the diseases most incident to republican government: And according to the degree of pleasure and pride we feel in being republicans, ought to be our zeal in cherishing the spirit and supporting the character of Federalists.

Publius
(James Madison)

Number 51

CHECKS AND BALANCES

To the People of the State of New York:

To What expedient, then, shall we finally resort, for maintaining in practice the necessary partition of power among the several departments, as laid down in the Constitution? The only answer that can be given is, that as all these exterior provisions are found to be inadequate, the defect must be supplied, by so contriving the interior structure of the government as that its several constituent parts may, by their mutual relations, be the means of keeping each other in their proper places. Without presuming to undertake a full development of this important idea, I will hazard a few general observations, which may perhaps place it in a clearer light, and enable us to form a more correct judgment of the principles and structure of the government planned by the convention.

In order to lay a due foundation for that separate and distinct exercise of the different powers of government, which to a certain extent is admitted on all hands to be essential to the preservation of liberty, it is evident that each department should have a will of its own; and consequently should be so constituted that the members of each should have as little agency as possible in the appointment of the members of the others. Were this principle rigorously adhered to, it would require that all the appointments for the supreme executive, legislative, and judiciary magistracies should be drawn from the same fountain of authority, the people, through channels having no communication whatever with one another. Perhaps such a plan of constructing the several departments would be less difficult in practice than it may in contemplation appear. Some difficulties, however, and some additional expense would attend the execution of it. Some deviations, therefore, from the principle must be admitted. In the constitution of the judiciary department in particular, it might be inexpedient to insist rigorously on the principle: first, because peculiar qualifications being essential in the members, the primary consideration ought to be to select that mode of choice which best secures these qualifications; secondly, because the permanent tenure by which the appointments are held in that department, must soon destroy all sense of dependence on the authority conferring them.

It is equally evident, that the members of each department should be as little dependent as possible on those of the others, for the emoluments annexed to their offices. Were the executive magistrate, or the judges, not independent of the legislature in this particular, their independence in every other would be merely nominal.

But the great security against a gradual concentration of the several powers in the same department, consists in giving to those who administer each department the necessary constitutional means and personal motives to resist encroachments of the others. The provision for defence must in this, as in all other cases, be made commensurate to the danger of attack. Ambition must be made to counteract ambition. The interest of the man must be connected with the constitutional rights of the place. It may be a reflection on human nature, that such devices should be necessary to control the abuses of government. But what is government itself, but the greatest of all reflections on human nature? If men were angels, no government would be necessary. If angels were to govern men, neither external nor internal controls on government would be necessary. In framing a government which is to be administered by men over men, the great difficulty lies in this: you must first enable the government to control the governed; and in the next place oblige it to control itself. A dependence on the people is, no doubt, the primary control on the government; but experience has taught mankind the necessity of auxiliary precautions.

This policy of supplying, by opposite and rival interests, the defect of better motives, might be traced through the whole system of human affairs, private as well as public. We see it particularly displayed in all the subordinate distributions of power, where the constant aim is to divide and arrange the several offices in such a manner as that each may be a check on the other—that the private interest of every individual may be a sentinel over the public rights. These inventions of prudence cannot be less requisite in the distribution of the supreme powers of the State.

But it is not possible to give to each department an equal power of self-defence. In republican government, the legislative authority necessarily predominates. The remedy for this inconveniency is to divide the legislature into different branches, and to render them, by different modes of election and different principles of action, as little connected with each other as the nature of their common functions and their common dependence on the society will admit. It may even be necessary to guard against dangerous encroachments by still further precautions. As the weight of the legislative authority requires that it should be thus divided, the weakness of the executive may require, on the other hand, that it should be fortified. An absolute negative on the legislature appears, at first view, to be the natural defence with which the executive magistrate should be armed. But perhaps it would be neither altogether safe not alone sufficient. On ordinary occasions it might not be exerted with the requisite firmness, and on extraordinary occasions it might be perfidiously abused. May not this defect of an absolute negative be supplied by some qualified connection between this weaker department and the weaker branch of the stronger department, by which the latter may be led to support the constitutional rights of the former, without being too much detached from the rights of its own department?

If the principles on which these observations are founded be just, as I persuade myself they are, and they be applied as a criterion to the several State constitutions, and to the federal Constitution, it will be found that if the latter does not perfectly correspond with them, the former are infinitely less able to bear such a test.

There are, moreover, two considerations particularly applicable to the federal system of America, which place that system in a very interesting point of view.

First. In a single republic, all the power surrendered by the people is submitted to the administration of a single government; and the usurpations are guarded against by a division of the government into distinct and separate departments. In the compound republic of America, the power surrendered by the people is first divided between two distinct governments, and then the portion allotted to each subdivided among distinct and separate departments. Hence a double security arises to the rights of the people. The different governments will control each other, at the same time that each will be controlled by itself.

Second. It is of great importance in a republic not only to guard the society against the oppression of its rulers, but to guard one part of the society against the injustice of the other part. Different interests necessarily exist in different classes of citizens. If a majority be united by a common interest, the rights of the minority will be insecure. There are but two methods of providing against this evil: the one by creating a will in the community independent of the majority—that is, of the society itself; the other, by comprehending in the society so many separate descriptions of citizens as will render an unjust combination of a majority of the whole very improbable, if not impracticable. The first method prevails in all governments possessing an hereditary or self-appointed authority. This, at best, is but a precarious security; because a power independent of the society may as well espouse the unjust views of the major, as the rightful interests of the minor party, and may possibly be turned against both parties. The second method will be exemplified in the federal republic of the United States. Whilst all authority in it will be derived from and dependent on the so-

ciety, the society itself will be broken into so many parts, interests and classes of citizens, that the rights of individuals, or of the minority, will be in little danger from interested combinations of the majority. In a free government the security for civil rights must be the same as that for religious rights. It consists in the one case in the multiplicity of interests, and in the other in the multiplicity of sects. The degree of security in both cases will depend on the number of interests and sects; and this may be presumed to depend on the extent of country and number of people comprehended under the same government. This view of the subject must particularly recommend a proper federal system to all the sincere and considerate friends of republican government, since it shows that in exact proportion as the territory of the Union may be formed into more circumscribed Confederacies, or States, oppressive combinations of a majority will be facilitated; the best security, under the republican forms, for the rights of every class of citizens, will be diminished; and consequently the stability and independence of some members of the government, the only other security, must be proportionally increased. Justice is the end of government. It is the end of civil society. It ever has been and ever will be pursued until it be obtained, or until liberty be lost in the pursuit. In a society under the forms of which the stronger faction can readily unite and oppress the weaker, anarchy may as truly be said to reign as in a state of nature, where the weaker individual is not secured against the violence of the stronger; and as, in the latter state, even the stronger individuals are prompted, by the uncertainty of their condition, to submit to a government which may protect the weak as well as themselves; so, in the former state, will the more powerful factions or parties be gradually induced, by a like motive, to wish for a government which will protect all parties, the weaker as well as the more powerful. It can be little doubted that if the State of Rhode Island was separated from the Confederacy and left to itself, the insecurity of rights under the popular form of government within such narrow limits would be displayed by such reiterated oppressions of factious majorities that some power altogether independent of the people would soon be called for by the voice of the very factions whose misrule had proved the necessity of it. In the extended republic of the United States, and among the great variety of interests, parties, and sects which it embraces, a coalition of a majority of the whole society could seldom take place on any other principles than those of justice and the general good; whilst there being thus less danger to a minor from the will of a major party, there must be less pretext, also, to provide for the security of the former, by introducing into the government a will not dependent on the latter, or, in other words, a will independent of the society itself. It is no less certain than it is important, notwithstanding the contrary opinions which have been entertained, that the larger the society, provided it lie within a practical sphere, the more duly capable it will be of self-government. And happily for the *republican cause*, the practicable sphere may be carried to a very great extent, by a judicious modification and mixture of the *federal principle*.

Publius
(James Madison)

Appendix E

THE CONSTITUTION OF THE UNITED STATES OF AMERICA*

We the People of the United States, in Order to form a more perfect Union, establish Justice, insure domestic Tranquility, provide for the common defence, promote the general Welfare, and secure the Blessings of Liberty to ourselves and our Posterity, do ordain and establish this Constitution for the United States of America.

Article I

SECTION 1

(General Legislative Powers)

All legislative Powers herein granted shall be vested in a Congress of the United States, which shall consist of a Senate and House of Representatives.

SECTION 2

(House of Representatives, Elections, Qualifications, Officers, and Impeachment Power)

The House of Representatives shall be composed of Members chosen every second Year by the People of the several States, and the Electors in each State shall have the Qualifications requisite for Electors of the most numerous Branch of the State Legislature.

No Person shall be a Representative who shall not have attained the Age of twenty-five Years, and been seven Years a Citizen of the United States, and who shall not, when elected, be an Inhabitant of that State in which he shall be chosen.

Representatives and direct Taxes shall be apportioned among the several States which may be included within this Union, according to their respective Numbers, *which shall be determined by adding to the whole Number of free Persons, including those bound to Service for a Term of Years, and excluding Indians not taxed, three fifths of all other Persons.* The actual Enumeration shall be made within three Years after the first Meeting of the Congress of the United States, and within every subsequent Term of ten Years, in such Manner as they shall by Law direct. The Number of Representatives shall not exceed one for every thirty Thousand, but each State shall have at least one Representative, and until each enumeration shall be made, the State of New Hampshire shall be entitled to chuse three, Massachusetts eight, Rhode-Island and Providence Plantations one, Connecticut five, New-York six, New Jersey four, Pennsylvania eight, Delaware one, Maryland six, Virginia ten, North Carolina five, South Carolina five, and Georgia three.

When vacancies happen in the Representation from any State, the Executive Authority thereof shall issue Writs of Election to fill such Vacancies.

The House of Representatives shall chuse their Speaker and other Officers; and shall have the sole Power of Impeachment.

SECTION 3

(The Senate: Election, Qualifications, Officers, and Impeachment Trials)

The Senate of the United States shall be composed of two Senators from each State, *chosen by the Legislature thereof*, for six Years; and each Senator shall have one Vote.

Immediately after they shall be assembled in Consequence of the first Election, they shall be divided as equally as may be into three Classes. The Seats of the Senators of the first Class shall be vacated at the Expiration of the second Year, of the second

*Provisions in italics have been repealed or modified by subsequent amendments.

Class at the Expiration of the fourth Year, and of the third Class at the Expiration of the sixth Year, so that one third may be chosen every second Year; *and if Vacancies happen by Resignation, or otherwise, during the Recess of the Legislature of any State, the Executive thereof may make temporary Appointments until the next Meeting of the Legislature, which shall then fill such Vacancies.*

No person shall be a Senator who shall not have attained to the Age of thirty Years, and been nine Years a Citizen of the United States, and who shall not, when elected, be an inhabitant of that State for which he shall be chosen.

The Vice President of the United States shall be President of the Senate, but shall have no Vote, unless they be equally divided.

The Senate shall chuse their other Officers, and also a President pro tempore, in the Absence of the Vice President, or when he shall exercise the Office of President of the United States.

The Senate shall have the sole Power to try all Impeachments. When sitting for that Purpose, they shall be on Oath or Affirmation. When the President of the United States is tried, the Chief Justice shall preside: And no Person shall be convicted without the Concurrence of two thirds of the Members present.

Judgment in Cases of Impeachment shall not extend further than to removal from Office, and disqualification to hold and enjoy any Office of honor, Trust or Profit under the United States; but the Party convicted shall nevertheless be liable and subject to Indictment, Trial, Judgment and Punishment, according to Law.

SECTION 4

(State Regulation of Congressional Elections)
The Times, Places and Manner of holding Elections for Senators and Representatives, shall be prescribed in each State by the Legislature thereof; but the Congress may at any time by Law make or alter such Regulations, except as to the Places of chusing Senators.

The Congress shall assemble at least once in every Year, *and such Meeting shall be on the first Monday in December, unless they shall by Law appoint a different Day.*

SECTION 5

(Congressional Rules and Procedures)
Each House shall be the Judge of the Elections, Returns and Qualifications of its own Members, and a Majority of each shall constitute a Quorum to do Business; but a smaller Number may adjourn from day to day, and may be authorized to compel the Attendance of absent Members, in such Manner, and under the Penalties as each House may provide.

Each House may determine the Rules of its Proceedings, punish its Members for disorderly Behavior, and, with the Concurrence of two thirds, expel a Member.

Each House shall keep a Journal of its Proceedings, and from time to time publish the same, excepting such Parts as may in their Judgment require Secrecy; and the Yeas and Nays of the members of either House on any question shall, at the Desire of one fifth of the present, be entered on the Journal.

Neither House, during the Session of Congress, shall, without the Consent of the other, adjourn for more than three days, nor to any other Place than that in which the two Houses shall be sitting.

SECTION 6

(Congressional Pay, Privileges, and Restrictions)
The Senators and Representatives shall receive a Compensation for their Services, to be ascertained by Law, and paid out of the Treasury of the United States. They shall in all Cases, except Treason, Felony and Breach of the Peace, be privileged from Arrest during their Attendance at the Session of their respective Houses, and in going to and returning from the same; and for any Speech or Debate in either House, they shall not be questioned in any other Place.

No Senator or Representative, shall, during the time for which he was elected, be appointed to any civil Office under the authority of the United States, which shall have been created, or the Emoluments whereof shall have been encreased during such time: and no Person holding any Office under the United States, shall be a Member of either House during his Continuance in Office.

SECTION 7

(Legislative Procedures)
All Bills for raising Revenue shall originate in the House of Representatives; but the Senate may propose or concur with Amendments as on other Bills.

Every Bill which shall have passed the House of Representatives and the Senate, shall, before it become a Law, be presented to the President of the United States; if he approve he shall sign it, but if not he shall return it, with his Objections to that House in which it shall have originated, who shall enter the Objections at large on their Journal, and proceed to reconsider it.

If after such Reconsideration two thirds of that House shall agree to pass the Bill, it shall be sent, together with the Objections, to the other House, by which it shall likewise be reconsidered, and if approved by two thirds of that House, it shall become a Law. But in all such Cases the Votes of both Houses shall be determined by Yeas and Nays, and the Names of the Persons voting for and against the Bill shall be entered on the Journal of each House respectively. If any Bill shall not be returned by the President within ten Days (Sundays excepted) after it shall have been presented to him, the Same shall be a Law, in like Manner as if he had signed it, unless the Congress by their Adjournment prevent its Return, in which Case it shall not be a Law.

Every Order, Resolution, or Vote to which the Concurrence of the Senate and House of Representatives may be necessary (except on a question of Adjournment) shall be presented to the President of the United States; and before the Same shall take Effect, shall be approved by him, or being disapproved by him, shall be repassed by two thirds of the Senate and House of Representatives, according to the Rules and Limitations prescribed in the Case of a Bill.

SECTION 8

(Powers of Congress)
The Congress shall have Power

To lay and collect Taxes, Duties, Imposts and Excises, to pay the Debts and provide for the common Defence and general Welfare of the United States; but all Duties, Imposts and Excises shall be uniform throughout the United States;

To borrow Money on the Credit of the United States;

To regulate Commerce with foreign Nations, and among the several States, and with the Indian Tribes;

To establish an uniform Rule of Naturalization, and uniform Laws on the subject of Bankruptcies throughout the United States;

To coin Money, regulate the Value thereof, and of foreign Coin, and fix the Standard of Weights and Measures;

To provide for the Punishment of counterfeiting the Securities and current Coin of the United States;

To establish Post Offices and post Roads;

To promote the Progress of Science and useful Arts, by securing for limited Times to Authors and Inventors the exclusive Right to their respective Writings and Discoveries;

To constitute Tribunals inferior to the supreme Court;

To define and Punish Piracies and Felonies committed on the high Seas, and Offences against the Law of Nations;

To declare War, grant Letters of Marque and Reprisal, and make Rules concerning Captures on Land and Water;

To raise and support Armies, but no Appropriation of Money to that Use shall be for a longer Term than two Years;

To provide and maintain a Navy;

To make Rules for the Government and Regulation of the land and naval forces;

To provide for calling for the Militia to execute the Laws of the Union, suppress Insurrections and repel Invasions;

To provide for organizing, arming, and disciplining, the Militia, and for governing such Part of them as may be employed in the Service of the United States, reserving to the States respectively, the Appointment of the Officers, and the Authority of training the Militia according to the discipline prescribed by Congress;

To exercise exclusive Legislation in all Cases whatsoever, over such District (not exceeding ten Miles square) as may, by Cession of particular States, and the Acceptance of Congress, become the Seat of the Government of the United States, and to exercise like Authority over all Places purchased by the Consent of the Legislature of the State in which the Same shall be, for the Erection of Forts, Magazines, Arsenals, dock-Yards, and other needful Buildings;—And

To make all Laws which shall be necessary and proper for carrying into Execution the foregoing Powers, and all other Powers vested by this Constitution in the Government of the United States, or in any Department or Officer thereof.

SECTION 9

(Restrictions on Congressional Power)
The Migration or Importation of such Persons as any of the States now existing shall think proper to admit, shall not be prohibited by the Congress prior to the Year one thousand eight hundred and eight, but a Tax or Duty may be imposed on such Importation, not exceeding ten dollars for each Person.

The privilege of the Writ of Habeas Corpus shall not be suspended, unless when in Cases of Rebellion or Invasion the public Safety may require it.

No Bill of Attainder or ex post facto Laws shall be passed.

No Capitation, or other direct, Tax shall be laid, unless in Proportion to the Census or Enumeration herein before directed to be taken.

No Tax or Duty shall be laid on Articles exported from any State.

No Preference shall be given by any Regulation of Commerce or Revenue to the Ports of one State over those of another; nor shall Vessels bound to, or from, one State, be obliged to enter, clear, or pay Duties in another.

No Money shall be drawn from the Treasury, but in Consequence of Appropriations made by Law; and a regular Statement and Account of the Receipts and Expenditures of all public Money shall be published from time to time.

No Title of Nobility shall be granted by the United States; And no Person holding any Office of Profit or Trust under them, shall, without the Consent of the Congress, accept of any present, Emolument, Office, or Title, of any kind whatever, from any King, Prince, or foreign State.

SECTION 10

(Restriction on the Powers of the States)
No State shall enter into any Treaty, Alliance, or Confederation; grant Letters of Marque and Reprisal; coin Money; emit Bills of Credit; make any Thing but gold and silver Coin a Tender in Payment of Debts; pass any Bill of Attainder, ex post facto Law, or Law impairing the Obligation of Contracts, or grant any Title of Nobility.

No State shall, without the Consent of the Congress, lay any Imposts or Duties on Imports or Exports, except what may be absolutely necessary for executing its inspection Laws: and the net Produce of all Duties and Imposts, laid by any State on Imports or Exports, shall be for the Use of the Treasury of the United States; and all such Laws shall be subject to the Revision and Control of the Congress.

No State shall, without the Consent of Congress, lay any Duty of Tonnage, keep Troops, or Ships of War in time of Peace, enter into any Agreement or Compact with another State, or with a foreign Power, or engage in War, unless actually invaded, or in such imminent Danger as will not admit of Delay.

Article II

SECTION 1

(Presidential Power, Election, and Qualifications)
The executive Power shall be vested in a President of the United States of America. He shall hold his Office during the Term of four Years and, together with the Vice President, chosen for the same Term, be elected as follows:

Each State shall appoint, in such Manner as the Legislature thereof may direct, a Number of Electors, equal to the whole Number of Senators and Representatives to which the State may be entitled in the Congress: but no Senator or Representative, or Person holding an Office of Trust or Profit under the United States, shall be appointed an Elector.

The electors shall meet in their respective States, and vote by ballot for two Persons, of whom one at least shall not be an Inhabitant of the same State with themselves. And they shall make a List of all the Persons voted for, and of the Number of Votes for each; which List they shall sign and certify, and transmit sealed to the Seat of the Government of the United States, directed to the President of the Senate. The President of the Senate shall, in the Presence of the Senate and House of Representatives, open all the Certificates, and the Votes shall then be counted. The Person having the greatest Number of Votes shall be the President, if such Number be a Majority of the whole Number of Electors appointed; and if there be more than one who have such Majority and have an equal Number of Votes, then the House of Representatives shall immediately chuse by Ballot one of them for President; and if no person have a Majority, then from the five highest on the List the said House shall in like Manner chuse the President. But in chusing the President, the Votes shall be taken by States, the Representation from each State having one Vote; A quorum for this Purpose shall consist of a Member or Members from two-thirds of the States, and a Majority of all the States shall be necessary to a Choice. In every Case, after the Choice of the President, the person having the greatest Number of Votes of the Electors shall be the Vice President. But if there should remain two or more who have equal vote, the Senate shall chuse from them by Ballot the Vice President.

The Congress may determine the Time of chusing the Electors, and the Day on which they shall give their Votes; which Day shall be the same throughout the United States.

No person except a natural born Citizen, or a Citizen of the United States, at the time of the Adoption of this Constitution, shall be eligible to the Office of President; neither shall any Person be eligible to that Office who shall not have attained to the

Age of thirty-five Years, and been fourteen Years a Resident within the United States.

In Case of the Removal of the President from Office, or of his Death, Resignation, or Inability to discharge the Powers and Duties of the said Office, the same shall devolve on the Vice President, and the Congress may by Law provide for the Case of Removal, Death, Resignation, or Inability, both of the President and Vice President, declaring what Officer shall then act as President, and such Officer shall act accordingly, until the Disability be removed, or a President shall be elected.

The President shall, at stated Times, receive for his Services, a Compensation, which shall neither be encreased nor diminished during the Period of which he shall have been elected, and he shall not receive within that Period any other Emolument from the United States, or any of them.

Before he enter on the Execution of his Office, he shall take the following oath or Affirmation:—"I do solemnly swear (or affirm) that I will faithfully execute the Office of President of the United States, and will to the best of my Ability, preserve, protect and defend the Constitution of the United States."

SECTION 2

(Powers of the President)
The President shall be the Commander in Chief of the Army and Navy of the United States, and of the Militia of the several States, when called into the actual Service of the United States, he may require the Opinion, in writing, of the principal Officer in each of the executive Departments, upon any Subject relating to the Duties of their respective Offices, and he shall have the Power to grant Reprieves and Pardons for Offences against the United States, except in Cases of Impeachment.

He shall have Power, by and with the Advice and Consent of the Senate to make Treaties, provided two thirds of the Senators present concur; and he shall nominate, and by and with the Advice and Consent of the Senate, shall appoint Ambassadors, other public Ministers and Consuls, Judges of the Supreme Court, and all other Offices of the United States, whose Appointments are not herein otherwise provided for, and which shall be established by Law: but the Congress may by Law vest the Appointment of such inferior Offices, as they think proper, in the President alone, in the Courts of Law, or in the Heads of Departments.

The President shall have Power to fill up all Vacancies that may happen during the Recess of the Senate, by granting Commissions which shall expire at the End of their next Session.

SECTION 3

(Presidential/Congressional Relationship)
He shall from time to time give to the Congress Information of the State of the Union, and recommend to their Consideration such Measures as he shall judge necessary and expedient; he may, on extraordinary Occasions, convene both Houses, or either of them, and in Case of Disagreement between them, with Respect to the Time of Adjournment, he may adjourn them to such Time as he shall think proper; he shall receive Ambassadors and other public Ministers; he shall take Care that the Laws be faithfully executed, and shall Commission all the Officers of the United States.

SECTION 4

(Impeachment)
The President, Vice President and all civil Officers of the United States, shall be removed from Office on Impeachment for, and Conviction of, Treason, Bribery, or other high Crimes and Misdemeanors.

Article III

SECTION 1

(Structure of the Judiciary)
The judicial Power of the United States, shall be vested in one supreme Court, and in such inferior Courts as the Congress may from time to time ordain and establish. The Judges, both of the supreme and inferior Courts, shall hold their Offices during good Behavior, and shall, at stated Times, receive for their Services, a Compensation, which shall not be diminished during their Continuance in Office.

SECTION 2

(Jurisdiction of Federal Courts)
The judicial Power shall extend to all Cases, in Law and Equity, arising under this Constitution, the Laws of the United States, and Treaties made, or which shall be made, under their Authority;—to all Cases affecting Ambassadors, other public Ministers and Consuls;—to all Cases of admiralty and maritime Jurisdiction;—to Controversies to which the United States shall be a party,—*between a State and Citizens of another state*;—between Citizens of different States;—between Citizens of the same State claiming

Lands under Grants of different States, and between a State, or the Citizens thereof, and foreign States, Citizens, or Subjects.

In all Cases affecting Ambassadors, other public Ministers and Consuls, and those in which a State shall be Party, the supreme Court shall have original Jurisdiction. In all the other Cases before mentioned, the supreme Court shall have appellate Jurisdiction, both as to Law and Fact. with such Exceptions, and under such Regulations as Congress shall make.

The Trial of all Crimes, except in Cases of Impeachment, shall be by Jury; and such Trial shall be held in the State where the said Crimes shall have been committed; but when not committed within any State, the Trial shall be at such Place or Places as the Congress may by Law have directed.

SECTION 3

(Treason)
Treason against the United States, shall consist only in levying War against them, or in adhering to their Enemies, giving them Aid and Comfort. No Person shall be convicted of Treason unless on the Testimony of two Witnesses to the same overt Act, or on Confession in open Court.

The Congress shall have Power to declare the Punishment of Treason, but no Attainder of Treason shall work Corruption of Blood, or Forfeiture except during the Life of the Person attainted.

Article IV

SECTION 1

(Faith and Credit Among States)
Full Faith and Credit shall be given in each State to the public Acts, Records, and judicial Proceedings of every other State. And the Congress may by general Laws prescribe the Manner in which such Acts, Records and Proceedings shall be proved, and the Effect thereof.

SECTION 2

(Privileges and Immunities)
The Citizens of each State shall be entitled to all Privileges and Immunities of Citizens in the several States.

A person charged in any State with Treason, Felony or other Crime, who shall flee from Justice, and be found in another State, shall on Demand of the executive Authority of the State from which he fled, be de-

livered up to be removed to the State having jurisdiction of the Crime.

No person held to Service or Labour in one State, under the Laws thereof, escaping into another, shall, in Consequence of any Law or Regulation therein, be discharged from such Service or Labour, but shall be delivered up on Claim of the Party to whom such Service or Labour may be due.

SECTION 3

(Admission of New States)
New States may be admitted by the Congress into this Union; but no new State shall be formed or erected within the Jurisdiction of any other State; nor any State be formed by the Junction of two or more States, or Parts of States, without the Consent of the Legislatures of the States concerned as well as of the Congress.

The Congress shall have Power to dispose of and make all needful Rules and Regulations respecting the Territory or other Property belonging to the United States; and nothing in this Constitution shall be so construed as to Prejudice any Claims of the United States, or of any particular State.

SECTION 4

(The States as Republican Governments)
The United States shall guarantee to every State in this Union a Republican Form of Government, and shall protect each of them against Invasion; and on Application of the Legislature, or of the Executive (when the Legislature cannot be convened) against domestic Violence.

Article V

(Amending the Constitution)
The Congress, whenever two thirds of both Houses shall deem it necessary, shall propose Amendments to this Constitution, or, on the Application of the Legislatures of two thirds of several States, shall call a Convention for proposing Amendments, which, in either Case, shall be valid to all Intents and Purposes, as Part of this Constitution, when ratified by the Legislatures of three fourths of the several States, or by Conventions in three fourths thereof, as the one or the other Mode of Ratification may be proposed by the Congress; Provided that no Amendment which may be made prior to the Year One thousand eight hundred and eight shall in any Manner affect the first and fourth Clauses in the Ninth Section of the first

Article; and that no State, without its Consent, shall be deprived of its equal Suffrage in the Senate.

Article VI

(Debts, Supremacy, and Oath)

All Debts contracted and Engagements entered into, before the Adoption of this Constitution, shall be as valid against the United States under the Constitution, as under the Confederation.

This Constitution, and the Laws of the United States which shall be made in Pursuance thereof; and all Treaties made, or which shall be made, under the Authority of the United States, shall be the supreme Law of the Land; and the Judges in every State shall be bound thereby, any Thing in the Constitution or Laws of any State to the Contrary notwithstanding.

The Senators and Representatives before mentioned, and the Members of the several State Legislatures, and all executive and judicial Officers, both of the United States and of the several States, shall be bound by Oath or Affirmation, to support this Constitution; but no religious Test shall ever be required as a Qualification to any Office or public Trust under the United States.

Article VII

(Ratification)

The Ratification of the Conventions of nine States, shall be sufficient for the Establishment of this Constitution between the States so ratifying the Same.

Done in Convention by the Unanimous Consent of the States present the Seventeenth Day of September in the Year of our Lord one thousand seven hundred and Eighty seven and of the Independence of the United States of America the Twelfth. In Witness whereof We have hereunto subscribed our Names.

G: WASHINGTON—Presidt, and Deputy from Virginia

New Hamphire	John Langdon
	Nicholas Gilman
Massachusetts	Nathaniel Gorham
	Rufus King
Connecticut	Wm Saml Johnson
	Roger Sherman
New York	Alexander Hamilton
New Jersey	Wil: Livingston
	David Brearley
	Wm Paterson
	Jona: Dayton
Pennsylvania	B Franklin
	Thomas Mifflin
	Robt Morris
	Geo. Clymer
	Thos, FitzSimons
	Jared Ingersoll
	James Wilson
	Gouv Morris
Delaware	Geo Read
	Gunning Bedfor Jun
	John Dickinson
	Richard Bassett
	Jaco: Broom
Maryland	James McHenry
	Dan of St. Thos. Jenifer
	Danl Carroll
Virginia	John Blair—
	James Madison Jr.
North Carolina	Wm Blount
	Richd Dobbs Spaight
	Hu Williamson
South Carolina	J. Rutledge
	Charles Cotesworth Pinckney
	Charles Pinckney
	Pierce Butler
Georgia	William Few
	Abr Baldwin

Appendix F

AMENDMENTS TO THE CONSTITUTION

(The first ten amendments, known as the Bill of Rights, were ratified and adopted on December 15, 1791.)

Amendment I

(Freedom of Religion, Speech, Press, Assembly, and Petition)

Congress shall make no law respecting an establishment of religion, or prohibiting the free exercise thereof; or abridging the freedom of speech, or of the press; or the right of the people peaceably to assemble, and to petition the Government for a redress of grievances.

Amendment II

(Freedom to Keep and Bear Arms)

A well regulated Militia, being necessary to the security of a free State, the right of the people to keep and bear Arms, shall not be infringed.

Amendment III

(Quartering of Soldiers)

No Soldier shall, in time of peace be quartered in any house, without the consent of the Owner, nor in time of war, but in manner to be prescribed by law.

Amendment IV

(Security from Unreasonable Searches and Seizures)

The right of the people to be secure in their persons, houses, papers, and effects, against unreasonable searches and seizures, shall not be violated, and no Warrants shall issue, but upon probable cause, supported by Oath or affirmation, and particularly describing the place to be searched, and the persons or things to be seized.

Amendment V

(Rights of Accused Persons in Criminal Cases)

No person shall be held to answer for a capital, or otherwise infamous crime, unless on a presentment or indictment of a Grand Jury, except in cases arising in the land or naval forces, or in the Militia, when in actual service in time of War or in public danger; nor shall any person be subject for the same offence to be twice put in jeopardy of life or limb; nor shall be compelled in any Criminal Case to be a witness against himself, nor be deprived of life, liberty, or property, without due process of law; nor shall private property be taken for public use, without just compensation.

Amendment VI

(Additional Rights of the Accused)

In all criminal prosecutions, the accused shall enjoy the right to a speedy and public trial, by an impartial jury of the State and district wherein the crime shall have been committed, which district shall have been previously ascertained by law, and to be informed of the nature and cause of the accusation; to be confronted with the witnesses against him; to have compulsory process for obtaining Witnesses in his favor, and to have the Assistance of Counsel for his defence.

Amendment VII

(Rights in Common Law Suits)

In suits at common law, where the value in controversy shall exceed twenty dollars, the right of trial by jury shall be preserved, and no fact tried by a jury shall be otherwise re-examined in any Court of the United States, than according to the rules of the common law.

Amendment VIII

(Bails, Fines, and Punishments)
Excessive bail shall not be required, nor excessive fines imposed, nor cruel and unusual punishments inflicted.

Amendment IX

(Retention of Rights of the People)
The enumeration in the Constitution, of certain rights, shall not be construed to deny or disparage others retained by the people.

Amendment X

(Reservation of Powers to the States or People)
The powers not delegated to the United States by the Constitution, nor prohibited by it to the States, are reserved to the States respectively, or to the people.

Amendment XI

(Ratified on January 8, 1798.)
(Restriction of Judicial Power)
The Judicial power of the United States shall not be construed to extend to any suit in law or equity, commenced or prosecuted against one of the United States by Citizens of another State, or by Citizens or Subjects of any Foreign State.

Amendment XII

(Ratified on September 25, 1804.)
(Election of President and Vice-President)
The Electors shall meet in their respective states and vote by ballot for President and Vice-President, one of whom, at least, shall not be an inhabitant of the same state with themselves; they shall name in their ballots the person voted for as President, and in distinct ballots the person voted for as Vice-President, and they shall make distinct lists of all persons voted for as President, and of all persons voted for as Vice-President, and of the number of votes for each, which lists they shall sign and certify, and transmit sealed to the seat of the government of the United States, directed to the President of the Senate;—The President of the Senate shall, in presence of the Senate and House of Representatives, open all the certificates and the votes shall then be counted;—The person having the greatest number of votes for President, shall be the President, if such number be a majority of the whole number of Electors appointed; and if no

person have such majority, then from the persons having the highest numbers not exceeding three on the list of those voted for as President, the House of Representatives shall choose immediately, by ballot, the President. But in choosing the President, the votes shall be taken by states, the representation from each state having one vote; a quorum for this purpose shall consist of a member or members from two thirds of the states, and a majority of all states shall be necessary to a choice. And if the House of Representatives shall not choose a President whenever the right of choice shall devolve upon them, *before the fourth day of March next following*, then the Vice-President shall act as President, as in the case of the death or other constitutional disability of the President. The person having the greatest number of votes as Vice-President, shall be the Vice-President, if such a number be a majority of the whole numbers of Electors appointed, and if no person have a majority, then from the two highest numbers on the list, the Senate shall choose the Vice-President; a quorum for the purpose shall consist of two-thirds of the whole number of Senators, and a majority of the whole number shall be necessary to a choice. But no person constitutionally ineligible to the office of President shall be eligible to that of Vice-President of the United States.

Amendment XIII

(Ratified on December 18, 1865.)

SECTION 1

(Abolition of Slavery)
Neither slavery nor involuntary servitude, except as a punishment for crime whereof the party shall have been duly convicted, shall exist within the United States, or any place subject to their jurisdiction.

SECTION 2

Congress shall have power to enforce this article by appropriate legislation.

Amendment XIV

(Ratified on July 28, 1868.)

SECTION 1

(Rights of Citizenship)
All persons born or naturalized in the United States, and subject to the jurisdiction thereof, are citizens of the United States and of the State wherein they

reside. No State shall make or enforce any law which shall abridge the privileges or immunities of citizens of the United States; nor shall any State deprive any person of life, liberty, or property, without due process of law; nor deny to any person within its jurisdiction the equal protection of the laws.

SECTION 2

(Representation in Congress)
Representatives shall be apportioned among the several States according to their respective numbers, counting the whole number of persons in each State, excluding Indians not taxed. But when the right to vote at any election for the choice of electors for President and Vice-President of the United States, Representatives in Congress, the Executive and Judicial officers of a State, or the members of the Legislature thereof, is denied to any of the male inhabitants of such State, being twenty-one years of age, and citizens of the United States, or in any way abridged, except for participation in rebellion, or other crime, the basis of representation therein shall be reduced in the proportion which the number of such male citizens shall bear to the whole number of male citizens twenty-one years of age in such State.

SECTION 3

(Restriction on Eligibility to Hold Office)
No person shall be a Senator or Representative in Congress, or elector of President and Vice-President, or hold any office, civil or military, under the United States, or under any State, who, having previously taken an oath, as a member of Congress, or as an officer of the United States, or as a member of any State legislature, or as an executive or judicial officer of any State, to support the Constitution of the United States, shall have engaged in insurrection or rebellion against the same, or given aid or comfort to the enemies thereof. But Congress may by a vote of two-thirds of each House, remove such disability.

SECTION 4

(Definition of Public Debts)
The validity of the public debt of the United States, authorized by law, including debts incurred for payment of pensions and bounties for services in suppressing insurrection or rebellion, shall not be questioned. But neither the United States nor any State shall assume or pay any debt or obligation incurred in aid of insurrection or rebellion against the United States, or any claim for the loss or emancipation of any slave; but all such debts, obligations and claims shall be held illegal and void.

SECTION 5

The Congress shall have power to enforce, by appropriate legislation, the provisions of this article.

Amendment XV

(Ratified on March 30, 1870.)

SECTION 1

(Black Suffrage)
The right of citizens of the United States to vote shall not be denied or abridged by the United States or by any State on account of race, color, or previous condition of servitude.

SECTION 2

The Congress shall have power to enforce this article by appropriate legislation.

Amendment XVI

(Ratified on February 25, 1913.)
(Personal Income Taxes)
The Congress shall have power to lay and collect taxes on incomes, from whatever source derived, without apportionment among the several States, and without regard to any census or enumeration.

Amendment XVII

(Ratified on May 31, 1913.)
(Popular Election of Senators)
The Senate of the United States shall be composed of two Senators from each State, elected by the people thereof, for six years; and each Senator shall have one vote. The electors in each State shall have the qualifications requisite for electors of the most numerous branch of the State Legislature.

When vacancies happen in the representation of any State in the Senate, the executive authority of such State shall issue writs of election to fill such vacancies; Provided, That the Legislature of any State may empower the executive thereof to make temporary appointment until the people fill the vacancies by election as the Legislature may direct.

This amendment shall not be so construed as to

affect the election or term of any Senator chosen before it becomes valid as part of the Constitution.

Amendment XVIII

(Ratified on January 29, 1919.)

SECTION 1

(Prohibition of Liquor)
After one year from the ratification of this article the manufacture, sale, or transportation of intoxicating liquors within, the importation thereof into or the exportation thereof from the United States and all territory subject to the jurisdiction thereof for beverage purposes is hereby prohibited.

SECTION 2

(Enforcement Power)
The Congress and the several states shall have concurrent power to enforce this article by appropriate legislation.

SECTION 3

(Provision for Ratification)
This article shall be inoperative unless it shall have been ratified as an amendment to the Constitution by the legislatures of the several states, as provided in the Constitution, within seven years from the date of the submission hereof to the states by the Congress.

Amendment XIX

(Ratified on August 26, 1920.)
(Women's Suffrage)
The right of the citizens of the United States to vote shall not be denied or abridged by the United States or by any state on account of sex.

Congress shall have power, by appropriate legislation, to enforce the provision of this article.

Amendment XX

(Ratified on February 6, 1933.)

SECTION 1

(Terms of Presidential and Vice-Presidential Office)
The terms of the President and Vice-President shall end at noon on the 20th day of January, and the terms of the Senators and Representatives at noon on the 3rd day of January, of the years in which such terms would have ended if this article had not been ratified; and the terms of their successors shall then begin.

SECTION 2

(Time of Convening Congress)
The Congress shall assemble at least once in every year, and such meeting shall begin at noon on the 3rd day of January, unless they shall by law appoint a different day.

SECTION 3

(Death of President-Elect)
If, at the time fixed for the beginning of the term of the President, the President-elect shall have died, the Vice-President elect shall become President. If a President shall not have been chosen before the time fixed for the beginning of his term, or if the President-elect shall have failed to qualify, then the Vice-President elect shall act as President until a President shall have qualified; and the Congress may by law provide for the case wherein neither a President-elect nor a Vice-President elect shall have qualified, declaring who shall then act as President, or the manner in which one who is to act shall be selected, and such person shall act accordingly until a President or Vice-President shall have qualified.

SECTION 4

(Presidential Succession)
The Congress may by law provide for the case of the death of any of the persons from whom the House of Representatives may choose a President whenever the right of choice shall have developed upon them, and for the case of the death of any of the persons from whom the Senate may choose a Vice-President whenever the right of choice shall have devolved upon them.

SECTION 5

Sections 1 and 2 shall take effect on the 15th day of October following the ratification of this article.

SECTION 6

This article shall be inoperative unless it shall have been ratified as an amendment to the Constitution by the legislatures of three-fourths of the several States within seven years from the date of its submission.

Amendment XXI

(Ratified on December 5, 1933.)

SECTION 1

(Repeal of Liquor Probibition)
The eighteenth article of amendment to the Constitution of the United States is hereby repealed.

SECTION 2

("Dry" States)
The transportation or importation into any State, Territory, or Possession of the United States for delivery or use therein of intoxicating liquors, in violation of the laws thereof, is hereby prohibited.

SECTION 3

This article shall be inoperative unless it shall have been ratified as an amendment to the Constitution by conventions in the several States, as provided in the Constitution, within seven years from the date of the submission hereof to the States by the Congress.

Amendment XXII

(Ratified on February 26, 1951.)

SECTION 1

(Limitation on Presidential Term in Office)
No person shall be elected to the office of the President more than twice, and no person who has held the office of President, or acted as President, for more than two years of a term to which some other person was elected President shall be elected to the Office of the President more than once. But this Article shall not apply to any person holding the office of President when this article was proposed by the Congress, and shall not prevent any person who may be holding the office of President, or acting as President, during the term within which this Article becomes operative from holding the office of President or acting as President during the remainder of such term.

SECTION 2

This Article shall be inoperative unless it shall have been ratified as an amendment to the Constitution by the legislatures of three-fourths of the several states within seven years from the date of its submission to the States by the Congress.

Amendment XXIII

(Ratified on March 29, 1961.)

SECTION 1

(Electoral Votes for the District of Columbia)
The District constituting the seat of Government of the United States shall appoint in such manner as the Congress may direct:

A number of electors of President and Vice-President equal to the whole number of Senators and Representatives in Congress to which the District would be entitled if it were a State, but in no event more than the least populous State; they shall be in addition to those appointed by the States, but they shall be considered, for the purposes of the election of President and Vice-President, to be electors appointed by a State; and they shall meet in the District and perform such duties as provided by the twelfth article of amendment.

SECTION 2

The Congress shall have power to enforce this article by appropriate legislation.

Amendment XXIV

(Ratified on January 23, 1964.)

SECTION 1

(Poll Tax Abolished)
The right of citizens of the United States to vote in any primary or other election for President or Vice-President, for electors for President or Vice-President, or for Senator or Representative in Congress, shall not be denied or abridged by the United States or any State by reasons of failure to pay any poll tax or other tax.

SECTION 2

The Congress shall have power to enforce this article by appropriate legislation.

Amendment XXV

(Ratified on February 10, 1967.)

SECTION 1

(Presidential Succession)
In case of the removal of the President from office or his death or resignation, the Vice-President shall become President.

SECTION 2

(Vice-Presidential Succession)

Whenever there is a vacancy in the office of the Vice-President, the President shall nominate a Vice-President who shall take the office upon confirmation by a majority vote of both houses of Congress.

SECTION 3

(Presidential Disability)

Whenever the President transmits to the President pro tempore of the Senate and the Speaker of the House of Representatives his written declaration that he is unable to discharge the powers and duties of his office, and until he transmits to them a written declaration to the contrary, such powers and duties shall be discharged by the Vice-President as Acting President.

SECTION 4

(Congressional Power to Declare and to End Presidential Disability)

Whenever the Vice-President and a majority of either the principal officers of the executive departments, or of such other body as Congress may by law provide, transmit to the President pro tempore of the Senate and the Speaker of the House of Representatives their written declaration that the President is unable to discharge the powers and duties of his office, the Vice-President shall immediately assume the powers and duties of the office as Acting President.

Thereafter, when the President transmits to the President pro tempore of the Senate and the Speaker of the House of Representatives his written declaration that no inability exists, he shall resume the powers and duties of his office unless the Vice-President and a majority of either the principal officers of the executive departments, or of such other body as

Congress may by law provide, transmit within four days to the President pro tempore of the Senate and the Speaker of the House of Representatives their written declaration that the President is unable to discharge the powers and duties of his office. Thereupon Congress shall decide the issue, assembling within 48 hours for that purpose if not in session. If the Congress, within 21 days after receipt of the latter written declaration, or, if Congress is not in session, within 21 days after Congress is required to assemble, determines by two-thirds vote of both houses that the President is unable to discharge the powers and duties of his office, the Vice-President shall continue to discharge the same as Acting President; otherwise, the President shall resume the powers and duties of his office.

Amendment XXVI

(Ratified on June 30, 1971.)

SECTION 1

The right of citizens of the United States who are eighteen years of age, or older, to vote shall not be denied or abridged by the United States or by any state on account of age.

SECTION 2

The Congress shall have power to enforce this article by appropriate legislation.

Amendment XXVII

(Ratified May 7, 1992.)

No law, varying the compensation for the services of Senators and Representatives, shall take effect, until an election of Representatives shall have intervened.

Appendix G

PRESIDENTS AND VICE PRESIDENTS OF THE UNITED STATES

President and Political Party	Born	Died	Age at Inauguration	Native of	Elected from	Term of Service	Vice President
George Washington	1732	1799	57	Va.	Va.	Apr. 30, 1789–Mar. 4, 1793	John Adams
George Washington (F)			61			Mar. 4, 1793–Mar. 4, 1797	John Adams
John Adams (F)	1735	1826	61	Mass.	Mass.	Mar. 4, 1797–Mar. 4, 1801	Thomas Jefferson
Thomas Jefferson (D-R)	1743	1826	57	Va.	Va.	Mar. 4, 1801–Mar. 4, 1805	Aaron Burr
Thomas Jefferson (D-R)			61			Mar. 4, 1805–Mar. 4, 1809	George Clinton
James Madison	1751	1836	57	Va.	Va.	Mar. 4, 1809–Mar. 4, 1813	George Clinton
James Madison			61			Mar. 4, 1813–Mar. 4, 1817	Elbridge Gerry
James Monroe (D-R)	1758	1831	58	Va.	Va.	Mar. 4, 1817–Mar. 4, 1821	Daniel D.Tompkins
James Monroe (D-R)			62			Mar. 4, 1821–Mar. 4, 1825	Daniel D.Tompkins
John Q. Adams (N-R)	1767	1848	57	Mass.	Mass.	Mar. 4, 1825–Mar. 4, 1829	John C. Calhoun
Andrew Jackson (D)	1767	1845	61	S.C.	Tenn.	Mar. 4, 1829–Mar. 4, 1833	John C. Calhoun*
Andrew Jackson (D)			65			Mar. 4, 1833–Mar. 4, 1837	Martin Van Buren
Martin Van Buren (D)	1782	1862	54	N.Y.	N.Y.	Mar. 4, 1837–Mar. 4, 1841	Richard M. Johnson
W. H. Harrison (W)	1773	1841	68	Va.	Ohio	Mar. 4, 1841–Apr. 4, 1841	John Tyler
John Tyler (W)	1790	1862	51	Va.	Va.	Apr. 6, 1841–Mar. 4, 1845	
James K. Polk (D)	1795	1849	49	N.C.	Tenn.	Mar. 4, 1845–Mar. 4, 1849	George M. Dallas
Zachary Taylor (W)	1784	1850	64	Va.	La.	Mar. 4, 1849–July 9, 1850	Millard Fillmore
Millard Fillmore (W)	1800	1874	50	N.Y.	N.Y.	July 10, 1850–Mar. 4, 1853	
Franklin Pierce (D)	1804	1869	48	N.H.	N.H.	Mar. 4, 1853–Mar. 4, 1857	William R. King**
James Buchanan (D)	1791	1868	65	Pa.	Pa.	Mar. 4, 1857–Mar. 4, 1861	John C. Breckinridge
Abraham Lincoln (R)	1809	1865	52	Ky.	Ill.	Mar. 4, 1861–Mar. 4, 1865	Hannibal Hamlin
Abraham Lincoln (R)			56			Mar. 4, 1865–Apr. 15, 1865	Andrew Johnson
Andrew Johnson (R)	1808	1875	56	N.C.	Tenn.	Apr. 15, 1865–Mar. 4, 1869	
Ulysses S. Grant (R)	1822	1885	46	Ohio	Ill.	Mar. 4, 1869–Mar. 4, 1873	Schuyler Colfax
Ulysses S. Grant (R)						Mar. 4, 1873–Mar. 4, 1877	Henry Wilson
Rutherford B. Hayes (R)	1822	1893	54	Ohio	Ohio	Mar. 4, 1877–Mar. 4, 1881	William A. Wheeler
James A. Garfield (R)	1831	1881	49	Ohio	Ohio	Mar. 4, 1881–Sept. 19, 1881	Chester A. Arthur

President (party)	Born	Died	Age	Native of	Elected from	Term of service	Vice President
Chester A. Arthur (R)	1830	1886	50	Vt.	N.Y.	Sept. 20, 1881–Mar. 4, 1885	
Grover Cleveland (D)	1837	1908	47	N.J.	N.Y.	Mar. 4, 1885–Mar. 4, 1889	Thomas A. Hendricks
Benjamin Harrison (R)	1833	1901	55	Ohio	Ind.	Mar. 4, 1889–Mar. 4, 1893	Levi P. Morton
Grover Cleveland (D)	1837	1908	55			Mar. 4, 1893–Mar. 4, 1897	Adlai E. Stevenson
William McKinley (R)	1843	1901	54	Ohio	Ohio	Mar. 4, 1897–Mar. 4, 1901	Garret A. Hobart
William McKinley (R)			58			Mar. 4, 1901–Sept. 14, 1901	Theodore Roosevelt
Theodore Roosevelt (R)	1858	1919	42	N.Y.	N.Y.	Sept. 14, 1901–Mar. 4, 1905	
Theodore Roosevelt (R)			46			Mar. 4, 1905–Mar. 4, 1909	Charles W. Fairbanks
William H. Taft (R)	1857	1930	51	Ohio	Ohio	Mar. 4, 1909–Mar. 4, 1913	James S. Sherman
Woodrow Wilson (D)	1856	1924	56	Va.	N.J.	Mar. 4, 1913–Mar. 4, 1917	Thomas R. Marshall
Woodrow Wilson (D)			60			Mar. 4, 1917–Mar. 4, 1921	Thomas R. Marshall
Warren G. Harding (R)	1865	1923	55	Ohio	Ohio	Mar. 4, 1921–Aug. 2, 1923	Calvin Coolidge
Calvin Coolidge (R)	1872	1933	51	Vt.	Mass.	Aug. 3, 1923–Mar. 4, 1925	
Calvin Coolidge (R)			52			Mar. 4, 1925–Mar. 4, 1929	Charles G. Dawes
Herbert Hoover (R)	1874	1964	54	Iowa	Calif.	Mar. 4, 1929–Mar. 4, 1933	Charles Curtis
Franklin D. Roosevelt (D)	1882	1945	51	N.Y.	N.Y.	Mar. 4, 1933–Jan. 20, 1937	John N. Garner
Franklin D. Roosevelt (D)			55			Jan. 20, 1937–Jan. 20, 1941	John N. Garner
Franklin D. Roosevelt (D)			59			Jan. 20, 1941–Jan. 20, 1945	Henry A. Wallace
Franklin D. Roosevelt (D)			63			Jan. 20, 1945–Apr. 12, 1945	Harry S Truman
Harry S Truman (D)	1884	1972	60	Mo.	Mo.	Apr. 12, 1945–Jan. 20, 1949	
Harry S Truman (D)			64			Jan. 20, 1949–Jan. 20, 1953	Alben W. Barkley
Dwight D. Eisenhower (R)	1890	1969	62	Texas	N.Y.	Jan. 20, 1953–Jan. 20, 1957	Richard M. Nixon
Dwight D. Eisenhower (R)			66		Pa.	Jan. 20, 1957–Jan. 20, 1961	Richard M. Nixon
John F. Kennedy (D)	1917	1963	43	Mass.	Mass.	Jan. 20, 1961–Nov. 22, 1963	Lyndon B. Johnson
Lyndon B. Johnson (D)	1908	1973	55	Texas	Texas	Nov. 22, 1963–Jan. 20, 1965	
Lyndon B. Johnson (D)			56			Jan. 20, 1965–Jan. 20, 1969	Hubert H. Humphrey
Richard M. Nixon (R)	1913	1994	56	Calif.	N.Y.	Jan. 20, 1969–Jan. 20, 1973	Spiro T. Agnew
Richard M. Nixon (R)			60		Calif.	Jan. 20, 1973–Aug. 9, 1974	Spiro T. Agnew* / Gerald R. Ford
Gerald R. Ford (R)	1913		61	Neb.	Mich.	Aug. 9, 1974–Jan. 20, 1977	Nelson A. Rockefeller
Jimmy Carter (D)	1924		52	Ga.	Ga.	Jan. 20, 1977–Jan. 20, 1981	Walter F. Mondale
Ronald Reagan (R)	1911	2004	69	Ill.	Calif.	Jan. 20, 1981–Jan. 20, 1985	George Bush
Ronald Reagan (R)			73			Jan. 20, 1985–Jan. 20, 1989	George Bush
George Bush (R)	1924		64	Mass.	Texas	Jan. 20, 1989–Jan. 20, 1993	James D. Quayle
William J. Clinton (D)	1946		46	Ark.	Ark.	Jan. 20, 1993–Jan. 20, 1997	Albert Gore
William J. Clinton (D)						Jan. 20, 1997–Jan. 20, 2001	Albert Gore
George W. Bush (R)	1946		54	Texas	Texas	Jan. 20, 2001–Jan. 20, 2005	Richard Cheney
George W. Bush (R)						Jan. 20, 2005–	Richard Cheney

Key to abbreviations: (D) Democratic, (D-R) Democrat-Republican, (F) Federalist, (N-R) National Republican, (R) Republican, (W) Whig.

Source: "National Party Conventions 1831–1980," *Congressional Quarterly* (1983): 212. Updated to present. *Resigned office. ** Died in office.

Glossary

administrative law   The rules and regulations issued by departments and agencies of the executive branch of government.

adversary system   A judicial process characterized by the conflict of two or more opposing parties before an impartial third party, the court.

advisory opinion   An opinion given by a court on a legal issue to the executive or legislative branches of government or to a private individual but not actually presented in a case brought by parties with adverse interests.

affirmative action   Programs created by government and private organizations that are designed to provide greater opportunities for women, African Americans, and other minority groups who have been victims of past discrimination.

agency   An organization within the federal bureaucracy that is headed by a single administrator and performs specialized functions but does not have departmental status.

agenda ("things to be done")   The list of issues to which government and nongovernmental actors are paying serious attention at any given time.

amendment   A formal addition to the Constitution that either changes one of its sections or adds matters that were not included in the original document.

amicus curiae **brief** ("friend of the court")   A written brief in support of one of the parties in a legal dispute that attempts to influence the decision of the court.

anarchy   A view of international affairs that holds that nations are free to act according to their interests as they define them since there is no institution or supreme authority in the world capable of defining rules of good conduct or punishing countries that violate these rules.

Antifederalists   Opponents of the Constitution of 1787 who wanted to preserve the authority of state governments.

appellate jurisdiction   The authority of a court to review on appeal the decisions of lower courts.

appropriation bill   A bill that allocates funds to a program of the executive branch of government.

Articles of Confederation   The document that created the United States' first central government. It was ratified in 1781 and remained in effect until 1788. Congress, the only branch of government created by the Articles, did not have the power to tax or to regulate commerce and was unable to address the economic problems of the nation.

authorization bill   A bill that permits the executive branch of government to undertake a specific program and limits the amount of money that may be spent on it.

balance of power   The theory in foreign affairs that holds that threats to the security of a country from another nation or a coalition of nations are best prevented by increasing armaments and by creating countervailing power through alliances with other countries.

ballot   A printed list of candidates for public office used for secret voting. The names may be printed on paper or appear on a voting machine.

bicameral legislature   A legislature composed of two separate chambers.

bill of attainder   An act of a legislature that singles out specific persons or groups and orders them to be punished without judicial trial. Such acts are prohibited by the Constitution.

bill of information   A method of obtaining an indictment in which the public prosecutor presents a written statement of the evidence to a judge or magistrate.

Bill of Rights   The first ten amendments to the Constitution, ratified in 1791. These amendments guarantee the basic rights of Americans.

blanket primary   A type of primary election in which voters do not have to declare a choice of political party and are free to vote in more than one primary (e.g., voting Republican for one office and Democratic for another).

block grant   A sum of money that is given by the national government to a state to be used for a broad, general purpose.

brief   A written argument submitted to the court by attorneys for the parties in a case.

bureau   The largest working subunit of an executive department that performs specific functions.

bureaucracy   A way of organizing people to achieve a specific goal; a means to get work done.

cabinet   A body that advises the president and serves to coordinate and implement governmental policy. It is

420

composed of the heads of the executive departments. Other high officials, including the vice president, may also attend cabinet meetings.

calendar Bills reported from a standing committee of Congress are assigned to a calendar, which is used to schedule debate on the floor of the House and the Senate.

casework The handling by members of Congress of the problems their constituents have with governmental agencies.

caucus A meeting of party members at the local or precinct level to select delegates to the national convention. Also, a meeting of all the members of one party in the House or the Senate.

centralized federalism A view of federalism, followed by President Lyndon Johnson during the 1960s, that believed that the national government should define public problems and provide national solutions that state and local governments must follow.

checks and balances A system of organizing the power of government in which the executive, legislative, and judicial branches possess some power over each other's activities, thus preventing arbitrary action by any one branch.

civil law Law that defines the legal rights of citizens and thereby provides rules for resolving disputes between individuals and/or corporations or between individuals and/or corporations and the government.

civil liberties The rights of the individual that are guaranteed by the United States Constitution.

civil rights The right of individuals not to be discriminated against on the basis of their race, sex, or nationality.

civil service A system of employing government workers that is based on merit and grants tenure to those employees.

class action A legal action brought by one or more individuals as representatives of a group of similarly situated persons.

closed primary A primary election in which participation is limited to voters who have formally registered as members of a particular political party.

cloture vote A procedure to end debate in a legislative body in order to obtain a vote on a bill that is being considered by that body.

coattail effect The ability of a popular presidential candidate to help elect legislative candidates of the same party in a presidential election.

collective security A view of international affairs that holds that the security of nations can best be attained through the creation of an international organization that can maintain world order by the cooperative efforts of its members against any acts of aggression.

commercial speech Advertising used for business purposes. The Supreme Court has granted First Amendment protection to certain forms of truthful commercial advertising when used by lawyers, doctors, other professionals, and corporations.

common law Law established by past judicial decisions, often referred to as "judge-made" law.

compelling interest A test used by the courts in interpreting some civil liberties and civil rights issues that require the government to produce very strong and convincing reasons to justify its policies.

concurrent powers Powers that are shared by the state and national governments.

concurring opinion A written opinion of a judge who agrees with the decision of the majority but feels that the majority opinion does not adequately express his or her own reasoning.

confederation A system in which the legal power of government is held by state governments; the central government has only the powers that have been given to it by those governments.

conference committee A joint committee composed of members from each house of Congress, whose purpose is to create a compromise version of a bill that has been passed by both houses in different forms.

Connecticut Compromise A compromise between the New Jersey and Virginia plans worked out at the Constitutional Convention. It was agreed that the national legislature would be bicameral, and representation in the House of Representatives would be based on population, but in the Senate each state would have equal representation.

Constitutional Convention A meeting in 1787 of fifty-five delegates selected by the states to revise the Articles of Confederation. The result of the Convention was, however, an entirely new constitution, which was ratified in 1788.

constitutional court A court authorized and created under the provisions of Article III, Section 1, of the Constitution.

constitutional democracy A form of democratic government that places limits on the power of a majority to act and defines those limits in a written constitution.

constitutional law Law based on the provisions of state and federal constitutions.

containment The policy followed by the United States and its allies after World War II of containing the threat posed by the Soviet Union and the spread of communism throughout the world.

convention A meeting of either elected or appointed members of a political party that may nominate candidates for public office, elect party officials and delegates, and write party platforms.

cooperative federalism A form of federalism that emphasizes cooperation between the national government and the states to achieve policy goals set by the national government.

corporatism The theory that holds that groups in society do not merely attempt to influence public policy but are themselves part of the decision-making and implementation system.

criminal law Law that defines acts that constitute a violation of the public order and provides specific punishments for those acts.

de facto **segregation**   Segregation ("in fact") that is a product of private actions and not of governmental policies.

defamation   Spoken or written words that are false and hold an individual up to public ridicule and contempt. (See **libel** and **slander**.)

defendant   The party against whom a legal suit is brought.

de jure **segregation**   Segregation ("by law") that has been created by the policies and actions of government.

delegated powers   Powers specifically granted by the Constitution to the federal government, especially those given to Congress by Article I, Section 8.

democracy   A system of government in which the policy decisions of the government rest on the freely given consent of the people and that guarantees certain basic rights such as freedom of speech and the right to vote.

department   The major administrative unit within the federal bureaucracy, headed by a secretary who is a member of the cabinet.

deregulation   A process by which supervisory laws and regulations are removed from various parts of the economy.

detente   The policy followed by the United States in the 1970s of favoring the normalization of relations with the Soviet Union.

direct democracy   A form of democracy in which the people themselves meet to discuss and decide issues of public policy.

discharge petition   A petition that requires the signatures of a majority (218) of the members of the House of Representatives to remove a bill from a standing committee and bring it to the floor of the House for consideration.

dissenting opinion   An opinion written by a judge to record disagreement with the majority decision and to express reasons for voting against it.

distributive policy   Those policies of government that provide tangible benefits to groups or individuals in a non-competitive manner.

double jeopardy   The retrial of an individual for a crime of which he or she has already been acquitted. Double jeopardy is prohibited by the Fifth Amendment in federal courts and by the due process clause of the Fourteenth Amendment in state prosecutions.

due process clause   Section 1 of the Fourteenth Amendment, which declares that no state ". . . shall . . . deprive any person of life, liberty, or property without due process of law. . . ." Also found in the Fifth Amendment to the Constitution.

electoral college   The name given to the group of electors chosen in each state in the November voting and who actually elect the president and the vice president.

elite theory   The theory that holds that public policy is made by a relatively small group of influential leaders who share common outlooks and goals.

English Bill of Rights   A list of the rights of Englishmen adopted by Parliament in 1689. Included in the list are the right to trial by jury and the right to petition the government for the redress of grievances.

equal protection clause   Section 1 of the Fourteenth Amendment, which declares that no state shall "deny to any person within its jurisdiction the equal protection of the laws."

equity   A system of law that provides relief in situations in which common law or statutory remedies are inadequate, especially through the issuance of injunctions to prevent injuries.

establishment clause   A provision of the First Amendment that limits the power of Congress to create a state religion or provide aid to any religion by legislation. This restriction also applies to state governments through the due process clause of the Fourteenth Amendment.

exclusionary rule of evidence   A requirement that any evidence in a criminal case obtained illegally by police cannot be used as evidence in a trial.

executive agreement   An international agreement between the United States and a foreign nation made by the president; unlike a treaty, it does not require the advice and consent of two-thirds of the Senate, but it has the same legal status as a treaty.

exit poll   A form of public-opinion polling in which sample voters are interviewed in front of polling places on election day to determine how they actually voted.

ex post facto law   A law that imposes a penalty for performing an act that was not considered criminal when it was committed, or that increases the punishment for a crime after it has been committed. Such laws are prohibited by the Constitution.

federalism   A system in which the legal power of government is divided between a central or national government and smaller units of state government, usually under the authority of a written constitution.

Federalists   Supporters of the Constitution of 1787 who favored a stronger national government.

felony   The more serious forms of crimes such as robbery or murder.

field service   The regional, state, and local subunits of the federal bureaucracy.

filibuster   The use of extended speaking by a minority in the Senate to prevent the passage of a bill favored by the majority.

First Continental Congress   A meeting of delegates from twelve colonies in 1774 for the purpose of coordinating colonial opposition to the policies of Great Britain.

fiscal policy   That area of public policy that seeks to control the economy through the raising and lowering of tax rates and levels of public expenditure.

free exercise clause   A provision of the First Amendment that prohibits the national government from restricting an individual's right to the free exercise of his or her religion, as long as the religious practices involved do not violate the law. The free exercise clause is also applicable to the states through the due process clause of the Fourteenth Amendment.

full faith and credit clause   A provision of Article IV,

Section 1, of the Constitution that requires states to honor the final civil rulings of other states.

general revenue sharing A system under which states and cities were given a certain portion of federal tax revenues to be used in financing their programs, with no strings attached.

gerrymandering The division of a state, county, or city into voting districts in such a way as to give an unfair advantage to one party in elections.

government The institutions and processes by which decisions or rules are made and enforced for all members of a society.

government corporation A governmental body that, under policy regulations established by Congress, provides a public service but is organized like a private business corporation.

grandfather clause A device used by southern states during the late nineteenth century and early twentieth century to disfranchise blacks. The grandfather clause excused most whites from taking literacy tests by allowing all who had voted before 1867, or whose ancestors had voted before that date, to vote in future elections without having to pass such a test.

grand jury A jury that decides whether there is enough evidence to indict and bring to trial a person accused of a criminal act. Grand jury indictment is required in federal cases involving capital or otherwise infamous crimes.

grant-in-aid A sum of money that is given by a higher level of government to a lower level to help finance programs.

group theory The theory that holds that public policy is a product of competition among groups in society.

guarantee clause Article IV, Section 4, of the Constitution, which provides that the United States "... shall guarantee to every state in this Union a republican form of government...."

hard money Campaign contributions made by either individuals or groups that are limited in amount by federal law.

hegemon The dominant nation in a particular geographic area.

House majority leader A legislator who is chosen by the majority party in the House of Representatives but is not a constitutional officer of that chamber. The majority leader serves as a spokesperson for that party and along with the Speaker of the House plans legislative strategy.

impact evaluation An examination designed to discover the extent to which a policy causes a change in the situation it is designed to address.

impeachment Indictment of the president, the vice president, federal judges, or other civil officers of the United States by the House of Representatives on charges of treason, bribery, and other high crimes and misdemeanors. Conviction and removal from office requires a two-thirds majority of the senators present to vote.

implementation The directed change that occurs over time following the adoption of a new policy by government.

implied powers Powers given to Congress in the necessary and proper clause of Article I, Section 8, of the Constitution that enable the federal government to carry out its delegated powers by any constitutional means.

impoundment A president's refusal to spend money that has been appropriated by an act of Congress. A 1974 law sharply limited the president's right to impound money.

Independent A voter who does not identify with a political party.

independent regulatory commission A government agency that is responsible for the regulation of a major sphere of the economy. It is headed by a number of commissioners who are appointed by the president, with the advice and consent of the Senate, for overlapping terms. The commissioners exercise executive, legislative, and judicial powers.

indictment A formal accusation of a named person with the commission of specific criminal acts; the indictment is made either by a grand jury or by a bill of information.

injunction A court order issued by an equity court forbidding a person or a group of persons to commit an act that they are attempting to commit, or restraining them from continuing to commit such an act, or requiring them to perform an act.

interest group An organization of people who share certain attitudes and interests and try to affect the political system by shaping public opinion, opposing or supporting candidates for public office, and influencing the decisions of government officials, especially legislators and administrators.

interstate compact An agreement between two or more states, adopted by the state legislatures and often approved by Congress, in which arrangements are made to deal with interstate problems.

interstate rendition clause Article IV, Section 2, of the Constitution, which provides that an individual who is charged with a crime in one state and is found in another state may be returned to the state with jurisdiction over the crime.

isolationism A theory of world affairs that holds that a nation's interests are best served by having a minimum involvement in world affairs and by avoiding all alliances with other countries.

issue A subject becomes an issue after the attention of policymakers is drawn to a particular problem that requires government action.

Jim Crow laws Laws that enforced the practice of segregation or discrimination against blacks in public places, employment, and other areas of social life.

joint committee A committee, composed of members from both the House and the Senate, that has been created to deal with issues that require joint consideration.

judicial activism The belief that the judiciary should be willing to exercise its authority to declare unconstitutional actions of the other branches of government and to establish new rules of public policy.

judicial review The power of a court, and especially the Supreme Court, to review the acts of legislative bodies and executive officials to determine whether those acts are consistent with the Constitution.

judicial self-restraint The belief that judges should exercise self-control in using their judicial power and should generally defer to the policies of the elected branches of the government.

jurisdiction The legal authority of a court to hear a particular kind of case.

law Principles and regulations established by a government that are applicable to the people and enforced by the government.

legislative court A court created by Congress under Article I, Section 8, of the Constitution.

legitimacy The belief that certain principles or rules are right and proper; according to Max Weber it is based on tradition, charisma, and legality.

libel Written material that publicly defames the character of an individual.

liberalism A view of international affairs that believes that capitalism and democracy working through international institutions can produce peaceful cooperation among nations.

line agency An agency that carries out government policies and provides various types of services.

line item veto The power of a chief executive to cancel specific items in an appropriation or tax bill. Most state governors possess this power and in 1996 Congress authorized its use by the president.

literacy test A written or oral test used to determine eligibility for voting. Used by southern states from the late nineteenth century until the 1960s to prevent African Americans from voting.

living constitution The judicial philosophy that believes that constitutions should be interpreted in light of present-day circumstances.

lobbying Attempting to influence government policy by persuading legislators to vote for or against a particular proposal or by convincing members of the executive branch of government that a particular program is or is not desirable. Lobbying is the primary method used by interest groups to affect public decisions.

Magna Charta An English document of 1215 stating that the king was to be bound by the law and was to respect the rights of his subjects.

majority opinion An opinion of a court that has the support of a majority of the members of the court.

majority rule A basic principle of democracy under which public policy is set by the freely given consent of the majority, either directly by the people or through elected officials, but limited by the recognition of certain basic rights of the minority.

material policies Those policies of government that provide tangible resources or power to their beneficiaries or impose costs on groups in society.

mercantilism The theory that wealth and power are connected and that a nation should pursue policies that are intended to increase its wealth.

merit system The civil service system established by the Pendleton Act in 1883, in which people compete for jobs in the federal government and are hired on the basis of ability as demonstrated in a standardized test.

minority leader A legislator, chosen by the minority party in each house of Congress, who serves as a chief strategist for the party and as spokesperson for the minority party's position on issues.

minority rights Those rights of the minority recognized in a democracy. These include the rights to vote, to run for political office, and to express dissenting political opinions. In the American system of government, these rights are found in the Constitution and especially in the Bill of Rights and the Fourteenth Amendment.

minor party A political party that lacks the power or resources to get its candidates elected but exists to oppose present policies and to advance its own ideas.

misdemeanor Less serious forms of crimes such as trespassing.

monetary policy That area of public policy that seeks to control the economy through the control of the money supply and the raising or lowering of interest rates.

Monroe Doctrine The doctrine stated by President James Monroe in 1823 that European nations would not be allowed to interfere with or colonize any country in the Western Hemisphere.

muckrackers American journalists in the first years of the twentieth century who sought to expose corruption and wrongdoing in corporations and government.

multilateralism The theory that the security of nation states can be secured not by the pursuit of national power and alliances but through international law and cooperation among nations in a democratically constituted international organization.

multiparty system A political system in which there are more than two major political parties.

national chair The top official in the national organization of a major political party, who acts as the party's national spokesperson.

national committee The executive committee of the national party. Its members, who serve four-year terms, are formally elected by the national convention but in reality are chosen by the state parties by such methods as direct primary or state convention, depending on state procedures.

national convention A national meeting, held by each major party every four years, at which elected or appointed delegates nominate candidates for president and vice president.

national supremacy The doctrine, set forth in Article VI of the Constitution, that the Constitution and all national laws and treaties are the supreme law of the land.

necessary and proper clause Article I, Section 8, of the Constitution, which provides that Congress can ". . . make all laws which shall be necessary and proper for carrying into execution . . ." its delegated powers and the powers of any other branch of the United States government.

New Jersey Plan An alternative to the Virginia Plan presented to the Constitutional Convention by William Paterson of New Jersey. It called for a unicameral legislature that would have the authority to tax and to regulate interstate commerce, a national executive office presided over by two people, and a national judiciary.

open primary A direct primary in which a voter may choose the party primary in which he or she wishes to vote without having to formally register as a party member.

original jurisdiction The authority of a trial court to hear a case "in the first instance."

override A situation in which a president vetoes a bill, and it must be returned to the Congress. If both houses of Congress then approve the bill by a two-thirds vote, the bill becomes law.

oversight The power of Congress to supervise the activities of executive departments and agencies.

party identification The loyalty of voters to a particular political party.

party platform A political party's statement of general policy, adopted at the party's national convention.

party unity vote Votes in Congress in which a majority of the members of one party vote on one side of an issue and the majority of members of the other party vote on the other side.

plaintiff The party who brings suit or initiates court action.

pluralism The theory that holds that public policy is dispersed among many individuals and groups.

pocket veto A form of veto power. Bills that are sent to the president during the ten-day period before the adjournment of a session of Congress automatically die unless the president signs the legislation.

policy agenda A list of proposals on problems that government officials are concerned with at a given time.

policy influential Persons who have expertise and access to the governmental decision-making process.

political action committee (PAC) A group created by labor unions, business corporations, or private individuals and groups to engage in political activities and campaign spending.

political culture The fundamental, widely supported values that hold a society together and give legitimacy to its political institutions.

political executive A government employee who is ap-

pointed by the president with the advice and consent of the Senate.

political opinion Attitudes expressed by members of a particular community on political issues.

political party An organization that attempts to influence the political system by gaining the support of voters and especially by getting its members elected or appointed to public office.

political power The influence of an individual or a group on the political behavior of others.

political socialization The process by which people form political opinions; it is influenced by group membership, social categories, and historical events and political issues.

politics A process by which values are authoritatively allocated for a society; a method of deciding who gets what from government.

poll tax A special tax, formerly used in the South as a requirement for voting, that prevented many blacks and poor whites from voting.

popular sovereignty The theory that the people are the source of all legal authority.

precinct The basic unit of party organization in many states, corresponding to the small local area in which elections are administered.

preemption The policy first announced by President George W. Bush that the United States would use military force to forestall or prevent hostile acts by its adversaries.

presidential primary A primary election used by a majority of states to select delegates to the presidential nominating conventions of the major political parties.

President of the Senate The presiding officer of the Senate, who is also the vice president of the United States.

President *Pro Tempore* ("for the time being") A senator who is elected by the majority party to preside in the absence of the President of the Senate.

primary An election in which voters select a political party's candidates for local, state, and national office and in some states select party officials, such as members of party committees, convention delegates, and other leaders.

prior restraint Censoring or preventing the publication of material before it is actually released.

privileges and immunities clause Article IV, Section 2, of the Constitution, which prohibits a state from discriminating against citizens of another state.

procedural policies Those policies of government that deal with the way something will be done and/or who will do it.

process evaluation An examination designed to discover the extent to which a policy is implemented according to the guidelines set forth in law.

professional associations Organizations of professionals—e.g., doctors, lawyers—that are primarily concerned with standards in their professions but that also function as interest groups on some public issues.

public hearing A meeting of a committee or a subcommittee of Congress at which members of the public are permitted to testify about proposed legislation.

public opinion The range of opinions expressed by citizens on any subject.

public policy Ongoing, goal-oriented action that deals with both real and perceived public problems.

ratification Legalization of a constitution or an amendment to a constitution by formal consent; to become legal by formal procedures defined in the document.

realism The theory of international affairs that holds that cooperation among nations is limited by competition among states and by the lack of any institution capable of enforcing good behavior.

realpolitik The unsentimental pursuit by a country of its national interest.

reapportionment The redrawing of legislative district lines on the basis of new population information supplied by the United States Bureau of the Census.

reasonableness test A standard used by the Supreme Court to interpret the equal protection clause of the Fourteenth Amendment. The Court assumes that the law in question is constitutional and will uphold it if the government can advance reasonable argument in its defense.

redistributive policy Those policies of government that reallocate resources among groups in society.

registration The procedure by which a person proves to an election official that he or she is qualified to vote.

regulatory policy Those rules established by government that embody rules of conduct enforced by sanctions.

removal power The power of the president to remove from office any appointed official who performs strictly executive functions.

representative democracy A form of democracy in which public officials who represent the people are elected by popular vote in free elections.

reserved powers Powers that are neither delegated to the national government nor denied to the states by the Constitution; they are "reserved" to the states or the people by the Tenth Amendment.

Roosevelt Corollary The doctrine set forth by President Theodore Roosevelt in 1904 that, when necessary, the United States had the right to interfere in the domestic affairs of any Latin American or Caribbean nation.

rule A special order, issued by the House Rules Committee, that determines when a bill will come up for debate and sets time limits on the debate.

runoff primary A second primary in which the two candidates receiving the highest number of votes for a party's nomination for local or state office compete with each other, both having failed to win a majority of votes in the first primary.

sampling A process used in public-opinion polling that involves choosing a relatively small number of cases to be studied for information about the larger population.

scientific polling A means of finding out about public opinion through the use of scientific methodology and mathematical probability.

Second Continental Congress The second meeting of colonial delegates in May 1775. Although it had no specific authority, the Second Continental Congress printed money, raised troops, coordinated colonial efforts in the war against England, and adopted the Declaration of Independence.

sedition Oral or written advocacy of rebellion against the government that is designed to overthrow the government.

select committee A congressional committee created to do a specific job, such as conducting an investigation into a specific problem. Also called a special committee.

selective engagement The theory that in the post–cold war era, the United States should not overextend itself in foreign affairs, but should limit its involvement to only those situations that affect vital national interests.

selective incorporation The process by which the U.S. Supreme Court incorporated most of the provisions of the Bill of Rights into the due process clause of the Fourteenth Amendment. The court selectively chose individual provisions rather than incorporate the entire Bill of Rights at one time.

self-government The political idea that people are sufficiently rational to govern themselves, and do not need to be ruled by kings or tyrants.

self-incrimination Being compelled to be a witness against oneself. Self-incrimination is prohibited by the Fifth Amendment and is applicable to the states through the due process clause of the Fourteenth Amendment.

Senate majority leader A legislator who is chosen by the majority party in the Senate but is not a constitutional officer of that chamber. The majority leader schedules the work of the Senate and is the main spokesperson of that party.

senatorial courtesy The informal rule under which the president must clear nominations for federal positions within a state with the senior senator from that state who is a member of the same party, or risk Senate rejection of those nominees.

seniority system The system under which chairs of congressional committees were appointed on the basis of length of service on a committee.

separate-but-equal doctrine The standard used by the Supreme Court to interpret the equal protection clause of the Fourteenth Amendment from 1896 until the mid-1950s. The requirement that a state must provide equal protection was held to be satisfied if the government provided separate facilities for blacks, as long as they were equal to those provided for whites.

separation of powers A system of organizing the legislative, executive, and judicial functions of government, characterized by the creation of independent institutions to perform those functions.

Shays's Rebellion A protest in 1786 against mortgage foreclosures and high taxes in Massachusetts led by Captain Daniel Shays.

single-issue interest group An interest group that is concerned with only one public issue.

skeptical scrutiny An approach to constitutional analysis used by courts in the area of gender discrimination. Laws based on gender are subjected to a skeptical examination and are usually found to be unconstitutional.

slander Spoken statements that publicly defame the character of an individual.

social contract An agreement by the people creating the political community and the government.

soft money Money given to political parties rather than to candidates during political campaigns. It is not subject to the financial restrictions found in the Federal Election Campaign Act.

Speaker of the House The presiding officer of the House of Representatives, nominated by the majority party and formally elected by all members of the House.

spoils system The system used in the early part of the nation's history to fill government jobs. Jobs were awarded to friends and supporters of the party in power.

staff agency An agency that gathers information and makes it available to the president.

standing committee A permanent congressional committee with authority to consider bills in specific areas.

stare decisis A legal rule that requires courts to apply existing precedents to cases involving similar facts.

statutory law Law written and enacted by a legislative body.

strict scrutiny An approach to constitutional analysis used by courts in the area of race discrimination. Laws based on race are subjected to the highest degree of examination by the court and are always found to be unconstitutional.

subgovernments Also known as "iron triangles." The theory that holds that government does not make policy choices on its own but endorses decisions made by sections of the government in alliance with interest groups. Subgovernments are coalitions of like-minded legislators, bureaucrats, and interest groups.

substantiality test A standard used by the Supreme Court in determining whether laws based on gender are constitutional. To pass this test, a law must serve "important governmental objectives" and be "substantially related to achievement of those objectives."

substantive policies Those policies of government that embody actual plans of action and provide individuals with advantages or disadvantages.

survey research A method of data collection in which information is obtained from individuals who have been selected to provide a basis for making inferences about the larger population.

symbolic policies Those policies of government that provide little or no tangible benefits but appeal to widely held values such as justice, equality, and patriotism.

symbolic speech The communication of ideas by certain acts (such as wearing an armband or flying a flag) to dramatize a person's beliefs.

telephone poll A type of public-opinion poll in which information is obtained by telephone interviews based on random selection of phone numbers.

terrorism Politically motivated violence against noncombatant targets by subnational groups.

textualism The belief that judges should interpret the provisions of a constitution according to the meaning of the language at the time the document was composed.

tracking poll A form of polling that interviews as many as a thousand persons on a daily basis in the weeks immediately preceding an election.

trade associations Business interest groups organized on the basis of a single industry, such as steel or coal.

treaty An international agreement negotiated by the president that requires the advice and consent of two-thirds of the Senate to become effective.

two-party system A political system in which only the candidates of two major political parties have any real chance of being elected to office.

unanimous consent agreement A procedure in the Senate to establish the terms for consideration of a bill and set limits on motions, amendments, and debate.

unilateralism The theory that a nation should act alone in international affairs without seeking the approval or cooperation of other countries.

unitary government A system in which the legal power of government is possessed by the national or central government.

veto The power of a president to reject a bill passed by Congress. A veto can be overridden by a two-thirds vote in both houses of Congress.

Virginia Plan The fifteen resolutions presented by Governor Edmund Randolph of Virginia to the Constitutional Convention. It influenced the decision to abandon the Articles of Confederation and write a new constitution. The plan called for a national government consisting of executive, legislative, and judicial branches. The legislature was to be bicameral, with representation based on population and taxes paid.

voir dire ("to see and to say") The process by which members of a trial jury are selected. Prospective jurors are questioned by the judge and/or attorneys who are handling the case.

voter turnout The percentage of eligible voters who actually cast ballots in an election.

ward A small local unit of political party organization concerned primarily with campaigns and elections.

welfare Services provided by government that cover a wide range of social and economic benefits such as health care and education.

whip An assistant floor leader who is appointed by his or her party and whose task is to keep party members informed on party-sponsored bills, notify the party leader regarding the support that may be expected when the bill comes to a vote, and obtain the voting support of as many party members as possible on key bills.

whistleblowers Corporate or government employees who make public the mistakes or misdeeds of their superiors.

white primary A device used before 1945 in the one-party southern states to prevent blacks from voting by denying them the right to participate in Democratic party primary elections.

writ of *certiorari* ("to be made certain") A discretionary writ granted by the Supreme Court directing a lower court to send up a case for review.

writ of *habeas corpus* ("you have the body") An order issued by a court requiring that the government bring an arrested or detained person before the court to determine whether that individual is being legally held. Habeas corpus is guaranteed by the Constitution.

writ of *mandamus* ("we command") A court order to a public official to perform an act that is legally required.

yellow journalism A form of tabloid journalism that seeks to increase sales by printing stories about sex, violence, and other sensational subjects rather than by reporting facts and information.

Photo Credits

CHAPTER 1: Google, 3; UPI/Corbis, 4; Daniel MacDonald/Stock Boston, 6; W. Wellstood/Library of Congress, 7; The Granger Collection, 9; The White House Photo Office, 13; James L. Shaffer/PhotoEdit, 15.

CHAPTER 2: Library of Congress, 24; Richard Frear/Photo Researchers, Inc., 25; Thomas Sully, *James Madison,* 1809. In the Collection of The Corcoran Gallery of Art, Gift of Frederick E. Church, Washington, D.C., 27; *George Washington,* Oil on Canvas, ca. 1790s, 53 x 43 cm. American 18th c. The Cleveland Museum of Art, Hinman B. Hurlbut Collection, 2552.21, 28; The Granger Collection, 35 Ankers Photographers/ Supreme Court Historical Society, 39.

CHAPTER 3: AP/Wide World Photos, 48; Robert Goldstein/Photo Researchers, Inc., 56; Tom McHugh/ Photo Researchers, Inc., 62.

CHAPTER 4: Bill Bachmann/Photo Researchers, Inc., 73; AP/Wide World Photos, 76; Paul Conklin/ PhotoEdit 78; AP/Wide World Photos, 87; Joel Page/ AP/Wide World Photos, 89; Netscape Communications, 91 (*top*); Netscape Communications, 91 (*bottom*).

CHAPTER 5: Stan Wakefield/Pearson Education/PH College, 109; Tom McCarthy/PhotoEdit, 114; AP/Wide World Photos, 122.

CHAPTER 6: Jim Cole/AP/Wide World Photos, 132; AP/Wide World Photos, 133; Ron Edmonds/ AP/Wide World Photos, 143; Corbis, 155.

CHAPTER 7: UPI/Corbis, 162; AP/Wide World Photos, 174.

CHAPTER 8: Steve Liss/Tim Life Pictures/Getty Images, 195; Pool/Getty Images, Inc.-Liason, 196; AP/Wide World Photos, 198; Michael Probst/AP/Wide World Photos, 203; AP/Wide World Photos, 206; AP/Wide World Photos, 210; Corbis, 212; Susan Biddle/The White House/The White House Photo Office, 217; Corbis, 219.

CHAPTER 9: AP/Wide World Photos, 233; Eddie McCrossan/U.S. Department of Defense Visual Information Center, 239; Ronald Zak/AP/Wide World Photos, 241; AP/Wide World Photos, 247.

CHAPTER 10: Corbis Digital Stock, 255; M. Granitsas/The Image Works, 260; Supreme Court Historical Society, 269; M. Reinstein/The Image Works, 272.

CHAPTER 11: SW Productions/Getty Images, Inc., 285; Gifford/Getty Images, Inc.-Liason, 286; Doug Kanter/AP/Wide World Photos, 291; Shepard Shehbell/Corbis/SABA Press Photos, Inc., 298; AP/Wide World Photos, 302; David Young–Wolff/ Getty Images, Inc.,–Stone Allstock, 303; Paul S. Conklin/PhotoEdit, 305.

CHAPTER 12: Library of Congress, 313; Fred Ward/Black Star, 314; Doug Mills/*The New York Times,* 316; AP/Wide World Photos, 317; Corbis, 321; Spencer Grant/PhotoEdit, 323; AP/Wide World Photos, 324; Arlene Collins, 330.

CHAPTER 13: UPI/Corbis, 347; Mike Theiler/ Reuters/Corbis, 350; UPI/Corbis, 353; AP/Wide World Photos, 355; Sam C. Pierson, Jr./Photo Researchers, Inc., 356.

CHAPTER 14: Lee Snider/The Image Works, 363; Corbis, 366; Corbis, 367; Corbis, 371; AP/ Wide World Photos, 376; AFP Photo/Ahmad Al-Rubaye/ Corbis, 377.

Name Index

A

Adams, John, 21, 43, 146, 194, 221, 222
Adams, John Quincy, 361
Adams, Samuel, 23
Agnew, Spiro, 169, 196
Ashcroft, John, 81, 247

B

Bakke, Allan, 331
Barber, James David, 220–21
Benton, Thomas, 188
Black, Hugo, 301
Blair, Tony, 233
Bork, Robert, 271–72
Bradley, Bill, 134
Brandeis, Louis, 265, 271
Brennan, William, 277
Breyer, Stephen G., 270–72
Brown, Oliver, 315
Bruner, Lynn, 248
Burger, Warren Earl, 266
Bush, George, 101, 142, 196, 199, 237
   defeat in 1992 election, 212
   diplomatic recognition of new
      nations of Eastern Europe and
      Central Asia, 199
   judicial appointments, 268, 270
   nomination of John Tower, 241
   Panama invasion, 166, 202
   pardons, 209
   tax increases, 350
   trade restrictions, 349
   vetoes, 208
   war with Iraq, 166, 203, 215
Bush, George W., 84, 89, 92, 195, 206,
   233
   anti-ballistic missile treaty, 200
   Congressional elections of 2002,
      150–51, 210
   election of, 80, 142, 146
   fiscal budgets 2002 and 2003, 165
   foreign policy, 166, 376–78

judicial appointments, 268–69
judicial nominees, 169
nomination of, 134
organizational style, 234
primary campaign, 132
removal of secretary of treasury and
   director of the National
   Economics Council, 205
Social Security reform, 343
television debate, 143
trade restrictions, 349
vetoes, 208
war on terrorism, 166, 204
war with Iraq, 204, 376–77

C

Cannon, Joseph, 175
Carr, E. H., 372
Carter, Jimmy, 101, 136, 142, 146–47,
   207
   Egypt/Israel peace agreement, 201
   executive agreement with Iran,
      201
   Iran hostages, 215
   recognition of People's Republic of
      China, 199
   television debates, 143
   vetoes, 208
Catt, Carrie Chapman, 324
Channing, William Ellery, 312–13
Chapman, Carrie, 324
Chase, Salmon Portland, 266
Chase, Samuel, 275
Cheney, Richard, 136, 222
Churchill, Sir Winston, 3
Claiborne, Harry, 275
Clinton, Bill, 36, 101, 134, 142, 150,
   195, 237, 242
   attempt at Israel/PLO peace
      agreement, 202
   budgets, 164
   Census Bureau proposal, 171

diplomatic recognition of Vietnam,
   199
foreign policy, 166, 375, 381
impeachment of, 37, 85, 169, 197,
   220, 266
and Jewish voters, 154
judicial appointments, 268, 270, 272
Justice Department nominations, 169
military actions, 166, 202, 215
Monica Lewinsky scandal, 85, 197,
   211, 217
NAFTA, 112–13
Nuclear Test Ban Treaty, 200, 381
organizational style, 234–35
pardons, 209
political skills, 220
press conferences, 211
reelection in 1996, 212
and Roman Catholic voters, 154
Social Security reform, 343
and Supreme Court, 213
tax increases, 350
televised speeches, 211
trade restrictions, 349
use of focus groups, 79–80
vetoes, 176, 208, 209
welfare reform, 63, 354, 355
Whitewater affair, 247
Clinton, Hilary Rodham, 235, 247
Clymer, George, 28
Coolidge, Calvin, 19, 208, 220
Corwin, Edward S., 165
Cox, Archibald, 214
Cuomo, Mario, 57

D

Daley, Richard, 109
Dawes, Charles G., 222
Dean, John, 214
de Gaulle, Charles, 3
Dole, Bob, 154
Dole, Elizabeth, 85

Subject Index

Minority leaders, 178-79
Minority rights, 9-10
Miranda v. Arizona (1966), 304-5
Misdemeanors, 256
Missouri Compromise, 312, 313
Mixed caucuses, 129
Monetary policy, 348-49, 351
Money supply, 348
Monroe Doctrine, 364-66
Moral equality, 13
Muckrakers, 72
Multilateralism, 374-75
Multiparty system, 101

N
NAACP v. Alabama (1958), 295
NARAL Pro-Choice America, 117, 121
National Abortion Rights Action League, 117
National Association for the Advancement of Colored People (NAACP), 117, 120, 315-17
National Association of Manufacturers, 116
National chair, 107
National convention functions of, 135-36
National conventions, 107, 134-36
adoption of, 130
delegate selection, 131-33
National Council of Churches, 117
National Education Association (NEA), 116
National Farmers' Union, 116
National government. *See* Federalism
National Grange, 116
National Labor Relations Act of 1935, 65
National Minimum Drinking Age Amendment, 50
National opinion leader role, 210-11
National Opinion Research Center (NORC), 77
National Organization for Women (NOW), 117, 325
National parties, 107, 109
National primary concept, 136
National Rifle Association (NRA), 115, 121
National Right to Life Committee, 117
National Security Act of 1947, 379
National security adviser, 201
National Security Council (NSC), 201, 237, 379
National Security Strategy of the United States, 378
National supremacy, 36, 39-40, 57-58

National Voter Registration Act (Motor Voter law) of 1993, 144
Natural law, 6
Natural rights, 6
Near v. Minnesota (1931), 289
Negative advertising, 87-88, 93
New Deal, 59-60, 63, 65, 154, 231, 278, 341
New England Confederation, 22
New Federalism, 62-65
New Jersey Plan, 29
News magazines, 248
Newspapers, 83-84, 88, 92, 248, 383
New York v. Quarles (1984), 305
New York Times Co., v. Sullivan, The (1964), 293-94
New York Times Co., v. United States, The (1971), 289
Nineteenth Amendment, 40, 42, 155, 311, 325
Nix v. Williams (1984), 299
Nominations
of presidential candidates, 131-36
delegate selection, 131-33
national convention, 134-36
preconvention campaign, 133-34
procedures, 129-31
Noneconomic interest groups, 117
North American Free Trade Agreement (NAFTA), 112-13
North Atlantic Treaty Organization (NATO), 369, 370
Nuclear Test Ban Treaty, 200, 381

O
Obscenity, 292
Office-block ballot, 144
Office of Management and Budget (OMB), 162-63, 235-36
Office of Personnel Management, 232
Omnibus Crime Control and Safe Streets Act of 1968, 300
Open primaries, 130
Opinions
freedom to express, 12
Supreme Court, 264-65
Oral arguments, 263-64
Organized opposition, 11-12
Original jurisdiction, 55, 258
Override of veto, 189
Oversight, legislative, 246-47
Oversight function, 168

P
Pardon power, 209
Paris, Treaty of (1783), 26

Parochial schools, aid to, 286-87
Party-column ballot, 144
Party identification, 110-12
Party leader role, 209-10
Party platforms, 135
Party unity votes, 113
Patronage, 207
Peer group role in political socialization, 72
Pendleton Act of 1883, 238
Pension reform, 349
Pentagon, 239
Pentagon Papers, 249, 289
Peremptory challenges, 303
Personality, 2-3
Personal Responsibility and Work Opportunity Reconciliation Act of 1996, 63-64, 354
Petition, freedom of, 289, 291-92
Philadelphia v. New Jersey (1978), 58
Plaintiff, 256
Planks, 135
Planned Parenthood v. Casey (1989), 327
Platforms, 135
Plessy v. Ferguson (1896), 265, 313, 314
Pluralism, 340
Policy adoption, 342, 344
Policy agenda, 184
Policy evaluation, 342, 345
Policy formulation, 342, 344
Policy implementation, 342, 344-45
Policy influentials, 383
Policy legitimation, 344
Policy representation, 167
Political action committees (PACs), 117-18, 138
Political campaigns. *See* Campaigns
Political culture, 71-72
Political events, role in political socialization, 74
Political executives, 240-42
Political opinion, 75
Political participation, 94-95
Political parties, 2, 11-12, 42-43, 99-113
composition of Congress by, 178
decline of party identification, 110-12
functions of, 100
in the legislature, 112-13
minor parties, 105-6
president as leader, 209-10
and reform, 113
structure of, 107-10
two-party system, 2, 12, 101-5, 113